# BIX
## MAN & LEGEND

# BIX

## MAN & LEGEND

*by*

## Richard M. Sudhalter
## &
## Philip R. Evans

*with William Dean-Myatt*

$\mathbb{A}$RLINGTON HOUSE·PUBLISHERS

NEW ROCHELLE, N. Y.

**Library of Congress Cataloging in Publication Data**

Sudhalter, Richard M
   Bix: man and legend.

   Discography: p.
   1. Beiderbecke, Bix, 1903-1931. 2. Beiderbecke,
Bix, 1903-1931.-Discography. 3. Jazz music.
I. Evans, Philip R., 1935-     joint author.
II. Title.
ML419.B25S8    788'.1'0924 [B]       74-6326
ISBN 0-87000-268-6

"All I've ever called the dear boy was Bix . . . just that name alone will make one stand up—also their ears. And when he played—why, the ears did the same thing . . ."

LOUIS ARMSTRONG, 1954

# Introduction

Leon Bix Beiderbecke played jazz on the Bb cornet and a variety of music, some of it defying categorization, on the piano. He came from Davenport, Iowa, and died at twenty-eight in New York of a combination of pneumonia and the effects of alcoholism. He flared briefly and brightly in the popular music world of the 1920s, and departed before he was able to explore any more than a fraction of his native talent. He was only on wide public view for about three years, yet his memory and influence among musicians still survive after nearly half a century.

This is the outline of the story. Beyond introducing Bix, it tells us nothing. Leave it, rather, for a veteran saxophonist of the era to hint at the rest:

"I remember the day we heard Bix was dead. It went around the musicians in whispers, as though nobody dared say it out loud. We couldn't believe it—it was like saying the Pope was dead. If it was true, if Bix was really gone, what the hell were we all going to do?"

The springtime years of jazz produced many outstanding players, some of them colorful personages in their own right. Why, of all of them, did the passing of this quiet, deferential young man provoke so widespread a feeling of almost apocalyptic bereavement among those who knew him or even merely admired him from afar? And by what process did the succeeding years turn him into what the British critic Benny Green has aptly termed "Jazz's number one saint?"

Part of it, of course, rests with his music. Phonograph records, relatively few of them, have left some indication for later generations; yet even they, according to the now grey and wistful emeritus flaming youths who heard him in the flesh, are but pale echo of the real thing. They hint at a blindingly silvery tone, tempered by melancholy even in moments of joyous abandon. There is ample evidence of a faultless ear and a contemplative, sophisticated musical intelligence. Perhaps most significant, they suggest the capacity to reach a listener and move him emotionally even at first contact.

But an understanding of why there had to be a Bix Beiderbecke legend comes only through matching up the musical legacy with the facts of his life, background and character. Inevitably, this means hacking away more than 40 years of underbrush, destroying the popularly accepted image to get at the person of fact, flesh and blood.

Not to fault the legend-spinners. Certainly jazz, as an artistic outgrowth of the 19th-century romantic tradition, had to have its tragic heroes, and Bix had all the qualifications. He appeared—and died—at the right time. He was different, revolutionary from a musical point of view. He was good-looking, personally charming and widely loved. And he was sufficiently incomprehensible to the majority of his fellow-jazzmen—no thinkers, they—to take on instant enigma status even in his brief lifetime. Enlightening, in this context, the trumpeter Wingy Manone's remark that Bix "was always wanting to try this or that, play over figures . . . never wanted us to have any fun."

So, for awhile, Bix Beiderbecke becomes jazz's Keats and its Rupert Brooke. But the 20th century has not been kind to the romantic tradition. For better or worse, the century's near-cataclysmic events have tempered even nostalgia with an unmistakable skepticism, a new spirit of inquiry. Nothing accepted out of hand, not ideas or personages, and least of all legends. Challenge and question—and categorical dismissal of whatever doesn't stand up.

As a result, ever less remains in half-light. Within the past year excellent, unsparing biographical studies have already dispelled much of the ambiguity surrounding the lives of such seminal figures as blues singer Bessie Smith and Charlie Parker, saxophonist and architect of modern jazz. Their biographers, casting off the trappings of conventional myth, have revealed people far more human for their flaws, far more extraordinary for those elements of their lives which are recognizably fallible, flesh and blood.

Inevitably, there were bound to be attempts to unravel the "young man with a horn." Otis Ferguson, writing in the magazine *New Republic* within a decade of Beiderbecke's death,[1] was able to articulate much of the feeling evoked by listening to Bix, lacing in some background information gathered from the cornetist's boyhood friends in Davenport. Edward J. Nichols' chapter in the pioneer anthology *Jazzmen*[2] soon after took a stab at documentation—but came to grief in its acceptance of some of the standard half-truths and rumors bandied about among musicians. Numerous "reminiscences" in such magazines as *Down Beat* and *Metronome* further clouded the issue by presenting often confused, fondly exaggerated nostalgia as fact.

By the late 1950s, when Charles Wareing and the late George Garlick of Britain compiled their biography, *Bugles for Beiderbecke*,[3] the situation was hopelessly muddled. Working at a remove, and with limited budget, Wareing and Garlick had little choice but to rely heavily on previously-published material—and in so doing compromised their own work from the start. But for all its shortcomings, *Bugles* was a courageous book. It sought, with the well-ordered logic of attorney Wareing's mind, to make sense of apparent contradiction, and to set Bix in a musical and social perspective.

Wareing was the first to perceive in print that Beiderbecke's membership in the Paul Whiteman orchestra was far from the commercial sellout and source of musical frustration which more parochial jazz scholars had always assumed it to be. He devoted space to careful examination of Bix's

1. Ferguson, Otis. "Young Man with a Horn," *New Republic*, LXXXVII (July 29, 1936), 354.
   Ferguson, Otis. "Young Man with a Horn Again," *New Republic*, CIII (Nov. 18, 1940), 693–95.
2. Ramsey, Frederic Jr., and Smith, Charles Edward. *Jazzmen*. New York, Harcourt, Brace and Co., 1939. pp. 143–160.
3. London, Sidgwick and Jackson, Ltd. 1958.

impact on fellow-musicians, to cornetists who absorbed facets of his innovative style.

Another Briton, the critic Burnett James, contributed a series of valuable musical insights in a brief book of his own, published in 1959 by Cassell in their "Kings of Jazz" series.[4] Though hindered by the by now more-or-less standard factual inaccuracies, James did display acute understanding of Bix the musician.

There have been other writings, some more successful than others. Richard Hadlock's treatise on Bix's records in *Jazz Masters of the Twenties*[5] contains many astute observations. Gunther Schuller's Bix chapter in *Early Jazz*[6] is especially good in its musicologist's defense of the Whiteman orchestra. A recent work from Italy, *The Bix Bands*,[7] offers painstaking discographical work marred by some faulty scholarship, not all of it the fault of the authors, who used previous writings as source material.

Autobiographies of the musicians themselves, among them Eddie Condon, Mezz Mezzrow, Bing Crosby and Hoagy Carmichael, offer generally colorful but not always strictly factual accounts of a jazzman's life during the 1920s. Their chief value is in their power to evoke the thoughts and feelings of the springtime years.

By the mid-1950s an alarming, though inevitable, development made it clear that time for writing a factually documented book about Bix was running short. The natural laws of attrition were beginning to catch up with the generation of the twenties, and the men and women who had known Bix Beiderbecke were starting, slowly, to die off. They were the primary sources, the only ones whose combined accounts, weighed against one another and pieced together, puzzle-fashion, could dispel the contradictions and half-truths.

With this in mind, Phil Evans and Bill Dean-Myatt began work in 1957, Dick Sudhalter the following year, contacting first the musicians whose names appear on the record personnels, then the Beiderbecke family, finally other figures known to have played with Bix or to have employed him. Our paths inevitably crossed, but it took several years for Evans and Sudhalter to get together as a partnership. Dean-Myatt, of Walsall, England, had attracted Evans' attention at the outset with a Bix discography in the British collectors' magazine *Matrix*. He and Evans soon agreed to work together.

Initial response was encouraging. Paul Whiteman offered help. Jean Goldkette, Hoagy Carmichael, Red Nichols—all were willing to talk, and to submit to endless, detailed questioning. All supplied names and addresses of others who "might have a thing or two to add," though their connections with Bix might not be so well-known.

So it began, an unending, ever-widening process of letter-writing, travel and interview, reading, phoning and taping, which consumed the next 15 years and still continues as this volume is published. For Evans, especially,

4. James, Burnett. *Bix Beiderbecke.* London, Cassell & Co. Ltd., 1959.
5. New York, Macmillan, 1965. pp. 76–105.
6. New York, Oxford University Press, 1968. pp. 187–194.
7. Castelli, Vittorio, Kaleveld, Evert, Pusateri, Liborio. *The Bix Bands.* Milan, Raretone, 1972.

it meant devotion of the best of his adult years to learning more about Bix Beiderbecke than any other single person on earth. There would be no reliance on past writings, though all had to be carefully read and absorbed to clarify the seams where fact blends into myth. All sources were to be primary—the story told, where possible, in their own words. Each account of an event to be weighed against the others, often by bringing narrators into direct contact with one another for the first time in years, to resolve apparent contradictions in their recollections.

There were unexpected benefits. For many years, alumni of the Paul Whiteman orchestra held annual parties at the home of Ferde Grofe in California, during which they reminisced freely about the early days. It was Evans' good fortune to be invited to several of these otherwise exclusive gatherings, and to be present as groups of Whiteman musicians discussed an event among themselves, catching one another up on errors and inaccuracies until a consensus emerged. At these parties, Evans was able to question at length men who had been reticent in correspondence about points of detail, or who simply preferred not to answer letters at all.

Similarities of attitude emerged, both here and elsewhere, chief among them a pronounced desire to protect Bix's name and reputation against denigration, especially over his alcoholism. Almost all displayed undisguised affection for him; detractors were few and far between. All were at pains to stress that the drinking should not be allowed to obscure a clear picture of the whole human being.

This kind of research also meant closer and deeper understanding of Bix's music. It meant acquiring full, complete collections of Bix's recordings, issued and unissued. Sudhalter was able to bring to bear experience as a jazz cornetist and trained musician in investigating the harmonic and melodic implications of Beiderbecke's piano compositions and recorded solos. Together the triumvirate, as it evolved during the 1960s, was able to investigate every lead which had even vaguely pointed to Bix's presence on a record. In each case, one of the three would acquire the disc in question through collector sources and disseminate tape copies to the other two; then discussion would begin. When the authors of *The Bix Bands* discovered a possible Beiderbecke solo on a Marion McKay Gennett recording made in late 1924, Dean-Myatt quickly came up with a copy, Evans found McKay still living in the midwest, and Sudhalter went to work both cross-checking the solo against Bix's other work of the period and exploring the possibility that it might have been the work of another cornetist.

As information rolled in and a picture of Bix began to take shape, it became clear that a special style would have to be evolved for the writing of the book. It would have to combine the reportage and quotation techniques of journalism with a quantity of more technical discussion not ordinarily of interest to the non-specialist reader, but indispensable all the same to the understanding of Bix and his impact. Frequently, moreover, sufficient information was available to reconstruct dialogue; this was done, then checked by submitting relevant passages to either persons directly involved or, where this was not possible, to sources close enough to them to know whether things happened as depicted.

Frequently, such portions would come back with marginal notes—corrections, additions of other information evoked in the reading. If, as was the case on one or two occasions, there were objections that a remark or action was out of character for the person described and would have to be changed, it was, and the passage was resubmitted to the critic.

Such techniques, and the time-lag involved in transatlantic collaboration, often cost valuable time and ran the constant risk of misunderstanding. That there was a minimum of friction, and very little crossing of wires, is all the more amazing in view of the fact that Sudhalter and Evans did not meet face to face until April 1972. Evans and Dean-Myatt have never met. Yet a singularity of purpose united us, bound us together in pursuit of a common goal. On those few occasions when disagreement occurred —usually over interpretation or presentation of information, never over matters not directly concerned with the mechanics of writing the book— someone was prepared to compromise in the interests of harmony.

Such teamwork extended into the actual writing of the book. Over eleven months, Evans fed a constant stream of raw material through the post to London, all the while keeping up a full volume of correspondence with sources and slotting new information into the shipments as it became available. A copy of each completed chapter would then be mailed to him, for copying and distribution among its sources for checking. Once critical comments were in, they were relayed back to me and my copy of the chapter in question would be duly amended. Far from being a particularly cumbersome process, this method quickly established its own rhythm.

Several editorial decisions were difficult to make. Whether, for example, it was necessary or even desirable to examine some of the more familiar bits of nonsense surrounding Bix's life, and marshal evidence to refute them. In the end it was decided not to: our primary purpose was to tell Bix's story. If an anecdote was based in fact, it would appear, correct, in its proper place in the narrative. If not, its omission would speak clearly enough. Too much space devoted to disproving mistakes, we decided, would hold up the flow of an already long book. Did Bix, for example, actually insert that Charleston figure in "Goose Pimples" to ruin an unsatisfactory take? The record itself, and a little musical common sense, offer answer enough: the two notes are harmonically correct, and coincide with the same figure as played on the piano by Frank Signorelli; there are no discernible "goofs" up to that point; and Bix leads out the final ensemble with a passion which hardly bespeaks dissatisfaction or an attempt at sabotage.

Some questions were not so easily resolved. Years of inquiry, for example, have shed no light on accounts of a reported friendship between Bix and Babe Ruth, home run king of the New York Yankees during the twenties. Knowing the Beiderbecke love for baseball, it is not hard to imagine him spending occasional afternoons at Yankee Stadium watching the Bambino, Lou Gehrig and the rest of Miller Huggins' stable of temperamental stars go through their paces. But of Ruth's alleged visits to the 44th Street Hotel, barely able to squeeze his massive bulk through the doorway, there remains no evidence.

The discography, too, presented some questions, usually of a technical nature. Our adoption, with some modifications, of Brian Rust's system of label and instrument abbreviations is based on the preeminence now accorded Rust's *Jazz Records 1897–1942* and other books as the standard reference works in their field.

We have restricted ourselves to 78 RPM issues in the discography, making exceptions only in those cases in which a selection has appeared for the first time on LP. LP issues are a continuing thing, and any attempt to keep an up-to-date listing, with records being produced in more countries than ever before, is doomed to be out of date by tomorrow. Sufficient, we feel, to have it known which selections have been issued, and to provide, through notation of significant solo passages, a handy key through which multiple versions or "takes" of the same number may be distinguished from one another.

A word, too, about photographs. We have attempted to include in the present volume as many hitherto-unpublished—or at least rarely-seen—photos of Bix as were obtainable. We have deliberately omitted many of the more familiar shots, in the conviction that no purpose would be served through inclusion of *every* available Bix photo. Special thanks in this area must be extended to Paul Mertz, who made available to us the stills from the exceedingly rare home movie shot by Charlie Horvath during the Jean Goldkette orchestra's travels in the east.

There are other photos, as yet unpublished, in existence. Some were all but impossible to trace. In at least one case, a rare shot of the Wolverines during Vic Berton's summer tenure with them, the owner asked a price for its use far beyond what the authors felt fair or reasonable. In another, the only extant print of an informal Wolverines pose was of such poor quality as to defeat any effort to reproduce it.

Bix research is, like the output of the sorcerer's apprentice, a continuing phenomenon. The authors would therefore welcome additional data unearthed as a result of publication of this book, with an eventual second edition in mind.

Our eternal thanks to all those, both living and dead, who have assisted us over the years with patience, generosity and a near-universal love for Bix Beiderbecke. It is to them that this book must be dedicated.

Richard M. Sudhalter

*London, England*
*November 5, 1973*

# Acknowledgments

The authors would like to thank the following persons without whose assistance—and seemingly inexhaustible patience in the face of prolonged and detailed questioning—this book would never have come about. Many of them are no longer living; it is our sincere hope that this work will make a small contribution to their immortality.

Sylvester Ahola
Walter C. Allen
Lillian Anderson (Sweden)
Larry Andrews
Phil Applin
Robert Archer
Louis Armstrong
Ed Arpee
Edwin (Squirrel) Ashcraft
Harry E. Avery
Vincent Bach
E. B. (Woody) Backensto
Roy F. Bargy
Dr. M. C. Barnard II
Floyd Bean
Charles B. Beiderbecke
Franco F. Bellacci (Italy)
Fred Bergin
George Bird
Louis Black
Elizabeth Blackwell
Marty Bloom
Milton (Mickey) Bloom
J. D. Bolton (England)
Robert Boucher
Tony Briglia
Carrie V. Brown
Ted (Steve) Brown
Vernon Brown
Earl Bruckman
Harry O. Brunn

Paul Burgess
Burton Historical Collection (Detroit Public Library)
Rupert Buttress (England)
Jorge Cajarville (Uruguay)
James (Jimmy) Caldwell
Dave Carey (England)
Hoagy Carmichael
Jess Carneol
Olin Carver
CBS Inc.
William Challis
John Chilton (England)
Helene Chmura
Pat Ciricillo
Alan M. Cohn
F. Mildred Colby
D. R. (Russ) Connor
Z. Jack Cornea
Al Cox
Ken Crawford, Jr.
Wally Curtis
Frank Cush
Jehangir B. Dalal (India)
John R. T. Davies (England)
Charles Davis
Pat Davis
Dave L. Dickinson (England)

Kurt Dieterle
Phil Dooley
Richard DuPage
Joe Duroe
Bud Ebel
Robert Effros
Chris Ellis (England)
Lennie Esterdahl
Herman (Hymie) Farberman
Fred (Fuzzy) Farrar
Chris Fletcher
E. C. Forman
Birgir Formo (Norway)
Bruce Foxman
Lawrence (Bud) Freeman
Irving (Izzy) Friedman
Jack Fulton
Harry Gale
Gene Gifford
Gene Gladson
Jean Goldkette
Benny Goodman
Jim Gordon
Russell Gray
Howard P. Greene
William T. Grimm
Ferde Grofe
Arthur Gronwall
Dr. John J. Habers
Clyde Hahn
Wilbur Hall
Merrill M. Hammond

Virgil M. Hancher (U. of Iowa)
Francis Hannaford
Kenneth J. Hansen
Ralph S. Harding (England)
Renee Murray Harris
Damon (Bud) Hassler
Wilbur (Bud) Hatch
Joe Haymes
Steve Heim
Alphonso Henry
Stan Hester
Robert Hilbert
William Hillpot
Curt Hitch
Art Hodes
Mrs. Edith Horvath
Horace Houck
Reagan Houston
Armand Hug
G. W. G. Hulme (England)
Edward Hunt
Malcolm Hunter (S. Africa)
Cecil Huntzinger
Clarence Hutchinrider
Don Ingle
C. M. Jenkins
Mel Jenssen
Oliver Johnson
Wayne Jones
Leonard Joy
Keeley Institute
Frank Kelly
Sylvan Kirsner
Manny Klein
Vera Cox Korn
George Kraslow
Gene Krupa
Art Kurth
Harold (Scrappy) Lambert
Otto Landau
Horst H. Lange (Germany)
D. Jas. (Nick) LaRocca
Fred Laufkoetter
David J. LeGate
Jim Lindsay
Dr. Rodney Long, M.R.C.S., L.R.C.P.
Walter Long
John MacKenzie

Daniel C. Mahony
Roy J. (Red) Maier
Matt Malneck
Charles Margulis
Anthony Marinaccio (Davenport, Iowa, public schools)
Luigi Martini (Italy)
Robert Mayhew
Leo McConville
Brad McCuen
Ann McGuire
Tom McIntosh
Marion McKay
R. Douglas McNamee
Jimmy McPartland
Dud Mecum
Violette Meikel
Julian S. Merigold
Paul M. Mertz
Eddie Miller
Victor Moore
Chauncey Morehouse
Dr. Fritz Morris
John Morris
Phil Napoleon
Louis Nauman
William Neill (Scotland)
Otis Neirouter
E. L. (Red) Nichols
Floyd O'Brien
Don O'Dette
Trave O'Hearn
F. C. (Cork) O'Keefe
Harold Olm
Harold O'Neal
William A. Paley
E. Clinton Parker
Georgia Patterson
Hollis Peavey
Tom Pletcher
John Powell
Charles Previn
Bill Priestley
Richard F. Putzier
Frank Quartell
Radio Corporation of America
John Randolph
William C. Rank
Billy Rauch
Dr. Herbert Reaver
Don Redman
Sidney (Happy) Reiss
Charles Rinker

John W. Rippin (England)
Paul Riseman
Irving Riskin
Bob Roberts (England)
Wayne Rohlf
Joseph Rushton
Charles (Pee Wee) Russell
Brian A. L. Rust (England)
David Rust
L. Stanley (Doc) Ryker
Norma Ryker
Chester Sableman
Andy Sannella
Tony Sbarbaro
Duncan Schiedt
Elmer Schoebel
Warren W. Scholl
Arthur Schutt
Andy Secrest
Irwin Shainman
Nat Shilkret
Mary Louise Beiderbecke Shoemaker
Estelle Shaffner Siebert
Rome Siemon
Edgardo Silvestri (Argentina)
Marlin Skiles
Dale Skinner
Charles Edward Smith
Harl Smith
Martin Smith (England)
Victor Smith
Oro (Tut) Soper
Mervyn Sorensen
Dr. Edmond Souchon
Jack Souther
Karl Spaeth
Byron Spaulding
Thomas K. Spence
Esten Spurrier
Dr. John Steiner
Rex Stewart
William Grant Still
Charles Strickfaden
Robert Strong
Albert W. Sudhalter
Joe Sullivan
Michael Sutcliffe (Australia)
Les Swanson

Ruth Shaffner Sweeney
Charles Teagarden
Jack Teagarden
Jack Teegen
Bessie Shaffner Ten-Broek
Tommy Thunen
Raymond Thurston
Richard Toll
Eric Townley (England)
Richardson Turner
Cornelia Marshall VandeWallen

George Van Eps
Joop Van Galen Last (Holland)
Omer Van Speybroeck
Ralph Venables (England)
Joe Venuti
Roy Voysey (England)
Howard Waters
Ruby Weinstein
C. K. (Bozy) White
Paul Whiteman
Paul Whiteman Collection (Williams College)

Bert Whyatt (England)
John Wiggin
Newell (Spiegle) Willcox
Jack Willett
Al Woodyatt
Laurie Wright (England)
W. Gordon Yadow
Otis Zirkle
Theo Zwicky (Switzerland)

# Prologue

They named the boy Leon Bix. At first there may have been the intention of calling him Bismark, after his father; but Bismark Herman Beiderbecke, so named in a new world's first-generation homage to an old, had
himself been "Bix" to family and friends since his youth in post-Civil War
Davenport, Iowa. His firstborn son, Charles Burnette, inherited the nickname. By the time Bismark's second son made his appearance in 1903, it
was as much an institution in the Beiderbecke family as were the Beiderbeckes in the city of Davenport.

Carl Beiderbecke, Bismark's father, had arrived in Iowa in the mid-
1850s, nearly two decades after Col. George Davenport founded his town
atop a long, sloping bluff overlooking a wide sweep of the Mississippi at
the only place where the big river flows east-west, rather than north-south.
Young Beiderbecke (the name in German means "by the brook") had left
Germany among thousands of Europeans drawn by the promise of a good
life in the new world. Landing at New Orleans, he made his way northward, following the muddy river back upstream until he happened on Col.
Davenport's fledgling community.

There he settled, and found immediate opportunity in a partnership
with Hermann Mueller, a fellow-immigrant, running a wholesale grocery
business. Later, he apparently sold out to Mueller and landed a job with
the First Chartered National Bank of Davenport, eventually becoming its
president.

His marriage to Louise Piper, a talented and well-educated German girl
four years his junior, confirmed Carl Beiderbecke's standing among
Davenport's rapidly-growing population. Success in business brought
prominence in community social affairs and cultural life; Carl, whose
family in Germany had taught him music at home, organized and led a
well-attended *Maennerchor*, which sang every Sunday at the Lutheran
Church and furnished entertainment for social events. Louise, by all accounts, was an accomplished pianist. Music in the Beiderbecke home was
adjudged a social grace, indispensable to a warm, close-knit family life.

Bismark Herman, third of Carl Beiderbecke's children, was born into
this environment on Tuesday, March 17—St. Patrick's Day—1868. A Beiderbecke family chronicle recounts with some humor how the day of his
birth nearly had a far-reaching effect on the boy's life:

> ... there perhaps was an Irish community in Davenport at about this time,
> and it is possible there was a festival in celebration of St. Patrick's Day, at
> which Carl Beiderbecke's musical group was scheduled to participate. A

third child was expected that day and it had been planned he should also be named Herman, if a boy, for his father's friend and partner in Beiderbecke and Mueller. The boy arrived on March 17 and he was first named Patrick Herman. But the Beiderbeckes now were Americans, and in fact Carl had named his first son for himself—Charles Thomas—and about this time Carl himself had become Charles Beiderbecke.

Patrick Herman was a good name and not too German, but it wasn't good enough for the Beiderbecke nurse and servant. She insisted that this fine German boy be named for the "Iron Chancellor." She won out, and this boy was christened Bismark Herman Beiderbecke.

In keeping with his increasing prosperity, Carl built a new house up on Seventh Street with a commanding view of the Mississippi, and the family settled in with enthusiasm. Their life was lively, the house full of young people much of the time. Each of the four Beiderbecke children had a separate circle of friends, and each was known almost exclusively by nickname. Charles, the eldest, was "Tally," daughter Otilia "Tilly"; Bismark rapidly became "Bix" and baby Louise "Lutie."

Music played a popular and pivotal role in their lives. America, as yet without recognizable indigenous cultural traditions, turned for inspiration to European artistic values, most notably those of German-dominated 19th century romanticism. Neil Leonard, in his *Jazz and the White Americans*,[1] expressed it thus:

> These immigrants who shaped our concert life were largely the products of this Germanic music tradition. They were inspired by the philosophical idealism of romantic critics and artists who had divided the universe into two realms. One was the material world, comprehensible and adjustable by means of the tools of science, observation and reason. The other was the supernatural, which according to the Platonic, Christian and other cosmic philosophies, was approachable only through art and religion . . . of all the arts, music in its proper form was the most spiritual, the farthest removed from the material world. Traditional academic music, particularly symphonic, which was the purest sort, had a social mission . . .

Within such families as Carl Beiderbecke's, the social mission was an article of faith, and Wagner, Brahms, Beethoven and Mozart its patron saints. Popular or "light" music, as heard in dance halls or on the paddlewheel excursion boats which plied their gaily-painted way up and down the river, was regarded at best with the tolerance of forced good nature. But the attitudes, hence the climate, in which Bismark and his brothers and sisters grew up were best summarized by the conductor Theodore Thomas, in his own *Musical Biography* of 1905:[2]

> A symphony orchestra shows the culture of a community . . . the man who does not understand Beethoven and has not been under his spell has not lived half his life. The master works of instrumental music are the language of the soul and express more than those of any other art. Light music, "popular" so-called, is the sensual side of the art and has more or less devil in it.

---

1. University of Chicago Press, 1962.
2. *Ibid.*

18

In the days following the Civil War, the songs of Stephen Foster and Dan Emmett, echoing a white view of Negro life and culture under slavery, were on everyone's lips, even those of the Beiderbecke children. For Bismark, "Old Black Joe" and "Swanee River" were tunes to play on the zither and sing on a typical autumn or winter evening, grouped around the piano with Tally and Tilly, Lutie and various of their friends. Often Adele Seiffert from down the street might drop in, bringing Max von Binzer, Albert Stibolt or, more and more often, a girlfriend who, unlike most of the Beiderbeckes' circle, was not of German descent.

Agatha Jane Hilton belonged no less to Davenport than did her well-to-do German friends. She was the daughter and only child of Bleigh Hilton, a Mississippi riverboat captain widowed shortly after her birth. His wife, Caroline Hill, had come west in a covered wagon from Greenville, Pennsylvania, near Pittsburgh, as one of the younger children in a large family, and had married Hilton against her parents' wish. Following her death, Hilton returned to the stern-wheelers, leaving his baby daughter in the care of his wife's unmarried elder sister Mary Ann and brother John, owner of a Davenport livery stable.

Agatha grew up a quiet, dark-haired beauty, possessed of a keen mind and the sort of quick talent for music which guaranteed her instant and lasting popularity. She studied piano and organ with the best teachers John Hill's money could provide, becoming an accomplished performer on both instruments. On Sundays, she played the organ at the Davenport First Presbyterian Church.

She was a welcome addition to musical evenings at the Beiderbecke home, and come Christmas found herself at the center of the family's *Weihnachtsfeier*. With Agatha at the piano, Bix took to the zither and Tillie her harp. Lutie whistled, and Carl and Louise joined in group singing of carols in German and English.

The beauty and poise of Bleigh Hilton's daughter were far from lost on young Bismark Beiderbecke, and after a courtship as ardent as it was brief he won her hand. They were married in 1894, and moved into a roomy new white frame house at 1934 Grand Avenue, in a peaceful residential neighborhood closer to downtown Davenport, but only a short ride by trolley or horseless carriage from Seventh Street.

It seemed a good, lasting existence, one of hammocks under shady trees and long summer evenings on the veranda, the clip-clop of the family buggy giving slowly way to the cough and sputter of the gasoline engine. Change, certainly, was in the air; Bix and Aggie were aware of it, accepted its inevitability secure and confident they could watch it come, live with it and adapt to it, all the while able to retain what they found good and warm in the past. What they could never have suspected was that one of their own children would become the embodiment of another sort of change—one so drastic and abrupt as to shatter the very coherence of so well-ordered a universe.

# Contents

The house at 1934 Grand Avenue, Davenport, Iowa, where Bix Beiderbecke was born on Tuesday, March 10, 1903.

PHOTO COURTESY MARY LOUISE SHOEMAKER

# Chapter 1

Bismark and Agatha Beiderbecke's two-story house on Grand Avenue blended Davenport's distinctively American life-style with a European flavor inherited from Carl and Louise. A front porch, running the width of the building, looked out over a sloping lawn to the President John Tyler Elementary School No. Nine across the street; the porch could be screened in during the summer, guaranteeing comfortable socializing during the long, sultry evenings. A gold ceramic tile fireplace, flanked by window seats, dominated the entranceway; the living room, at 27 feet by 14, was generously sized, as were three bedrooms and a floored attic upstairs.

Aggie lavished care on every room, and though already pregnant with their first child, set about with characteristic energy turning the house into a comfortable, welcoming home for Bismark as he plunged into business as a member of the firm at the East Davenport Lumber and Coal Company.

The child, a son, came along August 11, 1895, and was christened Charles Burnette, in "Opa" (Grandpa) Carl's honor. A daughter, born October 20, 1898, became Mary Louise, after Aggie's maiden aunt Mary Ann and "Oma" (Grandma) Louise.

There were now two Bix Beiderbeckes. Bismark's first-born son had picked up the nickname, occasioning some confusion until friends and relatives, for clarity's sake, dubbed Bismark "Big Bix" and Charles "Little Bix." So it was to last, until two o'clock the morning of Tuesday, March 10, 1903, and the birth of Bismark's and Aggie's second son.

In years to come, after the name Bix Beiderbecke had long since become immortal in a way "Big Bix" never envisioned, even the naming of the child on a cold March day in Davenport was to become subject for dispute. Many assumed "Bix" was still a nickname, and that the child was named Leon Bismark after his father. But there is too much evidence to the contrary: Davenport city records, newspaper clippings referring to him as Leon Bix with no quotation marks around the second name. Mary Louise was always emphatic on the point:

"Bix was named Bix. Let there be no mistake about that. Dad would not have allowed his baby to be named after him—but after much talk it was decided Leon (for no reason) and Bix, which is the nickname for Bismark, was the name of this baby."

More intriguing, perhaps, might be Bismark's reasoning in selecting the name. Did he reckon that the nickname he had borne most of his life, and which had already been passed on to one son, was suitably representative of a new world and century to bestow it formally on another? Certainly within this family it was sure invitation to confusion. Charles, who later dropped his "Little Bix" title altogether to become "Burnie," confirmed this:

"When Bix was born the folks named him Leon Bix Beiderbecke, and he was so christened in the First Presbyterian Church here in Davenport. When I got out of World War I and came home it was surely confusing with three Bixes. When the phone rang and someone asked for Bix, we would have to ask, 'Do you want the coal man (which was Dad), or the soldier (me) or the musician?'"

If Leon Beiderbecke's first three years were remarkable for anything at all, it was for their very lack of the remarkable. Davenport life, in the recollection of all, was a pleasant pastel of lazy routine, socializing and the shelter of close family groups at once both rooted in European tradition and full of the energy and enterprising spirit of the United States. Mary Louise retained a vivid memory of her father, a tall, handsome figure in a well-cut tweed suit, patting Queenie, the family horse, gently on the head while climbing down from the wagon at lunchtime every day. It is an image summing up a time, a vignette of turn-of-the-century middle America.

Thus, the Beiderbeckes. Young Leon, age two and "Bickie" to his mother for the time being, toddles out the front door, down the walk and out into the street, where he sits down happily between the trolley tracks. Mr. Musselmann, stopping his streetcar with a sigh, picks the tot up and gently returns him to one of the neighborhood children, who duly collects the usual nickel from Aggie Beiderbecke as the day's lucky finder of her wayward son.

Lazy summer afternoons and evenings, dry-cold winters full of ice-skating, sledding and snowball fights. Bismark still played his zither now and then, and under Agatha's tutelage Mary Louise was showing interest in, if not extraordinary flair for, the piano.

"Bickie" was still too small to be anything but a source of indulgent pleasure. Aggie, playing the parlor piano during an afternoon's relaxation, smiled as the baby waddled uncertainly into the room and attempted to "dance" to the music. Mary Louise, often present, remembered the toddler's delight at hearing his mother play "Oh, Mister Dooley," a popular tune of the day:

"Although he really couldn't walk, he could sit, and danced his legs till sometimes his derrière would walk itself under the bookcase, where he would cry until he was pulled out by a sympathetic person."

Accounts vary as to exactly when and how the boy first demonstrated the faultless ear and pitch sense which would someday become his music's hallmark. But around age four he somehow discovered that by standing on tiptoe in front of the piano, he could reach and press down keys to produce tones. Mary Louise spoke of a fumbling attempt to reproduce "Oh, Mister Dooley"; other, perhaps more socially self-conscious accounts make it the melody of Franz Liszt's *Hungarian Rhapsody No. 2.*

By the time he was five and a pupil in Miss Alice Robinson's kindergarten at Tyler School, Master Leon Bix Beiderbecke had a number of accomplishments to his credit. He could negotiate "Pop! Goes the Weasel," "Oats, Peas, Beans" and other simple melodies with one finger. And he could sing in tune. A school party on his fifth birthday rated an item in the *Davenport Daily Democrat;* probable consequence of the Beiderbeckes' position in Davenport life, the account reads like the society pages of the *New York Times,* attesting that "Yesterday was the fifth birthday of Master Leon Bix Beiderbecke, the bright little son of Mr. and Mrs. B. H. Beiderbecke." School, too, was a place to make music, and to savor the rewards it brought. Miss Robinson, walking out of her classroom one day, found the boy about to slide down the staircase bannister. "No!" she said, shaking a warning finger. Leon, already in motion, slid to the bottom, climbed off, and smiled at her. "Now what can I play for you?" he asked. Miss Robinson did not carry the matter further.

Neighbors, too, soon heard of Aggie Beiderbecke's "bright little son," and Mary Louise recalled that they put his talents to good use.

"On Sunday afternoons, while the neighboring girls entertained erstwhile beaux, Bix was frequently called in (to their homes) to render a few ditties. The beaux, anxious to impress, perhaps, gave nickels to our Bix. In the beginning, it was a one-fingered affair . . . later, the left hand pointer finger joined the right . . . as he grew, his hands grew, as did his repertoire. The octave in the right hand and a wooden-legged bass accompanied— all, of course, in the key of C."

These early years remain a potpourri of half-remembered family anecdotes in which the young Bix is at least part of the time regular kid, all beans and mischief and sticky fingers, playing ball with the gang, getting into rough-and-tumble scraps with every high-spirited dog in the neighborhood, and returning home at dusk stuffed full of applesauce, toast and cakes by Davenport townsfolk entranced with his good manners and fast-developing skill at the piano. The family, too, responded to his musicality with some enthusiasm. Their feelings at this early stage were doubtless mirrored in an advertisement run locally around the time by Schmidt's Music Company, of 111–113 West Third Street in Davenport, and clearly aimed at just such parents as Bismark and Agatha. According to its text,

> . . . through music, the child
> Enters into a world of beauty
> Expresses his inmost self
> Tastes the joy of creating
> Widens his sympathies
> Developes [sic] his mind
> Soothes and Refines His Spirit
> Adds grace to his body.

Agatha soon sought expert guidance in harnessing her son's obvious talents. One of her cousins was married to Albert Petersen, a competent cornetist and brass band conductor known to the Beiderbecke children as "Uncle Olie." Three of his sons had shown early promise, imparting to him the status of family talent scout and arbiter of musical precocity. He dropped over one day to hear Agatha's seven-year-old boy wonder go through his paces.

Olie could hardly contain his enthusiasm. "Agatha, this boy has something," he said. "Keep me informed about his progress—and whatever you do get him some piano lessons."

The Beiderbecke family, c. late 1904 or early 1905. L to R: Charles Burnette "Burnie" Beiderbecke, Bismark Herman Beiderbecke, Leon Bix (on his lap), Agatha Hilton Beiderbecke, Mary Louise.

PHOTO COURTESY WAYNE ROHLF

Bix at five.

PHOTO COURTESY WAYNE ROHLF

STATE OF IOWA.                                    COUNTY REGISTRAR
County of Scott                                   Vital Statistics

# Certification of Birth

Name___LEON BIX BEIDERBECKE___

I, ELMER JENS, do hereby certify that I am the Clerk of the District Court in and for said county and state, and as such official I have the possession and control of all records of births in and for said county, and am charged with the duty of keeping said records, that in Book___6___ Page___24___ of said birth records is found and appears the following entry in reference to the birth of the above named.

Name ___Leon Bix Beiderbecke___ Sex ___Male___

Date of Birth___March 10, 1903___

Place of Birth___Davenport___

Mother's full maiden name___Agatha J. Hilton___

Full name of Father___B. Her. Beiderbecke___

Name of Medical Attendant___Not shown___

Date of Filing Return___During the year 1903___

Given under my hand and official seal on this___30th___ day of___January___ A. D. 19 63

(SEAL)

Clerk of District Court

By _____
                                                  Deputy

About this time, the Grand Avenue Prodigy made the *Democrat* again, in a feature article headlined "SEVEN-YEAR-OLD BOY MUSICAL WONDER, Little Bickie Beiderbecke plays any selection he hears!"

Leon Bix Beiderbecke, aged seven years, is the most unusual and the most remarkably talented child in music that there is in this city. He has never taken a music lesson and he does not know one key from another, but he can play in completeness any selection, the air or tune of which he knows.

"Little Bickie," as his parents call him, has always had an ear for music. When he was two years old, Mrs. Beiderbecke says that the child was able with one of his chubby fingers to play the tune of "Yankee Doodle." It was not as distinct, by any means, as he can play now, but even then the tune could be detected as it was running through the child's mind. It must not be understood that he still plays with one finger and one hand. He plays every selection that he learns as completely in the bass and treble clef as it is written. In fact, so acute is his ear for music that if his mother plays a piece in another key than that in which "Bickie" has always played it, the child will sit down and play the piece in exactly the same key with proper bass accompaniment.

As a rule, however, if he hears and learns the air of a new piece he will play it in one or two, and perhaps three or four, flats. In fact, he plays most of his pieces in flats.

The child has a love for music. It is such a satisfaction and delight to him that if he is a little out of sorts, as any child occasionally is, his spirits are always brightened by a suggestion from his loving mother that they go to the parlor and play a little on the piano.

When "Bickie" is playing the piano, he never looks at the keys; he never watches his hands. To one watching and listening to the child playing the piano, it might seem that the child's mind was not on what he is playing, because his eyes are centered upon objects about the room or he is looking into space with apparently no thought of the piece he is playing. But a careful observation of that gaze and of the child indicates that his mind is absorbed in the music, in the melody that he is playing.

"Bickie" attends the Tyler school on Grand Avenue, across from the Beiderbecke home, and whenever Prof. Otto comes to the school he plays the violin and calls upon Bix to play the accompaniment on the piano.

Mrs. Beiderbecke is a gifted pianist and the child hears and has always heard music at the home. His mother is contemplating engaging an instructor, even at the child's tender age, for the reason that she fears that his playing will become too mechanical and that he will never fancy playing by note.

Clearly, young Bix had advanced by this time beyond the everything-in-C stage described by Mary Louise. Prof. Ernest Otto, musical director for the Davenport School system, conducted regular summer concert programs, many outdoors; he urged the Beiderbeckes to bring Bickie along. They did, but the boy, increasingly independent of mind and temperament, scarce concealed his boredom at such cultural force-feeding. He went his way, playing his tunes at the piano, and otherwise doing most of the things others of his age were doing.

Easy, and fun, to loll on the playground grass with other neighborhood boys during the hot summer days and evenings, listening to the sounds of Davenport changing before them. Evenings, especially, if you lay very still and strained your ears, you could hear the gay dancing music from the tall, brightly-painted riverboats down at the waterfront.

The Mississippi at Davenport is broad and muddy and slow-moving, ideal turnround and mooring point for excursion steamers up from New Orleans, Cape Girardeau and St. Louis. The young Louis Armstrong, playing the boats with Fate Marable as early as 1919, recalled that the Streckfus brothers kept most of their stern-wheelers moored at Nahant, outside Col. Davenport's former Iowa settlement, during the winters. But each Memorial Day the river became a carnival of boats and people and music, a flamboyance and reckless life style quite in contrast with the Beiderbeckes' sedate existence on Grand Avenue. It had been there from the start, of course, and the early settlers had welcomed its freedom and abandon. But a combination of time and cultural habit saw to it that Carl Beiderbecke and many of his contemporaries fashioned for themselves a life which in great measure reproduced the one they had left, though in a new setting. It was at all events an effective means of establishing visible class distinctions in a conspicuously classless society, one still redolent in many ways of the frontier. Through this supremely ironic process, a middle class aristocracy took shape in such communities as Davenport which preserved and perpetuated many of the particularly European values the settlers had thought to leave behind them in coming thousands of arduous miles to new shores.

Now, while still welcome and dynamic, the levee and its bustle were also coming to be viewed as a threat to the morality and cultural purity of the young, a potentially dangerous diversion and distraction, an insidious form of arousal confronting stolidly Victorian values. Miss Alice Barrow, teacher-investigator for educational and welfare organizations, spoke for the "silent majority" of the time when, after a study of the effect of jazz and ragtime music on midwestern towns in 1920, she wrote:

> The nature of the music and the crowd psychology working together bring to many individuals an unwholesome excitement. Boy-and-girl couples leave the (dance) hall in a state of dangerous disturbance. Any worker who has gone into the night to gather the facts of activities outside the dance hall is appalled, first of all perhaps, by the blatant disregard of even the elementary rules of civilization . . . We must expect a few casualties in social intercourse, but the modern dance is producing little short of holocaust . . .[3]

"Bickie" fast became "Bixie" among his growing circle of friends. He, Alphonso "Bay" Henry, Larry Andrews, Harry Schantz, Reed Severn and other youngsters looked to the levee as a fascinating unknown, all the more exciting for the bitterness with which some of their parents inveighed against its alleged evils. While there is little evidence that either Agatha or Bismark waxed particularly vehement about such matters, Bixie was nevertheless strongly advised not to wander down toward the river if he knew what was good for him.

Sometimes it was hard. There were evenings, Bay Henry said, when even up on Grand Avenue the music was so clear that it "could be heard like it was in your front parlor. Often Bixie, with two pieces of wood in

---

3. Leonard, *op. cit.*, pp. 34–35, 176.

Bix at eight with his mother.

Bix at about nine, near his home.

his hands . . . would sit there on the playground grass tapping out the rhythm he was hearing from the riverboats.

"In the summertime the excursion boats—the Quincy, St. Louis, St. Paul, J.S., Capitol or City of New Orleans—would ply the Mississippi from mouth to source, stopping here and there for a week at a time. Each boat had a steam calliope and a small band for dancing. When the boats moved up and down the river the steam calliopes and bands would pour forth that music, never to be forgotten . . . that was the music Bixie cherished."

A few weeks after beginning Miss Myrtle Petersen's third grade class at Tyler School, Bixie came down with an unusually severe case of "summer complaint"—chronic diarrhea—which soon gave way to scarlet fever. It meant too long an absence for him to return to the third grade, so the family withdrew him for the remainder of the 1911–1912 school year.

Aggie, anxious to keep her son's mind occupied as he recovered, took Al Petersen's advice at last and engaged a piano teacher, Prof. Charles Grade (Graw-deh) from Muscatine, 40 miles west of Davenport. The professor came once a week—and very soon found he had taken on a major problem. He would assign the boy a lesson to learn for the following week, gladly obliging when asked to play each selection over first "so I'll know how it sounds." The same musical memory which had recorded "Oh, Mister Dooley" from Agatha Beiderbecke's parlor performances now whirred quietly into operation, registering each selection note for note—slips and all; if the professor made a mistake in his demonstration, it showed up in the prodigy's own rendition the following week. It was probably this which finally tipped Grade off to what was going on; exasperated, he now demanded the boy learn his lessons "the right way," and to this end stubbornly refused any further "preview" performances. Instead, he forced Bixie to sight-read through each new lesson. This way, he told Aggie, he would have a means by which to judge his pupil's progress.

And progress it was—but not exactly as expected. Bixie worked out each selection, to be sure; but once having figured out more or less how it went, he merely filled in the detail from imagination. As a result, nothing came out the same way twice—a fact hardly appreciated by the Professor. For Grade, this was simply too much.

"I'm terribly sorry, Madam, but I do *not* believe I can teach your son anything further about the piano," he announced one day after a particularly imaginative hour's improvisation. "I play something for him, he plays it back—with 'improvements.' I do not think I can be of any further assistance to you or to him."

And with an emphatic squaring of shoulders he left, saying yes, the boy was indeed precocious, probably deeply gifted musically. But he was not yet old enough to relate the painstaking, often tedious business of learning to read music from printed notes, reproducing the ideas and even feelings of others, to his own way of "having fun" with the piano.

By summer 1912 Bix was well again, though hardly looking forward to returning to school. Most of his friends had been promoted a grade ahead of him during his long absence, and this meant new faces and a lot of book learning after a year's loafing. But come Monday, September 2, he was there, cowlicks plastered down with water and bay rum, a model child in blue velvet Lord Fauntleroy suit taking his place in Miss Blythe Bennett's third grade.

A year at home had been fun, and the daily round of the three R's soon proved anything but that. Little by little, school became just hours of clock-watching, and come 3:30 in the afternoon he was off and running for the playground or for home. Inevitable, now, that the music wafting up Grand Avenue on the lilac fragrance of a warm May night should draw him all the more strongly.

Sometimes, Mary Louise admitted, the river was about the only place around where the breezes were cool and the air fresh. "You know, in the Mississippi Valley we have these great bluffs which run along either side of the river, and the hot air settles down in there and gets mixed up with the steam from the river and—well, there's your day. The town is right there and sometimes it really got stifling. It was cooler up on the bluffs— or right down by the river, although we weren't allowed down there."

Allowed or not, Bix began to take private excursions down toward the levee, excursions which became more daring as he grew. Aggie fretted about it at first, but as the boy approached his twelfth birthday she seemed to adopt a boys-will-be-boys kind of resignation. Even this forbearance must have been strained the night a riverboat captain called from Muscatine to say he had found a lad on board his ship, which had cast off from Davenport earlier in the day. The boy had announced himself as Leon Bix Beiderbecke, of 1934 Grand Avenue, and volunteered his services as a calliope player. The captain, while acknowledging that the stowaway "played that thing like blue blazes," averred he was just a mite too young and would be sent home forthwith.

Another, much later, time, said Mary Louise, "we were just sitting down to dinner without him when the strains of 'Smiles' came floating up from a riverboat calliope. It must have been all of five miles away, but you could tell in a second who was playing it. He hadn't come home to supper, but at least, then, we knew where he was."

"Smiles" dates from 1919, meaning that Mary Louise's fondly-remembered tale concerns a rather older Bix. But it is consistent with an early-established pattern, even if her estimate of the distance from the levee to Grand Avenue is a bit generous.

On Sunday, June 28, 1914, nine days after Leon Bix Beiderbecke finished Miss Frances Martin's fourth grade, a Serbian zealot in the Bosnian city of Sarajevo shot the Archduke Franz Ferdinand, heir to the Austrian throne, and set in motion a chain of events which were to involve all Europe—and the world—in a war of unprecedented size and bloodshed. For the moment the United States tried to stay uninvolved, but within three years President Woodrow Wilson got Congress to declare war on Imperial Germany and the other Central Powers.

Charles "Little Bix" Beiderbecke, in his sophomore year at Iowa State College, followed most of his classmates and enlisted at once in the army. All the more important, given the state of the national temper, for Americans of German extraction to make open declaration of their loyalty. For Bismark Beiderbecke, named for the very German who had united the enemy, it was a time of mixed emotions: embarrassment at the name and ancestry in which he had always taken pride, yet a father's satisfaction at seeing his first-born son preparing to fight under the banner of the country which had received Carl Beiderbecke and allowed his progeny to prosper.

Bixie, age 14, took little notice. Davenport was a long way from Europe, and there was no radio or television to explode the Somme, the Argonne or Verdun into the parlors of the millions. Life went on more or less as usual. Aggie's younger son was fast growing into a handsome youth and a skilled, if still intuitive, pianist. The family was often far more deeply occupied with the pros and cons of giving Bix a formal musical education than with the war news in the headlines of the *Democrat*.

Music might indeed soothe and refine the spirit and develop the mind, but as Mary Louise remembered it, "It wasn't the music we regretted, but the professional part of it. Somehow we couldn't forget the old feeling instilled in us from Grandfather—that professional music wasn't exactly a gentlemanly art . . . we were growing more and more discouraged, as it looked to us as though we were going to have a musician in the family in spite of anything."

In January, 1917, while the United States teetered on the brink of war, events were taking place in New York City which would realize the family's worst fears. Five white musicians from New Orleans, billed as "the jasz band," opened January 27 in the "400 Club" room of the newly-completed Reisenweber Building at Columbus Circle, Eighth Avenue and 58th Street. After an initial period of uncertainty, the public responded with cheers to the music they played; it evoked marching bands and black ragtime piano "ticklers," society orchestras, folk songs and spirituals, the chaos of the machine age superimposed on the lazy traditions of the South. It clattered, rattled, jumped, sputtered, crooned and cried. It was played on the instruments of the marching band—cornet, clarinet, trombone, drums—with the piano thrown in to furnish harmonic and rhythmic support.

New Yorkers were tense and depressed at the prospect of war, and the new music, full of abandon and carefree gaiety, was just what they needed to let off steam. Within two weeks after its opening the band's name was up in lights over Columbus Circle and its music had been recorded, if with trepidation, by the prestigious Columbia Graphophone Company. The firm, far from convinced of the salability of the squeals and gargles which had forced one executive to slam his door in a fury at what he thought a practical joke, shelved the band's two titles in their files. The "jasz band," now known as the Original Dixieland Jass Band, turned up shortly afterwards on two selections issued by Columbia's chief competitor, the Victor Talking Machine Company. Victor's "Livery Stable Blues" and "Dixie Jass Band One Step" found their market ready and waiting; sales in the first three weeks exceeded Victor's—and the band's—wildest hopes. Columbia, realizing too late that it had missed a winning bet, exhumed its own coupling for issue; but by now the band belonged to Victor. Its recordings were distributed nationally. The Original Dixieland Jazz Band had arrived, and though Leon Bix Beiderbecke, just starting high school in Davenport, Iowa, did not yet know it, his destiny was now decided.

Bix at eleven with some Davenport pals.

Bix at about eleven with his class at Tyler Elementary School. Bix easily recognizable at far right, second row.

Charles Burnette Beiderbecke, Bix's elder brother, at his Davenport home in the late 1950s.

Vera Cox, age 16; Davenport High School photo.

# Chapter 2

World War I ended in armistice Monday, November 11, 1918, not a moment too soon for Lt. Charles Beiderbecke, by then an instructor at a Louisville, Kentucky, officers' training camp. Instead of waiting, uncertain, for assignment and possible combat "over there," he was now, exhilarated, on a train home to Davenport, a healthy wad of U.S. Army separation pay in his pocket. All at once, life looked every bit as sunny as the golden day rolling by outside the window, and "Little Bix" was in a mood to celebrate.

"I had a fair amount of loose cash with me," he said. "So a little while after I got home—must have been sometime into December—I bought a Columbia graphophone, the old windup type, and later a few records to go with it, and brought them home for the family."

Among the overtures and operatic arias was a "popular" oddity—the Original Dixieland Jazz Band's performances of its own one-step novelties "Tiger Rag" and "Skeleton Jangle," recorded in New York March 25 for the Victor Talking Machine Company. The record was the quintet's third for Victor, and like its predecessors was selling fast all over the country.

Neither Bismarck Beiderbecke nor his wife was particularly charmed by the blare and clatter of syncopated effect. But Leon Bix, now 15 and in his freshman year at Davenport High School, was intrigued. Here were five instruments playing successfully together without apparent planning, and certainly not chained to the tyranny of the printed note. Musical anarchy, if Professor Grade, Ernest Otto or Uncle Olie Petersen—or even Bismark and Agatha—were to be believed. Yet the music *worked*, it all seemed to fit. And it was fun. No clash or harsh discord. And at the center, driving "Tiger Rag" along with what must have seemed irresistible momentum, was a cornet. Bix did not know that he was the "D. J. LaRocca" to whom both titles were credited on the label, but he did know he liked the silvery edge of the tone coming strong and clean through the big speaker of the windup graphophone in the parlor.

Bix's reaction both surprised and vaguely alarmed Agatha. Where before he had been loath to practice any music with a view to learning it, the boy appeared to be doing just that with the noise (it could hardly, she thought, be called music) on this record. He set up the machine just to the left of the piano, then pushed the turntable speed lever back to its slowest point to pick out, note by note, the cornet's phrases. Then, having learned them, he again let the turntable spin at normal speed and played along on the piano.

This went on for several weeks, amid awkward silences and puzzled looks from parents, brother and sister. Aggie crossed her fingers: Bix had a way of becoming deeply absorbed in momentary preoccupations, passing interests which faded as rapidly as they appeared. She could only hope this, too, would soon pass.

One mid-January day he came banging in the front door with a whoop that brought his mother running.

"Look, Mother, isn't it just swell?" Agatha stopped and stared, heart sinking. Her son, gangling and beginning to tower over her, held out a dented, tarnished silver-plated cornet. "I borrowed it from Lee Ely, down the street. Isn't it great? Pretty, too." Lea Ely, (called "Lee"), a quiet, scholarly boy later to become a professor at Yale University, had long since given up early aspirations to be a cornetist, preferring the more easily accessible mandolin. His cornet had lain for months in a closet, unused and forgotten. Now, abruptly, it had a new home.

The next few days were a trial for the Beiderbecke household, Bix showing up early for breakfast to wolf down his shredded wheat, cocoa, toast and two eggs in a scramble to get to the cornet before he had to leave for school. Then, come afternoon, he was back in the straight-backed chair in front of the phonograph, trying with short, blasting—and for the most part wrong—notes to reproduce Dominick James "Nick" LaRocca's lead on "Tiger Rag" and "Skeleton Jangle."

More than once his parents, returning from a night out, found their son, in pajamas, huddled over the graphophone, listening.

Aggie worried lest the neighbors complain about all the blaring. Bismark grumbled but said little. Neither Mary Louise nor Charles, puzzled, knew what to make of it. At first, Bix found what he wanted by simple trial and error, pushing down different combinations of the instrument's three valves until the desired note came out, thus stumbling accidentally but logically on the unorthodox fingerings he was to use all his life. First he discovered that each valve, pressed down alone, would yield a different note; hence it was natural, once he began producing recognizable pitches, that he play concert "G" with the third valve, just as he played "A" with the middle one and "Ab" with the first. Only years later did he learn that for reasons of convenience and, occasionally, intonation, brass teachers recommend other, more complicated fingering patterns.

About two weeks after the siege began, and perhaps at Agatha's behest, Bix bought himself a cardboard straight mute at a Davenport music shop. "We all sighed with relief when that mute appeared," Mary Louise said. "Then, suddenly it seemed, as though a light had dawned, he was able to play, head up close to the graphophone, mute in place, so sweetly and quietly that we could read on the other side of the room without being disturbed."

Bix was developing into a handsome, well-built and personable young man, increasingly popular with the Davenport girls. One such was Vera Cox, whom he had met at school. He spent frequent afternoons at the Cox home, a few blocks from his own, inevitably winding up at the piano.

"He knew lots and lots of tunes," said Vera, a lifelong Davenport resident. "We would all sing when he played . . . he bounced up and down at the keyboard, and his fingers were always very straight, not the way I'd thought piano players played. My mother always had to shoo him out in order to get him home for supper."

36

Bix, too, was far from unaware of petite, pigtailed Vera. But what to do about it? "My, but he was shy . . . he often followed me home from school —but on the other side of the street, usually half a block behind me. He was very charming . . . his eyes sort of sparkled, and he always had something witty to say, never got angry."

Vera was there, beaming her pride and admiration, when Bix, Larry Andrews and a bunch of other Tyler kids got "Putzi" Trinkle, the janitor, to flood the big hill behind the school for sledding and skating. As Larry remembered it, "About five of us nuts who had no brains got out our skates and did stunts on them down the hill.

"Boy, could Bix ever skate! He was a natural athlete, all right. Douglas Fairbanks was just starting his run of pictures then and Bix could do all the things he could do in climbing, jumping and that sort of stuff. And I mean *do* them. I don't believe he ever had an overcoat, or at least I never saw him with one."

Larry, too, had taken a shine to Vera, occasioning a friendly rivalry between the two boys. "We shared her time. He'd skate with her one day at Central Park Lagoon, I'd do it the next. Later on, when we started dating, I'd take her to a picture show one night, he the next, and so on . . . actually there were two girls. Vera was the important one and Dorothy Albright was the fill-in, but there was no question that we both liked Vera best."

Summoning the courage to ask Vera out was, for Bix, a personal ordeal, and in keeping with his upbringing he did it by the rules. "He asked my mother first if it would be all right," she said. "His father came to call with him to make sure our parents had no objections . . . but after that he was always asking me out to parties and things.

"In those days, dating wasn't quite what it has come to mean today. The most important thing was to have fun together, often in large groups. In fact, very often Bix's sister, who was a few years older than he, would date Ferd Korn, the son of a local bakery owner, while he—Bix, that is—took me out. We never thought it possible that Ferd would become my husband." Vera married the baker's son some years later. Korn died in 1958.

If music, dating and hijinks on skates were Bix's kind of fun, schoolwork decidedly was not. He was having particular trouble with algebra, and grumbled bitterly at being forced to sit at the dining room table every evening to do it. Although the Beiderbeckes, because of family closeness and more substantial means, tended to remain aloof from social contact with those outside their immediate circle, Aggie decided it was time for direct action to boost her son's lackluster performance at his studies. At her encouragement, he and Larry began getting together after school for joint homework sessions. Andrews, son of an indifferently successful hardware salesman, was entranced at what seemed the unlimited opulence of the house on Grand Avenue.

One night at the Beiderbecke dining room table, he took to investigating a mysterious bulge in the carpet near where Agatha normally sat. "My folks didn't have any hired help, and I knew nothing of the wiles of push-buttons . . . but every so often the maid kept poking her head in the door—or possibly it was the cook; the help was being called in every time

I shifted my feet under the table, and Bix was getting the biggest kick out of it. But he didn't tell me what the button was until he'd had a good laugh and thought I should know."

On another occasion "he, I and my dad worked until about twelve one night at my home trying to figure out an algebra problem on a man delivering coal. The problem's full particulars I don't remember now, but it was comical to Bix that he couldn't get it, what with his father a coal dealer."

His efforts on the cornet were still fumbling and secret, but Bix's reputation as a pianist was growing fast among his fellow-students and their families. Inevitably, when a group of Davenport High students thought of organizing a little band to play for Friday afternoon tea dances in the gym, his name came up. Dorothy Albright's brother "Erkie," a pianist of more enthusiasm than ability, organized the first rehearsal in early March at his own home. Others taking part included Bob Struve, now showing promise as a trombonist, and Richard Fritz Putzier, who had just enrolled in Davenport High, on cornet.

Erkie and Bob had heard the Original Dixieland Jazz Band records, and jumped right into a clumsy attempt to reproduce "Tiger Rag." Putzier, already a trained player who sight-read well enough to accept paid engagements, sat puzzled, his shiny, silver-plated Conn Victor cornet across his lap. Then, tentatively, he tried a few notes.

"Frankly, I had, up to that time, never heard of this dixieland music. But as we played I began to get a bit of the idea and sort of liked it. Then, after about half an hour, someone looked out the window and said, 'Oh, here comes Bix.' I looked out. There was snow on the ground, I remember that. There, outside, was this boy in kneepants, cap and short overcoat hotfooting it toward the house. He came in all bright-eyed and enthusiastic and headed for the piano.

"I liked him immediately, but when he sat down and played I couldn't figure out exactly what he was doing. The other fellows seemed to get a great kick out of his playing, so I laughed along with them, though I wasn't exactly sure what I was laughing at."

Fritz and the kid in the cap took to each other at once, and Putzier became a frequent guest in his new friend's home. But Bix never once let on that he was working on the cornet. "He would sit down at the piano and play the various 'breaks' along with the records. He wanted me to listen to parts played by the cornet, clarinet and piano. I stayed with him many times overnight, but I never heard him mention this horn he got from Lee Ely, nor did I see it."

The little band soon learned enough tunes to fill a one- to two-hour tea dance, and were an immediate hit Friday afternoons in the high school gym. Youngsters came stag to the functions, boys entering through one door and girls another. Each paid ten cents admission, an easy way for any participating class to raise money. Bix, for once not asked to read music, found he could rely on his ear to "fake" the songs. The band set up in a corner of the gymnasium, and couples dancing by took to shouting encouragement to the young musicians. One such greeting produced an unexpected reaction.

"Come on, Bismark, make it hot!" Bix, engrossed in a solo, reddened. He whirled and leaped to his feet, glaring. "Who said that?" Putzier singled out Loring "Bob" Pollock, the Davenport High head cheerleader. There followed a few furious moments of half-whispered, angry dialogue between the two, band and students looking on in surprise, ending with Pollock striding sullenly away. "We couldn't hear what was said," Fritz reported, "but we'd all heard Bob call Bix Bismark and it was obvious Bix told him to lay off calling him by that name." World War I had left its mark.

Bix kept plugging away on the cornet, and by late spring had worked up enough confidence to approach Al Petersen for advice. Uncle Olie, whatever his reasons, was less than encouraging. "Why don't you try the violin first, and get yourself a good, solid musical foundation?" was the substance of his reply. Bix went home and practiced some more, dodging his mother's questions about the session. He never mentioned it again.

Come summer vacation, Fritz Putzier landed himself and his high school friends a job. The captain of the *Julia Belle Swain*, a Percy Swain lines excursion boat out of Peoria, Illinois, needed a band in a hurry to fill a cancelled summer booking; Putzier, Struve and three others took it, but Bix, still only 16, was adjudged too young by his parents and could not go along. Another Davenport High student, Adolphe de Lindholm, played the piano. The job ran from mid-July through the end of the first week of September, which meant that Struve and Putzier had to leave a week early in time to start school. They put it to Captain Swain—who refused to hear of it.

"All the same, we felt our schoolwork was more important than playing another week or two," said Fritz. "So Bob and I snuck off the boat about midnight one night at La Salle, Illinois, while they were unloading a large group of passengers. On arriving in Davenport the next morning, I got in touch with a fellow, a cornet player by the name of Ray Otto, and persuaded him to finish the season on the boat. Thus I salved my conscience for having let the good captain down. It all worked out fine."

Bix, though homebound, got down to the docks often enough to hear the bands coming in on the riverboats. The dancing and entertainment music some of these groups served up was a far cry from that of the Dixieland Jazz Band. But it was live and new, and full of the flavor of a culture far removed from Davenport and its Germanic traditions. In early August the big Streckfus stern-wheeler *Capitol* pulled in, bringing Fate Marable's orchestra from New Orleans with Warren "Baby" Dodds on drums, Johnny St. Cyr on banjo and the 19-year-old Louis Armstrong on cornet. Louis' assertions that Bix "was playing a lot of pretty cornet" at this time can be discounted, but it is likely the two young musicians met briefly during the *Capitol's* stay in Davenport.

"He was a cute little boy," said Armstrong, all of three years Bix's senior. "He'd come down to hear the bands, and then go home and practice what he heard. He and I became friends the first time we met—he was the type of youngster I admired all the way. No matter how good the solo was that he played, he wasn't very much satisfied with it. He never seemed satisfied with his efforts; this was true in later years, too, even while he was driving all the cats wild."

Tuesday, September 2, marked the start of Bix's junior year at Davenport High. As Principal George Edward Marshall droned his way through an opening day assembly address, Putzier delivered his own whispered account to Bix of his summertime adventures aboard the *Julia Belle*

*Swain.* He ended by mentioning offhand that he had played an all-day job Saturday which had strained his already sore embouchure and was therefore thinking of switching to saxophone and wanted to pick up a bit of cash by selling his Conn cornet. Bix almost leaped out of his auditorium seat in excitement.

"Sell it? You mean that? How much?" His whisper was clearly audible several rows away. Putzier grinned.

"Probably $35." Bix couldn't wait for the rest of the assembly, but unceremoniously grabbed Fritz by the arm and herded him into the music room across the hall. There the deal was consummated, Bix delivering a down payment of $15, the balance to be paid off in two monthly installments of $6, plus an $8 payment at the end.

"He still owes me that $8," Fritz reflected recently. "Never did get around to paying it."

The Conn Victor cornet, a "long model" with thumbscrew-operated tuning slide mounted on the bell section back of the valves for a quick shift of the instrument's basic pitch from Bb to A, was to be Bix Beiderbecke's horn for the next several years; returning Lee Ely's battered old instrument with thanks, he set right to work practicing the Conn around the house.

One evening not many weeks later he waylaid Fritz at the corner of Third and Brady as Putzier, now a C-melody saxophonist of rather more enthusiasm than actual proficiency, waited for a trolley to take him over to nearby Bettendorf to play a high school dance. "It must have been sometime in November, because it was quite cold," said Fritz. "Bix was wearing a knee-length sheepskin coat and the sort of squashed-in hat typical of those times among school kids.

"He asked me if he could come out and sit in at the dance. I, of course, told him we'd love to have him, though I knew he'd only had the cornet six or seven weeks and hardly expected him to hit a note higher than middle C.

"I went on to Bettendorf Town Hall, up to the second floor, and joined the four other fellows in the band and the dance got underway. About an hour later, while we were right in the middle of a number, I saw Bix come in through the door, which was in the opposite corner from where we were playing. Without even taking off his coat and hat he made a beeline for the band—didn't bother to skirt the dancers but just cut right through, the shortest route he could take. Still with coat and hat on, he opened his cornet case, took out the horn, and had at it."

Putzier and Bob Struve, also on the job, were astonished. Playing softly in the middle register, and not without some hesitancy, Bix was filling the gaps between their melody phrases with "those cute little passages for which he later became so famous. We couldn't believe what we were hearing. It was just great. Some 'blue' notes or 'clams,' yes—but he was hearing things, and it was only his lack of knowing the horn, and a weak lip, that prevented him from getting it all out the way he wanted to."

Bix's interpretation of the dixieland style was already a variant on what he had learned off the Victor records. He had used LaRocca's straight-ahead melody statements as a point of departure for what he called "phrasing around the lead"; he used the one- and two-bar spaces between the standard cornet phrases for connecting material, either introducing the phrases or extending them, making the lead more supple and more easily converted into an independent solo line. The style sprang largely from Larry Shields's clarinet "fill-ins" to LaRocca's lead in the Original Dixieland Jazz Band, and its application to a brass instrument was unprecedented in 1919. The result of such an approach, Bix explained to Davenport drummer Jack Teegan, was a closer-knit, more melodic ensemble. "The band comes with you better this way," was his verdict. Within the ODJB's dixieland idiom, as in the white American midwest, there was little direct contact with the blues tradition, and it is hardly surprising that even later, as a mature artist, Bix displayed little affinity for the blues. His few recorded blues choruses, though highly melodic and often adventuresome, demonstrate another set of musical preoccupations entirely.

The school year passed with little event. Bix picked up some cornet-playing friends in Lloyd Jennison "Jimmy" Hicks and Esten Spurrier, both boys about his own age. When Hicks and Teegan played at Turner Hall in Davenport, and later at the Linwood Inn roadhouse about ten miles out of town, Bix showed up, Conn Victor in hand, eager to sit in. This zeal, however, did not extend to his schoolwork, which was worse than ever. Bismark, in hopes that discipline might force an improvement, slapped restrictions on his son's evening activities and took to supervising homework sessions himself. "What *is* this thing he has, anyway?" he would ask, uncomprehending. For a while the lessons rallied. Aggie even did his botany for him to pull it up. But as soon as the supervision was relaxed things began to slide again. Ultimately the music would win out, just as it did when Bix was with Vera Cox.

"If we were on a date, and there was an orchestra playing, chances are I'd be left high and dry while Bix ran off to listen to the band," she said. Her exasperation with this state of affairs became more pronounced with the growing awareness that Bix Beiderbecke had blossomed into a most attractive young man. He now stood five feet nine inches tall, weighed a well-distributed 150 pounds. His hair, once nearly blond, had darkened to auburn, and had an appealing way of spilling in locks over his forehead. He played baseball and excelled at tennis, winning a Davenport Outing Club cup one year in tri-cities competition. It was a full, Norman Rockwell kind of mid-American life, ice skates in the winter and swimming in summer. And when brother Burnie came home from Iowa University sporting a Beta Theta Phi fraternity pin, Bix was dazzled. He borrowed both Burnie's pin and that of Mary Louise's sorority and took to wearing both, telling Vera he, too, would soon become a fraternity man.

Meanwhile Burnie, perhaps irked a bit by the popularity trailing in the wake of his kid brother's musicianship, took a brief fling at the C-melody saxophone. Bix, wandering in one day, asked if he could "see" the instrument—and within a short time had worked out enough of the fingering to produce a simple tune. While this is no monumental accomplishment on the saxophone, whose basic C-major scale is fingered logically and in easy sequence, it appears to have been enough to discourage the elder Beiderbecke son from pursuing the matter further.

Burnie was not without his own influence on Bix. One spring day, said Vera, "I was sitting on our front porch, when up walked Bix. His big brother had been joshing him because we'd been going out on dates and he hadn't 'made any time' with me. Well, here I was sitting on the porch swing, and he just came walking up to me with a sort of mischievous smile on his face. All of a sudden he leaned over and gave me just the smallest peck on the cheek. He whooped for joy and bounded off the porch, shouting, 'I did it, I did it,' and tore home."

Summer was coming on, and with it the promise of riverboats, music and lots of leisure time. Despite his floundering studies, Bix was in high spirits, something abundantly apparent Friday evening, May 28, when Davenport High School presented its end-of-term Concert and Vaudeville Night at the Grand Opera House under the direction of Miss Alice Roger. By now both students and teachers were well aware of Leon Beiderbecke's musical aptitude; besides singing tenor in the boys' glee club, he was given two featured spots on his new instrument. First he joined Miss Iren Kier, the school piano accompanist, and four fellow students to form the "Black Jazz Babies" for a selection called "Far Away in the South," then stayed onstage for "Ma Punkin Sue," billed as a "jazz specialty" and featuring the tap dancing of classmate Ray Moore. Vera Cox was there that night, and her reaction coupled astonishment and pride.

"It was the first time many of us had heard him play the cornet," she said. "It stunned everybody—nobody realized how good Bix had become since he'd started playing. He was quiet, you know, never made much of a show about things. At first I remember feeling almost embarrassed when I saw him up there; I was afraid he'd make a mistake and everybody would laugh at him. He really thought he didn't have any real talent, and was honestly surprised when he got to be famous."

Summer vacation began Friday, June 18. Bix was now a regular sight on the Davenport docks as, one by one, the big boats came in, among them the stern-wheelers *Capitol* and *Washington* and the giant Streckfus side-wheelers *J.S.* and *St. Paul,* all carrying groups with such fanciful names as the "Metropolitan Jaz-e-Jaz Band," the "Ten Palmerette Jazzerites" and the "Ten Alabama Jazz Kings." Most of the boats worked the river from New Orleans to St. Louis, some as far north as St. Paul and Rochester, Minnesota. Years the water was high, the *Capitol* and *Washington* ran trips up the Illinois River to Peoria, and sometimes as far east as the Ohio River. There was always music, and Bix's appetite for it grew the more he heard. He took to phoning Struve and Putzier regularly.

"Hey, let's go on out in the country and play a few licks," and off they went. Fritz recalled lazy, sunny afternoons, the three of them perched on the wooden railings of a bridge outside town, when "we'd just cut loose with the dixieland music. He, Bix, blew as loud as he wanted to and—well, isn't it just a shame we don't have tapes from some of those sessions? They were just terrific."

Little Bixie was growing up very, very quickly.

Neal Buckley's Novelty Orchestra, probably taken just before Bix joined in July-August 1920. L to R: Bob Struve (trombone); Dick Woolsey (drums); Richard Fritz Putzier (C-melody sax); Buckley (piano); Harvey Berry (violin).

# Chapter 3

Neal Buckley, a young local pianist with a good business head, had been using Struve and Putzier for dance jobs; now, with the idea of a steady group taking root in his mind, he gave in to their urging and started hiring Bix. The young cornetist's excitement at this turn of events leaks through an attempt at a casual tone in a letter written Saturday, July 10, to Vera, then visiting her grandparents in Vermont, Illinois. His crush on the popular Davenport beauty is obvious:

Dear Vera:
Received yours of the 8th with much satisfaction, as I feared that you would forget one so unimportant as I. Yes, I am working, but at an environment that I consider having a good time, playing for dances in a hot orchestra, making piles of jack in preparation for a good time next fall with you?
In answer to your question whether anything new had happened I must say that I am sorry to say that I was asked at three (3) parties at which I was to take you. One has passed, Doddy Dowd's at which I had to take Bunny Hansen at the last resort, but I was filled with disappointment, emotion and beer at not being able to take you. Next Thursday is Hillie Kohler's party at which I'm bound to take you. Now, Very, getting down to brass tacks will you come home Wednesday and meet me at Galesburg or someplace and I'll bring you home, then Friday I'll take you to Geo. von Maur's party. For the love of all good things wire one word YES and then I'll write all arrangements to meet you. Then if desired, I'll take you back to continue your visit. *Please* wire yes . . . I might be able to beat fate's time by having you here anyway, if you'll only consent. Of all bad luck, this is the worst—to have all these parties while your [*sic*] away. Hurry and wire. In regard to Bob Pearson [here follows a large inkblot—ed.] Can you beat that—blotting the paper then walking into it? Well, coming back to Bob, he may be all right the first time, but you know what I mean! Tell your grandmother that old friendship is the best and that you've decided that I'm about as good as anyone, which I hope is true—tell her you're coming back to me. Well, Very, must close. Please answer.

Yours anxiously,
LEE[4]

"Say Yes"

Bix, Struve and Putzier were along on Friday and Saturday, July 30 and 31, when Buckley's newly-named "Novelty Orchestra" played for two evenings of dancing at the Linwood Dance Pavilion, not far from Linwood

---

4. A nickname Bix used with Vera. Cf. p. 281.

Inn. The three horns were blending better, and the band was gaining a following; work was coming in, and by Monday, August 30, when Bix Beiderbecke enrolled for his junior year at Davenport High, they had more than their share of bookings.

He had been playing cornet little more than a year, and there were still frequent moments when he faltered, and the music did not come out quite as intended. Some of his legitimately-trained schoolmates regarded him first with bewilderment, then outright amusement, because he appeared to be playing all wrong. Wayne Rohlf, one of those who had learned trumpet the "right" way, first laughed at Bix's fumbling but later came to revere it. Esten Spurrier was learning, too, sometimes as much by Bix's mistakes as his own. "I'd had lessons, played in the high school orchestra and band for awhile, but it was boring," Spurrier, still living in Davenport, told the authors. "We were both lousy, I'm sure . . . just a couple of embryo punks. But I will say he had enthusiasm, loved it—no lip, but he played diligently. He did *not* develop in Davenport as a player; his acceptance was mainly among the youngsters who thought along the same lines."

Fritz Putzier cited a case in point. At a dance hall job in Durant, Iowa, the owner, an elderly German with a heavy accent, grimaced in mock pain as he listened to Bix struggling manfully through a "hot" chorus. "Dat cornet player off yourss," said the old man, "he *squeeks* on dat ting!"

He had a point, said Putzier. "I certainly recall lots of 'blue' notes that night. He, Bix, was sitting right next to me, and I quite frankly got a little tired of some of the things he was doing, for he still wasn't quite with it. He would blat 'em out, however, and I had to admire his courage, right or wrong."

Not all musicians, especially the seasoned professionals, were quite so understanding. Around the beginning of the school term, Bix began showing up regularly to listen to the band of pianist Carlisle Evans, one of Davenport's best of the era, featuring the able cornetist Bill Zimmerman. Spurrier was often along, and remembered Zimmerman as "a good, solid cornet. Nice, phrased lead. Remember, cornet players were not too venturesome in those days. Most of them, Zimmerman included, played this kind of phrased, but pretty straight, lead with lead-in notes, little play-ups to the lead phrases. But we liked to listen to Bill, and I'm sure we benefited.

"What a character that guy was, speaking of Zimmerman. Drank his share, as they all did. Used to show up in a tux with yellow brown shoes to match. Nut on cars, always taking them apart and putting 'em back together. Bix and I got a big kick out of him, fingernails and hands imbedded in grease; we used to call him the 'black hand cornet player.' "

Zimmerman left Evans in late 1920 to join Earl Burtnett in California; his chair was taken briefly by Harold "String" Oermann, who played mostly trumpet but liked to take a cornet along on jobs for occasional "semiclassical" solos. He, too, was adept at a phrased, but essentially straight, lead. The appearance of young Bix when the Evans band was playing usually meant being pestered with entreaties to borrow "String's" cornet and sit in.

"You want to know what those pros thought of us then?" asked Spurrier. "Well, Evans at that time used a violin player named Bob Schurr, or Shears, I'm not sure which, who stood in front. This Schurr had a real nasal, twangy voice, slow-like. He'd spot Bix comin' down the floor and say, real slow out of the side of his mouth, 'Hey, String, hide the li'l horn, here comes that goddamned Beiderbecke kid.' But despite that, once in awhile they let him sit in anyway."

Bandsmen working for trumpeter Tony Catalano on the Streckfus steamers recalled Bix cajoling the veteran New Orleans bandleader to "let him play a chorus now and then. I can still see him," said Catalano's drummer Earl Bruckman, "sitting between Tony and myself with Tony's horn between his knees . . . there were also times when Tony took the horn away from him because what he was playing didn't fit."

Bix plugged on undaunted. On Friday, November 5, the Buckley sextet became "Billy Greer's Melody Jazz Band" for a dance upriver at Sabula, Iowa, under the promotion and leadership of Greer, a Davenport drummer slightly older than Bix and his friends. The job went well, and afterwards Bix and Struve amused themselves—if not the townsfolk—by singing two-part "hot licks" on the railroad platform. Once the train arrived, Bix climbed into a front coach, curled up on a seat by an open window, and fell asleep, head propped on his cornet case. With a staccato hoot, the locomotive puffed out of Sabula station, belching black clouds of coal smoke and soot; one caught the sleeping Bix squarely in the face, blackening him like an end man in a minstrel show. Putzier and the others were hardly able to contain their mirth as a furious Bix leaped to his feet, wrestled the window shut, and set about wiping the soot off his face.

The Buckley band was now sufficiently popular to bid for, and win, a job at the Terrace Gardens restaurant in the new Kahl Building downtown, set to open Thursday, December 23. Bix was elated at the thought of his first steady job, and his fellow-musicians were no less delighted at having him along.

"Bix was just gaining experience," said Fritz Putzier. "By the time Buckley landed that Terrace Gardens job he was ready to go, and while not perfect by any means, Buck was anxious to have Bix as a permanent member to give the band the drive and kick that would make it really spark. There was something about that drive of his, and the enthusiasm, even when he didn't pull off what he wanted to do, that was stimulating to all of us.

"The Gardens, too, was a nice place . . . sort of like a night club, with a dance floor at ground level and probably five or six terraces coming off it, each with tables for dining and each table with a small lamp. Nice, and attractive."

Everything looked rosy—until, less than a week before the opening, the conductor of the pit orchestra in the Capitol Theater, also in the Kahl Building, placed an angry phone call to Davenport tri-cities Local 67, American Federation of Musicians. "This band of punk kids," as he called them, were not union members, and what the hell were they doing playing in the same building as a dues-paying union group? He refused to allow his men to play unless something were done. Union executive Roy Kautz, himself pit orchestra pianist at the Orpheum Theater and a man who had little time for either jazz or "ear" musicians, delivered an immediate ultimatum to Buckley: either the entire band joined the union on the spot or it couldn't have the job.

Struve and Putzier had no worries. All it took to get a union card was a brief audition in front of one or more officials from the local to demonstrate command of the instrument and sight reading. The problem, obviously, was Bix; he could hardly read at all, and, in the eyes of legitimately-trained musicians, played the cornet "backwards." He stood not a chance of passing. The only possibility, a slim one, would be a group audition; the date was duly set for December 21, two days before the Terrace Gardens opening.

"We worked up a few numbers and got them sounding okay," said Fritz. "Then on the day of the audition, we agreed to meet at Hickey's cigar store, Third and Harrison, before going on over to union headquarters. I guess we were all nervous, for we all arrived at the store almost an hour early. Bix was shaky, and insisted we have just one more rehearsal. As the YMCA was just a block up the street, at Fourth and Harrison, we decided to do as he suggested."

Came the long-dreaded moment, and Buckley's Novelty Orchestra filed quiet and nervous into the audition room, a drafty, bare, high-ceilinged rehearsal hall with a few chairs at one end and an upright piano at the other. A string of Harvey Berry's violin broke as he tuned it; Dick Woolsey took an inordinately long time to set up his drums. Kautz, a severe-looking man in starched collar and neat, trimmed moustache, more than exemplified Esten Spurrier's later disparagement of Davenport as a "*very* predominantly German town, whose music was *over* legitimate . . . a dotted eighth was a dotted eighth, and a vibrato was *verboten*, only excusable in a solo and then used sparingly . . . we punks who played jazz were frowned on and ridiculed as 'chassers,' German accent for 'jazzers.'"

The six young musicians played, soft and shivering, through their pair of carefully-memorized dance selections. Once or twice Kautz stopped them, to ask for a passage again. Perhaps something in their nervousness had aroused his suspicions, for when they had finished he produced a small stack of sheet music, handed it out, motioning Buckley away from the piano.

"Now, gentlemen, let us start with the violin, please." One by one, the supplicants stepped forward to sight-read an unfamiliar solo, with Kautz furnishing the piano accompaniment. All passed, until Bix's turn came up. Putzier held his breath.

"The piano part was just a chord-like accompaniment with embellishments," said Fritz. "Not knowing the melody, Bix picked out the notes of the piano part and made an effort to play along, a fraction of a second behind. It was, of course, nothing like the part he was supposed to play." Kautz soon stopped playing and shook his head. No point in going on. Bix had failed.

Back at Hickey's afterwards, the band tried to cheer him up—with little success. Buckley's Novelty Orchestra could have the Terrace Gardens job, but it would be without Bix Beiderbecke. His five fellow-musicians took a vote: no Bix, no job. They turned the engagement down.

The new year 1921 brought new excitement. Davenport was close enough to Chicago to snare some big-time show business entertainment, which often meant music. The Columbia Theater, downtown, was on the Orpheum circuit, and was often used as a proving ground for new acts before they moved on to the big city. The shows changed every Thursday, said Esten Spurrier, and "Bix and I usually played hookey if there was anything we wanted to listen to. If it was really good, we managed to take in additional shows during the run.

"Frank Westphal's orchestra made the circuit several times and had an up-and-coming trumpet who took off; we haunted them. Also Wingy Manone came through as a single, billed as 'the one-armed Indian,' and played very interestingly . . . but we didn't have the guts to be 'stagedoor Johnnies,' so we rarely met anyone.

"Now in late January, Bee Palmer, the 'shimmy queen,' was booked in, apparently on a tryout basis. She had this fabulous five-piece band in which Leon Roppolo [often erroneously spelled Rappolo—ed.] was on clarinet and Emmett Hardy from New Orleans on cornet. We didn't miss a performance, the music was so great. But the act apparently got a bad report as being risque and it didn't last." They moved on to Peoria, where they broke up, leaving the New Orleans musicians hunting for work. Hardy and Roppolo returned to Davenport, where they joined Carlisle Evans, opening at the Coliseum Dance Hall Sunday, February 13. Also in the personnel was the local banjoist Louis Black, to accompany Roppolo later that year to Chicago, where both became charter members of jazz history's second significant white jazz ensemble, the New Orleans Rhythm Kings.

Emmett Louis Hardy, born June 12, 1903, just outside New Orleans, was a few months Bix's junior, but there is little doubt that he had developed into a far more accomplished cornetist by age 17 than had the Davenport youth. He had worked in his home city with the legendary bands of Norman Brownlee and Jack "Papa" Laine, developing a style softer in tone and less forceful than the brash LaRocca. The cornetist of the Dixieland Jazz Band later dismissed Hardy altogether, claiming that "if this man had played anywhere and would have been some great man I would have known about him." This can be discounted; Hardy was still a boy when Nick LaRocca left New Orleans, and died of tuberculosis at 22 in 1925, the year the older man returned.

Hardy never recorded, but some musicians who heard him insisted that he was not only a dominant influence on the young Bix, but actually originated the Beiderbecke way of "playing around the lead."

Jack Willett, drummer with Evans during the Hardy-Roppolo stay, endorsed this viewpoint. "In my opinion and that of a couple of old-timers still around, Bix definitely was influenced by Emmett Hardy's playing, and I can say that Bix's style was very much like Hardy's. It is too bad Hardy had to die so young, as, in my opinion, he was one of the greatest, but didn't live long enough to become known very well."

The younger Davenport musicians disputed this. "Bix's way of 'phrasing 'round the lead' was his own idea," Wayne Rohlf stated categorically. Spurrier expanded on the point with the insight of both a friend of Bix and an accomplished, respected jazz cornetist along similar stylistic lines. To his ears Hardy, like Zimmerman, played essentially an embellished lead in the by-then established straight-ahead style of the Dixieland Band. "Hardy was good, all right, and we enjoyed listening to him. But as far as Bix getting a pattern of style that was the basis for later virtuosity—no. In this sense, the whole Hardy myth has always been inexplicable to me. Sure —Bix plucked the best from what he heard, saved it, and dovetailed it into a distinctive style. But it was his own."

Spurrier and other Davenporters felt that Paul Mares, trumpeter with

Bee Palmer, "The Shimmy Queen," taken around 1921.

Carlisle Evans' Jazz Band at the Davenport Coliseum Ballroom in spring 1921. L to R: Jack Willett (drums); Myron Neal (tenor sax); Evans (piano); Emmett Hardy (cornet); Leon Roppolo (clarinet); Louis Black (banjo); Tal Sexton (trombone).

the New Orleans Rhythm Kings, was a pioneer in breaking away from the conventional formula; perhaps influenced by Roppolo's legato clarinet style, he smoothed out much of his instrument's disjointed lead role with connecting notes and longer phrases. Frank Guarente, featured trumpet with the Georgians, a small jazz group within the society dance orchestra of Paul Specht, did much the same thing after absorbing at first hand the influence of many of the black New Orleans pioneers.

But it was only with the emergence of Louis Armstrong that the idea of the virtuoso jazz trumpet or cornet solo found definitive expression. With Armstrong, the instrument freed itself entirely from the restrictions of its original marching and circus-band role. When Bix heard Louis later in Chicago, Spurrier said, he realized that King Oliver's young protege had "departed greatly from all cornet players . . . in his ability to compose a close-knit, individual 32 measures with all phrases compatible with each other—all the while based on the fundamental tune and chord structure being played. It evoked amazement and envy in all of us."

In 1921, however, Louis Armstrong was still to be heard only in New Orleans and on an occasional riverboat, and Emmett Hardy was about the most exciting thing around for Bix and his Davenport High School cronies. They took their opportunities where they found them, hanging around the Coliseum, which Mary Louise remembered as "kinda tough, not the most high-class place." The Evans band worked four nights a week, off on Fridays. Sometimes Bix and friends could scrape up the 75¢ per person admission charge, sometimes not; but when the money wouldn't go around, they could always slip around to the side of the single-story wooden building to listen and watch through the big windows.

Despite its setback at Roy Kautz's hands, Buckley's Novelty Orchestra continued to get work, including regular dances at Hayne's Dancing School and out at Davenport's Forest Park Pavilion during May and June. Fritz had ample cause to remember their job there the evening of Friday, the 13th of May. Finishing a saxophone solo, he glanced down to see who had been applauding so vigorously. There, clarinet in hand, stood a thin, sallow figure: Leon Roppolo. "He asked if he might sit in . . . we were overcome. Couldn't figure out why he'd come to hear us. Maybe he wanted to see what we had, or maybe just wanted to noodle around; but boy, were we ever thrilled," said Fritz.

The Coliseum closed for the summer Monday, May 30, and with it the Carlisle Evans band's steady engagement in Davenport. After a few one-nighters, they opened for the summer at Electric Park, Waterloo, Iowa. But by now the two guests from New Orleans had the urge to wander. Emmett Hardy gave his notice and left on Sunday, June 19, to join trombonist George Brunies (later he spelled it Georg Brunis) and other friends from home playing for Albert "Doc" Wrixon, drummer and leader of the band aboard the Streckfus steamer *Capitol*, which had brought Louis Armstrong upriver two years before. A week later Roppolo, too, departed.

Bix Beiderbecke had meanwhile taken a significant professional step forward by joining the Plantation Jazz Orchestra on board what a Streckfus Lines advertisement of the time hailed as "the mammoth, non-sinkable steamer MAJESTIC." A stern-wheeler whose five decks could take on close to 2,500 passengers, it worked the upper Mississippi from St. Louis to Winona, Minnesota, often in shallow waters where the larger side-wheel

Esten Spurrier, taken in Davenport, summer 1973.

flagships *J.S.* and *St. Paul,* because of their heavy draughts, could not go except in high-water seasons.

"You are as safe as in your own home on this steel, non-sinkable up-to-date steamer," said the advertisements, and the *Majestic* lived up to the pledge. It catered to private parties, traveling from a temporary central berth such as Davenport to points up and downriver, charging each passenger between 75¢ and $1.00 for a 12–15 hour ride, depending on the size of the party.

The Streckfus family, brought up in the old packet trade, had the kind of experience and flair for business which guaranteed them rapid success on the big river. They hired bands both black and white, and worked them both hard—though, as more than one musician recalled, there *were* differences in treatment. "They liked to give orders," said one, "and when it came to the nigger bands they knew no questions would be asked. The boys were glad to play. But understand, we played day and night—lived and ate on the boat, dumped our dance crowd at 11:30 or midnight, then immediately took off upstream or downstream for the next town where a church or industrial group were ready to load for their annual excursion, anywhere from 6:30 A.M. onwards. With such confinement, the temperament of the white boys could be more difficult, and such independence was something the Streckfus people wanted not at all."

Esten Spurrier, who broke in on the boats about the time Bix signed on the *Majestic,* provided vivid detail to illustrate the Streckfus penchant for discipline. "When you worked for Streckfus you were told exactly what tempos to play. I don't recall now exactly, but like a one-step at 160 beats per minute, slow-drag at 60, normal foxtrot, say, around 120; and nothing was left to chance—a captain at any time would hold a stopwatch on the band and you didn't deviate. At that time, especially, this sort of discipline worked better with colored boys than with white." Rehearsals, said Spurrier, were another Streckfus obsession. "If a band had a morning off or a long jump and no daytime trip, the band was expected to rehearse. With few new tunes and the constant playing of the same repertoire, it could be really a bore."

Some of the more colorful band names were strictly Streckfus improvisations, often applied to two or three different groups in the same season. "Streckfus used all these trick names to draw the people—sometimes would kick the whole band off and replace them, using the same name," said Spurrier.

Rome Siemons (pronounced Simmons) and Wade Foster, both from the Davenport-Rock Island-Moline tri-cities area, led the Plantation Orchestra on the *Majestic.* Foster, from Moline, was at this time still a violinist; he later gained wide reputation throughout the middle west as a jazz clarinetist in the "Chicago" style pioneered by the late Frank Teschmacher. Siemons, a pianist, had hired Bob Struve a month earlier on trombone; when the *Majestic* docked at Davenport in late June, trumpet man Chet Ogden found a wire from his father calling him home, and Struve suggested Bix as a replacement. Siemons agreed.

"At that time he was just another kid who liked to play, and certainly not famous," the pianist said. "I guess he played pretty much the same way he did later, but we didn't take a lot of notice of it. He was just another one of us music nuts."

# MOONLIGHT CRUISE
## on
## STEAMER WASHINGTON

SUN. JULY 1

Leave Wheeling 8:15 p. m.
Return 11:30 p. m. Fare
only 75c.

ELDER'S CELEBRATED
DE LUXE ORCHESTRA

BEAUTIFUL ROOF GARDEN
TWO CAFETERIAS
SIX SPACIOUS DECKS

WE WILL BE LOOKING FOR
YOU ON THIS PALATIAL
STEAMER WHERE EVERY-
ONE ENJOYS A SAIL, AS IT
WILL BE A LONG TIME TO
THE NEXT ONE.

TICKETS ON SALE AT
STEAMER 8 P. M.

Advertisement for Streckfus
Line steamers on the
Mississippi during the 1920s.

PHOTO COURTESY
LENNIE ESTERDAHL

A race on the Mississippi near Davenport between the stern-wheeler *Homer Smith* and
another, taken from the afterdeck of the second vessel. c. 1920.

PHOTO COURTESY LENNIE ESTERDAHL

The *Majestic* ran excursions out of Davenport on Tuesday, June 21, then on the 25th, 28th, and 30th. Bix, unaccustomed to such long hours and hard blowing, developed a large sore on his upper lip. But, said Siemons, he was clearly delighted to be in the band, and pitched in with his usual enthusiasm. "He had this tremendous lift, you know. It made us want to play even harder than we did."

Esten Spurrier came aboard to visit. "I can still picture in my mind the band with Bix in it. They all wore these 'Yama Yama' suits, sort of harlequin suits, and sat on the right side of the boat."

Wednesday, June 30, the steamer was plowing its way upriver toward Sabula when a Mississippi squall blew up out of nowhere. It had been an unpredictable summer, full of sudden shifts of weather; and now, with a clap of thunder, the heavens split open and sheets of rain, driven by warm, howling wind, pelted the "mammoth, non-sinkable steamer." It rolled and creaked and shuddered, passengers huddling inside or scrambling to the railings to be sick; the band, if a trifle haphazardly, played on.

Suddenly there was a bone-jarring lurch and a loud splintering noise as the *Majestic* groaned to a halt, a large tree limb sticking up through its dance deck floor. The steamer, clearly, was not *all* steel. "We'd run aground," said Siemons. "There we were, stuck fast in the mud just offshore, wind blowin' like mad and the rain just showerin' down." Passengers, terrified that the boat might capsize, milled about the decks; women screamed and fainted. Some rushed to the railings to shout for help, their voices disappearing into the wind. The captain, moving from group to group, tried to restore order with assurances that the Mississippi was quite shallow at this point and everyone would get off safely. He turned at one point to the band. "Keep playing, gentlemen, or sure as shootin' we're a'gonna have a riot on our hands." Bix clapped cornet to mouth as Siemons stomped off "Tiger Rag."

Little by little the crew talked groups of men, women and children into the *Majestic's* lifeboats, which ferried them a few hundred feet across choppy but shallow water to shore. Finally, with the customers off and the wind beginning to slacken, the musicians, trousers rolled up and instruments brandished, safari-style, above their heads, left their impaled craft and waded ashore through waist-deep water and ooze.

Quickly refloated and repaired, the *Majestic* made it back to Davenport in time for Independence Day celebrations July 4—only to find trouble awaiting its young band. The entire personnel had joined the musicians' union in Louisiana, Missouri, shortly after taking the job and before the arrival of Bix and Struve. But all were from the tri-cities area, and when they got back to Davenport, Local 67 cracked down.

"We showed them our cards, but the union wouldn't honor them," said Siemons. "They felt we should have joined there." Bix, of course, had no card at all, and several local musicians still feel Kautz's men had come "gunning" for him, making innocent victims of the others. After a long, heated and ultimately fruitless argument, the band gave up the job, Siemons staying on to work the ship's calliope "because the new band's piano player couldn't play it." When the *Majestic* cast off from Davenport on Friday, July 8, the Plantation Jazz Orchestra was no longer aboard. Nor was Bix Beiderbecke.

Bix came home to surprising news—and a lucky break. Doc Wrixon and

The Streckfus steamer *Washington* at its winter berth at Nahant, outside Davenport, c. 1920.

Albert "Doc" Wrixon and his band aboard the steamer *Capitol*, summer 1921, immediately after Bix Beiderbecke's abrupt departure. L to R: Johnny Watson (trombone); I. V. "Bud" Shepherd (piano); A. A. "Happy" Conger (banjo); Omer Van Speybrouck (tenor sax); George Byron Webb (alto sax); Vic Sells (cornet); Grant Harris (clarinet); Wrixon (drums).

his coterie of New Orleans talent had fallen out; Hardy, Brunies, and several others had quit on the spot, leaving the bandleader to recruit instant replacements. He got pianist Bud Shepherd, Omer Van Speybroek on clarinet and saxophone and now, at only a few hours' notice, he got Bix Beiderbecke on cornet. The *Capitol* sailed from Davenport Wednesday, July 6, just two days after Bix had been forced to leave the *Majestic*. There was no time for the union to find out; he was on and gone before anyone realized he had even been home.

The old stern-wheeler worked the river from Hannibal, Missouri, deep in Huck Finn country, all the way up to Winona, Minnesota, east of Rochester. Most of the trade was in 24-hour charter jobs—all-day private excursions followed by an evening's dancing and entertainment in port.

Bix, relaxed and relieved, settled down to playing—only to be pitched into dismay once again when the boat stopped early the following week at Davenport. Two Local 67 officials were waiting on the pier and marched angrily down to Wrixon's cabin for a lengthy and loud harangue about "this goddam kid who can't even read well enough to get a card." Wrixon, an older, established musician who commanded considerable respect in the tri-cities area, stood his ground and faced the union men down. But the victory was a temporary one, and he knew it.

"Look, Bix," he said the next morning, as the *Capitol* chugged down-river in a rare moment of brilliant summer sunshine. "I can't go on like this. We'll be in Davenport again at the end of the week, and those guys are gonna be around again after your ass. They can get me in one helluva lot of hot water over you."

Bix, at the rail, stared down at the brown water, silver-flecked, churning under the bow. "Yeah. I know. Not fair to you, is it?"

"Nor to you, lad. You know I like you, and we all like the way you play. But I don't see how we can keep you, unless you get a card."

"Sure. But I stand as much chance in Davenport as—"

"Yeah. I know. I know. But I don't know what else to do." He'd wait and see what happened Saturday, he said. If "those guys" gave him any more trouble, Bix would have to go.

Saturday the big steamer tied up at Davenport levee—and there, as Wrixon had feared, was an even bigger union delegation, looking sufficiently determined to leave no doubt as to their purpose in coming.

"Guess that's it, Bix," the bandleader said as deckhands lowered the gangplank. "It's been great. Sorry." They shook hands, and Bix went below to pack his things while Wrixon received the Local 67 officials with smiles and promises to replace him at once with a union cornetist.

Though disappointed, Bix was far from shattered at the outcome of his first two flings on the boats. There would be plenty of chance to play with Buckley, come fall; and in the meantime, he managed to land his first featured billing, when the "Bix Beiderbecke Five" played a dance August 5 at Hayne's Dancing School.

Bismark Beiderbecke had watched his son's growing involvement in riverboats, jazz bands and suspect company with growing misgivings. Bix's academic prospects were dubious. He had finished his junior year with only 14 graduation credits after flunking several subjects, so he was ineligible to enroll as a senior when school opened in September. Worse yet, he seemed to care less and less about it. If he stayed on in Davenport he was

*The* famous photo of Bix Beiderbecke, taken Tuesday, August 30, 1921, in a Davenport studio while Bix was on his way to play with Ralph Miedke's Society Orchestra.

Richard Fritz Putzier, taken a few minutes later.

PHOTO COURTESY RICHARD PUTZIER

sure to flunk out of high school, and the family would lose him to the perilous world of professional music and a future uncertain at best. A university education and subsequent success in business would then be, once and for all, out of his reach.

At first, Aggie and her husband contemplated sending Bix to University High School at Iowa City, operated by Iowa State University especially to help such "difficult" cases—students who, though not lacking in intelligence or native ability, had strayed from the approved path and needed special attention.

Bix, meanwhile, was keeping only too busy. Ralph Miedke hired him for the grand opening on Tuesday, August 30, of the Moline State Trust and Savings Bank. The band was scheduled to play from 1 to 6 P.M., and for the first time in his life the younger Beiderbecke had to wear a tuxedo.

"How do I look, Mother?" he asked, turning in the bedroom mirror. Aggie, full of doubt over her son's future, had nevertheless to admit that he cut a handsome figure. Bix took the stairs two at a time, stopping only to grab his cornet. "Where are you off to?" his mother asked, puzzled. "It's only nine in the morning, and you don't have to play for another four hours."

Bix laughed. "Fritz and I are going to have our pictures taken in these li'l ol' fancy suits." And out the door he bounded. The photograph taken that August morning in 1921 has become the model by which Bix Beiderbecke is now recognized. All others are compared to it; even though later photos are more representative of what he looked like at the peak of his career, this early likeness remains one of the chief ingredients of the process which eventually turned the flesh-and-blood Davenport youth into the "Young Man with a Horn" of legend.

Clear-eyed, hair parted just off the middle in the fashion of the day, he contemplates the camera with an earnestness which seems to reflect the intensity of his dedication to music. The Conn Victor rests, proudly displayed, on his right thigh. There is a combination of elements in the face —seriousness, refinement and white-middle-class good manners, youth and romanticism; it is a face which could have been the stuff of a folk legend even if Bix Beiderbecke had never played a note. Few other photographs have captured so much in one click of a shutter.

Agatha and Bismark were still making inquiries, and after much soul-searching came to a decision at last. For reasons no longer known, they passed up University High School; instead, Bismark enrolled his wayward son in Lake Forest Academy, a boarding school outside Chicago with the kind of academic and disciplinary standards certain to guide Bix back on to an approved path. Mary Louise, moreover, was now teaching in Chicago, and could drop by periodically to keep an eye on her brother's progress.

Toward the end of the week of September 4, 1921, Bix Beiderbecke left Davenport for Lake Forest, located on its own verdant grounds about 35 miles north of Chicago. In sending him there, his parents had unwittingly furnished him an ideal launching pad into the very life from which they most wished to protect him.

The Lake Forest Academy "Lower Middle" class, autumn 1921. Bix at far left, middle row.

Lake Forest instrumental group. Prof. Koepke stands at the center of the rear row, with Bix and "Cy" Welge immediately to his right. Clinton Parker (trumpet) and Sid Stewart (saxophone) are easily identified in the front row.

# Chapter 4

A loud knock caught E. Clinton Parker in the final, impassioned solo cadenza of an air from Bellini's "Norma." Vaguely annoyed, he laid his new King trumpet on the bed and went to answer the door.

He found a young stranger about his own age, well-dressed, and sporting an expansive smile. "Hi, I'm Bix Beiderbecke." The newcomer extended his hand. "I live downstairs and just heard you playing. Mind if I come in?"

Late September, and the academic year 1921–22 at Lake Forest Academy was rolling into gear with its usual complement of new faces and uncertain adjustment to life away from home. Clinton Parker had just enrolled as a junior, and was still spending most of his time practicing in his new third-floor room in East House dormitory.

Bix Beiderbecke glanced first at the King trumpet, then at the Arban book on the music stand. "I'm in the school orchestra," he said, sitting on a corner of the bed. "We'd like to have you join us."

Parker brightened. "You play an instrument too?"

"Yep. Play cornet m'self."

This was puzzling. Nobody played cornet any more; his teacher, old Heinie Byers, had said trumpet was the thing nowadays. Cornet was old-hat, a brass-band relic. "Cornet? How come? Why not a trumpet?"

Beiderbecke laughed and picked up the King, holding it out at arm's length to let its silver finish catch the light. "Nope. Cornet's my baby, all right . . . I can do more dixieland on 'er." Clinton Parker had hardly ever heard the word "dixieland" used this way before, let alone the music it obviously described. His perplexity was apparent to his visitor, who suggested they continue the conversation at the upright piano in the parlor downstairs.

Bix himself had arrived at Lake Forest only two weeks before, but was already involved in nearly every musical organization on campus. As his mother had feared, his erratic performance at Davenport High School had left him without credits enough to enroll as a senior or even as a member of the "upper middle" class, the Academy's designation for its juniors. As a result, he was one of 31 students in the "lower middle," or sophomore class. But Headmaster John Wayne Richards, whose faculty of twelve instructors saw to the scholastic and disciplinary needs of Lake Forest's 129 students, assured Agatha and Bismark Beiderbecke that their son would be "well seen to here."

Within his first two weeks, Bix had auditioned successfully for the orchestra on cornet and gained a name as a versatile pianist. He lived two flights down from Clinton Parker, at the northwest corner of the ground floor of East House.

At the parlor piano he raced through "Ostrich Walk," "Tiger Rag" and a few other dixieland numbers; his newfound friend stood by in mute amazement, as Bix "imparted to me the mysteries of dixieland jazz." But the loud clearing of a throat brought the demonstration to an abrupt halt. "Gentlemen, you *will* excuse me—"

Beiderbecke and Parker whirled to face the tall, gaunt, bearded figure of Edmund J. "Sned" Rendtorff, Faculty Senior Master, whose apartment was next door to the parlor. "Please don't think me lacking in appreciation of music or any other of the fine arts, but I do think your time at this stage would be better used in more, shall we say, academic pursuits." So saying he melted back into the semigloom of his chambers, leaving the two new friends deflated but resolved to carry on at a less vulnerable time.

At Bix's urging, Clinton Parker auditioned for the Academy orchestra, much to the delight of its conductor, Prof. R. P. Koepke, who responded warmly to the new trumpeter's obvious training and good sight-reading.

Born in Strasbourg, France, and educated in Paris and Berlin, Koepke taught languages and supervised musical activities at Lake Forest. With his scrupulous attention to the printed note and lack of patience with such "irresponsibilities" as improvisation in music, he typified the sort of musician Esten Spurrier had denounced in Davenport as "overlegitimate." His orchestral repertoire drew heavily on hymns and such "popular" light music composers as Von Suppe, Offenbach and Lehar—all fetching a snort of "Stuffy!" from an impatient Bix Beiderbecke.

In his opening weeks of school Bix made few friends outside the ranks of campus musical groups. He spent some time with John Graydon and Howard Strahan, the only fellow-Iowans in his class, but it was soon clear that their interests did not coincide, and they drifted apart. Julian Street Merigold, a classmate of Clinton Parker's who also roomed in East House, said Bix made a routine of heading for the parlor piano after his last class every afternoon to work out progressions of unusual chords, going over patterns again and again until they made sense to him. Inevitably they would bring Rendtorff shambling out of his seclusion next door with the suggestion, usually laced liberally with sarcasm, that such activities hardly stood to enhance the Beiderbecke academic career.

Several Lake Forest staff members mentioned the new student's obsession with music to Latin Professor Arthur "Abe" Edgington, supervisor of the lower middle class; he, in turn, saw Bix, encouraging him to go out for sports, both to diversify his activities and, perhaps as a result, to promote a more serious interest in his studies. This, the professor found, was easier said than done.

"He was not like other boys," said Edward Arpee, author of the official history of Lake Forest Academy, published in 1944. "Book learning simply did not appeal to him. He was always in scholastic and disciplinary trouble. His interest in music meant everything to him, and other activities meant nothing."

For a time he appeared to take Edgington's advice, at least partially out of responsibility to his parents. Though neither large nor heavy enough for varsity football, Bix pitched into intramural competition, playing for the school "orange" team against the "black" in a series of four games. The

Orange won two, lost one and tied one, to capture their eighth straight series; classmates remembered young Beiderbecke as "a real scrapper" on the gridiron.

He was also beginning to orient himself socially. His charm and quiet good manners made him a frequent and popular guest at the home of Marie Sweet Findlay, staff member of the *Lake Forester* newspaper, for Sunday evening dinners.

But music still called the turn, and Clinton Parker well recalled Professor Koepke's fury when the two trumpet sectionmates, having completed a somewhat less than inspired reading of von Suppe's "Poet and Peasant" overture, decided to try out some two-part jazz breaks, devised by Bix, behind their music stands. He berated Clinton, especially, for allowing himself to fall prey to such "musical degeneracy."

Lake Forest, all red brick buildings and rolling lawns, was within easy reach of Chicago. Trains on the Chicago and Northwestern Railroad and North Shore Electric Line ran frequently, and as the autumn wore on and Bix's chafing at the constant discipline began to show, the appeal of the city and the music he might be able to hear there drew his thoughts.

Chicago in 1921 was still in the early stages of its heyday as a jazz gestation center. The Original Dixieland Band had been through as early as 1916, serving up what the newspaper *Vaudeville* hailed as "the wildest kind of music ever heard outside of a Comanche massacre." Their popular success spurred a growing influx of Southern musicians both black and white, among them the New Orleans trumpet man Paul Mares. In August he had joined Roppolo, Lou Black and George Brunies in backing Bee Palmer for a new act at a basement cabaret at 60 East Van Buren called the Friars' Inn. Steve Brown, who replaced the New Orleans bassist Arnold "Deacon" Loyocano in the group, remembered Miss Palmer as "a woman of about five feet, six inches, very well attired for a woman of the twenties, and possessed of a fine voice." When, after several weeks, she and her husband, pianist Al Siegel, departed, Mares rounded out his Friars' Society Orchestra with some Chicago musicians and settled in for a long residency at the cabaret.

By the time Bix Beiderbecke got around to wondering how he could get into Chicago to hear some jazz, the Friars' Society Orchestra—shortly to be renamed the New Orleans Rhythm Kings—was an organized, smoothly-functioning band. They were playing "Farewell Blues," "Tin Roof Blues," "Bugle Call Rag" and other original numbers later to become staples of the small band jazz repertoire begun by the Original Dixieland Band.

For the moment, however, Bix was stuck on the Lake Forest campus, and it was not long before he fell in with other students who shared his interests. By the end of October he had joined forces with Samuel Sidney "Sid" Stewart, Jr. and Walter Ernest "Cy" Welge in forming a small band, under the ever-watchful eye of Professor Koepke, to play at school dances.

Stewart, from Flint, Michigan, played C-melody saxophone. "I was the virtuoso sax type, going in for intricate runs, fast arpeggios, and flashy technique," he said in later years. "I specialized in showy stuff like Rudy Wiedoft's 'Saxophobia,' or 'Sax-o-trix,' most of which I'd learned off Wiedoft's records." Much to Sid's consternation, such razzle-dazzle hardly impressed Bix at all, but their shared interest in jazz made them fast

Lake Forest intramural football team. Bix front row, third from right.

Lake Forest combined musical groups. Bix in rear row, third from right.

at Academy dances. 'Big Dick' headed for the balcony. Miss Tremain looked horrified and all hell broke loose. For the balance of the evening the music was most proper . . ."

Reports of their son's growing involvement in music, to the exclusion of virtually all else, were reaching Bismark and Agatha Beiderbecke in Davenport, arousing no little concern. After some discussion, they wrote him separate letters, each lacing bits of family news and gossip with entreaties to pay greater attention to his studies. Bix's reply of Tuesday, November 8, leaves little doubt as to either the direction of his thinking at the time or the conflict building up within him between his sense of duty and his natural inclinations, though no direct mention is made of music:

Dearest Mom and Pop,

I received both your letters, mother's day before yesterday and Dad's today, and I'm going to answer both of them at once because it would be too late to try and answer each one separately. I wrote Burnie yesterday, did he get it? That was because you told me how he felt about my failure in not writing, but it was because I had written the last letter.

Mother I will surely send a note of regret for M. Weiss' wedding on the 12th at 4 P.M.

I believe I can safely say that my table manners are OK—I finished my incomplete in geom. & passed it with an absolute 100 can you believe that? In this school? I'm really trying in Eng. Hist. but it sure is hard for me—so damn much to remember & I sure have a blank of a memory.

In regard to Thanksgiving we get out Wed noon in time to catch the 12:28 out of there and have to be back at 10:00 Thursday night. I'd arrive in Dav. about 7 or 8 PM and have to leave the next day about 12 or 1.

As much as I'd love to, I don't suppose you'd think it worth while & I believe I don't think that I'll feel disappointed because it would cost too much "do" for having Xmas so near & I really think I can have a good time if you'll send me a little dough for the occasion—gee, all those stunts that require dough at the same time. I tell you Dad it is necessary that we have this Culver money because if one guy drops out they all do, I don't know why. But if you will send me not under $7 or over $10 for Culver and whatever you want to for a couple of shows and carfare and ahem, Thanksgiving including the price of a good Thanks. dinner, I sure would appreciate. Either send it all to the school or if you trust me to me, because it's kiddish to put it in the school treasury. After this, it is all over in regard to money & really the Culver trip seems to be the berries according to the kids here —they have about 3 cars and a driver on a special and the whole school goes. I can't imagine anything more fun.

Glad you have a girl "Mom," stick with her & I hope your teeth are all jake now. By the way, either you or dad have to write me a written permit that I can go to Chi over thanksgiving whether I'm coming home or not. If I don't come home Thanksgiving I'll stay at the Hamilton Club with those Patterson boys & will be safe as long as I'm with them—of course this is if I don't come home.

Well Dad I'll proceed to answer yours. I received the clipping and am not surprised because she's a beauty all right—give Aunt Tillie my love and also ma and all the folks and let me add on seeing that about the Culver game it is compulsory—absolutely because no one is allowed alone at the school.

friends, and the young cornetist from Iowa found in Stewart a willing—if not always completely comprehending—listener for his increasingly vehement views about how the music should be played. Where Sid went for technique, Bix was obsessive about clarity of tone, economy, and the conviction that every note of every phrase should mean something, and no throwaways. Sometimes Sid's patience with such categorical thinking wore thin.

"Know what's the matter with you?" he said to Bix one afternoon after some jamming in an East House dormitory room. "You're nothing but a note miser. Why don't you get just a little flashy stuff? It wouldn't hurt."

Bix lay back on the bed and grinned. "Sidney, my boy, the trouble with *you* is that you play so many notes but they mean so little." Stewart took the remark to heart; he never forgot it.

He and Bix, plus Cy Welge from nearby Evanston on drums, formed the nucleus of the combo, drawn from the ranks of the school orchestra, which played the Lake Forest Hallowe'en Dance Saturday night, October 29. *CAXY*, the Academy yearbook, described the year's first social event as "a taste of the pep and wholesome fun which always characterizes an Academy dance . . .

> The "gym" was appropriately bedecked—pumpkins, corn stalks, lanterns festooned with witches and cats and other usual Hallowe'en decorations, were in keeping with the spirit of the season. On the walls were branches of autumn leaves, especially beautiful in their russet and orange coloring. A shock of corn with hollow pumpkins, grotesquely illuminated by electric lights, occupied the center of the floor and added to the effect. "Bix" Beider-becke, one of our "home talent," and his orchestra furnished music which was declared to be unexcelled by his fellow students.

Julian Merigold offered a rather more restrained account of the ceedings in Lake Forest's autumnally decorated gymnasium. "The played from a small balcony, a recess in the wall just large enough the piano, a set of drums which Cy played, with room for a couple guys." Most of Lake Forest's young men drew their dates from F an exclusive girls' school not far away later attended by the ill-st actress, Jean Harlow. The girls would arrive as a group, under scrutiny of Miss Tremain, Ferry Hall's headmistress; she wo place during the evening beside Lake Forest headmaster ferred to affectionately among less reverent students as "B several of the other Academy administrators.

Again, Merigold: "The whole setting was, of course, all ve everything including the music in the best taste and ex manners and decorum for students of fashionable board band, with Bix in a most subdued role, worked discreetl of the days as "Coral Sea," "Humming," "Bright Eyes," Think of Me."

"Everything was going just fine," said Merigold pleased that the boys and girls were not holding o and that the behavior of all participating was pe best known to Bix and Cy, the band swung into a the way. That did it! The dancers let go with the

I sure will try in English history Dad and if I can will try to get out of exams so I can be with you a week early.

Tell Burnie that Vera's nuts about him and that he's not too old to get a date with her. The box of goodies will come in handy—well it's snowing like hell & a good day for studying of which I sure have a lot to do so I must close with everlasting love.

LB Beiderbecke

Please don't forget the permission to go to Chi Thanksgiving if I can't come home.

Bix went on the trip to Culver, a military academy in Indiana not without its own role in jazz history. Ernest Loring "Red" Nichols, a cornetist later to be profoundly influenced by the young Davenporter, had been a scholarship student there from December 1919 to September 1920, when he was dismissed for bad conduct.

The Lake Forest Thanksgiving recess was too brief to permit a trip home to Davenport; Bix got his written permission to go to "Chi," though it is not difficult to imagine Bismark's misgivings in granting it.

Once in the city at last, he made for the Friars' Inn. Roppolo and Lou Black knew him from Davenport, and welcomed him. Mike Fritzel, the manager, did not object; he had laid down a house rule that young musicians wanting to listen to the band could sit off to the side without trouble from the bouncers, as long as they kept quiet and didn't get in the way. The Friars' Inn was a popular haunt for many big Chicago underworld names. Dion "The Florist" O'Banion, gangland baron of the North Side, was a steady customer, as was the man who eventually did him in, Al "Scarface" Capone, brought to Chicago only a few months before as personal bodyguard to rackets czar Johnny Torrio.

The music fired Bix's imagination. The Rhythm Kings played more smoothly, with more finesse, than the Original Dixieland Band. But they swung none the less. In Paul Mares, they had a trumpeter who could lead the ensemble and play effective solos which would paraphrase the melody line rather than embellish it. Brunies was, if anything, a more imaginative anchor man on trombone than the ODJB's Eddie Edwards, and Roppolo could imbue the clarinet obligato line and solos with a somber and wistful quality in sharp contrast to the bright parade style of the Dixieland Band's Larry Shields. It was clear that Bix would have to find a way of getting into town more often, even if it meant leaving the Lake Forest campus illegally after lights-out at night. The idea disturbed him: he was still new at the Academy, and had promised his mother and father to work hard. He couldn't let them down, and certainly should not risk his future at school by taking chances. Yet he had to hear this music and he had to play; his parents refused either to understand or accept that.

Friday night he dropped in at the Black Cat Room, in the basement of the Edgewater Beach Hotel. Jimmy Caldwell, a pianist, had the regular five-piece combo there. Bix had met them less than a month before, when they played a weekend dance at Lake Forest. Four were students at Northwestern and Caldwell, tenor saxophonist Don Murray and drummer Virgil Leech were Sigma Chi fraternity brothers. Jimmie Fallis, the clarinetist, was in Sigma Nu.

"Bix had played a couple of numbers with us at Lake Forest, and we'd liked him. But he hadn't really cut loose—and I'd not been too happy about the whole idea of having him sit in because he was a high school kid and we were college students," Caldwell told the authors. "Don took to him right away, and started trying to get me to use Bix on some of our dates."

But the leader of "Caldwell's Jazz Jesters" resisted. "A high school kid just didn't fit into our plans, as I saw it," he said.

But Bix's few days in Chicago had made their impression on him. He'd heard the Rhythm Kings and he'd met a group of young musicians who shared his passion for jazz. It was an exhilarated, but at once deeply troubled Bix who returned to Lake Forest after Thanksgiving.

Two days later his and Sid's little band, now suddenly ringing just a bit clumsily in its cornetist's ears after his exposure to the music at the Friars' Inn, played at another school dance, Bix doubling at the keyboard for two-piano numbers. *CAXY* again bore witness to the enthusiasm of their reception by the students:

> The gym was very appropriately decorated in orange and black with multi-colored japanese lanterns giving a rainbow of light. LFA banners, pennants and pillows were, of course, much in evidence while on the wall facing the entrance to the gym, a huge black paper football with the inscription—champions 1921—served to increase the spirit of celebration.
>
> Under the leadership of two LFA students, Beiderbecke and Stewart, the orchestra turned out feats of musical skill which everyone declared excellent. As a privilege, the pianos were allowed to be moved from the balcony, where they generally are, to a corner of the dance floor. This greatly increased the tone and pep of the music and was well appreciated. The last dance brought to an end one of the peppiest and best social events ever given at the 'Cad.

Stewart, later to become a successful industrialist and civic leader in Flint, found Bix both intense about his music and articulate in conversation. They discussed at length what the young Iowan had heard in Chicago, Sid resolving that after the Christmas holidays they had to find a way of getting into the city without undue risk.

Interviewed before his death in the late 1960s, Stewart said he found puzzling the notion that Bix was at all shy or withdrawn during his school years. "Quite the contrary—I remember him as being extremely witty, tending to run toward sarcasm. He was extremely extroverted, with a keen sense of humor. He was an intelligent fellow, and a good athlete, but his primary interest was playing that horn."

Christmas vacation brought Bix back to Davenport and into touch again with Spurrier, Putzier and other hometown jazz friends. His glowing account of a night spent listening to the Rhythm Kings found an eager audience—all of which strengthened his determination, once back at school, to get into Chicago more often. Even as the "Bix-Wally Orchestra" was winning praise for its performance at the Academy "Pre-Mid" prom in mid-January, Bix and his cronies were planning far more ambitious undertakings.

They agreed on one fundamental point—their group had to capture, as closely as possible, the sound of the Rhythm Kings. But this would take a lot more experience than they were getting by jamming in dormitory rooms or playing for occasional Academy dances. The only solution was to begin accepting some of the offers trickling in from other schools and social organizations around the Chicago area.

This they did, and by the time the "Cy-Bix Orchestra" played an informal dance to help kick off Lake Forest's Midwinter Weekend festivities Friday night, February 17, they were well into the market for off-campus work.

Bix had also been active on his own. When Jimmie Caldwell expanded his quintet January 26 for a senior prom at Senn High School in Chicago, Bix was among those he brought in—and he never regretted it. "He really came into his own that night," said Caldwell. "He had those kids cheering and screaming. We had Harry Gale on drums that night. Although he too was in high school, he could really play.

"Well, Bix showed up with his cornet wrapped in newspaper. He didn't have a tux, so we sat him behind the grand piano so people wouldn't notice him. But as the evening progressed, he got better and better, and the kids started screaming for him so much that we had to move him down front. Every time he took a solo, they'd go wild. It was eerie. He was the hit of the evening."

Caldwell, much to Don Murray's glee, was converted. He agreed to use the high school cornetist whenever possible, but Bix was not always able to get off the Lake Forest campus, he said, and would only be able to make it once in awhile.

He was along for a dance early in February at Ferry Hall. "The old girl at Ferry Hall"—presumably Miss Tremain—"wanted a violin, piano, and other soft music instruments," said Caldwell. "She didn't want a clarinet or trumpet. I told her about this nice boy from Lake Forest, and how well-mannered he was, etc., and she said he would do."

Predictably, Bix wasn't long in turning on the jazz, and by intermission time had the temperature markedly on the rise. "At the intermission," said Caldwell, "the old gal grabbed me and marched me behind the palm plants. She said, 'That *nice boy* of yours is exciting my girls! Make him stop.' I told her that he was playing what he felt and it would be hard to calm him down. 'Do it,' she said."

Caldwell tried, and Bix agreed to restrain things—but to no avail. The next set turned out as had its predecessor, and this time Miss Tremain had had enough. "She told me Bix could no longer play for her girls, so he had to sit out the rest of the night."

Midwinter Weekend began with a concert featuring the Academy's combined musical groups performing for students, their parents and friends. Prof. Koepke, anxious to impress, chose Clinton Parker to render the program's only wind instrument solo, a now-forgotten salon piece entitled "In Old Madrid." Parker had good, if painful, cause to remember the evening in vivid detail. "The time for my solo arrived, and I got up to play," he said. "Prof. Koepke, at the piano, started the accompaniment, I raised my instrument to begin—but no sound came out! I had what is called 'cotton-mouth,' a drying-up of the salivary glands caused by nervousness or stage fright. It feels as though the cheeks are stuffed with cotton and nothing will vibrate, so no tone comes out of the trumpet.

"I had to sit down, and after that every time Prof. Koepke met me he spluttered, 'Trumpet player—bah!' "

Koepke's cavalier treatment of his former favorite seemed to Clinton's friends an injustice which could hardly go unavenged. One morning not long after the cotton-mouth episode, Bix, Parker and several others stole down to the cottage at the other end of the campus where the professor lived. "We fastened a pail of ice water above his front door, and when he came out it tipped and deluged him with its contents. For four days, the angry professor hibernated in his cottage, refusing to come out."

After the concert Friday night, Lake Forest's student body presented their *Academy Follies of 1922.* Bix took part in two of the ten sketches, singing two numbers with a barbershop quartet, then accompanying Sid Stewart at the piano for a performance of Rudy Wiedoft's "Saxophobia." Afterwards, according to Lake Forest's yearbook, *CAXY,* "Bix-Wally's lived up to their reputation by turning out wonderful music" at an informal dance in the gym.

Saturday night brought a quite unexpected break. Bix had no date for the big prom. His parents were home in Davenport, and there seemed nothing to stop him from wandering over and listening to the band brought in from Chicago to provide the music. It was called Bill Grimm's Varsity Five. Grimm, the pianist, remembered the night well.

"As the evening progressed, I noticed this one young chap standing close by, first leaning on the piano, then listening to the sax or drums. It became obvious he didn't have a date, but was just standing as close as he could to the music."

The band took a short break, and Grimm got up from the keyboard to stretch his legs. The kid sat down and started to chord—softly, gently, nice full progressions. He looked up.

"Hope you don't mind."

Grimm laughed. "Hell, no. Play the rest of the set if you like. It's steaming in this place. I can stand the rest."

"Thanks just the same, but I'd rather sit in a little later with my horn."

"Horn? You play something else?" Grimm was puzzled and fascinated at the idea of a youngster who just materialized out of the woodwork and sat down to play knocked-out chord sequences at the piano—then started talking about being a horn player.

"Play cornet. Mind if I sit in? I won't make trouble."

Grimm was dubious. To a lot of guys, sitting in was just an excuse to make a lot of noise. He didn't know this kid from Adam. "Well, y'know we have these orchestrations and things, and it might sound funny if you came up without rehearsing—"

"I won't get in the way," the kid said, a note of stubbornness creeping into the soft midwest voice. For some inexplicable reason, Grimm believed him. "After a short while he returned with his cornet, and when I tried to offer him a sheet of cornet music he waved it away. I thought this was odd, and wondered what I was in for."

He soon found out. In the first number, then another and another after that, the cornet found the notes the arranger had left out, and played choruses that left the Varsity Five chuckling and grinning. "He wasn't interfering with our music—in fact he was improving it quite a bit. We encouraged him to take choruses on his cornet. What came out of his horn amazed me, as he had a sense of perfect harmony, could fake any piece we played and, I learned, couldn't read a note.

"As the evening wore on and Bix took breaks which, I must admit, inspired us no end, I suggested that if he wanted to join the band for a dance we were playing the next week at a fraternity house in Northwestern University, I'd be happy to have him join us. He readily agreed, and that was the beginning of Bix playing with Bill Grimm's Varsity Five for a period of about two years."

Around the same time, Bix launched his first offensive on the Chicago jazz scene. Marty Bloom, pianist-leader of the band at Red Callahan's on North Clark Street, looked up in surprise onc late February evening to see a pair of unlikely figures lurking in the shadows of the rear entrance to the side of the bandstand. "There were these two skinny kids standing there listening to us," he said. "They each had what proved to be trumpets under their arms, wrapped in newspaper. Bix introduced himself and his friend, and told us he'd heard about us and would like to sit in. He was emphatic in saying he could play okay, but had never played with our kind of organized jazz band.

"He said he was enrolled at Lake Forest Academy but was unhappy there, wanted to blow it all off and start playing. But his family wanted him to get an education. We let him play the rest of the sets, and the band and I got a bang out of his phrasing."

From early March, around the time Bix won a second team varsity letter on basketball at Lake Forest and decided to go out for baseball, the clandestine trips to Chicago after lights out became more frequent. His room in East House was near the fire escape door, and from there it was only a few steps to the grass and freedom. "Sned" Rendtorff's lodgings were around the opposite side of the building; it was unlikely he would hear Bix stealing out, his instrument wrapped in a newspaper for handy carrying.

Paul Mares had to chuckle at Bix's fervent entreaties to let him sit in during the late evening at Friars' Inn, when the band was beginning to tire. "He kept pestering us to play 'Angry,' because it was the only one of our numbers he knew well at the time," the trumpeter said. Elmer Schoebel, pianist with the orchestra, was emphatic in his recollection that the musicians had decided reservations about Bix's as-yet unformed style. "It didn't really work out with the group that well," Schoebel said. "We'd let him sit in occasionally for a number, but we didn't encourage him."

One time Sid Stewart accompanied Bix on one of his nocturnal expeditions. They hit the Friars', then headed for the College Inn in the Sherman Hotel, where the Isham Jones orchestra featured Louis Panico, an 18-year-old trumpeter with an "advanced" concept who had already created considerable stir with his composition, "Wabash Blues." After an early beginning as a "hot" man, Panico later succumbed to commercial temptation and became a specialist in muted gimmicks and technical tricks. Stewart and Bix "sat there for hours and just listened. We thought it was just wonderful . . . and it quickly became clear to me that Bix was destined for a career in professional music. It was as inevitable as death."

Just how often Bix slipped out of East House to catch the North Shore Electric into the city is not certain, nor whether Stewart, Parker or Welge went with him more than once. Julian Merigold, looking back at the circumstances of life at Lake Forest, said he thought that "everybody overestimates the number of times Bix went into Chicago . . . He was short on money for such things, and it took money for all those trips . . . I also question that he was accompanied by Stewart or Welge more than once or twice because an exodus of that kind from East House certainly couldn't have gotten by Abe Edgington or Sned Rendtorff."

By mid-April, when Bix won a place on the Lake Forest baseball team as a utility outfielder, he had more cash in his pocket, a consequence of increased off-campus playing activity with the Cy-Bix Orchestra and occasional weekends with Grimm. But his studies were slumping badly, drawing worried letters from Aggie.

One night, sitting in with Bloom, he remarked that things were looking so dire he would not be surprised if he flunked out at the end of the term. All he wanted to do now, he said, was play. "He told me his marks were punk, and it was only a matter of time before his school days ended . . . I went out to the bar and told Callahan I wanted to add Bix, and he okayed it," Bloom said.

"Bix showed up the following night and played, continuing for a number of weeks . . . he played all night and liked it, meaning that his schooling would have to suffer. He started to miss classes, and was in the doghouse with the school, and eventually with his old man, too."

The long nights were indeed beginning to tell. Bix was showing up late, sometimes not at all, for morning classes. Fellow students and faculty members also noticed another development: he sometimes appeared with what was clearly a hangover.

But thanks to jobs with Grimm and Caldwell, and to other sitting-in activities, Bix was making friends with a widening circle of collegiate musicians, not much older than he, who shared his love for music. They included three other Northwestern undergraduates, clarinetist Jimmy Hartwell, tenor saxophonist George Johnson, and Vic Moore, who played drums. They turned up in an ever-shifting combination of groups which also included Murray, son of a Methodist minister from Illinois, and Wilford "Min" Leibrook, from Hamilton, Ohio, who had switched to brass bass after an early false start as a cornetist. All swiftly became admirers of "that high-school kid" from Lake Forest.

Several of them ran into him at Friars' Inn the night George Johnson brought along his pal Hoagland "Hoagy" Carmichael, a sophomore at the University of Indiana, who remembered Beiderbecke as an "extremely young kid in a belted pile coat and cracked patent leather shoes."

As Bix's circle of friends widened, so did his ambitions for the Cy-Bix Orchestra. He and Welge paid cash for an advertisement to be run in CAXY when it appeared in June, informing one and all that the band would be available for dance engagements even after the end of the 1921–22 academic year. But the good money and the best jazz opportunities were elsewhere, and when Lake Forest officials got around to engaging a group for its junior prom Saturday, May 6, Bix and Cy had to turn them down, explaining that they had already accepted an engagement that night over in Gary, Indiana, on the other side of Chicago.

Headmaster Richards, duly informed, hit the ceiling. He summoned Koepke, whose responsibilities were supposed to include absolute control over *all* musical activity on the Lake Forest campus. The Professor shrugged helplessly and pleaded innocence. The boys had long since ceased to heed his advice, he said, and mostly because of young Beider-

Lake Forest baseball team, spring 1922. Bix center front.

Lake Forest Glee Club. Bix, though not a member, strolled over as the picture was being taken and stands at the back, far left.　

Lake Forest faculty group photograph, showing Prof. Koepke (front row, second from left), Edmund "Sned" Rendtorff, senior master (front row, third from left), and headmaster John Wayne Richards (front row, center).

becke. The lad was not a positive influence on his fellow students, and otherwise promising young musicians such as Clinton Parker had been led into most distressing ways by Beiderbecke's obsession with "all that jazz business."

"Big Dick" had heard all he wanted to hear. He issued orders that the Cy-Bix Orchestra was to be confined to campus after its Gary date, following up with a stern warning that more severe action could be expected "unless you gentlemen come to your senses." The headmaster ordered his faculty and staff to keep a special eye on young Beiderbecke, reporting any suspicious behavior, absence from classes or other potential trouble.

All the band members, even a relatively contrite Parker, felt Richards' sentence harsh and unjust. Disgruntlement set in quickly, and one morning during the week of May 7 Bix called a council of war in one of the dorm rooms before morning chapel service. The purpose, Cy Welge explained, was to reaffirm that nothing "Big Dick" said or did would stay the Cy-Bix Orchestra on its road to recognition and musical success. Someone proposed sealing the agreement with a toast, offering as a libation a large bottle of Ed Pinaud's Face Lotion, 85% alcohol and non-toxic. Trombonist Morris Rising and one other bandsman made the rounds of neighboring rooms, collecting a few glasses, which they then filled half full of water. Then Bix, with great solemnity, poured the colorless lotion into each. The liquid turned milk-white, Parker said, in the manner of Ouzo or Pernod.

"Placing clothespins on our noses, we then prostrated ourselves on the floor and swallowed the mixture in the glasses, one to a member, in one gulp." Then, suitably fortified, the musicians reeled off toward the chapel to play hymns for an unsuspecting student body and faculty. What happened next went into the annals of Lake Forest's unofficial history—and remained vivid in Clinton Parker's memory throughout his life.

"By the time we had reached 'Rock of Ages,' the closing hymn, the Pinaud-and-water potion had begun to work mightily. We were, in a word, tight. At a signal from Bix, the entire orchestra lit into 'Rock of Ages' in syncopated dixieland style; he played the lead and took all the 'breaks,' I keeping up an accompaniment with a 'jazz obligato.' The trombone whooped and swayed, the saxophone moaned and the clarinet shrieked, while Bix made his cornet cry like a baby. Cy Welge almost punctured his drums with enthusiasm."

Headmaster Richards sat as if turned to stone in his place at the side of the platform, only the deepening crimson of his face betraying his gathering rage. Suddenly, with a wrath which hushed orchestra and audience at a stroke, he rose to his feet, arms spread wide. "Stop this! Stop this minute, all of you! Stop."

They stopped, struck sober by his rage. Richards curtly dismissed the assembly, then turned to the group of now subdued young musicians. Bix bit his lip.

"I should like to know," the headmaster said in a suddenly very soft voice, "what the meaning of this spectacle might be." No sound. Clinton thought fondly of Friars' Inn. "No . . . I do not expect any of you to reply. But I have a very good idea indeed who is behind all this, and they—or he—will be dealt with. In the meantime, gentlemen, I have no choice but to place you all on probation until further notice." And, turning on his heel, he stalked out.

Probation meant an effective end to the Cy-Bix Orchestra. Rehearsals and dormitory jam sessions were out, especially with the headmaster's edict strictly enforced by an ever-more-caustic Sned Rendtorff. The senior master's nightly checks of the offenders' lodgings, instituted at "Big Dick's" orders, all but ruled out evening escape to Chicago. Bix sulked in his room, attending classes only sporadically. This was reported to Richards, who decided the time had come to root out the source of disruption in Lake Forest's otherwise tranquil existence. He summoned Bix on Wednesday, May 17, for a final admonitory talk. The youth was nowhere to be found. That afternoon Rendtorff was advised to double his vigilance at East House, especially during the evening hours.

Two nights later, Sned checked around the rooms after lights out and found Beiderbecke's empty. He said nothing, but the following evening installed himself quietly in the shadows at the base of the dormitory fire escape. He did not have long to wait. Slowly, silently, the first-story door opened, and a figure carrying a paper parcel slipped out and down the few steps to the lawn. As he reached the bottom, Rendtorff stepped out of the darkness.

"Ah, good evening, Mr. Beiderbecke. Lovely evening for a stroll, don't you think?" Bix froze, then began a halting attempt at explanation—only to be cut off in mid-sentence by the senior master. "I think for your own sake it would be wiser not to say anything. You may tell it to Headmaster Richards tomorrow. Good night, sir."

The Lake Forest faculty met in emergency session Sunday morning to hear reports from Rendtorff, Koepke, Richards and others who had followed the steady decline of Leon Beiderbecke's academic and disciplinary performance. Several said they were alarmed that he sometimes appeared to have been drinking. All agreed that despite his musical gifts, deeply admired even by some of those most critical of him, young Beiderbecke was not a good influence on his fellow scholars and would not benefit from continued attendance at Lake Forest.

Richards, in the chair, put it to a vote. The result was a foregone conclusion: Bix would have to go, for "persistently being out of his room after lights." The drinking, though a factor, would not be mentioned officially in deference to his family.

It fell to Rendtorff to break the news. To his surprise, Bix accepted the decision without objection, apologizing for having caused the senior master any undue embarrassment, and set immediately to packing his bags.

The following morning, May 22, Bix said his goodbyes to Stewart, Welge, Parker and the rest, turned in his East House door key to Rendtorff and caught a train for Chicago. He had gone to Lake Forest in an attempt to fit into his parents' plans for his future; from the start it had not been what he wanted. Now, at least for a time, he was free to go where he could play jazz.

Bix with Bill Grimm group on the beach at Michigan City. L to R: Grimm, Don Murray, Bix and Ray Landis.                    PHOTO COURTESY WILLIAM T. GRIMM

Bix with Davenport pianist Ed Meikel at White Lake, Michigan, July 1922.

# Chapter 5

Out of school and short on cash, Bix set about hunting up work as soon as he got into Chicago. Bill Grimm's phone didn't answer, and Vic Moore was out of town. So he tried Marty Bloom—and hit paydirt.

"Hey, no kidding!" The pianist's delighted response to news of Bix's expulsion all but bowled him over. "That's the best news I've had all week. Listen to this." Little more than a week before, he said, he had run into the head of the Orpheum Theaters "Orpheum Time" revues and got to talking ideas about future productions. With Bix more or less in mind, Marty had suggested building one of Orpheum's prestige "office acts" around a jazz theme, featuring an all-star hot band, lavish sets, a chorus line and star singers and dancers. The act could work a 35-week booking around the Orpheum circuit. Doubts about Bix's availability, Marty said, had prevented him from pushing the plan harder. Now, with his star cornetist free, that seemed resolved.

"Bix went for the idea, and I got right to work organizing the band," said Bloom. "That part was a cinch—Bix's playing prowess was already the subject at many a bull session among jazzmen in Chicago. I don't recall exactly whom I got, but I do remember that Wingy Manone was one of them."

Bloom had played Orpheum Time revues before, and had little trouble selling the idea and cornering the musical directorship, then using the company's big rehearsal hall in the State-Lake Building to whip his hand-picked outfit into shape. He and Bix, in the meantime, saw a good deal of one another. Late evenings usually found them drinking down the street from Red Callahan's at a tiny speakeasy with a battered old upright piano in one corner. Bix, at his friend's prompting, sooner or later wound up taking the front off it and  sitting down to demonstrate something he had just learned from a roll—a new composition by Roy Bargy called "Foolish Child."

"He told me he learned it by freezing the movement of the roll at spots which were tough to pick up solely by ear, then laying his hands on the depressed keys to memorize chord formation," said Bloom. "If you can get hold of one of those player piano rolls of 'Foolish Child,' you'll understand why he chose it, for it was a rendition far out and ahead of its time in artistry." Bargy, star of the Benson Orchestra of Chicago, was later to help an older, more ambitious Bix with difficult chord sequences and voicings when both were members of the Paul Whiteman orchestra.

The new band sounded even better than Bloom had dared hope. Bix's playing had improved over the previous few months; his lip was stronger, his attack more forceful. His natural relaxation, perhaps benefiting from being able to play for once without worrying about the effect on his history or geometry performance, gave the band just the lift it needed.

"Bix was broke by then," said Marty, "so I started feeding him his sawbucks on a draw basis, for without him—well, no band. And boy, it sure was worth it. I brought B. B. Kahane, one of the Orpheum circuit officers, up to hear us, and he flipped after just one set—so much so that I was able to put the bite on him for an advance. I had some dough, but I needed the bread for Bix."

It was too good to last. In the nearly two weeks since Bix's dismissal from Lake Forest, Headmaster Richards had been in touch several times with Bismark and Agatha. They had not had a letter from their son for more than a week, and now, thanks to "Big Dick," it was only too clear why. It took little further sleuthing to determine where Bix was. Bismark packed a bag and caught the afternoon train to Chicago.

Bix, meanwhile, was caught up in the exhilaration of rehearsing days for the coming tour, then going out in the evenings to jam. He got through at last to Bill Grimm, who was building a going business out of booking bands for private engagements around the Chicago suburbs, especially in Evanston and other areas where the money was good. Grimm had an idea.

"Hey, Bix, ever played on a boat before?"

"Sure. Did the *Majestic* and the *Capitol* last summer. Why d'you ask?"

"Got something you might like." Bill had landed a concession on the Lake Michigan summer boats, doing daily excursions to Michigan City and other spots along the lake shore. He and Don Murray were looking for another horn for their own five-piecer aboard the *Michigan City*, starting almost immediately.

Bix liked the idea, but told Grimm he was already committed to Marty Bloom. The leader of the Varsity Five was undeterred. "Okay, pal, but in case you just happen to find yourself free, give me a call."

Came final rehearsal day, and the Bloom band was running down one of its big feature numbers when the door at the back of the hall opened and a stranger came in. "He was well-attired, graying—what I'd have called a typical sort of well-to-do Iowan," said Bloom. "He just stood there, with a faint smile on his kisser, listening as we finished this tune, with Bix riding it out on top. I pointed him out casually to Bix when we finished. He looked over in this guy's direction and sort of gasped, 'Oh oh, he tracked me down!'

"I didn't like the sound of *that* at all. 'Who is he?' I said. 'It's Dad,' he said, and went over to talk to him. We took a rest, but I was fearing the worst. It was all innocent enough on the surface, but I had this strange feeling of impending doom."

Bix ended his conversation with his father with a shrug, and "sure enough, he came back to me and said, 'I'm sorry to have to do this to you, but I've got to go back to Davenport with my father. You better count me out. There are good guys around town that play. Don't break up the band on my account.'

"As Bix evaporated through the door, I turned to the guys and told them it was nice knowing them. I went back to the Orpheum office and broke the news to Kahane, thanked him for the use of the hall, and gave him back his dough. I relocated in New York right after this disappointment, and didn't see Bix again for years."

Bix accompanied his father back to Davenport, but it is pure conjecture what passed between them. Bismark and Agatha were at a loss what to do with him now that he was out of Lake Forest. In any case it was summer, so the school issue would have to be held in abeyance for the time being. Rather than have Bix hanging listlessly around Davenport, constant reminder of the family's dilemma and social embarrassment, his parents consented to allow him to play throughout the rest of June, July and August.

Bill Grimm wasn't even surprised when Bix landed back in town a few days later.

"Ready to play now?" he said.

"Sure. When do we start?" The answer was immediately, and Bix, accordingly, joined Grimm, Don Murray, banjoist Frank Lehman and drummer Ray Landis doing one round-trip a day on the Graham and Morton Lines' *Michigan City.*

Nor was this all. Sid Stewart came up with a summer job at the White Lake Yacht Club in White Lake, Michigan, about 20 miles north of Muskegon. Davenporter Ed Meikel was on piano. Bix answered Sid's entreaties to join with a promise to make it on weekends when he could, and it is certain that he was there during the first two or three days of July. The Yacht Club ballroom had two pianos, Stewart recalled, which meant that Bix, when he did show up, spent his evenings in tandem between cornet and keyboard.

Chicago, too, offered a bright development. King Joe Oliver, the New Orleans cornetist, had brought his Creole band back from the coast and opened over at the Lincoln Gardens, 459 East 31st Street, corner of Cottage Grove Avenue. "Our boat docked in Chicago each evening around 7:30," said Grimm. "That left us free to roam and do as we wished until the boat sailed at 10 A.M. the next day.

"I suppose I got to know Bix most intimately when we played on the excursion boat each day. He was often a bit sleepy in the morning, especially after one of those evening jaunts, but he never failed to play inspiring horn. And I can still visualize his part-smile, with twinkling, squinted eyes, which became his trademark before ill-health set in."

Suddenly everyone in sight seemed anxious to hire Bix Beiderbecke. Vic Moore turned up at the pier just before ten one morning with an offer of his own. He had a chance to do a few Saturdays with a quartet at the Delavan Lake Country Club, Wisconsin summer hideaway for well-to-do Chicago executives. On piano, and leading, was Wilbur "Bud" Hatch, who had just graduated from the University of Chicago and was killing time until the start of a new job around the New Year in California.

"Vic made up the quartet most of the time with Jules van Gende on sax," said Hatch, later to become a major name in musical direction for West Coast television. "It was strictly a non-arrangement, faking foursome . . . choruses only, except for the dixieland repertoire, when we'd stick with the complete tune or routine. On the choruses, we'd give out with the melody the first time around, and from then on it would be every man for himself. This was where Bix really shone—I can state emphatically that he was considerably ahead of the period in his conception, especially of harmony."

Bix played his first date with the Moore-Hatch quartet Saturday, August 12. "He was an exuberant boy," the pianist said, "very extroverted, sort of a playboy type—but music was certainly his life." Sometimes annoyingly so: whenever the band took a break, Bix made straight for the piano to experiment with chords. He had discovered, instinctively and by ear, the possibilities in extending standard progressions by adding their ninth and eleventh voices, thereby also increasing possibilities for inversion and voicing. Hatch, though admiring, took a dim view of such doodling. "This became something of a sore point with me . . . it was my firm conviction then and for many years later that private parties prefer a bit of silence in between dances to having to listen to extraneous music, be it piano or what have you. But with Bix one suggestion was never sufficient, and you can imagine how often I became one frustrated leader trying to keep that talented gentleman in line. In retrospect, though, I'd have to admit that Bix was hearing some of the musical sounds that eventually found their way into his compositions."

It was the same personnel the following Saturday—with one exception, a stranger Moore had picked up at the last moment to fill the saxophone chair. "Vic was a horrible procrastinator when it came to getting men," Hatch said. "We'd usually go up Saturday noon by train on the crowded tourist special, and this invariably meant a last-minute scramble to get his men.

"Well, this particular time Jules couldn't make it—had some other engagement; so Vic brought along a guy he'd met that same morning walking along Michigan Avenue carrying a sax case. Without bothering to ask whether the guy had ever played a dance job, Vic practically dragged him on the train as it was pulling out. It took us about four bars of the first tune that night to know this guy had had about three lessons. So Vic paid him off and the rest of the evening Bix, Vic and I functioned as a trio—and that night there was lots of piano melody, believe me."

Larry Andrews and tenor saxophonist Ray Eisele rattled in from Davenport one afternoon in Larry's beat-up, topless, fenderless Model T Ford. They found Bix a willing and worldly guide to Chicago jazz life. Their evening began with Papa Joe Oliver, the Dodds brothers and, most exciting, Oliver's young protege Louis Armstrong on second cornet. Louis, fresh up from New Orleans, had just joined the Creole band. For Andrews it was heady stuff, and his memory of the night retained even the vivid image of another "King": the bouncer, King Jones. "That guy musta stood about seven feet tall," said Larry.

They went on, Bix in the lead, to the College Inn to hear Louis Panico, who had been taking "lessons" in jazz playing from Papa Joe. Like his namesake before him, this second Louis greeted Bix's arrival with a whoop. "Bix! You old son of a bitch . . . c'mon over here!" Andrews and Eisele were speechless; the boyhood chum had become a celebrity. Panico showed Bix the new trumpet he'd been given by the Conn factory to endorse and try out on the job. His own, in its case, lay at the back of the stand. "C'mon, Bix, blow a couple with me," said Louis, pointing to the horn. Bix obliged, filling the Davenporters with awe.

The Delavan Lake season wound up on August 26, the lake boats on

Labor Day, little more than a week later. Bix and Jimmy Hartwell, who had been playing on one of the other boats, took off for Indianapolis, the clarinetist's home town. Then, after a brief stay, Bix headed at last for 1934 Grand Avenue, Davenport. But if Bismark and Aggie still nursed any notions that their son was home to stay, or had undergone any change of heart about his music, they were in for a rapid disillusionment.

He'd scarcely had time to unpack his bag when the telephone rang. It was Pee Wee Rank, who had played drums with Bix on the *Majestic* the summer before. He had a chance to take a band to Syracuse, New York, for two months, at $75 a week per man, and had already asked fellow Davenporters Wayne "Doc" Hostetter and Johnny Eberhardt on reeds and violins. He needed a cornet. Bix's answer was an enthusiastic yes, and the next day the four of them were on a train for Chicago, where they were to meet the band's banjoist, a skinny, fast-talking kid from Goodland, Indiana, named Eddie Condon.

Condon was a protege of Hollis Peavey, known throughout the midwest as leader of Peavey's Jazz Bandits and a man with a sharp eye for turning talent into money. He'd picked up Condon, taught him some fancy chord sequences on the tenor banjo, and bought him his first union card down in Waterloo, Iowa, for $5. In his own autobiography, *We Called It Music,*[5] Condon recounted in vivid detail his first meeting with the "kid in a cap with the peak broken" at Chicago's La Salle Street Station. In Condon's eyes, Beiderbecke's outstanding feature appeared to be "a green overcoat from the walk-up-one-and-save-ten district; the collar was off his neck. He had a round face and eyes that had no desire to focus on what was in front of him."

They made the usual rounds, first to the College Inn to see Panico, then to the Friars' for a few sets by the Rhythm Kings. Condon's reaction quickly changed from derisive scepticism to the same kind of stunned astonishment Andrews and Eisele had betrayed at Bix's popularity with such pace-setting musicians.

Billed as the "Royal Harmonists of Indiana," Pee Wee's little band opened September 21 at Harry E. Morton's Alhambra Ballroom, 275 James Street, in Syracuse. They found lodgings at the Snowdon Apartments, a rooming house up the way at 400 James, and settled in for a two-month stay. The job produced little of extraordinary interest, save for two things: Bix's growing skill with pinball machines, and an advertisement in the *Syracuse Herald and Post Standard* for Friday, October 6, announcing that the eight-piece instrumental group would present "their interpretation from a famous opera" at 10:30 that evening, and again the following night. No review of either performance appeared in the newspaper.

With the end of October and of the Alhambra job, Condon, Eberhardt and the others struck out at once for Chicago; but "Doc" Hostetter had other ideas. Syracuse, he reminded Bix one night, was a lot closer to New York than the young cornetist had been before. It would be a shame to pass up the opportunity to get into the city and listen. The Original Dixieland Band were appearing nightly at Sixti Busoni's Balconnades Ballroom, 66th Street and Columbus Avenue. There was also the Original Memphis

5. 1947; Holt, Rinehart & Winston, New York.

Five, its musical foster-child, with the technically accomplished Phil Napoleon on trumpet. The temptation was too strong; Bix agreed, and the two caught a train for New York.

They checked into a hotel not far from Columbus Avenue. Bix, giddy with excitement, could hardly sit still. "Hot in here," he said. He rolled up the shade and opened the front window, which looked directly across a U-shaped courtyard to the other wing of the hotel—and burst out laughing.

"Hey, Doc, come over here a second." Hostetter peered over his shoulder. In the room directly opposite, a man and woman were writhing nude on a double bed; taking a quick window count, Bix headed for the door. "Be right back," he said.

Seconds later he returned, and picked up the phone. "Hey, what the devil are you up to? Are you nuts?" Hostetter was beginning to have his doubts about the entire situation. "C'mon, Bix, cut it out." Bix got the operator, and asked for the room across the courtyard. He stood and watched as the man, annoyed, rolled off his partner's body and reached for the telephone.

"Hello down there!" Bix boomed into the mouthpiece. "This is God, and I've been watching you. Shame! Shame!" Dismayed, the recipient of this message looked about—to meet only the inquiring gaze of the woman on the bed—then, to Bix's and Doc's merriment, slammed the phone back down on its cradle.

With evening they were off to find jazz. First stop, inevitably, was the Balconnades—but only after a detour to pick up a jug of gin. Bix met Nick LaRocca with undisguised hero-worship, and the elder cornetist obviously relished it. In later years, LaRocca insisted he had met Bix some years earlier, while the Dixieland Band was still at Reisenweber's. He "recalled" that Beiderbecke, then a boy of 15, came alone to New York in 1918 and hung around the band for several days until "I began to worry about him and had to send him home as I knew I could have been charged with the harboring of a minor." No amount of research has been able to substantiate this alleged visit; there is no account of a prolonged absence from Davenport in either 1918 or 1919. Bix only heard the ODJB records for the first time following Burnie's return from the army in late 1918. Tony Sbarboro, drummer in the Dixieland Band, discounted the possibility of such a visit entirely.

But this November night in 1922, a slightly tipsy Bix was indeed sitting by the bandstand as his idol counted off "Tiger Rag." Contrary to LaRocca's assertion that he was quick to welcome Bix and respond to his playing, Hostetter said it took an exhaustive sales pitch to even arouse the older man's curiosity. Finally, late in the evening, he agreed to hear what the kid could do. Motioning Bix to the stand, he called the band's new medley of "Margie" and pianist J. Russell Robinson's composition "Singin' the Blues."

"While I played the melody of 'Singin' the Blues,'" said LaRocca, "he used this countermelody which had parts in it that Mr. Hoagy Carmichael later incorporated into his song, 'Stardust.' Now when I say this countermelody was similar I mean this man derived his idea or drew on Bix ideas as I had heard this boy play similar. Please do not construe that I try to take this credit away from Mr. Carmichael, as he is the composer, but there are many people who get ideas from others."

In later years, Hoagy acknowledged Bix as chief inspiration for "Stardust," especially the verse, which when played at about the same tempo as Beiderbecke's 1927 recording of "Singin' the Blues," takes on the melodic shape of a characteristic Bix solo. Also, "Singin' the Blues" and the refrain of "Stardust" begin in the same chordal position; this, coupled with Bix's affinity for both songs, makes more than likely a countermelody to "Singin' the Blues" incorporating elements of either Hoagy's verse or chorus—or both.

LaRocca was impressed with the newcomer from the midwest—all the while careful to remind posterity that "it was none other than the ODJB that Bix derived his own style from; playing along with the records of the ODJB he built this himself, and all the others styled themselves on him."

Among the musicians at the Balconnades that night was Artie Seaberg, who had replaced Larry Shields as clarinetist with the ODJB. He and Bix were about the same age, and took to one another immediately. At a table after the music was over, Bix and Doc answered in glowing terms all LaRocca's and Eddie Edwards' questions about Chicago, the Friars' Inn, and its resident jazz ensemble. These men had known Roppolo and the Brunies family in New Orleans, but had lost contact when they came north. LaRocca, especially, asked in detail about chances to play in Chicago—with good reason. The backlash against jazz and "wild" living which had emerged across America immediately after World War I was gaining ground in New York. Parents and teachers, clergymen and politicians by turns denounced a music which seemed to threaten a new and dangerous permissiveness among the young. The New York Commissioner of Licenses, wholly in sympathy with such thinking, outlawed all jazz and dancing on Broadway after midnight, cutting down both the hours during which jazz could be played and the money musicians could command for playing it. Though the band could still work for Busoni at the Balconnades, the Danceland at 95th and Broadway, or other similar houses, the midnight curfew had wiped out the latenight dancing crowd which was the Dixieland Band's bread and butter. LaRocca, ever the astute business head, sensed tough times ahead, and looked to Chicago as a place where the mobs could keep the booze and good times flowing without interference from politicians, parents or meddling pedagogues.

Bix, more than a little intimidated, was only too pleased to oblige LaRocca's queries, and promised to approach Mike Fritzel as soon as he got back to Chicago.

Bix's first week in New York dissolved in a chaos of sitting-in, running to catch taxis and trains to auditions which somehow never materialized, and more bootleg booze than the 19-year-old Iowan had ever consumed in one brief period of time. Somewhere in the blur, perhaps running to catch an elevated train, he tripped and dropped the Conn Victor, denting its tuning slide. The repair bill occasioned a loan from Artie Seaberg to shore up his new friend's diminishing cash supply.

He met Phil Napoleon, whose pure "legitimate" tone and control of his instrument were a revelation after LaRocca's more primitive approach. "In those days I didn't know if I'd be a concert musician or whether I should play jazz," Napoleon reminisced recently. "But Bix—well, he liked what I did. I'd take him aside and show him what I was doing.

"He used to come around and ask me if he could come along to the studios with us. What the hell, there was nothing wrong with that. And we showed him how we did things. Then one time, later, we had to go out to Gennett in Richmond, Indiana, and he had evidently gone home to Davenport, Iowa—and damned if he doesn't walk in on us there."

Finally, with money running out and time getting short, Bix and Hostetter said their farewells and took a train back to Chicago. Doc continued on back to Davenport, while Bix immediately picked up a fraternity house job with pianist Charles "Murph" Podalsky at Northwestern University's homecoming weekend.

He dropped in at the Friars' Inn to find trouble brewing. Discord within the Rhythm Kings made it plain that the band would not be together as a working unit much longer, and Fritzel was on the lookout for a star jazz act to follow them. He showed interest in Nick LaRocca's plans to come west. They talked.

Bix boarded a Monday morning train for home November 20, and as the Rock Island Line express puffed its way across the central Illinois cornfields, he wrote to LaRocca:

Dear Nick: -
Am on my way home from Chi and I thot I'd take this opportunity to write you the dope.
I saw Mike Fritzel last night and he sure seemed impressed when I told him about you boys wanting to come to Chi and that you would consider the Friars Inn if everything—"Do" and hours were satisfactory—I sure poured it on thick, well Nick Mike wanted to know the dope in regard to the money you boys wanted etc. and I said that you would write him the full particulars that I just didn't know. All I knew was that you were the best band in the country. Well he expects a letter from you Nick. I'm sending your address to him so he can write you—I was supposed to meet him today at 3 but I left early so I left your address addressed to him at Friars.
You write him about what combination you'll have and everything else. I told him that you just made a record which pleased him—his address is Mike Fritzel, Friar's Inn, Chi.
Well Nick I wish you the best of luck—give the boys my best and tell that clarinette player to expect some "do" right soon and also tell him he's the best boy I've ever met.
Sincerely,
B. Beiderbecke
Ropollo and the band are leaving in about a week they aren't going to New York for awhile—Rap also sends you Eddie and Tony his regards.

Fresh back from the fast, bright world of New York and Chicago, Bix was ill-prepared for the family ultimatum which awaited him in Davenport. Since he had shown no further interest in continuing his schooling, his father said, he would have to go to work. And what better place to begin than the East Davenport Coal and Lumber Company, starting at once. There would be no professional "jazzers" in Bismark Herman Beiderbecke's family, and that was that.

# Chapter 6

Bix started work the first week in December. His chores around his father's office included weighing coal before loading it on delivery wagons, taking deposits to the bank and, inevitably, collecting bills. Within a week he was chafing at the boredom and the enforced routine of the regular hours. He missed music. He could sit in around town evenings with Carlisle Evans or Bill Greer, but his still-unresolved difficulties with Local 67 kept him off anything but occasional pickup dates, most of those out of town.

Bud Hatch called. Could Bix work a society party for him outside Chicago? Agatha could offer no further resistance. The day of the job he boarded a train for Chicago eager for the chance to get away, if only for a day. And there was a bonus: he'd wanted to buy a new cornet for some time to replace Putzier's old Conn. This day he had finally taken the plunge and bought a Martin in a big, sturdy case.

"Bix's train was delayed in arriving," said Hatch, "and we had to start our dance without a trumpet. When he finally did get there, much to our relief, he took his horn out of the case, took a breath and blew—and nothing came out. He'd bought a new horn that day before leaving Davenport, and decided to lubricate his valves while on the train, but instead of taking them out one by one to oil, took them all out at once and then proceeded to put them back in all wrong.

"Believe it or not, and regardless of what anyone may tell you about valves being numbered, these were not. I'll never forget the scene—we all took turns holding up the horn, pushing down a valve, and trying to match up the holes so the air would go through. I can assure you that Bix during all this was the least worried member of the group—including the guests. We finally got it to work, and it turned out to be a very successful evening despite all the confusion."

Bill Grimm, too, proved himself a friend in need. A high school fraternity in his home town of Dubuque, Iowa, signed him up for its Christmas dance. "We had a little larger band than usual—seven or eight pieces, I believe—as I wanted to impress the people of my home town with my orchestra. I got Don Murray, and Bix as well."

It snowed heavily across Iowa that day "and Bix's train was late. But he made it just in time; although we had no time to rehearse with this larger unit, the boys were so inspired to have Bix with us that I was highly complimented by my Dubuque friends for having such good music. We had a party with old friends afterwards . . . stayed the night in a big dormitory-type room in the Julien Dubuque Hotel, where the dance was held."

Bismark Beiderbecke realized as well as his son did that having Bix at home working under his watchful eye, but coming and going to band jobs with increasing frequency, was at best an unstable situation. Bix clearly regarded the lumber and coal depot as little better than a prison, and both parents were coming around to acknowledging what was only too clear: given the first opportunity, their son would again be off to play, and nothing his family could do or say was going to stop him. As spring came on the parental strictures relaxed, and Bix was back and forth regularly between Davenport and Chicago, sometimes with Esten Spurrier in tow.

"I recall one time that the Benson Orchestra of Chicago, a Victor recording orchestra under the direction of Don Bestor, came to town," said Spurrier. "I remember Bix saying that I had to hear the cornet player and a guy named Frank Trumbauer on C-melody; I don't know who the cornet player was, but he was good."

Eddie Condon, meanwhile, had again hooked up with Hollis Peavey, this time for a season at the Arcadia Ballroom in St. Paul; and it was not long before the banjoist's fabled gift of gab shifted into gear with glowing tales of the Alhambra and the kid from Davenport who could make a cornet sound "like a girl saying yes." Iowa trombonist Tal Sexton seconded the motion, and Peavey wrote to Bix in Davenport to offer him the Arcadia job at $65 a week.

Bix surprised even himself with his response. "Make it $75 and I'll come," he said. Peavey, taken aback, nevertheless agreed. It all seemed set; Bix would come up and join the band within a week, said Peavey, but then "the trumpet player that I was letting go went to the owner of the ballroom and cried on his shoulder, and the boss requested me to keep him on and not take Bix.

"Bix was okay about it—said he was going to study up some more and learn what the third valve on his cornet was for, or something polite to that effect." The Jazz Bandits carried on without Bix Beiderbecke.

Warm weather brought increased musical activity to the tri-cities area. The riverboat season soon got into full swing, and Bix was a frequent sitter-in with Tony Catalano, Wrixon and other Streckfus regulars. He dropped in at the Linwood Inn, on the road to Muscatine, to play with the Hawkeye Melody Boys, a band from Grinnell, Iowa. Their pianist, Floyd Bean, recalled seeing him arrive, cornet in a brown bag under his arm, to an enthusiastic greeting. Such evenings usually ended with Bix at the piano and Bean hanging over his shoulder, trading chord sequence ideas. Bean, who later lived for a time in Davenport before making his name as a dixieland pianist in Chicago, affirmed that Bix "taught me a good deal" during these sessions.

Gradually, Bismark Beiderbecke despaired of fighting a rearguard action. Though anything but pleased at the outcome of his attempt to keep Bix at home and working, he was under no illusions. By the beginning of July, the East Davenport Coal and Lumber Company had lost a temporary weighing clerk and bill collector, and Bix Beiderbecke was back in Chicago, eager to play. He phoned Dale Skinner, who had played tenor sax in Vic Benning's six-piece relief band at Friars' Inn back in the Rhythm Kings days. Skinner, establishing himself around town as a leader and arranger of stock orchestrations, issued a prompt invitation to move in with him on Kenmore Street, near Wilson Avenue.

"We'd left the Friars' Inn early that spring and opened at the Valentino Inn, at 22 E. Adams Street, between State and Wabash," said Skinner. "In June I took over the band and reorganized." The New Orleans Rhythm Kings had split up as a working group after leaving Friars' Inn despite efforts by Mares and Roppolo to hold it together with replacement personnel. Losses of key men were too great. The rhythm section of Elmer Schoebel, Lou Black, Steve Brown and Frank Snyder had moved together over to the Midway Gardens, where Schoebel became house bandleader. By March 12, and the NORK's second scheduled record date for Gennett, Mares had to content himself with Mel Stitzel, the Midway Gardens' second pianist, and Ben Pollack on drums.

Skinner, reorganizing in June, picked up George Brunies and Kyle Pierce, a pianist who had jobbed around with several of the Rhythm Kings. He got the veteran New Orleans bass and tuba man Martin Abraham, better known as "Chink Martin"; he auditioned, but for financial reasons did not hire, a young collegiate banjoist named Bob Gillette, who had been a frequent visitor at the Friars'. Gillette knew Bix and was a friend of Murray, Glenn Scoville, George Johnson, Vic Moore and the other second-generation jazzmen loosely associated through both Bill Grimm and other groups loosely centered on the Northwestern campus. Skinner rounded out his group with Gene Cafferelli on trumpet and Bill Paley on drums.

Bix dropped his bag at Kenmore Street, grabbed some supper at a ham-'n'-eggs joint around the corner, and made for the Valentino Inn. He got a warm welcome, and before long was on the stand. The late Charlie Margulis, later to sit beside Beiderbecke in the trumpet section of Paul Whiteman's orchestra, was in the audience. At one point, he said, the newcomer held the cornet in his right hand and fingered with his left, to demonstrate the way Nick LaRocca did it.

The musicians liked what they heard. Bix had improved since the days when he pestered a long-suffering Mares to play "Angry." Even Brunies, a hardened veteran at age 23, was enthusiastic. Skinner gave Cafferelli his notice and hired Bix.

He fit in well. The awkwardness which had often marred his early style was all but gone. The tone had taken on a lustre, and there were times when ideas would tumble out with a flow which made even Mares sound stodgy. Bix was beginning to punctuate his choruses with unusual intervals, and excursions into the sixth and ninth voices of chords, in ways unheard of among jazzmen of 1923. Inevitably, during intermissions, he made for the piano. A favorite number, said Skinner, was "No No Nora," a pop song by Gus Kahn, Ernie Erdman and Ted Fio Rito with an ever-shifting chord sequence which lent itself well to Bix's piano variations.

But if Skinner, Brunies and the others were lavish in their praise, Dan Baroni, owner of the Valentino, definitely was not. He complained that the new man was playing "wrong notes" and making the whole group sound "out of tune."

"I tried to explain to Dan about Bix's advanced ideas in harmony, his use of intervals and chords, but he wouldn't hear of it," said Skinner. So Bix was warned discreetly to play things "a bit straighter" whenever the owner was in sight. Inevitably he would forget—only to draw new, more vociferous Baroni complaints. Finally, at the end of Bix's second week, the roof fell in.

"Get rid of that guy, y'hear?" Baroni barked at Skinner one night. "I don't want him around any more. He's bad for my business. He drives me nuts with his bum notes, and he plays outa tune and makes the whole band sound like shit. I want 'im out."

Again, Skinner tried to explain. Bix was a truly original talent, might someday be recognized as an important musician. Baroni waved him aside.

"All the same to me, brother. Either he goes or you all do. And that's final!"

There was nothing for Skinner to do but break the news to Bix and give him a week's notice, then rehire Cafferelli. The decision hardly seemed to affect Bix's spirits. He played, if anything, better during his final week, unhampered by any need to sound "respectable" for Danny Baroni's benefit.

Paul Mares, fresh back from New York, organized a reconstituted New Orleans Rhythm Kings for two days of recording for Gennett at Richmond, Indiana. Roppollo was along, but the original Schoebel-Brown-Black-Snyder rhythm team, by now well-established at the Midway Gardens under Schoebel's leadership, was either unable or unwilling to take part. So the trumpeter took Brunies, Chink Martin and Kyle Pierce from Skinner's group and added Bob Gillette on banjo. He got Jack Pettis, who had played C-melody sax on the first Friar's Society Orchestra records the previous August; and, perhaps on Gillette's recommendation, he hired two extra saxophonists, Murray and Scoville. Ben Pollack on drums rounded out the band.

As if a four-man reed section were not enough of a departure, the date also included the flamboyant New Orleans pianist Ferdinand "Jelly Roll" Morton. Morton's connection with the Melrose Music Company, plus the fact that several of the arranged selections performed on the date were Melrose publications and included several Morton compositions, betray the organizational hand of the publishing firm in the background.

The band assembled in the Gennett studios, an ancient clapboard and brick building beside a railroad track, on Tuesday and Wednesday, July 17 and 18, 1923, to record eight titles. Morton did six more as solos, then Pierce another two, neither of them issued. Roppolo and Martin teamed up for a pair of guitar duets; these, too, remained unissued, though test pressings of both are rumored to exist.

Not only was the session racially mixed, but this two-day burst of recording also teamed the first-generation New Orleans men—Mares, Brunies, Roppolo, Martin—with a group of their Chicago disciples. With both fellow Skinner bandsmen and personal friends along, and a chance to watch his heroes, the Rhythm Kings, in action again, it is unlikely that Bix passed up the opportunity to go out with them to Richmond for two summer days of jazz.

But Bix was fresh out of a job. He turned again to Bill Grimm, midway through a second season on the boats. The setup was about the same as it had been the previous summer, but Don Murray had left for Detroit and a job with Jean Goldkette's orchestra, and Jimmy Hartwell was committed to an out-of-town job, said Grimm, and "since all the college musicians I knew had gone home for the summer, we were really shorthanded and in a jam.

"Harry Gale said he knew a saxophone player and would ask him down the next day. Sure enough, a little lad still wearing short pants and black stockings accompanied Frank to the boat. I took one look at him and said to myself, 'This will never do. What'll people think?' But just then the boat's whistle sounded and I knew we were about to take off, so I told the little fellow to jump aboard and we would make a day of it. He couldn't read much music, either, but he could play any piece we knew and also played the clarinet. He was so good I offered him a regular job, provided he could locate a pair of long pants. He said he had long pants with his Sunday suit and he would ask his mother if he could wear it every day.

"His mother approved, and Benny Goodman played with us all that summer."

There was another new face, a familiar one. Ray Landis had been replaced by a young drummer whose checkered blazer, matching cap and preference for plus-fours set him off from the other, more conventionally-dressed musicians: Bix's pal from the Caldwell band, Harry Gale.

"Harry could have been the greatest drummer ever," said banjoist Lehman, "but he never got the recognition, nor was he around too often. The big problem was his negligence—sometimes he'd come on a job without drums, hoping someone else would have left theirs." Bix and Gale liked one another on sight; they remained friends throughout the rest of Bix's life. When, five years later, Gale dropped in unexpectedly on a Frank Trumbauer recording session to see Bix, he wound up behind the drums, and in so doing confounded generations of record collectors to whom his name was unfamiliar.

Both Bix and Harry, said Lehman, were "really good dressers, sharp as a tack. Bix especially—good looking clothes, the real Joe College type. You hear stories about his being sloppy, unkempt, etc. Well, all I can say is that while I was around him it was just the opposite; he was very neat and well-kept."

Though still smarting at his dismissal from the Valentino Inn Band, Bix settled gratefully back into the lake boat routine. Both the fleet and Grimm's concession had expanded since 1922, and business was good. Graham and Morton were doing especially well with twice-a-day runs across 30 miles of water to Benton Harbor, in the southwest corner of the state of Michigan. The trip included a glimpse of the House of David colony, which had made headlines some months before after authorities exposed a sex-ring operating behind the facade of a religious cult. Elmer Schoebel's "House of David Blues," written and recorded at the height of the furor over "King Ben" and his virgin concubines, was already a major hit.

Monday, September 3, was Labor Day, and marked the end of the lake boat season. Bix hung on for a few days, working a date or two with Grimm, then hopped a train home to Davenport and a pleasant surprise. Aggie Beiderbecke, pondering her son's future, had begun to come to terms with a number of all-too-apparent realities. Not only was it clear that he was hell-bent on becoming a professional musician despite any opposition she or Bismark might mount, but, even more important, he was clearly very good at what he did and in growing demand among orchestras specializing in his music. It was not *her* music or Bismark's, nor that of Ernest Otto or Professor Koepke or Uncle Olie Petersen. But music it was, and Bix's failure to win a union card—and the musical respect that went with it—in his own home town was hurting him. It was, she reflected, keeping him away from home when he could be playing around the tri-cities area, and it had already cost him a number of good opportunities. He had lost the Terrace Gardens job, the *Majestic,* the *Capitol* and heaven knew how many others, simply because the grayer heads of Local 67 would not accept the possibility that a "jazzer" could be a musician too.

Aggie telephoned Al Petersen and asked her cousin to have a chat with the gentlemen of the examining board, Roy Kautz included. "I thought it might be easier for Bix here than in Chicago," was her explanation in later years. Uncle Olie, far from entirely convinced but in this case allowing family loyalty to dominate, made a point of talking to board members Ben Ebeling, Ernest Otto and Frank Fich immediately about young Beider-becke.

"The kid might be light on reading," he said, "but he does have some talent as a jazzer. Be too bad to turn him down again." After lengthy and heated discussion, and not a little grumbling, he won their assent to examine the "jazzer" again. Come Monday, the first of October, Bix Beider-becke turned up, neat and smiling—and hornless—at the union audition hall.

"Where's the cornet, Bix?" Ebeling said, perplexed. Bix grinned.

"Oh, that. Hope you don't mind, but I thought I'd take the exam on piano." Whereupon he seated himself at the keyboard, played through two "light" classical selections, and passed without so much as a question from the thunderstruck examiners.

The word got around, and new offers, better ones, began to come in. Bix went down to St. Louis in early November to do a theatre job with a group led by the drummer Charles Cotterell. From there it was directly on to Chicago.

Three months before, events had been set in motion which were to have profound effects on the Davenport cornetist. Drummer Bernie Cummins, leading the band at the Stockton Club, a roadhouse outside Hamilton, Ohio, was offered a job beginning Labor Day at the Toadstool Inn in Cincinnati. He took it, over protests from his trumpet player and musical director, George "Red" Bird, that the band was not yet ready. Bird, seeing in the Stockton a good chance for himself to set out on his own, gave his notice to Cummins.

"The Stockton Club was a pretty rugged operation," said Bird. "Bootleg-ging, gambling, the works. It was managed by a Damon Runyon character we knew only as 'Chappie.' He liked me, and asked what he should do. I said he could hire another band, or I would organize one for him. He told me to organize one."

Bird took "Chappie," co-manager Gerald Chapman, at his word, and set out for Chicago to put together a band of his own. In doing so, he unknow-ingly set the stage in jazz history for the coming of Leon Bix Beiderbecke.

The Wolverine Orchestra during its engagement at Doyle's Dancing Academy, Cincinnati, January-February 1924. L to R: Vic Moore (drums); George Johnson (tenor sax); Jimmy Hartwell (clarinet); Dick Voynow (piano); Bix (cornet); Al Gandee (trombone); Min Leibrook (sousaphone); Bob Gillette (banjo).    PHOTO COURTESY MARY LOUISE SHOEMAKER

Same band, same day, alternate pose. L to R: Gandee, Moore, Gillette, Voynow, Hartwell, Beiderbecke, Johnson, Leibrook.    PHOTO COURTESY "BUD" EBEL

# Chapter 7

If nothing else, the Stockton Club was easy to find. It faced on to a lonely stretch of U.S. Route 4 about seven miles south of Hamilton, an easy 20-mile drive up from Cincinnati. Its setup was a cliche of Prohibition-era America. The ground floor of the two-story frame house was split into halves, one for a gambling casino, the other a cafe operation specializing in food of dubious quality and high-grade bootleg booze. Backed by five Ohio millionaires, the Stockton quickly became a popular hangout for gangland figures and thrill-seekers alike, the presence of the former more often than not enhancing the *frisson* for the latter. There was a dance floor on the cafe side, where the band played from nine in the evening until three in the morning. The upstairs housed caretakers and other club staff.

Both Chappie and his fellow-manager, a man remembered only as McCarthy, had won reputations for toughness sufficient to get their club nicknamed "Little Chicago" among the locals. But both shared a soft spot for musicians, and treated those in their employ accordingly.

"Red" Bird returned promptly from Chicago with the nucleus of a band in tow, recruited one or two men locally, and was ready to open. Jimmy Hartwell and the drummer, Bob Conzelman, knew each other from gigs with Jess Brown and Bill Grimm. Dudley C. "Dud" Mecum, the pianist, had already made his name as composer of "Angry" and other popular songs. Gene Huls on banjo and Clyde Reynolds on trombone, plus Ole Vangsness on tuba and bass sax, completed the personnel. They opened in late September, and, as Bird remembered it, "the band was a better dixie band than the Cummins band had been. At any rate, Chappie was happy with it, as were the customers . . . we were playing pretty good by the end of September."

From the start, however, there were the seeds of discontent. Bird, for all his enthusiasm and organizational talent, was not really a jazz trumpeter, and Hartwell, used to musically faster company, was far from reticent about expressing his impatience both with the leader and the band's jazz standards. "Right off," said Mecum, "Jimmy didn't like Red's trumpet or any of the rest of the local guys. So he started plugging this Chicago bunch he knew."

Just what decided Bird to leave is not clear; but whether because of tension within the band or an offer to join the Jean Goldkette orchestra in his home city of Detroit, the trumpeter gave his notice in mid-November. His leavetaking was far from acrimonious. "I'll go see Chappie," he told Hartwell, "and tell him I want to quit. Then you can take over, and

I'll stick around till you can get a band together that suits him and suits you."

This was the chance Hartwell had been waiting for ever since meeting Bix Beiderbecke more than a year before. He dumped Huls and Reynolds, then wired Chicago for Bix, Bobby Gillette and Abe Sholdelenko, a tenor sax man who worked regularly as "Abe Cholden" with Grimm and others on the collegiate circuit. Cholden wired back that he could only do a week, but could get George Johnson, whom Bix knew from Northwestern, as a replacement. Hartwell unveiled the new personnel during the last week in November, with Bird staying on alongside Bix for a few days to ensure continuity.

Predictably, the repertoire now swung over sharply to ODJB and Rhythm Kings jazz numbers—much to the delight of both Chappie and McCarthy. Even George Reagan, who ran the crap table and as a matter of principle refused to let the musicians take part ("You guys ain't rich enough to afford it"), poked his head in frequently to listen.

The band all lived at the YMCA in Hamilton, a few miles down the road. For Bix especially, it was a new and intriguing kind of existence. He'd never run across characters like Chappie and McCarthy before. Even the way they battered the English language was something to hear. He wondered, amused, what Agatha might have thought if she could have heard McCarthy use the word "joint" to mean anything otherwise denoted by an ordinary noun. One of Bix's first nights there, McCarthy had stood by the stand as they jammed Jelly Roll Morton's "Wolverine Blues," finally cupping his hands to yell up at Bix, "Hey, kid, whyntcha take a chorus on the joint?"—meaning the song.

Nor were Chappie or the others any slouches when it came to colorful behavior. One especially intriguing figure was Roscoe Ales, who had grown up in vaudeville, knew all the famous show business personalities, and got along especially well with musicians—not least because he ran the Stockton's bootlegging concession. His comings and goings were shrouded in secrecy. Roscoe turned up and vanished at irregular, unpredictable intervals—but always had time for an anecdote about Jolson as a kid, or Eddie Cantor, or some other big vaudeville name.

For the new band's repertoire, the accent was decidedly on loosely-organized jam ensembles and solos, with a minimum of arrangement. Bix insisted—and Dud Mecum willingly agreed—that "Angry" become a staple item. But when it came to anything which required "straight" playing —waltzes, tangos or anything not easily rendered by a dixieland ensemble, things tended to flounder. Only Mecum could read any music at all, and in an effort to remedy the situation took to calling rehearsals a couple of afternoons a week. They were generally chaotic affairs, with Bix functioning as informal musical director. "The boys learned pieces four bars at a time," said Dud. "You know—Bix would give each guy his note, then they'd play four bars and stop. Then he'd give notes again, they'd play four more, and so on. It was tedious going, but there seemed no other way."

One number which got into the Stockton band's repertoire this way was "Wolverine Blues." It sounded good; more important still, it sounded coherent, nearly arranged, and as a result was played frequently. Unschooled jazzmen shun rehearsal and routine at the best of times. Now, with a few such numbers worked out, there seemed even less point in rehearsing new things. Interest dropped off—and Dud Mecum's discontent grew.

"They played 'Wolverine Blues' so much that I said one day as a rib, 'Why don't you guys just call yourselves the Wolverine Band?' " They took him at his word; the name, to Mecum's surprise, stuck. But he did not. By early December he had had enough of the nonstop dixieland and general musical laziness to begin thinking of quitting. The sole compensation to remaining lay in Bix himself. The cornetist's interest in the piano had taken on new dimensions over the preceding months. His noodling with chord sequences at the keyboard showed an awareness of music outside the scope of jazz, especially that of the impressionists, with their whole-tone scalic patterns and exploration of chords of the ninth and eleventh.

Bix had even found himself a piano teacher. Shortly after his arrival at the Stockton, looking through the *Hamilton Evening Journal* he had come across an advertisement for piano lessons given by a Miss Priscilla Holbrock. He phoned for an appointment, and went to see her—only to find a very pretty girl of his own age.

"He was completely surprised," said Bob Conzelman, "and she was just as shocked, because she had felt her ad would bring in children from the ages of nine through twelve. But she agreed to accept Bix." He went to her once, sometimes twice a week, but his "lessons," George Bird said, "consisted of listening to her play the works of Eastwood Lane and other modern composers of that time."

Before too long, said Conzelman, "the situation was reversed—she was sitting and listening to him play." And eventually—perhaps inevitably—Bix started dating her. Priscilla later fixed Conzelman up with her best friend, the daughter of the Cincinnati Symphony's tympanist, and the two couples double-dated.

The "piano lessons" soon fell by the wayside—apart from Bix's enhanced interest in some of the works Priscilla had played for him. He bought a folio of Eastwood Lane piano pieces and, whenever he found Dud Mecum free, beseeched him to play from it. On one occasion, the two even made tentative steps toward collaboration on writing a song.

But the tribulations still outweighed such satisfactions, and Mecum finally made up his mind to go. He left at mid-month, but only after Bix, suddenly shy and hesitant, had presented him with his copy of the Eastwood Lane folio "just as a reminder. I liked Bix very, very much," the pianist said.

George Johnson came up with just the man to take over at the keyboard. Richard F. "Dick" Voynow had played with them in Charles Cotterell's band in St. Louis and impressed them both. Hartwell was quick to agree, and Voynow became regular pianist of the Stockton Club band—newly renamed the Wolverine Orchestra as a consequence of Mecum's jest.

News of the reorganization, and of Bix's presence, began to circulate. Cincinnati musicians drove up to listen, among them drummer "Bud" Ebel, banjoist Carl Clauve and the 17-year-old cornetist "Wild Bill" Davison, all working in the highly popular band led jointly by Howard Chubb and Elie Steinberg. "Clauve and I would finish up at midnight," said Ebel, "and head right for the Stockton in Clauve's Model T to hear Bix and the band, then wait for him and bring him back to Cincy with us. The three of us were together constantly, and often liked to jam a bit as we travelled."

They showed up during the last set one night just before Christmas. It had been snowing heavily, and the Model T had taken more than two hours to cover the twenty miles. Even so, Bix needed little coaxing to join them. "We set out for Cincy," said Ebel, "and were almost there when we decided to stop on Paddock Road to have a little nip from the jug and jam a bit. Clauve, who was bothered by bladder trouble and couldn't hold his water too long, had to get out of the car to relieve himself."

Enter, in this unlikely setting, Bix Beiderbecke's loose pivot tooth. As a boy, wrestling with a friend on the front lawn, Bix had been thrown to the ground and had broken one of his front teeth. A Davenport dentist fashioned a removable false tooth, slotted at the sides to fit neatly into place. It might never have bothered Bix again, save for his habit of playing with it, removing it and slotting it back in when at all nervous. It had eventually become loose in his mouth, so that a cough or sudden jerk of his head might dislodge it.

In later years, Bud Ebel remembered Clauve as the man with the loose tooth. While it is possible that both men shared the same affliction, it appears more likely that it was Bix who, moments later, climbed out of the Model T to join Clauve at the roadside, coughed loudly, and "all of a sudden started yelling for help . . . he'd coughed the tooth out of his mouth into the snow. So all three of us wound up crawling around in the dark looking for this thing. Finally found it, somehow."

Their troubles were far from over. Paddock Hill had turned slippery with snow and ice, and the friction of the Model T's spinning back wheels as it struggled up the slope finally blew both tires. "We got out again to take a look. We were parked next to a streetcar track, and decided the only way we were going to make it up the hill at all was to take the tires off altogether, place the rims on the tracks and back up—which we started to do. We were going along real good, when over the top of the hill comes a streetcar and starts down." The trio, though by this time more than a bit tight, got the Ford off the tracks in record time.

The Wolverine Orchestra's maiden engagement came to an abrupt, if spectacular, end on New Year's Eve. The crowd packing the Stockton that night included rival gangsters from Hamilton and Cincinnati, and McCarthy and Chappie, wise to potential trouble, had laid down strict ground rules: Hamiltonians in one section of the club, the boys from Cincy in another. No contact, no trouble.

Things appeared to be going well. The building was noisy with revelry until sometime in the wee hours, when two of the Hamilton mob ventured into Cincinnati territory. The actual remark which struck fire is long-forgotten—if indeed it was ever known—but somebody started punching, and within minutes all precautions had gone out the window in an eruption of fists and flying bottles.

The seven musicians were relaxing in the band room when Chappie burst in, coat ripped, face red. "Hey, youse guys, they're really jiggin' out there! Get your asses in and play!"

They made it to the stand, but by now things were getting wild. "It was really a dandy," said a newly-arrived Bud Ebel, "with most of the band hiding in back of chairs, or anything that would give them cover" as glasses, dishes, chairs and other missiles rained around them. A moment later Chappie came storming through the room at the head of a gang of goons, his own "peacemaking squad." He made straight for the bandstand, grabbing Hartwell by the sleeve. "I said play, so you guys play!" he yelled over the din. "And keep on playing till I tell ya to quit!" The clarinetist hesitated, then ducked to avoid an airborne beer bottle. "I mean it, kid. You play!" snarled Chappie, and melted back into the fray.

Whether the band actually did, as George Johnson later asserted, play "China Boy" or anything else for more than an hour as the melee swirled about them will probably never be known. But by 4 A.M. at least twelve of the combatants had been cut and bruised. A report in the *Evening Journal* for January 2, under the headline "Free for All Brawl at Stockton Club New Year's Morning," said one man was "definitely known to have been seriously injured. According to the reports of neighbors, one person was said to have been taken to Mercy Hospital . . . hospital authorities deny that such a person was brought there."

The newspaper quoted witnesses as saying the rioters "threw all caution to the four winds and ended their New Year's pursuit for pleasure with a free-for-all fight." Many persons, it said, were seen in Hamilton area restaurants New Year's Day "with bandages about their heads, and with scars and bruises." The newspaper concluded by noting, without explanation, that "no report of the matter has reached the hands of the county authorities or the police and no investigation of the matter has been made . . ."

The brawl did close the Stockton club for the time being, leaving the Wolverine Orchestra fresh out of a job. Bix, despondent, suggested returning to Chicago to look for work. Conzelman decided that was a good idea in any case—and quit on the spot. Hartwell, more patient, dropped by the Toadstool Inn in Cincinnati to talk to Bernie Cummins, who had offered to help if he could even while the Stockton seemed a sure bet to continue through the winter.

He hit paydirt. In no time flat, Cummins had fixed up a contract for them at Doyle's Dancing Academy, downtown at the northwest corner of Court and Central Avenue, third floor, starting Monday, January 14. Now, with nearly two weeks to kill, they packed themselves and their instruments into one beat-up Phaeton open touring car and drove back to Chicago, where Palmer Cody, a jazz fan who ran a cavernous upstairs dime-a-dance palace at Sheridan and Argyle called the Cascades Ballroom, agreed to use them as second band for a week.

There were a couple of new faces in the Wolverine Orchestra when it opened at Doyle's. Ole Vangsness had decided to stay in Chicago and forget music for the time being while he established a practice as a dentist. Bix, meanwhile, had talked Vic Moore into coming in on drums. Moore's rhythm had a natural lift, and he and Bob Gillette were no strangers to one another in a rhythm section. Cincinnatian Eddie Johnson filled in before Moore arrived.

No replacement had yet turned up for Vangsness. But for the moment, at the insistence of the management at Doyle's, they took on a trombone player named Al Gandee. While nothing spectacular musically, he did add "bottom" to the ensembles and allow Bix to work for awhile with a full dixieland front line. The basslessness was soon remedied when Wilford "Min" Leibrook, a Hamiltonian who had played tuba and bass sax occasionally in Chicago and had sat in at the Stockton, dropped by to announce that his latest theater job had finished and he was at liberty. They hired him on the spot.

The new lineup meant a fuller sound. Bix's lead was more confident, and the band responded. But the Wolverines made little impact on the regular patrons at Doyle's, largely working girls and non-collegiate youngsters out for weekend recreation. The high school and college crowds went elsewhere, and with them the kind of appreciation which would have assured the new group instant acclaim. Doyle's Dancing Academy was far from the campuses and country clubs, and the Wolverines were more often than not just "that band playing now up at Doyle's." The hall's most enthusiastic patrons, by far, were the musicians who came just to listen.

From the beginning, there was ample indication how good things could be. Four days after opening at Doyle's, the Wolverines landed their first campus dance job, a junior prom to be held Friday, January 25, at Miami University in Oxford, Ohio, about forty miles north of Cincinnati. They were promised $175 for the evening, and split the bill with the Ohio Nine Collegians of Defiance, Wild Bill Davison's home town.

Not without some nervousness at such a debut, the Wolverines warmed up after supper at Phi Delta Theta fraternity house, then crossed the street to Herron gymnasium for their first exposure to a collegiate audience.

Francis A. Hannaford, a Miami senior and jazz fan, attended the prom. An evening of listening to this unknown band convinced him and his fellow undergraduate enthusiasts that something new and very exciting was in the wind.

Early in the evening the two groups worked in rotation. But it wasn't long before the Ohio Collegians dropped out, giving Bix and his friends the limelight. "The dancers seemed really stimulated by their new emphasis on rhythm," said Hannaford. "It was a departure from all the bands we had heard before. As a matter of fact, after the dance two student musicians from the leading campus band, the Campus Owls, were pretty voluble in their praise. John Sloat, the banjoist, I especially remember—he raved over their new kind of stressed rhythm. He called it 'sock time,' meaning that all the instruments in the band emphasized each of the four beats of the measure, whereas only the rhythm sections of other bands had done it in the past.

"Frank Smith, who played trumpet with the Owls and later became a professional musician himself with bands like that of Ace Brigode, was impressed by Bix's tone and surety of timing. Both of them resolved to incorporate what they'd heard into the music of the Owls."

The Wolverines' new feeling owed equal debt to Bix's growing skill at turning even the dixieland lead into a flowing melodic line, and to Bobby Gillette's rhythmic lift on the banjo, tighter and more thrusting than the relaxed timekeeping of the NORK's Louis Black. The band was far from perfect, as even its fans were quick to point out. Johnson and Gandee occasionally played wrong notes, and stumbled across each other's lines in ensembles. Vic Moore, so solid in the rhythm section, rushed breaks. But the music had a new feeling of urgency, smoother than the jerky syncopations of the Original Dixieland Band but crisper than the lilt of the Rhythm Kings.

The Wolverines, too, began to realize they were on to something different. Just how different became clear on Monday, February 18, when the eight musicians left Cincinnati at 3:30 A.M., after a characteristically dispiriting night at Doyle's, to drive 125 miles out to Richmond, Indiana, for their first recording date on the Starr Piano Company's Gennett label.

Gennett plays a uniquely seminal role in early history of jazz on record. As the first label to operate something approaching a liberal policy toward jazzmen of both races, it managed to attract many of the most important artists and groups of the early 1920s.

It had come into being as a tiny division of the Starr Piano Company, reportedly the first such firm west of the Alleghenies. Starr went into recording in 1915, issuing records on its own Starr label until independent dealers, conscious of social snobberies, began to balk at use of the name, hitherto identified only with pianos and record players.

The label was promptly changed to Gennett, after Harry Gennett, a key figure in the company since 1893. But the new operation also catapulted Gennett records straight into trouble. Victor, ever jealous of its own established market, brought suit against Starr for patent infringement in the use of a record-cutting stylus. Starr went to court, using movies of the record-cutting process to illustrate its case before the jury. This marked the first acceptance of motion pictures as courtroom evidence. After six trials, the U.S. Supreme Court ruled in Starr's favor.

Gennett did its recording in two studios, one at 9–11 East 37th Street in Manhattan, the other at Richmond, building up a highly successful business both out of marketing its own records independently and supplying mail order houses by leasing Gennett masters to a host of other labels in the United States and Britain.

Gennett had entered the jazz field almost by accident. Fred Wiggens, who managed Starr's Chicago music store, dropped into the Friars' Inn, just around the corner, one evening and heard a band that sent him scurrying back to his telephone to call Fred Gennett, one of Harry's three sons. Gennett listened sceptically—but he listened. He respected Wiggens as a man with a good ear for new talent, and one whose instincts had never failed him in the past.

"You got to hear them, Fred, they're really something."

"Yeah. Sure. But what do they *do?*"

"Well, they play hot. You know—one-steps, all that. But they're really good, and I think we can use them. Come on up and hear them."

Far from convinced, but intrigued nonetheless, Fred Gennett boarded a train for Chicago the next morning. Evening found the two of them in attendance at the basement cabaret listening to the Friars' Society Orchestra. After more fast talking by Wiggens a deal was closed. Mares, Roppolo and friends joined William Jennings Bryan, the Cincinnati Symphony Orchestra, assorted Ku Klux Klan orators and sacred music singers as Gennett recording artists.

The idea caught on, and Wiggens reaped two rewards: control of Gennett's sales and artists division, and a free hand in determining who got to record for the label. Shortly thereafter, King Oliver's Creole Jazz Band, with the newly-arrived Louis Armstrong, came out to Richmond. And on February 18, 1924, the Wolverine Orchestra pulled up to the big building by the railroad track, instruments spilling off the sides of the Phaeton, ready for their debut on wax.

Hartwell and Voynow had purchased a day's recording time, Wiggens' way of giving untried talent a break while covering his costs, and the band had spent the night in earnest discussion of how they would sound when the moment came. "In truth, none of us had the faintest idea," George Johnson said later.

The studio was itself a perplexing setup. A plain, board-panelled room down at the far end of Starr's main piano assembly building, it looked, in the words of Indiana bandleader Charlie Davis, "like an afterthought or an accidental happening." On the back wall, just below the words "Gennett Records" in old English script, two horns were suspended to pick up the sound. Even getting at them to take a solo, as Bix soon found out, was more often than not an invitation to a catastrophe like tripping over some fellow-bandsman's feet or kicking something over in the process.

The room was poorly ventilated, and the combination of the steam locomotives puffing by outside and the creaking equipment within, forever going out of adjustment or simply breaking down when cold weather hardened the heavy gear grease in the turntable mechanism, guaranteed that no recording session would go uninterrupted for long.

The Wolverines recorded four titles that day, only two of which Wiggens considered fit for release. But "Jazz Me Blues" and "Fidgety Feet," issued back-to-back on Gennett record No. 5408, stand as the earliest known documentation of Bix's cornet style, and as such merit close scrutiny.

The opening chorus of "Fidgety Feet" illustrates what Fran Hannaford and his friends meant by "sock time." Rather than simply playing atop their rhythmic support, the horns give the impression of playing *with* and *to* it, producing a momentum hitherto unheard on jazz records. Neither performance is fully relaxed, and Bix's fast, pronounced vibrato on "Fidgety Feet" betrays some nervousness; but his mid-ensemble cornet break is warm-toned and original, establishing him from the start as a player of greater creative potential than either of his mentors, LaRocca or Mares, and easily the standout member of the Wolverines.

His full-chorus solo on "Jazz Me Blues" is even more enlightening, rolling lightheartedly along on Gillette's four-to-the-bar rhythm. The phrases in bars five and six make adventuresome use of a triplet and introduce the idea of the complementary phrase couplet, both to become basic elements of Bix's later style. Both occur again in the same solo, culminating in the four-part breaks of bars 13–16. Esten Spurrier termed this structural idea the "correlated chorus," and maintained that it began with the early solo work of Louis Armstrong.

"Louis departed greatly from all cornet players," said Spurrier, "in his ability to compose a close-knit individual 32 measures with all phrases compatible with each other . . . so Bix and I always credited Louis as being the father of the correlated chorus: play two measures, then two related, making four measures, on which you played another four measures related to the first four, and so on ad infinitum to the end of the chorus.

So the secret was simple—a series of related phrases." Certainly, Armstrong's solos on such 1924 Fletcher Henderson recordings as "Go 'Long Mule" indicate he was aware of the principle.

Bix was particularly partial to the middle register of the cornet, said Spurrier; and a cornet it remained, even after most other brassmen, following Armstrong's lead, had gone over to trumpet and begun to exploit its wider expressive latitudes. "We both discovered that the range we favored within a chorus was almost normal vocal range, that the chorus had to be expressed as though it were being sung—in vocal terms. Neither of us ever played a sustained high note series, we believed, because the throat had a tendency to close; a high note had to be reached for, outside vocal range. You'll notice that on many of Bix's choruses he lunges out for them, then back into vocal range."

Both qualities—complementary or "correlated" phrasing and cultivation of the vocal, "singing" middle-range of the cornet—are on display in Bix's "Jazz Me Blues" solo, along with an already discernible inclination for unusual accidentals and inner chordal voices. It is a pioneer record, introducing a musician of great originality with a pace-setting band. And it astonished even the Wolverines themselves. Each, as George Johnson recalled, was listening hard to himself as the first playbacks came out, through the big horn on the wall, and "I honestly believe that at that moment, and not at any time before, was born in each of us the idea that as a unit, we had something different in the music line. I doubt that any of us realized until that moment how different in style and how dissimilar in effect our results were from the music of the Friars' band that had knocked us all out—and not long before. Coming at us out of that horn, it sounded like the music of another band, not at all like it sounded on the job."

This growing musical awareness was hardly restricted to jazz. Johnson, Moore and Bix had become regular patrons of the Cincinnati Symphony's Saturday matinee concerts. In the absence of more detailed accounts of Bix's non-jazz musical preoccupations at this time, there is always Johnson, quoted by Hoagy, telling all and sundry at the Friar's Inn that Bix, when still at Lake Forest, was "nuts about Ravel and Debussy's stuff." The piano "lessons" with Priscilla Holbrock in Hamilton appear to have developed things still further. Bix was clearly attracted by many of the same elements in those composers which were showing up in his own piano and cornet work: the fuller emotive qualities of chords of the ninth and eleventh, and the formation of melodies which used these voices as part of their fundamental vocabulary. Debussy's *Prelude to the Afternoon of a Faun* and Ravel's *Pavane pour Une Infante Defunte* come quickly to mind among the shorter works.

The Wolverines had been at Doyle's three months but had caused a far greater stir among local musicians than among the paying customers. With the exception of an offer to do a broadcast or two over radio station WLW, there seemed little point in staying around Cincinnati. George Johnson had received a letter from Hoagy Carmichael talking about the possibility of booking the band for a few weekend dances at Indiana University during the spring. But nothing definite.

Jimmy Hartwell came up with a piece of news from his home town. The

101

Northeast corner of Court and Central Avenue, Cincinnati, taken November 28, 1965. Doyle's Dancing Academy occupied the third floor of the corner building. The alley immediately to the right is the one into which the Wolverines lowered their instruments in making their March 1924 getaway.　　　　　**PHOTO COURTESY FRANCIS S. HANNAFORD**

The Wolverine Orchestra in the Gennett studios, Richmond, Indiana, February 18, 1924, on their first record date. L to R: Leibrook, Hartwell, Johnson, Gillette, Moore, Voynow, Bix, Gandee.

Indianapolis Athletic Club was looking for a band to play for its full program of social functions. Auditions would be held around the first of April.

That did it. Agreement was instantaneous. The band gave its notice to Doyle the next morning—only to be told in no uncertain terms that their contract was long-term and binding, and that a departure now was simply out of the question. To emphasize his point, Doyle forbade the musicians to remove their instruments from the building after closing hours.

The prospect of being chained to the dancing academy indefinitely was too much to bear, and an escape strategy was not long in coming. On Monday night, March 31, Dick Voynow stayed late, spreading sheets of manuscript paper across the piano and insisting that he had arrangements to do and no other time in which he could work on them undisturbed. After hanging around for nearly an hour, the caretaker checked the windows, then left him alone with an admonition to "make sure all the doors are locked when you leave."

Once the building was empty and silent, Voynow opened a back window and peered down.

"Hey! You there?" Bix, hidden in the shadows of the alley three stories below, confirmed all were present. Voynow opened the piano lid and took out a length of clothesline; he tied one end of Leibrook's sousaphone and eased the heavy instrument out the window, lowering it gently to the ground. At one point, the horn clanged noisily against the side of the brick building.

"Hey, watch what the hell you're doing!" its owner barked from the darkness—only to fetch an angry "Shhhh!" from Hartwell and Bix. The drums followed, with Moore stage-managing the operation lest his prize bass drum, newly hand-painted with a mountain lake scene and wired up with flashing lights within, come to grief during its descent.

At last all the instruments, plus Voynow, were out and safe. From then on, said George Johnson, it was easy. "Early morning found us in Indianapolis"; all but Cincinnatian Gandee, who seemed almost grateful to see the last of his enforced compatriots. Apart from a guest appearance by George Brunies on one of their records some months later, the Wolverines never again used a trombone.

The Athletic Club audition failed to pan out. For the moment there was no word from Hoagy. That meant, as Bobby Gillette acidly observed, that "we have just joined the swelling ranks of the unemployed." Good to be free of the nightly grind at Doyle's, but the future of the Wolverine Orchestra looked at best questionable.

The weekend brought a break. The band of Charlie Davis, a local favorite, was opening an extended run at the Ohio Theater, playing for movies and doing occasional onstage backing for barbershop quartets, solo singers and an array of local entertainers. The Wolverines decided to hear what kind of music Davis had to offer.

The decision proved a fortuitous one. Davis' group had just worked up a brand new number and dropped it into the first half of the program. He called it "Copenhagen"—and it fetched a reaction from the Wolverines which not even its composer had expected.

"When those boys heard that tune their stage whispers could be heard clear to the box office," recalled Davis. "Bix almost yelled at us, 'Hey, what is it?' and Jimmy Hartwell, their magnificent clarinetist, added, 'Hey, do it one more time!' When we took a rest they came down front in a body, wanting to know, 'Hey, whassat? Where'd ya get that tune? Please play it some more.' "

Davis, pleased at the attention, explained that the title of the tune did *not* refer to the Danish capital, but to the brand of chawin' tobacco his sousaphone player, Ole Olsen, kept in one cheek while pumping out bass notes with the band.

They talked awhile, and it soon became clear to Davis that the Wolverines were short on work prospects, and even shorter on cash. "It became evident that these fellows needed some 'walk around and eatin' money,' so Uncle Fritz Morris, our violinist and treasurer, happily supplied a few dollars each. Our boys chipped in some of the Jasper Corn all musicians usually kept in stock in those days—and gave sky-high praise to Blacker's chili parlor next door, suggesting they give it a try.

"For the record, Jasper Corn was a distillate of the finest Indiana grain corn and barley, boiled into a sour mash, run through the hidden stills of the southern counties and jugged with the original esters at somewhere around 193 proof. The back-hills folks agreed that a draft of full-strength Jasper could cure colds and fever, pleurisy, croup, malaria and sometimes even pneumonia. Certain matrons even claimed a woman ready to deliver with her pains a minute or two apart, upon taking a cupful of Jasper, undiluted, would produce her yelling offspring with never a need for twilight sleep, sodium amatyl or other of the allied nostrums. The boys in our band, without exception, preferred Jasper over bathtub gin—and for good reason. This preference dated from recent 'alky' purchases made from Sammy Kolinsky, our friendly bootlegger . . . purchases which we suspected had been cut down in proof. Maybe Sammy had made three outa two, or maybe yet changing three to four. Who knows?

"But Bix needed no help in forming his opinion of Jasper Corn. He found it a magnificent restorative, a superb stimulant for his lazy appetite which started juices flowing like sap in a Vermont sugar-bush. And so stimulated he planted himself on the corner stool at Blacker's, ordering chili three ways (macaroni, beans and chili). He liked it dry, without too much gravy. He would then drench it with Heinz's catsup; and together with a bowl of oyster crackers—and an additional bowl appropriated from the next place setting—it made a fairly well-balanced meal of protein, carbohydrates and some vitamins.

"Bix didn't mind the waiter eyeing him with utter disbelief, and completely oblivious of any undue attention he would finish his chili, winding up the meal with a dessert of oyster crackers generously laced with chili."

This ritual went on for three days, said Davis. On the fourth day, Bix bounced in for lunch to find a new sign up over Blacker's counter:

Chili three ways . . . . . . 25¢
Chili three ways (with catsup) . 60¢

Morris couldn't go on giving Bix and his friends spending money indefinitely, and for the moment there appeared to be no work in sight. So the Wolverines decided to drive back to Hamilton, where they had open welcome at the YMCA and Min Leibrook's family could see to it that their eating expenses stayed low.

"Don't worry, fellas," Charlie Davis called through cupped hands as the Wolverines climbed aboard the Phaeton. "I'll rustle you up some work in a few days. I'll be in touch." The band returned to Hamilton more than a little sceptical; but Charlie soon proved himself the best good luck charm they'd had since Bernie Cummins. A day or two after their arrival back in Ohio came a telegram: Davis was scheduled to play the Butler College junior prom on April 18. He'd talked the organizers into taking the Wolverines on as a second band, to alternate with his own group in the main ballroom and do separate sets in the smaller south room of the Athletic Club. He'd also landed them four nights in Marion, Indiana, right afterwards.

Cy Milders, who later sang with Davis' band, remembered the looks on the young musicians' faces when the wire arrived. "Bix and all the band just jumped for joy. I can see him in that old blue sweater—I think he wore it for ten years without cleaning it. He said to me, 'We're on our way at last—through the efforts of Charlie Davis!' "

The result, hailed by the Butler campus newspaper *The Collegian* as "the greatest social event in Butler's history," was everything Doyle's should have been but never was. It convinced the seven musicians once and for all that they had something very special, something totally their own.

Davis' own account of the evening's events is characteristically colorful:

"The prom started off in the fashion of the times. We played a set or two kinda soft and sweet-like . . . the boys held the little gals real tight, swaying gracefully with the music and not covering too much territory in the swaying. A regulation dreamy affair . . . our band turn ended with a few polite handclaps, quite reserved and bordering on the delicate. Then the Wolverines started.

"Bix and the boys crashed into the 'Jazz Me Blues' and for eight bars everyone stood kinda stunned-like. Then the place started to rock . . . the poet man must have got his inspiration—when he talked about the 'dawn coming up like thunder' he must have been listening with the kids. The afterbeat swayed the whole building. The excitement built with the kids forgetting about poise and delicacy and jiving like at a football rally. We never saw anything like it. Soon the dancers gathered around Bix and Jimmy and George listening, with their ears practically in the horns, following every hot lick, laughing at every solo break and roaring king-sized appreciation at every hot chorus. This was a spectacle . . . Bix was something to watch as well as something to hear!"

George Johnson summed up the band's feeling about the evening in one short sentence: "We realized," he said, "that we were at last in the right place."

If Davis had been a godsend for the Wolverines, so had they been for him. He was committed to do the summer season at Gar Lawrence's and Otto Ray's Rainbow Casino gardens, but then had a better offer from Harry Page's Fairview Dance Pavilion over at Manito, Illinois. "The Casino management wanted to keep us, and probably for good reason: the Casino catered to the middle-aged bathtub gin crowd that were good spenders; a crowd that liked a good dance rhythm—not too loud, not too fast, and here and there a good vocal. They liked a pretty waltz now and then, and they liked to chin around with the boys in the band and be a little folksy once in a while. Our lads filled this bill in fine fashion. The management couldn't be faulted for wanting to keep a good thing agoin' —but Harry Page wanted us too.

"Fritz Morris solved this problem in a rather subtle fashion. He very quietly planted the story of the prom—how the Wolverines had creamed the Davis lads in the battle of the bands, and finally how, if engaged for the summer, they would build a sizable clientele so big he'd need an armored truck to make the bank deposit. That did it! The Wolverines were engaged for the summer at Casino Gardens."

Suddenly things looked better than Bix had dared hope. The night after the Butler prom he and the Wolverines drove over to Marion, Indiana, for three nights at the Luna Lite Theater, then a civic hall dance on the fourth. Hoagy, too, had kept his promise. A senior at the University of Indiana, Hoagland Howard Carmichael was formally studying law, but seemed far more interested in both playing and talking jazz. Indiana was fertile jazz country, and collegiate fans abounded. New groups were cropping up all the time, most of them—Hoagy's own included—modelled on Bix and the Wolverines and, through them, on the foundations laid by the Rhythm Kings and the Dixieland Band before them.

Some, like Curt Hitch's Happy Harmonists, made it into the Gennett studios and consequently the history books. Others—and veteran fans and musicians insist there were many—were not so fortunate, though none the less good. As the veteran collector-historian Merrill Hammond, himself a former drummer, remarked, "There was a whole separate style of midwest jazz playing, and no one seems to remember that. It flourished in and around Indiana, Illinois and Ohio long before the so-called 'Chicago style' became well-known."

Hoagy considered it his mission to bring the Wolverines to the Bloomington campus as soon as possible—and to make sure their reception there was nothing short of ecstatic. He talked them up among the students, organized pilgrimages to hear them play in Indianapolis and Marion, and finally came across with the promised weekend jobs for them at university fraternity houses and various social functions. He and his crowd, decked out in raccoon coats and quoting lines from P.G. Wodehouse or from their own sage-in-residence, Bill Moenkhaus, were as good a public relations outfit as Bix, Johnson and friends could ask. The Wolverine Orchestra, it seemed, had struck gold at last.

The Wolverines examining a Gennett test pressing during the summer of 1924. Location unknown; perhaps at Palace Theater, Indianapolis. L to R: George Johnson, Bob Gillette, Bix and Vic Berton, front; Jimmy Hartwell, Min Leibrook and Dick Voynow, rear.

The Wolverine Orchestra at the Cinderella Ballroom, New York, September 1924. L ro R: Voynow, Gillette, Johnson, Leibrook, Vic Moore, Hartwell and Bix.

# Chapter 8

For the next month the Wolverines virtually set up headquarters on the Indiana University campus. Hoagy had done his homework; every weekend a different fraternity house featured what the *Indianapolis News* cheerfully described as the "exponents of Sock-time rhythm." And when they did a formal at Kappa Sigma, Carmichael's own fraternity, the reception was euphorically red-carpet.

Hoagy and Bix spent most of their leisure time in each other's company, often listening to Stravinsky's *The Firebird* or *Petrouchka*, sharing a jug, talking in dreamy circles. They joined the gang that hung out down at the Book Nook, a campus bookshop-turned-refreshment parlor which provided a focal point for the more casual side of the University's social life. As Carmichael has reminisced,[6] it played host to everything from deep philosophical discussion to the most disorganized of jam sessions. Bix fit in at once with Bill Moenkhaus, Wad Allen and the rest of Hoagy's circle of rugged individualists, quickly establishing, in just one memorable conversation, his ability to think just as imaginatively as they.

Bix clearly relished the campus life, and his mood as the Phaeton chugged east along Indiana Route 40 on May 6, bound for Richmond and the Wolverines' second Gennett record date, was sheer exuberance. Everything was falling into place: the band sounded better than ever, and the kids were rioting to hear them play. Musicians, too. Curt Hitch's Happy Harmonists from Evansville, down at the far southwest corner of the state, had come over to hear them at Kappa Sig and gone away dazzled. Right there, on the spot, said Hitch, he and his cornetist, Fred Rollison, "had decided to change our orchestra from Original Dixieland style to Wolverine style." They'd watched and listened in awe as Bix and his friends stomped off Charlie Davis' "Copenhagen" on the back of a truck riding from sorority house to sorority house, serenading the girls. "When we heard that, Bix at his very best playing in the open air, we were sold more than ever on the Wolverines."

Davis, Bix mused aloud to Bobby Gillette, was a good guy. He'd gotten them work, shared "Copenhagen" with them, even landed them a job at the Rainbow Casino Gardens in Indianapolis at the end of the month. A godfather.

"Yeah," said Gillette, watching the farmland roll by. "But you could've gone easier on the chili."

---

6. Carmichael, Hoagy, *Sometimes I Wonder*. New York, Farrar, Straus and Giroux, 1965, pp. 54–56, 68–69, 129–134.

The record date was a good one. They did five titles, four of them polished enough to issue. Hoagy had written a band piece for them with some good break stuff in it and a couple of strains for variety. He'd called it "Free Wheeling." Bix liked everything but the name—and had talked the composer into retitling it "Riverboat Shuffle." They did Walter Donaldson's "Oh Baby" and a thing by Indiana sax man Charlie Naset called "Susie." And finally, "Copenhagen."

Thanks to George Johnson, Charlie's tune emerged from the day's labors just a bit different from the way it had gone in. The arrangement involved both George and Jimmy Hartwell playing a chorus apiece on twelve-bar blues chords. "We did three takes of it," said Johnson. "I played a different solo on it every time. Each one, of course, was strictly ad lib." But when the Wolverines' "Copenhagen" hit the market several months later, it was enough of a hit for Melrose Music to have Jelly Roll Morton transcribe the issued version from the disc and publish a stock arrangement with the clarinet and tenor solos written out. Clarinetists quickly departed from all but the opening bars of Hartwell's solo, but Johnson's remained intact: saxophonists playing "Copenhagen" as late as the middle 1930s were still reproducing his figures as though they belonged to the composition. "Imagine," George told an interviewer in 1938, "how it would have been if one of the other versions we did that day had been issued."

The records made by the Wolverines that May Tuesday in 1924 caught the spirit of the moment: seven young men, flushed with success and good living and being young at a time when it was a very good thing to be young and carefree. Their music sings across the years, Bix's tone on his full-chorus "Riverboat Shuffle" solo floating sure and warm out of an Indiana spring. It is an ineffably gentle solo—as gentle, said Hoagy, as its creator. "That's the thing about him that's been lost. He was charming, could be talkative, witty—sometimes even biting. But there was this gentle quality about him. That's what came across most."

> Rainbow Casino Gardens
> Opening Our Outdoor Gardens
> The Rainbow Terrace
> The Charlie Davis Wolverines

The Casino Gardens job began on May 29 with all the excitement of a Bloomington campus fraternity dance. Charlie Davis, out playing for Page at Lake Manito, got what he called "kind of a blow by blow account" of the night from Katie Wilson, a childhood friend studying at Butler at the time. Katie recapped it all years later in a letter to Charlie:

"As you boys know, I danced the junior prom with George, and we never had a better time. We both thought the Wolverines were fantastic . . . and that Bix—well, he was the greatest. All our crowd liked 'em so well we crashed their opening at the Casino without reservations and were tickled pink when we got tables. They had a wonderful crowd. The Hatfields were there with a party of about twenty, buying up a storm with their fresh bath-tub mix. I heard they'd got some VAT 69 labels from Sammy (Kolinsky). The Woodes were there with a good-sized party and even Miss Larue, Bill's secretary (no one can understand why he keeps her on—she's a louzy speller). Old Doc Stone was there with his whole family (his kids had talked him into coming), and I'll bet I could name forty couples from the junior class out at school who wanted a repeat performance of the PROM. And that's just exactly what it was . . . more jumpin', more jivin', etc. A great opening.

"George insisted that we go again Monday to the Casino. We gotta hear the boys—whatta band. I didn't want to go on account of nobody does much business on Monday and with a slim crowd, not too much fun. I did think the Wolverines played their hearts out, but the zip didn't seem the same as Saturday. OK—no sweat! But George insisted on making reservations for the next Saturday."

A nice time to be young and alive. The crowds coming in to hear them at the Gardens, afternoons free to laze around in the country, or even slip into the roof ballroom of the Lincoln Hotel, where they were staying, and play on the big pipe-organ.

Just short of three weeks after Bix and the Wolverines opened at the Casino Gardens, Fritz Morris got a long-distance phone call at Manito from Gar Lawrence. He didn't sound happy. "Hey, Fritz, you gotta help me. These boys don't draw flies, and our business has gone down to nothin'. The river spots are getting all the trade. What the heck am I gonna do with these boys? Gotta let 'em go."

Morris, taken aback, stalled for time. "Quit talkin' a minute, Gar, and lemme think."

"Don't think too long, Fritzie. Just get the hell back down here and play us back in business—and quick. Like right now, f'rinstance."

Morris thought—and came up with a compromise solution. The Miami Lucky Seven, popular with *all* the crowds because they could play it quiet *and* turn on the heat a bit when the occasion demanded, were free. Why not book them in until Charlie's band closed out at the Fairview? Then they'd come back to Indy and pull Gar's bank account out of the red.

Davis knew the Casino Gardens crowd, the folks who "liked a good dance rhythm, not too loud, not too fast . . . a pretty waltz now and then." And what might have knocked 'em out on the campus at Bloomington or for the kids at the Butler prom hardly went down night after night with their parents. Katie had seen the signs at the end of the first week, as she spelled out in her letter to Charlie:

"Saturday, somehow, didn't ring the bells and blow the whistles like before. The Hatfields were there again but with a smaller group, but I had an idea his ulcer was acting up again because Herby wasn't his jovial self and wasn't doin' too much dancin'. We didn't make plans to come next week; George wanted to try one of the other spots, and I was surprised because none of the river clubs had anything like the famous music of the Wolverines.

"Their music is not for the night after night clientele of the Casino Gardens. You've got scads of old geezers who want a good steak, a baked potato and a salad, together with some soft music which won't disturb their meal and won't excite their wives into the dancing urge. And the kids (the ones who have enough allowance to pay the cover) hear 'em a couple of times or maybe three or four and they's had it . . . they are ready for a change.

"Put the Wolverines in spots where the folks come in from the hinterlands for some of the spice and action of the BIG CITY and they'll kill 'em. Give these boys the visiting crowds and they'll send the customers back home again to Indiana with nothin' but rave notices, boasting they'd heard Bix Beiderbecke and his wonderful Wolverines."

By the last week in June the Wolverines were finished at Casino Gardens. But the job, with all its disappointment, had brought one positive development in the form of a flashy Chicagoan named Vic Berton. Berton played drums—and he was good. His 28 years had already seen experience ranging from the Chicago Symphony Orchestra through John Philip Sousa into jazz bands, pit orchestras and even leadership of the house group at the Merry Gardens. He'd heard "Jazz Me Blues," and, intrigued, had come along to hear some more. The Wolverines, he told Voynow with the air of a big-time pro, were even better than they themselves thought they were.

"Listen, take it from me, you guys are just great. You gotta be heard." Berton's fame so eclipsed anything the Wolverines or even Bix had yet known that they felt compelled to hear out his proposal for what he called "our little partnership": he would take over management of the band, at least for the summer, handling the bookings and playing drums. He had connections throughout Illinois, Indiana, Ohio, even down into West Virginia. He could get work.

"Just leave it to me," he said. "You guys'll *kill* them."

Fine, said Bix. But there were going to be problems. If Berton moved in on drums, there would be no place for Vic Moore, mainstay of the band sound. He and Gillette, working as a team, had made the whole "sock time" idea possible. Without Vic—well, said Bix, Berton might be good and fast, but Vic Moore was the Wolverines' drummer.

"Let's try him out," said Hartwell. It seemed a fair idea, especially in view of the work situation, and by June 20, when the Wolverines drove over to Richmond for another Gennett date, Berton was in. For a week or two they carried two drummers, while they made up their minds what to do. Berton booked them into the Palace Theater in Indianapolis as the "Vic Berton Wolverine Orchestra," followed by a short tour of vaudeville houses in Louisville, Terre Haute and other cities. He had a deal lined up with his cousin, Louis Glueck, who was on the parks board in Gary, to use the Wolverines during August at the new Marquette Park Pavilion. They could also do the Gay Mill dancehall at Miller Beach, right nearby.

But what to do about Vic Moore? Vic himself came up with the answer. After watching Berton in action on the June 20 record date, he took his souvenir test pressing of "Tiger Rag" and announced that he was returning to Chicago for a "vacation," and would rejoin after Labor Day, if they wanted him.

The three titles recorded on June 20 show the beginnings of a pattern which was to culminate before the end of the year in Bix's departure from the Wolverine Orchestra. His solos on "I Need Some Pettin'," "Royal Garden Blues" and even a tense, scrambling "Tiger Rag" show him already in motion while his colleagues are standing still. There is little change in Jimmy Hartwell's clarinet playing between "Fidgety Feet" in February and "Sensation," recorded seven months later. But the Bix Beiderbecke who takes the first solo chorus on "I Need Some Pettin'" is already using notes and figure constructions more ambitious than anything he would have attempted in his days at Doyle's. The tone is big and round, with a new ring clearly audible even through the acoustical recording.

Red Nichols, on his way out to Walled Lake, Michigan, to join Dick Bowen and his "Blue Streak Orchestra of New York," heard somewhere in eastern Indiana that the Wolverines were playing nearby, and went bumping down a series of rutted dirt roads to catch them and sit in. It was the first time he had heard Bix in person; the encounter shaped the rest of his long musical career.

Nichols had come to hear of the Wolverine Orchestra—and of its 21-year-old cornetist—in an entertainingly roundabout fashion. On June 26 he had recorded a pop tune, "You'll Never Get to Heaven With Those Eyes," for Victor with George Olsen's orchestra. Arranger Eddie Kilfeather had given Red a full-chorus solo, a note-for-note transcription of Bix's "Jazz Me Blues" solo on the Wolverines' Gennett.

Red, intrigued, asked Kilfeather what it was. When, less than a month later, he saw them advertised in Indiana, he could not pass up a chance to hear this new band in the flesh.

On into August. Eugene Swartz, a senior at the University of Illinois, was working as a lifeguard at Gary municipal beach. Like many a midwest collegiate jazz fan, he had fallen under the spell of the Wolverines that spring, discarding his C-melody saxophone for a tuba—and a chance to play two-to-the-bar oompah in a campus combo. He had seen posters announcing the Wolverines' August 2 opening at Marquette Park, but was nevertheless astonished one morning to catch sight of George Johnson, Vic Berton and Bix Beiderbecke tramping across the sand toward the lake for a before-lunch swim.

"I found out they were living in a couple of cottages up in the dunes not far away, and got to know them all pretty well during this time," he said. "I took to coming over to the pavilion evenings to listen to them play, then took off with them afterwards." The pavilion, a bare brick shell with open sides, all but engulfed the band in the evening's early hours. But by 10 P.M., said Gene, there were usually large and enthusiastic crowds, liberally peppered with musicians and collegians, Hoagy and his gang among them.

"After 1 A.M., when dancing at the pavilion ended every night, we sometimes went over to Indiana Harbor, a part of the city of East Chicago, Indiana, about ten miles from Gary," Swartz said. "There was an all-night cabaret there called the Martinique Inn; they served the usual moonshine drinks of the era and had a small band. Bix liked to go there but seldom took his horn."

The late clarinetist-saxophonist Milton "Mezz" Mezzrow led the house band at the Martinique. As Swartz recalled it, Bix usually moved right in "at the piano, and most of the time it would turn out to be an all-night session. You may have heard a lot of tales about Bix being on the wild side, but at least in the time I knew him I don't think that this was true. We all used to drink—but certainly not to excess." Swartz did admit, however, that "it was some of the Wolverines that first introduced the gang I ran with to marijuana, but this was more a thrill process than a habit. You tried it and forgot about it. It certainly wasn't an habitual thing."

Neither Berton nor Mezzrow was any novice at smoking "muggles." Mezz dwelt long and lovingly on it in his autobiography, *Really the Blues*.

Berton was to have the rather dubious distinction, seven years later, of being "busted" with Louis Armstrong when they were caught sharing a joint in a Los Angeles parking lot. Louis, loath to put his fast-growing career at risk through further brushes with the law, gave up all use of "gage" on the spot, as he later related to the British jazz critic Max Jones.

Bix, from all accounts, never even got beyond a tentative first flirtation. Drummer Harry Gale was one of several close friends categorical on this point:

"As you know, Bix came from an excellent family and reflected gentle and fine instincts in his behavior," Gale told the authors in a 1973 letter. "Yes, we're all aware of his drinking problem. However, nothing annoys me more than when I hear people mention that Bix used marijuana and stronger stuff. Nothing could be further from the truth! Bix strongly opposed such use and frowned upon other musicians who used pot. It was Bix's opinion and is my own to this day that a musician does not play well under the influence of marijuana."

Vic Berton's thirteen-year-old kid brother Ralph, who grew up to become a respected author and scholar, spent the month with the band in one of the dune cottages, and by his own account followed Bix around in rapt hero-worship. He has written extensively and euphorically of sitting "glued to a chair hard by the bandstand" to watch his hero's every expression. His account of these weeks, lengthily serialized abroad and published in the United States in 1974 by Harper and Row, captures the flavor of a 1924 summer spent with little to do but be young and able to pour all of youth's energies into making music.

Bix, he of the twinkling brown eyes and ready smile, attracted his share of female admirers, as both Berton and Swartz attested. "There was one," said Gene, "who had gotten quite a crush on him and followed the band everywhere. I'm not certain where she came from—it might have been Indianapolis. Her name was Gladys, and while Bix would spend the occasional night with her she never achieved permanent bunk status by being allowed to move into his cottage."

Through all the giddiness, some thought still had to be given to the future. Prospects for work after August looked slim, and Vic Berton had run out of surefire ideas for booking "his" Wolverines.

Min Leibrook wrote to his friend Harl Smith, who played drums in one of Paul Specht's dance bands and managed Specht's booking office in New York's Hilton Building at 48th and Broadway, to ask about bringing the Wolverines to New York. Smith, as it happened, was in a position to help. A Mr. Josephs, one of two brothers who managed the newly-opened Cinderella Ballroom across the street, had been in to talk music and business. He had hired the popular dance band of Arthur Lange in an effort to pull some of the dancing crowds away from the Roseland, three blocks up Broadway at 51st Street. "But instead, business was lousy," said Smith.

"I'd had this letter from Min, whom I knew from Ohio, and he told me about the band, how they'd like to come to New York, and so forth. I talked them up to the Cinderella guy, and he decided to buy them, and run two bands . . . continuous music . . . and I am positive that that was the beginning of that policy at that time."

The Cinderella came as good news, and was soon chief topic of conversation at Miller Beach. With the pavilion job due to end on Labor Day, the bleak outlook of only a few weeks before had been replaced with anticipation of a job on Broadway, and the fame it could mean for the Wolverines and for Bix.

They wired Vic Moore and he came at once. With Labor Day, the Wolverine Orchestra, its two drummers, Vic Berton's kid brother and a well-to-do hanger-on named Lloyd "Babe" Jones set out in two old touring cars for the long haul east to New York City.

The trip overland took four days and most of the nights, punctuated by flat tires, potentially fatal accidents narrowly avoided, and occasional roadside stops "just to jam a number or two." Accounts of this odyssey vary as to time, route and events, but it is clear that money was in short supply and that Babe Jones picked up at least some of the Wolverines' running costs en route. Ralph Berton tells of having been accompanied at least part of the way by "several stray sweethearts of the band," perhaps anticipating the preoccupations of the groupie culture by half a century.

Jones's family owned a large country house not far from Keuka Lake, one of the Finger Lakes in New York State, where Hoagy and Johnson had played the summer of '23 with violinist Tommy Bassett. Accordingly, he offered to put the road-weary musicians up for a few days to relax before the final sprint into the city. They accepted only too gratefully. One of the cars had skidded and turned over outside Buffalo, nerves were taut, and towing and repairs had just about cleaned out the band exchequer. Tired and irritable, they burst in the front door and collapsed onto anything in sight which was soft, be it couch, bed or rug.

Once in Manhattan, the Wolverines moved in on whatever friends and acquaintances they could, until their first Cinderella paycheck allowed them to take hotel rooms. Bix stayed a few days with the Berton family, which had relocated in New York some time before.

New York was full of good jazz and crack musicians, and the Wolverines went out looking for their share in the little time they had before opening at the Cinderella. The whole septet was in the audience Sunday evening, September 7, when Ray Miller's band, with Frankie Trumbauer on C-melody sax and Milfred "Miff" Mole on trombone, did a concert at the Hippodrome theater.

Miff's chorus on an up-tempo "Limehouse Blues" drew such stamping and whistling from the gallery that ushers moved in fast to eject what they thought were rowdies heckling the band. Backstage afterwards, the "rowdies" introduced themselves to Miff, and he laughed in relief. "Jeez, I thought you guys were giving me the bird."

Quickly redubbed "The Personality Kids" for the engagement, the Wolverines opened Friday at the Cinderella opposite Willie Creager's dance band and proved an instant hit. The dancers caught on to their "sock time" from the start, and the word got around fast among musicians that a new band was in town, and that they were something special.

A lot of the New Yorkers came around to listen out of little more than curiosity. They'd heard it all, from the Dixieland Band on, and didn't surprise easily. Many had even heard the Gennett records and came with an idea of what to expect. But according to Richardson "Dick" Turner, a trumpet-playing Yale undergraduate, Bix's way of doing things knocked out even the sophisticates.

Flanked by a party of ten Ivy League friends, Turner went down to 48th and Broadway a few nights after the opening to hear it for himself. "There must have been about 50–60 musicians standing around, hats in hand. No one was dancing just then—everyone was listening to the Wolverines playing. It is impossible for me to express properly the electric thrill this bunch produced, except to say that I think it was at least partly due to watching them, actually seeing them playing their music."

Records by white New York musicians at this time provide ample explanation of the Wolverines' impact. If the New Yorkers were high on technique and polish, their jazz seldom exceeded the limits prescribed by public taste for "novelty music." A "hot" man such as Mole or Trumbauer might get half a chorus worth of solo space in a dance band arrangement; small Memphis Five-type groups might distill Dixieland Band numbers and pop tunes into peppy "syncopation"; but it was a rare thing to hear a full seven-piece white band devoted to playing jazz *as* jazz, with no compromises. The Wolverines, with Bix's lead flashing the way, were like a beacon for Turner and his friends, something brand new, indescribably exciting.

Ironically, another historic jazz moment, very much a parallel one, was occurring a few blocks up Broadway at Roseland about the time the Wolverines opened at the Cinderella. Louis Armstrong had just come east to join Fletcher Henderson's big band, and black musicians were swarming to hear him in the same numbers—and with the same awe—as the whites were going to hear Bix. Armstrong turned jazz brass playing on its ear, all but eclipsing even the individual styles developed by Joe Smith, Jabbo Smith and other Negro brassmen on the New York scene.

As for the Wolverines, they even *looked* different. Bix "played in an unorthodox way," said Turner. "He shook the horn with all fingers up, and played leaning over at the floor at about a 45° angle. They'd take about ten 'last' choruses on each tune, standing around the drummer and playing at him. It was frantic." The audience this night also included at least two significant guests. The first, in an expensive polo coat, was a roly-poly fiddle player from Denver whose band's popular music style hardly earned him his sobriquet "King of Jazz." But Paul Whiteman knew talent when he heard it, and came away from the Cinderella with an admiration for Bix Beiderbecke which only three years later would bring the younger man into his brass section and the front ranks of the big time.

Another spectator, no less enthusiastic, represented Bix's past as clearly as did Whiteman his future. Nick LaRocca listened to about three numbers and was heard to remark, "Well, I guess I'll have to go home and get my *cor*net," pronouncing the instrument's name the British way, accent on the first syllable.

Harl Smith came up to hear them. "Business had picked up at once," he said. "It was sensational. People would stand around and listen to the other orchestra; then, the minute the Wolverines would play, the floor was packed."

Dick Turner went around backstage to meet the band. "Bix was quite pale, even then, probably due to his all-night activities. But he was very kind to us, and showed this wonderful, often biting sense of humor. We discovered we had a good bit in common: we both enjoyed P. G. Wodehouse, thought a lot of the same things were funny. We agreed that we'd have to see more of each other, which, of course, we did." The friendship

116

sealed that night lasted until Bix's death seven years later.

The trade press more than matched the enthusiasm shown for the Wolverines by New York jazzmen. Writing in *Variety* for Wednesday, September 24, reviewer Abel Green averred that

> ... as a torrid unit it need doff the mythical chapeau to no one. Their sense of rhythm and tempo is ultra for this type of dance music, and their unquestionable favor with the dance fans speaks for itself ... the band has struck favor from the start! Out west they recorded for the Gennett disks, but although less than a week on Broadway they have had 'dates' with a number of minor companies, with the Brunswick also interested.

Vic Moore, asked in later years about these alleged other record dates, said the reference was probably journalistic license for the sake of plugging the band, which was recording only for Gennett.

Nor was enthusiasm about the new cornet star confined to the pros in New York. The rapid development of Bix Beiderbecke had intrigued Jean Goldkette, the Detroit bandleader who had lured Don Murray away from the lake boats the summer before and had a reputation as a man who appreciated jazz talent.

Born in France and trained as a concert pianist in Greece and Russia, he had come to the United States in 1911 in search of a career in the concert halls of the new world. To pick up money in the meantime, he played in dance bands led by Edgar Benson, founder of the Benson Orchestra of Chicago, one of the Victor Talking Machine Company's most popular recording attractions. Benson, taking note of his new pianist's continental accent and charm, decided to try him out as a front man for Benson office bands. He achieved quick popularity and before long made the jump to Detroit, with bands and a booking agency of his own, à la Benson. Like his former boss, he had an eye for organization and an acute business instinct—and like Benson he was quick to realize and exploit the commercial potential of having jazz players in his groups. By mid-1924 he had snared Murray, trombonists Bill Rank and Tommy Dorsey, and Tommy's saxophone-playing elder brother Jimmy, for the thirteen-piece orchestra at his Graystone Ballroom.

The Graystone itself Goldkette had built into what its own house newsletter, *Graystone Topics,* would later extoll as ...

> The most beautiful ballroom in the middle west if not in all the land. The Graystone is ravishingly beautiful. From the main entrance to the farthest corner of the spacious ballroom it is bewildering and bewitching, a maze of color as radiant and varied as the rainbow and as perfectly harmonized and gracefully blended.
>
> The entrance lobby is purely Spanish in design. The walls are stuccoed in a soft, creamy tan tint, and the ceiling is resplendent in a canopy of satiny fabric. Characteristic of Spanish decoration and architectural art are wall niches in unexpected places, pedestals, miniature trees, and flower-adorned fountains, and the whole scene is enriched by subdued vari-colored lights ...
>
> The mezzanine around the entire ballroom is canopied and replete with inviting chairs and divans where guests may rest or lounge while enjoying the music and a full view of the dancers below ...

As the word got around about the sensational new cornetist from Iowa, Jean Goldkette's curiosity increased. He made it his point to listen to the Wolverines' Gennett records, and heard just enough to convince him that it would be worthwhile to hear young Beiderbecke in person, and see how he fared over the grind of an evening's job playing for dancers.

Goldkette came to New York and, unannounced and unrecognized, visited the Cinderella. He made his decision on the spot, went backstage, introduced himself and made Bix an offer to come back to Detroit and join the Goldkette Victor Recording Orchestra. The money would be good, far better than Bix could hope to earn with the Wolverines.

The cornetist sat down and looked for a long time at the dapper little man with the round spectacles. Finally, he spoke.

"Can I have a little while to think about it? Do I have to tell you yes or no right now?" Goldkette assured him he did not, and could take his time deciding, then wire his answer.

A hard decision to make. New York was exciting, and it had welcomed him. Name musicians were coming around to sit in and listen. Red Nichols, especially, had become a fervent admirer since his encounter with the band in Indiana. Bix's tone and attack were already becoming discernible in Nichols' own playing.

In New York Bix could go up to Roseland and hear Louis with Henderson, or walk a block up Broadway to the Kentucky Club, on 49th Street, where Edward Kennedy "Duke" Ellington, a pianist from Washington, had a good little band. Up on Pelham Parkway, at their own Ramblers Inn Roadhouse, the California Ramblers played hot dance music with Bobby Davis on alto sax, Bill "Jazz" Moore on trumpet and the widely-admired Adrian Rollini playing things on the ponderous bass sax that most other jazzmen couldn't even execute on alto or tenor. Harlem offered such lavish jazz-flavored revue productions as Noble Sissle's and Eubie Blake's "Chocolate Dandies." The Lafayette Theater, at 131st Street and Seventh Avenue, was featuring the beautiful Florence Mills in the "Plantation Revue," backed by an all-star hot band. And Bix's special favorite among the black singers, Ethel Waters, had just returned from a stay in Chicago.

The Cinderella itself was not without its appeal. The management had picked up on the growing craze for the Charleston, a syncopated dance step around in one form or another since the first decade of the century, but which had only really caught on after being featured by the chorus line in the Broadway show *Runnin' Wild* the year before to music by the Harlem piano master James P. Johnson. Now, all at once, everyone was doing it, and no band interested in commercial success could afford to ignore it. The Charleston beat cropped up overnight in arrangements played by the California Ramblers; even their Columbia recording of "Copenhagen," otherwise faithful to Jelly Roll's transcription of the Wolverines' Gennett, managed to sneak a Charleston sequence into the first strain.

Within weeks, the Cinderella had become the place to head for if you wanted to Charleston. Things got fast and furious—and, inevitably, a bit on the wild side for more conventional older dancers. As George Johnson ruefully remarked, "Those who did not dance it, and some of those who did, found a crowded floor a disadvantage, objecting to the danger to life and limb in the shape of flying feet, and soon the situation changed. The

Charleston dancers came to the Cinderella and the rest of the dancers who liked less violence went elsewhere."

Yet Goldkette's offer had been attractive. After days of agonizing about it and discussing it with the others in the band, Bix cabled his yes to Detroit. He did so with the blessing of his fellow-Wolverines, by now resigned to the realization that their cornetist was destined for bigger things.

Then, by a coincidence supreme in its irony, the roof fell in at the Cinderella. Josephs decided that the Charleston trade was driving away too many of the cash customers, and only a drastic change in policy would reverse the tide. That meant dumping the Wolverines. He broke the news bluntly: their contract would not be picked up after the initial three-month period.

Through connections in Florida dating back to the winter they'd spent there with Hoagy, Johnson and Moore set up a deal that would take the band down to Palm Springs that December—but without Bix. They'd have to get a replacement in a hurry.

The first choice was probably the most logical. If the New Orleans Rhythm Kings had been the Wolverines' first inspiration, why not try to snare their ex-trumpet man, Paul Mares? He was at home in New Orleans and not doing much. Dick Voynow, who had resumed managerial duties when Vic Berton faded out of the picture, wired him an offer to join. Mares turned it down but suggested a promising young Crescent City trumpet man who, he said, would be a natural to fill Bix Beiderbecke's shoes. Mares, as one of the group of white New Orleans musicians who in later years persistently attributed Bix's style to Emmett Hardy, may well simply have underestimated the demands of the Wolverines. He sent Joseph "Sharkey" Bonano, who duly arrived at the Cinderella brimful of confidence and bravado.

He lasted just short of two hours. He knew hardly any of the band's repertoire, even appeared to have trouble picking up the songs as he went along. In later years, George Johnson remembered little of him save his fire-engine-red long underwear. "I doubt if any man ever made a faster round trip," said the saxophonist.

"How about Rollison?" somebody ventured the morning after Sharkey's abrupt departure. Fred Rollison, Curt Hitch's cornet man, had developed a rolling melodic style heavily influenced by—if less dynamic than—that of Bix. Voynow sent another wire.

"When I walked on to the bandstand that Sunday night it was an unforgettable thrill," Rollison said in 1966. "The place was packed with all the leading musicians and publishers in New York. I struck off with a tune I knew by heart and got a good hand, but after a couple more tunes I began to hit rough sledding. The Wolverines had a book of head arrangements numbering over 85 standards, and about 25 pop tunes, and they didn't have the time for me to learn them all."

Exit Rollison. But now that he was in New York, he decided to hang around for a few days anyway while Bix, Gillette and Hartwell showed him what delights the big city had to offer.

Still no replacement. In later years, Red Nichols disclaimed any assertion that he, too, was approached for the job. Nichols, just establishing himself as a freelancer and recording-studio regular, had no intention of giving it all up—certainly not to go to Florida. Besides, he said, at $50 a side for records alone he was making far more than the Wolverines could offer him.

Vic Moore came up with a name. The summer before he'd heard about a high school kid playing on one of the lake boats. He was young, very green—but he played clean and a bit like Bix. "Have him come," said the star of the Wolverines, and a telegram went out to Jimmy McPartland: "CAN YOU JOIN WOLVERINES IN NEW YORK REPLACING BIX BEIDERBECKE AT SALARY OF EIGHT-SEVEN DOLLARS FIFTY PER WEEK QUERYMARK ANSWER IMMEDIATELY STOP." McPartland didn't take long to make up his mind. Within a day, the 17-year-old cornetist's answer was in hand: "SEND TRANSPORTATION STOP I ACCEPT JOB." Voynow sent him $32.50, exact railway fare from Chicago to New York, and McPartland headed east, toting a dented old silver cornet with clanking valves, plus one battered suitcase.

The Wolverines, meanwhile, had one more Gennett record date to do before Bix left. Fred Rollison, by now enjoying himself thoroughly in the big city, came along to watch them do two pop tunes, "Tia Juana" and "Big Boy"—both liberally sprinkled with Charleston beats. Bix, said Rollison, had an idea. "He dreamed up a cornet duet for 'Big Boy' featuring the two of us, but although we practiced it incessantly, Bix was never satisfied and kept changing it. Eventually, just as we were ready to cut the tune, he decided to scrap the duet altogether and substituted his piano solo in its place. I stood by, holding his cornet as he played the passage."

The next two days were frantic. McPartland, a husky, curly-haired kid with a bluff manner and big smile, got in early the next morning, grabbed a few hours' sleep, and turned up full of energy for an afternoon rehearsal called by Voynow. Jimmy Hartwell suggested running down a couple of choruses of each tune in quick sequence, in order to avoid a recurrence of what had happened with Sharkey and Rollison.

"I was very nervous," said McPartland in recollection. "Of course I had memorized some of the band's arrangements from their records, and when Dick asked me what I wanted to play I said, 'Anything.'" For good measure, he reeled off a few samples.

"You know all those?" Hartwell was openly sceptical.

"Sure," said the newcomer, cockier now. Voynow counted off "Jazz Me Blues" and the audition began, Bix sitting off to the side, listening. "I played their routines, took my solo where Bix used to take his, and when the number was finished, Bix patted me on the back and said, 'Great, kid.' He called me 'kid' for the next couple of years, even though he was only four years older than I. We did a few more tunes and I was in, then and there. I started feeling a helluva lot better, relieved, all the more so when Bix said to me, 'Hey, kid, I like you. Tell you what—why don't you move in with me and I'll show you all the stuff you need?'"

McPartland moved in, and the next couple of afternoons found the two together, Bix "showing me the tunes and coaching me in stuff he used in his playing. It was funny—every morning, as soon as we rolled out of bed, we'd get our horns out and he'd show me phrasing and certain little figures, some of which I still play. He told me, 'You may be playing along, and if your mind goes blank you can always fill in with one of these. They sound good anywhere.'

120

Jimmy McPartland, cornet replacement when Bix left the Wolverines in October 1924.    PHOTO BY R. M. SUDHALTER

Ray Miller, whose band of 1924 included Miff Mole (trombone), Frank Trumbauer (C-melody sax), and Rube Bloom (piano).

PHOTO COURTESY MELODY MAKER

Joseph "Sharkey" Bonano, the trumpeter sent from New Orleans on Paul Mares's recommendation to replace Bix.

PHOTO COURTESY MELODY MAKER

"Then at night we'd go to the Cinderella and play the tunes together. First he'd take the lead, then have me take over while he played a second part to break me in."

Nor was Bix's patronage limited to tips on phrasing. McPartland's beat-up cornet, its intonation none too certain, began to prove irksome to his host. Bix handed him his newest Conn Victor one afternoon to try, and the young Chicagoan was converted. "You need a horn like this," said Bix. "C'mon with me."

After stopping to hit Voynow for some money, they headed for the C. G. Conn showrooms. Four or five Victor models later, Bix found one he liked, and with a "Hey, kid, this is the one for you," presented it to his new protege. McPartland, flabbergasted, protested. "Look, kid," said Bix, affecting the same world-weary tone he'd used to relate his schoolboy exploits three years earlier to Putzier and other Davenport pals, "I like you, you're a good guy. You sound like I do but you don't copy me. You play your own stuff. So take the horn and blow it."

Bix left the Wolverines on Friday, the 10th of October. McPartland made two sides with them for Gennett in December, and the music tells its own story: the lift and buoyancy gone, the weaknesses of the rhythm section now on glaring display. Bix had taken the magic with him.

Miff Mole, Frank Trumbauer and Rube Bloom, all members of Ray Miller's band, had set up their own date for Gennett and asked Bix to come along before he left town. He, in turn, got Moore and Min Leibrook for the rhythm section. They recorded Saturday afternoon, and in a sense "I'm Glad," a Trumbauer original, and Bloom's up-tempo "Flock o' Blues" stand as milestones on Bix Beiderbecke's march upward. Some of the Wolverines' energy shows up, but there is also a new sophistication and ensemble looseness never achieved by the larger group.

Trumbauer, musical director for the day, decided in the interests of good relations with Ray Miller, who was under contract to Brunswick, not to have the coupling issued under his own name. Bix eagerly snapped up his call for suggestions as to what to call the pickup group.

"How about the Davenport Six?"

Silence in the studio. Miff Mole suppressed a giggle. They really took civic pride seriously out there in the corn country. "Okay, Bix. We'll call it the Davenport Six. Right, fellers?"

Nobody objected, and Bix left the studio happy. Only when the record came out did he learn that his city-slicker friends had pulled a fast one on him. The group's name celebrated an Iowa community all right, but one directly across the state from Davenport. It was called the Sioux City Six.

Time to leave for Detroit. He filled in Sunday night for Harry Gluck with the New Orleans Jazz Band, which also featured the fluent clarinet of Sidney Arodin. Then, all high hopes and just a little trepidation, Bix Beiderbecke boarded a Monday morning train for Detroit and what looked for all the world like a jump at last into the big time.

Bix at the wedding of his sister, Mary Louise, to Theodore Shoemaker at Davenport Outing Club, November 8, 1924. Bix is in the rear row, second from left. Brother Burnie is in the rear row, third from right, standing immediately behind Mary Louise.

# Chapter 9

Jean Goldkette, said the *Detroit Sunday News*, "has just returned from a tour of the eastern cities, in which he has gathered many ideas which are to be employed by his orchestra this winter." One such idea brought a new face, that of Bix Beiderbecke, into the Goldkette ensemble for its 1924–25 season at the Graystone Ballroom, downtown at 4237 Woodward. Bix deposited his union card with Detroit's Local 5 on Wednesday, October 15, the morning after his arrival from New York and three days after the report in the *News*. He listed himself as staying with William and Freda Kraft at 5323 Parker Avenue.

From the start, when he turned up for work Wednesday evening, the going was far from easy. The Goldkette book was scored for four brass—two trumpets and two trombones—giving Bix more sight reading to cope with than he had ever had in one place. The band's weekly 10 P.M. broadcasts over station WWJ demanded a constant flow of new material. Fred "Fuzzy" Farrar, first trumpet and brass section leader, helped where he could, but it soon became clear that Bix was in over his head. If there was a hot chorus to be played he was on firm ground, but the rest of the time he floundered. Somehow he got by, with Farrar helping out in the section and fellow-jazzmen Tommy Dorsey and Don Murray cheering him on when he soloed. But something had to give, and it took a domineering, pear-shaped Victor recording director named Edward T. King to bring things to a crisis.

King had been with the Victor Talking Machine Company since the early days of the World War. Working out of New York, he combined the functions of the modern-day artist-and-repertoire man with occasional stints as conductor, piano accompanist and even auxiliary percussionist on Victor records. He was a man of firm, if none too catholic, tastes, and hot jazz of the sort Bix Beiderbecke played was definitely not among them. This, coupled with King's absolute and unchallenged authority over recording sessions under his supervision, was to have irreversibly damaging consequences for Bix and for a later Jean Goldkette orchestra. But Eddie King's distaste for jazz hardly kept him from realizing that a bit of it could sell records. As a result, he allowed a measure of hot improvisation on popular or dance band records as long as the melody was clearly in evidence and "things don't get out of hand."

Victor sent King, a pair of technicians and a truckload of portable recording equipment on a swing through Minneapolis, Detroit and Cleveland in the autumn of 1924 with an eye to recording as many bands, orchestras and soloists as possible. The company had not yet begun recording operations in Chicago, and this was the most practical means of reaching attractions which seldom if ever came east to New York or Camden. Within two years, the advent of electrical recording would make such field trips unnecessary, as recording studios sprang up in most major U.S. cities. King had recorded the Goldkette orchestra during a two-day session in March under much the same circumstances, and the records had sold well.

The Victor crew arrived in Detroit during the weekend and set up its equipment at the Detroit Athletic Club, the hall used with considerable success during the March sessions. Monday morning the Goldkette Graystone orchestra, this time with Bix, turned up to begin another two-day spate of recordings.

Their first number of the day was a reworked stock arrangement of "I Didn't Know," a pop tune which seemed likely to catch on nationally. The entire second chorus was given over as a solo to Bix, showcasing the arrival of the star of the Wolverines. The band ran it down, Eddie King standing quietly off to the side. When they finished, he summoned Charlie Horvath, drummer and band manager, for a conference.

"Who the hell's that kid on the cornet?" His tone augured ill.

"That's Bix Beiderbecke." Horvath kept talking. "We got him from the Wolverines. He's the last word these days, hottest thing around. Big hit on the campuses."

King scowled and snapped his suspenders. "Yeah? Well, let the college kids have 'im, then. That's not the kind of jazz we want here. Take him off it." Horvath protested. King shook his head. But when Horvath started to do a slow burn, King appeared to change his mind.

"All right, all right, let him play. But keep him under control."

The recording began. They did one take, Bix taking a full chorus. No good, said King. Too long. A half-chorus was plenty. On take two Tommy Dorsey blew the melody for 16 bars with the saxophones reading the arrangement behind him. Bix got the last 16. This version survived, to be issued nearly half a century later; it brings Bix's tone ringing across far more clearly than had the primitive Gennetts. But by now King had had enough.

"I said take 'im off, and I mean take 'im off!" he thundered at Horvath. "Give the solo to your first man and tell him to play it properly!" Farrar played it straight. Bix sat as if struck. King, said pianist Paul Mertz, was satisfied.

"He just didn't like that kind of jazz from the very first hearing," said Mertz. "He probably tolerated a couple of takes so as not to be too brutal in yanking away the plum. He then changed the spot over to Farrar for the Henry Busse type of polite trumpet he preferred."

Bix "was stunned and heartbroken. We were all pretty crestfallen, as we thought he was just the greatest, despite his reading trouble." Mertz's memory of this session helped a number of jazz historians, including the authors, to unearth this lost recording and get it issued at last in 1960. By that time, the stamper in Victor's vaults had been damaged through decay, but RCA issued the selection anyway for its historical value. No other version of "I Didn't Know" from this session ever saw issue.

Bix took no further part in Monday's recordings, but sat unhappy at the back of the hall while the band ran through "I Want to See My Tennessee" and Irving Berlin's "Remember." But the next day, said Mertz, he was back.

"We were doing a symphonic arrangement of Borowski's 'Adoration' written by George Crozier, who had played trombone with us earlier. Bix loved this arrangement, but it was only scored for two trumpets, and Goldkette had Tex Brusstar handling the second part. Bix begged to have a third part added in spots that he could handle, so that he could honestly claim to have participated.

"Goldkette, King and Horvath went along with the notion . . . a rather sparse third trumpet part was cued in, and since Bix couldn't read even that worth a damn, the fingering was written for him above each note. So Bix made the record, and was elated no end."

"Adoration" was pressed but never released commercially. Each band member got a test pressing as a souvenir. "Mine," said Mertz, "was promptly broken when I carefully laid it on a car seat and someone sat on it."

The clash with King over "I Didn't Know" hardly affected Bix's stature in the eyes of Murray, Rank, Dorsey and the others in Goldkette's jazz-oriented band. But it brought the leader face to face with a problem he had been trying to avoid for some time. Bix's continued presence was becoming a liability, both for the group and for the cornetist himself. It meant paying an extra trumpet to play the parts, leaving Bix there just for solos. Jazz formed only a part of the band's repertoire, meaning that Bix was playing only sporadically, something that was doing neither his embouchure nor his development as a jazzman any good. Goldkette discussed the problem with Horvath. Both, reluctantly, agreed Bix would have to go. Goldkette's planning called for switching Joe Venuti, Tommy Dorsey and some of the others to the band being formed to open the new Book-Cadillac Hotel on Monday, the 8th of December. The resulting reorganization would be as painless a time as any to drop Bix from the regular personnel.

"But I don't want to let him out of my sight," the leader added as an afterthought. "He's going to be very good indeed; mark my words."

Goldkette broke the news to Bix himself, cushioning it with some fatherly—and heartfelt—advice. "Go out and get some experience, Bix. Brush up your reading, learn more about music so you can be an advantage to any ensemble you join. The jazzing is all well and good, but there are other skills you have to master." He promised to use the young cornetist whenever possible and to "keep an eye on you." Ultimately, perhaps, there might again be a place in the Victor recording orchestra for this most promising of jazzmen.

But come December 8th, Bix was out. No more Wolverines, no more Goldkette. Just a young Iowan with a cornet and a growing reputation, and nowhere in particular to go. He flipped a coin, and struck out for Indianapolis. There, at least, he had friends. Hoagy was there; Charlie Davis was still around. It shouldn't be too tough to come up with some sort of work.

Carmichael had no jobs—but he offered what seemed, for the moment, the next-best thing. The girl he'd been dating had a friend; perhaps she'd fix Bix up. It was worth a try, anyway.

She pulled it off, and a day or two later Bix went out for the first time with Cornelia Marshall, who worked in the New York Central Railroad office downtown. He took to dropping down to the office about closing time and walking her home.

"He was a very kind and sweet person, and at all times a perfect gentleman," Cornelia said in a 1973 reminiscence. So perfect a gentleman sometimes as to be exasperating. One night he showed up early at the Marshall home on East Ohio Street and, while Cornelia dressed upstairs, passed the time in conversation with May Marshall, her mother, in the parlor. "My mother asked him to play something for her on the piano. He sat down and played for quite some time and visited with her, and seemed in no hurry. All this time, I found out, he had a taxi waiting, and you can imagine my embarrassment. He just sat and played what he wanted to and seemed to be thoroughly enjoying himself. Needless to say, my mother loved it— and so, I must admit, did I."

Carmichael suggested a double date, an evening of dining and dancing at the Roof Garden of the Severin Hotel.

Bix perked up. "Who's playing up there?"

"Charlie Davis and Fritz Morris."

"Hey, no kidding! What're we waiting for?" He phoned the Marshall home, and, characteristically, spent nearly ten minutes chatting with May Marshall before even getting around to asking whether her daughter was in. She was—and her answer to his invitation was an enthusiastic yes.

Davis and Morris were as tickled to see Bix again as he was to see them. And as usual, Charlie had a new tune to plug. "Listen to this 'un, boy. It'll kill you."

It nearly did, said Cornelia. Cy Milders, whom Bix had known in Hamilton, sang it. The title was "I'll See You in My Dreams," and it was by Isham Jones and Gus Kahn. "Both Bix and Hoagy fell in love with the words and music and predicted it would be a big hit. I always think of Bix, even now, when I hear that tune."

That night at the Roof Garden was to have other, long-lasting significance for Cornelia Marshall. Playing alto and baritone saxophones with Davis was Karl VandeWalle, later to become her husband.

All the dates with Cornelia and good times with Hoagy were not helping find Bix work. He sat in at a few places around town, to universally warm receptions. But no jobs. The only glimmer of a break came the night he ran into Jack Tillson, a drummer and sometime singer he had met during the Casino Gardens engagement.

Tillson had an idea. It might not make Bix any money, but it was sure to be fun. He'd just had an offer to join Marion McKay, leader of a band popular throughout the midwest and loosely affiliated with the Jean Goldkette office. McKay wanted Tillson in Richmond on the 17th to record with his band for Gennett.

"Why don't you come along?" he said. "Bet McKay won't mind if you show up. All the guys in the band know you."

Bix turned up with Tillson for the date—and to the expected welcome. With a minimum of coaxing he took a 16-bar solo on McKay's record of "Doo Wacka Doo," collecting $30 for his trouble. Asked by the authors whether his regular trumpet man took offense at the sudden inclusion of a stranger, McKay laughed. "Hell, no. Bix already had a great reputation among the musicians, and they were proud to have him along. Our man just read the arrangements and Bix did the solo. All the boys were flattered to death to have him there."

There seemed little point to hanging around Indianapolis any longer. The work was simply not there. Too, Bix was having serious doubts about the whole professional music business. One minute he was the talk of New York, or playing a solo with Jean Goldkette's orchestra. Then, nothing. Here and gone, a will o' the wisp. Maybe Goldkette was right—he should stop for awhile and get some solid grounding in music. Study.

Toward the end of December Bix returned to Davenport and presented himself to Bismark and Aggie with what appeared to be a change of heart. Yes, he would now go back to school and attempt to pick up his education where he'd dropped it nearly three years before. At nearly 22, he was too old to go back to high school; but Burnie had said he thought it possible to enroll at the University of Iowa as an "unclassified" student, taking a kind of expanded freshman program which would yield sufficient credits to bring the student up to college level by the end of the school year. Bismark Beiderbecke made inquires, found this to be true, and gave his blessing.

Even as his parents were heaving a sigh of relief at this turn of events, Bix was already dropping in around town to hear what was happening musically. Over at the Garden Theater, opening Sunday, December 28, was a band from Iowa City, seat of the University. Bix listened to Merton "Bromo" Sulser and His Collegians for a set, and an idea was born. He went over to the stand to greet an old pal, trumpeter Chet Ogden, then introduced himself to Sulser and pianist Cecil Huntzinger, the band's co-leader. "He told us he was thinking of coming to school at Iowa and wondered if we might be able to use him if he did," said Huntzinger. Naturally, we were very flattered that he wanted to work with us, and assured him that we could use him, although we only worked Friday and Saturday nights at home and the pay was only $5 a night, later raised to $7. Bix sort of smiled and said that was all right with him."

Sulser's Davenport engagement closed January 3, and the musicians returned to Iowa City highly skeptical that they would ever again lay eyes on Bix Beiderbecke. It must have been a gag—but yet, said Cec Huntzinger, he showed up the first night, cornet in a brown paper bag under his arm.

"The boys were just flabbergasted, just as they had been with his first request. By now, Bix had a reputation amongst musicians—especially just coming off the Wolverines, who had a growing following due to their records. For a musician of Bix's calibre to actually be playing with us for dough like that was a shock, to say the least. But there he was, big as life."

Bix moved into a rooming house on Dubuque Street, a few doors down from Beta Theta Pi, Burnie's old fraternity. He was in Sulser's band Friday evening, January 16, when it took the stand for the University's Lions Charity Ball opposite Chuck Sullivan's orchestra in the men's gym. Next morning's *Daily Iowan* took lavish note, headlining its review: "A Sensation—at the charity ball last night: BEIDERBECKE, trumpeter extraordinary!"

Saturday evening the Sulser Collegians opened with Bix at the Blue Goose Ballroom of the Burkley Hotel, 9 West Washington Street. "Tubby"

Griffin, center and captain of the University football team, had leased the Goose weekends for dances he was promoting, and had engaged Bromo's band for the entire season. As word of Bix's presence got around among the student body, attendance at Tubb's dances picked up noticeably.

Though enrollment day was still two weeks off, Bix was already a familiar sight in campus student haunts, said Huntzinger. And he made friends quickly, a cheerful figure in an old blue sweater, "with his horn in a paper bag in one hand and a gallon tin of 'A,' as we called it, in the other. It was near-beer, the only malt beverage available, spiked with whatever he could lay his hands on. But it was all great fun. After the jobs on Fridays and Saturdays, we'd all go over to the Iowa Cafe across the street from the campus and jam a bit for some eats. The guy who ran it, Don Kastner, had once been a tenor sax player and still loved to hear the music. We had open invite to come there and jam after hours whenever we wanted.

"Funny, though. Bix seldom wanted to play his horn at those times. He seemed much happier at the piano. Maybe he'd blow a couple on cornet, then make for the keyboard. He was doing some of the stuff then that later became his 'In a Mist'—funny chords and sequences, interesting patterns. But he didn't have any name for it."

The band seldom worked early in the week, so Bix took the opportunity to do some travelling before the school term began. He was back in Detroit around January 19, the Monday after the Blue Goose opening, to say hello at the Graystone and drop in on the opening of the Detroit automobile show. From there he went to Richmond, where he talked Gennett's recording director Ezra "Wick" Wickemeyer into letting him do a record date under his own name. After another weekend at the Goose he was off again, this time to Indianapolis, where Hoagy Carmichael was still home with his family after the Christmas holidays.

"Hey, we're doing some records tomorrow in Richmond. Want to come along?" Carmichael's yes was a foregone conclusion. They spent the rest of Sunday together, winding up late that evening at the Ohio Theatre, where the Wolverines had first jammed with Charlie Davis a year before. It all seemed suddenly very long ago.

They played some four-hand piano on "Royal Garden Blues" and other dixieland tunes. Then, well after midnight, with Hoagy at the wheel of his new Ford—"a Christmas present to myself"—they set out.

"Who's on the date?" Carmichael asked as they followed the straight ribbon of road toward Richmond. Bix took a thoughtful gulp out of something swaddled in a paper bag. "Ought to be good. Gonna record in slow-drag style, and I've got some guys who can really go." Mostly Goldkette chums. He had written to Tom Dorsey, Mertz, Don Murray and banjoist Howard "Howdy" Quicksell, plus a freelance Detroit drummer named Tom Gargano. They'd be doing an as yet untitled tune Bix had worked out at home, plus LaRocca's "Toddlin' Blues" and one or two others. Dorsey had guaranteed, moreover, that "the guys are bringing three quarts along."

Night slowly became day over a flat Indiana countryside still blanketed in snow, trees dark against a lavender dawn sky, no sign of life save an occasional wisp of smoke from the chimney of a still darkened farmhouse. A quiet world, and a time for contemplation. Bix laughed, and slipped his horn out of its bag. "Hey, Hoagy, pull over a minute, will you?" Hoagy did,

Sulser's Iowa Collegians, March 19, 1924, ten months before Bix joined. Personnel, L to R: Paul Lindemeyer (trumpet); Mal ———— (banjo); Herb Jones (trumpet); Don Emery (piano); Carl Moller (trombone); Bromo (leader/violin); Arnold Olson (brass bass); Armand J. "Dick" Dickeson (drums); Russ Brobeil (sax); Cecil Huntzinger (piano); Bill Sunstrum (sax); Clarence Parizek (sax & violin); Hobe Dawson (sax). According to Huntzinger, this was an augmented personnel. The basic band was usually seven or eight men at most.

PHOTO COURTESY CECIL HUNTZINGER

Bix Beiderbecke and His Rhythm Jugglers recording for Gennett in Richmond, Indiana, January 26, 1925. L to R: Don Murray (clarinet); Howdy Quicksell (banjo); Tom Gargano (drums); Paul Mertz (piano); Bix (cornet); Tommy Dorsey (trombone).

PHOTO COURTESY MARY LOUISE SHOEMAKER

and Bix blew a single phrase across a silent field. Hoagy produced his own battered trumpet from under the seat and blew white breath on it to warm it up. For at least a few moments they played quietly together. Hoagy never forgot the feeling of the moment, and chronicled it in both his autobiographical books.[7] The magic remains.

From all reports the recording date itself was something considerably less than magical, despite the title of one of the selections waxed that day. Quicksell showed up too late to play on the two first titles, which turned out to be the only ones issued. By the time the band got to "Magic Blues," only magic would have salvaged the results. But the two selections released by Gennett under the name "Bix Beiderbecke and His Rhythm Jugglers" are lazy, good-natured performances, showing Bix in a relaxed, if not especially adventuresome frame of mind. Tommy Dorsey dubbed Bix's original "Davenport Blues," and the name stuck.

The final tune of the day bore the title "No One Knows What It's All About," and that, said Paul Mertz, was "pretty appropriate. It had a tricky tempo change in the middle, and by now we were all pretty well lubricated and kept muffing that tempo change. We never really got it right."

Bix returned directly to Iowa City to work the weekend with Sulser. Then Monday morning, at last, he enrolled at the University of Iowa as an "unclassified student." His curriculum, predictably, mirrored Goldkette's advice to ground himself more thoroughly in music. Seven of his 14 credit hours were devoted to courses in music theory, piano, and the history of the romantic and modern periods. Thursday's *Daily Iowan* announced that Bix had pledged Beta Theta Pi and moved into the fraternity's house at 804 North Dubuque.

No sooner was he settled in than he was off again, this time to appear with a Goldkette group at Ann Arbor for the University of Michigan's annual spring J-Hop, alternating with the Benson Orchestra of Chicago and with Arnold Johnson's Harmony Boys from the Edgwater Beach Hotel. Then back to school, and at an interview with the University freshman guidance counsellor Bix aired his discontent at having to clutter four hours of his program with a "religion and ethics" course. A terse entry in the University files records both the counsellor's reply and, with it, the school administration's views of what the new student should be doing with his time.

> Had $400 with him when he came. Gets money from home. Asked to drop religion and take more music. Is not registered for military training, physical education and freshman lectures. Was told to do so promptly. Plays one night a week.

The answer to his request was a resounding no, and just four days later Bix was out. Clearly, the freshman counsellor's attempt to temper his involvement in music undermined his newfound determination to educate himself. He could see no practical purpose in "religion and ethics," military training or even physical education. His attendance at classes dropped off, and Thursday night, according to Cecil Huntzinger, Bix and

---

7. *Op. cit.* Also Carmichael, Hoagy, *The Stardust Road.* New York, Rinehart and Co., 1946.

a rather noisy bunch of friends, among them a promising football player named Bill Flechenstein, got into some heavy drinking at Reichart's Cafe, on the fringes of the Iowa campus. Bix's mood got progressively uglier. Somewhere along the line things started to get rough, and a small riot erupted, with Beiderbecke and Flechenstein at its epicenter. "Tables were overturned, and there was a general disturbance," said Huntzinger. "Both Bix and Flechenstein, who later played pro football for the Chicago Bears, were expelled the next day."

Listless, undecided, he hung around Iowa City for a few days, then went back to Detroit, withdrew his union card, and headed for New York. It seemed the only option. School was now out of the question; he couldn't go back to Davenport and face his parents. Relations on that front were at an all-time low. Goldkette, for the moment, was out of the question, and the Wolverines, gradually disintegrating down in Florida, were a thing of his past. At least New York offered a chance to play, musicians who were sympathetic, and a lot of distance between Bix and anything to do with Iowa.

Once in town he phoned some friends. Jimmy Dorsey, who had also been with Goldkette, was now playing alongside brother Tommy and Red Nichols in the California Ramblers. Jimmy mentioned Bix's arrival to Herb Weil, a young drummer from over near New Rochelle who subbed for Stan King now and then with the Ramblers. Weil and his high school pals, including the bass saxophonist Spencer Clark, spent most of their spare time hanging around the band. Clark worshipped Adrian Rollini, the Ramblers' bass sax man and musical guiding spirit, an adulation which shaped his own playing over a lifetime.

The youngsters had landed a spring dance job at the exclusive Orienta Beach Club at Orienta Point in Mamaroneck through Spence's father, chairman of the entertainment committee. "I knew Bix was around and not doing anything," said Weil, "so I got Jimmy [Dorsey] to hire him for us. I picked him up in New York and brought him out for the gig. He must have had a horrible time, though we had even gone so far as to learn 'Riverboat Shuffle' in his honor. But he was so brought down by what I must admit was our mediocre musicianship that he played things very cool, casual, acting generally disinterested in the entire affair."

When the evening was over, Bix asked Weil to drive him over to the Ramblers Inn. "When he got there he barged up to the bandstand and practically begged to sit in. He took about nine choruses on the very first tune, getting it all out of his system, poor guy."

The Ramblers welcomed him aboard with a standing invitation to come up and play with them whenever he felt the urge.

"Hey, where you staying?" Red Nichols asked as they were packing up. Bix looked apologetic.

"Haven't found anywhere yet. I'll probably grab a hotel room somewhere. That oughta be okay for a week or two."

"Why not come over and stay with me?" said Red. "I've got a room at the Pasadena, up by Columbus Circle. Oughta be fun. Whatcha got for luggage?"

Bix grinned a bit sheepishly, and pointed to a small suitcase in the corner, fetching a laugh from Nichols. "That all?"

"Yep. I travel light."

The agreement was sealed with a handshake, and Bix moved into the Pasadena Hotel, at 60th and Broadway, the next day. The little suitcase, it turned out, contained a change of underwear, socks, a tie, and a few handkerchiefs. The cornet, as ever, traveled in a paper bag. Nichols, charmed and amused, had a piano moved into the room for a week "and we had a ball. During that period, I've got to admit, we were loaded pretty much of the time, and I do remember that I had record dates for Sam Lanin during that time, as well as the Ramblers, and, unless I recall wrongly, one for Joe Candullo. How I got through them in that condition I'll never know.

"There was this one morning that we hadn't been to bed and I was really afraid that I couldn't get through the date, so I asked Bix to go along with me and help me out. In return I'd split the money with him. He agreed. Who this was for I'll probably never know, cause it was a case of the blind leading the blind."[8]

Red and Bix were together constantly for the next week or so. As Frank Cush, lead trumpet with the Ramblers, recalled, the two often came to work at the Ramblers Inn together. "As you know, Bix didn't read very well, but in spite of this he worked out fine, all things considered. Don't forget, he had terrific talent. His ear was tops—he'd just have to hear something once and he had it. Most of the things we did at that time were worked out from the printed scores. In fact, it was a difficult spot for anyone to walk in cold for any chair in the band. But that ear never let Bix down.

"He was a funny guy. I don't think that I ever saw him with a cornet case. He just tucked his horn under his arm and off he went. And for a schooled person to watch him play was pretty odd. No one had ever showed Bix how to finger the legit way, so he just started pushing valves and things came out. For example, a schooled person would always finger an 'A'—that's 'G' concert—with the first and second valves. Bix just as often used the third. Most people will play a middle 'D' ('C' concert) with first only; he used first and third. But for all that, I have to say that not many people in those days knocked us out. But Bix—he did."[9]

Bix's ten days in New York passed in a whirlwind of jazz, gin and plain high spirits. He and Red visited Tommy and Jimmy Dorsey's home out at City Island, where Mother Dorsey cooked dinner for everyone. Then there was the day, as Bix later related to Les Swanson, when he and Nichols were cruising down Riverside Drive in Red's new Jewett sports car ("Try to pass it on a hill," said the advertisements) and wheeled to a stop at a red light. Two stylishly-dressed girls stepped off the curb. Nichols leaned out the window.

"Going downtown, gals?" he said in what passed for a come-hither voice. They fluttered their eyelashes and nodded "Yeah, big boy" as the light changed. "Okay—we'll meet you down there," said Red, and floored the accelerator, leaving the two maids coughing and cursing at the inter-

---

8. This purported joint recording has spurred years of speculation and investigation among record collectors and chroniclers of the period. The recent discovery of a check for $25, made out to Bix by Sam Lanin on October 20, 1927, has complicated things even further. Full discussion of this matter, with all available documentation and recording information, will be found in the chronology and discography sections of this volume.
9. A detailed discussion of this subject will be found elsewhere in this volume.

134

section. Bix, said Swanson, thought it was funny, though "just a bit crude."

In later years Nichols told a curious story about the fate of the small upright piano he and Bix had in the room at the Pasadena. A frequent visitor was Joe Venuti, jazz violinist and notorious gagster. Venuti was just in from Detroit, where he had been with Goldkette, to join the New York dance orchestra led by Roger Wolfe Kahn, son of millionaire banker Otto Kahn. Venuti, said Red, wondered aloud one day what the "predominant key of the piano was. I told him I thought it was 'C,' but he disagreed. He said if all the keys were hit at once, how could you tell which key would dominate?" Venuti announced he knew a way to find out, and that as of that moment he was taking bets on it. The whole issue sounded intriguing enough so that every musician to whom he mentioned it during the next few days offered to place a $5 bet on it. The decision would be made in Red's room at the end of the week.

Came the day, and a number of colleagues, Bix included, assembled in the room. Venuti, abetted by a couple of the more muscular among them, carried the upright over to the window, lifted it, and before the horrified Nichols could object, dropped it into the alley. "It landed with an enormous crash, with snapping of piano wires and whatnot, but there was no hint of any pitch," said Red. Joe went around the room, returning $5 to each investor. Nichols, stunned, kept asking why on earth he'd done it, and who was going to pay for the ruined piano.

"What the hell are you crying about, Redhead?" said the violinst. "I gave you your $5 back, didn't I?"

For all the hijinks, the time Bix and Nichols spent together had a deep and lasting musical effect on the Utah-born cornetist. Red's style took on more and more of Bix's phrasing and tone, though never freeing itself from a feeling of emotional detachment. A Nichols solo always reflected mannerisms arrived at methodically, through design, while Bix sounded spontaneous, emotionally more in touch with his music. Together they listened to records and traded fingering and embouchure ideas.

But despite the fun, Bix had no intention of staying much longer in New York. In Chicago there were more people he knew and who knew him. Chief among them was Dale Skinner, and it was Skinner Bix looked up when he got back to the lakeside city in a snowstorm around the beginning of the week of March 22. The saxophonist was working in a band led by pianist Charlie Straight at the Rendez-vous Cafe, at 622 West Diversey Avenue, corner of Broadway. "Bix stopped by one night to see me," Skinner told the authors. "We had a back room at the Rendez-vous which we used for broadcasting. It had burlap-covered walls—we called it the 'potato-sack studio.' It had a piano, and Bix played a thing he'd worked out —it later became 'In a Mist'—for me. He said he needed work and I told him I might be able to get him into the band with us, although we already had two trumpet men."

Easier said than done. As lead alto man Bob Strong recalled, Henry Horn, managing director of the Rendez-vous, "wasn't really much interested in adding a man to the band, so we had to figure out a way to handle it. Bix was well known by now, and we figured to get lots of kicks by having him in the band. The answer was in the hours we worked. You see, the regular band worked from seven till one, playing both for dancing and for the floor show, with the last show finishing about one. Then the band was cut to one sax, trumpet, perhaps trombone or tuba, piano and drums, and this was called the relief band. They played until five or so in the morning. Many of the guys in our band didn't care to stay over, but wanted to go home and go to bed. So there was a chance to bring outside guys in. That's how we got Bix in."

Art Gronwall came in for Straight on piano. Don Morgan, from the big band, played drums, sometimes replaced by Danny Alvin or Bob Conzelman. Skinner and Joe Gist alternated on reeds, with Gist sometimes filling in on tuba. "This took care of part of Bix's salary," said Strong. "Then the rest of the band kicked in $10 a week apiece just to have him with us." Eventually Bix wound up playing with both bands, as featured cornet with the relief group and as an extra man in the larger group.

He started work on Monday, March 23, moving in next door at the Rienzi Hotel. "It was great to have him in the band," said Skinner, "even though he brought the brass section to four and we had no arrangements scored for three trumpets. But I sat in front of him and can attest that he always found a part—he had an uncanny ear, and never doubled another man." Once again through Skinner's help Bix had found a band which appreciated his talents. Even Gene Cafferelli, whom he had displaced at the Valentino Inn two years before, welcomed him and, judging from later recorded examples of his own solo work, had fallen under his spell.

The Straight band did seven nights a week, and the Rendez-vous was always packed, even after hours. The late Dr. Edmond Souchon, New Orleans physician, banjoist and jazz historian, dropped in one April evening. He had just acquired both an M.D. certificate and a new wife, and music, he said, "was running a very bad second at the time to a biological urge. But I remember the place clearly—it was a sort of elongated rectangle, with tables and such, and a dance floor. The band was at the end.

"The Straight orchestra was quite a large one for the time, and was okay as far as Yankee dance bands went. But it was a far cry from Joe Oliver's band, which we were hearing on the South Side at about the same time." The intermission or relief band, said Souchon, played more for listening than for dancing, "and nobody ever got up to try to dance. They were playing what sounded to me like a very strange, advanced sort of music, and although I could see some sort of resemblance to what we in New Orleans called ragtime, or even early jazz, it was a far piece removed from what we were raised on. I recall very vividly that the trumpeter or cornetist would spend as much time at the piano as he would blowing his horn. His chording, too, was way away from the beaten path, and didn't especially bowl me over at the time. It took me a good many years to appreciate Bix. At the time it just sounded strange."

Bix had corresponded on and off with Cornelia since leaving Indianapolis, but they had seen little of each other since the winter. Cornelia, still working for the New York Central, decided to use her railroad pass to remedy the situation. Early in April she sent him a special delivery letter expressing her determination to come to Chicago the following Sunday, her day off, for a day's visit. Bix's reply was not long in coming:

Cornelia Dear:
This is the first time I've had a chance to answer your special, hon, and I'm

on the job at the Rendezvous now doing it. There's been a rehearsal every day and playing nights. But I sure want to make it a point to get this letter off to you in time for you to come to Chi Sunday. I'm sure tickled to hear you're coming and I'll sure meet you, dear.

There's so much noise in hear [*sic*] Cornelia that I can't concentrate and as there's nothing to say (except that I can't wait to see you) I may as well sign off.

Wire me your time of arrival, & I'll be there to meet you sweetheart.

Love,
Bix

"I recall arriving at an ungodly hour for him, I'm sure, on a Sunday morning," said Cornelia. "After eating breakfast and taking a ride, we decided to go to church. My being a good Methodist, we found a large and beautiful Methodist church, and he really enjoyed the whole service, especially the organ and choir music. That afternoon we drove all over Chicago in an open car, seeing all the places of interest, which was quite a treat for me. The weather was lovely and I had a beautiful new Spring coat, so we kept the top down. We had dinner at the nightclub where he worked, and after dinner he took me to the train as he had to get back to work and I had to get home.

"We corresponded for awhile after that, and then like all young people we drifted apart. He was a very quiet, very sweet and unassuming person."

According to Dale Skinner, all the tales of Bix keeping wild west novels on his music stand at rehearsals and even in the evenings were probably true. "He needed no music, you know." Bix, said Dale, was a natural, whose ear enhanced any arrangement the band played.

Bob Strong disagreed. "Bix couldn't read at all, and actually was of little use to the band. Sure, he played fantastic choruses on the old tunes he knew, but even the new ones where we gave him spots he was not too quick to knock us out." But Bix was learning all the time, and gradually acquiring the experience Goldkette had advised him to get. And the Detroit bandleader was never far away: Goldkette "borrowed" Bix from Straight to play with the Graystone band on Friday, May 1, at the 1925 Indiana University Junior Prom. An article in the April 26 *Indiana Daily Student* hailed the 22-year-old Iowan as "the best cornet player in the United States" and recalled his triumphs at Bloomington with the Wolverines the year before. Another article at about the same time promised that "Goldkette's personnel of 13 men will be used in the principal numbers, but to the half dozen comprising Bix's group will be left the task of presenting jazz to the Hoosiers." Goldkette, characteristically, had been quick to see the advantages of the band-within-a-band formula pioneered by the Georgians out of Paul Specht's orchestra and the "Goofus Five" drawn from the California Ramblers.

Under the headline, "JAZZMANIA INSPIRES GOLDKETTE MUSICIAN TO WRITE HARMONIES," a campus writer drew attention to Bix's Gennett recording of 'Davenport Blues' as "one of the cleverest hits of the year. Written in deference to that fickle goddess, Jazzmania, the piece carries with it the spirit of the age. If syncopation expresses American life, the 'Davenport Blues' is a current history."

On May Day itself, the same newspaper waxed ecstatic, if orthographically a trifle wayward, with a more detailed preview of the Goldkette orchestra:

> . . . the masters are apt and many. The great Jean Goldkette will direct them
> . . . there will be the sighing fiddler Charles Hammell; the sputtering first
> trumpeter Bix Beiderbecke, aided by the blares of Fred Farrar and Ray
> Lodwig; the grunting, snorting trombones of Thomas Dorsen [*sic*] and William Rank; the rippling piano driven madly onward by William Krenz; the
> strumming banjo of Howard Trucksell [*sic*]; the wailing, moaning saxophones of the Indianian Stanley Ryper [*sic*], C. H. Hutchins and Dorial
> [*sic*] Murray; and finally the staccato boom of the master drummer Charles
> Horwath [*sic*] . . .

Besides getting the names of Dorsey, Quicksell, Ryker, Murray and Horvath wrong, the author was also guilty of the popular misconception which makes of the cornet soloist a section leader. But the article did indicate that Bix and his music still commanded an enthusiastic following on the Indiana campus.

Then it was back to the Rendez-vous and Straight. Among frequent after-hours visitors was the trumpeter and vocalist Phil Dooley, who fronted the band over at the Merry Gardens where Art Gronwall worked in the early evenings before shuttling over to play with the Rendez-vous relief group. Bix, said Dooley, was playing better than ever before, but he was also drinking more. "When he didn't drink he was the nicest and most generous guy—that's why he had so many friends and was respected, not only for his talent but as a regular guy. But when he drank, his whole personality changed, and many times he would get insulting. But there was always someone around to square it off and protect him, like myself. I admired him for his talent and because I knew he was a good guy."

There was a bowling alley not far from the Cafe, and Bix talked Skinner into a few afternoon sessions. "He loved it, bowled about 180 average, which wasn't bad." The rest of his free time and energy was usually wrapped up in music, but not, Phil Dooley maintained, exclusively in jazz. "Bix always talked about modern music, and said records of works by Stravinsky, Ravel and Sibelius fascinated him. We'd be together in the 'Potato Sack studio' and some cat would play something and Bix would listen and say, 'Man, that's great . . . but how about adding this or that?' and then get wrapped up in funny cadences and things. Or he'd make an abrupt ending, then jump on to another chord. He liked tunes like 'Poor Little Me' and 'Railroad Man'; on piano, he played mostly in 'C,' but his favorite cornet key was 'Eb.' "

Sometime early in June Bix heard again from Goldkette. With the summer season just getting into action, a number of smaller Goldkette units were working at resort areas along the Michigan Lake shore. Trumpeter Nat Natoli, a Goldkette anchor man, needed a second trumpet in the group he was leading at Albert Tollentino's Lakeside Casino in Walled Lake, Michigan, about 40 miles out of Detroit. Bix could go up there for $50 a week plus room and board; it was $25 less than what the rest of Natoli's sidemen were making. But it was, Bix reminded himself, a possible avenue back to Detroit and the Graystone.

He talked it over with Straight, and finally gave his notice and left on the second of July. Cafferelli and Rex Maupin stayed on in the main band, with Francis "Muggsy" Spanier filling in on cornet with the relief group.

Natoli's band worked every night except Monday, playing well-mannered dance music for middle-aged couples. Bix, characteristically, soon sought diversion. Only eight miles up the road, at Island Lake, a group billed as "The Breeze Blowers" were doing six nights a week at the Blue Lantern Inn. On his first free Monday evening, Bix dropped up to listen —and to his astonishment found most of Goldkette's Victor orchestra, including Murray, Bill Rank, Jimmy Dorsey and a new addition, the former New Orleans Rhythm Kings bassist Steve Brown. Paul Mertz was on piano, Stanley "Doc" Ryker on lead alto sax, Howdy Quicksell on banjo and Chauncey Morehouse, from New York, at the drums. It was, in preview, the basic personnel of what little more than a year later was to become Goldkette's greatest orchestra.

Running the musical side of things as assistant ballroom boss, while acting as pro tem proprietor of a small grocery store on the property, was Fred Bergin, Goldkette's longtime office manager from Detroit. Bergin took over at the piano when Mertz left some time later to return to Detroit and a job at the Book-Cadillac Hotel.

"Bix liked our band better," said Bergin. "He knew the guys, and came down whenever he could to sit in or just hang around with them. At that time we had Jimmy Criswell on second trumpet."

But it wasn't too long, he said, before the hoped-for happened. Around the middle of July Criswell left the Island Lake unit and Bix, "much to everyone's delight," replaced him.

"Tommy Dorsey was originally supposed to be on the job, too. But he'd had this idea to round up some guys in Detroit and re-form the original Scranton Sirens and return to Pennsylvania," Bergin said.

Bix moved in with Bergin, Quicksell and Murray in a room under the pavilion, which jutted out over the water. "There was a pump organ in the hotel that he loved to play. One day, looking out at the beach, he saw a sandpiper running along the sand. It knocked him out. 'Look at that rhythm,' he said, and started laughing. Before we knew it he was at the piano, trying to give a musical impression of what he'd seen."

Joining the Island Lake band meant a $10 a week raise for Bix, plus free room and board. "There was a slot machine in the hotel. He always drew any cash that he had to have in advance, and when payday came, he took the balance in nickels. He then, honest to God, moved the slot machine out under a nice shady tree and pulled the crank until the money was gone.

"Funny, that. At one point that month Goldkette came up, and Bix hit him for a raise. Jean asked him right off what on earth he wanted the money for. Bix said he didn't know exactly, but he thought he ought to have more."

Goldkette, said Bergin, looked at Bix quizzically. "You know, Bix," he said at length, "I don't see any very good reason to give you a raise since you'd put it all in the slot machine and I own the machine and would get it all back anyway."

Bix, said Bergin, blushed with embarrassment but had to agree.

The summer brought other, far-reaching developments. Tommy Dorsey sent for "the brother" to come east and join him in his attempt to revive the Pennsylvania band which had given them both their professional start. Dorsey went, leaving Goldkette looking for a saxophone player to fill in at Island Lake.

"Jean had had his eye on Frank Trumbauer for a long time, even when Tram was featured saxophone soloist with the Benson Orchestra and, after that, with Ray Miller," said Bergin. "Now, Tram had left Miller and was freelancing around. Jean talked him into replacing Jimmy in our band."

Trumbauer came, said Bergin. "One reason I remember him there was because of his skill with knives. He was part Indian, I think, and used to give the guys in the band exhibitions of throwing knives at trees."

He stayed into August. Goldkette came up to offer him a permanent job both playing in and directing one of his bands. But Trumbauer already had a line on something else, an autumn engagement at the Arcadia Ballroom in St. Louis, which sounded too good to pass up. A month of playing alongside Bix had convinced him, too, that the star of the Wolverines had been no fluke. He wanted Bix in St. Louis with him.

But there was a catch. As a member of the St. Louis musicians' union Local 2, Trumbauer would be obliged to hire local men for the Arcadia job. This rule would have cheated him both of having Bix in the band and making use of another union regulation which categorized a group with even one imported musician as a "traveling band," eligible for 30% higher scale than locals could make.

The rule had a loophole, however, and Tram went for it at once. If Bix could be seen to be on the move, drifting from location to location and finally coming to rest in St. Louis by chance before the job was scheduled to begin, Trumbauer could approach the union at the appropriate time, claiming to have found no cornetist who fit the needs of his band and asking permission to use Bix. If the union said yes, the band would qualify for the higher scale and Tram would have his man.

Accordingly, Bix and Tram left Island Lake about the same time in mid-August, the cornetist heading west to St. Louis and the saxophonist going back to New York to do a record date and tidy up a few business ends before returning to Missouri.

Bix dropped his transfer at Local 2 on Saturday, August 15, registering at the Majestic Hotel. Three days later Karl Spaeth, a tenor saxophonist from Detroit, rolled into town and took a room at the Coronado. He, too, was to have a chair in the Trumbauer Arcadia group. Both men began working "casuals" around town as though they had no specific engagement in mind. Karl did a job on the big Streckfus side-wheeler *J.S.*, and Bix picked up some work with Ted Jansen, who did three nights a week and occasional specials out at Westlake park.

Ray Thurston, who ultimately got the trombone chair in the Arcadia band, recalled Jansen as "a very tin-eared drummer who at that time booked more work than any leader around here. He always made it his business to hire anyone who came to town on at least one job. In fact, just about every musician in St. Louis had worked at least one dance job for Ted."

The real reason for Bix's and Spaeth's presence in St. Louis was the worst-kept secret in town, it seems, even before Joe Ternes, owner of the Arcadia, let slip that Trumbauer was signed and that Beiderbecke and Spaeth were to be in his band. Trombonist Vernon Brown, also working for Jansen at the time, recalled that rumors began circulating shortly *before* Bix arrived.

By the time Trumbauer himself showed up during the last week of August, there was no longer any doubt in anyone's mind. A new band was in the making, and with it an unexpected, deeply fateful turn of events for Bix Beiderbecke.

Frank Trumbauer's Orchestra, Arcadia Ballroom, St. Louis, autumn 1925. L to R: Ray Thurston (trombone); Marty Livingston (vocals); Pee Wee Russell (clarinet/alto sax); Trumbauer (C-melody sax, but sitting behind bass sax for the photograph); Dee Orr (drums); Bix; Damon "Bud" Hassler (saxophone & arranger); Louis Feldman (piano); Dan Gaebe (bass); Wayne Jacobson (banjo).                       PHOTO COURTESY RUTH SHAFFNER SWEENEY

# Chapter 10

"Well, Ruthie, how about it?"

The sound of her elder sister's voice reached Ruth Shaffner deep in a reverie compounded of equal parts of boredom with the novel on her lap and absent contemplation of the weekend just coming up.

"Ruthie, are you listening? Are we going tonight or not? Make up your mind, will you?"

Going. Tonight. Ruth's mind snapped back into focus. Friday night. She, Estelle and Bess were going dancing at the Arcadia to hear Frank Trumbauer's new band. Really hot stuff, with this dreamy cornet player . . .

"How about it, Ruthie?" Bess was getting impatient.

"Sure, Bess. Wouldn't miss it for the world."

Ruth, Estelle and Bess Shaffner had come to St. Louis three years before from Pittsfield, in farm country Illinois. All had found jobs, Ruth as a $9-a-week receptionist for Dr. Hiram C. Clark, a podiatrist. The sisters shared flat 106 of the Sheridan Apartments at 4471 Olive Street.

The Arcadia, down the street at numbers 3515–3523, was not only the biggest ballroom in town; it was nearby, and a good place to go together on double, sometimes triple dates. Each of the three Shaffner girls, petite brunettes all, had long since acquired a full complement of male admirers.

Ruth, just five feet tall and weighing a gossamer 98 pounds, was 19 and, in one admirer's words, "as cute as a bug's ear." She loved to dance and be where people were. It remained for Bess, as eldest sister, to keep occasional rein on her taste for fun and good company. But a Friday evening at the Arcadia, with a new band, was something none of the girls would miss.

The Arcadia Ballroom, a hangarlike wooden building with a stone facade, had begun life in the early days of the century as Dreamland, and adopted its new name shortly after World War I. Its recessed dance floor, one step down, ran the entire length of the hall and was ringed by what Ruth recalled as "a kind of bannister." Across the north end of the room, opposite the front entrance, was a large stage. Here the ballroom's featured band played from 8:30 to half past midnight every night but Monday, and did a Sunday matinee for younger dancers. Off to the left was a second, smaller bandstand for the relief band, a six-piece dixieland group from New Orleans which had opened as the "Crescent City Jazzers" but soon become the "Arcadian Serenaders" for obvious reasons.

It was shortly after nine when the Shaffner girls got to the Arcadia. Trumbauer's band was playing "Clarinet Marmalade." Ruth spotted Car-

The Arcadia Ballroom, Olive Street, St. Louis, c. 1925.

The Shaffner sisters, 45 years later. L to R: Estelle, Ruth, Bess.

rie Spradling over by the stage. Carrie had met the new cornet player, and promised to introduce him. Just as the sisters joined her, he stood to take a fast-tempo solo—tone clear and ringing, forceful yet sweet of quality, not harsh; and, Ruth reflected, he was very good-looking indeed. About five-ten, she guessed. Well-built. Brown hair and, like her, brown eyes. He smiled a lot, and seemed to be having fun. Carrie took a look at Ruth's expression and laughed. "Don't worry, Ruthie, I'll introduce you when they take their break. His name's Bix Beiderbecke and he's from Iowa. He's nice—sorta shy, but he's a sweetheart."

The band had opened on Tuesday, September 8, after a flurry of rehearsals and a few preliminary personnel changes. Ray Thurston had replaced the teenager Irving Kordick on trombone at $80 a week, third highest salary in the group next to Bix's $90 and Tram's $125 leader's fee. Other St. Louis sidemen, including Charles "Pee Wee" Russell on clarinet and alto sax, got $75. Trumbauer, Spaeth and Russell were the reed section, with Lou Feldman at the piano, Wayne Jacobson on banjo and Edgar "Eggie" Krewinhaus on drums, later replaced by Pee Wee's friend Dee Orr, from Texas. Trumbauer had been unable to find a suitable tuba player, so he brought in Anton "John" Casertani, of the St. Louis Symphony, on string bass.

Trumbauer counted off Dud Mecum's "Angry" and Ruth found herself unable to take her eyes off the young man with the cornet. His every motion was interesting. When, a few bars before his solo, he began wiping his mouth with the back of his sleeve, she turned to Carrie.

"Why does he keep doing that?" she whispered.

"Haven't the faintest idea. Why don't you ask him yourself?" As it happened, Ruth never got around to asking. Bix came bounding down the steps from the stage. "Hi there, Carrie, how's the kid?"

"Bix, meet a friend of mine. Ruth Shaffner, this is Bix Beiderbecke." Ruth smiled as demurely as possible and offered her hand. Bix just stared; then, abruptly, grabbed it, beaming. "Ah, yes. Hello there. My pleasure . . . yes indeed, my pleasure indeed." They chatted a few minutes, both laughing a little too readily, Ruth talking more and faster than was her habit. Then, suddenly, it was time to play again and he was off.

"Words can't express how wonderful he seemed to me," Ruth said in later years. "He was so handsome, and had a smile that was just out of this world . . ."

Life at the Arcadia looked musically promising. The Serenaders' 19-year-old cornetist, Sterling "Bozo" Bose, had absorbed his jazz in New Orleans but took to Bix at once. He replaced Wingy Manone, who had left after prolonged personal friction with the other sidemen. Bose and Bix became pals, keen both in their taste for jazz and for the same dubious quality of bootleg booze.

Relations within the Trumbauer band were equally cordial, and Bix's room at the Majestic soon became a center for easy socializing. He had a windup record player, Karl Spaeth said, and "when we all got high we'd go up to the room and listen to records of Stravinsky's *The Firebird* and *Petrouchka* to the glow of a dim red light. Bix, of course, was a great one to partake of any nectar that would induce an 'out of this world' feeling . . . nowadays they have rockets, but all we had then was moonshine." Bix, said Spaeth, "was a great drinker, and we split many a jug listening to his favorite recordings in the room." Ray Thurston, too, found it "too bad that Bix had to be such a terrific drinker . . . and the liquor was terrible. Even the best moonshine was rotgut . . ." To the 18-year-old Vernon Brown, playing trombone alongside Fred Laufketter in the Missouri Cotton Pickers over at Tremps' Ballroom on Delmar, it seemed Bix "could consume more liquor than anyone I have ever come in contact with." Brown, who later replaced Thurston in the Arcadia band, was amazed at Bix's seeming ability to play coherently even when drunk.

Ruth Shaffner, now an ever-more-frequent visitor to the Arcadia, saw none of this. "True, he did drink. But I would call it socially and for amusement . . . I only saw him *once* when he had had too much. He was too much of a gentleman."

And it was Bix the gentleman, always a little shy, who captivated her. "As far as I knew he was first a gentleman and second a talented musician," she said. "We got to know each other a lot better toward the end of September, and I found him a kindly, fun-loving person, with a great sense of humor and a personality plus—and a handsome man." Around this time they started dating regularly, going out together to dinner or to after-hours cafes such as "Joe's," across the street from the Arcadia; "Ethel's" ("It was a flat and had only beer"); the Eastern Cafe at Grand and Olive for wee hours breakfasts; or to their favorite, a combined restaurant and speakeasy called "Larry's." "They served beer and very good food there, but after they closed the restaurant for the night Bix and I would go there, others too. They had a back room with tables and a piano, and Bix would play the piano. Other musicians played, too—there was always a certain bunch who went there. It wasn't a dark place, especially, but I do remember we always entered by the rear door. That was at 18th and Washington; it's now a parking lot."

Ruth was quick to contest suggestions that Bix was anything less than immaculate and fastidious about personal hygiene when in her presence. "I never saw Bix when he wasn't clean," she said. "Always clean-shaven, fingernails, not a hair out of place, teeth brushed. Even his shoes were always shined, and I might add that if his tie wasn't just right, he'd buy a new one . . . All those stories about his lack of cleanliness—that really hurts, it's so far from being true. I never saw him in a soiled tuxedo, never saw him ragged or crumpled or whatever else. He was a very clean person, took as many baths or showers as anyone else."

Whatever the case, Bix was clearly stuck on the brown-eyed girl from Illinois, and she on him. Mondays, with the band free for the day, the couple would board a bus—"he never owned a car"—and head for the movies or, before the season ended, for Sportsman's Park to see the St. Louis Cardinals play. Bix's passion for baseball had survived his Lake Forest days. His idol was the Cardinals' home-run clouting second baseman Rogers "The Rajah" Hornsby. Others, including such musicians as Vernon Brown and Pee Wee Russell, went to ball games with Bix from time to time. Each, said Brown, "had a jug in his inside coat pocket and a soda straw, which was a neat way of consuming the contents unnoticed by anyone."

Around the beginning of October, Ruth Shaffner began keeping a diary.

Its daily entries[10] chart her deepening attachment to the young man from Iowa, and how Ruth was beginning to adjust her day-to-day existence to the lopsided hours and pace of a jazz musician's life. Often with Estelle and a none-too-approving Bess in tow, she would arrive at the Arcadia late in the evening, and by prior arrangement with the bouncer, Frank "Big Red" Schiezer, get in free and go to a specially-reserved table near the stage. Come 12:30, Trumbauer ("he liked to be called just Frank—hated the name Frankie") would pack up promptly and go home to Mitzi, his wife, and their two-year-old son Bill. But for Bix and Ruth the evening was just starting; by now Estelle was seeing Pee Wee, and double-dating was frequent. Bessie participated only sporadically after hours. As a rule she retired early, and occasionally, when she felt the need, appointed herself chaperone and guardian of her sisters' virtue.

"Now listen here, Bix Beiderbecke," she remonstrated at the door one especially late weeknight, "don't you know my sister is a working girl and can't be kept out all hours of the night? She needs her sleep. *You* can sleep all day, but Ruth has to be ready for work in just a few hours." Bix, cowed, stared at his shoes. "If you plan to take Ruth out from now on, young man, you can bring her home at a reasonable hour." So saying, she stalked into the bedroom and Bix, after a hasty goodnight, beat his retreat down the stairs.

Bessie's bark, it turned out, was considerably fiercer than her bite. A few days later the sisters invited a still-hesitant cornetist to a fried chicken dinner and all was forgiven. "It was one of his favorite dishes," said Ruth. "He absolutely loved chicken and french fries or ham and french fries. My family, you know, lived on a farm, and cured their own ham and pork. Dad would send us a ham, and pork sausage, and all that. The hams were much different from hams today, and Bix was crazy about them."

On Wednesday, November 4, Bix and Sterling Bose moved into room 608 at the Coronado Hotel, just three blocks from the Arcadia and a lot closer to the Sheridan Apartments than the Majestic had been. The week also brought two other developments. First, Anton Casertani left to begin the winter symphony season. His replacement was Dan Gaebe, a tall, shambling, good-natured St. Louisian whose chief instrument was tuba but who had started to develop on string bass as well. Karl Spaeth, too, decided to go. "It was purely a matter of domestic problems," he said. "I had a mother and a home in Detroit. I couldn't live in two places on the $75 a week Tram was paying me." He returned to Detroit and joined Ray Miller. His replacement was Damon "Bud" Hassler, a classically-trained musician who had worked in the violin section of the St. Louis Symphony and knew the theoretical side of music. He had met Bix on dates with Jansen and Gill and taken an immediate interest in him, all the more so after discovering their shared interest in modern concert music.

Hassler had met Pee Wee Russell earlier in 1925 while the clarinetist and his friend from Texas, pianist Terry Shand, were with Herb Berger's orchestra at the Coronado Hotel. Around that time Berger's trombone chair became free, and Shand wrote to a trombonist he knew in Texas who, he said, could more than fill it. Less than a week later Weldon "Jack"

10. See "Chronology" later in this volume.

Teagarden rolled into town—only to find himself trapped in the same union bind which was nearly to prevent Trumbauer several months later from using Bix. Teagarden had not bothered to come in quietly and work the obligatory "casuals" first, but instead showed up ready to join Berger —only to be turned down flat by the union. Predictably, he did a few jobs with Jansen and one or two others, then he and Shand elected to move on. Hassler recalled that "neither of them could read music, and after a few trial jobs they couldn't get any work. So a gang of the local dance band men took up a collection so they could buy gas to get back down South. They had come with their wives and were stranded in a cheap rooming house, but they had this Model T Ford which eventually got them back to Texas."

Until now, most of Bix's spare time musical occupations had been with jazz. When he wasn't seeing Ruth, he and Pee Wee sought out black musicians active on the other side of town. Over at John Estes' Chauffeurs' Club at 3133 Pine Boulevard, the regulars included the trumpet-saxophone doubler Charlie Creath, who had been active for more than a decade on Streckfus riverboats with the Kentucky-born pianist Fate Marable. St. Louis, a major port of call for the big boats, had always been a musical way-station for black jazzmen. Among musicians either resident or often in town were the trombonist Albert Wynn, clarinet men Horace Eubanks and William Thornton Blue, cornetist Dewey Jackson and trumpeter Leonard Davis, later a mainstay of Charlie Johnson's big band at Small's Paradise in New York. They played a rough-hewn but vigorous kind of jazz, directly descended from the New Orleans beginnings but not as refined as what was happening on the South Side of Chicago. Thornton Blue's spiky, acid clarinet typified the style and was itself a standout.

"St. Louis was pretty segregated at this time," said Hassler, "but the common interest in jazz that we had with the Negro musicians dissolved many of the social barriers. We wouldn't have dared play in public with them, but after hours was another story."

Even though the American Federation of Musicians maintained two strictly segregated locals, the St. Louis color bar appeared far less rigid than in many other cities further north. Such interracial jamming was common, and when Creath recorded four sides for the Okeh company on November 3, he used Sonny Lee, a white trombone man from Texas who later joined Bix and Tram at the Arcadia. The Chauffeurs' Club won its own small immortality through "Chauffeurs' Shuffle," recorded for Okeh May 14, 1926, by a group led by the clarinet and alto sax man Jimmy Powell.

After the symphony season began, Bix and Pee Wee expanded their activities to include Friday afternoon matinee concerts at the Odeon Building. Bud Hassler found out about it and started going along as musical tour guide and walking encyclopedia. "I had explained to Bix about some of the works he'd heard, and he decided he wanted me to go with him from then on. I guess we went to a half dozen concerts during the season this way, Bix with a jug in his jacket pocket and a straw sticking out of it. 'Big Red' Schiezer—Bix, for some reason, called him 'Ponzi'—wasn't only the bouncer, but a bootlegger too, and Bix always left the ballroom with a couple of pints.

"Bix had a really remarkable ear, jazz or no. He had perfect pitch and could distinguish A-440 from A-444 without preparation. There were two such tuning bars in a local music store, and he could easily tell one from the other. If you struck a handful of notes on a piano, at random or not, he could call every note at once.

"Apart from this talent, which he sort of took for granted, Bix was just another ordinary guy, with a keen sense of humor. Liked to date girls, even liked to play a bit of golf (when he was sober enough to get up during the day) and would have certainly laughed at the thought of ever becoming the almost legendary figure that he is today."

The Trumbauer band made no recordings during its stay at the Arcadia, curious in view of Okeh's recording activities in St. Louis at the time. Even the Serenaders, though the ballroom's relief group, recorded on October 26 using Trumbauer's vocalist Marty Livingston. They are intriguing records, showing young Sterling Bose midway between his New Orleans roots and a singing style immediately associable with Bix. Cliff Holman's alto sax, moreover, strongly reflects Trumbauer's approach on the slightly larger C-melody. Bose's lead on "Angry" rolls along atop the rhythm in a way reminiscent of the Beiderbecke of Wolverine days.

Ironically, said Thurston, Bose was the only member of the Serenaders who could read music while Bix, his idol, was the only man in the Trumbauer group who could not. "When we rehearsed, the rest of us would use music but Bix would have to learn the melodies by memory. Before we played anything on the job that was not a jam tune, he always asked me what the first tone was . . . but once he started a number his memory was perfect and his playing unerring. Hah! When you started to tell him about notes he'd say, 'Talk to me in concert; it's the only way I understand.' He thought only in terms of concert pitch, thought of his horn as a concert instrument, with valves one and three as 'C' instead of 'D' the way most trumpet players think of them. Partially because of this, he rarely played open tones; instead he'd rely to a marked degree on the first and third together and third alone. This produced a sort of 'jug tone' effect, and gave his phrasing and articulation a different effect from the orthodox players, and beautiful it was to hear.

"He had no range at all. High 'G' concert—played, by the way, with third valve rather than the standard one and two—was about the limit and not too many of them. But his playing was remarkably accurate. He never sounded strained or lost. He could play anything that he could think."[11]

The weather turned cold the first week of November. Bix was now spending the better part of his free time in Ruth's company. Whatever dating he had done prior to meeting Ruth appears to have trailed off as his romance with her gained momentum. They were all but inseparable. They went to films together ("He usually chose what we saw"); bowled, often with other bandsmen and their dates; took long walks together. On

---

11. The various accounts of Bix vigorously wiping his mouth before playing, coupled with Vernon Brown's recollection of a night when the cornetist, drunk, was "unable to find his embouchure" with the mouthpiece, indicate that Bix played on what brassmen refer to as a "dry" embouchure. This means, as it indicates, that the lips are dry, not moistened, when the mouthpiece is applied, making it necessary to "lock" or "slot" it into its customary position, finding the proper seating through trial and error. This method, long since discarded by responsible teachers because of its inconvenience, has also been known to have an inhibiting effect on the range and endurance of the player.

rainy or snowy days, there was indoor golf at the Coronado Hotel.

And around this time they became lovers. In later life Ruth was reluctant to discuss this side of their relationship in depth or detail, save to confirm that Bix was the first man to whom she had given herself. "We were deeply attached to one another . . . he was deeply affectionate. No one could make love like he did . . . I could just sit and look at him . . . it was a feeling I can't explain. I had many dates with Bix before anything was discussed about sex. It was a feeling. No one could resist . . . it was a mutual decision. Everything we did, or places we would go, it was a mutual thing . . . I was certain of Bix's love for me by the way he treated me, and the love he showed for me. What else can I say? He was so considerate, thoughtful . . . I know he loved me. I would have died for him.

"He wasn't the type to talk about his previous life—I mean girls . . . I believed the things he said to me and it simply meant he was in love with me . . . you know, I consider the most important part of my life was my life with him . . ."

She was proud to be seen with him, to be known as his girl. He, in turn, was proud to be able to take her backstage when they went to the movies and introduce her to musicians he knew in the pit orchestras. They loved to talk, to discuss things, said Ruth; all except two subjects: music and his family in Davenport. "He never said much about them or his school days —except for his sister. He was pretty proud of her, and crazy about her."

And the music? "Funny about that, now that I think of it. Although I heard him play the piano many times, and he could. play any piece I wanted him to, he never told me who his favorite composer was, or anything like that. I never even asked him if he took lessons. As far as I was concerned, he didn't need any—he could simply hear a piece and play it by ear. As for music itself—aside from saying he liked Ethel Waters' singing, he never talked about it with me."

But he did with Bud Hassler. The more often they attended concerts, the more Bix wanted to know about the theoretical side of what he was hearing. By this time, said Hassler, Bix had formed distinct, if somewhat one-sided, tastes within the symphonic repertoire. "His favorite composers were Debussy, especially for the *Prelude to the Afternoon of a Faun,* Ravel for the *Daphnis and Chloe* suites, and Stravinsky for the ballets, especially *Petrouchka* and *The Firebird.* He felt that Beethoven, though heroic in stature, lacked the same sense of intricate cadence and resolution in harmonic structure; in other words, he felt that he could hear many missing parts in Beethoven's orchestration."

Some Beiderbecke judgments, he said, were far more categorical. Mozart? "Childish." Brahms? "Pedantic and repetitive." Chopin and Liszt were "beer and chocolate soda, respectively." In the main, said Hassler, only the impressionists and modern tonal composers captured Bix's imagination, especially harmonically. "I tried to explain the classical masters and what they were driving at, but he wasn't much impressed. Tchaikovsky as an orchestrator could hold his attention, but not, for example, Mendelssohn. In fact, one Friday night after we had heard the *'Italian'* *Symphony* Bix started faking in the themes of the last movement into some dixieland thing we were playing. I gave him a funny look and said, 'Hey, you feel pretty long-haired tonight, don't you?' and he laughed and said, 'Mendelssohn doesn't sound any better to me even in the 'Jazz Me Blues.' "

Perhaps as a result of his friendship with Hassler, Bix announced one November day that he was going up to see Joe Gustat, first trumpet with the symphony, about taking lessons and "maybe developing some legit technique." Gustat, said Hassler, was well-known to jazzmen as "a scholarly guy, a profound musician, a great technician, one of the best—and a good guy along with it. He headed the Gustat Institute of Music in downtown St. Louis, where most of the first-chair symphony men taught."

The old man greeted Bix warmly. He had heard the Wolverines' records and had even gone to see the Arcadia band. He more than reciprocated Bix's admiration for him. "Play for me," he said, settling into a chair in a studio cluttered with instrument cases and trumpets of more sizes and shapes than Bix Beiderbecke had ever seen before.

Bix played. They talked. He played some more and Gustat demonstrated some technical points for him. "Look, Bix," he said at length, "let's not kid ourselves. From a symphony man's viewpoint you play all wrong. Totally and completely. Your fingering is all backwards—I'm not sure I even understand how you get some of those notes to come out in tune. I certainly couldn't that way. Your whole way of phrasing wouldn't fit in a symphony orchestra. Your attack is completely unconventional, and you use vibrato in a way—well, you'd have to abandon it altogether if you studied legitimate playing. Frankly, I don't think it would be worth it to you. Trying to change someone like you would be putting a wild animal in a cage—and to what end?"

Bix's face betrayed his discouragement. "But I want to learn to play properly. And I want to learn how to read. And—"

"Reading you can learn anywhere. All it takes is work. But why change what you've developed? Look at me—I'm a musician in a cage." Bix started to interrupt, but Gustat waved him aside. "No—I mean it. I've been trained that way all my life, and I've been playing the trumpet a good many years. All I know is what's written on the page they hand me—portions of Beethoven or Brahms or whoever. I'm on their leashes. You won't believe this, maybe you'll never understand it, but I envy you. You have a great, God-given gift, and many of us would easily consider trading what we have for what you have. Be proud of it, my boy, don't try to change it."

What passed through the mind of Bismark and Agatha Beiderbecke's son in that moment will never be known, but it is hardly difficult to guess. Here was Joseph Gustat, a man the Beiderbecke family would have instantly admired, directly contradicting one of the most basic articles of their musical and social creed. He was saying that Bix's jazz, far from being frivolous or degenerate, represented a new form of virtuosity, perhaps deplored under the values of the middle class but deeply admired by the practitioners of the very music the Davenporters found acceptable. Gustat's endorsement could only feed Bix's growing sense of conflict between conditioning and personal inclination, a conflict which was to reassert itself far more strongly in his association with the Paul Whiteman orchestra and subsequent personal disintegration. But here were the ingredients: the shaping of attitudes by family and education, pitted against a direction dictated by talent and interest; this, with Bix's gradual realization of how severely his theoretical and technical shortcomings as a self-taught musician could impede his development within his chosen idiom, presented a dilemma which proved, in the end, insoluble.

There was now little doubt in anyone's mind that Bix Beiderbecke was a major, even revolutionary, jazz talent. Hassler, working beside both men nightly, compared him and Trumbauer. The saxophonist had achieved a widespread following through his work with Ray Miller and the Benson Orchestra. His solo on the 1924 record of "San" with the Mound City Blue Blowers had become a set piece imitated note-for-note by any saxophonist aspiring to recognition as a jazzman. Trumbauer, not Bix, was the attraction of the Arcadia band. Yet for Hassler and many others, Bix was the more interesting figure.

"Tram, as great as he was, played mostly 'prop' stuff—in other words, the same licks, however original, a million times over. Formulae, attractive because they were different, but formulae nevertheless. But not Bix —he played a million things that will never be repeated . . . To get a perspective on the guy, you had to hear the way the trumpeters played *before* him and *after* him. The criterion for a jazzman before him was how many mutes he carried. Hell, Bix didn't even *own* a mute. He made them all change—and that includes Louis, Red Nichols, Oliver, Louis Panico, Frankie Quartell, and all the others. They just followed the road Bix built."

Vernon Brown waxed no less ecstatic, and rather more vivid, on his reaction to playing alongside Bix: "I don't mean to be dramatic, but it was like a bud opening up its petals into a flower. It was a shock to have heard, for the first time, anyone with that kind of natural ability."

Even allowing for a certain amount of hyperbole in such paeans, it seems safe to say that Bix was making a substantial impact on the jazz and dance music fraternity. Both Hassler and Tommy Satterfield, house arranger at the Missouri Theater down the street from the Arcadia, were intrigued by the constant musical push-pull going on within him, and by his attempts at the keyboard to incorporate elements of one music into another. Satterfield, too, later joined Paul Whiteman, and tailored many outstanding scores to reflect ideas he and Bix had discussed during St. Louis days.

After several sessions with Gustat, Bix resolved to do something about his reading. He started with an ultimatum to Bud Hassler, who by now was doing most of the Trumbauer band's arranging: no more parts written in concert. "Give me regular Bb parts. I've got to learn to read properly." Many of Hassler's arrangements came about in bits and pieces, usually the result of routines worked out on the stand. Someone would throw out an idea, another would pick it up, and it developed from there. Trumbauer had been deeply impressed by some of Rube Bloom's "advanced" scores for the Ray Miller band, and he and Hassler began to experiment with five-part voicing incorporating major seventh, ninth and eleventh chords. Bud remembered one arrangement of the pop tune "I Ain't Got Nobody," built around descending whole-tone scales voiced in five parts for two brass and three reeds.

With Bix as unofficial ringleader, the band was just as quick to toss out popular conventions of the day if they didn't fit the "advanced" thinking. No more ending tunes on tonic seventh chords, a commonplace with jazzbands since the heyday of the ODJB. Bix, said Hassler, dismissed such trite devices as "corny" or "cornfed." "He was a great one for inventing terms like that. 'Cornfed' was a special favorite of his; I'd never heard the term used like that before, but I can't say it actually originated with him. I'd not be surprised, though." Other jazz slang, such as calling wrong or muffed notes 'clams,' also appears to have begun with Bix, according to musicians who worked with him. One of Ray Thurston's fondest memories was of Bix expressing his contempt for a given piece of "corn" by sticking his tongue out, hayseed-style, and rubbing his thumb up and down against it while going "ts-ts-ts" or "a-zick-a-zick-a-zicka . . ." Sometimes as a gag he would play deliberately corny choruses, "and he was damned good at it, funny as all getout."

Then, as now, jazzmen were among the first to develop new "in" words and phrases unfamiliar to the general public. Eventually they would find their way into common usage—by which time the musicians had long since discarded them and moved on to new ones. Marijuana, brought up the Mississippi by musicians and riverboat roustabouts and still all but unknown to the general public, was "muggles" or "gage" or "mouta," shortened to "mout." Wingy Manone, said Hassler, was one of several who had a regular supply brought up to St. Louis on the Streckfus boats. Use among musicians was widespread, though far more casual than was the case in later years. Even in 1925, a musician high on "mout" would be apt to play "far out." After 1927, regular smokers took to addressing one another as "Lindbergh" to indicate that they were flying high. And "mout" was cheap: the average price per joint in the speakeasies around the riverfront was about a dime.

Ruth Shaffner knew, wished to know, none of this. Bix was her romance, perhaps her future husband. He reciprocated her love; little else mattered. He was fun to be with, courteous and considerate to a fault. And, she reflected, he could be as mischievous as a schoolboy. When, on Wednesday, November 18, a week before Thanksgiving, the Arcadia staged a "barnyard dance," complete to dressing the band in overalls, Ruth went along for the fun. Highlight of the evening was the presentation of a turkey to a member of the audience, selected allegedly at random. With a roll of Dee Orr's drums, Trumbauer stepped to the microphone to announce that the lucky winner was none other than—

"Me. I was so embarrassed. They'd arranged it, of course. Although I was flattered, I just didn't think it was right, and I told Bix so." The bird was later re-awarded to someone else at Ruth's behest.

Thanksgiving came and went, and December arrived snowy and cold in the usual round of Arcadian evenings, Friday afternoon symphony concerts, and good times snatched and shared where and when they could be. Then, on Saturday, December 12, Bix's phone rang. It was Ruth.

"Can we go out alone tonight? Nobody along? I have to talk to you."

"Well sure, Ruthie. What's up?"

"I'd rather not say now. I'll tell you tonight."

They went out together after the job. The air was clean and crisp and very cold, and the snow crunched under their feet as they walked down Olive Street. Several times Ruth started to speak, then stopped. They walked on, holding hands, Bix staring at his feet.

"Bix?"

"Mmmm?"

"Love me?"

"Sure. What's the matter? Why do you ask?"

"Sure you won't be mad?" She looked up at him, eyes moist. He smiled. That same smile, soft brown eyes sparkling and dancing.

"Positive."

They stopped. "Bix, I'm late. For my—well, you know. I'm more than a week overdue."

It took a few seconds to sink in. Then, quietly, he wrapped an arm around her shoulder and they walked on. "Any chance it could be—you know, just late?" Ruth shrugged.

"I don't know. It might come tomorrow, next week. I just don't know. But I don't *feel* the way it usually feels just before. Oh Bix, I'm so scared." She began to weep softly. He drew her to him, kissed her softly on the forehead, then the tip of her nose.

"Wait a few days. Don't worry about it. If nothing happens, then we'll talk about it again and decide what to do."

"Bix?" she said again.

"Yup."

"Would you—well, marry me? Would you let me have our baby?"

"Sure. Sure. But don't worry about that now, hon. We'll see next week. Okay?"

Ruth went home that night deeply troubled, and confided her fears to Estelle with hesitation and bitter self-castigation. Gently, Estelle calmed her down. There were two simple possibilities, she said: either she was pregnant or she was not. In either case, Ruth was going to have to make up her mind once and for all about Bix Beiderbecke.

"Look at it this way, Ruthie. He's a lovely boy, nice and kind. A real gentleman." Ruth nodded. But he was also a musician, always on the move, living a kind of life which was okay if you were young and unattached and carefree, but terribly unstable when a home and family had to depend on him. Casting her lot with Bix would mean living the way Frank Trumbauer and his wife lived. Home promptly after the job every night, no fun, no freedom. Just responsibility and instability—and endless waiting. Could Bix Beiderbecke get used to that? Could she?

"But he *loves* me! And I love him," Ruth blurted out. "I won't let him just up and go away. And besides, he wouldn't do anything like that anyway."

Estelle thought a moment. "Look, Ruthie, tell you what. Whether you're pregnant or not, we'll all go home for Christmas together. It'll give you a chance to think about it all, and maybe we can even talk about it with Mom and Dad. They could—"

"No!" Ruth shook her head violently. "They'd never understand. They're so strict. They'd think of a thousand reasons why not. They wouldn't understand at all. Nobody understands but Bix."

"I think they might." Estelle pressed for her way. "You can't just go ahead and do something like marry somebody, or have a baby or anything, without thinking about it and talking about it first. If Bix says he'll marry you, it means that he cares, doesn't it? A lot of men would just push you away if they thought you were pregnant, pretend not to know you any more. He's not like that, is he? So he deserves thinking about."

The next ten days brought confirmation of what Ruth had suspected: she was pregnant with Bix Beiderbecke's child. Thoughts and emotions raced in confusion through her mind: pride at this consummation of her love for Bix, yet fear of her family's—even Estelle's—reactions. Embarrassment at the social difficulties which awaited her, yet overwhelming affection for the man who had brought love into her life.

The sisters left for home on Wednesday, December 23. On the railroad platform, Bix and Ruth first solemnly exchanged Christmas presents, he giving her a giant box of chocolates, she presenting him with a pair of gold cufflinks. They kissed; he held her for a long time.

"It'll be all right, Ruthie," he whispered. "You'll see." He kissed the tears as they rolled down her cheeks. The train started to move. Ruth scampered up the steps just in time, and the conductor clanged the door shut behind her. She waved.

Bix stood a long time on the platform until the train had disappeared in the distance. Then, hands deep in pockets, he turned and walked slowly out of the station.

A dime-store photograph of Ruth Shaffner, c. 1925.

Wingy Manone recording at the Okeh studios in Chicago in November 1925. The band is "Mannone's San Sue Strutters." They recorded eight sides in eight hours—none of them subsequently issued. L to R: Jerry Bump (trombone); Min Leibrook (sousaphone); Lennie Esterdahl (banjo); Earl McDowell (drums); Wingy (trumpet); George Harper (alto sax); Paul Fried (piano).

# Chapter 11

Bix's mind was in turmoil, and spending the holidays in St. Louis without Ruth was hardly a calming prospect. He hadn't been home in months; now seemed as good a time as any to go and visit the family, and by doing so to get away and think.

He played Christmas and New Year's Eve with the band, then took off for Davenport on New Year's Day. First, though, he dropped around to the bowling alley at Grand and Olive, latest hangout for white jazzmen working around town. Some of the regulars were there.

"Hey, Bix," Vernon Brown yelled, seeing Beiderbecke amble in. "You gonna be back in time for Thursday?" Bix looked puzzled, and Brown laughed. "Bet you forgot all about it. You guys are bowling against us. Without you, you guys are a pushover. It'd hardly be fair contest."

Bix clapped a hand on the trombonist's shoulder. "Have no fear, Brownie, m'boy. I'll be there just to whip you all. Count on it."

Brown was still with the Missouri Cotton Pickers, renamed "Tremps' Troubadours" by leader Joe Lechner for their engagement at Tremps' Ballroom. They had started a three-team bowling league with Trumbauer's band and the Serenaders. "We all used to meet there after our jobs were over at night and bowl from about one until four or five in the morning," said Brown. "Bix was a better than fair bowler, made about 180 on the average."

Bix was as good as his word. The Trumbauer team was just getting up to bowl early Thursday morning when the door opened and "in walked Bix as relaxed and cool as you please. He'd come directly from the railroad station, hadn't even stopped at his hotel."

The following afternoon he called Ruth. She'd been back since Sunday, she said, and had waited for his return.

"Well, Ruthie, how about it?"

"About what?"

"You know. Us. I mean—"

"Can't it wait until tonight, Bix? I mean, it's so hard over the telephone . . ."

"Sure, suppose so." Concern edged his voice. "You *will* come down tonight, won't you?"

Ruth arrived early at the Arcadia and stayed most of the evening listening. Bix was his usual self, animated and genial as ever, greeting friend and stranger alike with a "How's it going down there? Great to see you." Ruth had to laugh—half the time he never remembered their names. But he couldn't bring himself to fluff anyone off. Dear Bix.

One visitor stood out. He was a slight, tough little ex-jockey, also a St. Louisian, named Bill McKenzie. The musicians called him "Red," and welcomed him as one of them. He played no instrument, but sang jazz choruses into a comb wrapped in tissue paper. He had teamed two years before with Dick Slevin, who played kazoo, and Jack Bland, banjo-strumming native of the ragtime city of Sedalia, Missouri, to form a "Novelty Jazz Trio." They changed the name to "Mound City Blue Blowers," in celebration of St. Louis, for their February 1924 Brunswick recording debut. Trumbauer had helped to make a name for both them and himself by recording "San" with them. Without Tram, but with Eddie Lang on guitar, the group had toured the U.S. Theater circuit and played London. McKenzie had heard Bix with the Wolverines and later dropped in on one of their Gennett record dates. Later, as an Okeh company talent scout, he had a key role in winning recording contracts for a number of jazz artists, Bix among them.

"I don't know, Bix. I don't know what to do," Ruth said as their cab headed for the busy west end after the job. She had not discussed him, marriage or the baby with her parents. She had not brought the subject up at all.

"I just couldn't," she said. "It would have been so wrong. I mean, my parents are—well, they're very strict, churchgoing people. They'd never have understood."

Bix sat quiet for a moment, hands folded in his lap like a schoolboy as Ruth talked on, her voice calm, measured, even. "I've thought about it a lot, and I just don't think it'd be right to have the baby. It won't work. It's just—well, impossible."

"Impossible is a ridiculous word." He was getting cross. Ruth could tell, though his voice never rose. "Nothing's impossible, Ruthie. It's just a question of whether you want something enough . . ."

"I—I don't understand what you mean."

"Sure you do. It's our baby. Yours and mine. It would be wrong to us and wrong to the baby to—to do anything about not having it. Ruthie, don't you see? A baby's a wonderful thing. It's ours. We made it. Together. Nobody's going to hold that against you."

He was smiling at her, that damnable smile that always made her melt, made the tears well up behind her eyes. "I thought about it while I was home this week," he was saying. "You know, all about Tram and Mitzi and the way they live, getting married and bringing up kids. I couldn't get over the feeling that it was intended that we should be together. That's the really important thing, that we love—"

"Oh, Bix!" Ruth's confusion and indecision evaporated in a flash of annoyance. "Don't you understand? Don't you know more about life than that? It's just not the same for a girl as for a man. You—you could go away any time, be free and happy. And nobody's going to remember or bother you or hold it against you if you decide one day you're tired of me and want to move on to somebody else. But I can't do that. I'd have to come home and listen to people talking about what a fool I was to give myself to a travelling jazz musician, what a disappointment I was as a daughter, or a Christian, or just a person."

"But Ruthie—"

"No, wait—let me finish. You're a man. You never hear any of—"

"But we'd go together . . ."

"Sure. For awhile. But would it really last? What if I did have your child, and then you weren't there any more? Oh, Bix, it'd be so wrong. We're too young to ruin our lives like that. You're only twenty-two and you can't be tied down; I'm not even twenty yet."

She paused. Bix looked at her, uncertain what to say. Ruth kept talking. "I think we have to make a fresh start, go back to the way things were, where we can have fun, and—"

"You mean—" Bix stared at her, incredulous. She slumped in her seat, avoiding his gaze. In the darkness he couldn't see her tears.

They left it there, each promising to think about it and then talk again. About a week later, Ruth took two weeks off from her job at Dr. Clark's to "rest up"—only a week after returning from a vacation at her parents' farm in Illinois. In later years she remained close-mouthed about this fortnight; but it is not difficult to infer her thoughts. By the time she and Bix went out again, on Saturday, January 30, Ruth's pregnancy, and the crisis it had triggered, were things of the past.

"If only I could relive my life," she said recently. "I was so young, and didn't know what the outcome of it all would be. Bix tried so hard to persuade me, but all I could see was how impossible it all was because of my family and everything. I've shed so many tears over this . . . I loved him so much I would have been very, very happy."

Bix appeared to become more introspective. He took to discussing religion and philosophy with Hassler, long, running argumentations often spanning whole evenings and lasting into the early hours of the morning —to the occasional bewilderment of fellow-bandsmen. "You should have heard them go at it," said Ray Thurston. "Bud, you know, was a free-thinker, while Bix always held on to his strict Presbyterian principles. They argued about all sorts of things, and Bix appeared very serious at such times.

"He was pretty orthodox about religion. Not that he ever got up out of his bed to go to church—he wasn't that type. But he stayed completely loyal to his family rearing and always argued this line with Hassler, who was pretty damn good at expressing his free ideas. You could almost say Bix's thinking about religion was as orthodox as his horn playing was unorthodox."

The Arcadia band, meanwhile, was getting better and better, and Bix along with it. Hassler's arrangements were increasingly ambitious, and word about the group's modern sound had filtered back to Chicago. Musicians passing through came round to listen.

Thurston quit about this time to front his own group, a decision he later had cause to regret. "I suppose one of the things that prompted me was the thought that both Tram and Bix would eventually go back to some other band as sidemen themselves, which was later borne out. Trumbauer was angry with me when I left, because I didn't give him much notice. I suppose he was right about that. Also, I have to confess that I was kind of fed up with the heavy drinking that went on all the time in the band.

"Funny, that I should remember this, but Tram never did pay me my last week's salary. He still owes me $83 after all these years."

Sonny Lee stepped in briefly to fill the chair vacated by Thurston, until Vernon Brown, recruited from Lechner's band via the bowling alley, joined as full-time replacement. He found himself part of a closely-knit musical team, sparked by the partnership between Bix and Tram. Trumbauer specialized in C-melody sax, using alto only in section work. His dry, humorous style contrasted well with the earnest intensity of Bix's playing. Often the two men swapped phrases on solo choruses, evolving "chase" sequences of startling empathy. It was a device they were later to exploit with great success as members of Paul Whiteman's orchestra. One would play a two- or four-bar phrase, and the other would answer with a paraphrase or variation on it. The effect on the listener was of two contrasting sides of the same personality. Chester Sableman, a St. Louis businessman who frequented the Arcadia, got "an enormous kick out of watching the two of them trying to outdo one another. Frank might stand up and take off on something terrific, only to have Bix play it back at him practically the same, with just enough variation to make it interesting. Sometimes Bix went first, and Frank would come back at him. They were a terrific team, and it was a thrill to watch and listen to them."

At the end of January the band took a weekend off to drive 150 miles to Carbondale, Illinois, Trumbauer's birthplace, to play a widely-advertised Elks' Club evening. The *Carbondale Free Press* heralded the event with a glut of stories about the home town boy who remained loyal even after he had moved to St. Louis as a child. "Though the orchestra would cost more than the Elks could afford to pay," said the paper, "Trambauer [*sic*] is coming because Carbondale is his boyhood home." The praise—and the misspellings of his name—continued. Saturday morning, January 30, after the date, it was:

> Frank Trumbaur's [*sic*] orchestra that played at the Elks' Club last night in the town of his boyhood was hailed as the best jazz orchestra ever to play within the walls of the Elks' Dance Hall. Dancers who filled the hall to capacity from Carbondale and many southern Illinois towns heard the orchestra and acclaimed the music superior to any they have heard played here. Trumbaur [*sic*] and his orchestra, which he, in his characteristic modest manner says "is not mine but our band. It is the result of cooperation and about the only reason I call it mine is because I pay them off."

The *Free Press* waxed even more ecstatic (and spelled Trumbauer's name wrong yet another way) after the band did a return engagement on Friday, February 26: "Frank Trombaur, Carbondale's pride in the jazz world, the boy who struggled from an urchin to his place in this line of entertainment which has in modern days become a dignified profession, played for the second time last night in his home town for a dance at the Elks' Club . . . the dancers were even more enthusiastic than the first time and the orchestra played its best."

Around the same time, Trumbauer's mother, who had taught him to play the saxophone, sent a letter to the *Free Press* talking at length of Frank's family background, as different from that of Bix as were their musical styles, and dispelling the notion, apparently prevalent in Carbondale, that he was an orphan.

> . . . Frank had no father to help him since he was 11 years of age. I have fulfilled the duties of both mother and father with the able assistance of my good mother and father, Mr. and Mrs. H. B. Crowell . . . Nineteen years ago,

I left home (Carbondale) and came to St. Louis to earn a living for Frank and myself. With a fair knowledge of music, I went to work in the small theaters and studied after work hours for four years and completed my piano work, gained a reputation as a fair pianist, then took over the work of the larger theaters at the piano. For nine years (many times with a bed made on three chairs behind my piano in the pit for Frank to sleep on until my work was done), for I kept him with me a great deal. Then I took up the saxophone and have become one of St. Louis' leading saxophone teachers and the only lady director of a saxophone orchestra in the city. Let me say I planned and instructed Frank's future until he was 19 years of age . . . From then on Frank has gained by enormous bounds into the realms of stardom (as you know) by his own hard study and untiring efforts . . .

The letter was signed Mrs. William H. Stevenson, 2304A Russell Boulevard, St. Louis.

The second Carbondale trip was not without incident. About halfway there, said Vernon Brown, "Bix realized he'd left his cornet case on the bandstand at the Arcadia. We'd left in a hurry after the job, and he'd had it ready to go, all right, but then walked off without it. Trumbauer said not to worry: he had an old friend whose son played cornet in the school band there." Sure enough, Tram got hold of the horn and Bix played it "and promptly fell in love with it. But the kid's father wouldn't sell it to him because there was a sentimental attachment to it. It was an heirloom of some sort that had been used by the kid's grandfather."

After the Elks' Club dance most of the band members went with the mayor of Carbondale out to his country house, where they drank and shot craps until dawn. Bix, said Brown, was in a gambling mood and "came out the big winner." They rode back the next afternoon in Dan Gaebe's car, Bix and Brownie sitting in the back seat and munching coconut-covered chocolate cookies in between gulps of mash. "That really slew me. He must have eaten half the bag by himself, chasing each cookie with a jolt of whiskey. It's never ceased to amaze me how a guy could consume cookies—cookies, for Pete's sakes—with a whiskey chaser. He was quite a guy, in more ways than one."

February and March settled back into familiar routine: the band doing evenings at the Arcadia, Bix and Ruth dating after hours and on days off. They still talked about getting married, but now there was a hesitancy, an unwillingness to talk in specifics. The prospect of a future together had edged imperceptibly into the abstract, away from "when" into "if." Ruth's recollections of the time are a mosaic of vignette episodes: Bix sitting with the sisters in a cafe dunking doughnuts in a cup of coffee, "the first time we'd ever seen anybody do that"; Bix disregarding a quarantine blockade to visit Bess in the hospital during a siege of scarlet fever.

On Monday, March 29, Bix went to Detroit for the day to talk to Jean Goldkette. The Arcadia was due to close for the summer on May 3, and Goldkette had been in touch about using Bix and Tram, plus several of the other band members, during the summer holiday. Then, at the end of April, Charlie Horvath journeyed to St. Louis with an offer. The Goldkette Victor Orchestra needed someone to front it and act as musical director while Goldkette concentrated on the business side. With the booking agency growing rapidly and the music school well-established in Detroit, he had his hands full. But whoever took over the Victor band would have to be personable, respected, reliable—and a topflight musician. Trumbauer filled the bill, said Horvath, if he wanted it. Bix, as expected, would also join as featured cornet soloist, this time for good.

Trumbauer accepted at once.

Goldkette's plan was first to play a string of prom dates with the full, reorganized group, then split it into two smaller bands, adding a few outsiders, for a pair of summer resort jobs. One, at Island Lake, Michigan, would be largely Goldkette's regular personnel playing scaled down versions of the Graystone band's arrangements; the other, at Hudson Lake, Indiana, about 20 miles from South Bend, would contain the new complement of hot men plus Dee Orr, Dan Gaebe, Sonny Lee and Pee Wee Russell from the Arcadia.

It meant, too, that Bix and Ruth would be separated. They were spending most of every day with each other now, she trying to hold back the clock, his loyalty to her being inexorably submerged by enthusiasm at the prospect of rejoining Goldkette. The days whirled by: Bix and Ruth walking and talking, endlessly discussing a conditional-tense future; Bix full of animation about Goldkette's orchestra; a final goodbye round at "Ethel's," another at "Joe's"; then, at the last, moments of quiet in each other's arms, Ruth sobbing gently.

"Hey, hey, Ruthie. None of that," kissing eyes moist with tears. "That just makes it hurt all the more. I'll be back. You know that. It's not as if I were going away forever."

"Will you really come back? Really? Or are you just going to—"

"Sshhh . . ." He closed her lips with a kiss.

"But I—oh, Bix, I'm so scared."

"No, no . . . don't be scared. I'll be back sooner than you think . . . I'll just be gone a little while, and I won't be far away. Don't worry . . ."

The Arcadia closed Monday, May 3. Three nights later Bix and Ruth parted for the last time. She cried herself to sleep—only to be awakened in the morning by the telephone. "Hey, Ruthie, I'm still here. We're not leaving until later this afternoon. Come on down." Typical Bix, she thought. For all the sadness, the idea brought a laugh. Typical. Big goodbye Thursday night, surprise phone call Friday morning. Impossible, ridiculous Bix. Frustrating, endlessly charming Bix. She and Estelle met him outside "Joe's" almost as though nothing were different. "We didn't speak much. He just held my hand. That was enough."

Then, at last, it was really time. He climbed into Dee Orr's convertible and they were off, leaving Estelle and Ruth in the sunshine on the corner outside the Arcadia Ballroom, now quiet and empty and boarded up.

"He *will* be back, won't he?" It was more a plea for reassurance than a question. Estelle shrugged.

"I don't know. Maybe he will. I'm sure he *wants* to. But he wants to play, too. I just don't know, Ruthie."

"Well, I do. He will. I know it. I just feel it," said Ruth, resolute. They started home, Estelle wrapping a reassuring arm around her sister's shoulder. Better, she thought, to leave unspoken the conviction growing in her mind that Bix Beiderbecke was gone for good.

The Casino at Hudson Lake, Indiana, renamed the Blue Lantern Inn by Jean Goldkette. Bix and Trumbauer played here with a Goldkette unit in the summer of 1926.

The full Goldkette Graystone Ballroom Orchestra, autumn 1926, on the front lawn of the Hillcrest Inn, Southboro, Massachusetts, headquarters for the band's New England tour. L to R: (seated) Ray Lodwig, Bill Challis, Newell "Spiegle" Willcox, Fred "Fuzzy" Farrar, Bill Rank. Bix, kneeling at the end, appears to have moved his head as the shutter snapped, blurring his face. Rear, standing: Howdy Quicksell, Chauncey Morehouse, Irving Riskin, "Doc" Ryker, Don Murray, Frank Trumbauer (with cap), Steve Brown (holding bass).

# Chapter 12

Teetering precariously atop a rickety stepladder, Jean Goldkette hooked a large blue-painted glass lantern onto a nail above the entrance to the long frame building.

"How's it look, boys?" he called. Charlie Horvath and his brother-in-law, Frank Fellows, broke off discussing the weather with Mrs. Victor Smith and surveyed Goldkette's handiwork.

"Not bad at all, Jean," said Horvath. "Ought to be just the thing."

"Yeah. Looks great, Jean," Fellows chimed in, more in reference to the building's fresh coat of glistening white paint than to his boss's blue lantern.

"I don't like it," said Mrs. Smith. Goldkette nearly lost his balance. Clinging to the portico with one hand, he hastily straightened round, wire-rimmed spectacles on his nose with the other. "Now, Mrs. Smith, don't you worry. Our little venture will be a great success. That I guarantee you. You must have a little faith."

She would take some convincing. Her husband had put up this building in 1922 at Hudson Lake, Indiana, 90 miles east of Chicago, on the South Shore Electric Railway between South Bend and Michigan City. He'd called it the Casino and let the people in free for dancing every spring and summer. Folks liked it here, and they always came back. But Victor Smith had died suddenly March 10, only a week before the Casino's St. Patrick's Day opening for the 1926 season. His widow had decided to carry on for the time being, but long-term prospects looked uncertain at best.

Goldkette and his managers, Horvath and Fellows, had come up for St. Patrick's Day and found it packed, more than 600 couples on the polished wood floor, the lights of fishing boats twinkling on the lake outside. Impressed, he offered to rent the hall for the summer season, taking an option to buy. Mrs. Smith accepted. Now it was May, and Goldkette was there to make ready for the summer—and to change the Casino's name to the "Blue Lantern."

"I was sure he'd made a mistake," Mrs. Smith said. "The place was always known under its old name, and all the trolley-buses in Chicago had advertisements with that name. Also, we'd never charged admission fees. But the first thing he did when he arrived was to start charging $1.50 admission. For a long time afterwards, even after we'd changed the name back and dropped the charge, people asked us about it."

Opposite the Casino, also on the lake front, stood a hotel built in 1885 by Victor Smith's father. The family lived there, said Mrs. Smith, but a small yellow cottage in a field out behind the building could also be made available to Goldkette to house employees or musicians who worked at the Blue Lantern during the summer.

Goldkette clambered uncertainly down the ladder. "Have no fear, Mrs. Smith. My boys will be here in about two weeks to give you a positively gala opening night for our partnership on the 22nd. Take my word for it, Madam, I guarantee you will be pleased." He returned to Detroit, leaving Horvath in charge.

Friday evening, May 21, Goldkette's Victor Recording Orchestra, newly revamped to include Bix Beiderbecke and Frank Trumbauer, did its final Graystone Ballroom broadcast of the summer over WCX. It was picked up by WSBT, the station of the *South Bend Tribune*, which served the Hudson Lake area, to acquaint the Casino's clientele with what it could expect musically during June, July and August.

After the show the band split into two units for the summer. One, with Don Murray, Ray Lodwig, Steve Brown on bass and Bill Rank on trombone among the personnel, went up to Island Lake. The other, with Bix, Tram, Dee Orr, Gaebe, Pee Wee Russell and Sonny Lee joining Goldkette regulars Fuzzy Farrar, Doc Ryker and pianist Irving "Itzy" Riskin, plus Frank Di Prima on banjo, whom Trumbauer knew from the Ray Miller band, drove up to Hudson Lake.

Bix and Tram had joined the orchestra in Terre Haute, Indiana, on Thursday, May 13, for the Rose Polytechnic Institute Junior Prom. With the memory of his 1924 experiences still vivid in his mind, Bix regarded his return to the band at a princely $100 a week as a triumph, and the enthusiasm was more than mutual. "Everybody liked him," said alto saxophonist Ryker. "He was such a nice fellow, easy to get along with. He still couldn't read well, but he could fake. He could always find another note . . . no matter how many notes were played, he'd always find one that somebody else didn't have."

Ryker, newly-married, was one of several musicians who brought their wives along for the summer. They took bungalows some distance from the Blue Lantern, further down the lake shore, leaving the single men—Bix, Pee Wee, Orr, Riskin and Lee, plus Gaebe, who left his wife in St. Louis —to room together in the yellow cottage behind the hotel. It came with two mascots: a cow which took no note at all of either their coming or going, and a rooster which, said Riskin, "crowed in 32nd notes as we walked back in the early morning after the jobs. We dubbed it the corny rooster."

From Bix's point of view, the cottage had one undeniable advantage: an ancient, out-of-tune but still playable Knabe square "salon" piano. "He was delighted with it," said Itzy. "His greatest pleasure, from the start, was to have me play him to sleep with Debussy, Stravinsky, and such American composers as McDowell and Eastwood Lane. Whenever I got to an interesting harmony he'd just lie there in bed and moan."

Bix and Pee Wee took the first initiative in exploring the area. Before long they had even come up with a source of cheap booze. Two elderly spinsters on a nearby farm brewed their own corn mash and, it seems, supplied every musician in the area. Evans Neirouter, who as "Slim Evans" played saxophone alongside Wild Bill Davison that summer in a Wolverinestyle band at Hamilton Lake, not far distant, recalled similar periodic trips to "the sisters" for their weekly mash supply.

This brew, plus a single bottle of milk every day, was the sole liquid refreshment for the yellow cottage. "You can be certain who did the cooking and clearing up after meals," said Riskin. "No sooner had those guys finished a meal than they'd be off to visit the spinsters for jugs of that awful stuff."

Come June the weather turned hot, and the band settled in for a long, lazy sojourn. "It was a wonderful summer," said Doc Ryker's wife Norma. "On a balmy night, you could hear the music out over the lake. Freddy Farrar had the most beautiful tone for waltzes, probably the loveliest I've ever heard. It was just a beautiful place to be."

May Prindeville, whose family lived down the road, recalled that "we could hear music from the cottage all day long. I wouldn't say they ran wild or anything like that . . . no, they were just simply happy and very gay. We were always seeing them fishing and swimming in the lake."

None of the six bothered to do any real cleaning. Half-empty open cans and milk bottles began to accumulate, and with them hordes of flies to add to the ever-present mosquitoes. On a hot summer morning, the buzz of the insects made sleep all but impossible. Bix contributed enough mosquito netting to cover each man as he slept. But the disorder—and the smell—only got worse. Doc Ryker dropped in, had a look, and reported back to Norma, whereupon she and Edith Horvath trooped over one Sunday afternoon while the band was playing, to see for themselves. "It was just frightful," said Norma. "They'd let everything slide. It'd got so dirty that Edith and I swore right there we'd have to go in once a week just to clean up. They had all sorts of sardine cans and dozens of half-empty bottles of milk on the porch. They'd just let them stand there and go sour."

Edith ran back to the cottage the Rykers and the Horvaths shared, returning with a large, shallow-sided wash basin. "She dumped all the sour milk into it and started down the steps of the cottage, intending to go over and heave it into the lake," Norma said, "but don't you think she slipped with it as she was going down the stairs of that old cottage? What a mess!"

Lapses in personal hygiene were more easily—if summarily—dealt with. Neither Bix nor Pee Wee seemed overinclined to bathe or shower regularly, said Doc Ryker, apart from an occasional swim in the lake. With Ruth and Stella far away, both men seemed intent on shedding any burden of presentability their relationships with the sisters had placed on them. The other single musicians, perhaps a trifle more fastidious, "couldn't get Bix to take a bath, so they'd get him out in a rowboat and dump him in . . . Pee Wee was the same way," said Doc.

Norma cut in with a laugh. "I think the real reason they didn't want to bathe was that none of the cottages had a bath. The bath house was up in the hotel, and you had to pay 25¢ to use it. I don't think either Bix or Pee Wee could see spending their money on such luxuries."

The band worked every night except Monday, with all-day and evening sessions on Sundays to accommodate the big excursion crowds down for the day from Chicago. It was a long haul, and Bix was only too glad to spell Riskin occasionally at the piano. The combination of good musical company—in essence an extension of the Arcadia band—and the lazy, relaxed atmosphere, was having startling effect on Bix's playing. "He really came into his own that summer," said Dee Orr. "His tone became as dazzling as some incandescent metal . . . he and Frank used to take whole choruses together, with their eyes closed—and right! You know, Bix played his very best that summer, and there's not a single record of them then either. He —Bix—used to like to sit by the drums and piano, one leg crossed over the other, under that terrific glaring light on the stand."

Mrs. Smith's teenage son Buddy—Victor, Jr.—also got to know the musicians up at the yellow cottage, but he was one of the few to venture close. Riskin recalled, not without a measure of irony, that even Trumbauer, with whom Bix had developed so close a musical rapport, "warned his wife not to mix with us, and didn't even want her to meet us on a harmless social level." Young Smith proved more intrepid. One day, he said, Bix, Farrar, Gaebe and he went bass fishing on the lake right after work. "Gaebe was a giant of a man, and was careless enough to stand up in the boat—which promptly capsized, Fred losing his rod and all his fishing tackle. Bix was the only one to have a real good laugh about it, while the others all looked as if they were going to a funeral.

"At that time, incidentally, I was a scout, and when Bix learned that I wanted to learn how to play the bugle, he gave me one of his mouthpieces."

The band did several broadcasts over WSBT, each accompanied by a story in the *Tribune* praising the various musicians. One such review of a program aired on Monday, June 21, put it thus, under the headline, "Goldkette Orchestra gives great concert":

> ... Music such as is seldom heard from any radio station was sent on the ether last night from WSBT by Jean Goldkette's Blue Lantern Orchestra, under the direction of Frank Trumbauer. The band presented a carefully thought-out program of numbers, including concert arrangements, symphonic dance arrangements, "hot" tunes, a medley of old dance numbers, and piano, saxophone, trumpet and banjo solos.
>
> From the very first number, a special arrangement of "Five Foot Two, Eyes of Blue," to the last strains of "Home Sweet Home," the Goldkette organization demonstrated very thoroughly that it is one of the most capable dance orchestras in America. Solos from various members of the organization brought rounds of applause from the large crowd gathered in the studio and complimentary telephone calls from those listening in . . .
>
> ... "Bix" Beiderbecke varied the program with a unique piano solo, "The Legend of Lonesome Lake," by Eastwood Lane. Mr. Beiderbecke, who plays the trumpet with the band, is also an accomplished pianist . . .
>
> ... Jean Goldkette's orchestra plays every night except Monday at the Blue Lantern, Hudson Lake, Indiana. An orchestra as great as this one cannot help please the dancing public, and those who have not danced to the orchestra owe it to themselves to do so . . .

The band was now splitting evenings with Joe Dockstader's Indianans from South Bend, who had played the Casino before Goldkette sent his own group up from Detroit. Despite the *Tribune*'s superlatives, and perhaps predictably, in view of Mrs. Smith's remarks, the Dockstader band proved consistently more popular with the crowds. As Buddy Smith saw it, "The music the [Goldkette] guys played was just simply beyond the regulars. They preferred the Indianans. That's probably why business was pretty bad all summer. Weekends there were a lot of people who came up from Chicago, South Bend and Michigan City, but evenings during the week there was nobody."

Among the weekend visitors was a steady stream of Chicago musicians coming to sit in and get out of the city heat for a day or two. Frequent faces included Mezz Mezzrow, Benny Goodman, Jimmy McPartland and drummer Dave Tough. The invasion usually began late Saturday evenings and slackened off 24 hours later. As in St. Louis, it was generally an unending cycle of booze, "mout" and music, with Riskin trying to grab some sleep in the next room. "Sunday was a tough day," he said, "and I just didn't have the energy to cope with it unless I got some sleep."

Back in St. Louis, Ruth Shaffner had heard next to nothing from Bix since his departure. He had assured her he would be back, and she had taken that on faith. Yet there was only silence. Then, on a Monday in mid-June, the telephone rang.

"Hi, Ruthie. It's me." The voice made her heart leap.

"Bix? Is it really you? Where on earth are you?"

"I'm here. In St. Louis. Get ready, we're going places."

"Going places" meant Westlake Park, an amusement park outside St. Louis famed for a towering roller coaster which the Shaffner girls had dubbed "the mountain ride. When you got to the top, it would drop straight down." On this afternoon, Bix and Pee Wee joined Ruth and Estelle, and Bess came along with her boyfriend and future husband, Barrent Ten Broek, Jr.

They all sat squashed together in the same creaking, wobbling car, taking the plunges with screams and laughter. As they neared the end of the ascent for the "mountain ride," Bix stood up to reach in his hip pocket for a pint flask he had brought along. Just then the car lurched over the top, throwing him off balance.

"Bix, for goodness' sake, sit down!" Ruth shrieked over the noise, even as Bix was pitched forcefully back into his seat, flask still in his pocket.

"Hey, silly," he whispered as they hurtled down the incline. "Did you really think I was going to bail out?" Despite herself, Ruth laughed.

Shortly after his whirlwind visit to St. Louis, Bix went with most of the Hudson Lake band to Detroit and combined with the Island Lake contingent to play at what Irving Riskin remembered as "some swanky affair. I don't remember a lot about it, except for thousands of little lights in the garden where we played, arranged to simulate fireflies. Tram, by the way, planned to go by air—he was quite air-minded, and went into it a lot more deeply later. The rest of us didn't care much for the idea, so we drove down."

None of the musicians involved in this event was able to remember its date or place. But Bix withdrew his card from the Detroit union local on Friday, June 18, an indication that the engagement may have taken place during this weekend.

The summer rolled lazily on. Trumbauer enlivened Fourth of July celebrations at the Blue Lantern by turning up for work in a full cowboy outfit. "It had an angora sweater covered in stains," said Mrs. Smith, "and it was horrible." Crystal Hawkins, a girl from down the road, famed in the region for her fondness for good times and bootleg hooch, ran a three-day nonstop party at the cottage. In the words of one interested non-participant,

"I'll bet when it was through she knew that gang better than anyone else around did." And, said Buddy Smith, there was the afternoon Bix, sitting at the piano after rehearsal, was asked by a couple of local enthusiasts to play for them so they "could watch how he did it. One of them offered him $20 for just a couple of minutes' instruction, but Bix said no, he wanted to go swimming with the gang. I was amazed that he would turn down the money."

Until now Dan Gaebe's car had been the sole means of transport for the residents of the yellow cottage. Bix and Pee Wee, deciding more freedom was needed, pooled their resources and put down $60 in nearby LaPorte on a 1916 Buick roadster, then set off for home lighthearted and more than a bit sloshed. They weren't halfway there when something in the motor gave a loud clang, and the Buick rolled sputtering to a stop and died.

"Aw, shit," said Pee Wee. Bix, in the driver's seat, shook his head solemnly and stood in place, holding aloft a jug of the spinsters' best mash.

"No, my dear fellow," he said in a mock English accent. "You simply *must* see these things in the correct spirit. A valiant and time-honored warrior has breathed its last in our service. We must drink to its eternal rest." He followed the toast with a long, celebratory draught.

"Aw, shit," said Pee Wee.

The two of them were singing lustily when they rolled up, towed by a farmer's pickup truck, to the front entrance of the Blue Lantern at 10:30 P.M. Arm in arm they reeled in—to find a none-too-amused Jean Goldkette waiting to greet them. He had decided on this night to pay one of his rare visits to Hudson Lake to hear how his star sidemen were faring. "Good evening, gentlemen," he said, straightening his spectacles. "I do hope— really I do—that I've not interrupted anything. Do carry on, please."

After one or two unsuccessful attempts at repair, Bix and Pee Wee gave the Buick up as a lost cause and parked it permanently in the field adjoining the cottage, where it kept the cow and the rooster company for the rest of the summer as an occasional outdoor shaving stand, with built-in mirror. There it remained until the outbreak of the Korean War nearly a quarter-century later, when it was sold for scrap iron.

The Goldkette band's departure from Hudson Lake was as abrupt as the summer preceding it had been lazy. On Thursday, August 26, the *South Bend Tribune* announced a contest:

> So interested is Frank Trumbauer, the orchestra's leader in what WSBT listeners think of his band that he is offering five prizes for the five best letters on the subject, "my opinion of your orchestra." Arrangements have been made to print in the *Tribune* the five prize-winning letters, and the prizes will be awarded at the WSBT-Blue Lantern Radio Frolic, which will be held at the Blue Lantern, Hudson Lake, Indiana, Saturday, Sept. 4 . . . the concert [the following] Monday night will perhaps be the last broadcast by this band from the Tribune station, as the season at the Blue Lantern will soon close and the orchestra will leave this territory . . .

Then, just three days later, in the *Tribune* for Sunday, August 29:

> Art Haerens' orchestra, under the direction of Myron Walz, will be the orchestra feature of the program broadcast Monday night from the *Tribune* station. The broadcast by Jean Goldkette's Blue Lantern Orchestra, under

Frank Trumbauer's direction, which was scheduled for Monday, had to be cancelled due to the fact that the Goldkette organization is leaving the Blue Lantern at Hudson Lake to play an engagement in New York City.

Goldkette's plans to take his star-packed ensemble on tour in the East had firmed up. Its first dates in New England were scheduled for the latter half of September, less than a month off. The tour was to climax with a run at Roseland Ballroom, in which Goldkette's orchestra would be pitted against that of Fletcher Henderson, itself full of top musicians. But apart from a few dates just before the summer, the full, revised Goldkette band had not yet played together as a unit. They were short on arrangements suitably showcasing Bix, Trumbauer and the other hot men. There was plenty of hard rehearsing to be done and precious little time in which to do it.

The men added for the summer went their respective ways. Orr, Gaebe and DiPrima hardly appear again in the history books. Sonny Lee went from Gene Rodemich's St. Louis dance orchestra through a succession of big bands—notably those of Isham Jones, Bunny Berigan and Jimmy Dorsey—to a position of respect as one of the most accomplished trombone men of the next two decades. Bix, Tram, Ryker, Riskin and Farrar, meanwhile, returned to the Graystone Ballroom and a crash rehearsal program for the tour.

It was tough going. Steve Brown, once the bass-playing anchor man of the New Orleans Rhythm Kings and the Midway Gardens Orchestra, had joined Goldkette September 15, 1925, around the time Bix and Trumbauer were just opening in St. Louis. Brown had spent the summer with the Island Lake band, and "when we came back together again at the Graystone we found that each unit had developed a different style. It was hell. We had to rehearse lots to iron things out."

Even then, the ironing hardly came easy, said Itzy Riskin, because of an undercurrent of competition between the two factions and a stubborn resistance to Trumbauer among some of Goldkette's old guard. "It was hard to pin down, but there was a subtle psychological battle to see whose style would predominate. Tram, especially, complained to me on a couple of occasions about the cold shoulder he was getting from the rest of the boys."

The Hudson Lake band had been used to working as a team, with a fund of specially-tailored "advanced" routines left over from their year at the Arcadia. The Island Lake group relied on standard Goldkette arrangements, most of them by George Crozier and Russ Morgan, a trombone player who had fronted the band on its first swing east in 1925. But with such jazzmen as Murray, Rank and the indomitable Brown, it was at no loss to play in the hot manner, as such early 1926 Victor recordings as "Dinah" demonstrate. At least once an evening, Brown would come out front for a feature number, in which he slapped and snapped the bass strings with enormous drive and great showmanship, to the delight of the crowds. But the band's style tended as much toward conventional "hot dance" music as the Hudson Lake unit's approach had veered away from it. In view of this it is easy to understand Riskin's repeated references to rivalry within the reconstituted orchestra between the "Eastern" style of Island Lake and the "Western" accent of the ex-Arcadians.

Trumbauer supervised the rehearsals, and got none too easy a ride from the Eastern loyalists. He would order a cut in a given arrangement—only to have Quicksell or Murray produce a pair of scissors and actually cut out the portion to be deleted. If at a later time Trumbauer decided to reintroduce the same section, the culprits would protest that "you told us to cut that part out, so we cut it out," holding up tattered, ribboned sheets of manuscript paper.

Ironically, it was Bix himself who helped heal the breach. "It was hard not to like him," said Doc Ryker. "He always had something nice to say. Like, we'd play through a portion that gave him trouble, and instead of getting irritable or nasty he'd kind of laugh and say something like, 'I ain't got much technique, but I sure have a lousy tone.' Things like that broke the ice and fostered a real spirit of cooperation in the band."

Bix was one of the boys, but he was also close to Trumbauer in ways largely determined by their musical affinity. Thin and gaunt, vaguely Mephistophelian of feature, Tram was Bix's diametric opposite in most respects. Order regulated his life as much as disorder and impulse characterized Bix's. When Goldkette regulars bristled at Tram's attempts to impose a schoolteacher's discipline on what he viewed as an unruly ensemble, Bix stepped in and soothed tempers. When Trumbauer, disgusted at the lack of cooperation, threatened to quit, Bix reminded him none too gently that "this is—or can be—the best damn band in the country. Are you going to walk out on that?"

Yet Tram always remained on the outside, always apart, and ever with an alert eye to commercial potential. Even Ryker, who split section leads with him ("He took the hot stuff, I took the sweet") and admired his musicianship deeply, betrayed a touch of irony in describing him as "the kind of guy who'd play a tune through, then take it home and come up with something good after working on it. But put him cold on a recording date and he didn't always come up with something."

But Trumbauer was beginning to come up with something simply by rehearsing the Goldkette Victor Orchestra regularly. By the time the group jumped down to Cincinnati for a couple of nights at the Swiss Gardens, the rhythm was coming across with an attractive lift. Bix and Tram shone in solo spots; Murray's clarinet laced the ensembles. Brown's bass kicked things along with a slap technique which, through use of across-the-bar-line syncopations, was to open the way to a more elastic concept of playing time. "At that time most bands were using tuba," Doc Ryker said. "It was much stiffer, more metronomic. But Steve introduced an entirely different sort of idea. In some ways he was the real star of that band. He'd get out in front and do a feature, and everybody—all the dancers—would stop and watch. He'd go into a Charleston and they'd all go wild."

During the Cincinnati job Newell "Spiegle" Willcox, who had left Goldkette at the beginning of the summer to take a lucrative season with Henry Thies, returned to the trombone section—only to have to drop out again temporarily a few days later because his wife, Helen, was due to give birth to their first child. He took her home to Cortland, New York, where she gave birth to a son on Sunday, September 12.

On the same day, Bix, Murray, Riskin and a few of the others, spending a day off in Chicago, drove out to Lincoln Field, a racetrack at Crete, just outside the city. Murray took a look at the day's card and whooped with delight.

"Hey, get a load of this!" he said to the others. "There's a nag running today name of 'Helen's Babe.' Whatcha think of *that?*"

"Personally," said Bix, adopting the English accent he'd worked up since reading a collection of P.G. Wodehouse's golf stories, "I think it's well worth laying a spot of capital on, what?"

Murray collected a few dollars from each man and placed it all on Helen's Babe. "This has to be a good omen," he said.

"It'd better be," Riskin shot back. "You just copped my last five bucks."

It was. The horse won, and around the time Helen Willcox was giving birth far away in upper New York State, Spiegle's bandmates were on their way back into Chicago, counting a good day's winnings, close to $200.

Jean Goldkette's Victor Orchestra left by train for the East no more than three days later. They had a few one-nighters scheduled along the way, and were due back at Southboro, Massachusetts, just west of Boston, on Tuesday, September 21, to set up headquarters in a country hotel called the Hillcrest Inn. Their New England promoter, J. A. Lyons, had made Southboro the hub of an itinerary which would take the band out for a day at a time, then back to the Hillcrest. In the meantime, they would begin afternoon rehearsals immediately for an October 6 opening at Roseland.

Willcox, unable to make the first few dates due to the birth of his son, wired Tommy Dorsey to fill in for him. Dorsey duly set out for Boston with careful instructions to head for the town of "Muttings-on-Crow," allegedly "just outside the city." It took him a fruitless day's searching to discover that Spiegle had been talking about Nutting's-on-the-Charles, a rambling old wooden ballroom overlooking the Charles River in suburban Waltham, Massachusetts.

J. A. Lyons was standing on the platform when the train carrying the Jean Goldkette orchestra pulled into Southboro station just before 10 o'clock the morning of the 21st. Behind him, parked by the building, was a green bus bearing the insignia of the Framingham Taxi Company and emblazoned with a banner reading "Jean Goldkette Orchestra, New England Tour, J. A. Lyons, Mgr."

"Well, boys, looks like we've arrived," said Bill Rank, head out the coach window. "They've even decorated the station house for us." Strung across the front of the building was a giant cloth streamer proclaiming "Welcome Jean Goldkette Orchestra, the Paul Whiteman of the West."

"Hey, Don, get a load of that," Bix called to Murray. "These folks think Detroit's in the West. Guess that puts Davenport somewhere in China, huh?"

Murray looked up from the sports page of his morning paper. "That's funny. You don't *look* like Paul Whiteman."

"Maybe all together we do," said Quicksell. He glanced over at Fuzzy Farrar, still asleep in a rear seat. "And *he's* got the moustache!"

Hillcrest Inn was more a country house than a hotel, steeped in the natural elegance of New England tradition. An item the next day in the *Marlboro Enterprise* quoted band members as saying they felt "at home, rather than in a hostelry, and the reports they had received as to the aloofness of New Englanders have not been substantiated."

Again, in the *Enterprise* for Saturday, September 25:

... the greatest dance attraction ever presented to the dancing public of New England will be staged at Lyonhurst this evening, when Jean Goldkette and his famous Victor Recording Orchestra of Detroit, Mich., "The Paul Whiteman of the West," will compete in a super battle of music with Mal Hallett and his famous jazz orchestra, considered by musical critics as New England's greatest jazz band ... the biggest crowd of the year at any dance hall is expected at Lyonhurst this evening, and the management has now added much more parking space to take care of the motorists from far and near.

The band had been to New England the year before with Russ Morgan directing, but a lot had happened in a year, and word of the presence of Bix, Tram, Brown and the others had preceded their coming. A publicity broadcast over station WTAG in Marlboro whetted local appetites even more sharply. When the band opened at Lyonhurst Saturday night the musicians present all but outnumbered the dancing customers. Al Sudhalter, a 21-year-old Boston alto sax man who had fallen hard under the spell of Trumbauer and Jimmy Dorsey, was among them.

"You couldn't move, there were so many musicians there," he said. It was the same again a few nights later at the Music Box, on Huntington Avenue in downtown Boston. Again, Sudhalter was there.

"Sometimes, when I had the admission price, I'd go in to take my place among the musicians clustered around the stand. When I didn't, I could always go around into the back alley. Since the windows in back of the orchestra were open, it seemed as if one were right there with the band."

The Goldkette band played several nights at the Music Box, and Sudhalter recalled one, especially, when "the lines of musicians in front of the bandstand ran about 15 to 16 deep. And when Bix stood up to take a four-bar break, the great yell that went up from all the musicians would dwarf the wildest screaming of the teenage set for the Beatles.

"They had arrangements of 'My Pretty Girl' and 'Tiger Rag' which were great, but the ones that really knocked us out were 'Baby Face' and 'Blue Room,' both of them advanced, beautifully written, and played with enormous spirit."

"Baby Face" and "Blue Room" were the work of William H. "Bill" Challis, a 22-year-old saxophone player from Wilkes Barre, Pennsylvania, who had met Farrar, Riskin and Russ Morgan when all were in the Scranton Sirens, a Pennsylvania dance band famed as a musical incubator for big-time talent. Both Dorsey brothers were also Sirens alumni.

He had submitted "Baby Face" to the Goldkette office as a trial score, his second, after a visit to Detroit early in 1926 as a member of Dave Harmon's band. When the Graystone unit came through Wilkes Barre on its way east, Challis went along to listen—and was knocked out to hear his arrangement propelled along by Brown's slapped bass, with biting section work and leaping solos by Bix and Tram.

"Gee, it sounded just great to me," Challis recalled. "Especially when the improvised spots were filled in by these guys. I went up and introduced myself to Ray Lodwig, who seemed to be more or less in charge at the time. He said to send some more stuff, so I did 'Blue Room' and sent it to them. When the band went up to New England they rehearsed it and started to play it on jobs.

"Then, out of the blue, I get a call from Horvath to come and join the

The Goldkette orchestra on tour in New England. Atop bus, L to R: Challis, Willcox, Riskin, Bix, Murray, Quicksell, Ryker, Morehouse, Farrar, Lodwig, Rank, Trumbauer. Brown is on the hood, presumably "riding shotgun." PHOTO COURTESY MARY LOUISE SHOEMAKER

Another scene on the New England tour. L to R: Trumbauer, Murray, Challis, Riskin, Morehouse, Bix, Rank, Lodwig, Farrar, Brown, Willcox, Ryker, Quicksell.

PHOTO COURTESY MARY LOUISE SHOEMAKER

band up around Boston. I said, 'What do you want me to do, play or arrange?' He said, 'Oh, bring your horns along anyway.' "

Challis showed up at the Hillcrest that week toting an armful of saxophone cases. But by then Horvath had made up his mind that he wanted the newcomer to "forget the saxophones. Sax players are a dime a dozen, and we have all of 'em we need." He motioned Challis to an easy chair in front of the six-foot-high fireplace. "What we really need is arrangements. We're really hurting for scores. All we have is seven or eight, plus your stuff and a bunch of concert things George Crozier did for us. So why don't you just concentrate on making arrangements? You can play later."

Just then Trumbauer came loping downstairs. "Hey, Charlie, got a moment?" Horvath shook his head yes. Trumbauer touched a bandage on his face. "This thing is giving me a bit of trouble, Charlie. How about a couple of days off so I can have it taken off?" "It" was a mole under Tram's left eye which had first appeared in St. Louis and had been growing ever since. A doctor had advised having it removed surgically. Horvath shook his head.

"Can't it wait until after Roseland, Frank? We're in enough of a pickle as it is, without having to worry about you not being there."

Trumbauer shrugged. "Okay, but right afterwards, okay?"

"Sure, Frank. And hey, before you go, let me introduce you to Bill Challis." They had met before, in Wilkes Barre; Horvath had not been there. They shook hands again anyway. "Frank, why don't you take Bill for a little walk and tell him what we need by way of arrangements from him?"

They walked. Arrangements weren't just a problem, said Tram, they were a catastrophe. "Odds and ends, assorted stuff from different places. But we're supposed to be going down to play against Fletcher Henderson's boys, and we're going to look like yokels unless we have something better to show for ourselves than this.

"Rehearsals—jeez, half the band won't listen to anything and just want to cut up all the time. Bix is drinking much too much—but I can't tell *him* that. He just laughs and changes the subject."

They stopped. Trumbauer put his hand on Challis' shoulder. "Look. Do you realize that this could be the best damn orchestra in the whole world? I know that. Bix knows it—he kept me from quitting awhile back by reminding me of it. But Christ, trying to keep all those kids in line is going to be the death of me yet."

Challis listened in silence. Then, at last, he laughed softly. "Looks as though my work's cut out for me," he said. "When do I start?"

He got down to work that afternoon. When the band boarded the bus for an evening in Boston or Worcester or Waltham, Challis stayed behind, and one by one the arrangements took shape. They got run down immediately during the afternoon rehearsals under Tram's ever-strict supervision. They bore the same stamp as "Blue Room" and "Baby Face"—intelligent, harmonically adventuresome, plenty of room left for soloists. Bix took to them and to Challis right away—a liking instantly reciprocated by the newcomer.

"We hit it off right from the start," said Challis. "He used to come up to my room and discuss the band. He'd say, 'Gee, we have a great band, but don't you think it needs this and that?' and such. Sometimes we'd sit

176

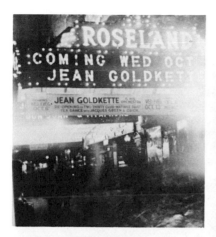

Roseland heralds the October 6, 1926, opening of the Goldkette orchestra and a return engagement by the Fletcher Henderson band a week later.

PHOTO COURTESY
PAUL MERTZ & HAZEL HORVATH

Don Murray, Bix and Howdy Quicksell "horsing around" on a stuffed animal, location unknown, late 1926.　PHOTO COURTESY RED NICHOLS

Doc and Norma Ryker on a visit to London in 1971.　PHOTO BY R. M. SUDHALTER

Bix and Goldkette sidemen during a jam session captured in a home movie, probably during New England tour, autumn 1926. L to R: unknown, Quicksell (with banjo); Lodwig (trumpet); Riskin; Murray (with clarinet); Brown (with bass); unknown; Willcox (trombone); Rank (trombone); Trumbauer (saxophone). Bix is seated, cornet to mouth, cross-legged at the front.

PHOTO COURTESY PAUL MERTZ AND HAZEL HORVATH

**LEON "BIX" BEIDERBECK**
Trumpet

**STEVE BROWN**
String Bass and Tuba

**FRED FARRAR**
Trumpet

**RAY LUDWIG**
Trumpet

**CHAUNCY MOOREHOUSE**
Drums and Tympani

**DONALD MURRAY**
Sax and Clarinet

**HOWARD QUICKSELL**
Banjo.

**WILLIAM RANK**
Trombone

**IRVING RISKIN**
Pianist

**STANLEY "DOC" RYKER**
Saxophone

**FRANK TRUMBAUER**
Saxophone

**NEWELL WILCOX**
Trombone

Personnel of the Jean Goldkette Orchestra, complete with misspelled names, from *Graystone Topics,* house organ of the ballroom.

PHOTO COURTESY STEVE BROWN

Paul Mertz shared the Goldkette piano chair with Irving Riskin.

Jean Goldkette in January 1927.

Same session, same home movie. Front, L to R: Quicksell, Bix, Farrar, Rank. Rear, L to R: Lodwig, Riskin, Murray, Brown, Willcox, Trumbauer.

down together and play over ideas he had at the piano. We talked—idly, then—about someday getting together for transcribing sessions, him playing and me writing the stuff down. But that didn't happen until later, except for the opening part of what ultimately became 'In a Mist,' which we got down in sketch form up there."

A visitor turned up during afternoon rehearsal. Harry Akst, songwriter, plugger and sometime pianist, had done the music for "Dinah" and cornered himself a hit both through Ethel Waters' vocal version for Columbia and the instrumental by the Goldkette band for Victor. He had collaborated with Benny Fields on "Baby Face"—but by his own admission had never expected to hear it played like this.

"He sat in with us at the piano and was amazed at our beat," said Riskin. Akst arranged with Horvath that vaudevillian Benny Davis would probably visit the band at Roseland to do "Baby Face" as a feature. Could the band handle it?

Challis laughed. "Yeah. We'll handle it," he said.

Rehearsals began to bear fruit, but some resentment for Trumbauer still lingered. Ray Lodwig, who had usually counted off the numbers and functioned as "concert master" before Tram's coming—and still asserted his prerogatives from time to time, as Challis' experiences in Wilkes Barre showed—resented the authority given an outsider. He made his dissatisfaction clear to Horvath.

"I can't take it, Charlie," he said after a dispute over tempo ended up in a quarrel during a rehearsal. "That guy's gonna ruin us, with all his orders and discipline. He treats us like kids. It's like school or the army or something."

Tram's version was slightly different, though his mood was no less angry. "Ray is one of those guys who just won't cooperate. As long as they don't, we might as well not even bother trying."

Horvath, ever the peacemaker, worked out a compromise which both men accepted. Tram would continue to front the band, but tempi would be chosen in collaboration with Lodwig, and would be counted off by the trumpet player.

Nor was this the only friction produced by the forced regimen of traveling, living and playing together. Even the daily bus-job-bus routine was bound to frazzle nerves, as Spiegle Willcox well recalled. "One time—I don't know whether Bix pushed me or I pushed him, but there we were all of a sudden in the aisle of the bus one night after the job, sort of wrestling each other around. I know I was using all my strength and that guy was strong. Nothing resulted—just a short flare of temper. It was forgotten as quickly as it had come up, and turned into a case of who could apologize the most, Bix or me. We both agreed that it was due to that damn bus. Not Bix's fault and not mine. It was the damn bus's fault."

The tour was going well. The "Paul Whiteman of the West" was packing in good crowds wherever the band appeared. Musicians came to hear Trumbauer and pick up his tricks, to marvel at Bix's tone and phrasing, and to stomp for more every time Steve Brown "took to the window" with a slap bass solo. Generally, promoter Lyons rode with them in the bus and acted as sometime master of ceremonies on the jobs. "He was always with us," said Bill Rank, "and always beaming with pride. Except one time. We were somewhere around Boston, playing a dance where the crowd was a

180

bit older and—well, they didn't really appreciate us. Lyons, who'd had a couple of drinks by this time, was getting mad about the lack of response from the dancers. So he hops on the stage, asks Chauncey [Morehouse] for a drum roll, and steps forward. 'Ladies and gentlemen,' he says, 'you are lucky to have here tonight the best goddamn band in the country, and I hope you appreciate it!' Well, that was all we needed. We were finished for that night."

The Goldkette orchestra played Lyonhurst for the last time Saturday night, October 2, closing out their New England stay. The band's reputation had grown enormously over the two weeks, and spread down through Rhode Island and Connecticut to New York. The late Rex Stewart, playing cornet with Fletcher Henderson's band at Roseland, recalled it well. "We kept hearing things about those guys, about how they'd stood everybody upside down up there in New England, and had all these fantastic new-sounding arrangements and all. We'd met Horvath when we played the Graystone some months before, and he'd told us then we'd get cut by these guys. But this didn't mean much to us, so we didn't take it too seriously. We figured, 'Ah hell, they haven't had any real competition up there. Wait'll they get down here. We'll grind 'em up in little pieces."

On Monday, October 4, the twelve musicians, Challis and Horvath checked out of the Hillcrest Inn, took their leave of J.A. Lyons, and boarded the train for New York City and an appointment with jazz history.

Jean Goldkette in the 1950s.

Publicity photograph taken at the Graystone Ballroom, c. March 1927. Heavy retouching appears to have been done to fill in features "washed out" by unshaded photoflash. The extra violins were usually added, said Paul Mertz, when playing for "older audiences on special occasions." Front row, L to R: Don Murray, Danny Polo, Doc Ryker (reeds); Chris Fletcher, Jack McGay (violins and reeds); Howdy Quicksell (banjo). Rear: Willcox and Rank (trombones); Bix, Lodwig and Farrar (trumpets and cornet); Marlin Skiles (piano); Frank Trumbauer, standing and leaning on piano. Steve Brown and Chauncey Morehouse are at the far rear.

# Chapter 13

At the first murmur of anticipation from the crowd, Rex Stewart leaned forward and tapped Coleman Hawkins on the shoulder.

"Hey, man, what if these cats really *are* good? I mean—well, we ain't heard 'em yet, have we?"

The star tenor saxophonist of the Fletcher Henderson band glanced across to Roseland Ballroom's second bandstand, where a lone banner announced the arrival of Jean Goldkette's Victor Recording Orchestra from Detroit. He laughed.

"Man, them cats don't show me nothin'. Bunch o' li'l ol' white boys from out there where all that corn grows. Nope. Ain't got nothin' to say to me."

Stewart, 19 and still nervous in the cornet chair only recently vacated by his idol, Louis Armstrong, was less confident. "I don't know, man. Remember what that cat told us in Detroit."

Some weeks before, Henderson's star-studded band had played the Graystone Ballroom on a swing through the midwest. Officials of the Goldkette office, Charlie Horvath among them, had come to listen and admire their ensemble drive and solo strength. But Horvath had also had a word of warning for the musicians who billed themselves as the "world's greatest dance orchestra."

"Don't get too cocky about being the best, boys," he told Hawkins, clarinetist Buster Bailey and several of the others. "You haven't heard our Graystone band yet—and when you do you're gonna be in for one helluva shock."

Wednesday, October 6, and if there was to be any shock it would be this night. The Henderson band, resident at Roseland, was billed to play a "battle of music" with Goldkette's proteges, fresh from a successful tour of New England. Henderson himself, cool, aloof, was far from concerned. With the brash Stewart balancing Joe Smith's lyricism in the trumpets, and Hawkins and Bailey in the sax section, Henderson was confident his musicians would make quick and merciless work of any aspirant to leadership in the hot dance music domain. Even the absence this night of his brilliant lead alto sax man and arranger, Don Redman, hardly ruffled his quiet assurance.

The Henderson band, arrayed on the left of Roseland's long stage, played its first half-hour set with fire and polish, featuring both Rex and Joe Smith on Fletcher's up-tempo "Stampede." At one point Stewart peered out into the sea of faces packing the big dance floor.

"Lord a-mercy, them penguins is sure out there tonight," he said, as lines of musicians in tuxedos pressed in close to the stage. Russell "Pop"

Smith, Henderson's veteran lead trumpet man and Joe Smith's elder brother, shook his head. "Now don't you go frettin' about all those cats, li'l Rex," he said. "You just play that horn an' worry 'bout soundin' good, hear?"

Stewart wasn't the only one surveying the crowd and worrying. In the wings, waiting to go on, Bill Rank took a look and retreated backstage to where Bix was sitting, removing and reinserting a newly-acquired false tooth. "Hey, Bix, quit playing with that thing and come get a load of this. The place is just full of musicians. What the hell are we going to do out there, anyway? Those guys are *good* . . . I think I want to go home to Detroit."

Bix popped the tooth back into his mouth. "Relax," he said. "We're better. We'll do just fine." His manner, Rank reflected, was absurdly calm. If only he'd leave that blasted tooth alone.

"Aren't you even a little nervous?"

Bix snapped the tooth out into his hand. "Sure. We all are. But don't worry—we'll show 'em anyway."

Then, at last, time to go on. Time to put some music behind the big buildup and the "Paul Whiteman of the West" ballyhoo. Ballrooms in small New England towns were one thing, but Roseland, at the corner of 51st and Broadway, was quite another.

Trumbauer strolled up, sax gleaming on a strap around his neck. "We'll open with something they won't expect," he said. Bix, Rank and the others looked at one another, puzzled. "These boys have been dishing up all their hot stuff, probably because they've heard we play hot. Well, let's give them and the people something different before we get down to business."

They filed out and took their places on the right of the stage. Henderson's musicians, sweating under the colored spotlights, stayed in place to listen. "Shee-it," said Charlie Green. "Zat all? Zat *all?* Just a bunch of fine-lookin' li'l college boys? Now ain't they just *too* cute . . ."

"I don't know," said Rex. "I just gotta feeling . . ."

Trumbauer held up his hand for silence. The crowd, hushed now, pressed in tight around the stage. Hawkins slouched back in his chair. Stewart bit his fingernails. Then Lodwig's foot stamped time on the floor and they were off—into a George Crozier arrangement of the Spanish 6/8 march "Valencia."

The Henderson men sat up as one in astonishment. "Valencia?" What was this? Goldkette's band was supposed to be full of hot players. Fletcher had especially chosen arrangements in his first set to show off his band's ability to play stomping, exciting jazz. And here was the competition playing a 6/8 march! What started as a ripple of amused laughter in the crowd quickly spread and swelled to open approval. Someone clapped; with a roar the crowd picked it up and applause broke like summer thunder across the ballroom, punctuated by cheers and whistling. Up front, Trumbauer grinned as Farrar's strong lead whipped smartly into the coda. When it was over the applause and cheering went on.

Tram cupped his hands. "Okay, boys," he called. "Let's give 'em the business." And before the ovation had subsided, Jean Goldkette's Victor Orchestra hit "Tiger Rag" for all it was worth, and the battle was on. "Baby Face" followed "Blue Room" followed "My Pretty Girl," as they worked down the new Challis scores, interspersing them with waltzes and even an occasional tango, all played with lift and polish. Each number brought the house down—and left Henderson's musicians shaking their heads in disbelief.

"I mean, put it this way," Rex Stewart said in later years. "We were supposed to be the kings, the greatest thing in New York. We had the best men, the best arrangements. Everything. Then, suddenly, up pops this band of Johnny-come-latelies from out in the sticks—white boys on top of it—and they just *creamed* us. Stayed on for 45 minutes, instead of half an hour, and they would've stayed on forever, the way the crowd was cheering 'em on.

"It was pretty humiliating for us, and when the time came for us to go back on, we didn't really know what we should play. They'd covered it all, and they were swingin' like mad. Bix, for Pete's sakes. You know, I worshipped Louis at that time, tried to walk like him, talk like him, even dress like him. He was God to me, and to all the other cats too. Then, all of a sudden, comes this white boy from out west, playin' stuff all his own. Didn't sound like Louis or anybody else. But just so pretty. And that *tone* he got. Knocked us all out.

"We kept makin' excuses, but we knew we'd been licked. That was all there was to it."

Nor was Stewart's recollection by any means isolated. One day in 1962, Irving Riskin ran into Don Redman and Benny Carter on a street in Hollywood. He got to reminiscing with both saxophonists about the Roseland battles.

"Boy, that band was just great," said Redman, who had returned for the encounter on October 13.

"It wasn't just great," said Carter, his replacement at the October 6 opening. "It was frightening."

"That made me feel," said Riskin, "that we must have had a pretty good band."

Opening night was hardly without incident. In the middle of one of the later sets, Lodwig was just counting off an arrangement when Bix raised his hand and signalled a halt.

"What's the matter, Bix?" Tram called.

"Damn tooth." Bix was down on all fours, groping around in the semi-darkness under rows of chairs and music stands. One by one, the others joined him in the search for the new tooth, which had apparently again worked its way loose as a result of all the removal and reinsertion. Finally, after what seemed an eternity, Spiegle Willcox spotted it under his chair and the music continued.

"The next day Bix went off to the dentist's and had a permanent tooth put in there so he could play and not worry about it," said Rank. "We were just as relieved about it as he was, and that night at work the manager of the Roseland Ballroom came forward during one of our sets, asked Chauncey [Morehouse] for a drum roll, and announced he had a presentation for Bix. Bix came out front, and the manager presented him with a large wooden tooth, about six inches by ten, painted white and inscribed 'To Bix.' Everybody got a big laugh out of that."

Later that evening, by arrangement with the Remick music publishing house, vaudeville trouper Benny Davis put in an appearance to plug "Baby Face." During a band break, Challis sketched out a quick modulation into Davis' key and slotted two vocal choruses into his "Baby Face" arrangement, just before Bix's cornet solo.

Always popular with the crowds, Davis went on to cheering and applause. Dick Turner, among the hundreds pressing close to the stage, recalled that he "sang several wonderful choruses with lively animation, very much à la Eddie Cantor, and although it may be hard to imagine now, it was just wonderful and catchy and full of rhythm.

"But then—what a moment! Bix swung right into three straight choruses after Benny and just went crazy. I don't know what the magic to a cornet player is after a good vocal, but Bix had it—he was on fire, and I think I can state now that if I could turn back the clock on just one moment in Bix's life I'd rather hear that impromptu flight again than anything else I ever heard him do."

The band's initial apprehension about playing at Roseland had completely evaporated in the cheers of the crowds, and when the Henderson band took off for Detroit for a week at the Graystone, the Goldkette musicians settled right in, in Spiegle Willcox's words, "as if we owned the place." They had taken New York by storm in what *Orchestra World* magazine termed a "riot of glory":

> Henderson was somewhat handicapped by the absence of his first alto man . . . Roger Wolfe Kahn conducted Goldkette's outfit through several numbers . . . Benny Davis sang some of his new songs, with Harry Akst at the piano . . . Miff Mole sat in and played a few torrid choruses . . . Thomas "Fats" Waller, the piano wizard, relieved Fletcher once in awhile, and the boys and girls stopped dancing to watch his fingers ramble . . . The absence of Jean Goldkette was keenly felt . . . Whoever is responsible for the Goldkette arrangements should be elected to the hall of fame. They are nothing short of marvelous . . . Most everyone who is anything at all in the music business was present . . . There was [*sic*] two big fights this week, both between white and colored contenders . . . Wills-Sharkey; Henderson-Goldkette!

Musicians were coming to listen and learn, and then going away to imitate—often, said Doc Ryker, with amusing results.

"It was pretty funny—when we hit New York most of the bands there were only using two trumpets. But here they saw this band with three, and not knowing the reason why we carried three, they all went out and got an extra trumpet. The truth was, of course, that we carried three men because Bix couldn't read well enough to cut the second book, so we had Fuzzy and Ray playing the two formal written parts, with Bix improvising a third and filling in and taking the hot solos. But nobody in New York realized that. They all thought our stuff was written for five brass.

"Similar thing with Steve on bass. At that time all the bands were using tuba, but when they heard him, heard what he could do, they all started switching to string bass. None of 'em could equal the way he slapped that thing, though."

If the most talked about band in New York had any difficulty at Roseland at all, it was over the length of some of their numbers. "If I remember correctly, the patrons had to pay for each individual dance," said Irv Riskin. "So we had to play short dances, which we didn't go for sometimes; and we got tremendous applause at the ends of numbers, which put the management in a peculiar spot, because they sold tickets for ten cents a

186

dance and so much valuable time was lost in the applause. I'll tell you something funny. There was this one thing we used to play, quite bright —forget the title now—and there were always one or two couples who ran out on the dance floor ahead of the rest so that they could do a few wide swirls before the floor got crowded. These dancers amused Bix, especially, and he used to laugh right out loud. After awhile, though, they began to annoy him, so he'd stand up and point his cornet at them, while Chauncey would simulate, on his drums, the rat-a-tat of a machine gun."

Early the following week the band was due to do its first record date for Victor since the coming of Bix and Tram. "We had big plans," said Challis. "We were going to record some tunes we felt would really help establish us and set New York on its ear." An article in *Billboard* promised records which "will scorch the wall paper off the studio walls." Certainly, Goldkette's twelve men were capable of doing just that. They played with a drive surpassing anything heard in the big city before their coming. The Challis arrangements were clicking well, perfectly tailored to the styles of Bix, Tram and the other soloists. It was all swinging together, and going down well with the crowds and the musical fraternity alike. But no one, amidst all the euphoria, had reckoned with one name in the hierarchy of the Victor Talking Machine Company, a name which was to plague Bix Beiderbecke throughout much of his brief career on records.

"It was Eddie King," said Challis. "We'd forgotten all about him. Nobody in the band liked him, and when we went to Victor a few days before the date to check out the tunes we'd selected with them, we discovered King had already selected the songs *he* wanted us to play. He gave 'em to Horvath, who gave 'em to me with an apology and said to arrange them as best I could. But boy, were they ever dogs! Charlie argued with him, and told him the tunes weren't what the band did nor what they wanted. But King won the argument. After all, they owned the record company.

"He told Charlie that if we didn't like his selection he'd find another band to do the tunes. So we got together for one rehearsal before the recording date, and you should have seen the guys' faces. I mean, these songs were just the worst! 'Idolizing you is all that seems worth while'— crap like that. I felt the best thing to do was to leave spots blank for the guys to fill in with solos, hoping to salvage something that way. But the songs were so lousy . . . there was one really putrid one called 'Hush-a-bye.' King was convinced it'd sell, but we thought it was just so punk. Even if it had been good, I wouldn't have liked it."

The other musicians were no less vocal in denouncing the insult they felt King had dealt them. "I suppose," said Riskin, "that our bosses were so thrilled to get a chance to record for Victor that they accepted anything . . . I suppose we were way over their heads, and they did this to try to get us down to what they thought was a commercial level." Or, as Doc Ryker more succinctly put it, "The way it seemed, Eddie King thought only stodgy old folks bought phonograph records."

There were five songs to do, and two dates in which to record them. No one seemed particularly enthusiastic when the musicians arrived at the studio after lunch on Thursday, October 12; but Bix, said Challis, was downright tense. "King, too, seemed uneasy. He avoided speaking to Bix at all—turned away whenever he came near. Bix, too, wasn't in any hurry to give that guy the time of day." Not until years later did Challis learn of what had happened the first time Bix and King had met in a recording studio.

The date got started shortly after 1:30 P.M. with "Idolizing," a sentimental pop tune which left Challis little room for showing off anything the band could do save play the melody. He gave the only substantial solo, the song's 16-bar verse, to Bix. Another, briefer spot fell to Joe Venuti, brought in for the date by King along with his partner, guitarist Eddie Lang, because "people know who they are, and they'll help sell the records." Venuti played it straight, leaving Lang to fill in an obligato behind Frank Bessinger's vocal.

"You should have seen this King guy," said Challis. "He looked like a bull, a short bull, with a bull-like head coming down to this huge can. He'd sit out in front of the band with a gripe and a grouchy look on his face."

"Yeah, was he ever corny," Riskin added. "The day[12] we recorded 'Dinah,' I had a piano vamp intro and wasn't playing crisp enough for him, so he came over to the piano and played it ever so corny, with exaggerations, so that all the boys could hardly refrain from laughter."

With King out front, Bix's nerves were on edge. He fluffed a note badly on the first run-through of "Idolizing," then settled down and got it the second time through sheer determination. But nothing caught fire. Tram didn't solo at all! Steve Brown was confined only to a metronomic bowed two-to-the-bar, tuba fashion, throughout. Bessinger, brought in by King, rendered his period vocal in a tenor voice best described as adenoidal. "Bessinger and Frank Marvin and those guys might have been very dependable when the down beat was given, came in on the right beat and all, but they weren't for us," said Riskin. "They didn't fit the sort of thing we did. One of the reasons our records never showed off what we could do had to do with this—they muddied our new, fresh sound and drive with dull name singers who might have had much experience in recording but were out of place with us. On one date, for Pete's sakes, they even gave us the veritable Methuselah of recording artists, old Billy Murray."

But Paul Mertz, who was in and out of Goldkette bands from the start and who had his share of tribulations with King as a member of the Graystone unit, held a rather more moderate view. "It seems to me," he told the authors, "that King, while having a substantial voice in the selection, probably had to heed the wishes of others higher up in the Victor organization. In the overall, he didn't do too badly by the Goldkette band when one takes into consideration that Whiteman had first choice as an international attraction. Goldkette was still more or less in the 'regional' category—and until January 1926 there had been a hiatus in Goldkette recording since those November 1924 sessions."

The closest the Goldkette band got to playing jazz on this record date was a Challis arrangement of "Sunday" which gave Rank and Murray a bit of blowing space and featured a brass chorus led by Bix. But a good part of the record was given over to the Keller Sisters and Lynch ("He was their brother," said Riskin), a decidedly third-rate vaudeville song-and-dance act.

The Henderson band got back to New York the day after Goldkette's first Victor session, and for the next two weeks the two bands shared

12. January 28, 1926.

Roseland's long bandstand, one picking up the other's last number without a break in accordance with the ballroom's continuous music policy. It was this policy which, two years before, the Cinderella Ballroom farther down Broadway had tried to emulate by bringing a new, unknown band called the Wolverines to New York.

Now the star of the Wolverines was the young man to watch in Jean Goldkette's brass section—and that, Bix Beiderbecke reflected as he got off the bus at Cooper Square, was no bad thing. But today was more important still. Eastwood Lane, composer of *Adirondack Sketches* and other favorites of Bix's, worked here, in the offices of the Carl Fischer music company at number 62. The opportunity to meet his idol was not to be passed up, but Bix was not at all certain how he would be received. "Maybe he thinks jazz is for the birds," he thought, getting into the elevator cage. "Then he won't want to bother seeing me." As things turned out, Lane knew a fair amount about jazz, knew who Bix was and admired him. The votary found himself accorded the reception of a peer. Their meeting was warm and cordial, ending in a lengthy discussion of theories of composition and harmony, and the composer made Bix the gift of several pieces of sheet music.

The Goldkette orchestra finished at Roseland on October 17, and with the promise from manager Louis J. Becker of a return engagement in January, headed west to do the winter season at the Graystone. They took rooms at various Detroit hotels, Bix opting for the Billinghurst on West Willis along with Murray, Quicksell and Rank, largely because it was within easy walking distance of the ballroom. They opened Friday, November 5, and three days later Bix took a train to Davenport for a day to be best man at Burnie's wedding to Mary Dennison Neelans in Maquoketa, about 40 miles north of the tri-cities.

The music was at its most relaxed during November and December, Challis adding new arrangements to the book as fast as he could turn them out. Riskin left briefly to go to Toledo, where he took an active hand in organizing and arranging for Goldkette's new "Orange Blossom" band, later to become the Casa Loma Orchestra. His place was taken by Paul Mertz.

Good music spurred high spirits, and inevitably band pranksters Murray, Quicksell and Mertz weren't long in getting into mischief: Mertz getting waylaid by the hotel detective as he tried to carry a ladder doused with chocolate syrup up to Challis' room, purpose obscure; Murray and Quicksell festooning their room with street signs, lanterns, construction horses and anything else they saw fit to "appropriate" off the street; Bix banging out "My Country, 'Tis of Thee" in two keys at once on the piano in the Graystone's band room, ending on an outrageously wrong chord; band members dealing each other hotfoots onstand during hot numbers.

And sometimes, Steve Brown observed, humor even sprang out of near catastrophe. "Bix would just throw his trousers over a chair when he went to sleep in his hotel room. It was a tiny room, and you could just about reach the chair from the window. Well, one night he did this, leaving a quart bottle of gin on the dresser. The window opened, and somebody reached in after his wallet, which was in the pants pocket. Bix woke up just in time, grabbed the quart and beamed the guy over the head with it.

Bix with Ernest "Red" Ingle during the Goldkette band's engagement at Castle Farms, Cincinnati, June 1927.                                         PHOTO COURTESY DON INGLE

"But after the police took care of the situation Bix was sore—because he'd lost all of his quart."

In its issue of Saturday, December 18, the weekly *Graystone Topics*, "published exclusively in the interests of the Graystone, Detroit's smartest ballroom," ran the following item:

> Paul Whiteman, personal friend of Jean Goldkette and the Jean Goldkette organization, as also are the members of his celebrated orchestra, while appearing at the Detroit Theatre recently, paid the Graystone a much-appreciated visit and were unstinting in their praise of the dance music rendered by our Victor band. Mr. Whiteman is a truly great musician and fair and liberal in his judgment of others in his field. He did not hesitate in declaring ours to be the greatest dance orchestra now before the public and frankly compared the individual abilities of its members with those of the most widely recognized artists in the world of music.

Whiteman, ever the astute businessman, had good reasons for visiting the Graystone. His reputation as "King of Jazz," won early at a time when public understanding of the word was sketchy at best, had to be preserved. In purely commercial terms this meant keeping a complement of hot men in the ranks of his large dance orchestra. It meant being ever watchful for new talent, original styles, potential Whiteman sidemen. The rotund ex-violinist from Colorado knew about Bix Beiderbecke. He had been in the audience on opening night at the Cinderella in 1924 and had made it his business to hear the Goldkette band during its stay at Roseland. He was impressed with Trumbauer's playing, and even more with the saxophonist's ability to take charge of a potentially unruly band and turn it into a tightly disciplined unit. Consequently, it was Tram whom Whiteman approached first with an offer to leave Goldkette and join his "symphonic jazz" orchestra. Trumbauer, though flattered, turned him down with an apology. The Graystone band was simply too good to leave now, he said, and it was getting better all the time; no one yet knew how good it would wind up. "I think I'd just as soon stay with it for awhile, Paul," he said. Whiteman nodded grudging assent. "We'll talk again, Frank," he said.

Whiteman went away empty-handed from the Graystone, but hardly without prospects.

In the months that followed, Red Nichols, Vic Berton, and the Dorseys found featured chairs in his band, some only briefly, some for long and comfortable stays. But Goldkette's collection of star sidemen was never far from his mind.

Goldkette introduced Bix to the "King of Jazz." The cornetist took the bandleader's hand with a shy smile. "What should I call you? I don't know what to call you. Paul? Mr. Whiteman?"

"He really meant that," said Challis. "You know how Paul was; he had a lot of dignity and carried a lot of weight . . . and Bix didn't know how to address him—and said so. That's not the sort of thing you'd expect from just any musician . . . usually it'd be just 'Hi ya, Paul' and that's that."

Tram later told Bix of Whiteman's offer, and of his interest in several of Goldkette's prize men, him included. "Yeah," said Bix with mock nonchalance, "I heard he was here getting his kicks."

With Christmas approaching, Paul Mertz found himself unable to carry the dual load of music supervisor at Detroit University during the day and pianist with Goldkette in the evenings. He dropped out for a week on Sunday, December 19, to help direct the University's Christmas operetta, for which he had written the score. His replacement, Marlin Skiles, not yet 20 and still inexperienced, confessed himself somewhat in awe of the band and of its sidemen, especially Bix.

"He was a very singular sort of guy," the pianist said. "It wouldn't be uncommon at the finish of the night's work to have the band leave the stand with Bix still sitting in his chair eating popcorn. Or after they finished at night the five brass players would converge on the dressing room and take great pleasure in blaring out "Stars and Stripes Forever" with each instrument playing one half tone lower than the other. A more cacophonous sound I don't think I've ever heard."

The band was due back in New York at the end of January, but this time enthusiasm and confidence had supplanted any uncertainty. Their weekly broadcasts over station WJR were being picked up in the East, enhancing an already illustrious reputation. All of which had a salutary effect on the individual musicians: Bix was spending more and more time at the piano up at Goldkette's music school, or the small organ Quicksell kept in his hotel room for working out arrangements and songs. Trumbauer had the time and zest to concentrate on his flying. Rank built his best crystal radio set yet and boasted to his bandmates one night that he had at last "done the impossible. I actually pulled in KDKA in Pittsburgh."

On days off it was easy to talk Tram into driving Bix, Challis, Murray and others over to Chicago to catch Ben Pollack's new band at the Southmoor Hotel and hear the ever-improving Benny Goodman, now 17 years old, on clarinet, Joseph "Fud" Livingston on tenor and Glenn Miller on trombone. Both Miller and Livingston were gaining respectable names as arrangers as well as instrumentalists. Livingston, especially, had become a byword among musicians for his experiments with modern harmonies and unusual voicings. He had himself been a Goldkette sideman during 1925.

During one such Chicago jaunt, Bix and his Goldkette pals dropped in on the Sunset Cafe, 35th and Calumet, to hear Louis Armstrong fronting the big band of Carroll Dickerson. Slim Evans, who had known Bix since the Stockton Club days, was there too. "There were a lot of 'em sitting at this big round table in front of the bandstand," he said, "including a good number of trumpet and cornet men. I remember Wingy, Muggsy and Bix, among others."

All were fascinated at Armstrong's ability to play chorus after chorus on any given melody, always with new variations and seemingly never with repetition. When he dropped by the table to greet "the cats," Wingy cornered him. "Hey, Pops, how do you play so many choruses the way you do?" Armstrong stopped, squinted at the array of jazz brassmen hanging on his answer, then grinned broadly, displaying a mouthful of dazzlingly white teeth.

"Well, I tell you . . . the first chorus I plays the melody. The second chorus I plays the melody round the melody, and the third chorus I routines." Bix, said Evans, was "knocked out. Later, we all wound up at the Rendez-vous on the north side, listening to Charley Straight's band. Bix blew—he knew all the cats. Then across the street to some apartment he knew filled with quiet lushes passing the bottles and listening to classical music—*The Planets, Petrouchka,* and all that—until noon and time to cut out. What a night!

"Same thing happened when Bix was in Detroit. Music day and night —after hours was always listening time . . ."

Goldkette's musicians returned to New York on Sunday, January 22, and opened at Roseland two days later, again sharing the stand with Henderson. This time, the New Yorkers knew what to expect. "We weren't about to be taken twice," said Buster Bailey. "We really tore the place down, played over our heads. But those guys were also getting better all the time, too. You can bet there was a lot of great music that night."

Recurrent gum trouble which had been plaguing Don Murray for weeks flared at last into a severe case of trenchmouth just before the start of a recording marathon set up by the Victor Company to stockpile ample quantities of music by a band which had turned out to be one of its hottest properties. Don phoned Jimmy Dorsey, who had been by the Graystone a month before with Whiteman and Whiteman's manager, Jimmy Gillespie. Dorsey, himself a Goldkette alumnus, agreed to sit in for a week and recommended a more permanent replacement in Danny Polo. A native of Clinton, Indiana, Polo had worked at the Midway Gardens with Elmer Schoebel and with Ben Bernie's dance band. He fit in beautifully—so well that many of his solos on Goldkette records of this period were long mistaken by collectors for Murray's.

To everyone's relief, Eddie King did not appear at any of the four Goldkette recording dates between January 28 and February 3. Nat Shilkret, a Victor executive and bandleader highly sympathetic to jazz and its practitioners, supervised three, and it is no accident that these dates yielded such spirited and characteristic numbers as Charlie Fulcher's "My Pretty Girl," in a composite arrangement by Murray, Dorsey, Riskin and Challis, and "I'm Gonna Meet My Sweetie Now." There were even solo spots for Bix, Tram and Rank, plus some stinging Brown bass on the otherwise quite forgettable pop song, "Hoosier Sweetheart." Challis enhanced this score with a private musicians' joke. Three times in the Bix-led brass ensemble following Tram's solo he inserted a five-note, downward-sloping phrase widely understood by musicians of the day to mean "Oh, you horse's ass." With Eddie King not present, it is doubtful the gag was directed at any person in particular. It is more likely an expression of Challis' attitude at having to score so corny a tune and that of his bandmates at having to play it, while such pace-setting arrangements as "Blue Room" and "Baby Face" went unrecorded.

On Tuesday, February 1, the band cut "My Pretty Girl," then went on to what could have been its greatest record—Fletcher Henderson's "Stampede," arranged by Don Redman. Henderson had recorded it for Columbia the previous autumn, around the time Goldkette's band opened at Roseland, and was calling it nearly every night. Bix and the other newcomers admired it enough to talk Henderson into trading it to them in return for one or two Challis scores.

This apparent about-face in Victor policy, said Paul Mertz, was clearly linked with the enthusiasm of audience response at Roseland to the Goldkette unit's hot side. As a result, he said, the company decided on an "experiment in sales value. As the last entry on one of the sessions, we were asked to select several numbers from our book. We played them there and then without further ado. At the time I frankly didn't know whether we were making test waxes or actual takes. But the numbers were 'My Pretty Girl,' 'Stampede,' my own 'Hurricane' and possibly, but I'm not sure, 'I've Found A New Baby,' "

The Goldkette record of "Stampede" was never issued, though it is uncertain whether this was due to Eddie King's intervention or to the fact that Victor already had a version of the same number, by the Savoy Bearcats, in its current catalogue.

A hearing of Henderson's 1926 "Stampede" gives a small idea of what was lost to jazz history with the loss of the Goldkette version. The arrangement opens with a burst of hot cornet trading four-bar phrases with the full ensemble. Rex Stewart, who played the solo with considerable fire, told the authors his efforts were "nothing much" in comparison to Bix's treatment of the same material in live performances during the band's January, 1927, stay at Roseland. According to various Goldkette sidemen, Trumbauer and Rank were also featured.

It was a heady time, a world-in-the-palm-of-my-hand time, for Bix and his Goldkette bandmates. Sometimes, said Paul Mertz, enthusiasm got the better of them. "I roomed with Bix at the beginning, over at the 44th Street Hotel, which became his stamping ground whenever he was in New York. But I had to work undisturbed at my arranging, and things just got too frantic. I finally had to move out. Bix didn't resent it. He understood —especially in view of the night he and Miff Mole came in while I was working like hell to finish a score and they, higher than a kite, proceeded to have a wrestling match—all in fun, of course.

"What a time, though. The impressions still remain fresh . . . my first meeting with Fletcher Henderson . . . Bix, Red Nichols and I tossing off a few at the bar of the speakeasy in the Roseland Building (the Goldkette gang used to duck down the fire-escape stairs to the joint while the Henderson band was spelling us) . . . meeting Oscar Levant, just returned from a sojourn in Europe, and, at the Kentucky Club after hours, giving a group of us Goldketters an impromptu recital of Debussy and Ravel music, with Bix just about swooning . . . and, oh yes, the flop we made in (I think) Springfield, playing against McEnelly's straight-type band, the local favorites . . . years later Frankie Carle told me he was the pianist in that band . . ."

These early February days caught Bix and Tram at a peak of creativity. Together and separately they were the talk of the popular music world. On the strength of this, Red McKenzie, comb-playing leader of the Mound City Blue Blowers, talked Tommy Rockwell of Okeh Records into giving Trumbauer a date for the label under his own name, using Goldkette musicians. Accordingly, the day after the band's fourth and last Victor date of the series, Trumbauer took Rank, Bix, Jimmy Dorsey, Mertz, Morehouse and Eddie Lang into the Okeh studios to do his own double-tonguing sax feature "Trumbology," plus two numbers associated with the Original Dixieland Jazz Band, Larry Shields's "Clarinet Marmalade" and "Singin' the Blues" by J. Russell Robinson and Con Conrad, introduced by the ODJB in 1920 as an interlude in their Victor record of "Margie" by the same composers.

It is this date, "Singin' the Blues" in particular, which marks the arrival of Bix Beiderbecke's name in the pantheon of immortal jazz soloists. His influence among musicians was already widespread. Only a scant three months after the first Roseland engagement, most white trumpet and cornet men in the big city had consciously altered their styles in emulation of Goldkette's 23-year-old soloist. Said Chauncey Morehouse, "You couldn't go anywhere in New York without hearing some guy trying to play like Bix. They copied his tone, his attack, his figures. Some guys tried to take his stuff right off the records. Others just came and listened. It was amazing."

Much the same held true for Tram among saxophonists. But Bix was the man of the hour. He had expanded his early notion of "playing 'round the lead" into a style of individuality and great creativity. It was, first, a white man's style, with its roots as much in European harmonic and melodic soil as in that of the Mississippi. The tone was that of the brass band cornetist, of Uncle Olie Petersen and all he valued—clean, ringing, every note struck head-on, with none of the half-valve effects, growls, buzzes or other "dirty" tricks common to black brass soloists. It functioned best not in the blues idiom, but on songs with appealing melodies and interesting chord structures, paraphrasing a given melodic line into a new, usually superior one bearing the natural structure of "correlated" phrasing.

"Singin' the Blues" epitomizes this idea. Bix's first four bars consist of two one-bar phrase fragments, perfectly matched and closely related, then a two-bar phrase which incorporates them into a coherent statement. Bars five and six extend the thought of the first four, only to have the entire idea wrapped up with a final two-bar phrase in bars seven and eight, preparing the ground for a new idea sequence. These eight bars, built around a descending sequence of half notes played against conventional G7 and C7 harmonies, manage to use the ninth voices of both chords in a manner so matter-of-fact as to create the impression things had always been done this way. This, and the consistent use of augmented chords in the first eight bars, are in fact innovations, breaking new ground by widening the basic harmonic vocabulary to create an expanded frame of reference. The band continues to play conventional four-voice chords, leaving Bix to hear and execute on his own.

The solo's first 16 bars build logically to a break consisting largely of a descending run of 16 notes which manage, again, to substitute a dominant ninth chord for the seventh by simply taking its presence for granted. For the remainder of the 32 bars Bix moves through a series of emotionally evocative, vocal phrases to an emphatic and poignant conclusion, built around a chromatic ascent to the dominant which was a Beiderbecke hallmark. It is one of those mannerisms most recognizable as Bix, and therefore most often seized upon by other, lesser cornetists attempting to evoke the superficials of his sound and phrasing.

Tram's saxophone solo fetched as much praise in 1927 and was as widely imitated as was Bix's. But history takes an unsparing view: Trumbauer used unusual intervals and constructions, but did so firmly within the musical conventions of his day. The "funny notes" were deliberate and for effect, commanding attention for their audacity and usually their wit. Trumbauer's end-of-chorus break typifies this treatment. It is chromatic in structure, tossing out a quick series of displaced accents in eighth-note triplets. It is something to be "figured out" and mastered through practice, in this regard not dissimilar to the double-tongue trickery of "Trumbology"—easy to understand, hard to do. But with the devices stripped away, Trumbauer's "Singin' the Blues" solo is very much of its time, superbly conceived and executed, but second-best in that it does not take for granted the advances which Bix's effort takes for granted. Heard as a whole, however, the record is a pioneer effort in its introduction of the concept of a "jazz ballad"—a slow or medium-tempo piece played gently and sweetly, but not cloyingly, with no loss of muscle. An elementary concept now, it was unheard-of in 1927. Lang's guitar accompaniment and countermelodies added immeasurably to the ballad feel of the number.

The other side of the record, "Clarinet Marmalade," was based on a routine worked out at the Arcadia and notated by Challis. Again, Bix and Tram are the stars of the performance, with Rank, Dorsey and Mertz contributing good but clearly dated solos, and Quicksell's banjo substituted for Lang. The same Bix-Tram relationship apparent on "Singin' the Blues" is in evidence here, with Bix demonstrating nimble, accurate valve technique and unerring harmonic instinct even at fast tempo.

Like Louis Armstrong's "West End Blues," recorded more than a year later, these two Bix-Tram titles are one of the landmarks in the history of jazz on record. It exposes a new and major instrumental talent, a new concept of how to play jazz, and foreshadows much of the harmonic development of the music in decades to come. Beiderbecke's "Singin' the Blues" solo, more than merely great jazz, is extemporaneous composition of considerable merit. Rex Stewart and Bobby Hackett are numbered among the cornetists who have paid it homage on record. On August 2, 1934, the veteran American vaudeville and cabaret entertainer Marion Harris recorded a performance of the song in which she did not state the original melody at all, but instead set her own lyrics first to Bix's cornet solo, then to Tram's saxophone chorus. This, Miss Harris' last known record, anticipated by two decades the work of Lambert, Hendricks and Ross, King Pleasure, and others. Even now, nearly half a century later, the Beiderbecke solo stands up to analysis from any viewpoint. Had Bix Beiderbecke never recorded again, his place in this century's musical history would have been secure on the basis of this one superb solo.

The Goldkette orchestra ended its second Roseland season on Sunday, February 6, moving up to Springfield, Massachusetts, and three days at Cook's Butterfly Ballroom. It was here that McEnelly and company took advantage of home town loyalties and copped most of the applause, though as Mertz remembered, "Our bandstand was ringed by a smaller number of the patrons who appreciated us to the ovation level." No matter—Roseland had done the trick. The band could now return to the Graystone secure in the knowledge that they were simply the best there was—truly, in Doc Ryker's words, "a band like nothing you ever heard."

Jean Goldkette orchestra, April-May 1927. Standing, L to R: unknown, Farrar, Quicksell, Brown, Riskin, Willcox, unknown, Ryker. Seated: Murray, Trumbauer, Lodwig, Rank, Bix, Morehouse, Sheasby.                                                                PHOTO COURTESY STEVE BROWN

The full Goldkette orchestra shortly before it broke up. L to R (front): Lodwig, Farrar, Bix, Morehouse, Murray, Trumbauer, Ryker, Willcox, Rank. Rear: Riskin, Brown, Quicksell.

# Chapter 14

Fame has its price. When the Jean Goldkette Victor Recording Orchestra had again settled in at the Graystone Ballroom, Bix dropped in on his boss for an informal chat.

"I now make $100 a week," he said, clearing his throat in introduction.

"Yes, Bix. I know that."

"Well, it seems to me that—I mean, I've been thinking that—"

Goldkette sat back and removed his spectacles. "You've been thinking you'd like a raise, is that it?"

Bix, taken aback, blushed. "Well, I—"

"Oh come, Bix. Do calm down. I've known you wanted an increase for some time now, and have just been waiting for you to bring it up." The bandleader's accent made the statement all the more intimidating.

"You have? I mean—well, I was just thinking that if I could get a raise to $125 I'll never ask for anything again in my life."

Goldkette laughed. He was happy to grant his star cornetist's request despite concern at the band's rapidly soaring budget. The Graystone orchestra might well be among the very best in the business, but it was also getting to be among the most expensive. Weekly costs were now running well over $3,000, and Charley Horvath was beginning to complain that Goldkette was slicing deep into the Graystone's profits to meet the payroll of the Victor band. Such an overhead could only be offset through increased work, and Goldkette had turned his attention to setting up one-nighters throughout late spring and early summer across Ohio and Pennsylvania, with side trips to New York to record for Victor and over to St. Louis in July for a week at Loew's State Theater.

Tram had another Okeh date coming up as well, and Bix had expressed definite ideas about the sort of material he wanted to do to follow up "Singin' the Blues." One night after the job he dragged Bill Challis up to a practice room at Goldkette's Music School to teach him the ODJB's "Ostrich Walk."

"I'd never heard the tune before," the arranger said. "So Bix sat down at the piano with me and played out each part with one finger, while I sketched out lines to harmonize. We worked all night on it, he playing a phrase and saying, 'Have the sax play this,' or 'Let's have it this way,' or some such. That place on the record where the whole band repeats one note with different accents—that started with Bix banging out the rhythm with one finger at the piano."

The "Ostrich Walk" arrangement wound up in two incarnations: one, a small group effort, for use at Okeh, the other an expanded version for the full Goldkette band. The 16-bar sax section chorus immediately preceding Bix's entry on the Trumbauer record was Tram's solo in the large unit's performances of the tune.

With Murray recovered and Riskin also back in the fold, Goldkette closed out his Detroit winter season on Sunday, April 10, with one of his annual concert performances, appearing as piano soloist and conductor of the augmented orchestra on George Gershwin's *Rhapsody in Blue* and other show-pieces, recalling Goldkette's New England billing as "The Paul Whiteman of the West." He drew on his ties with the Detroit Symphony to bring in a few string players to join new members Ernest "Red" Ingle, Chris Fletcher and Eddy Sheasby, who was now splitting leadership chores with Trumbauer.

The addition of all three men was indicative of trouble brewing in the Goldkette office. Ingle, a saxophonist, was a natural comic; he later became a featured member of the Spike Jones comedy troupe. Fletcher, who played violin and a bit of banjo, could sing in the kind of quavery tenor which would have gladdened Eddie King's heart. Goldkette, over Horvath's objections, reasoned that they would enhance the band's commercial potential.

Sheasby was another story. By this time, financial difficulties showed signs of opening a rift between Goldkette and Horvath. Trumbauer, who had been fronting, was, in Fred Bergin's words, "a Horvath man, and not exactly what Jean thought was needed in front of the band. By the time we are talking about, Jean had taken over the duties of booker and manager of the band somewhat independent of Horvath.

"I'm sure you know Jean's background was classical, and he made yearly appearances with the Detroit Symphony as a piano soloist. But the few times he tried to direct the Victor band were quite unsatisfactory both for him and the band. Among other things, he did not feel popular phrasing, and would more often than not go right on beating after the band had finished. Furthermore, he was unable to announce or talk to the audience due to his accent. He was aware of these shortcomings and would only consent to appearing with the band when there was no way to get out of it."

Prior to Trumbauer's coming, trombonist Russ Morgan had fronted and also contributed arrangements. Goldkette, said Bergin, felt his loss. The idea, too, of Trumbauer in front of the band did not entirely conform to his idea of the band image. "Jean had always been *very* impressed with an arrangement Sheasby did on 'Roses of Picardy,' featuring a very effective 16-bar crescendo passage," said Bergin. So Sheasby came in, and fronted most of the time. Trumbauer took the change without complaint, Bergin said, "because Tram was a great gentleman and Jean was a *most* convincing talker."

Leading a band was one thing, but playing with it as piano soloist quite another, and Goldkette pitched into preparations for his April 10 concert with an energy which startled his sidemen.

"He rehearsed us really hard for that big night," said Bill Challis. "He was doing the *Rhapsody*, but also featured himself on 'Maple Leaf Rag.' On the numbers where Jean played piano he had V. P. Coffey, chief viola in the Symphony, as conductor."

The concert was held at the Detroit Athletic Club, scene of Bix's first run-in with Eddie King more than two years before. "Well, here we were on the big night, with Jean conducting like mad, really hanging out the paper. We're building to a big crescendo on some number or other and down comes the baton for the big blast—and only the piccolo is playing. The guys had it rigged that way. Jean, though embarrassed, took it in good spirits."

Then they hit the road. Goldkette, meanwhile, was full of plans which, if successful, might well bail the Graystone orchestra out of its financial straits. That winter he had met a Negro drummer named William McKinney, whose "Synco Jazz Band" had been working throughout Michigan and Ohio and who was looking for a break into the big time. Goldkette, deeply impressed by the possibilities opened up by the Fletcher Henderson band in performing to an all-white dancing market, put a proposal to McKinney. He was interested in establishing a black band at the Graystone, playing in the Henderson style, whenever his own group was out of town. McKinney could have the job, provided he was willing and able to build the Synco Jazz Band into a high-caliber unit. He told McKinney to "go out and get yourself the best men you can find for the job."

The process took several months. McKinney formed his unit around a core of musicians from Virginia and West Virginia, including Cuba Austin on drums, John Nesbitt on trumpet and George "Fathead" Thomas on saxes and vocals. The band opened its residency at the Graystone billed as "McKinney's Cotton Pickers." With the addition of Henderson's Don Redman in mid-1927 as lead saxophone, director and chief arranger, the band was on its way straight to the top. Nesbitt's admiration for Bix's playing was clearly apparent in his work on McKinney records made the following year. The two became friends, even to secreting their jugs in the same cranny outside the back door of the ballroom.

After an opening round of dates in southern Ohio, the Graystone band arrived in Bloomington, Indiana, early Friday, April 22, for the University Junior Prom. As ever, Hoagy Carmichael and his friends turned out in style to welcome them, and Hoagy, the eternal student, was voluble as ever over the music in general, Bix in particular. "What a screwy person he was," said Doc Ryker in lingering awe. "He'd played around a lot, liked Bix and the fellows. But wow! Somebody'd take a hot break he liked and you could never tell what he was going to do. He'd roll around on the floor or throw a chair or most anything. And he had all those kids in the school copying the things he did. They were all crazy down there."

Such high-spirited fun caught the band's mood exactly. As they swung up and down the eastern seaboard, with occasional incursions into Ohio, life with the Goldkette band became an endless cavalcade of uninhibited music and adolescent pranks, as when Murray and Quicksell "disappeared" briefly during a stop at Penn State —only to turn up touring the campus on freshly-purchased roller skates.

En route to a date in Connecticut, the full band stopped off at Camden, New Jersey, and recorded "Slow River," then headed northward. Bix, Trumbauer and several of the others went into New York to do "Ostrich Walk" and a hastily-sketched head arrangement on "Riverboat Shuffle" for Okeh. They recorded again four days later, this time putting down three titles: Riskin's arrangement of "I'm Comin' Virginia" and "Way Down Yonder in New Orleans" as scored by Don Murray, both featuring long and beautifully-conceived Bix solos, and finally a trio number with Bix at the piano, Tram on C-melody and Ed Lang on guitar. It used the chord sequence, but not the melody, of the popular favorite, "I'd Climb the Highest Mountain," retitled "For No Reason at All in C" for this occasion.

On Sunday, May 29, the Goldkette band moved back west to Cincinnati to open at A. J. "Toots" Marshall's Castle Farms. As at Roseland, their reception was ecstatic, with crowds overflowing into the street and whooping at every solo by Bix, Tram or the others. Euphoria seemed to be in the air, probably brought on at least in part by news that "Lucky Lindy," the youthful Charles A. Lindbergh, had flown the Atlantic solo earlier that week in his monoplane, "Spirit of St. Louis."

Musicians by the score, many remembering Bix from Wolverine days at Doyle's, turned out to listen and add their cheers to the tumult. One, leader of a band of teenagers, cornered Bix between sets and begged him to come along later in the week and listen to them. "We know all your arrangements from the records," he said. "The boys would get a real kick if you'd come along. Won't you?"

Bix was hardly disposed to turn down such a request. He and some of the others went—and found to their amazement that the band's arranger had indeed copied down everything from the Goldkette and Trumbauer recordings, even Jimmy Dorsey's clinkers in his "Clarinet Marmalade" solo.

"That really knocked us out," said Riskin. "Finally they got up enough nerve to ask Bix to sit in, and they played "Clarinet Marmalade" again. He was reading the arrangement along okay until he came to his own solo. And wouldn't you know—when he tried to read what he himself had played on the record, he faltered. Couldn't cut it. He told us later he never realized how difficult some of the stuff he played in solos was until he actually tried to read it. What a laugh!"

The band was held over beyond its scheduled two weeks at Castle Farms, and the crowds kept packing the ballroom nightly. Sheasby was doing most of the fronting, allowing Tram to work in the section and concentrate on his solo playing. Eddy had shown himself on several occasions to be a man of unusually volatile temper, especially after drinking, and he was none too popular even with the musicians. This became painfully apparent during the last week at Castle Farms. As Bill Rank recalled it, a three-member French variety act, name now forgotten, appeared on the bill with the Goldkette orchestra. "We had to back them for several of their routines. Well, one night after the show they had a few choice words to say about their dissatisfaction with the way the band had backed them. They were unable to speak a word of English, so it was all in French. But their meaning was only too clear.

"Well, Sheasby got the drift of it, and he just went through the roof. He went charging up to them and challenged each member of the troupe to a fight. He made a lot of noise about it, and ended up by storming out in a huff."

That seemed the end of the matter, though Sheasby's mood when the band closed at the end of the month was still sullen and withdrawn. As usual, though, he packed the band trunks with arrangements and equipment and saw them on to the train taking them to St. Louis for the July 2 opening at Loew's State.

"On the stage," said the *St. Louis Globe-Democrat* for Sunday, July 3

> is Jean Goldkette's orchestra, that comes out of Detroit with one of the greatest reputations ever built by a dance orchestra. Eastern critics have been unstinted [*sic*] in their praise, the city of Detroit and the State of Michigan have taken official cognizance of their several eastern tours through telegrams of congratulation from the Detroit mayor and the Michigan governor. The band is what is known among dancers as a "hot" orchestra, but it also has the ability to play straight scores and arrangements second to none in the country.

But when the highly-praised Graystone Ballroom orchestra arrived at the Theater to unpack its gear and set up for the evening show, Eddy Sheasby was nowhere to be found. He had vanished without a trace—and the band's entire library with him. Challis' revolutionary scores, all Crozier's and Russ Morgan's earlier efforts—all gone.

Trumbauer put in a frantic telephone call to Goldkette in Detroit.

"My God, Jean, what are we going to do? We're stuck here—and we're supposed to be headlining the bill."

Goldkette, though embarrassed, was hardly surprised. "Sheasby, plain and simple, was a drunkard," he later explained. "You might well guess what that meant. I first saw him again six or seven years later, and predictably he had no explanation to offer."

Fred Bergin offered the beginning of one. "I suppose Sheasby reasoned that in some way he had been 'put upon' and decided to take 'his' arrangements with him when he made his exit. Actually only a few numbers in the library were his. I don't know whether or not the books were ever recovered. It seems to me that if they had been, Jean would have made some of the arrangements available to the Orange Blossom band or to the Vagabonds, which I led sometimes at the Graystone. I can vouch that neither band ever got any and I would have been the first to ask for some of those fine Challis scores."

Meanwhile here was the Jean Goldkette Graystone orchestra, acclaimed as perhaps the country's greatest, without a stitch of music. "Because St. Louis was Frank's [Trumbauer's] home town, I told him to take over again fronting the band and fake half a dozen 'oldies' and jazz favorites," said Goldkette. "Then I got on the phone and called Cleveland, Indianapolis and other cities on our tour and cancelled out the entire itinerary. *Variety* called it the greatest flop of the greatest band attraction. Certainly it was the most embarrassing of all the incidents."

The band went on, using such reliables as "My Pretty Girl" and "Tiger Rag," and for a day or two the music swung with all the familiar verve. But after a review in the *St. Louis Star* remarked that the Goldkette aggregation "shows plenty of jazz talent but registers too much starch" onstage, theater manager Harry Greenman hit them with an ultimatum: the music wasn't enough. It didn't entertain the customers enough. Might be okay for a ballroom or for other musicians, but people came to the theater (he pronounced it "thee-ay-ter," one of the band recalled) to have a good time. The band would have to supplement its music with some entertainment, perhaps a few comedy skits. Make the folks laugh, keep 'em happy.

Riskin, hearing the news, collapsed in a chair, a hand clapped to his forehead. "Who does he think we are, anyway? The Keystone Cops?"

"Might end up that way," Murray observed. "We've got to be serious about this."

Riskin winced. "Yeah, that's just the trouble. Why the hell didn't we bring Ingle along?"

In the end, they all pooled ideas and came up with a few none too inspired comedy routines. "How terrible we were," said Riskin. "I'm embarrassed just to remember it. In one, I came out on stage with a newspaper and stood there reading it, singing 'My Wild Irish Rose' badly behind it. Chauncey 'shot' me by hitting his snare drum and I fell down. Then somebody, I don't remember who, came out and dragged me off.

"Or another bit. We're playing 'Tiger Rag,' and Don Murray stands up with a hot water bottle and takes a break by hitting it with a mallet. No sound, of course. I don't think the manager appreciated this style of comedy. He came down at the end of the first show and all that stuff went out, but fast."

The next night, however, Morehouse found a sound-effects pistol in the pit and shot it off during the same "Tiger Rag" break, startling both audience and band. Greenman, said Itzy, "really liked that. He insisted we repeat it each night."

Ruth Shaffner, meanwhile, had no idea Bix was back in St. Louis. He hadn't written or called, and she had missed the newspaper advertisements, which billed the Goldkette band in small print under a big spread for *Altars of Desire*, a Metro-Goldwyn-Mayer film starring Mae Murray, plus a "fourth of July novelty: *Our Flag*, in Technicolor, with Francis X. Bushman, Enid Bennett, Johnnie Walker, and Alice Calhoun."

Despite his promise to return to her, Bix had stopped writing to Ruth around the time the Goldkette orchestra went east for its New England tour and first Roseland opening. But he had remained in her thoughts, along with the hope, now waning, that he would indeed come back.

The day of the Goldkette opening at Loew's State, she and Rose Meyers, a girl friend, were coming home from work. It was hot, and the humidity was oppressive, but the girls were looking forward to the Fourth of July holiday weekend. "We were walking across the parking lot to her red convertible, which was parked out behind the theater. All of a sudden my heart just flipped over. It couldn't be! I nearly fainted."

"Hi there, Ruthie. How's the kid?" Impossible. There, handsome beyond words in a spotless white linen suit, smiling that same smile. Bix, after all this time. Bix, just as she remembered him.

They made a date, and over the next few days Ruth Shaffner saw *Altars of Desire* enough times to emblazon its every melodramatic scene on her memory for life. She clapped and cheered herself hoarse when the orchestra swung into "My Pretty Girl" and every other tune on which Bix stood up to solo. Then at night, after the show, just as in the Arcadia days hardly more than a year before, they went out to the old places, did the things they'd always done. It seemed, at least for the moment, as though no time had gone by at all, as though Bix and Tram were still at the Arcadia and it was *her* Bix Beiderbecke standing up to take those glittering solos.

"Funny thing," she said in recollection, "I don't recall any gun being shot off by Chauncey. But at that time he could have shot off a cannon and I wouldn't have noticed. My eyes were fixed on Bix."

Stage entertainment was hardly the Goldkette band's *metier*. The comedy routines were a disaster, and Greenman simply wasn't interested in a band that did nothing but sit there and play hot music. On July 8th he let them go. Again, Bix and Ruth spent a lingering goodbye, full of promises to stay in touch, and that someday . . .

They left it at that.

By now Goldkette had succeeded in rebooking a few one-nighters in Ohio and Michigan, bringing the band back to the Graystone toward the end of July. But the future looked ominous. Things had changed at the Graystone, and even Charley Horvath was having second thoughts, as Fred Bergin recalled.

McKinney's Cotton Pickers, the Orange Blossoms and the Vagabonds had all gained good followings at the ballroom, and "the payroll of each of these bands was somewhere around a third of the Victor band. It became apparent that business didn't suffer when the Victor band went out and one of the three came in. This was particularly important because Horvath had embarked on a facelifting program for the building that was to last until the Depression stopped it. He had heard rumors, one from Wayne King, that Andrew Karzas was interested in building another Trianon (ballroom) in Detroit, and Charley reasoned that the best way to keep him out was to make the Graystone so beautiful that it would be unprofitable for an adventure of that type by Karzas.

"We'll never know if he was right or not, since the weekly gross of the Graystone, which had been running along at about $12,000 a week, dropped to $6,000 by the last week in September, 1929, and went steadily down from there, leaving Jean with thousands of dollars of debts that he was never able to pay. Unfortunately he was too proud to take bankruptcy or even put the Graystone Corporation through the wringer.

"So the financial prop that was always under the Victor band was gradually removed, and the man who had put the band together originally and had been its first leader, Charley, had found a new toy—the rebuilding of the Graystone. Without his constant support and effort, the band was doomed."

Goldkette was at his wit's end. Thus when Francis "Cork" O'Keefe, partner with Tommy Rockwell in the newly-formed Rockwell-O'Keefe booking agency, telephoned to say he wanted to come out from New York to talk with Goldkette about the Victor orchestra, the leader's reply was an effusive yes.

O'Keefe had plans. First on his list was a month for the band at Young's Million Dollar Pier, on the boardwalk at Atlantic City. After that, Goldkette chimed in, they could move to New York for another stint at Roseland, and he was working at landing the featured band spot at the new Club New Yorker, due to open in the fall at what had for a while been the old Paul Whiteman Club, at 48th and Broadway on the site of the now defunct Cinderella.

But Goldkette's concern remained. His deficit was enormous, and the uncertainty of the winter season deeply disturbing. The Graystone facelift alone would cost him $150,000-plus, and the Victor band showed little sign of financial health. Ultimately, he told O'Keefe, he might have to consider an alternative hitherto unthinkable: dissolve the Graystone band altogether and lay more stress on operations which cost less and were paying for themselves. McKinney's, the Orange Blossoms and the Vagabonds were doing fine, and there was a new outfit being formed at the Pla-mor Ballroom in Kansas City with Hoagy Carmichael and ex-Arcadian Sterling Bose, plus old reliable Nat Natoli, along lines inspired by the Graystone ensemble but at a fraction of the cost. Goldkette weighed the consequences of such a move as he and most of his musicians boarded the train for Atlantic City and their August 8 opening.

Bix, characteristically, was not on board. Cork O'Keefe had mentioned in passing that he wanted to travel down with Jean, but didn't know what to do with his new Jordan roadster, which he'd driven out from New York. Bix volunteered at once to drive it to the New Jersey resort.

"It'll be a cinch," he told a not-altogether-convinced Bill Challis. "We take off tomorrow morning at five, right? We take the ferry to Buffalo, then drive straight down through Pennsylvania. Ought to be a snap."

At four the following morning, Challis stood shivering on the ferry dock, waiting for Bix to show up with the car. Come 4:30, and no Bix. The ferry pulled in and started to load. Still no sign of Bix. Challis went to a phone booth and called the Billinghurst. Bix's room didn't answer. Finally, with much creaking and a long, mournful blast of its whistle, the ship was gone, leaving a nonplussed Challis standing on the pier watching the sky pass from black to greyish-pink to blue and wondering whether to be angry or worried at his friend's failure to appear. He waited around another half hour, then went back to the Billinghurst.

Bix was there, stretched out across the bed sleeping. His face was bruised, and his right eye had been blackened.

"Hey, pal, what the hell happened?" Challis, genuinely startled, struggled to get Bix awake, his anger forgotten. As soon as Bix was able to talk he explained. On his way to the dock he had been set upon by thugs, beaten up and robbed at gunpoint. There seemed no way to tell Bill, and it was less of a distance back to the hotel than to the pier, so he had come back. He started to apologize. Challis cut him short. "Forget it, pal. Just that you're okay. Right now we've got to figure out another way to go and get moving. We got a job to make, remember."

Within hours they were off at last, this time by a later ferry to Cleveland, to drive through Ohio and part of Pennsylvania into southern New Jersey. All went well, Challis said, until just outside Harrisburg, Pennsylvania, when Bix decided to open the Jordan up a bit and see what she could do. As though by prearranged signal, a motorcycle patrolman materialized behind them and waved them over.

"Hey, buddy," he barked at Bix, "how long you been driving?"

Bix, black eye turning bright purple, managed a wan smile. "Since five this morning, I'd guess," he said.

The cop, said Challis, was neither sympathetic nor amused at what he doubtless took as a feeble attempt at a joke. He presented Bix with a speeding ticket and roared off in a swirl of dust.

Rumors of a breakup had preceded the Goldkette band to Atlantic City, and it seemed that every musician dropping in to hear them was asking the same questions. Was it true? What were Bix and Tram going to do? Were they going with Whiteman after all? Goldkette emphatically denied all the stories, and assured questioners that business had seldom been better. But such protestations rang hollow. The rumors persisted, and the arrival of Adrian Rollini on something clearly more than a social call hardly helped quell them. Rollini, no slouch on the business end of the music scene, had left the Ramblers and was contemplating forming an all-star band of his own with the best hot talent he could find. He had an inside track, he said, on the Club New Yorker, and the word was out that he, not Goldkette, would land the job. He also had irons in the fire for records and radio and other possibilities. The Goldkette band wouldn't last long, he said. Everybody knew that. Why not pitch their lot in with him on what seemed a surefire venture?

Goldkette pleaded for time. Roseland was a certainty, he said, and he felt sure that he could land the New Yorker too, despite what Rollini said. "All I ask is a couple of weeks, gentlemen," he said. "If this doesn't materialize, then we will indeed have to disband, and you will be free to accept whatever commitments you like."

The musicians agreed to hang on. "There was this enormous spirit," said Doc Ryker. "We were like a team, you know. Everyone had enormous respect for everyone else, and tremendous loyalty. We didn't want to see it fold, and were only too willing to give Jean every chance to pull it out."

Rollini went back to Manhattan determined to land the New Yorker. The Goldkette band, meanwhile, appeared nightly at Young's, surrounded by forebodings of breakup and financial disaster, with the name of Paul Whiteman continually cropping up as a potential next employer for the star sidemen. Such speculations hardly suffered when Whiteman himself turned up at the Million Dollar Pier one night, again flanked by Jimmy Dorsey and by manager and general business head Jimmy Gillespie. "Pops" and his full orchestra were playing Philadelphia as part of a long tour for the Paramount-Publix Theater chain, and he was indeed in the market for hot talent and still interested in Goldkette's men. Nichols and the other "Pennies" had long since departed from the troupe, preferring to clean up on the freelance and recording market.

A hot August night, and a capacity crowd of high-spirited vacationers thronged the Million Dollar Pier. Bix caught sight of Whiteman's portly figure moments after it swept in through the door. He walked over during a break and they shook hands. "You know," said the cornetist in mock puzzlement, "your name *does* sound familiar somehow."

Bix and Challis echoed Goldkette's suggestion that the "King of Jazz" conduct the Graystone band for a selection. Whiteman respectfully declined. "I don't know any of your arrangements, fellows. I'd just get in the way."

Goldkette cut in. "Not at all, Paul. I think it would be a splendid idea, and the people would love it. Go right ahead. Just count off and the boys will do the rest."

In the end Whiteman consented. Borrowing Goldkette's long baton, he "directed" the band through an arrangement of W.C.Handy's "St. Louis Blues." "There was some difficulty in keeping together for the first half chorus or so," said Challis. "His directing took some getting used to. But

207

the crowd ate it up. They hollered for more, and so we gave 'em 'Tiger' and they went wild. All the while, Jean was standing off to one side watching, and looking pretty unhappy. I think he knew, then and there, that the end wasn't far off."

Afterwards, Whiteman repeated his offer to Bix and Tram. He asked Challis as well. Bix brought up the New Yorker, and the possibility that either Goldkette or Rollini would land it. Whiteman, who had run the last club at the spot, snorted. "That place! I wouldn't give you a nickel for their chances. They have pretty shaky backing, and whoever gets it won't be there long, I can guarantee. I wouldn't give that one even a week, boys."

In the end, Bix and Tram decided to stick things out with Goldkette. But Challis was thinking ahead. He gave Whiteman a tentative yes. "Let's talk about it on the phone in a day or two, shall we?" said the bandleader, sure he had made at least one catch this night.

The full Goldkette band drove up to New York on Tuesday, August 21, for a date at Victor—only to have it cancelled, inexplicably, by telegram after they had rehearsed four numbers. The next day Rank, Ryker and one or two of the others spent the afternoon at the Edison studios recording for Joe Herlihy on the first of two dates involving Goldkette musicians. Research has established that Bix did not participate in either date, but the presence of Rank, Murray, Ryker and Trumbauer has been ascertained.

Thursday saw the Trumbauer group, plus Rollini and Lang, back at Okeh to do three sides. One, "Three Blind Mice," was an original by Chauncey, arranged by Challis and Tram. But the other two titles, "Blue River" and "There's a Cradle in Caroline," heralded what appeared to be a change in policy. Both were pop tunes, dressed up in arrangements far more commercial than anything Trumbauer had done on record to date, and both featuring the nasal vocalizing of Seger Ellis, a highly capable pianist who had developed singing as a lucrative sideline. It appeared a concession to the Eddie King dictum that jazz alone simply did not sell phonograph records; and Trumbauer, if he wanted to record regularly for Okeh, was going to have to sell his share of records. Where bands and singers recording for the "race" or colored market could afford not to compromise, Tram's records were going to a public far more attuned to Whiteman, Roger Wolfe Kahn or the vo-do-dee-o antics of the California Ramblers than to Louis Armstrong or even the advanced arrangements of Bill Challis. But even the banalities of "Blue River" ("Can we both forget that bright summer night, in our little canoe/when your blue eyes lost their light, and we whispered adoo . . .") left room for Bix to play what amounted to a solo behind Ellis' vocal (displaying next to no acknowledgement of the singer's presence), then to dominate the final ensemble chorus with an impassioned lead.

Again on Friday the full Goldkette band trooped into Victor's Liederkranz Hall studio, said Challis, "determined to turn out some really hot stuff. We were all pretty sure by then that the band would break up right after the Roseland job, so we wanted to get some of our best things down on record while there was still time."

As before, they rehearsed four numbers, including a Challis score on "Everybody Loves My Baby" featuring Bix. And again, as before, a telegram at the last moment cancelled the date without explanation. It was as though a jinx had fallen over the band in its twilight hour, determined

208

to prevent it from leaving any truly representative trace of what had caused a musical revolution during each of its visits to New York.

Then came the final bombshell: news that Rollini had secured the New Yorker job, edging out Goldkette. "Now will you come?" he asked Bix, Tram, Rank and Chauncey. And this time the answer, reluctantly, was yes. Rollini turned to Challis. "How about you, Bill? Want to play third alto and do the arrangements?" Challis was astonished. Apart from filling in briefly while Trumbauer was in the hospital having his cosmetic surgery done, he had all but abandoned playing the saxophone. But by his own admission, Challis was "a big Trumbauer admirer, and Bix was always after me to play. Right then and there I suspected his hand in all this." But it wasn't that easy. Whiteman had offered him good money to join his entourage as staff arranger alongside Tommy Satterfield and "symphonic jazz" master Ferde Grofe. Rollini's offer had simply come too late.

"I'll have to mull it a bit, Adrian," he said. "But don't get your hopes up."

The Goldkette musicians returned to Atlantic City with mixed emotions, some looking forward to working with Rollini but all deeply regretful that their days as an orchestra were numbered. They were sounding better than ever; most of the ground lost through Sheasby's departure had been regained through rehearsal. In Fred Bergin's words, "They knew all the tunes by heart anyway."

Goldkette was in Detroit, still trying vainly to negotiate further bookings, but hope was fading fast. Challis made up his mind, told Jean he was going—Goldkette graciously waived any requirement that he give longer notice—told Rollini no thanks, and prepared to leave for New York to join Whiteman at the Paramount Theater after a fortnight's rest in Wilkes Barre. At Tram's suggestion, the full band held a meeting before work one afternoon to discuss the situation. They decided to ask Goldkette to reorganize the band after half a year, or however long it took him to line up enough work to make such a venture financially worthwhile. It was a plan doomed from the start, as the leader soon told them.

Then, at last, there was Roseland, and a prelude to the end. Bix took his place in the trumpet section early Thursday night and peered out at the lines of faces already assembling in front of the stand. Right off he spied a friend.

"I say, old boy," he called in an exaggerated upper-crust English accent, "did you know I now belong to the school of Nastikoff?"

Dick Turner let out a peal of laughter. "Nastikoff no good," he shot back. "I spit me of Nastikoff."

This reference to P. G. Wodehouse, an enthusiasm they shared, pleased Bix. Good to see Turner here tonight. Nice fellow; heart in the right place about music.

"Hey, Bix, you seen the new one?"

"No; what's it about, old boy? Jeeves and all that sort of rot, what?"

"Not at all, my dear chap. More golf stories. The last, very last word. Called *Heart of a Goof*. Quite the rage, you know."

"Not as good as *Cuthbert*, surely?"

"Better, old top. Better. You simply *must* ask the oldest member to tell you about Rollo Podmash."

Turner and Bix had discovered their common regard for Wodehouse at their first meeting in 1924, when the Wolverines played the Cinderella.

Whenever Bix came to New York, Dick made it a point to be on hand. This time, especially, their reunion was cause for celebration. "We'd become good buddies by then," said Turner. "Even double-dated now and then. Once, I remember, we went out on a foursome, and the blind date he got was Ruby Keeler. He saw quite a bit of her after that, I think."

Ruby Keeler, later to marry Al Jolson, refused in later life to answer any questions about her association with Bix or anyone else in the "old days."

At the end of nearly each set during the Goldkette band's final ten days at Roseland, Bix made straight for Turner's table. He seldom got there without a struggle. "Hordes of admirers would congregate around him. You know how possessive someone feels about an artist they have worshipped on record and then actually met. Well, that was the case here. All sorts of characters, guys from Princeton or some New England prep school —and he always had this gracious way of handling it by some device such as, 'Hi there, boys, how's all the gang up there?' and then he'd tell me he had no idea who the hell they were. And he was utterly confused about what they were talking about when they referred to some chorus he'd played."

Sometimes, said Turner, "we'd sit by the hour up in his hotel room with a jug, taking turns reading from the golf stories[13] out loud until we cried from laughing—enhanced, of course, by the alcohol. Sometimes we went out to a movie, or decided to go on the town and hear the bands then current.

"His appearance everywhere created a stir. Every musician in town knew him—yet he could rarely remember them and never by name. He was invariably asked to sit in." On one such occasion, Rank and Murray joined them for a drunken odyssey uptown to the Cotton Club, where they all sat in with Duke Ellington's orchestra.

Turner and Bix played golf a few times, but "he was worse than I, which was pretty bad. We halved many holes at ten—he insisted on betting every hole and never had a penny to pay up. A true goof."

Frank Trumbauer, meanwhile, had been busy planning. He had firmed up his contractual arrangements with Okeh and had even been talking with Tom Rockwell about recording Bix's piano inventions. During the first trio date Bix had warmed up with what sounded sufficiently like a finished concert piece to get Rockwell interested. It didn't have a name yet, he said, but it did possess recognizable form and structural identity.

"Think we can get him to record something like that?" Rockwell asked.

Trumbauer flashed a particularly Faustian smile. "Leave it to me, Tom. We'll see," he said. Both agreed that such a recording would be worthwhile both for the originality of the music and for the novelty of presenting Bix Beiderbecke, cornetist, in a new and unexpected setting.

Bix himself, however, was less certain. "Aw c'mon, Frank," he complained as they climbed the steps of the Okeh-Odeon Building at 11 Union Square. "I'm not a pianist. All I do is noodle. That's not the kind of stuff they want to record."

Trumbauer refused to be swayed. "Let's let *them* decide that, okay, Bix?"

---

13. Wodehouse's golf stories were available chiefly in two anthologies: *The Clicking of Cuthbert*, published in 1922, and *The Heart of a Goof*, in 1926.

After some halfhearted protest, Bix agreed. The equipment was set up. He sat down at the piano and ran briefly through a piece built around a descending sequence of ninth chords, strongly redolent of moments in the works of both Debussy and Ravel, until it gave way abruptly to a passage which was far more openly jazz-flavored. Here he broke it off. "Okay, let's try one now," he said.

He did one take, but ran over the allotted time. Tram suggested a remedy. "You just play. I'll tap you on the shoulder fifteen seconds before you have to finish, and you wind it up. Okay?"

It worked. Bix combined the two sequences with several other passages he had worked out, tacked on a coda after getting the signal from Tram, and Okeh wrapped up the finished product for pressing.

"Whatcha want to call it?" the recording engineer asked, pencil poised. Bix shrugged.

"No name. Never thought of giving any of that stuff a name."

"Well, you guys are back here in a week. How about coming up with something by then?"

Bix laughed. "Sure. I'll give you a great and poetical name by then, my dear chap," he said in his best Wodehouse manner, and left with Trumbauer to catch the first rehearsal of Rollini's new band at the New Yorker.

The only new face in evidence when he walked in was a tall, sandy-haired Finn from Gloucester, Massachusetts, named Sylvester Ahola. He had been working with Peter Van Steeden's band around New York after an apprenticeship which included the California Ramblers, Paul Specht and other name groups before being snapped up by Rollini for the lead book. He was also able to turn out respectable jazz choruses if needed, a talent which would stand him in good stead later during an extended stay in England.

Trumbauer introduced Ahola and noticed that the idea of playing alongside a schooled brassman who also knew his way around hot music seemed at once to intimidate Bix.

"Pleased and honored to meet you," said the New Englander, dubbed "Hooley" by friends, perhaps after the Finnish word *huuli*, which meant "the embouchure." Bix smiled almost shyly and took his hand.

"Hell, I'm only a musical degenerate," he said. The remark drew a warm laugh from Ahola.

"That may or may not be, but you do play passable hot choruses."

This time it was Bix's turn to grin. They would get along fine, he thought.

Rollini pitched into rehearsals with a vengeance. In addition to a nucleus of Goldkette sidemen, he had brought in Venuti and Lang, Frank Signorelli at the piano, and Bobby Davis, former star of the Ramblers' reed section, to fill the chair Challis had turned down.

Amid all this activity the Goldkette band met at Liederkranz Hall to record one last time for Victor. The mood, Doc Ryker recalled, was far from what could have been expected from a lame-duck aggregation. "On the contrary, all the boys felt they wanted to get something really good down on record, something that'd show the band at its best," he said. They had tried twice now to do just that, both times thwarted by last-minute directives from on high. This time, as things turned out, was different. One of the two numbers they were scheduled to do was a bouncy tune called "Clementine (from New Orleans)," working from a published "stock" orchestration. With Challis gone, a custom-tailored score was out of the question. But everyone, Doc Ryker said, had suggestions for small alterations which would turn the stock into something special.

"We rehearsed quite awhile before we did it," Ryker said. "I sent the brass section out to one room, the saxes to another, to work out their choruses. I think, in fact, that they went to the ladies' room." The result was a pasteup job based only loosely on the original, with bits and pieces by Tram, Murray and Howdy incorporated. It featured a three-part sax section chorus, giving way to Bix's longest solo on any Goldkette recording —a full chorus over sustained band chords, with Venuti taking the release. By any standard, "Clementine" is an extraordinary record, and a departure from all Goldkette Victor performances before it. The band, lifted by Lang's guitar, sings along with a freshness and rich tonal balance rare on any recording of the 1920s and a rhythmic relaxation looking a good decade into the future. Bix fills in during the ensembles with the charm of a highspirited schoolboy, and his solo, simple in construction, refashions a new tune out of the old with the same natural grace which turned "Singin' the Blues" into a piece of jazz history.

Truly, said Ryker, a record to remember. "You bet," Rank added. "It was undoubtedly the best record we ever made. It should have been, because it took us all day. Everyone contributed to it as we went along. It was our last will and testament—and a great one at that."

The Rollini band, meanwhile, kept up a gruelling rehearsal schedule, working through the day until it was time for the Goldkette musicians to go to work at Roseland, then meeting afterwards at the New Yorker to drill until early morning.

Then, at last, it was September 18, Sunday night. For the last time the Jean Goldkette Graystone Ballroom Orchestra took its place on the bandstand at Roseland. Hard to believe, said Murray, that it had been only a year since Bix and Tram joined and turned a good band into a great one.

This night there was no rousing sendoff, no final "riot of glory" for the history books. Instead, in a burst of commonly-felt nostalgia, the band dipped into the back of its memory to pull out all the old Crozier arrangements, such light classics and sentimental favorites as "Under the Leaves," "To a Wild Rose" and even, at Bix's special behest, "Adoration."

"We played them all," said Rank. "We could do a very good job on those as well as on the jazz things. As to why—we just felt it was something we wanted to do, that's all." The dancers may have wondered, but there was no doubt in the mind of any man in the band.

At the end, when the last note had been played, there was nothing left to do but sign and exchange copies of the latest band photograph, showing twelve musicians in evening dress grouped around a Victor console talking machine, with a bigger-than-life statue of "Nipper" out in front.

"Looking back," Goldkette wrote in a 1958 letter to the authors, "one finds it difficult to comment on the band's performance or analyze what made it unique. Much better, I think, to say only that I deemed it a privilege and an honor to have known and worked with every man in it. They were all outstanding musicians and gentlemen to the core.

"It is on the basis of such things as these that history will pass her judgment."

212

Bix and Don Murray fooling around on
the Boardwalk.

PHOTO COURTESY PAUL MERTZ,
TAKEN BY RISKIN

Goldkette musicians and friends on the Boardwalk in Atlantic City shortly after the band's
August 8, 1927, opening at Young's Million Dollar Pier. L to R: Don Murray, unknown, Bix,
Sam Lanin, Quicksell, Lodwig. PHOTO COURTESY IRVING RISKIN

Adrian Rollini's band at the Club New Yorker on September 16, 1927, six days before the club opening. Seated, L to R: Sylvester Ahola (trumpet); Bill Rank (trombone); Bix (cornet); Frank Trumbauer (saxes); Don Murray (saxes); Frank Signorelli (piano). Standing, L to R: Eddie Lang (guitar and banjo); Chauncey Morehouse (drums); Rollini; Bobby Davis (saxes); Joe Venuti (violin). PHOTO COURTESY BILL RANK

# Chapter 15

An hour before opening time at the Club New Yorker. Adrian Rollini's new band running down a few final numbers. Waiters scurrying back and forth to align gleaming silver on white tablecloths. Master of ceremonies Frank Fay and comedienne Patsy Kelly standing off to one side, mugging through bits of their floor-show dialogue.

Sylvester Ahola glanced up, startled, from his first trumpet book just as a sheet of flame flashed with a roar across a wall draped in paper bunting. "My God, look out!" he yelled. Musicians and staff dived for safety.

"Somebody get some water!"

"To hell with the water! We gotta open in a few minutes! Hey Mario! Tony! Where the hell are all you guys?"

A burly waiter advanced, flailing a metal tray at the flames. Others joined him, and the blaze was soon out, leaving heaps of charred paper and a few black stains on the wall.

Less than five minutes had elapsed. Ahola slumped in his chair. "Boy, was I scared!" he said to Bix, sitting pale and quiet beside him. Bix shook his head dazedly and began picking up the pieces of manuscript paper scattered under his chair.

September 22, 1927. The night of the Long Count, when Gene Tunney survived what should have been Jack Dempsey's knockout punch to hang on to his long-disputed world heavyweight championship. Talk of Babe Ruth's mounting home-run tally in the air. Opening night at the Club New Yorker, and the management decided not to call the fire department, but instead to stash the burned bunting, cover the stains and let the customers in anyway. Bix shook aside his stupor.

"Yeah," he said to Ahola after a long silence. "Really took me by surprise. This place could have gone up—" with a snap of his fingers—"just like that."

The band was billed on the club marquee as "The New Yorkers." Rollini had succeeded in negotiating $1,750 a week for them and was able to pay Bix better money than he had been pulling down with Goldkette. Venuti fronted the ten-piece unit but Rollini called the tunes from behind the big bass sax. The book was small: a potpourri of Challis carryovers along with carefully-reworked stocks, plus some special material for the floor show. But every man was a solo talent, and there was a strong spirit of team effort held over from the Goldkette ensemble.

"We had a jazz group that played one or two sets each evening," Ahola told the authors. "They used outline arrangements with plenty of solos. Bix, Tram, Murray, Rank, Signorelli, Morehouse, Rollini, Lang, Venuti—

that is, without me. The management let the band play anything, and it was largely the Goldkette sound as it sounded at Roseland. I feel the jazz was over the people's heads, by and large. As I was playing Red Nichols style myself, they even let me take a chorus now and then.

"Bix, always, was modest, very unassuming. His lack of ability to read well bothered him. In fact, to tell the truth, all of them had some trouble reading new material, and I remember thinking the Boston musicians were really far ahead of those so-called famous musicians."

From the very first night, attendance at the New Yorker fell well below the management's expectations. Most of the patrons, it seemed, were fellow musicians. As Ahola remarked wryly Friday night in his diary, "I guess this will be a musicians' hangout all right." Among the visitors were bandleaders Jacques Renard, Art Landry and Paul Specht, with many of their sidemen. Pianists Newell Chase, Frankie Dunn and Phil Wall dropped down from Boston to see Hooley, as did multi-talent reed virtuoso Andy Jacobson. Nat Shilkret came by. So did Roger Wolfe Kahn. Roger had filled his own band with jazz talent on the pattern set by Goldkette, and paid good salaries to the likes of Miff Mole and trumpeter Leo McConville, an avowed Bix admirer.

If business at the club was less than promising, there was at least enough recording to keep the band busy—though little of it appeared to be coming from Rollini. On Wednesday, September 28, the full personnel went to Okeh to do three titles, two of them originals; both Fud Livingston's "Humpty Dumpty" and Morehouse's "Krazy Kat" work freely and comfortably with the modern chords basic to Bix Beiderbecke's musical vocabulary.

No one, it appeared, bothered to remind Ahola of the exact time of the session. He never showed up, leaving Bix to play solos *and* negotiate the often tricky lead parts himself. He did a creditable job on both, turning out passages on both numbers which float across the often ambitious harmonies with ease and grace.

The following day some of Rollini's men took part in a Harmony record date Sam Lanin had contracted during a visit to Atlantic City in August. Bix, Tram, Murray, Venuti and Rank joined a crew of Lanin regulars, including trumpeter Herman "Hymie" Farberman and bassist Joe Tarto, for two pop tunes, "There Ain't No Land Like Dixieland to Me" and, again, "There's a Cradle in Caroline." The records, though unremarkable on the whole, show Bix an effortless master of warm, easy-flowing ideas, sung through his horn's middle register.

Back to Okeh on Friday for two commercial titles by the full band with vocals by Irving Kaufman, who had also done the Lanin date. The songs ("Just an Hour of Love with You" and "I'm Wonderin' Who") are of dismal quality, the arrangements pedestrian. Predictably, the band sounds far from its best, hardly recognizable as the group which had handled the felicities of "Krazy Kat" just two days before. The two titles appeared abroad as "Frankie Trumbauer's Augmented Orchestra, with Bix, Lang, Rollini and Venuti, with Special Vocal Chorus"; but at home they bore the name of Benny Meroff, a Chicago bandleader under contract to Okeh. Bill Rank ventured the theory that Meroff "probably had one more session to do to fulfil his contract and couldn't make it, so Okeh used our date for that."

More recording still. Bix returned to Okeh the following Wednesday with Murray, Rank, Signorelli, Morehouse and Rollini to do three titles under his own leadership, the first since "Davenport Blues" more than two years before. As he recalled the story to Spurrier, the first person he spied upon arrival was the recording man who had supervised the piano solo session.

"How about that title, Bix? Thought of something yet?"

"Gosh, I don't know," he answered, parking himself at the keyboard. In truth he hadn't given the matter a moment's thought. "Don't ask me that one today, man, I'm just in a fog."

With all the predictability of the commercially-conditioned mind, the official—whose name has been lost to recollection—recoiled in delight. "Hey! That's perfect! We'll call it 'In a Fog.'"

Bix, said Spurrier, scarcely hid his annoyance. "Aw c'mon, man. That's corny. And besides, it sounds all wrong—all heavy, like a guy with a hangover. That's not the way I hear it."

"I like it," the Okeh man repeated. "Unless you can come up with something better, it stays in."

"After kicking it around for awhile," said Spurrier, "the word 'Mist' replaced 'Fog.' Bix said he thought it more in keeping with his feeling for the thing. So 'Mist' it was and 'Mist' it stayed."

The recording session itself turned out to be a dixieland romp, with Bix dipping into the ODJB repertoire for "At the Jazz Band Ball," "Jazz Me Blues" and "Royal Garden Blues," which he had done three years before with the Wolverines. Though the music hardly reflects it, the session was hard work. Everyone, Bill Rank recalled, was tired, slightly hung over and grumpy, and at one point Bix showed it. "He was taking a solo, and the recording engineer motioned from the booth that he was too far from the mike. I gave Bix a slight shove to move him in closer, and he stopped playing and said, 'Hey, don't push me!' Needless to say, it ruined the master."

The records turned out well—and established a standard against which all subsequent performances of these songs have been judged, and on which many have been modelled. Bits of the routines on "Jazz Me Blues" and the others have found their way into the standard dixieland band approach to the songs. Bix's solos are models of relaxation, structural intelligence and tonal clarity.

Things at the Club New Yorker, however, were slipping badly now, and it seemed only a matter of days before the band got its notice. On Saturday, October 8, the management dropped the entire dinner show, leaving the band free to double with Frank Fay and Patsy Kelly at the Strand Theater in *Midnight at the New Yorker*.

"That week or two at the Strand was really something," said Sylvester Ahola. "We didn't have an act, nor had we memorized anything. We used ordinary backstage chairs for music stands. Venuti was a clown—we even played an overture: no music, no key, no name, no nothing, with him pointing out the solos and Bix taking a long cadenza on the celeste." The "celeste" was in reality a Kramer Miniature Grand Piano given to the band for advertising purposes by the manufacturer and mentioned on Strand Theater programs.

As usual, there was mischief-making and practical jokes. Venuti picked

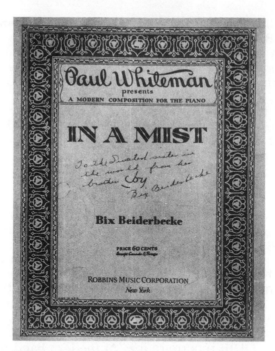

Original sheet music autographed by the composer
for his sister, Mary Louise Shoemaker.

Bill Rank, on a visit to London in 1967, surrounded by members of the Anglo-American
Alliance with whom he recorded while there. Author Sudhalter is holding the cornet.

up an ancient U.S. cavalry horn in a pawnshop and presented it to Bix with orders to "play hot on it." Bix obliged, Venuti said, and "did a damn good job, too."

Ahola provides an intriguing sidelight to the week at the Strand. "I'm an old-time radio ham, W1 PU, one of the first around New England, and the other day I contacted a ham in Connecticut, W1 OFU, a drummer who was around at that time, although I haven't met him. Well, he saw us at the Strand and remembers Bix playing a chorus into a big five-foot megaphone held between his knees and resting on the floor. It seems to me it was the arrangement of 'Clementine' as recorded by Goldkette."

Ahola's diary traces the demise of Adrian Rollini's New Yorkers from that point on:

"Oct. 9—Sunday—No business tonight.

"Oct. 10—Business very sad at the New Yorker. It looks as if the place is going on the rocks. Eddie Lang still not here. Quicksell is on banjo, which is a break for him.

"Oct. 12.—Joe Venuti didn't show up for the first show at all. Cafe going on the blink all night.

"Oct. 13— . . . Adrian broke the sad news of the club closing Saturday night. Hope we get our money . . .

"Oct. 14—Friday—Don Murray brings eggs onstage and we clown with them as it is Frank Fay's gag. Took movies of dirigible and New Yorker entrance and Strand entrance. Finished up at the Strand today. Adrian gives us the news about the place closing.

"Oct. 15—Saturday—Close at the New Yorker . . . Adrian wants boys to give him a week in which to book band. We all promise.

"Oct. 18—Saw Trumbauer but nothing doing yet. I guess no hope."

Paul Whiteman's prediction had come true; he had only underestimated how long the New Yorker would last. It had taken almost a month to fold.

Ahola, man of many hobbies, adds a further, tantalizing postscript. Like Charlie Horvath, he was an early experimenter with home movies shot on a 16-millimeter hand-crank camera. "I have movies of Rollini," he said, "but it's a shame I missed Bix. But they slept all day. In those days there were mighty few 16-millimeter movie cameras, so I missed the boat on a real scoop. But I do have a shot of the two marquees, the Strand and the New Yorker at night, with the lights and the signs for evidence."

Bix, Tram and the others were now on their own, picking up what freelance work they could. Willard Robison, songwriter and leader of his own "Deep River Orchestra," came through with some radio broadcasts and a record date for Pathe. Issued under Robison's name and under that of the "Chicago Loopers," the three titles made that day are among the most elusive of Beiderbecke recordings. One, a remake of Morehouse's "Three Blind Mice," shows Bix at a height of creative inventiveness, using upper chordal voices, unusual intervals and chromatics with aplomb, then almost casually ending his chorus on one of the two issued takes on a major seventh, a startling and audacious departure for 1927. Yet Bix pulls it off, and attracts no undue attention in doing so; the note is the natural resolution of its phrase. Again, Bix has taken for granted a musical frame of reference far broader than that of most of his contemporaries.

But such musical satisfactions hardly laid to rest Trumbauer's concern at the prospect of indefinite freelancing. Tram resolved to develop some manner of longer-term arrangement, even if it did not directly involve Bix, in order to make staying around New York economically viable.

To this end he approached Red Nichols with a proposal. Nichols had by now established himself as a constantly sought-after, highly paid recording-studio regular in New York. He combined solid reading and technical skills with an ability to turn out polished, convincing hot solos, winning praise even from such veterans as Hymie Farberman:

"I was very much impressed with Red's style and ability. It was a pleasure to have him alongside. His playing was very colorful and smooth. He could blend with whomever he played with, and like most good players, he developed and improved as he went along."

Nichols had also made a few enemies. Some, including many dedicated jazzmen, resented his nonstop hustling for work, others his ever-acute ear for the business gimmick. Bix, despite his personal liking for Nichols, nevertheless found his jazz solo work overstudied and emotionally bloodless.

Such criticism appeared not to deter Trumbauer. Nichols himself offered vivid recollection of Tram's scheme for a collaboration between them:

"Tram was out of work. He came to me with an idea. He had a record contract with Okeh, and suggested we work on a partnership deal. We'd take a tune, record it with a company that I had connections with, then jump down to Okeh and record the same tune under his name. This we did [on October 26] with 'Sugar.' In the morning, I wangled a deal with Victor Records. We had Tram, Rollini, Rank, etc. from his gang. Well, that afternoon we went down to Okeh to make the recording. Tommy Rockwell was in the studio and he blew his stack. I gathered he didn't like me because he objected to Tram using me. He said he would honor the recording date but Tram had to use Bix. Tram argued that Bix was in bad shape that day. Tommy said either Bix or no date. I left the studio. As I understand it, Tram found Bix in a speakeasy and he was plastered. He brought him to the studio to show Tommy. Made no difference to him. Bix had to do the date. When Tram heard the playbacks he was furious, and stomped out of the studio. Tommy decided to fix Tram, so he issued 'Sugar' using the name of a friend of his for the band. Tram didn't know about it until later and was furious with Tommy forever after. The record, on top of it, wasn't very good."

The friend whose name Rockwell used was a Minnesota trombonist named Russell Gray, with whom he had played drums in a Minneapolis boys' band in 1915. Charlie Margulis, later to sit alongside Bix in Paul Whiteman's brass section, was on trumpet in the Minneapolis band. Asked about this record, Gray told the authors he had never met either Bix or Trumbauer, and that Rockwell "never could even carry a tune." Gray said a meeting with Rockwell during a business trip to New York was the first he knew of his name being used on the Okeh record. It was the second time, said Rockwell. The first had been a recording by the Goofus Five, a small jazz unit from the California Ramblers, also with Rollini in the personnel.

"Sugar" offers yet further mysteries for the listener. The eight-bar cornet or trumpet solo following the vocal bears little resemblance, stylistically or tonally, to any of Bix's recorded work. No other trumpet player

Red Nichols, c. 1927.

Bill Rank posing in New York around 1927.

is listed in the personnel, though two are clearly audible in the closing bars of the final ensemble. Sylvester Ahola's diary bears no entry to corroborate any supposition that he might have been summoned on short notice to fill in for a Bix well under the weather. British collectors more familiar with Hooley's jazz improvisations on literally hundreds of records made in London between 1928 and 1931 have expressed doubt that he could be the soloist here.

Who, then? The trumpet-playing brothers Bob and "Bo" Ashford had taken part on the Nichols Victor date that morning. "Bo" later became jazz trumpet soloist with Casa Loma, then with a band led by Ozzie Nelson. But virtually no examples of his style exist on record for comparison. The identity of the man who took the solo while Bix noodled in the corner of the studio may remain eternally unresolved.

Bix's first small-group session for Okeh was ready for issue under the name "New Orleans Lucky Seven" and Rockwell, pleased with the result, asked that the same group do another three titles in the same manner. They obliged during the October 25 session, along with "A Good Man Is Hard to Find" and "Cryin' All Day" by the larger group, the latter title written by Tram and Morehouse around the opening figure of Trumbauer's "Singin' the Blues" saxophone solo in an effort to capitalize on the success of the earlier record. Bix contributes intense, moving solos to each performance, turning out one after another the most creative works of his brief career on records. Each solo displays in faultless balance the qualities which distinguished the style as the sole original alternative to the principles laid down by Louis Armstrong in these same years. In its "correlated" structure, tonal clarity and blending of European and American musical values, it is clearly a white man's music—but an original one, and unmistakably jazz. Where Armstrong and the generations of trumpeters following him gave free vent to a rhapsodic, emotionally open romanticism, Bix instinctively adopted a classicist's methods to harness a no less romantic sensibility, the mind holding the emotions in balance. But there is no loss of forcefulness, as many of Beiderbecke's critics appear to have overlooked.

Admittedly, such qualities are better suited to some kinds of material than to others. Bix is supremely at home on songs with appealing melodies and interesting harmonic structures; but his few recorded excursions into the blues generally emerge as engaging tunes, capturing little of the power or substance of the idiom. He solos strongly and with conviction on his Okeh recordings of "Royal Garden Blues" and "Goose Pimples," riding the latter title out in a burst of emotional intensity. Yet the impression left by such playing is far from the blues of Armstrong, Tommy Ladnier or even the admittedly lyrical Joe Smith, accompanist to Bessie Smith.

The uncertainty of the freelance existence began to affect Bix as well as Trumbauer, and it was to Tram that he turned in search of greater security. This, said Esten Spurrier, was to be a pattern in the continuing relationship between the two musicians. "Bix in a way had grown to like and expect a sort of predictable existence—you know, knowing who he was playing with and where. After he and Frank hooked up together, Bix relied on him to make deals for both of them, as spokesman and as a sort of security blanket."

The friendship had become increasingly complex since the days in St.

Louis, and Bix spoke of it often in letters to Spurrier and on periodic visits home. "Of course there were points of disagreement. Bix was always impatient with all the frilly intros, segnis and endings on Frank's arrangements of jazz tunes. And Frank never really accepted Bix's refusal to play set choruses, as he did. Frank always said—even to me on several occasions —that no matter how competent Bix was, his insistence on completely extemporaneous choruses always added to his nervousness in recording.

"But on those duets between them—they called them 'chase choruses' —when one of them would play a phrase and the other another answering him, Bix always said he tried for some terrific things as a challenge to Frank and always got such a kick out of Frank's replies. Bix thought some of the best licks Frank ever played were on chases, and that he should have been more extemporaneous. Frank, on the other hand, spent some time with me here in Davenport one year, and I remember him telling of his trepidation on recording those choruses. But he remembered, on hearing some of them over, that he rose to the challenge and came up with things he didn't know were in him."

Trumbauer had just about decided what he thought the next move should be. While Adrian Rollini and his tenor sax-playing kid brother Arthur, Bobby Davis and Sylvester Ahola were on the high seas bound for England and jobs with high-paying London hotel dance bands, Trumbauer was negotiating with Jimmy Gillespie. Paul Whiteman's offer to Tram was still open, Gillespie said; and, largely through Bill Challis' continued lobbying, it included Bix, too.

Sometime during the week of October 23, while Bix and Tram were finishing out their Okeh recording commitments, they came to an agreement with Gillespie. Not many hours after the "Sugar" session, an illustrious jazz partnership entered a new phase as Bix Beiderbecke and Frank Trumbauer boarded an airplane for Indianapolis to join the orchestra of Paul Whiteman.

Nathaniel "Nat" Shilkret, Victor bandleader and A & R man, c. 1928.

# Chapter 16

Paul Whiteman was a big man, and he was used to doing things big. Born in Denver on March 28, 1890, he had made his first musical mark early and well, playing violin and viola in two major symphony orchestras before his 25th birthday. His first flirtations with dance music were equally successful, and before long he was leading a band at the Ambassador Hotel in Atlantic City whose discipline and polish quickly became the talk of the music business. Many of its performances were spiced with the flavor, if not the essence, of the music of the Dixieland Jazz Band. The customers might well feel they were doing something vaguely naughty in dancing to Whiteman's music, but they were doing it in an unimpeachably civilized way. It could furnish novelty, but not offend conservative tastes in doing so.

Whiteman seemed blessed with a quick business head and an unerring instinct for dishing up what the public wanted at exactly the time the public discovered it wanted it. His records for the Victor Talking Machine Company were instant hits. By 1922 he could command an unprecedented $25,000 for six nights at the Trianon Ballroom in Chicago. The Whiteman orchestra played the Palais Royale in New York City, was featured in *George White's Scandals* and the *Ziegfeld Follies,* then did an astounding 13 weeks at the Palace Theater, all to consistently packed houses. By the mid-1920s, Paul Whiteman had toured Europe twice and assured himself a permanent niche in American popular music history by giving the young George Gershwin's *Rhapsody in Blue* for piano and orchestra its world premiere February 24, 1924, in an "Experiment in Modern Music" concert at New York's Aeolian Hall.

The concert, apart from establishing Gershwin's reputation as a composer and pianist, also helped make Whiteman a household name, the "King of Jazz" for millions of white Americans who had never heard of King Oliver, Jelly Roll Morton, Fletcher Henderson or the other pioneer black musicians. The very image of his rotund, avuncular face, moustache neatly trimmed and hairline inexorably receding, became inextricably associated in the public mind with the new music.

Whiteman more than lived up to his image. A big, jovial man of close to 300 pounds, he made no secret of the fact that his sidemen were the best-paid in the business, travelled in the most comfortable trains and coaches, stayed in the best hotels. Quite in keeping, the 1929 newspaper account which rather breathlessly enumerated Whiteman's "thirty musicians, a manager, a secretary, a complete stage crew, a piano tuner, a valet (Williams)," among the personnel, and "two special pullmans, and a sixty-foot baggage car . . . two concert grand pianos, scenery, platforms, electrical equipment, eighty-seven trunks, thirty-five chairs and music stands." Everything, from travelling to publicity to the *Rhapsody in Blue*, was cast on the grand scale, always with an air of luxurious high living and sense of occasion.

If Gershwin's attempt to fuse American and European forms sounds self-consciously pretentious today, and if the recordings of many of Paul Whiteman's early orchestras bear little resemblance to the real jazz of Oliver, the NORK or the Wolverines, they did reach a far wider public. They made that public aware of jazz music, and laid the foundation for fuller understanding by creating a climate for acceptance.

Whiteman was no fool. The "King of Jazz" title might be a travesty in the eyes of black *and* white musicians playing music far more worthy of the name for a fraction of the salary, but it is to Whiteman's eternal credit that the enormous influence he wielded in the entertainment business was ultimately coupled with determination to turn out music of a consistently high standard; that the affluence went to lure the best available men into the ever-swelling ranks of his concert orchestra.

Nor was this pure altruism. Although his "King" reputation owed as much to the inflated "modernistic" concert works of Ferde Grofe as to actual improvised hot music, Whiteman saw to it that his entourage usually included the best white jazzmen his freely-spent money could buy. He bid for Red Nichols' Five Pennies in early 1927 and got the leader plus Vic Berton. Neither of them stayed long; Nichols said in later years that he felt "buried" in the vast ensemble and preferred the freelancer's life. Jimmy and later Tommy Dorsey came in later that year and remained for longer hitches.

Whiteman was still very much in the market for jazz talent by autumn, and Jimmy Dorsey kept after his boss about the impending breakup of the Jean Goldkette orchestra. It might, he said, be the answer to Whiteman's problems. At Dorsey's urging, Pops went to hear Goldkette's band twice —first at the Graystone Ballroom in Detroit, then again in Atlantic City, each time with the saxophonist at one elbow and manager Jimmy Gillespie at the other. He was immediately taken with Frank Trumbauer, a sax virtuoso widely admired as a hot soloist yet equally capable of tackling the toughest scores with the best of the Whiteman reed section. Bix Beiderbecke, however, was another story. As a jazzman he was unsurpassed, Whiteman allowed. Tone, phrasing, personality—he had it all. But he was far from a technically proficient player. His reading was poor, and he had none of the background in concert playing which the "King of Jazz" valued so highly in his musicians.

Yet many of Whiteman's own men spoke glowingly of him. Bill Challis, who had joined the arranging staff while Goldkette was still at Million Dollar Pier, all but worshipped him. Trumbauer seemed to regard him at once as musical mentor and wayward son.

Finally, as leaders invariably will, Whiteman heeded his advisers. Beiderbecke and Trumbauer joined a troupe which already dwarfed any other of its kind in the entertainment business. Their coming brought the band alone, exclusive of singers, to 27 members: eight brass, eight saxophones including the virtuoso alto and clarinet soloist Chester "Chet" Hazlett, five violins, two pianists, tuba, Goldkette alumnus Steve Brown on string bass, plus banjo and drums. It boosted Whiteman's weekly payroll to just short of $10,000, three times the figure which had all but bankrupted Jean Goldkette and forced him to disband the Graystone Orchestra.

It also represented, said Esten Spurrier, a complete about-face from attitudes expressed by Bix and Tram during the brief heyday of the Goldkette band. "Bix always told me that when Goldkette was big among all the jazz group they always 'farted off' Whiteman, and the conversations would end, 'I wouldn't play with him for big dough if he asked me.'" But when the Goldkette band folded and the New Yorker fizzled and Whiteman offered Bix and Tram $200 a week each to join his band, "what a turnaround he and Frank made. They were actually flattered and pleased to have the offer, so the former statements, oft-repeated, went out the window.

"When they were negotiating salary, etc., all went well and Bix said that in his usual pattern Frank made the decisions and Bix just bobbed his knob in assent—until the price of recording came up. The offer was made of $50 a side. Frank was in the midst of agreeing and suddenly—Bix said later he could never figure out why he did it—he said no! It had to be $67.50 a side. Frank flipped! Couldn't believe the worm had turned. Bix had never done anything but go along. He said Frank showed his fright, lest that be the straw that broke the camel's back. But surprisingly, Whiteman's manager agreed and that was that.

"I thought this kind of funny and out of character when I heard it, so I asked Tram about it and he confirmed it. Said he was sure Bix had blown the works, said he could have punched him in the nose 'cause Bix and Frank had built this thing up, really wanted the job, and Bix's demand was not made in the most tactful manner."

After the Whiteman band's opening set at the Indiana Theater, Bix placed a long-distance call to Davenport. Bismark answered the telephone. His manner was cool, distant. Bix, flushed with excitement, hardly noticed.

"See, Dad? You said that if I became a professional musician I should only play with the best." Bismark said nothing. "Well, Dad, I just finished my first set with Paul Whiteman, the best in the country. What do you think of *that?*"

Little is known of Bismark Beiderbecke's response to this news, save that it was far less enthusiastic than his son had hoped. For the rest of his life, until his death in 1940, Beiderbecke *père* never fully reconciled himself to the path Bix had chosen. He blamed his son's early death on what he held to be the inevitable consequences of the professional musician's life: as "Opa" Carl had said, no fit life for a gentleman.

Closer at hand, however, the euphoria of the moment and the adulation of colleagues were sufficient to allow Bix to shrug off any disappointment at this lukewarm response to his good fortune. Bob Mayhew, kid brother of Whiteman saxophone stalwarts Nye and Jack, had joined Pops' trumpet section after Red Nichols departed, largely on his brothers' recommendations. Though not yet 20, he had turned in workmanlike hot solos on a number of Whiteman records and was cutting his section parts adeptly. Bix's arrival in the band meant the bulk of the solo work would now fall to another, but Mayhew was far from discouraged. If anything, he was overawed at having a hot music celebrity sitting next to him. Bix, perhaps sensing this, broke the ice right away.

"So you're the little son of a gun that *I'm* supposed to sound like, eh?" he said, tousling the youth's hair.

"After that," said Bob, "I'd have gone to the ends of the earth for him."

During the evening, whenever a solo came up, Bix deferred to Mayhew. "You go ahead. I want to listen to the band a bit. I'll play later." And Bobby would play the solo.

"Later," in fact, only came when Mayhew forced the issue by clapping his horn stubbornly in his lap at solo time and smiling over at the new-comer. Bix, momentarily flustered, quickly got the point and, resigned, stood to play the solos. The two got along well, Mayhew thrilled at blowing alongside his idol, and Bix only too flattered at the admiration. And their relationship, said Mayhew, was not without its amusing moments.

"He had this constant craving for peanuts—even chewed them during shows, which meant that he had to clean his horn pretty often. I remember, too, that somebody in Europe had sent him a small B-flat cornet, hand-made. I tried it and was knocked out—it was the most beautifully in-tune horn I'd ever played. I tried for months, it seemed, to buy it from Bix, but he wouldn't sell. Well, one day I made it—but in the screwiest of ways. He called me aside and told me he was desperate for some peanuts and said—maybe he was joking—that if I'd get him some he'd give me that cornet. I was out the door like a shot—and when I came back, peanuts in hand, he honored his bargain and I got the cornet."

Still more attention for Bix, this time from Hoagy Carmichael, who was at the Indiana Theater for opening night. Afterwards, Bix introduced him to Whiteman. To Hoagy's astonishment, Pops had not only heard of him but had admired his Gennett recording of his own "Washboard Blues" with Hitch's Happy Harmonists. At Bix's and Jimmy Dorsey's prompting, he played and sang it for Whiteman at a backstage piano—and was immediately drafted to do the same on a record by the Whiteman orchestra in less than a month's time. Nervous but thrilled, Hoagy agreed, and arranged to meet the band when it arrived in Chicago November 7th to open at the Chicago Theater.

Whiteman closed in Indianapolis the following night and headed west for St. Louis and a week at the Ambassador Theater. Again, Bix neglected to tell Ruth Shaffner of his coming.

"THE KING OF JAZZ HIMSELF," headlined an advertisement in the *St. Louis Post-Dispatch*. "Yes sir, he's back, in an all new program:

| NOT MERELY | IN PERSON |
|---|---|
| but the | with his world |
| super jazz | famous Victor |
| that made | Record Orchestra |
| Paul America's | including Paul's |
| greatest | Rhythm Boys and |
| attraction | their little piano |

What a show—On the Screen
"Lonesome Ladies"
A First National Picture
with Lewis Stone and
Anna Q. Nilsson

"So successful is Whiteman's trip proving to be," wrote the *St. Louis Star*, "that it is expected that he will shatter the local attendance record of last season when 113,000 persons paid $57,000 to hear the rajah of syncopation."

"Stella! Hey, Stella! Look out!"

Estelle Shaffner, lost in thought as she ambled down Seventh Street by the Ambassador Theater, glanced up just in time to avoid colliding with a familiar figure.

"Bix! Bix Beiderbecke. What are you doing here?" she shrieked as he hefted her two feet off the ground.

"I'm here with Paul. See?" He pointed to a poster advertising the Whiteman orchestra. "How's the kid, hey? How's Ruthie?"

"Well, Bix, I—"

"Hey, Stel, how'd you like to meet a wonderful fellow?" Stella blushed. "I said that I'd love to," she said, "so he took me over to the Mayfair Hotel and introduced me to Bing Crosby. And my, but he was handsome. Blue eyes, blond, wavy hair.

"It was all so funny. When I bumped into Bix like that I was on my lunch hour from my job as a salesgirl for, of all things, Philadelphia Cream Cheese. It was a new product then, and I was one of several hired to plug it. Well, after I met Bing and we made a date for the evening, I went back to work, sold all my samples in no time, got off work a couple of hours early, and rushed out and bought a whole new outfit. I must have really talked a blue streak to sell all that cream cheese that fast."

Bix and Bing had taken immediately to one another. They appeared to share an easygoing approach to most of life's tribulations, as well as a fondness and near-awesome capacity for bootleg gin. But the making of music was something else; both took it seriously, and Crosby often confessed himself in awe of Bix's absorption in and knowledge of the world of concert music.

That evening Bix and Ruth, reunited, joined Bing and Stella after work and made the rounds of some favorite haunts, ending up at "The Wedge" which was just the old "Joe's" renamed and under new management. There was a band, Estelle said. Bix sat in on cornet and Bing sang a few numbers.

Inevitably, when Whiteman closed in St. Louis and declared a couple of days off prior to opening in Chicago, Bix stayed behind with Ruth. He'd put on a bit of weight and grown a cute little Paul Whiteman moustache, she thought. But he was still the same sweet, utterly frustrating Bix. Two days whirled by before their eyes, and then, again, it was time to go. Bix and Ruth, forever standing on railroad platforms. Talk of marriage, of someday and wait for me. Ruth beginning now to wonder about it all. Gotta get established with Paul, Ruthie, but I'll be back for you. Be patient. Patient? Second choice again. Music first, and Bix's way now clearly up, a star in the ascendant. Ruth Shaffner felt the magic of Arcadia nights begin to slip away.

"Don't worry, Bix. It's all right. I'll wait." Even as hope, little by little, started to die in her heart.

Off and running, for a week at the Chicago Theater, and all the musicians coming to listen to their heroes.

The Jazz King is here in a Giant Stage Production: augmented orchestra, singers, smashing stage tableaux, comedians, color settings, new melodies, new comedy stunts, jazz, jokes, smashing thunder, and beautiful, beautiful music.

Thus the *Chicago Daily News* for opening day, November 7. A contemporary review mentioned that the highlight of the program was "Ulderico Marcelli's arrangement of the *William Tell Overture* (in jazz time) . . . featured with great success at the Tivoli and Uptown Theaters recently." Some Whiteman musicians recalled ending their Chicago programs with an all-out, gala performance of Tchaikowsky's *1812 Overture*. While this is possible, they may be thinking of the band's return to the Chicago Theater in mid-1928, so colorfully described elsewhere by Louis Armstrong.

After the show, Bix and the Dorseys, with Hoagy in tow, went over to jam at Sam Beers's "My Cellar," known among musicians as the "Three Deuces" after its address, 222 North State Street. The name was also, said Mezz Mezzrow, a parody on "Four Deuces," one of Chicago's biggest syndicate-run brothels. They jammed all night. Chicago pianist Oro "Tut" Soper was among the throngs of jazzmen packed into the place. "It was a madhouse," said Soper, "with at least a hundred musicians present and all seemingly wanting to sit in and play. I played two old warhorses, 'Royal Garden Blues' and "Jazz Me Blues.' Later on, Jess Stacy and Eddie Condon showed up, as did George Wettling, Gene Krupa, Don Carter—all drummers—plus Joe Sullivan. The music and blues went on until five or six in the morning."

A greatly reduced Whiteman orchestra assembled at Victor's Chicago studio at 9 A.M. Friday morning, November 18, just two weeks later, to do Hoagy's "Washboard Blues." Even before a note was played there was trouble. "I'd pared down the instrumentation quite a bit to get the effect I wanted," Bill Challis said, "and Henry Busse was not included. Busse found out about it and hit the ceiling. He went to Paul and said he had a contract that called for him to make every Whiteman record. I told Paul that my contract allowed me freedom in arranging." This clash posed Whiteman with a dilemma. Busse had been his trumpeter back in the Palais Royale days and had stuck with him all the way, through good times and bad. The two men were close personal friends, and Busse's muted effects had made such recordings as "Hot Lips" and "When Day Is Done" big sellers for the Whiteman band. Though sneered at by jazzmen, all the more for his reputation as a hot trumpet man in the eyes of Whiteman's public, Busse was regarded as an indispensable cog in the machine, and pulled down a salary to match. Yet Bill Challis had joined the "King of Jazz" on the strength of his accomplishments as a modern, forward-thinking arranger of jazz scores.

Whiteman thought about it, and ultimately decided in Challis' favor. The decision set ill with Busse, sowing a dissatisfaction and sense of injury which was to culminate several months later in his departure from the band.

The veteran trumpeter seethed all the more when he discovered Whiteman's arrangers starting to write Bix into concert scores in which there was no hot requirement. It had all started, said Esten Spurrier, when Bix, during a rehearsal, played over perfectly a passage which had stumped the reedman to whom it had been assigned. "So Bix told me they let him play it on the recording; it was his ice-breaker. Before, whether because of resentment on the part of Grofe or even Bix's $67.50 fee for recordings, they'd left him out. Now he was in. Bix played it for me, but I can't remember which record it was on."

Busse stayed out of "Washboard Blues." Hoagy, tense, showed up early, and was carefully running down his lyrics when the musicians began to arrive—Bing Crosby among them. "Bing kept hanging around near the piano, listening to me rehearse the number, and I wondered why," said Carmichael. "Paul later explained that he wanted Bing to be my substitute in case I broke down on the vocal job."

Bix and the Dorseys do a one-chorus up-tempo ensemble midway through "Washboard Blues," negotiating its unconventional melody and irregular bar structure with ease. The rest is given over to Hoagy's oddly appealing Indiana twang. Leroy Shield, who had supervised several of the Goldkette band sessions, was at the controls, and when they finished the first—and ultimately issued—take, said Carmichael, he came out and "I'd have sworn there were tears in his eyes."

Whiteman had meanwhile moved from the Chicago Theater to the Uptown, and now transferred yet again to the Tivoli. He was still packing them in, and had taken to spotting Bix and the Dorseys in a small hot combination out in front for a few numbers each night, an unexpected bonus for the jazz fans in the audience. The rest of the Whiteman act was by now an entertainment tradition, complete to trombonist Willy Hall playing "Stars and Stripes Forever" on a bicycle pump. Hall, like Busse, was a valued part of the troupe—and like the trumpeter he was one of the few who drew the maximum band salary of $350 weekly. Only arranger Ferde Grofe, at $375, topped them.

The combination of Hall's onstage antics and his favored status in the band made him a natural target for practical jokes, said Steve Brown. "But he was such a good sport about it . . . pretended it was all in the act. Things like guys putting talcum powder in his bicycle pump, or sometimes water, along with powder in his trombone. This would put him in a white cloud, or almost drown him. Yet he managed to finish the act and laugh about it."

Whiteman's "Rhythm Boys," too, were a surefire stage success, said Brown. Alton Rinker and Harry Lillis "Bing" Crosby had joined early in 1927 as a "hot piano–singing novelty duo." The step to star billing came with the addition of Harry Barris a short time later. "Rinker played piano, and Barris and Crosby would stand beside it, Bing with a cymbal in his hand, beating on it with a drumstick, while Harry slammed the top of this little piano of theirs in rhythm to their songs. Of course Harry could play piano if needed, but he never played in the act or recorded on piano with the band while I was with Paul."

Bix got his first chance to shine on a Whiteman record November 23, when the orchestra cut a Challis arrangement of Walter Donaldson's "Changes" for Victor, spotting 16 bars of muted cornet. Two days later he was featured on an equally sympathetic treatment of "Mary," a pop tune in which arranger Matty Malneck struck an effective compromise between the old guard and the jazz newcomers, to the advantage of both. He assigned solo space to both Busse and Bix, successfully exploiting the wide contrasts between them by pitting Bix-led brass against Busse's "straight" muted lead. Even more than the more widely-praised

"Changes" (on which Bix's solo so enthralled Tommy Dorsey that the trombonist begged him to "play it the same way on every take." Bix didn't —and produced two fine issued solos), "Mary" underscores the impact of Bix's arrival on the tonal possibilities of the Whiteman ensemble.

After Busse states the melody for the opening chorus in his muted "When Day Is Done" style, imparting to the proceedings the slightly stilted air of an early-twenties dance band, Bix charges in on his heels, leading the brass through the verse, tone cutting clean and silvery, with Brown's brass lifting the rhythm. A Crosby vocal, a Trumbauer-led sax section interlude, and Bix is back for an eight-bar statement completely redefining the essence of the song. Busse then returns, still muted, to lead the record out, with Bix and the brass punching counterpoint around him. Two breaks by Tram end the performance. It is a landmark both for Bix and the Whiteman band, a watershed separating old and new. Busse's days are clearly numbered; his contribution, even in the wider context of 1927, now sounds archaic, dated. Bix's way is the way ahead.

About the time the band closed at the Tivoli and headed east, Tommy Dorsey turned in his notice. Challis immediately suggested Whiteman replace him with Bill Rank, who had gone to work for Nat Shilkret in the pit band at the Strand Theater when the New Yorkers broke up. Pops said yes, and another Goldkette alumnus took over a chair in his band. Rank joined in Pittsburgh on December 12; he was to stay for a decade.

Whiteman's troupe worked its way east toward New York, playing concerts and one-nighters. Bix, Tram and the others found Pops a generous and, on the whole, easygoing boss, and only strict on one point, according to Steve Brown: "The only way Paul would fire someone would be if one broke his rule, which was, 'when playing shows, banquets, conventions, everyone must be on their toes. No drinking.' But when we played for a dance, Paul would help the boys in drinking. He did not care for such jobs."

Respect for the "King of Jazz" extended beyond the music world. He had become, in the manner of film stars and athletic champions, a superstar, an international celebrity. It was therefore wholly in character that Whiteman, upon arrival in Lansing, Michigan, for a concert and dance, should pay a courtesy call on Governor Fred W. Green, then be taken by his host on an inspection tour of the latest Ford production models.

A review in the *Michigan State Journal* of the Whiteman troupe in action took note first, inevitably, of Willy Hall, who played

> "Stars and Stripes Forever" on a bicycle pump which cannot, or at least the pumper pretends it can't, play the high note just before the close. Wilbur Hall also did a "screaming" two-horn solo with his two feet assisting.
>
> "Rhythm Boys" are new to Lansing. Two baby pianos whose lids go wham assist in the act, and there is jazz, dancing, singing, talking and much fun. Saxophone, vocal and even stringed solos were given. (Banjoist not featured. Two years before there had been.) A ventriloquist was in the act. Stringed bass being spanked with flat of the hand rather than bowed . . .

And again, on December 3: "The Whiteman band plays newer pieces with greater zest than ever before. Lansing audience puffed up with gaiety by glorified jazz. 'My boys can do anything, comedy falls to playing a dozen instruments, singing base [*sic*] and falsetto.' "

On east through Ohio, Pennsylvania and to Baltimore for six days at the Century Theater, and a pleasant surprise for Bix. His popularity among white collegiate audiences had spread with the records of the Wolverines, and he was now as much a hero on the campuses of Princeton and Yale as he had been at Bloomington. In the autumn of 1925, Edwin "Squirrel" Ashcraft, a Princeton undergraduate with a law career in his future and hot jazz on his mind, had used these same records to persuade a classmate named Bill Priestley to take time out from his guitar playing to learn cornet. Ashcraft and Priestley soon moved to the center of a well-established jazz cult at Princeton whose devotion to Bix, Trumbauer and their associates was only marginally less fanatical than that of Carmichael and friends.

Nor was jazz appreciation a new phenomenon on the New Jersey campus. As far back as 1923, Herb Sanford, later to become a respected author and radio–TV producer, had played piano in a Princeton Triangle Club jazz group. Dick Turner ("one of the greatest of college trumpet players," said Sanford) had sat in with them on a record in the winter of 1926, shortly after the Jean Goldkette Victor Orchestra had swept away most of their preconceived notions of how jazz should be played and left them all, Turner most notably, Bix devotees for life.

The Ashcraft-Priestley Princeton band took on a polish and musical sophistication unlike anything attained by the earlier groups. Arrangements were strongly Challis-flavored. Priestley's cornet, though limited in range and technique, captured some of Bix's melodic felicity. He was far and away the best of the Bix-influenced collegiate brassmen until the appearance of the magnificent but still virtually unrecognized Bob Bruce with Carl Webster's Yale band of 1929.

*Napoleon Passes* was the Princeton Triangle Club show for the school year 1927–28, and come Christmas holidays it went on the road for out-of-town engagements. Squirrel and Bill could hardly contain their excitement at the prospect of a December 22 opening at the Lyric Theater in Baltimore. Bix and Tram were in town with Whiteman, and in the afternoon, between shows, the Princetonians made a beeline for the Century. "They played their latest record for us backstage," Priestley said. "It was a test pressing of 'Changes' and 'Mary.' Later that evening, Bix, Tram and Jimmy Dorsey came to our show after their last performance, arriving in time to hear us in our stage bit. Our arrangements, mainly by Squirrel and myself, were very much influenced by Wolverine and Goldkette arrangements. After the show we had a jam session with them which produced, I must admit, much more fun than music."

At last, after doing New Year's Eve at the Bellevue-Stratford Hotel in Philadelphia, the Whiteman orchestra arrived in New York to begin a period of intensive recording activity brought on by Whiteman's decision to leave Victor for Columbia after an unprecedentedly fruitful eight-year association.

The reasons for the shift appear rooted in rivalry with Nat Shilkret over who recorded what material. Whiteman had for years assumed first crack at whatever songs he wanted, and the fact that Shilkret was more and more often recording many of the same selections, thus undermining what Whiteman saw as his personal market, angered the "King of Jazz." Whatever the case, by the time Whiteman arrived back in New York the decision had been made. Columbia, complete with a new, custom-designed label that pictured Whiteman himself, was waiting for termination of Whiteman's Victor contract in late spring. In the meantime, the Victor management determined to make maximum use of the orchestra in the last four months of its contract, stockpiling enough Whiteman records to counter any Columbia bid to take over the market for a good time to come.

On Wednesday, the 4th of January, Pops and his musicians assembled in Liederkranz Hall for the first of 32 record dates which were to turn out some of the best music of their leader's long career, featuring Bix and Trumbauer in settings highly congenial to their individual styles.

More than three decades of jazz criticism have made a running cliche of denigrating Bix's work with Whiteman. Too little space to "stretch out," overblown arrangements, unswinging rhythm sections, unworthy musicians as accompanists, unsuitable material to play, inadequate recording techniques—whatever the viewpoint motivating such charges, most of them are demonstrably untrue, at least during the orchestra's Victor period. Their assumption of a single absolute standard in judging jazz performance is borne out neither by the facts of jazz history nor by the testimony of the jazzmen who made it. There seems, at root, a tendency to judge Paul Whiteman and his musicians more in terms of commercial success and the "King of Jazz" sobriquet than on the actual merits of the music.

This is unfair. Jazz, once beyond its infancy, must stand or fall as a music among musics, subject to standards of excellence wholly as demanding as those of more established forms. To suggest that a Bix or Trumbauer solo on one of these Whiteman Victor recordings is any less decidedly jazz—or in any way less good—than one by Louis Armstrong or Coleman Hawkins ignores the fundamental variegation which is one of the music's basic strengths. Admittedly, Whiteman's was not a jazz ensemble in any strict sense of the word; nor did it set out to be. It was a popular-music orchestra, comprising men widely acknowledged as some of the finest instrumental virtuosi of their day outside the world of the symphony. That some of them were virtuoso jazzmen hardly set them apart—it merely enhanced their value as components in a musical kaleidoscope. Chester Hazlett won nearly universal admiration for the beauty of his tone on both saxophone and clarinet, for his effortless development of the latter instrument's "subtone" or *chalumeau* register, and for a flawless sense of dynamic and nuance. Frank Trumbauer could boast similar laurels within the ranks of musicians dedicated to playing jazz.

But if jazz was but one of several contributory elements in Whiteman's musical picture, it was none the less "authentic" or valid for such a role. In Bill Challis, he had an arranger whose work was easily on a par with that of Don Redman and other outstanding black jazz orchestrators. Admiration among such men was mutual, as close study of their influences upon one another reveals. Tom Satterfield and Matty Malneck, while less firmly rooted in an exclusively jazz milieu, could nevertheless produce consistently interesting and highly musical scores, freer of cliche than many recorded by bands with purer jazz pedigrees.

As a musical formula it worked, and well. The orchestra as heard on this series of Victor records played with a polish, euphony of sound and engaging rhythmic lift which, as Gunther Schuller has remarked, made people *listen* to popular music—jazz included—as well as dance to it. On record after record—"Changes," "Mary," "Lonely Melody," "Louisiana," "Back in Your Own Back Yard," "Coquette" and the magnificent "You Took Advantage of Me," to name but a few, the sheer quality of sound and balance are to be deeply admired—as they were by most musicians of the day, regardless of color or stylistic persuasion.

Such distinguished solo talents as Trumbauer, the Dorseys, Rank and especially Bix were for Whiteman a priceless ingredient—to be enhanced, set with maximum attractiveness within the overall musical fabric. Thus, again and again, the Challis, Satterfield and Malneck scores function as detailed, ingeniously conceived musical frames for Bix's solo efforts. Whether a full-chorus excursion, as on Challis' "Dardanella," or just two brief spots on "Back Yard," the orchestra builds carefully to a moment of perfect tension release in the ringing attack and silvery tone which were the Beiderbecke hallmark. On Malneck's treatment of "From Monday On," Bix charges out of the Rhythm Boys' jiving on a fiercely declamatory high Bb, announcing a full-chorus obligato so forceful as to take over the function of melody statement, reducing the saxophone section "lead" to accompanying status. Multiple takes of the various selections only show that it was the essence of Bix's musical personality, rather than any specific notes he played, which could turn such small miracles.

He is all over the Whiteman records of this period. Whether popping in for an eight-bar study in balanced phrasing on "There Ain't No Sweet Man" or leading the brass through a scored Challis paraphrase of a Beiderbecke solo on "Coquette," his personality—and to a rather lesser degree that of Trumbauer—dominates each performance. There is little to impugn here; Bix was in superior musical company, realizing ambitions and musical values formed in his mind long before he became involved with jazz. While he might well have sounded magnificent playing alongside the young white Chicago musicians with whom he often jammed at the Deuces after hours (and whom he doubtless inspired to considerable heights), Bix was essentially not one of them. His involvement with jazz was already showing signs of undergoing transformations far from the ken of such less complex men as Eddie Condon, Muggsy Spanier or Jimmy McPartland. As his weeks with Whiteman stretched into months, he turned increasingly to the piano, and to the possibilities inherent in modern harmony.

This was logical, and in keeping with already-discernible preoccupations. There is little difference, in essence, between Bix Beiderbecke, age 21, begging Charlie Horvath and Jean Goldkette for a third trumpet part in "Adoration," and Bix Beiderbecke, age 25, full of deep pride at having successfully executed the difficult solo passage in the second movement of Gershwin's *Concerto in F* on the Whiteman recording. Both belong to a pattern, a clear musical course, of which "In a Mist" also forms a key part, which extended far beyond "Jazz Me Blues" into areas Bix Beiderbecke was only beginning to comprehend, and then only by blind instinct.

For the moment, life with Whiteman was treating him well, and he could hardly get enough of it. He was rooming with Steve Brown, to whom it invariably seemed that "that boy could find the time to do everything but sleep. He'd always be coming in while I was going out—which was about noon. He was like a bee, jumping from one flower to another . . ." According to Brown, Bix seldom recalled which recordings he had made with Whiteman, and often said he did not feel his tone had been fully captured by the recording techniques. "Many times we'd hear records just released, things he'd played on, and he'd say, 'Did I play that?' "

The recording marathon continued. Trumbauer landed an Okeh date on January 9 and included Min Leibrook, Bix's old sidekick from Wolverine days, on bass sax. Leibrook joined the Whiteman orchestra soon after in one of several personnel changes. Three days later a small unit out of the orchestra did a new version of the old Whiteman arrangement of "San," updated by Challis with some modern touches and a three-cornet chorus for Bix, Margulis and Jimmy Dorsey. "It was one of those days when everything went wrong," said the arranger. "I got to the studio early, only to find I'd left the music at home in my apartment. Then the piano player —I forget who was supposed to be on it—didn't turn up at all. So I played the piano. They moved me way back, away from the mike, so I wouldn't bother anyone, and I played—strictly oom-cha stuff. It took us quite a few times through to get a good take. Even on the one that was issued first we rushed it out of the intro, which was slow and out of tempo."

On January 26, in one of its periodic experiments at combining the talents of star performers, Victor teamed the Whiteman orchestra with Thomas "Fats" Waller at the Camden studios. They rehearsed "Whispering" as an organ solo with band accompaniment, but cut no masters. Unfortunately, little is remembered of this unsuccessful union, and Victor's books do not list it.

Personnel changes in the band were inevitable. Things were getting unwieldy. The saxophone section could not be kept at eight; there were not enough parts in the arrangements. Steve Brown decided to return to the midwest and turned in his notice at the beginning of February. The Mayhew brothers departed, followed by Jimmy Dorsey, who preferred to freelance for the time being and work with Tommy on forming a jointly-led band of their own. His replacement was Irving "Izzy" Friedman from Linton, Indiana, who had been working around New York and knew Bix, Tram and several of the others. Roy "Red" Mayer, who later altered the spelling of his surname to "Maier," came in shortly before Hal McLean left the saxophone section.

But perhaps the most important addition of all was Roy Bargy, star of the Benson Orchestra of Chicago and Isham Jones's College Inn band, pianist, songwriter and arranger. He was a figure as deeply admired by Bix and the other hot men as by the straight musicians. Whiteman had sought him out and hired him in a fit of disgust with Harry Perrella, whose drinking on the stand had violated his boss's prime rule of performance decorum.

Bargy reported for work while the band was in Harrisburg for a one-night stand. Pops, characteristically, had forgotten he had hired him, and greeted him warmly with a "Hello there, Roy. What are *you* doing in *this* place?" Reminded of his oversight, Whiteman bade the newcomer welcome. "Just stick around for a few days and listen to the band. We'll get things straightened out in a couple of days."

Both Tom Satterfield and Harry Perrella took alarmed note of Bargy's arrival, each fearing it would be he who would now be let go. As White-

236

man musicians later recalled, both pianists went on "a real bender" that night to console one another—with the result that only Harry Barris, of the Rhythm Boys, was in decent enough shape to play piano in the band the next night.

Bargy provides an amusing sidelight to life with Whiteman. "The band uniforms at that time were hand-tailored and very expensive," he said. "There were two of them, and I was able to buy mine from one of the Mayhews—Bob, I think—and wore them without alteration." This reminded him, in turn, of the time Bix, through an oversight, packed his own uniforms in his trunk and sent them ahead while the band was on the road. He wound up borrowing one from lead trombonist Boyce Cullen, appearing onstage in an ill-fitting tuxedo to the amusement of all, Whiteman included.

The coming of Bargy was significant for Bix, whose admiration for him as both pianist and composer went back to the young cornetist's early days in Chicago. Bix turned to him ever more frequently for assistance in working out harmonic progressions at the piano. Sometimes, Bargy recalled, Bix was content to just sit and listen to him play, determined to soak up every chord.

The recordings continued through April and May, and there was little time, it seemed, for Bix to do anything but play, drink and, sometimes, sleep or eat. With all the new numbers coming at them ("Paul seemed to be recording just anything that was presented to him," said Friedman), there was plenty of rehearsing to be done on top of the record dates and one-nighters. Whiteman chose Liederkranz Hall, largely because its acoustics were favorable to the band and because most of the recordings were actually made there. One of the few outsiders to attend these rehearsals was Dick Turner. "The public was barred, but Bix asked me up anyway," he said. "I remember this one time—right after a long stretch of rehearsing—Pops called a 15-minute break and told Bix to 'take a couple on the piano.' He sat down and played 'In a Mist' first and then on and on with lovely things of his own. I'm not sure they had names, doubt it in fact, but they had lovely phrases and runs and things. It didn't seem that many of the assembled musicians (and they were the best) had ever heard him on piano before. I know I hadn't. But everyone was just enraptured and just looked at one another and shook their heads."

Just how profoundly Bix had been affected by the composers he admired and emulated was made clear during Whiteman's March 12 recording date at Liederkranz Hall. The band had just finished running down Tommy Satterfield's arrangement of "When" when Frank Trumbauer turned in his seat, caught Bix's attention, and nodded at an expensively dressed, bearded man, obviously not an American, who had entered and was standing with a group of Victor officials listening to the music.

"Say, Bix, any idea who that is?" Tram's smile betrayed immediately that he knew something Bix had better know too, and fast.

"Nope. Looks French to me."

"Very astute, old boy. That's Maurice Ravel."

Maurice Ravel. Bix gulped. Ravel, whose music he all but worshipped. A key figure in the French Impressionist school, master orchestrator, harmonic innovator, composer of *Ma Mère l'Oye* and the *Daphnis and Chloe* suites; this man's genius had produced the monumental orchestral setting of Moussorgsky's *Pictures at an Exhibition.*

"Oh, my God," said Bix. "It really is."

"Why don't you ask him for his autograph?" said Charlie Margulis, amused at his section mate's unconcealed awe. Bix shook his head.

"I couldn't. I mean, I wouldn't dare . . ."

Just then Tom Satterfield strode across the floor, a piece of manuscript paper and a pen in hand. He and the composer shook hands and spoke briefly; then Ravel, smiling, wrote something on the sheet. "Guess it didn't bother *him,* Bix," said Margulis.

Especially for the visitor's benefit, Whiteman kept the band on after the date to play through Grofe's *Metropolis* fantasy and his orchestration of Victor Herbert's *Suite of Serenades,* both of them scheduled for recording around this time. "I recall that Ravel seemed politely interested," said Roy Bargy, "but not overly enthusiastic about either composition. But he did seem to appreciate the musicianship of the players."

That evening, Bix, Bargy and other Whiteman sidemen went to hear Ravel conduct the New York Philharmonic, and later spotted the composer in a speakeasy. This time Bix was not too shy to try an approach, but advanced on his table with an air of almost fierce determination.

"Excuse me, sir. I'm Bix Beiderbecke. May I sit down?" Ravel, presumably too surprised to even think of a reason why not, indicated an empty chair. The two were soon engrossed in animated conversation, which began with Bix saying, quite audible several tables away, "I love everything you've ever done." It is not certain whether the two men saw one another again, though at least one account has Ravel visiting Bix's flat in 1931 to listen to him play his own piano works.

More recording dates, and a few innovations. Trumbauer's Okeh record of "Borneo," a pop novelty by Walter Donaldson arranged by Challis, included a Bix-Tram chase of the kind they had been doing since their Arcadia days. It was the first such musical conversation between the two men captured on record, apart from a somewhat formal exchange of eight-bar fragments on the New Yorkers' "Just an Hour of Love with You" the autumn before. "Borneo" affords a brief but tantalizing glimpse into the tight musical rapport underpinning the personal relationship between Bix and Trumbauer. Here, ironically, the real-life roles are reversed. Bix is all earnestness, serious and sober, setting out his two-bar statements with declamatory tone and attack, often cutting in impatiently on Trumbauer's dry, sometimes whimsical paraphrases. Easy to see in Trumbauer's work here the qualities which helped form the style of Lester Young, the first black tenor saxophone player to provide a viable alternative to the massive-toned, rhapsodic style of the instrument's jazz pioneer, Coleman Hawkins.

Straight man and buffoon, yet with supreme understanding of each other unparalleled elsewhere in the jazz of its time, save perhaps in the accompaniments of the cornetist Joe Smith and trombonist Charlie Green to Bessie Smith's blues singing. There is even a moment, at the end of the release of "Borneo," when Bix's lines and Tram's come together for two bars in the interval of a fourth, with the effect of wry comment on the proceedings to date and, perhaps, even on the absurdity of the song and its lyrics (". . . Wild Man Sam with his clothes all torn-eo, toot-toot-toots on his Bamboo horn-eo, and the bamboo babies start to sway . . ."). And

238

when Bix leaves three beats vacant in his next figure to let the effect sink in, Trumbauer obligingly follows suit. Until the stunning "You Took Advantage of Me" with Whiteman only two weeks later, this duet was the high-water mark in the Bix-Tram relationship, and an invaluable musical insight into both men.

Bix's small-group dixieland records for Okeh were doing well, and Tom Rockwell wanted more. On April 17, Bix, Izzy Friedman, Rank and three Whiteman bandmates went to Union Square to do "Somebody Stole My Gal" and the new Rodgers and Hart hit, "Thou Swell." Friedman recalled the date with affection. "I don't think Bix even thought about the fact that they wanted us to always include the verses to these tunes until we actually got into the studio and began running them down. Then it turned out that nobody knew the verse to 'Somebody Stole My Gal'"—so I improvised one." The Whiteman orchestra had just begun rehearsing Satterfield's concert arrangement of "My Melancholy Baby," a song with an especially tuneful verse section. Friedman merely borrowed it, with a few embellishments, for use on "Somebody Stole My Gal."

Paul Whiteman's musicians were showing their fatigue when, at last, they trooped into Liederkranz Hall for the final date under their Victor contract. There was little effort to conceal the grumbling and general unrest. Personal frictions were at an all-time high after nearly four unbroken months of making records. Among those most annoyed was Henry Busse. The onetime trumpet star of the orchestra had been given precious little featured solo space, restricted to bits on "Mary," "Love Nest" and one or two other scores. This he found humiliation enough, but to have to sit by and watch Bix, a technically unschooled player, being given one solo plum after another by Challis, Malneck and Satterfield was worse yet.

His resentment flared after the band had finished a Satterfield score on "Do I Hear You Saying," with a full-chorus solo spot for Trumbauer. Accounts differ as to how the quarrel erupted and what was said, but in the end Busse and drummer Hal McDonald, another veteran of Palais Royale days, exchanged loud and bitter words with Whiteman. Pops, under ordinary circumstances a good-natured and easygoing boss, lost his temper and fired both men on the spot. They stormed out, leaving two empty chairs with one number left to record.

Whiteman called things off for the rest of the day. When the bandsmen returned the following morning they found George Marsh, also a former Whiteman sideman, at the drums and Harry "Goldie" Goldfield, previously featured soloist with Jan Garber's dance band, in the trumpet section. Among Goldfield's attributes was his ability to turn in an uncannily accurate imitation of Busse, a talent which was to stand him in good stead in the months to come.

With these adjustments, the band went on to finish the date with Rodgers' and Hart's "You Took Advantage of Me" in a performance which marks the peak of Bix's association with Frank Trumbauer on records. As on "Borneo," they were left a full chorus for a chase. This time Bix used a straight mute, and they broke the structure up even more conversationally. Bix leads off with two bars, and Tram takes two. Bix comments for one, Tram for one, and they wind up the eight-bar episode with two bars together, obvious outgrowth of the "Borneo" exchange. They repeat the pattern in the second eight, split the release four bars each, then pull a variant on the "Borneo" trick in the last eight bars. Bix plays a humorous upward rip to begin his figure, and Tram follows with an even more exaggerated one of his own. They end the dialogue in four bars of unmistakably amiable chat. The mood befits the piece. It is, on the whole, a far lighter-hearted affair than "Borneo," catching both men in high spirits. Bing Crosby, entering immediately afterwards, catches the mood exactly, voice brimming with obvious pleasure at what has just gone on.

The sheer aplomb and total understanding in these two chase choruses go far toward explaining the near-hysterical adulation accorded Bix and Tram by so many jazzmen of the twenties. It is only to be regretted that, due to the conservatism of such figures as Eddie King, similar duets on Goldkette arrangements were never recorded. Now, with Whiteman calling the shots and clearly happy at the exposure his arranging staff was giving Bix and Trumbauer, there was every reason to believe the transfer to Columbia would afford the partnership increased opportunity to exploit its potential.

Though Whiteman, in Izzy Friedman's words, "never thought there was much future in records," he nevertheless saw to it that his switchover was attended by maximum publicity. A Fox-Movietone newsreel showed a clock ticking off one minute past midnight, heralding the end of Paul Whiteman on Victor and the beginning of the orchestra's long-awaited association with Columbia.

Columbia executives had been watching the four-month Victor recording marathon with growing concern. They saw a big Victor sales push in the offing, backed with dozens of Whiteman records. The only way to offset this, they reasoned, was to amass a Whiteman stockpile of their own, and deal a steady stream of brand-new "King of Jazz" records, adorned with their specially-designed orange, green and robin's-egg-blue "picture" label, to make it clear that the Paul Whiteman orchestra was Columbia property. They scheduled the first of 14 record dates for the day after the orchestra returned to New York from a successful two weeks at Loew's Metropolitan Theater in Boston.

Bix, especially, was happy. He was playing well, surrounded by top-flight men who clearly admired him as deeply as he did them. He was being given featured spots on scores by three sympathetic arrangers, and even being written occasionally into more and more difficult Grofe productions.

He and Friedman showed up together at the Columbia studios shortly before nine o'clock the morning of Saturday, May 12. Bill Rank was waiting at the studio door, and he didn't look happy.

"Hey, Bix, we got problems." He nodded in the direction of the glassed-in control room. "Take a look at who's gonna be supervising our sessions in this joint."

Bix, curious, walked in to get a better look. He froze on the spot and went white. "No! Oh, my God, no!"

There, sitting behind the glass, was the familiar pear-shaped figure of Eddie King.

# Paul Whiteman
## and His Orchestra

*Contents*

*Personalia*

**Paul Whiteman**
Known in America as the "King of Jazz," and accepted in Great Britain as the master of modern rhythmic music. Paul is a self-made man and a self-taught musician, originally a violinist, but now undoubtedly a brilliant conductor. His orchestra has always set a peerless standard for legitimate musical qualifications and has been for many years the initiator of all that is best in ideas and progress. The "jazz" *maestro* has visited England twice with his famous orchestra, and on both occasions left an indelible mark on British dance musicianship.

**Paul Whiteman's Rhythm Boys**
The "hottest" thing in harmonised rhythmic vocalism. These three *voices* seem able to do all that a complete orchestra can do. Their range of tone colours, rhythmic phrasing, comedy, and orchestration are works of great musical craftsmanship. Only known in this country by their records, but famous, nevertheless, through them.

**Paul Whiteman's Orchestra**
The most universally acclaimed orchestra in the world. As a concert band or "hot" dance band, it possesses a distinction and finish which cannot be surpassed by even the world's best symphony orchestras; in fact, its members are all brilliant and thoroughly well - schooled musicians, who would be equally at home with legitimate music. Whiteman records sell all over the world.

**Frankie Trumbauer**
Paul Whiteman's "hot" saxophonist. Leader of his own recording bands, "Frankie" has for years set the standard in saxophone style. Many of his choruses and ideas are "lifted" bodily from his records to be played by his admirers in their own bands.

**Chester Hazlett**
Solo saxophonist of Paul Whiteman's Orchestra, Chester Hazlett possesses the most beautiful silvery tone and the virtuosity of a concert platform artist. Noted, among other achievements, for his "sub-tone" clarinet playing, which has aroused much discussion in the musical world.

**Leon ("Bix") Beiderbecke**
Universally acknowledged to be supreme in the field of "hot" trumpeters and one of the most prolific recorders. He allies to a beautiful style what has become generally known as the "Bix" tone, the ability to feature which is the aim of his trumpet-playing admirers.

**Charles Margulis**
Solo trumpet and a musician of vast technique and orchestral solidity. He is one of those musicians, so typical of the Whiteman personnel, who could take first trumpet in any other orchestra in the world, straight or rhythmic.

**Ed Lang**
Pioneer of the Spanish guitar in the dance band, and a profound musician. Has certainly made more records as a guitarist than any other in the business, and for years has kept himself right in the forefront of the world's "star" plucked-string instrumentalists. A stylist to and of the finger tips, and an initiator of new ideas.

**Jack Fulton (Jr.)**
Trombonist and vocalist. An excellent musician, Jack Fulton also enjoys great distinction as a singer. His renderings of "Romana," "Little Spanish Town," "Lover, Come Back to Me," "Sweet Sue," etc., are still looked upon as the "classics" of Paul Whiteman's records.

Special *Melody Maker* supplement on the Whiteman orchestra, 1928.

ALL PHOTOS IN THIS SECTION COURTESY MELODY MAKER

# Chapter 17

Bix's shock at encountering his onetime tormenter gave way quickly to cool appraisal. Eddie King might have moved on in the world, but so had he, and the Bix Beiderbecke who was now featured cornet soloist with Paul Whiteman bore little resemblance to the apprehensive kid who had trembled through "I Didn't Know" three and a half years before. No point in getting rattled; King was just a funny, fussy little man, and Paul Whiteman's orchestra wrote its own ticket, here no less than at Victor. Bix strode into the studio.

"Good morning, Mr. King." King looked up, startled.

"Eh? Ah, yes. Good morning, Beiderbecke. Good to see you again." That was all there was to it. Bix soon forgot his apprehensiveness as the band dug in for another siege of recording, this time with a heavy emphasis on concert works. A few Challis scores, notably a good one on Willard Robison's "Tain't So, Honey, Tain't So," punctuated an almost unbroken diet of Grofe production numbers.

"Tain't So" offered its share of recording studio problems. Bing Crosby had to enter with no introductory chord, and kept losing his note—until Challis came up with a dime-store pitchpipe. Bix fluffed a number of solo entries, ruining several takes. Things kept going wrong, Jack Fulton said, until the ninth take. "It got to the point where all Paul had to do was to produce the sheet music and the guys would wince—you know, 'Oh no, not *that* again.'" Finally, on June 10, it went right, with Bix contributing a solo which numbers among his most creative, full of a rhythmic elasticity rare in early jazz forms.

The association with Columbia was producing problems in some unforeseen areas. The orchestra was recording heavily, but the increased clarity of the Columbia equipment appeared less sympathetic to the band sound on the whole than had been the case at Victor. Even allowing for experimentation with balance and placement over the first few sessions, the ensemble warmth captured on the Victor records—and the ringing sound of Bix's cornet in solo—appear not to have survived the move to Columbia.

At least part of the trouble, in the view of the respected British sound engineer, musician and critic John R. T. Davies, lay in technical contrasts between Victor and Columbia recording.

"It is understandable," he told the authors, "that an orchestra should receive a different treatment in each studio, but there is also a discernible difference in recording characteristics. With Victor, a "hump" around the 600 cycle-per-second area brings a fullness containing an exaggeration of

## PAUL WHITEMAN and HIS ORCHESTRA

Personnel according to Key : 1 Paul Whiteman, 2 Chester Gaylord (Vocalist) 3 Ed. Pinder (Trumpet) 4 Roy Bargy (Piano), 5 Skin Young (Vocalist), 6 Lon Hayton (Piano), 7 Mifford Lolbrook (Bass Saxophone and other Basses), 8 Rube Crozier (Saxophone), 9 Charles Strickladden (Saxophone), 10 Kurt Dieterle (Violin), 11 Frank Trumbauer (Saxophone), 12 Mischa Russell (Violin), 13 Izzy Friedman (Tenor Saxophone and Clarinet), 14 Bill Rank (Saxophone), 15 Matt Malneck (Violin), 16 Jack Fulton (Trombone and Vocalist), 17 Charles Margulis (Trumpet), 18 Mike Pingatore (Banjo), 19 "Bix" Beiderbecke (Trumpet), 20 Wilbur Hall (Trombone and Comedian), 21 George Marsh (Drums), 22 Boyce Cullen (Trombone), 23 Mike Trafficante (Bass), 24 "Red" Maier (Saxophone and Flute), 25 Harry Goldie ( Goldfield (Trumpet) 26 Chester Hazlett (Saxophone)

Key to Personnel

## PAUL WHITEMAN'S RHYTHM BOYS
### AL RINKER—HARRY BARRIS—"BING" CROSBY

LEON ("BIX") BEIDERBECKE

CHARLES MARGULIS

PAUL WHITEMAN

FRANKIE
TRUMBAUER

CHESTER
HAZLETT

ED
LANG

JACK
FULTON (Jr.)

studio resonances, which—while imparting a great warmth to the recording—tend also to confuse the sound somewhat. The Columbia recordings, on the other hand, have a similar 'hump' in an area about an octave higher, a pre-emphasis which yields a certain presence, yes, but with a slightly clinical harshness in reproduction.

"In the first instance the tone of Bix's horn is full, round and open, emanating from well down in the throat of the instrument; in the second, that same tone, while still clear, enjoys none of the sympathy abundantly evident in the Victors, the audible beginnings of the sound appearing to be only in the bell, or flared section, of the instrument."

Davies subjected several Whiteman Victors and Columbias of spring, 1928, to similar experimental changes of characteristic, straightening out the humps and opening the tonal ranges of the top and bottom of each. His conclusions: "The Columbias remain clinical, while the Victors unfold deliciously into airy vistas of sound, with truly excellent separation, presence, fullness and intelligibility barely hinted at in even the best reissues available to date. It is in such recordings as these that the full majesty of Bix Beiderbecke's sound is captured." Some later Columbias, Davies added, appeared to approach the sympathetic bias of the Victors, though with no discernible regularity.

The band was not ranging far afield while its glut of Columbia recording dates continued. Nearly the sole exception was a two-week stretch at the end of May which took them to Detroit, then home by way of Buffalo, New York. The Detroit engagement, a week at the Capitol Theater, afforded Bix an unexpected reunion with Esten Spurrier, one the other Davenport cornetist never forgot:

"In the spring of 1928, probably May, Marion McKay and his Victor recording orchestra had come from California, where they played Fatty Arbuckle's then famous "Plantation" in Culver City and were booked into the Oriole Terrace, Detroit. Well, McKay had also booked for the summer a famous eating and dancing resort at Long Lake, near Flint, Michigan. Then he got a much better offer at a lake near Jackson, Michigan. Being hungry, he wanted to keep both summer jobs. So his drummer, Red Curtis, knowing that I was in Davenport for the winter and that Davenport always had good bands and musicians, suggested that I front the band at Long Lake and after a few days McKay would get called to California on account of sickness or some silly reason, actually going to Jackson, and I would complete the Long Lake season.

"I took Jimmy Hicks's band from Davenport with me and we went to Detroit for preliminaries—picking up McKay's recording arrangements, rehearsing, and all that. Well, much to my surprise and delight, I found Paul Whiteman was doing a stage engagement at the Capitol. Because Bix and I were friends, I had to get him to come out to the Oriole Terrace so all the guys could meet him, maybe even get him to play a tune or two, especially since Detroit was Bix's old stomping ground and everybody knew him. I just knew it was asking the impossible—that it would be an imposition, so I took off for the Capitol Theater alone, not wishing anyone to witness my rebuff. I got there just before the band went on, saw Bix for only a couple of minutes, and he said to meet him after the show at their hotel out on John R. Street—which I did, and apologetically stated my mission. I told him I'd understand if he couldn't make it, but if he could just peek in for a minute and shake some hands it'd be just terrific. He said he'd sure try.

"I went back to the band, told them not to expect Bix, but that he'd try to get over for awhile even though busy, but that we wouldn't ask him to play. Imagine my surprise when Bix and a buddy from the band whom I don't remember walked in and Bix had his horn under his arm. I was almost speechless, but asked him how he got away. He said he knew it meant a lot to me, that he couldn't think of me losing face, and had brought his horn for two reasons: so we could play together and besides, the guys would have felt let down if he hadn't played. So he spent the rest of the night there and let whatever other commitment he'd made slide. Had a great time . . . how could I ever forget such a tremendous show of friendship and loyalty?"

Back in New York, Bix ran into Jimmy McPartland, by then solo cornet with Ben Pollack, at a Park Avenue cocktail party. The Pollack band was out of work, and money was short. Said McPartland: "Eight of us, including the Goodman brothers, were in one hotel room, and we were really scuffling for food. I told Bix I thought it was all pretty ironic—here I could get all the drinks I wanted for free, but didn't have enough money for a sandwich. He took me over into a corner and pulled out $200. I told him $10 was enough. He laughed. 'Don't worry about it, kid. You'll be making some money soon. Then, when you can see your way clear, you can pay me back.'"

Whiteman's recording activities ended for the summer with "Tchaikowskiana," a medley of themes by the Russian composer orchestrated by Herman Hand, who shortly thereafter went from a French horn chair in the pit of the Paramount Theater to writing musical scores for sound movies. Whiteman had promised his musicians a vacation at the end of July, but first there was the prospect of more than a month out of town, most of it in Chicago, doing the usual circuit: Chicago Theater, then the Uptown, and finally the Tivoli.

Bix felt no pain at the idea. Chicago had places to jam, old friends, good musicians by the dozen eager to play at any hour of day or night. Louis Armstrong, too, was by now well established around town, splitting his time between the big bands of Clarence Jones and Carroll Dickerson, playing ballrooms and theaters. Bix hardly could have expected Louis to take time out to come and hear him with Whiteman, but this is exactly what happened; the trumpeter showed up for the first show at the Chicago to hear the kid from Davenport "blow some of these big-time arrangements." Among the selections Louis remembered most vividly were "From Monday On" (". . . those pretty notes he blew went right through me . . .") and "the overture by the name of 1812." In the Tchaikowsky piece's closing bars, said Louis, "they started up shooting cannons, ringing bells, sirens howling like mad . . . but you could still hear my boy, blowin' right through it with that pure tone of his. No matter how loud the other cats were blowin', he cut right on through.

"Afterwards I had to go backstage and say hello to him. And that's something I don't usually do. You know, some people don't act the same —oh, I don't know . . . maybe it's nervous tension or something . . . but not Bix. He received me with opened arms. I told him that I was playing over at the Sunset Cafe out on the South Side. When he finished work that

Bix, sporting a brand-new moustache, became a featured soloist with the Paul Whiteman orchestra in late 1927. PHOTO COURTESY MARY LOUISE SHOEMAKER

night he came directly to the place and stayed till the customers left. Then we locked all the doors and had ourselves a nice little jam session . . . Bix and his friends, and my gang. Hmmm . . . I've never heard such good music since. Bix had a way of expressing himself—his music would want to make you go right up to the bandstand, shake his hand and make yourself known."

Other present that night have corroborated the substance of Louis' recollections about this memorable jam session—all except for the location. Louis was working regularly with Dickerson at the Savoy Ballroom, having left the Sunset around the end of 1927. He was still there, however, during the Whiteman orchestra's November 1927 run at the same three Chicago theaters. In view of this, it is not unjustified to assume that Louis thought of the Sunset in recollecting events which actually occurred either at the Savoy or perhaps even another South Side location.

At all events it was a session to remember. Bix brought with him Rank, Friedman and Bargy; the presence of Earl "Fatha" Hines in Dickerson's band suggests that Whiteman's pianist spent most of the time listening rather than playing. Other Dickerson hot men of the time included Jimmy Strong on clarinet and Fred Robinson on trombone, both of whom appear on Armstrong's classic recording of "West End Blues."

This night, said Friedman, both Bix and Louis played their horns, "but it wasn't a cutting session, not in the least. It was a real blending of ideas. We just played with these guys like old friends." Bargy, especially, remembered a ferocious version of "Tiger Rag" on which Louis "played 20 or more choruses, each one higher than the last, which broke things up completely."

"Yeah," said Friedman. "He really got right up there, didn't he? Bix, of course, took a different approach, but they blended." At one point Armstrong, grinning, watched Friedman negotiating an up-tempo solo. "Man, aren't you the technician," he drawled, not without a bit of tongue-in-cheek. The nickname "Technician" stuck with its recipient for years.

The Chicago run might have freed the full Whiteman orchestra from the rigors of the recording studio, but not Bix and Tram. On Thursday, July 5, remembered by one and all as the hottest day of the summer, the whole Trumbauer group stripped to their underwear in the Okeh Chicago studios while recording "Bless You! Sister" and "Dusky Stevedore." Dee Orr and Harry Gale, both drummers and both key figures in Bix Beiderbecke's early career, turned up to watch—and promptly were drafted for duty: Gale to play drums, Orr to sing.

Another studio guest in these summer days was brother Burnie, fresh in from Davenport for a reunion with Bix. "I sat under the piano most of the time," he said, "just to keep out of the way and because it was cooler under there. I don't remember a lot about it, save for how amazed I was that no one knew before they started recording just what numbers were to be recorded." The truth of this bit of information is readily apparent in the first 16 bars of "Dusky Stevedore's" opening chorus, where Bix misreads his melody line, misplacing each figure by two beats but using his unerring ear to alter its cadence resolutions to fit. He did it so well, it appears, that Okeh decided to release the master anyway.

With the end of the Chicago run Whiteman broke up the band for a two-week vacation. Bix, back in Davenport, jumped promptly into a round of visits and sitting in around town. Herbert Ross Reaver, then working his way through chiropractic school by playing banjo in various Davenport bands, recalled Bix's arrival one night at Eagles Hall "fairly early in the evening, and he sat in for one tune and took several choruses. I can't recall the tune except that it was thrilling to feed him chords . . . it was at intermission time that I actually met him and shook his hand. We all stood around and talked with him and his companion, after which they left. I was so struck by his kindness. We were discussing various records of his. Although I was a nobody from the musicianship standpoint compared to him and most of the others in the group, he paid courteous attention to my views on some of his recorded choruses. In other words, he treated me as a musical equal, and I deeply appreciated that."

Sunday afternoons Bix made a point of going aboard the 112-foot double-decker ferry *W. J. Quinlan,* fording the Mississippi between Davenport and Rock Island, to see trumpeter Tony Catalano. On at least one such occasion, Reaver was working with Catalano's "Iowans" when Bix showed up. "He seemed especially pleased to see Tony and Tony to see him," the banjoist said. "After he left, Tony remarked that the first time he used Bix on a job, he, Tony, had to show him how to tune his horn."

The Whiteman orchestra reassembled in New York in mid-August, then hit the road for a quick series of one-nighters through Pennsylvania and New York State up into New England. Its chief task at this point was to break in new scores for a two-month autumn tour of 23 states and into Canada. It was to begin, characteristically, with a Carnegie Hall concert spotlighting Grofe's new scoring of George Gershwin's *Concerto in F.* While Bix and the others relaxed, Roy Bargy had spent his vacation learning and polishing the piano part to the work, written in 1925 and originally designated *A New York Concerto* by the composer.

Columbia, faced with the prospect of having its new star attraction unavailable for nine weeks in the middle of the autumn season, booked the orchestra into its New York studios beginning Tuesday, September 4, for another solid month of making records. Among the first items up for consideration was the *Concerto in F.*

Grofe had rescored the piece from its original orchestration by William Dailey, who, according to the program notes at the work's December 3, 1925, premier, had written "for full symphony orchestra and used no saxophones, muted brass or other jazz tricks . . ."

Whiteman's attempts to direct the work for recording ran into trouble right from the start, said Bargy. "He wasn't too familiar with it, and had some trouble with the last movement, especially the first time through, so he asked Bill Dailey to conduct the remakes. I was happy about that because that movement is difficult and the conductor can throw the soloist a curve with tempos too fast or too slow." As was typical of him, the "King of Jazz" paid close attention while Dailey took the orchestra through its paces, and by Carnegie Hall time was ready to direct the *Concerto* with authority.

A week in Boston in mid-September brought a welcome break in the daily recording routine—and afforded Bix the opportunity to develop a new pastime. "He decided, just like that, to participate more in joining the boys in the band who played a lot of golf," said violinist-golfer Kurt Dieterle. "On this occasion we were playing the Metropolitan Theater in

Boston, doing four shows a day, and the golfers would get up early and get in 18 holes before starting work. Bix showed up one time, and before you knew it was joining us every morning." Trudging across the links with Dieterle, Hazlett, Tram, Friedman, Rinker, Crosby and company was hardly enough to make a good golfer out of Bix, said Bill Challis, "but being out in the fresh air certainly didn't do him any harm either, you can be sure. And he really enjoyed it. Later, when he sank a hole-in-one while we were playing up Rochester way—a real beauty, 220 yards clean—he never let anyone forget it."

Each record date seemed to be saved from drudgery by some memorable or humorous happening. For a Grofe concert arrangement of "Gypsy," a quasi-Hungarian tune penned by Malneck and ex-New Yorker pianist Frank Signorelli, Bix and a couple of cronies imported a cimbalom player from a Hungarian restaurant not far from the studio. The instrument, played with hammers on open strings, is indigenous to East European Gypsy music. No one ever bothered to take the player's name down, though he is featured throughout the record. On "Sweet Sue," made the same day, Bix, playing his full-chorus solo, caught one of his fingers between valves and wound up playing nearly four bars with the first valve depressed, Jack Fulton said. This passage, toward the end of the solo, sounds characteristically unruffled, with no hint of anything amiss save in Bix's selection of notes playable with the cornet's first valve.

Surprisingly, the weeks of recording had brought little interference from Eddie King. Most Whiteman bandsmen, Bix included, either tolerated him with natural courtesy or simply ignored him. But, Bill Challis recalled wryly, there were times when even that was not possible. One of Columbia's contingency plans in view of the forthcoming Whiteman tour called for making a two-sided 12-inch record of Christmas carols for release in time for the 1928 holiday season. King, in charge of the session, decided to "help out" by supplying organ and sleigh-bell effects on both a Grofe Christmas Melodies medley and Challis' own concert scoring of "Silent Night, Holy Night."

"Would you believe it—we were there the whole day working on that stuff," said Bill. "It was so laughable and so funny—but not funny, really. There was a lot of tension in the band. Nobody felt like making things like that. But King wanted to put 'em out and boy, was he a stubborn guy! So he starts off the record with sleigh bells. Then you're coming into church, with organ and chimes and everything. He's playin' away at the organ, then he turns around and a quartet starts to hum 'O Holy Night' and all sorts of things happen. Well, we'd been at this thing since nine o'clock in the morning, and they just couldn't time it out right. So out comes King and says, 'Let's try it again.' Well, by this time the guys were really beat, tired. You know, there's a point where you get almost to exhaustion, where you can't do anything further without seeming tremendously funny. You just burst out laughing—everybody laughs and you can't do a thing. Best thing is to break it up—start another day, 'cause no matter how hard you try you'll never get it back to that point.

"But no, not King. Off he goes again with his damned sleigh bells, and by this time everybody was sick and tired of sleigh bells. And he starts off with his organ, and by this time everybody's sick and tired of that li'l funny-sounding organ. And just before he's ready to turn around and give

251

January 20.
1928    SALARIES. -
        PAUL WHITEMAN ORCHESTRA
    WEEK ENDING JAN. Jan. 20-28.
        MOSQUE THEATRE- NEWARK, N.J.

PAYROLL 3

| Name | | Instrument | | Amount | Signature |
|---|---|---|---|---|---|
| MAYER, | RED | sax | " | 175 | |
| BARRIS, | HARRY | piano | " | 150 | |
| BIEDERBECKE, | Bix | trumpet | " | 300 | |
| BOUMAN, | J. | violin | " | 145 | |
| BROWN, | S. | bass | " | 175 | |
| BUSSE, | HENRY | trumpet | " | 350 | |
| CROSBY, | BING | vocal | " | 150 | |
| CULLEN, | B. | trombone | " | 150 | |
| DIETERLE, | K. | violin | " | 175 | |
| DORSEY, | JIMMY | sax | " | 200 | |
| FULTON, | J. | trombone | " | 200 | |
| GAYLORD, | C. | violin | " | 200 | |
| HALL, | WILBUR | trombone | " | 350 | |
| HAZLETT | C. | sax | " | 350 | |
| CROZIER, | R. | sax | " | 175 | |
| McDONALD, | H. | drums | " | 175 | |
| McLEAN, | HAL | sax | " | 200 | |
| MALNECK, | MATTY | violin | " | 150 | |
| MAYHEW | BROS. | sax | " | 350 | |
| PERRELLA, | H. | piano | " | 300 | |
| PERRY, | MARIO | accordian | " | 180 | |
| PINGITORE, | MIKE | banjo | " | 300 | |
| RINKER, | AL | piano | " | 150 | |
| RUSSELL, | M. | violin | " | 150 | |
| SATTERFIELD, | TOM | piano | " | 150 | |
| STRICKFADEN, | C. | sax | " | 200 | |
| TRAFFICANTE, | MIKE | bass-tuba | " | 175 | |
| YOUNG, | A. | banjo-vocal | " | 200 | |
| MARGULIS, | C. | trumpet | " | 175 | |
| GILLESPIE | J.F. | manager | " | 350 | |
| GROFE, | FERDE | arranger | " | 375 | |
| CHALLIS | B. | arranger | " | 175 | |
| LORENZEN, | M. | stage | " | 110 | |
| BLACK, | W. | valet | " | 50 | |
| TRUMBAUER, | FRANK | sax | " | 200 | |
| RANK, | W. | trombone | " | 200 | |

Paul Whiteman orchestra weekly payroll ledger sheet from January 20, 1928.

the downbeat for 'Adeste Fideles,' Chet [Hazlett] just breaks it all up, gives out with a great big horse-whinny on his sax. It's just human nature—the guy just couldn't stand any more. You start making fun of everything and everybody."

King, undeterred, called an intermission and told the band to be back promptly after lunch to do "Silent Night, Holy Night." This, said Challis, was the last straw. Came the afternoon session, and "none of us could have been serious if our lives had depended on it. Especially Chet—he was the big practical joker, and he had a field day on this one. By this time, King was in charge of the whole works. No one in the control room, so he was doing it all himself. He'd come dashing out of the control room, stop the band, go back in. He was back and forth all the time, and it was getting ridiculous." During a break, while a couple of the musicians diverted his attention, Hazlett and one or two others tied the back of King's suspenders to one of the lead weights used to balance the turntable mechanism. "It almost pulled his trousers off when the thing started moving—and you should have seen the look on his face."

It was a considerably subdued Eddie King who supervised the next Whiteman studio session two days later—with a resultant lift in the band's spirits. Jack Fulton recalled being so happy with the way the arrangement of "I Can't Give You Anything but Love" had worked out that he burst into an impromptu chorus of it afterwards on the street corner outside— and was startled to hear a cornet pick up an obligato right behind him. He whirled—and found Bix, grinning, standing in the doorway, horn to mouth.

With less than a month remaining before the tour, Whiteman booked the orchestra on some more one-nighters through Pennsylvania, West Virginia and Ohio, ending with a dry run of the concert program in Bogota, New Jersey, close to New York but sufficiently off the beaten path to be an ideal testing ground. First stop was Harrisburg. While most of the band went down by train, Bix, Fulton, Dieterle and fellow violinist Mischa Russell hired a big seven-passenger Packard sedan and drove.

"When we got in," said Fulton, "we stopped into a diner for a bite to eat. We were all famished. There were these two guys arguing pretty heatedly over Alfred E. Smith and Herbert Hoover, the two candidates for the election coming up that November. We all got our licks in, egging on the two arguers." This particular political debate was to have an unforeseen and not altogether pleasant aftermath. "When we came out we found that somebody had slashed one of our tires. The way we figured it, the Packard must have belonged to a bootlegger at one time, because it was absolutely full of secret compartments and funny places that looked ideal for stashing booze." Bix, Russell and Dieterle stood watching, puffing cigarettes, while Fulton, sweaty and grumbling, changed the tire. "It really exhausted me. When I finished, we went directly to our hotel and I went up to my room to lie down." He was roused a few moments later by a knock on the door.

"Jack? You there?"

It was Bix. "Yeah, man, c'mon in. What's on your mind?"

After some hemming and hawing, Bix blurted it out. He was conscience-stricken at not having helped with the tire. He apologized repeatedly and at length. "I told him it was all right, and that I wasn't mad or anything.

But he didn't believe me. He kept insisting that I must be annoyed, and to please forgive him. I told him, in the end, that the only thing that *would* annoy me was his endless apologizing, and to knock it off. He quit after that."

Dick Turner showed up in time to catch the band that evening at the Harrisburg Coliseum. "What a huge place *that* was," he said. "And my God, when Bix and Tram played their chase routine on "You Took Advantage of Me,' I thought the crowd would shout the roof off. They really sounded terrific.

"After the job, the two of us, Bix and I, hunted up a bottle joint. Bix waxed very loquacious under the spell of the booze, and for the first time I heard many of his personal views on music and life. Among other things, he said again and again that Louis [Armstrong] was the only current musician he'd go out of his way to hear."

Bix was by then more and more often "under the spell of the booze." From all accounts he had developed a near-limitless capacity to drink and remain in apparent command of his faculties. At least part of the reason he—and many fellow musicians—drank so heavily lay simply in the fact that alcohol, Prohibition or no, was readily available in considerable quantity, if not in outstanding quality. Musicians drank; it was a social factor in their lives, making the upside-down life of playing by night and sleeping by day, and the wearying effects of constant travel, however luxurious, more bearable.

It is difficult to pinpoint when Bix's drinking passed the point of conviviality on its headlong plunge into excess and, finally, addiction. Those of his colleagues who survived have been discernibly close-mouthed about it, preferring to skirt the subject altogether or, at best, dismiss it with a regretful shake of the head. What can be said with safety is that by the time the Paul Whiteman orchestra left on its 1928 grand tour, Bix Beiderbecke was drinking more than he should. The state of his health upon his return to New York more than bears this out.

"Bix's one bad trait," said Bargy, "was that he could not control his drinking, and that undoubtedly led to his early death. He was a gentle soul, a true gentleman who had great respect for good women and never got out of line in their company; always ready to praise other musicians, unwilling to knock even the bad ones. His one failing was the alcohol—he just could not handle the stuff."

But why? Easier, at first glance, to isolate what was *not* responsible. Bix's own remarks, coupled with the recollections of many colleagues and friends, should be enough to dispel any notion that he was "driven to drink" by the alleged frustrations of not being able to give free rein to his creativity as a jazz cornetist within the Whiteman orchestra.

"I remember him telling me how much he liked the Whiteman band, how he looked on it as a terrific musical education. He was learning from the musicians, and he got a big kick out of the arrangements Paul had. He really enjoyed himself—felt that it was the best means to learning his profession." Thus Jack Teagarden, a musician astute enough to realize from the outset that Bix, no matter how gifted a jazz improviser, was not the sort of jazzman who, in another colleague's apt phrase, "just had to play that horn or croak." His telephone call home to Davenport the night of his debut with Whiteman neatly sums up Bix's attitude toward being a member of the "King's" court. He was with the best, and was playing alongside musicians whose technical mastery of their craft filled him with awe. As Whiteman's musical plans became more ambitious, so did Bix's sense of challenge; and when he coped, satisfaction increased. Roy Bargy's recollection that Bix was "thrilled beyond words" at having recorded the solo trumpet part in the second movement of the *Concerto in F,* and recorded it with flawless execution, is perfectly in keeping.

As Bix's interest in piano and composition deepened, it led to ever bolder explorations of his own musical frontiers—and ever more acute awareness of their limitations. There are indications that he became increasingly dissatisfied at his own shortcomings over the months with Whiteman, more conscious of what he could *not* do. His reference to himself as "just a musical degenerate" on meeting Sylvester Ahola finds its echo in a much later, discouraged Bix, his health shot, confessing to Vera Cox in a Davenport street that he felt all his accomplishments as a jazz musician were meaningless. He was caught between two musical worlds, feeling loyalty to both.

But there was the growing conviction that in his life with Whiteman he would find a deeper satisfaction. Certainly his ability to read music had improved enormously in the "King's" brass section—he was now coping regularly with reasonably tricky scores which would have overwhelmed him even at the time he joined the band. The *Concerto in F* itself is a case in point. Toward the end of his second movement, Gershwin had written a long, legato solo for trumpet over chromatic woodwind chords. On the Whiteman record it fell not to Charlie Margulis to play, as might have been expected, but to Bix.

"I think we'd better make it clear right here and now," said Roy Bargy, "that Bix, in addition to being a great creative jazz player, had become a good sight-reader, able to hold his own in any brass section." His performance on the issued *Concerto* record seems to bear this out. He handles the long, high, taxing solo with ease and grace, negotiating the drop of a 13th from concert F above the staff to low Ab three times with an assurance and accuracy which give the lie to decades of assertion that Bix never learned to read well or never became an accomplished cornetist in any non-jazz sense.

When, in a Harrisburg hotel room, Dick Turner picked up Bix's new gold-plated Bach cornet and played, note-for-note, the Beiderbecke chorus from the Wolverines' 1924 "Riverboat Shuffle," Bix was little short of annoyed. "What on earth did you play *that* for?" he demanded.

Turner, astonished, explained that it was his favorite Bix solo—a remark which puzzled and upset the cornetist. For him, the Wolverines records were crude, musically simple-minded, one-dimensional and without depth. Perhaps, he told the flabbergasted collegian, "the years will forget them." Ironically, Bix retained great affection for the music of the Original Dixieland Band, his first inspiration; but there is the suspicion that this was as much nostalgia as expression of actual taste.

Then, too, there was Davenport. Despite his apparent rebellion against his home town and its way of life, there is little indication that Bix ever really eschewed its deeper values. But in becoming a professional musician over his parents' objections and attempts to stay his course, Bix had violated the Davenport code, and most of his adult life may be viewed as a long unconscious struggle to eradicate a sense of guilt by striving for "respectability" within his chosen field. It is arguable that his deep enjoyment of membership in the Whiteman orchestra—and his obsession with regaining his place in it after being forced by illness to leave—are closely related to Bix's inability to come to terms with this inner conflict. There was little hope of flexibility or real understanding from Bismark or Agatha; they were too intrinsic a part of Davenport and its culture for significant insight. Nor was Bix's understanding of himself and his circumstances sufficient to cope. His ultimate destruction, viewed in this light, was all but inevitable.

He and Turner spent most of the following day on the golf links, Bix, as usual, showing more enthusiasm than skill. But this failed to deter him from betting money on every hole they played. "We were both terrible," said Turner. "Up around 100 most of the time. But he insisted on betting anyway. Naturally, he never paid off." In the end, Bix missed the Whiteman train to Erie, and found himself stranded in Harrisburg, dead broke. "All he had was a $300 check from Okeh and nobody would cash it," Turner said. "I finally lent him $30 to get to Erie."

"Paul Whiteman Presents," the program for the 1928 tour, received its premier performance Sunday night, October 7, at Carnegie Hall. It took in facets of the orchestra's personality ranging from "Yes, Jazz Is Savage," a capsule history of jazz featuring Bix, Bill Rank and Izzy Friedman in a dixieland setting, through arrangements of "Sugar" and "Tiger Rag" to such straight items as Chet Hazlett playing his own "Valse Inspiration" on the alto saxophone. Both Gershwin's *Concerto in F* and Grofe's *Metropolis* suite were accorded featured spots. Even Willy Hall got a chance to display his bicycle pump and other paraphernalia on "Free Air: Variations Based on Noises from a Garbage," as scored in quasi-baroque style by Grofe.

For the Carnegie Hall concert, Whiteman scheduled one additional selection, coming immediately after *Metropolis* on the program: Bix Beiderbecke at the piano, playing "In a Mist" accompanied by Bargy and Hayton at separate grands of their own. Each man was invited to choose his own piano for the performance, said Bargy. "The Steinway Company housed the pianos for Carnegie Hall; it was just a short distance away. So we went down, all three of us, that afternoon to pick out our instruments. I'll never forget it. On top of each piano was a name card showing which artist always used such and such a piano. I spotted one with the name 'Rachmaninoff' on it and so I chose that one. He was my idol. I forget which ones Lennie and Bix selected.

"Those pianos sure took up a lot of room onstage. Well, I was in for the shock of my life when that concert began. Right at the start, I looked out over the crowd—the place was packed—and there, in a front box, was Sergei Rachmaninoff himself, big as life! Imagine that—my idol, right out there, and me playing on his piano! Brother, was I ever scared!"

The program went off without incident, and when the time came for "In a Mist," it was a determined Bix who left the brass section and walked forward to where his concert grand had been wheeled out for him. There, in Carnegie Hall, with the eyes of thousands on him, Bix Beiderbecke, self-taught pianist, playing a composition he himself had written, with two pianists he deeply admired providing discreet accompaniment. It is only too possible to speculate on what was in his mind at this supreme moment. Roy Bargy provides some small insight:

"Everyone applauded loud and long, and Paul called for Bix to come forward and take a bow. He did, with a sort of nervous yet characteristically polite 'Thank you,' made a real quick dip toward the audience for a bow, and hurried back to the section, as though embarrassed about the whole thing."

The tour proper began the next day with a concert scheduled in Norfolk, Virginia. Bix, atypically for him, was among the first to arrive at Pennsylvania Station, lugging a big old leather valise with underwear, socks and a couple of changes of clothing stuffed inside.

"Hey, Bix, whatcha got in there, a refrigerator?" Jack Fulton called, laughing. Bix, embarrassed, grinned weakly.

"Never hurts to have a little extra room, just in case," he said barely audibly, face red. The remark proved his undoing. As Bix sipped a cup of coffee in a station snack shop, valise momentarily unguarded with the rest of the band luggage on the platform, Fulton and Trumbauer deftly snapped it open and slid in a 25-lb. brake shoe Tram had picked up off a siding. Once on the move, they forgot about the whole thing, Fulton said, until a few days later "when Bix started complaining that there must be something wrong with him because he was getting weak. We asked him why and he said, 'Well, things are getting so I can hardly lift my suitcase any more.' We had all we could do not to fall all over ourselves laughing. It took him a good week, poor guy, to discover the brake shoe, and then he took it in good spirits."

A band on the road, especially one as flamboyant as Whiteman's with its extravagant comforts and collection of temperamental individualists, is bound to produce its share of anecdotal reminiscence. Stories of this tour, some more solidly based in fact than others, abound. Some are well-documented recollections, such as the gala party thrown for the band by Mary Louise Shoemaker, Bix's sister, in Atlanta. "She kept asking me to sing, 'I Can't Give You Anything but Love,' couldn't get enough of it," said Fulton. "I wound up pretty hoarse as a result."

On to Memphis, and a chance meeting with the orchestra of Whiteman's former clarinet star, Ross Gorman. On trumpet was Wayne Rohlf, Bix's Davenport friend. "I hurried over to the Peabody Hotel where Bix was rooming and looked for him in the dining room but couldn't find him," said Wayne. "I called his room. He was there, all right. Said he'd decided to skip dinner because he wasn't feeling too well. But he said to wait—he'd be right down. Bix was like that, you know. Finally he and Tram came down and they had a test pressing of 'Margie' with them that Bix wanted to hear. Spud Murphy, who was in Gorman's band too, had a record player, so we borrowed it and played the record. It was a great time."

The band hit New Orleans on Sunday, October 28, and among the musicians flocking backstage at the St. Charles Theater during intermission to see Bix and Tram were two early Beiderbecke heroes, Paul Mares and Nick LaRocca. He greeted both men with warmth and great deference, according to pianist Armand Hug, and immediately asked after the health of Leon Roppolo, who had suffered a breakdown and been committed to a mental institution for treatment.

As they were talking, Whiteman strolled by. Drummer Monk Hazel, never one to mince words, waylaid the portly bandleader and announced for all to hear that "if you don't let Bix play more this half we'll tear this place down."

"Don't worry, boys," said Pops. "He'll have plenty to do this time."

After the show, Bix, Tram and Izzy joined Hug, Hazel and the youthful tenor sax man Eddie Miller for a session at Mares's place. In Friedman's recollection, the former Rhythm Kings trumpet star "was playing very little at this time—I think he was in the fur business." Mares had indeed left music temporarily to go into his family's business in wholesale muskrat pelts.

During the session, Hug asked Bix for some help in working out the chords to "In a Mist," and Bix gladly obliged. "He stood in back of me and put his hands over my shoulders and played the parts for me. Believe me, I shall never forget that piano lesson . . ."

Back on the train, an incident which was to leave its mark on the memory of every member of the orchestra. It was 6:45 A.M., the morning after the concert in Tulsa. Roy Bargy, shivering with a small knot of musicians on the platform waiting to board the train to Ponca City, Oklahoma, was surprised to see a cab pull up and Bix step out. "He got out and looked at the boys as if to say, 'This time, I made it.' Being no doubt more than a little punchy at that ungodly hour, he walked right on to and through this darkened train and into another one on the next track facing exactly the other way, but also due to leave at seven. When we boarded our train a few minutes later, nobody noticed that Bix wasn't with us. I guess we assumed he was in the men's room or sleeping somewhere."

Sleeping he was, but in a train now heading rapidly southeast, instead of northwest to Ponca City. A conductor shook him awake and asked to see his ticket. "I'm with the band," he mumbled irritably, and turned over. "They've got all the tickets."

"Hey, mister, ain't no band on this-heah train. What y'all talkin' about?"

No band? Bix shook himself awake. No band? Suddenly a half-remembered encounter on the platform took terrible shape in his mind. "You mean—I mean, doesn't this—this *isn't* the train to Ponca City?"

The conductor laughed. "Not on your tintype, sonny boy," he drawled. "Y'all's headin' the 'xact wrong way."

A perplexed Bix got off at the next station and began hunting up ways to get back to Ponca City in time for Whiteman's afternoon show. There were no trains due until much too late in the day to be of any use. A car was out of the question. But a filling-station attendant not far from the station came up with an idea. "Got a feller over yonder got his own biplane. Mebbe he'd fly y'all up there."

Izzy Friedman, travelling with the Whiteman entourage on the *right* train, takes up the story from there. "He sent a telegram to Paul—it was delivered while we were on the train—saying he was going to fly and would certainly be there in time for the concert. When we got into Ponca City, quite a few of us made a beeline out to the airport, such as it was— it looked as though it had until very recently been just another cornfield —to witness his arrival.

"Pretty soon this reconverted 'Jenny,' 1919 vintage, appears out of a deep blue sky, circles and makes a very good landing. We all rushed up to the plane, an open cockpit job, as Bix and the pilot climbed out. As they both hit the ground, Bix put his arms around the guy and shouted to us, 'He's the best damned pilot in the world!' And with that the pilot took two steps toward us and fell flat on his face. He was so loaded we had to support him to our cars and take them both to the hotel. He and Bix had been taking alternate sips of corn mash up there, and while Bix was able to hold it, the pilot didn't waken until seven that evening. He was Paul's guest all the rest of the evening and we went out to the field the next day to see him off."

But the story hardly ended there, Jack Fulton recalled. "Bix played the afternoon performance just fine, but while waiting for the evening one to begin he found a place somewhere backstage and decided to stretch out for awhile. When he awoke, he found he'd slept through the evening concert. Everybody had been hunting high and low for him, but this place he found was off at the other end of the building, and he hadn't heard a thing. Paul levied a fine on him, as he would any musician who missed a performance. But how ironic, after all that effort to get there in time! And there he was, in the building all the while."

The band swung north, toward Iowa. There was little time off, just a lot of traveling and at least one concert, sometimes two, every day. The pace seemed to be getting to Bix; he complained of frequent nausea and weakness in his legs. He was often fatigued and sometimes, especially while on the train, irritable. "He stayed in his berth as much as possible," Fulton said. "He hated the train, felt that trains had it in for him. He told me once, 'This train can go a hundred miles on a straight course while I'm in bed or sitting down, but all I have to do is get up or try to walk down the aisle and it'll whip 'round a curve and send me sprawling!'"

Sick or not, he appeared just often enough to frustrate Fulton, Bargy and the four other regulars in the Whiteman band running poker game: "Skin" Young, Friedman, Mischa Russell and Kurt Dieterle. "We had this rule, understood among us, that Bix couldn't play," the trombonist said. "He always won. No matter what we did, nobody could beat him. Well, sometimes if one guy would have to go to the bathroom or something, he'd ask Bix to sit in for a few minutes. I can still see this in my mind—he'd pick up all his cards at once from the table, cup both hands together, the cards held in his palms, then look around real slow at the other guys at the table. He'd slowly squeeze the cards apart, and after each card would look again at the other players, studying their faces. Took him forever to get those cards apart—it drove us nuts.

"Nine times out of ten, when we asked him, 'How many cards?' he'd say, very quietly, 'I'll play these.' It was nerve-wracking. By the time the man whose place he took would return, Bix would have all the money that had been on the table, and the game was over."

When the orchestra arrived in Clinton, Iowa, for two concerts, half of Davenport, only 30 miles distant, turned out to hear their home town boy. As the *Clinton Herald* noted, "a large crowd was attracted to the concert this afternoon, including many visitors from out of Clinton." One faded newspaper clipping, source unknown, describing these two concerts, mentioned that "one musician was given an enthusiastic ovation after every appearance." Only brother Burnie was on hand to represent the Beiderbecke family, but Wayne Rohlf, just home from his tour with Gorman, came along. "When the curtain went up after intermission, the band started to play a big symphonic introduction [to Tchaikowskiana—ed.] and Charlie Margulis blew some awfully sour notes. He stopped playing, looked at his trumpet, and discovered that someone had pulled out his tuning slide during the break. The band broke up, but finished the number as Paul did a slow burn, getting redder and redder. From where I sat, Bix looked guilty."

Finally, after a series of dates in Ohio and upstate New York, and one quick foray into Canada for a concert at Toronto's Massey Hall, the Whiteman orchestra headed for home. Bix, by now, was clearly not well. The nausea and weakness in his legs were getting more persistent, and he had caught a cold he seemed unable to shake. He remained with the band for six days of recording immediately after arrival back in New York, but finally gave in to Whiteman's urging and dropped out for a rest on Sunday, December 16. He entered a hospital in Astoria, Long Island, where his "cold" was diagnosed as pneumonia.

The clouds were beginning to gather.

The Whiteman trumpet section, mid-1928. L to R: Eddie Pinder, Bix, Charlie Margulis, Harry "Goldie" Goldfield. Taken from an advertisement for Holton instruments.

Whiteman orchestra on stage, autumn 1928. Rear row, L to R: Boyce Cullen, Wilbur Hall, Bill Rank, Jack Fulton (trombones); John Bowman, Charles Gaylord, Matty Malneck, Mischa Russell (violins). Middle row, L to R: Eddie Pinder, Bix, Mike Trafficante, Min Leibrook, Mike Pingitore, Austin "Skin" Young, Kurt Dieterle. Front row: Harry Goldfield, Charlie Margulis, Chet Hazlett, Frank Trumbauer, Irving Friedman, Charles Strickfaden, "Red" Mayer, Rube Crozier. Floor: Roy Bargy, George Marsh, Whiteman, Lennie Hayton.

PHOTO COURTESY ROY BARGY

Frank Trumbauer combining his two favorite pastimes, music and aviation, c. 1929–30.

# Chapter 18

He was back on the tenth of January, in time for a Whiteman recording date—and a sentimental reunion. Bee Palmer, whose arrival in Davenport just seven years before had added a new dimension to Bix Beiderbecke's life, was now a fixture on the New York social scene. Her parties and jam sessions were the talk of the entertainment business, and Whiteman's men numbered among the regular guests. More than one had kept after his boss to use her on a record date, and finally Pops assented: she would do two titles under his sponsorship, backed by a small hot group out of the band, with arrangements by Challis. Bix and Tram would have the featured spots.

After plowing through a Grofe extravaganza called "Chinese Lullaby" and Challis' straightforward score on "Cradle of Love," most of the band took a break while Bix, Tram, Friedman, Rank, Charlie Strickfaden and the rhythm section ran down "Singin' the Blues" and "Don't Leave Me Daddy" with Miss Palmer. On guitar was Edwin "Snoozer"Quinn, picked up by Whiteman in New Orleans. In addition to his chores in the band, Quinn's job also included accompanying Whiteman to social functions, where he was always on call to back whomever Pops chose to bring along.

From Challis' standpoint, "Singin' the Blues" offered excellent possibilities. He fashioned an arrangement based loosely on Trumbauer's 1927 Okeh record, and featuring Bix. Both tunes went well, the musicians recalled, and they were scheduled for issue on Columbia's Whiteman label under the legend "Paul Whiteman presents Bee Palmer with the Frank Trumbauer orchestra." What went wrong nobody knows, but the coupling remained, unissued, in Columbia's vaults. All trace of it is lost today, save the rumor that test pressings still exist.

Realistically, though, it is hardly likely that Bix was at anything approaching his best here. Though back with the band, he was far from well. Hospitalization had forced an unexpected cut in his consumption of alcohol—and if anything, he felt all the worse for being on the wagon. He was still weak—the effects, he presumed, of his bout with pneumonia. There were nights, even now, when he felt too shaky, not physically up to playing. Mickey Bloom and Manny Klein, who had filled in for him in December, did several evenings on short notice. He was smoking a lot, puffing nervously on cigarette after cigarette. Fellow-bandsmen found him jumpy, irritable, moodier than the Bix of old. He complained of trouble sleeping.

The band did a week in Cincinnati, then opened at the Palace Theater in Cleveland on Sunday, January 20. On opening day they all checked into the most luxurious hotel in town, the Cleveland. Exact details of what happened then may never be fully known. Whiteman musicians, almost to a man, have been uniformly reluctant to discuss it, preferring to dwell instead on the healthy, creative Bix of earlier days.

Bill Rank: "He cracked up, that's all. Just went to pieces; broke up a roomful of furniture in the hotel."

Roy Bargy: "It was a breakdown, all right, a major one. He was unable to make our evening performance. Paul took charge, and got him a doctor. As far as I remember, he was left at the hotel in the care of a male nurse."

The pattern of this breakdown, set against the course of events leading up to it, leaves little doubt that by January of 1929 Bix Beiderbecke had become addicted to alcohol. In connection with this, the authors consulted a number of physicians, both in the United States and Britain. These included Dr. Rodney Long, M.R.C.S., L.R.C.P., a leading British authority on alcoholic disorders. Dr. Long, frequent contributor to medical journals on developments in the treatment of alcoholism, was fully briefed on the known events of Bix Beiderbecke's life, especially the deterioration of his health from mid-1928 onward.

His view concurred with that of past medical opinion that Bix's Cleveland "breakdown" was in all probability an acute attack of delirium tremens, perhaps brought on by abrupt withdrawal of alcohol from a system already weakened by illness and in generally rundown condition.

Bix may well have regarded his hospitalization as a godsend—an opportunity to go on the wagon without having to take the difficult initial step himself. Released from the hospital, he may have decided to use the momentum of a week or more without a drink to stay sober and buckle down to the challenge of his ever-increasing responsibilities with Whiteman.

Ironically, this very determination may have helped bring on his Cleveland attack, in the form of a withdrawal fit. Pneumonia was not watched with x-ray technology and treated with the same exactitude in 1929 as is the case today. It is, therefore, not unlikely that Bix was released from Astoria as soon as his condition appeared to stablize. He may have continued to harbor pneumonia sub-clinically for some time thereafter, even developing a permanent proneness to it. The constant sapping of his bodily strength by such an illness may have left him particularly prone to the seizure at the Cleveland Hotel.

"A withdrawal fit in these circumstances," Dr. Long told the authors, "is by no means inconsistent with this man's history up to this time."

The Whiteman orchestra left Cleveland the weekend of January 26–27. Bix remained at the hotel, in the care of the male nurse. An item in the *Cleveland Press* of the day before makes it clear that Whiteman expected him to go from there home to Davenport for a brief rest, returning in time for the orchestra's first broadcast under sponsorship of Old Gold cigarettes on February 5. Whiteman, meanwhile, arrived in Detroit lacking a hot soloist in the trumpet section. At Min Leibrook's suggestion, the "King of Jazz" once again turned to Jean Goldkette for help. One of Goldkette's most promising young musicians was a cornetist named Andy Secrest, a native of Muncie, Indiana, who had played with the bands of Ted Weems and Ray Miller before joining the unit formed by Goldkette for the Plamor job in Kansas City.

Not yet 22, Secrest had fallen hard under Bix's spell. On at least one record made by this particular Goldkette ensemble, an otherwise wholly forgettable version of "Here Comes the Showboat," Secrest and his two sectionmates, Sterling Bose and Nat Natoli, can be heard swapping two-bar phrases. The influence of Beiderbecke on all three men is striking.

Secrest, moreover, was a quick and sure reader, making him, for Whiteman's purposes, the ideal stand-in: capable of holding his own on the arrangements, yet able to simulate the sound and style of Bix in solo spots. Whiteman arranged with an ever-helpful Goldkette to "borrow" the young Indianan for his orchestra's four-day stint at the General Motors Research Building in Detroit. The new man's performance over those four days was enough for the King of Jazz. He knew a good piece of insurance when he saw it, and without consulting Secrest purchased the cornetist's contract from Goldkette at the end of the Detroit engagement. When the orchestra returned to New York, Andy Secrest returned with them.

"Let me say this about my style at that time," Secrest told the authors. "I don't want anyone to say that I copied Bix. I didn't. That is, I didn't take his solos off note for note, or anything like that. You could say I was a pupil of his. I idolized the guy, first heard him play with the Wolverines in 1924. I thought his style and tone were way ahead of the times. I started playing that way because it was the style that I wanted to obtain, and by the time I joined the [Whiteman] band I sounded a good deal like him."

Once back in New York, a group of Whiteman's musicians, Izzy Friedman among them, went directly from Grand Central Station to the 44th Street Hotel to grab some sleep. But as the clarinetist walked in, a worried-looking desk clerk called him aside.

"Thank God you guys are back. I thought you'd never arrive . . ."

"Why? What's up?"

"It's that friend of yours—what's his name? The trumpet player."

"Bix?"

"Yeah. That's the one."

No point in courting gossip, Friedman thought. "He's not with us, won't be for awhile. He got sick on the road, and went home for a few days to—"

"The hell he did, mister. That's what I wanted to tell you. He's here, upstairs, and he's in terrible shape."

Friedman, startled, called over Boyce Cullen and a couple of the others while the little man in the rumpled green uniform blurted it all out. "He came in late last night. He was hurt, clutching himself here—low down. I couldn't see much, but it looked like he was bleeding. I tried to—"

He never finished the sentence. As one, Izzy in the lead, the musicians took off running for the stairs. They found Bix in the bathroom of the room he shared with Friedman, doubled over the sink in pain, holding a blood-soaked towel to his lower abdominal region. He had gone greenish-white. His eyes were glazed. He was bruised and his face was cut. He was trembling violently. He had vomited into the sink, and every new spasm convulsed him with fresh pain.

Tears streaming down his cheeks, Friedman knelt by his friend's side. "Bix, for God's sakes, what happened? Who did this?" Bix only shook his head.

They laid him on the bed and phoned Whiteman. "I'll be right there with the doctor," he said, and hung up.

Exactly what happened to Bix Beiderbecke that night has never been clarified. His own account of it was sketchy, blurred. He had managed to elude his male nurse at the Cleveland Hotel shortly after the band left for Detroit. He had simply walked out, he said, and caught the first train he could for New York. Somewhere along the line, perhaps convinced that going on the wagon had in some way brought on the trouble in Cleveland, he picked up a jug of gin and, once back in town, hit the first speakeasy he found.

From here the trail becomes indistinct. Some accounts speak of Bix and an unidentified companion having a run-in with sailors, and one of them shoving the jagged end of a broken bottle into Bix's gut during the fight. Other, potentially more sinister versions suggest that Bix, who occasionally dated showgirls and others associated with the entertainment world, had somehow angered a small-time hoodlum, who specifically came after him to exact revenge. Given the circumstances—his return to New York after an absence, his physically debilitated condition over these weeks—this hypothesis appears unlikely.

Too, the nature of his injury has never been exactly established. According to some, his attackers rammed the bottle into his abdomen. Others said the groin. One story, circulated widely among musicians, maintained that it was the other end of the bottle and another end of Bix's anatomy.

Whatever the exact facts, Whiteman's reaction when he arrived moments later with both the doctor and Bill Challis in tow was clearly remembered. "This is terrible," he said. "I want this man sent home immediately." He turned to Challis. "Make sure he's on that train, too. Get me? Don't let him out of your sight until the train pulls out of the station. Understand?"

Challis understood, and as soon as Bix was strong enough to get up and about, escorted him to Grand Central and put him on a train for home. He was still shaky, and could not walk without using a cane. Bix bore the effects of this injury the rest of his life. Eventually he was able to discard the cane, but he never lost a noticeable limp. Also, the attack appeared to have shaken his self-confidence, something already under siege on a strictly musical front.

A few days at home, however, appeared to set him back on his feet. On February 5, the day of Paul Whiteman's first weekly Columbia network broadcast for Old Gold cigarettes, Bix dropped a brief note to Tommy Rockwell at Okeh. Its tone strongly indicates that he felt he had let people down and was anxious to make amends:

Dear Tom:
    Guess you know that I've been through quite a siege and I thought I'd write you and tell you that I'm practically over it and will be in N.Y. in a couple weeks so be prepared for some bigger and better Okeh records.
    Here's hoping I see you in a week or so.

Sincerely,
Bix Beiderbecke

On evidence, it seems Whiteman was expecting him back soon as well. Grofe's arrangements of "Lover, Come Back to Me" and "Marianna," finished in the early hours of February 4 and 6 respectively for a February 7 recording date, include parts labelled "Bix."

But he remained in Davenport for the rest of February. Few outside his immediate family knew any more than what they read in the *Davenport Sunday Democrat* on February 10, which began an interview with the hometown celebrity by informing its readers that the "world's hottest cornetist of Paul Whiteman's Orchestra" was "convalescing from a recent illness at the home of his parents, Mr. and Mrs. B. H. Beiderbecke, 1934 Grand Avenue."

The full text of this article, reproduced elsewhere in this volume, reflects little more than the convoluted view of jazz and its practitioners taken by American journalism of 1929:

> Plinky-planky-plinky moans! Crooning tones!
> Ear-tickling, piercing, soul-wrenching
> melodies—that's jazz!

This first visit home brought another shock, one which Bix later recounted to Esten Spurrier. "He'd always sent a copy of every record he made home to the folks—a terrific collection and all brand new. He was proud of them and of being with Whiteman." But with a few days at home, he took to browsing around the house—and found the entire collection in their original mailing boxes, unopened. "That sort of hurt him, though he didn't say a lot about it," said Spurrier.

The Whiteman orchestra, meanwhile, settled back into its New York routine with Andy Secrest handling most of Bix's solo spots. He was doing well in reproducing the superficials, at least, of his mentor's style. But there were few of the startling turns of phrase or audacious harmonic twists which earmarked a Bix solo. Secrest's harmonic frame of reference was conventional, unadventurous. He lacked Beiderbecke's rhythmic lift, with the result that many of the Trumbauer records of this time on which he is featured tend to plod, something they seldom did with Bix present.

But things in the Whiteman band were changing, and Secrest's contribution in a role of ever-diminishing prominence was sufficient for the moment with the arrangements, even those by Challis, making less and less use of the jazz element in the personnel. The balance so clearly in evidence on the Victor records of only a year before had begun to shift. Where "Mary" had served up Bix as a main course, a score such as Hayton's "Nobody's Sweetheart" used him as little more than a garnish. No more cornet trios to punctuate and lift otherwise straitlaced readings of pop tunes. Since Steve Brown's departure, the string bass had been used far less prominently, even to back jazz soloists. The reappearance of the tuba in this role often all but threw the overall orchestral sound back half a decade.

"Nobody's Sweetheart," finally recorded that October, gives clear indication of what had happened. Opening with a full-chorus obligato for Secrest's muted cornet, it soon becomes embroiled in thematic allusions

# 'Jazz Is Musical Humor,' Says Davenport Composer and Cornetist of Whiteman's Ba

### Believes Humor of Jazz is Many-Sided; Classifi Catch-as-Catch can Music as "Sweet" and "He but Prefers the "Hot" More Than Purring Resp tability of the "Sweet"

P LINKY-PLANKY-PLINKY moans! Crooning ton
Ear-tickling, piercing, soul-wrenching melod
—that's jazz!

Put them all together and what have you?

"Musical humor," says the world's hottest cornetist
Paul Whiteman's orchestra, Leon "Bix" Beiderbecke, w
is convalescencing from a recent illness at the home of
parents, Mr. and Mrs. B. H. Beiderbecke, 1934 Gr
avenue.

And "Bixie," as his friends all call him, should know! For a year and a half he has played with the king of jazz orchestra on Whiteman's special concert tour and filled every little niche and cranny with a catch-as-catch-can tricks of melodic figures and spent hours in the recording library of phonograph and music companies recording his own compositions.

"Jazz is musical humor," he says. "The noun jazz describes a modern American technique for the playing of any music, accompanied by noise called harmony, and interpolated instrumental effects. It also describes music exhibiting influence of that technique which has as its traditional object to secure the effects of surprise, or in the broadest sense, humor."

### Those "Barrel-House" Tones!

Tracing the origin of jazz back to the gay nineties when Dixieland musicians played negrotic "barrel-house" tones into "bowlers" and blew moaning saxophones into jugs and lengths of gaspipe, Mr. Beiderbecke pointed to the date Feb. 12, 1924 when Paul Whiteman gave the first jazz concert ever given in Aeolian hall, New York, and by cacophonic combinations proved what a change came over the face of Melusina and Terpsichore in a decade.

"The jazz band's chief stim of course, was the rise of the n "blues" and their exploitation the negro song-writer, W. C. dy," the cornetist stated.

"They at once were melanc and humorous, and dealt excl ly with the singer's own en and philosophy. Their experin were convert. In today's jazz are open. The visual effe comic instruments and bodily tortions of the musicians is dispensable, a part of jazz it

Mr. Beiderbecke classifies as "sweet" and "hot." He the "hot," which slightly mo the original pandemonium of "Livery Stable Blues," more the purring respectability of "sweet," whose hush and mu throb is heard behind a balus of potted palms at debu dances.

### Humor "As You Like It

"The humor of jazz is rich many-sided," he said. "Som it is obvious enough to ma dog laugh. Some is subtle, mouthed, or back-handed. It turns bitter, agonized, and g que. Even in the hands of composers it involuntarily ref the half-forgotten suffering o negro. Jazz has both white black elements, and each in respects has influenced the o It's recent phase seems to

**LEON "BIX" BEIDERBECKE**

light of the white race's sophistication upon the anguish of the ...k."

...Bixie," as his boyhood gang ...ed him, practically grew up ... music. His grandfather, the ... Charles Beiderbecke, was a ...poser and pianist of no little ...e, and his mother, before her ...riage, was organist at the First ...byterian church in Davenport. ...usic was in the air at the ...erbecke home— "Bixie" took ...o lessons for a time from two ... instructors, not more than a ...e in all. When he arrived at ...school at Lake Forest, Ill., he ... dripping arpeggios and moon...over Chopin's nocturnes like ... mere high-brow.

**Goodbye Grieg and Lizst!**

...17 he became interested in ...in insidious and perverse in...ons which crept into popular ...c, so he bought himself a cor...and laid aside his Grieg and

...e boys told me to put more ...ican punch into melodies," he ..."A copy of 'Yes, We Have

and I was told to play like a he man."

He did. Figuratively speaking he taught the cornet to laugh by unexpected thrills, to moan by sudden perky blares, to do stunts, and to hold its head up high. He emphasized exact tempo and decisive rhythm.

After completing his course at Lake Forest, he enrolled in the school of music at the State University of Iowa. Here he droned, "one, two, three, four" on the piano while he transposed and translated notes and melodies into orchestral scores.

With his "huddle system," came the desire to start an orchestra and in the fall of 1925, he organized a motley crowd of ex-collegiates and called them the "Wolverines."

From Chicago to New York the itinerant orchestra played. Later looking for new and lucrative fields to conquer, "Bixie" played for six months with Charlie Straight's orchestra in Chicago and three years with Gene Goldkette's band in Detroit, which broadcast programs over station WGN.

**We Want More!**

It was on one of the musical tours of that organization that Paul Whiteman heard him play and urged him to join his orchestra. But contracts are contracts and not until his contract was up did he make the change.

Since joining Whiteman's orchestra "Bixie" has played one of the three concert pianos besides being cornetist, and director of one of the Whiteman orchestras.

Among the most recent compositions recorded are "Thou Swell," "Tu Tan Elegante," and "In a Mist," in which "Bixie" is featured in a piano solo.

"We have great times traveling about," he said—the "boys" are airplane crazy and movie-shy. We have a new Travelair plane and several are learning to pilot.

"Might come in handy some time," he laughed, "in case we oversleep and miss the train, but we're generally on time. In fact one time we were a bit ahead of the Uptown theatre in Chicago and the curtain went up without warning. 'Be nonchalent!' was employed and we picked up our instruments and started to play."

Article in *Davenport Sunday Democrat*, February 10, 1929, "interviewing" Bix during his first recuperatory period at home after his breakdown in Cleveland.

PHOTO COURTESY LENNIE ESTERDAHL

to Stravinsky's *Petrouchka* and Delibes' ballet *Sylvia*. Hayton's small musical joke is anything but subtle: if Stravinsky's puppet-hero is nothing else, he is nobody's sweetheart; Sylvia, by contrast, hardly lacks for admirers. Entertaining, perhaps—but such use of material, even though interspersed with good solos by Secrest, Friedman and Trumbauer, betrays a banality never present on the Challis and Satterfield scores of the Victor period.

Bix returned from Davenport on Monday, March 4. To Andy Secret's astonishment, Whiteman dropped not him, but Eddie Pinder, from the band. "I was completely floored," he said. "I was nervous as anything, just sitting next to Bix. He was my idol. The master. At that time the Whiteman band was *the* band, and all the musicians would come to hear us. Consequently, the guys in the band were fighting for solo spots so the rest of the musicians, out in the audience, could see us being featured. We loved to show off, but when Bix came back he insisted that *I* take the solos. He seemed to get a kick out of hearing me play. He was a very gentle person, you know—so gentle that I really felt that if I didn't take the solos he would personally feel hurt.

"With night after night of sitting next to him, I guess I absorbed his style. He so influenced me that I subconsciously was becoming another Bix-styled horn and playing ideas that I'd associate with him. But believe me, it was due to my worship for the guy, not trying to copy and cash in on his fame. Let's face it—he was the master. I was just overawed at being next to him."

It is easy to sympathize with Secrest's plight. Perhaps more than any other white jazzman of his period, he has suffered the curse of living in another man's shadow. Where Sterling Bose, Jimmy McPartland, Red Nichols and others who consciously modelled themselves after Bix nonetheless achieved a good measure of acclaim on their own merits, Secrest has for decades been one of jazz's "unpersons." It is almost as though he were being tacitly punished for the circumstances into which he found himself drawn when Whiteman took him on.

The job was certainly a mixed blessing. To play with Paul Whiteman was honor enough, but to play alongside, and eventually replace, Bix Beiderbecke was dazzling for the 21-year-old midwesterner. Such events soon forced him into a comparison unfair by any standard. He was young and relatively inexperienced, his style still in the formative stages. Yet he was being paid top money by the leader of the biggest dance band in the business to sound as much as possible like the man who had been his inspiration. Little surprise that Secrest's solos on Whiteman and Trumbauer records of this period hardly stand critical comparison to Bix's. Judged by any objective standard, most are perfectly acceptable: well executed and conceived, played with good tone and engaging lilt. Were it not for the shade of Bix hovering over them, determining even the role of the instrument within the arrangements, Secrest's efforts might now be praised as those of a first-rate hot man in the making.

Later, as an older, more experienced musician, Andy Secrest demonstrated an individual musical personality which, while owing much to Bix, was as much his own voice as were those of Bose, McPartland or Nichols. His solos on such Bing Crosby recordings as the 1937 Decca "Smarty," with John Scott Trotter's orchestra, are excellent jazz cornet playing by any standard. But jazz history has taken little note of such developments. For most of the music's public Andy Secrest has remained, unjustly, the man who was unable to assume instant immortality as a surrogate Bix Beiderbecke. That he should have been penalized for this over an entire career is, in an objective critical view, unpardonable.

Old Gold had launched its weekly Whiteman radio broadcasts on CBS in direct competition to a similar National Broadcasting Company variety show sponsored by Lucky Strike and featuring an orchestra led by B.A. Rolfe, a trumpeter famed for his ability to play "sweet" solos in the highest register of his horn. Whiteman's sponsors, the Lorillard Tobacco Company, demanded a constant turnover of fresh material, including instrumental novelties in the style popularized by Rolfe's 60-piece ensemble.

"If any of our tunes sounded Rolfe-like," said Roy Bargy, "there was a reason for it. Our big competition was Lucky Strike on NBC, with Rolfe conducting that big band loaded with banjos, accordions and xylophones. Paul threw one in on purpose once in a while to sound like B.A."

Lorillard also insisted that the "King of Jazz" lend his broadcasts the personal touch, as Rolfe had been doing, by speaking to his audience direct on the air. At this Whiteman balked. "I'm a bandleader, not an announcer," he told a Lorillard executive. This was soon to change. Lorillard persevered, and on May 21 Whiteman opened the show with a few words about his orchestra's preparations for its forthcoming trip to the West Coast to begin filming *King of Jazz*, conceived as a film biography of Whiteman himself. Audience response to his remarks was so favorable that he took to doing master-of-ceremonies chores more often. Years later, with his bandleading days far behind him, Whiteman reached new generations of radio and television audiences as m.c. of a succession of popular shows.

Competition determined the rules. Rolfe played more numbers per show than Whiteman—drawing none-too-subtle suggestions from Lorillard that introductions be pared and time between selections shortened to cram as much as possible into the hour. Lennie Hayton recalled with amusement altering his "China Boy" arrangement to begin with a single C-augmented chord in line with the new policy.

The Rolfe camp, too, felt the effects of the network battle. The band's pianist and arranger at the time was none other than Irving "Itzy" Riskin, compatriot of Bix and Tram from Goldkette days. "The arrangements were loud and fast, good and corny," said Itzy, "but the checks came in regularly, and good sized, so I stuck with it." One day Rolfe summoned Riskin into his office. He was happy with the pianist's work, he said, but he had heard a record which seemed just the sort of sound he wanted to achieve with his own orchestra. Would Riskin mind listening to it and perhaps seeing if he could adapt some of its ideas for the Lucky Strike broadcasts? Wondering what he was in for, Itzy said he'd try.

"Imagine my astonishment—my utter shock—as he played for me the Goldkette record, our record, of 'Idolizing,' with that dreadful vocal and Bix doing the verse."

"Do you like it?" Rolfe asked.

Riskin thought a moment. "It's very difficult for me to say, B.A.," he ventured at last. "You see, I'm playing piano on it, and I am fully aware of the style. I was there when it all happened." Rolfe, said Itzy, was "just

Andy Secrest, young cornetist from Indiana hired by Whiteman to fill in for Bix during the latter's illness.

amazed. He never again tried to influence me in the arranging department."

Whiteman opened on the fourth of May at the Pavilion Royale in Valley Stream, Long Island, owned by the same concern which operated the Palais Royale, scene of his first Manhattan triumph nearly a decade before. For Bix, only fresh back in the brass section and still none too long on endurance, this and the constant broadcasting and recording were just too much. With some hesitation—and, as it turned out later, considerable guilt —he asked Trumbauer to drop him from all small-band Okeh dates, "at least for awhile." He had to call on all his strength and energy to keep up with the Whiteman schedule. Reluctantly, Tram agreed. Secrest did the hot work from then on—and the records tell the rest of the story. Trumbauer appears even to have attempted a "chase" chorus with Secrest on his recording of "Reachin' for Someone." It is, predictably, a failure. Without Bix, the entire style was living on borrowed time, and the decline or stylistic metamorphosis of its principal performers from this time onward bears all too eloquent witness to its dependence on the originator's creative influence.

The Whiteman orchestra left for the West Coast May 23 aboard the Old Gold Special, a train outfitted to carry the "King of Jazz" and his entourage across the United States in a splendor befitting Whiteman's reputation for luxurious living. Each man slept in a spacious, comfortable berth. There were extra dining cars, observation cars and lounges. If the trip would be nothing else it would be supremely comfortable.

The train headed out west, stopping almost daily for concerts. Whiteman was on the bill at the May 30 Memorial Day race at the Indianapolis Speedway. As Roy Bargy recalled it, "We were towed around the track before the start of the race, then parked on the infield near the first turn, where we watched the race. And brother, was it hot!"

Then St. Louis, and a phone call to Ruth. "He asked me to come over to the Mayfair Hotel to see him, which I did. He looked bad, but he wasn't drinking," she said. "I thought I detected a slight limp, but he wasn't using a cane when I saw him." Ruth did not come out to the Washington University Field House to hear the band, "but afterwards we went out to some of our favorite places.

"Next morning we had a good breakfast and lunch, and went to the station early so he wouldn't miss the train. When we got there there wasn't a musician in sight, so I got on the train with him. It was a very long train —that I remember well. He didn't seem unhappy, particularly, but he looked very bad. I was terribly worried about him and told him so. He just smiled—the way he always did when you tried to tell him something—and said it'd be all right, not to worry."

Somewhere northwest of Kansas City the Old Gold Special ran into the torrential rains which had been raking the American plains states all spring, bringing widespread flooding to thousands of acres of farmland and disrupting traffic and communications. Most scheduled trains across Kansas and Nebraska were either subject to indefinite delays or cancelled outright. It was only through a lot of hard talking—and not a few frayed tempers—that Whiteman persuaded railroad officials in Omaha to let the Old Gold Special keep to its rigid timetable by pushing on the same day to Lincoln, Nebraska, for an afternoon concert.

All Lincoln, it seemed, had converged on Burlington Station to watch the long train come in, and police had thrown up barriers to keep the crowd from flooding over on to the platform. Among the throng were Esten Spurrier, Lennie Esterdahl and a group of fellow-musicians who had been passing through and decided to stay over and see Bix. Watching the crowd press forward, Spurrier had grave doubts about the whole project.

"It seemed an impossibility, a fool's errand. How in heck, with the hustle and bustle of a train unloading, guys scattered through cars, and all that, could we ever even get close to him?"

Suddenly there was a hush, and slowly, almost ghostlike in its silence, "the train came sneaking into the station, and a very bleak looking, unoccupied-looking object it was, too. And this you *can't* believe: no conductor in view, no brakeman. Nobody—except, down about four or five cars, some guy had opened the door, raised the step cover and was standing there like he owned the train. As the car came closer, I recognized him and almost fainted. My problem, miraculously, was over."

Within seconds Bix had spotted the pair of familiar Davenport faces in the sea of people, and broke into a grin. He swung himself down as the train lurched to a halt, pumping every hand in sight. He looked genuinely grateful to find friends waiting, and willingly answered their questions like a politician at a press conference.

"He told us the going was so slow that all through the night they'd proceeded at a snail's pace, the water being over and covering the rails and roadbed for miles and miles. Since there was no way to know whether the roadbed had washed out, men walked in front of the engine, testing every step of the way to the end of their section, when the section crews from the next section would take over and complete their section. When the roadbed again became visible, the train would continue on slow order."

Musicians were beginning now to alight from the coaches. The crowd, catching sight of them, surged forward. "See you guys later," said Bix, and disappeared again inside the train. What happened next was pure pandemonium, as a front-page article in the following morning's *Lincoln Star* described under the banner headline, "Unruly Crowd of 5,000 nearly disrupts Whiteman's Concert":

A crowd of more than 5,000 persons battled with police and guards for a glimpse of the jazz king, nearly disrupting the thirty-minute concert of Paul Whiteman's orchestra at the Burlington Station Sunday evening.

Whiteman lost several buttons of his coat and was cut off inside the station for a time from members of his band who had taken places on the platform outside of the building. After several attempts to force through the crowd had failed, the musicians were called back into the station.

The crowd surged after the musicians. Several women fainted in the jam. Attempts of every member of the police department except the desk sergeant and driver failed to control the crowd in its frantic effort to see Whiteman.

A line of milling, pushing spectators thronged past doors of the building throughout the concert in an effort to see Whiteman. Inside the building every inch of standing space was taken. Some had climbed to the sill in front of the ticket windows, onto benches, and other places of vantage. Very few could see Whiteman because of the jam. The Jazz King directed the first

The Whiteman orchestra immediately before its departure for California in May 1929. L to R: Min Leibrook, Mike Pingitore, Mike Trafficante, Irving Friedman, Boyce Cullen, Wilbur Hall, Red Mayer, Ted Husing (announcer, at microphone), Bill Rank, Bernie Daly (sax), Roy Bargy, Whiteman, Margulis, Hazlett, Goldfield, Trumbauer, Hayton, Secrest, Strickfaden, Bix, Dieterle, Gaylord, Russell, Bowman, Malneck. Standing, rear: Ferde Grofe, Challis, one unknown, George Marsh (behind drums), unknown, Harry Barris, Alton Rinker, Bing Crosby.

Bix and Trumbauer before entraining for West Coast, spring 1929.

piece and only a portion of the second selection, "Stars and Stripes," then turned over the direction of the orchestra to an assistant. A chance to hear some of the "softer" Whiteman pieces was prevented by the shouts and noise of the crowd.

After the tumult had passed, said Lennie Esterdahl, he and Spurrier and a few of the others "spent about 45 minutes with Bix and Min Leibrook on the train in their Pullman car visiting and having a couple of blasts. Bix was indeed using a cane, but not depending on it. We also chatted with Chester Hazlett, Izzy Friedman, whom I had become acquainted with in 1925, Wilbur Hall and several others, including Trumbauer."

They were sitting around talking, said Spurrier, when "all of a sudden Bix asked us, 'Hey, any of you guys smoke Old Golds?' Answer affirmative. He reached up to the baggage rack and uncovered about a dozen cartons of Old Golds and passed them around with what, to me, was one of his cute characteristics. He explained that in the club car there were thousands of cartons of Old Golds, and that all you had to do is ask for a carton and you received one.

"Bix said he couldn't stand Old Golds. I can't recall his brand at the time, but all the other brands were available in single packs only. So Bix said that it being an Old Gold tour and Old Gold's graciousness, he always felt a little ashamed to just get his own brand. He had therefore devised his own technique. He'd belly up to the counter with enthusiasm, ask for a carton of Old Golds, then start to turn and walk away, but turn as an afterthought and say, 'Oh! I believe I'll also have a pack of—whatever his brand was."

On to Denver, and the sort of hometown festivities to be expected in honor of the son of Wilberforce J. Whiteman, director of Music Education for the entire Denver Public School system. The band's arrival was a major civic event, with full coverage by newspapers and radio, a tour of the city for the entire band ("Some of us skipped it and played golf," Roy Bargy admitted), and finally an evening at the Whiteman family farm, as the *Rocky Mountain News* faithfully reported, "for an old-fashioned dinner. Mrs. Whiteman had prepared a huge feast of fried chicken, baked hams, biscuits and all the country trimmings for Paul's homecoming."

The combination of fresh mountain air, good food and a bit of relaxation seemed to revive Bix's spirits. His mood during a rehearsal the next morning at the Shirley-Savoy Hotel reminded his bandmates of the Bix of old, before the skies had begun to darken.

"Hey, pass me a clam," he called when lead trombonist Cullen, a friend and drinking partner, fluffed an entrance. The word appeared to have been Bix's invention; but it caught on, and before long rehearsals came to be known as "clambakes" among the Whiteman musicians. He was in equally good shape for Whiteman's regular Old Gold broadcast that night, aired at 6 P.M. Central Standard Time over Denver station KLZ. He and Tram tore with all the old spark through a chase chorus on "Glad Rag Doll"; then Bix, a derby hung over the end of his cornet, slashed out choruses on "Sweet Georgia Brown" and "Runnin' Wild" with a fire and determination that startled everyone.

After a stop in Salt Lake City, California was just a jump across the Rockies, and the Whiteman aggregation rolled into San Francisco revitalized, ready for the long weeks of filming ahead. They did a week's warmup

Irving Friedman, Bix (in hat), and Whiteman en route to California, spring 1929.

Whiteman orchestra en route to California, June 1929. L to R: Whiteman, Chet Hazlett, Roy Bargy, Kurt Dieterle, Wilbur Hall, Mischa Russell, Bix, Jack Fulton, Lennie Hayton, Austin Young, Harry Goldfield (with moustache) immediately behind John Bowman, then Rube Crozier, Boyce Cullen (with hat and cigarette) and George Marsh. Rear: Charlie Margulis (with moustache and black vest), with Red Mayer beside him. Above them Bill Rank, with Irving Friedman at the top. (Frank Trumbauer and Charles Strickfaden not shown; Bargy believes Trumbauer was the photographer.) Far right, Hugo Haas of the William Morris agency.

at the Pantages Theater, then rode the Old Gold Special back down the coast to Los Angeles, and a reception rivalling those accorded visiting foreign statesmen and political dignitaries. A report in the *Los Angeles Examiner* for Saturday, June 15, captures the atmosphere surrounding the "King of Jazz" on his arrival. In its sheer ballyhoo and sense of occasion, it is pure Hollywood:

> Four worlds will rally today to greet Paul Whiteman, when the noted bandmaster and his associates arrive in Los Angeles.
>      Cinema, stage, the silversheet [?] and lyric forces will all be represented at the Southern Pacific Station at 9:30 this morning.

Alexander Pantages himself, impresario and owner of the Pantages Theater chain, led the welcoming committee, which also included Carl Laemmle, president of Universal Pictures, Paul Fejos, signed to direct *King of Jazz,* and such screen luminaries as Laura LaPlante, Reginald Denny, Joseph Schildkraut, Otis Harlan, Glenn Tryon, Kathryn Crawford, and John Boles, who wound up with a prominent role in the film, finished more than a year later.

> Following a reception at the station . . . the entire group will sweep in full parade form up to the City Hall, where Mayor Cryer will be waiting with the keys to the city as a welcome signal to the honored guest. Following the greeting by city officials, the parade will speed down Spring to Seventh Street and up Seventh to the Pantages Theater, where the musicians will disband to see that their flutes and saxophones are properly ensconced in the star dressing rooms of the theater.

Whiteman opened at the Los Angeles Pantages for a week's run, while working out final preparations with Universal for filming his biography. Fritz Putzier, in town on business, came around to see Bix backstage during intermission on the band's second night. Bix greeted his old friend with a warm handshake.

"We went out into the alley to talk. He was still nervous, chain-smoking cigarettes one after the other. He still didn't look at all good—he had this terrible pallor about him. But he said he was happy about the trip—looked on it as a vacation, a chance to soak up the sunshine and rest. I told him I thought that was the right idea—that relaxation and fresh air would do wonders for him and his health."

Something well worth hoping for. But, as Fritz soon found out, it was not to be.

Arrival in Los Angeles, June 1929. Whiteman inspects the fleet of automobiles rented to take his musicians on a parade downtown to the Pantages Theater. George Marsh and Wilbur Hall visible in next car.

PHOTO COURTESY OTTO LANDAU

Whiteman band breakfasting in Denver June 3, 1929. Whiteman sits between his parents at the far end. Eddie Lang is third from left, followed by Charlie Margulis and Bernie Daly. Right side, R to L: Boyce Cullen, Wilbur Hall, George Marsh, Joe Venuti, Mike Trafficante, Bix, Otto Landau; others obscured. PHOTO COURTESY IRVING FRIEDMAN

# Chapter 19

A piece of disheartening news during the early stages of the Pantages run cast a pall over the remainder of Bix's stay in California. Don Murray, friend, colleague and kindred spirit since the lake boat days, had been killed in Hollywood earlier in the month while the Whiteman Orchestra was still working its way west. Murray had been with Ted Lewis' band, and had come to California in the spring to film the Lewis talkie, *Is Everybody Happy?*. He and Bix had lost touch with one another some time before.

"We stopped at some town in New Mexico and I picked up a Los Angeles newspaper," said Bill Rank. "On the front page was a headline, 'Musician dies,' and when I read who it was I was very saddened. As for Bix, he didn't seem to show much emotion upon hearing about Don—but Bix was never very demonstrative about his emotions. He kept things very much to himself.

"After we arrived in Los Angeles, I contacted one of Lewis' men and he told me the story. Don was living in an apartment and he was going out to the grocery store. Some friends of his were driving by and stopped to talk. Don was standing on the running board of the car, and somehow fell backwards; his head struck the curbing, fracturing his skull. He died in the hospital."

According to Paul Mertz, Murray might have recovered. "Charlie Horvath told me years later that Don's prospects for recovery were good . . . but Don had some booze sneaked into his hospital room . . . and the reaction was drastic. He died as a consequence."

Finishing up at the Pantages, the Whiteman orchestra was left now with little to do but wait—until the planners at Universal came up with a format and script for *King of Jazz*. The unprecedented success of *The Jazz Singer* in late 1927 and *Lights of New York* shortly thereafter had opened up limitless possibilities for the movie industry, and the Whiteman film, as the first musical in the new two-color Technicolor process, was expected to push out the frontiers even farther. It had to be good—and Universal was sparing no effort to guarantee that it would be. Charles MacArthur, co-author with Ben Hecht of the hit play *The Front Page*, was pulled off another assignment to join the scriptwriting team in an effort to find a formula which would satisfy both the studio and Whiteman. Each time the team turned out a rough draft, a copy was forwarded to Ferde Grofe, who accordingly sketched out score ideas—only to be told, sometimes within hours, that that version had been scrapped and another would be forthcoming.

Things started to get out of hand until Whiteman, furious, announced that Grofe would no longer be available—until Universal presented him with a finished, approved script.

The band, meanwhile, was far less troubled by the situation. Its only firm commitment was the regular Old Gold radio show, aired at 5 P.M. every Tuesday, Pacific Standard Time, over Los Angeles station KMTR. Otherwise there was unlimited time to loaf and soak in the sunshine, reporting to the studio each afternoon at two "just in case." Evenings brought parties, Hollywood night life, sometimes jam sessions.

In Joe Venuti's case, boredom inevitably bred mischief. One afternoon he turned up on the lot with a fox on a leash. He had caught it the day before up in Laurel Canyon. He called for silence.

"Gentlemen, meet Mr. Reynard Vomit! Reynard would like it known that he can outrace any dog in the house."

Inevitably, somebody came up with a dog, and the two animals were led to the starting line. At Izzy Friedman's "Go!" Venuti snapped open the leash—and Reynard Vomit took off running for the hills, never to be seen again.

In the interests of diplomacy, Universal had extended visiting privileges to the Whiteman musicians. They could walk around the lot all they wished, watching filming in progress—as long as they were quiet and didn't get in the way.

"Hey, get a load of that!" Venuti summoned Friedman, Boyce Cullen and a small group of other strollers to where a love scene was in progress against a quasi-oriental backdrop. The director, megaphone in hand, turned a baleful eye on the interlopers. "Cut!" he thundered. "May we *please* have quiet on the set? We are filming in sound. Please remember that." Venuti said nothing, but waited until the cameras began cranking for another take. Then he let out a deafening razzberry which broke up the scene, the actors, his fellow-musicians—and sent one enraged director storming over to the head office with bitter complaints about rowdies on the set.

It happened again, with another director, and yet another, until, as Venuti himself recalled with undisguised amusement, "every director in the place was bitching about us upsetting their filming." Universal responded by banning the entire Whiteman orchestra from the lot until shooting actually began.

Most of the band had been living within easy travelling distance of the studios to facilitate commuting when the filming did begin. Now, with things apparently at a stalemate, there seemed no need to stay around. Bargy, Fulton and Hazlett took houses in the Hollywood Hills, while Tram, Secrest and some of the others preferred to remain closer to town. Bix and Boyce Cullen, sharing a flat near the studio, found a place up in Laurel Canyon, a piece of crumbling once-upon-a-time extravagance bearing passing resemblance to a Spanish hacienda, and moved in.

One of the first things Whiteman had done upon arrival was to arrange for each of his musicians who wanted one to buy a car. "They were all Fords," said Andy Secrest. "We purchased them—paid for them ourselves, by the way—from Tommy Thompson at the Nerney Ford Agency on Santa Monica Boulevard. I'll bet that was the largest order that guy ever had. Imagine, 30 guys coming down at once and buying cars from him!"

Bix's Ford was bright violet, and like all the others had a canvas cover on the spare tire emblazoned with Whiteman's caricatured head. Sure identification for any cop or highway patrolman in California, as Roy Mayer, Bing Crosby and Mischa Russell soon found out. After all three had been nabbed for speeding, most of the covers disappeared. "The cops were on the lookout for us," said Bargy, "and with those things identification was a cinch."

Putzier's pleas notwithstanding, Bix appeared to be doing anything but resting and soaking up the sun. His isolation up in the canyon just meant that fewer people could keep tabs on him. "He was drinking pretty heavily again," said Secrest. "We really thought he'd taken the cure at home, but he'd apparently just rested or something, because it didn't slow him down." Andy went up to the house several times to see "the master." Once it almost cost him his life. "There was this steep dirt road getting up there, with lots of hairpin turns and things. Really tough going, heckuva time getting up and down. One night, when I left, I backed clean off the side of the road and fell twenty feet to the next ledge. The car landed upside down—but by some miracle I wasn't hurt."

Hoagy Carmichael turned up unexpectedly, lured west by the prospect of opportunities opening up for songwriters in sound movies. He adds a tantalizing insight into Bix's behavior during these weeks. According to Carmichael, Agatha Beiderbecke came to Los Angeles to visit her son, perhaps in an attempt to coax him back to Davenport for a more protracted period of recovery. Whatever the case, said Carmichael, she apparently only saw Bix once. "It wasn't something he wanted to discuss, and I didn't feel right bringing it up. I think there was conflict between them, despite their close attachment."

He did come down for some of the numerous parties to which Paul Whiteman, superstar—and often his musicians—were constantly being invited. At one, Pops was introduced to—and promptly fell for—a film actress named Margaret Livingston. Many proposals, bouquets of flowers, and one monumental crash diet later, he married her.

Jascha Heifetz, whose admiration for Joe Venuti's violin virtuosity was exceeded only by Joe's worship of his, invited the band to one of his parties just to listen to Venuti play. Accordingly, Whiteman featured him in number after number, almost to the exclusion of the other soloists.

"Those parties were fun," said Bargy. "After those first couple, Paul always brought some of us along to entertain—the Rhythm Boys, Venuti and Lang, Jack Fulton, me, lots of the others. We were treated more like guests than hired help—and usually had more fun than anybody."

Actor Richard Barthelmess threw a big one, with such celebrities as Charlie Chaplin, Douglas Fairbanks and Mary Pickford on the guest list. At one point early in the evening, Bill Rank slipped around to the back door and let Hoagy Carmichael in. Hoagy later described the high point of the evening as the Whiteman band playing "Weary River," theme song for Barthelmess' latest film, Bargy doing his *Rhapsody in Blue* feature, and a couple of jazz numbers, "Sweet Sue" among them, spotting Bix. Whiteman's musicians, too, remembered the evening—chiefly for the fun of watching Carmichael in action. "Before you knew it," said Bill Rank, "Hoagy was dancing with every female star and starlet in the place. That was some party, all right."

They played for Buster Keaton, then for Marion Davies at her palatial mansion overlooking the beach at Santa Monica. "All the big stars of the day were there," said Bargy. "Pickford, Fairbanks, Barthelmess—and of course William Randolph Hearst, Marion's boyfriend, who picked up the check. The band arrived by bus and were admitted only through the side entrance. Whiteman, as an invited guest, was allowed to use the front door, of course. This sort of treatment hacked the guys plenty, as we were pretty spoiled by a lot of attention in other quarters.

"We were stuck in a room off the swimming pool until time to play. Joe Venuti called the chef on the house phone and said, 'Send down 30 steaks at once!' The chef sent a waiter instead, so no steaks. Joe also—wouldn't you know it?—offered to jump in the pool with his tuxedo on for a buck apiece from the boys. He actually started the collection—but we were called upstairs to play before he could make good. He would've done it, though."

This time, at least, the band had the last laugh. When the time came for George Marsh to carry his drums out—again by the side door—it seemed that half the band materialized to help him lug the heavy cases out to the bus. And heavy they were—packed to brimming with every bottle of booze 30 musicians had been able to lay their hands on. "We had a party of our own later," said Rank, "and wound up toasting Miss Davies with her own liquor."

The month came to a tragic end. Driving out to Santa Barbara on the Roosevelt Highway a few days after the Davies party, Joe Venuti's Ford collided head-on with a car carrying two elderly ladies from Illinois on their first vacation trip to the West Coast. Mario Perry, Whiteman's long-time accordion and violin stalwart, was rushed to a nearby hospital, suffering from multiple internal injuries. Venuti's bowing arm was found to be fractured at the wrist. Within two days Perry was dead, and "Four-string Joe" was out of action, his entire future as a violinist now in doubt.

Bix found a diversion. Mark Hellinger, journalist, author, friend of literary lions and entertainment celebrities, had arrived in Los Angeles in his bullet-proof Cadillac, a new wife at his side. He set up court at a beach house down the coast, and both Beiderbecke and Carmichael were occasional visitors. Bix, well-enough read to surprise Eddie Condon one day with an astonishingly concise two-sentence explanation of the works and life-style of Marcel Proust, seemed to relish the endless discussions about Faulkner, Hemingway, Dos Passos and other contemporary writers. Hellinger's parties, too, were the talk of the movie colony, and Bix and Hoagy appear to have attended their share.

Al Rinker of the Rhythm Boys threw one of his own at his sister's apartment on the first Saturday in August. His reasons were as much business as pleasure. Mildred Rinker had come down from the state of Washington with the Fanchon and Marco stage revue and had sung on a few broadcasts over KMTR. A big woman, of part American Indian extraction, she possessed a small, rounded singing voice which had won her a lot of admirers—but not much work. By the time the Whiteman orchestra arrived in California, she had just about decided to give up the whole idea of being a singer and settle down to home life with her husband, Benny Stafford.

Her brother insisted that she audition for Whiteman, and began talking her up to the boss. To little avail. Whiteman had heard dozens of would-be vocalists, sisters of friends and friends of friends, all looking for the big break. They came a dime a dozen, and he'd long since established a personal policy of keeping the door to any such approach firmly shut.

Stalemate—until Al Rinker hit on a foolproof strategy to lure Pops into a situation where it would be impossible *not* to hear Mildred sing. A party was the answer. Mildred and Stafford invited almost the entire Whiteman band—except its leader.

"Don't worry," Bing Crosby confided to her on the telephone Saturday afternoon. "He'll be here. He can't stand being left out. His curiosity'll get the better of him, wait and see."

He was right. Whiteman showed up midway through the evening. Mildred greeted him with a motherly hug—Whiteman, at nearly 300 pounds, was more than a match for her—and ushered him into the kitchen for a taste of her own home-distilled brew.

As he stood there, chatting idly with Stafford, Bix and Izzy Friedman, Lennie Hayton sat down calmly at the living room piano. "Sing, Millie," said brother Al. "Now's your chance." Hayton chorded in "What Can I Say, Dear, After I Say I'm Sorry?" with Eddie Lang joining in on guitar. Mildred sang—and out in the kitchen the King of Jazz stopped drinking to listen.

"Who the *hell* is that?" He listened some more to the voice, pure, mellow, just sweet enough, unbelievably delicate coming out of so massive a woman. The phrasing tasteful and sure, utterly professional, yet personal. Unlike any voice Paul Whiteman had heard before. "My God," he said, heading for the living room, "that's absolutely gorgeous."

Thus, in the best showbiz tradition, did Paul Whiteman "discover" and hire the singer who just three days later joined his orchestra as Mildred Bailey, first woman to sing regularly with a band, just as Crosby had been the first man. She made her debut on Tuesday night's Old Gold show, doing the vocal on Bargy's arrangement of "Moanin' Low." Before the end of the broadcast, Whiteman took the microphone to announce that a fan had telephoned KMTR to say he thought it was the "best number he'd ever heard us do. Listening to this girl's voice myself, I'm tempted to agree."

Mildred became a regular at the parties. "She was like one of the guys," said Bill Rank, "but a sort of mother-hen to boot." He especially treasured the memory of one night when she appeared "in black silk pajamas. In some way she split the pants down the front. She was really heavy, you know—and was really in a spot until they rounded up a needle and thread and made the necessary repairs."

Paul Mertz was also in town, drawn like Hoagy by the lure of writing music for talking pictures. He, too, marvelled at Mildred's voice; her interpretation of his own "I'm Glad There Is You" thrilled him as much as her vocal on Hoagy's "Rockin' Chair," written expressly for her, had thrilled Carmichael.

Mildred took a special shine to Bix. Though able to hold her own with the best when it came to a salty retort or locker-room joke, she seemed to change when in his presence. She cooed over him, chiding him if he failed to take care of himself. If he played especially well, there was always a hug and a kiss on the cheek. If he showed up hung over or unkempt, she might scold him like a country schoolmarm.

Whiteman, meanwhile, was making no progress with Universal. There was still no script, and no prospect of one in sight. With the band stuck out on the coast, inactive, for more than two months, other leaders had begun to zero in on the popularity and market of America's top popular orchestra. Finally Whiteman lowered the boom: he was taking the band back East, to open at the end of the month at the Pavilion Royale. He would return only when Universal had a script ready and shooting could begin. So the Paul Whiteman orchestra, its grand pianos, risers, music stands, 87 trunks and sundry paraphernalia—plus a hitchhiker named Carmichael—boarded the Old Gold Special and returned, non-stop this time, to New York.

Fritz Putzier came to the railroad station to see his friend off. "I got there early after finding out which train was theirs, and wandered over to the Whiteman special," he said. "I struck up a conversation with Harry Goldfield, and when Goldie learned that I was a friend of Bix's, he told me that Bix hadn't been taking care of himself and it had caused a deep hurt in the musicians to see it happening. Finally Bix came down the walkway, heading for the train—and he was using a cane. I was shocked. He seemed intent on making certain that he boarded the train. His only conversation was a mumbled greeting—not at all like him—and a quick handshake. Then he said something like 'I've gotta get on the train,' and disappeared. He looked awful, and was clearly embarrassed to meet me in that shape. I told him to take care of himself."

The incident left Putzier deeply shaken. Bix had not benefitted from sunshine, rest or anything else.

Bix is hardly visible through events at this time. From the guarded accounts of fellow-bandsmen it is possible to infer that he was again off the wagon, and that his performance was becoming erratic. His increased use of a derby and other devices to mute his tone, something he had done only occasionally before, betrays possible technical problems.[14]

Warren Scholl, who had camped by his radio set every Tuesday night since the start of the Old Gold broadcasts, faithfully transcribing the program notes which appear in the chronology section of this volume, came down to the Pavilion Royale on Whiteman's second night back. To his dismay, Bix was not even in the brass section. He was sitting, dressed in his tuxedo, at a table off to the side. He did not appear in even one of the 25 selections the band played before Scholl's departure at 10 P.M.

On those occasions when he did play and felt good, the old magic could still be there. Al Rinker remembered one night at the Pavilion when a Beiderbecke chorus drew an ovation from the band itself. But such moments were fewer and further between. More often it was the other way, as the time violinist Otto Landau remembered, when "Bix came out to the Pavilion in pretty bad shape. He'd forgotten to bring his horn with him, and of course there was hell to pay. Paul was wild. But we still had a little time, so I suggested to Paul that if he'd let me go out and ring some

---

14. Such muffling has two beneficial effects for the player of a trumpet or cornet. First, obviously, it disguises impurities of tone. Second, and perhaps even more significant, it provides added resistance to the flow of air coming out of the instrument, allowing the player a buffer which works as a steadying influence on below-par muscle and breath control. Blowing into a hat, or even, as has been described, a sheet of paper held over the bell of his horn, would have allowed Bix to conceal deterioration in his control of his instrument.

doorbells I might be able to find someone in the neighborhood who owned a trumpet.

"So I went, and sure enough, after a couple of blocks a man came up with a battered old cornet, green with age and with a lot of dents in it. But the valves worked—and when I explained the predicament, he said I could have it. So I took it back with me and Bix borrowed a mouthpiece and played it—played it as only he could."

Whiteman was dumbfounded.

It was clear to all that something was going to give, and probably very soon. Bix was turning up late, sometimes not at all, for jobs. His playing was more erratic than ever. When, on the 9th of September, the band went into Columbia's studios to record Grofe's arrangement of Irving Berlin's "Waiting at the End of the Road," Bix ruined three out of four takes with fluffed entries to his eight-bar solo. Whiteman, troubled, gave him relatively little to do on the next day's Old Gold broadcast, then advised him to "take a couple of days off. Relax. Get some sleep. We're back at Columbia on Friday. You should feel a lot better by then."

If anything, he felt worse when he took his place Friday morning for another crack at "Waiting at the End of the Road." His face was puffy, with a pasty, unhealthy pallor. He moved slowly, seemed only half-awake.

"My God, I feel rotten," he said to Secrest as they warmed up. "I'm so exhausted I don't know how I'll ever make it through the day. I feel as though all my strength has been drained out of me."

They began. Two more takes fluffed outright, though not this time through any fault of Bix's. They then got a good one, and Whiteman signalled to try one more, just for insurance. This time they played the arrangement, with its interpolated quotes from the "Going Home" theme of Dvorak's *New World Symphony*, impeccably. Bix's solo was clean, open-toned, betraying nothing of how he was feeling.

Then on to "When You're Counting the Stars Alone," another Grofe score set up in much the same way, giving Bix another eight-bar release in the last chorus.

One take down, he finally caved in. "Sorry, man, but I just can't make it," he mumbled to a worried Secrest. "Gotta lie down. Feel just awful. Take it, will you?" Secrest played the solo and finished the date. To this day, his part, on file in the Paul Whiteman archive at Williams College, bears the pencilled instruction "Get ready for solo/Jump to other part."

Bix, said Andy, felt so bad he "just went over into a corner and pushed a couple of chairs together, right there in the studio, then lay down on them and went to sleep."

He spent all of Saturday in his hotel room. Sometime during the afternoon, Whiteman, Kurt Dieterle and Mischa Russell came up to see him. He was stretched out on the bed, fully dressed, pale but composed.

"How's it going, boy?" Paul asked with forced joviality, his eyes doing a quick inventory of the room.

Bix grinned. "Couldn't be better, Paul. I'm in the pink of condition. Just a little tired, that's all."

"Bix, be serious. Have you had anything to drink today?"

Bix seemed hurt. "Nope. How could I? Haven't been out of the room all day."

As Whiteman turned to say something to Dieterle, standing behind him, his foot struck something lying half-concealed under a corner of the bed. Bix started as if struck. Whiteman bent over and picked up an empty bottle.

"Better come clean, Bix. Where'd you get it?" Bix closed his eyes and lay back on the pillow. He was quiet for a very long time. When the words finally came they came hard, as though his whole body were fighting against uttering them.

"Bellboy got it . . . slip him half a buck . . . goes 'round the corner for a pint . . ." His voice trailed off. Whiteman sat down heavily on the bed, head in hands. For a long time nobody spoke, Kurt and Mischa standing silent by the door, Bix staring blankly up at the ceiling.

Then, very gently, Pops set the empty bottle on the bedside table. "Bix, I'm sending you home. And I don't want you coming back until you're absolutely straight. I mean completely. Cured. No more halfway measures and no more funny business. You keep up this way and you're going to kill yourself. It's no good."

The next morning Whiteman himself, with Dieterle in tow, took Bix to Grand Central and put him aboard a train for Iowa. They shook hands on the platform.

"Your chair will always be there, Bix. Don't worry about that. You can have it back any time you want it, but you have to straighten yourself out first. Do it. Rest. See a doctor if you have to. Do what you have to do—and then get in touch with me anytime you're ready."

The last thing Paul Whiteman saw as the train moved slowly out of the station was Bix Beiderbecke's pale, wan face staring straight ahead, pressed hard against a window already smeared with his own tears.

"I kept him on with full pay for a couple of months, then on half pay for about four or five. I then realized that Bix would never return, and, reluctantly, I took him off the payroll completely."

# Chapter 20

Bix's departure hardly caught the Whiteman orchestra unprepared, but it created an unexpected problem for Bill Challis. For weeks, while the band was out on the Coast, he had been trying to sell Vincent Youmans on the idea of allowing Whiteman to record the hit title song from his show, "Great Day," and a companion number, "Without a Song," as a vehicle for Crosby.

Youmans resisted. He distrusted jazz and popular bands in general, Ferde Grofe in particular. The composer of *Metropolis* and the *Grand Canyon Suite*, he said, always changed the basic harmonies of the songs he arranged and distorted their character with an avalanche of "symphonic jazz" bombast. For Youmans, releasing "Great Day" to Whiteman meant exposing it to Grofe. No, thanks.

Challis kept after him, offering to do the scores himself along lines faithful to the composer's wishes, and promising as a bonus that "this great lyrical cornetist"—Bix—would play the only improvised solo. Beiderbecke, he added, was no run-of-the-mill "jazzer." He would not distort the melody, he would enhance it.

Eventually won over, Youmans consented, and the Whiteman orchestra began to rehearse Challis's arrangements of "Great Day" and "Without a Song" for its October 9 Columbia recording date.

But now with Bix gone the prospect of having another man, no matter how competent, handling the long solo was worrisome. Full of misgivings, Bill tried to get the "Great Day" project shelved for the time being, or even scrapped entirely. But Whiteman vetoed this. He had brought Secrest into the orchestra for just such contingencies. Andy could handle the solo.

They went ahead, Secrest taking a competent but hardly inspiring solo. Youmans, as feared, was livid, and attempted to block release of the record. Challis, saddened, could only lament later that it "could have been the finest recorded solo of Bix's career."

Bix, back in Davenport, was in bad shape. This time even rest and constant family attention seemed to make no difference. He seldom went out and Agatha, presumably at his request, discouraged callers. He still complained of weakness and pains in his legs. Sometimes, at night, he had trouble breathing. Family doctors advised that he be hospitalized, perhaps in a sanatorium where his condition could be treated under strict supervision.

It was a moment Aggie and Bismark had dreaded. Bix was sick, yes. A cold, fatigue or exhaustion brought on by the pace with Whiteman; all that could be lived with, explained away. But now there was the irrefutable fact of hospitalization and treatment for alcoholism. The word itself was socially a taboo—enough to blight the family's carefully-tailored respectability in the community. In years to come, sister Mary Louise would steadfastly refuse to use it, avowing that her brother came to grief only "because he drank too much."

Monday morning, October 14, Burnie drove Bix the 130 miles to Dwight, Illinois, to register him at the Keeley Institute, known throughout the midwest for its success in the treatment of alcoholism. Bix went without objection.

Treatment at Keeley was voluntary; a patient could not be kept against his will. When he felt he wanted to go, he left. No questions asked, no resistance from the staff. There were several such institutes across the United States, all based on roughly the same therapeutic technique: rapid withdrawal of the supply of alcohol, then aftercare in as relaxed and controlled an atmosphere as possible, to put a hesitant or potentially hostile patient at his ease. At Keeley, the doctors explained, addiction to alcohol was viewed as both a psychological and physical disorder, so no effort was spared to avoid causes of pressure or tension.

It was not until 1935, six years later, that Alcoholics Anonymous opened the way to public discussion of addiction and group therapy as treatment. Such latter-day techniques as aversion or deterrent therapy were still decades off. Within the context of 1929, the very word "alcoholism" still evoked—as indeed it yet does in some quarters of society—the Victorian image of the drunkard, a social outcast, a figure at once pitiable and contemptible. In the minds of the Beiderbeckes and of their Davenport peers, Bix's affliction could only be viewed as a taint, a source of shame to be kept secret at all cost from public view.

Bix stayed at the sanatorium five weeks, one longer than the normal course of treatment. The hospital administration gave this account of his time there:

> On October 14, 1929, we admitted a patient who gave his name as L. B. Beiderbecke of 1934 Grand Avenue, Davenport, Iowa. He gave his age as 29 [sic] and his occupation as a musician.
>
> His medical history includes mention of the fact that he had had pneumonia in December of 1928 and also delirium tremens at about the same time. He complained of neuritis in his legs and extreme weakness which was said to have dated from December, 1928.
>
> On physical examination he was found to be in very poor condition and the examining physician noted on the record that there was a good possibility the patient would lapse into delirium tremens.
>
> He was a cooperative patient and made a very good recovery, although the physician who closed the file was very guarded in his prognosis.
>
> The record is not clear as to who paid Mr. Beiderbecke's account.
>
> Mr. L. B. Beiderbecke was discharged from treatment at the Keeley Institute on November 18, 1929. Inasmuch as four weeks was the minimum and usual duration of his treatment at that time, it would appear that Mr. Beiderbecke's progress was slower or his condition more serious than that of the average patient.

Burnie said he thought Bix stayed a week in a private home before returning to Davenport, but there is no trace of his whereabouts during that time. He arrived home early the last week in November to join his family for Thanksgiving dinner.

The change in him was startling. Before his hospitalization Bix had shown no interest in playing or even in seeing Davenport friends who telephoned or visited the house looking for him. Now he appeared outgoing, optimistic and cheerful.

The telephone rang. Bix answered it. Esten Spurrier.

"Hey, what're you doing back in town? I thought you were out on the road with whatsisname."

Spurrier was silent for a moment. "Didn't your mother tell you I'd called? I phoned a couple of times to ask how you were. Told her to be sure and tell you I'd called and to phone me back when you felt up to it."

"Nope. She never said a thing. Funny. She must've forgotten."

Spurrier, remembering the conversation, outlined another interpretation to the authors. "I guess they couldn't stomach my being a musician. They had this thing about musicians, especially now. Bix was always something of a black sheep in their eyes because of the music. His fame—yeah, of course it was known to them, and was probably just about as acceptable as if he had been a famous bookie. But now he was feeling better, and we were together from then on almost daily, playing records, shooting the bull (Bix was informed on more subjects than most people realized), he playing the piano a lot because he liked it and I was a good audience."

Bix talked at length about his piano compositions. And one morning not long afterwards, "he called me bright and early, said he wanted to pick me up and go to his house, had a surprise for me. No hint of any surprise all the way home, just 'Wait.' When we arrived, he immediately sat down at the piano and played through a complete composition and told me he was going to call it 'Candlelights' because it seemed to capture the nostalgic feel of an intimate group at a dinner party. The glow of good eating, social drinking with candles.

"Anyway, he said he'd composed three bridge passages but couldn't decide which one to use, and that I had to select the best. So I listened to all three, liked all three. But Bix was adamant: the bridge had to be picked by me, so I finally selected one."

The two friends spent hours together listening to records—many of them Bix's own. "He never got tired of recounting the little occurrences during recordings where someone got mixed up—wrong drumbeats or something, or of Frank Trumbauer's foibles and little persnickety introductions, interludes and endings. Soup to nuts."

Spurrier had gone to work at the new Danceland ballroom at Fourth and Scott with a band led by another boyhood chum, Jimmy Hicks, who had developed into a strong, if none too subtle, hot trumpeter. On trombone was Bob Struve, alumnus of Erkie Albright's first high school band, Buckley's Novelty Orchestra, and the Plantation Orchestra on board the *Majestic*.

"We were doing three or four nights a week, and I got the bright idea of asking Bix if he would play with us, provided we could fix it up. He said he wasn't sure he should, but in the end he agreed. I immediately went to Hicks with my bill of goods, to see if Al Norgardt, the manager, would buy it: 'Famous Bix Beiderbecke, featured trumpet with Paul Whiteman,' etc.

"Well, Hicks said if I went with him we'd give it a try. So we did, and after a long session, Norgardt bought it. Union scale was then $6.00 per night, but we got Bix $15, and so we were all set —or so we thought."

A day or two later, the *Davenport Democrat* ran an advertisement for Danceland along the "featured trumpet with Paul Whiteman" line and, said Spurrier, "the roof caved in. Bix was mortified about trading on Paul's name, said 'The old man wouldn't like it,' and refused to hear of it. He could be one stubborn Dutchman when he made up his mind, believe me."

Hicks and Spurrier went back to Norgardt and explained the situation. The manager altered his advertising to carry such slogans as "come out and hear Bix." Even this bothered him. "Forget that stuff," he told Hicks. "I just want to be one of the boys, that's all."

It was a difficult time for Bix. He was determined to return to Whiteman's brass section, but not before he was strong enough and had enough grip on himself to undo his embarrassment at what had happened in Cleveland, then the scene in his hotel room when Paul had found the bottle. He was feeling better, no doubt of that. The Keeley "cure" appeared to have worked, at least for the moment. Now, Whiteman or no, he was still a cornetist and had to play, especially after weeks of inactivity. He would never get back into shape by *not* playing.

Fritz Putzier arrived home, and upon finding Bix around Davenport, came chugging up to the house on Grand Avenue one brilliant sunny morning at the wheel of his father's brand new Buick sedan. He honked the horn. Bix, grinning in a maroon turtleneck sweater, bounded down the snow-covered walk to greet him. Only just the trace of a limp.

"How's it goin', pal?" He climbed into the warm car and stamped the powdered snow off his shoes. "What's the latest?"

Just like old times, as if the dark days in New York and California had never existed. Putzier could hardly believe it. Bix looked rested. His eyes had some of the old sparkle and he talked with animation, first about Davenport friends, then, gradually, about life with Whiteman, being on the road, the hours, the strain and the pressure.

"He didn't say he regretted anything or felt he had tossed his chances away," said Fritz. "He said he was glad to hear about the progress of certain of our friends; and he said it in a way, a pensive look in his eyes, that made me suddenly realize he may have felt he had chosen a way of life quite different from that of the average man. No regrets, really—just that perhaps our way of life may have all at once appeared more substantial to him.

"It was a very quiet, very friendly chat, typical of two old friends discussing the past while sitting in the front seat of an automobile, the sun shining on us and the view outside one of a typical winter day in Iowa."

Whatever Bix was thinking now about Davenport and its life-style, he appeared to be thriving on it. Stopping into Hickey's cigar store later the same week he ran into Larry Andrews, onetime kindergarten playmate, ice-skating partner and rival for the affections of Vera Cox.

Bix lit up his pipe, a new acquisition, and they talked. After about ten minutes they were joined by Trave O'Hearn, a bandleader from Illinois who had fallen for a Davenport girl and decided to settle there and get married.

"He asked us both if we'd like to play a job," Andrews said. I thought he had a lot of guts to ask Bix, but was even more surprised when Bix said, 'Sure, if Larry can play too.' It was a neat thing to do, considering the punk state of my banjo playing."

The events of the months just past had shaken Bix's confidence and left him insecure about himself and the future. In Andrews, Putzier and their friends, faces in a Davenport apparently unchanged by time, he had constant reminders of stability, things with which he was able, for the moment, to identify.

Bix and Larry showed up together for the first of several gigs with O'Hearn's eleven-piece band, a Kappa Delta fraternity dance December 23 at the Hotel Blackhawk in downtown Davenport. To celebrate the occasion, the leader produced his own arrangement of "Singin' the Blues" based closely on the 1927 Okeh record Bix had made with Trumbauer. Written into Ed Sidebotham's lead trumpet part was a note-for-note scoring of Bix's famous chorus.

O'Hearn called "Singin' the Blues" early in the evening. The saxophones were reading through the opening chorus, Trumbauer's solo from the record voiced in three parts, when Sidebotham leaned over to Bix, snatched his second part, and dropped the lead sheet on the music stand in its place.

"Your solo, Bix. You take it."

Bix, startled, froze. Musicians there that night swore he stared at the page without any recognition of what he was being asked to play. Frantic, he looked first at Sidebotham, then out front at O'Hearn. Both beamed back in expectation. Four bars gone, rhythm marking time and the saxes laying down a chord cushion. Eight bars, and no move from Bix. Then, nearly sixteen in, he stood, resolute, to play a fresh solo on the theme. It bore no resemblance to the recorded version but, said pianist Les Swanson, it was just as good. They all laughed about it later, "and I can tell you, Bix laughed as hard as anyone," Swanson said.

Throughout the evening, Bix and Larry carried on a running conversation, half serious, half wisecracks and schoolboy jokes from earlier days. At one point Andrews admired some of the girls on the dance floor. Bix affected an exaggeratedly world-weary manner.

"Well, Larry, old boy, I'll tell you," puffing on the pipe. "After you play behind the Follies, where they pick the most beautiful girls out of thousands, then you ride on a train from New York to California with them, you get so that the girls don't interest you much." Andrews' reaction to this discourse is lost to posterity.

More music, more chat, and "Hey, Larry, whatever became of Vera?"

"Didn't you hear? She married the baker's boy, Ferdie Korn."

As if on cue, Vera and the baker's boy danced by. Bix lowered his horn and glanced, incredulous, at Andrews. Both burst out laughing.

After the job, Bix hung around a while to talk to Struve, Swanson and some of the others. A few non-musician friends wandered up, and inevitably there were requests for him to play "some of those modern things" on the piano. Bix glanced quickly, almost furtively, at the door.

"Is everybody out of here?" he asked. Les assured him the hall was empty. Bix sat down behind the baby grand and began chording his way through "I'd Climb the Highest Mountain," a personal favorite which had formed the basis for his trio record of "For No Reason at All in C" with Trumbauer and Eddie Lang.

"We all had an inferiority complex playing alongside him at the start, but we soon lost that," Swanson said. "He just seemed to want to play, to be 'one of the boys.' Around that time there were some other local musicians who had been out in the big time briefly, either in Chicago or New York, and would come back with that 'superior' attitude, trying to run the band and all that.

"But not Bix. On the dates I played with him I never heard him so much as request a single number, nor did he ever ask for a chorus."

Larry booked most of Trave's band for a job of his own, a Frigidaire factory employees Christmas dance at the Blackhawk on December 27. Bix went along in high spirits. Just how high became apparent after first trumpeter Harry Rathjens, whom Andrews described as "a German band-type player," decided to try his own luck at a hot jazz chorus. Corny, said Larry, was hardly the word for it.

Bix, deadpan, leaned over to his banjo-playing friend.

"Hey, Larry, can Harry take a joke?"

"S'pose so, but whatcha got in mind?"

"Think I'll do a little takeoff." And a number or two later Bix did just that, tossing off a caricature full of triple-tonguing, razzamatazz and beer-garden polka rhythms so faithful to the original, Andrews said, that "I don't believe it could have been more perfect had a record been made of Harry's performance and replayed, except that Bix's tone was the same bell tone he used in all his playing."

New Year's Eve with O'Hearn's band again, this time at the Elks' Club across the Mississippi in Rock Island. At Larry's behest, Bix played "In a Mist" on the piano during intermission, ending with several full chords he termed "my M. F. chords." When Andrews looked puzzled, Bix laughed. "That means 'Mit feeling,' " he said.

Bix continued with Hicks at Danceland through January and February, always courteous and punctual, playing better each time. His strength and confidence were returning, and with them the old conflict. He spoke more and more often of regaining his place with Whiteman. But the memory of the pressure, the pace which had led to the crackup in a Cleveland hotel room—all that was still fresh in his mind.

He talked about it with Spurrier. "He spoke with horror of the visions, the snakes and animals and things in the middle of a seizure of DTs; of being disoriented, never wanting to go through it again. He said he had no recollection at all of his trip home.

"We had a very close sort of relationship—I was almost like a father-confessor sometimes, it seemed. The fact that I was married, had a couple of kids and an apparent happy existence did make an impression. I think Bix really enjoyed being put, at home, for the time being and talking of the varied things stable people did. I don't think we ever talked about girl friends. Bix was always liked by the gals, and had that big baby-eyed appeal. But other than mentioning that someday he looked forward to finding the right girl—marrying and getting off the travel bit . . . Later, he wrote me from New York saying he thought he *had* found the right one. But by then it was too late."

The idea of stability and home must have been on Bix's mind a lot over the holiday season. Shortly after New Year's, Vera Cox had a surprise visitor at her parents' home.

"It was Bix. I was visiting my parents then with my baby son. We were living out in Pella, Iowa, and had come to town to spend the holidays with them. Bix—well, he was the same old Bix. Came to call on me 'to see the baby.' "

Same old Bix, still a touch shy, still the kid who had stolen his first kiss on the porch swing back when life was still colored blue and gold and there was always tomorrow. They walked a bit, past rows of comfortable, substantial, warm Davenport homes with holly on the doors and decorated Christmas trees still in the windows. "He told me he didn't really *feel* famous. He told me, 'I don't know where I'm going from here.' "

"It was almost as though he longed to be just a young boy again, riding his bike no hands down the hill near our house to show off for me, or sledding near the school. Now here he was back from New York, with a funny little moustache, and looking kind of fat and not at all healthy. He kept on saying he felt he'd reached the top and there was no other height to reach, therefore the only direction was down, and that he was afraid sometimes. It wasn't said despairingly, I believe. Just matter of fact."

"Bix insisted on seeing our baby. Even then, even after all those years, he still called me 'Lorry,' my middle name, and he liked the name Lee, the baby's name, because he said it sounded like a blending of Leon and Lorry. He used to sign his letters to me 'Lee' when we were kids.

"We talked about a lot of things. He talked about Paul Whiteman, and how Whiteman had been a kind boss but had never set the right tempos. He laughed about that. He even said—I think trying just a bit to impress me—that he'd dated Ruby Keeler, but that he'd lost out to Al Jolson."

Whiteman was increasingly on his mind. The band was again in California, and this time filming on *King of Jazz* had gone ahead without a hitch, but with an entirely new format. The screen biography idea had been jettisoned. Instead, Universal had recast the picture as a musical variety show. The band had several featured spots, including Bargy playing *Rhapsody in Blue* against a lavishly-designed set based on multiple shades of blue. Venuti and Lang had a feature, as did Willy Hall, the Rhythm Boys and a few of the others.

"This was the first movie in which the music was recorded first and then the film shot to the sound track," said Bargy. They shot the band first, then I had two or three weeks off before they were ready for me. The piano had dummy strings and made no sound . . ."

Not being in the film, said Spurrier, was "a kind of hurt for Bix, though he never said much about it."

Sometime during these weeks, perhaps at the height of his preoccupation with Davenport, Putzier, Spurrier and all the others who were settling down to raise families, Bix telephoned Ruth Shaffner. He spent a long time talking to her and Estelle, ending with a promise to come to St. Louis within the next few weeks to renew old ties.

While Ruth waited, Bix did some serious thinking. He couldn't see her again without first having something to show for it, something to tell her, the prospect of some sort of future. He could hardly base an offer of marriage on occasional jobs around Davenport.

Ruth wrote, asking when he planned to come; but by the time her letter arrived, Bix Beiderbecke was on his way to New York. He had decided that he was well enough to take the risk—to make contact with Whiteman for the first time in five months and explore his chances for rejoining the orchestra and offering Ruth a future.

First stop on the trip east was Chicago, and a visit to the Three Deuces. Wingy Manone, leading the band, spotted him the minute he walked in, Bach cornet in a black corduroy drawstring bag under his arm. "Ladies and gentlemen, a big hand for the one and only Bix Beiderbecke," the trumpeter bawled through the microphone as the blue-white spotlight fell square on Bix. "C'mon up here with us, man, and blow a couple." The applause rocked the little room as Bix, looking almost sheepish, climbed on to the stand. Art Hodes, sitting in the crowd, took over from Tut Soper at the piano as Wingy counted off "At the Jazz Band Ball."

Just like it had been, Bix blowing it ahead clean and free, and notes tumbling out almost the way they had, once upon a carefree midwest time. "The people were knocked out, absolutely spellbound," said Hodes. "Bix, too, seemed to be enjoying himself thoroughly. He'd been out of action for awhile, we'd heard, and was clearly glad to be back."

Later, when things had quieted down, he played the piano, running through "Candlelights" and another new one, which he called "Flashes," for the enraptured musicians. "It got late," said Hodes, "but they wouldn't let him off, even with the porters standing by to clean up. What a night!"

On to New York, and a surprise visit to Bill Challis at his sister's apartment on Riverside Drive. He wanted to talk with a friend before tackling the Whiteman office. Challis scarcely hid his delight at the cornetist's new enthusiasm and improved appearance. He'd gone a little pulpy, true, but his complexion was closer to normal. They talked openly about the drinking. Bix was on the wagon and would stay there, he said. He hadn't touched a drink in months, and he was feeling good.

"He looked good. My God, he looked good," the arranger said. "He made you want to hope it would all work out well for him."

So armed, Bix went up to see Jimmy Gillespie at the Whiteman office. "How the hell are you, Bix?" clapping a fatherly arm around his shoulders. "How's the boy?"

"Like a million bucks. Jim, I want to go back with Paul."

They discussed it. The band was due to finish filming at the end of the month and jump directly into a new, long tour which would take them halfway back across the United States, up into Canada and eventually to Europe. He could join them when they hit Chicago around the middle of April.

There had been changes. The October 1929 market crash had knocked the financial bottom out of the entertainment business along with the rest of the American economy. Bands could still work, but the big money was no longer there. Even Paul Whiteman had been forced to reassess his commercial potential and view each sideman as an investment, able to offer maximum value for money. So the proprietor of the biggest band of them all had decided that immediately after the premiere of *King of Jazz* at New York's Roxy Theater in May, he would have to chop his inflated budget by paring his personnel to 18 men. This meant a lot of long-time, faithful faces would have to go, and there would be room for only one hot man in the trumpet section.

"What about Andy?" Bix said.

"What about him?" Gillespie replied. "It's your chair. You know how Pops feels about you. All you have to do is say the word and bang! Andy's out and you're back in."

He returned to Chicago elated, and checked in at the Sherman Hotel for a few days. He didn't have to be back in Davenport until February 14, and was determined to have some fun. He phoned Phil Dooley, a friend from his days with Charlie Straight.

"I visited him at the Sherman," Dooley told the authors. "I brought my German shepherd dog along, as I knew Bix liked dogs. He'd been home in Davenport, resting, and he looked pretty good—he'd filled out and was in better shape. He said he was on his way to rejoin Whiteman, so I took the opportunity to give him some of the tunes I'd written. He said he'd try to get them played.

"He told me he'd had a busted spleen. From what I gathered from the conversation, he may have gotten into a jam alone, no one around knowing who he was, and no one to protect him. Something must have happened to him."

Ted Weems had the band over at the Granada Cafe, on Chicago's tough South Side, doing arrangements by Joe Haymes. "Bix had heard the band on the radio a few times in Davenport and wanted to meet Joe because he liked the arrangements. So I called Joe, and he told the guys in the band Bix was coming out to the Granada."

Weems had some good men, including clarinetist Don Watt, Country Washburn on bass and Orm Downes on drums. Haymes's arrangements were not unlike those of Bill Challis, and Bix gratefully accepted the leader's invitation to sit in on cornet, filling the gaps between the arranged phrases and taking the jazz solos. He sounded fresh and sure, and the Weems sidemen were knocked out.

The Granada's manager, a small-time hood named Al Quodbach, heard it with other ears. For one sudden, terrifying moment it was Dan Baroni and the Valentino Inn all over again.

"Get that guy outa here!" he bellowed at Weems during a break. "He doesn't even know the songs right. How come he keeps screwin' up the melody with all them wrong notes?" Bix sat alongside Weems's trumpet-playing brother Art, shaking his head in disbelief as the bandleader tried to explain that this was no tinhorn cornball trumpet man, but the great Bix Beiderbecke, star of Paul Whiteman's orchestra, idol of jazzmen coast to coast.

"I don't give a good goddam if he's Lucky Lindy. I said get him outa here or you can take your whole fuckin' band and leave now!" Weems started to argue, but Bix shook his head no. He dropped the Bach back into the drawstring bag and hopped off the stand.

"No point in asking for trouble, Ted. Thanks for everything." He left, with Weems promising to give the management "a piece of my mind" about the incident.

Weems, an old pro in the band business who had dealt with much tougher nuts than Al Quodbach, went over his boss's head to the syndicate men who controlled the Granada and other of Chicago's Prohibition-era nightspots. They knew about Whiteman and, surprisingly enough, about Bix Beiderbecke. They promised to have "a little talk" with Quodbach.

Little is known of this tête-a-tête, but when Bix returned to the Granada a night or two later, he got the red-carpet treatment, with as much sitting in as he wanted. Even a suddenly jovial Quodbach applauded his solos.

Haymes, listening to him play, had an idea. He was to take a band of his own into the Mayo Hotel in Tulsa, Oklahoma, March 9, playing arrangements very much in a Challis-Whiteman vein, and Bix would be an ideal component. All it took was asking. Bix agreed to sit in on a couple of rehearsals while he was in town, especially now that it was clear that Whiteman's arrival was going to be delayed.

"He told me he wanted to get himself back in shape to rejoin the old man, and welcomed the chance to play," said Haymes. "He went along a time or two—but he kept having nervous spells, during which it was sometimes hard for him to finish a chorus, especially on piano. He'd just stop—you know, drop his hands and say, 'I'm too nervous, I can't go on.' Something like that. He seemed unsure of himself on the arrangements, too, though his reading seemed okay."

Bix did the first week in March with drummer Bob Tyldesley's Kentucky Reveillers in the tri-cities area. Though based in Muscatine, Tyldesley had used Wayne Rohlf and other Davenport musicians from time to time. Now he was short a cornet, and Bix offered to fill in as a favor. They opened on Saturday night, March 1, at the Roof Garden of the LeClaire Hotel in Moline. Several of Tyldesley's men remembered the night with no little embarrassment. Bix, still pacing himself, dropped out during some of the ensemble backing parts—only to have Archie Long, the band's sousaphone player and librarian, prod him in the back.

"Hey there, Beiderbecke," he growled. "In this band we play *all* the figures." Bix, with characteristic good manners, apologized rather than cause trouble. Later it was Tyldesley's turn to apologize, after berating his red-faced bassist.

Bix was seldom without reminders of illness. Thursday evening Wayne Rohlf, playing in the stage band at Davenport's Capitol Orpheum Theater, took a note from a messenger boy who had slipped in, breathless, through the stage door. It was from Bix, asking his friend to "please come over to the LeClaire Hotel, Moline, after the show and work in my place. I'm sick."

"All the fellows in the band were laughing," said Wayne, "and I thought it was a gag, so I went straight home after the show. A couple of days later I met Bix on the street, and he bawled me out—in his usual gentlemanly and half-kidding manner—for not showing up."

Ruth, meanwhile, had heard nothing from Bix since his telephone call. Now, with something definite to tell her, he wrote on March 18:

> Dear Ruth:
> I could kick myself all over the place for not having written to you before, you old sweet thing, but honestly I've been out of town, and sort of taking advantage of the first vacation I've had in eight years, and I really did receive your letter late.
> I'm joining Paul again in two weeks in Chicago, from where we go to New

York, and then possibly London, England, for a few weeks to be present at the premiere of the picture "King of Jazz Revue."

I'm sorry I couldn't get to St. Louis but I really couldn't make it, Ruth, it seemed that every town led me further away from St. Louis because I went east for business purposes. When I talked to you and Stella that night I really thought that I would be in St. Louis that next week but things happened that took me in opposite directions.

I'm entirely well again and haven't had a drink of anything intoxicating for over six months and it looks like I'm going to lay off for good. I made a promise to the folks and that goes—imagine me a teetotaler. It's a fact.

Well, Ruth, I guess it will be a long time before I'll see you again, I only wish that we could re-live those two days in your apartment before I go to Europe. Do you remember when I was indisposed, and you, Stella and Bess took care of me?

At any rate I'll see you at the first opportunity, may that be soon—the best of everything to your sisters and love to you.

Whiteman finished filming *King of Jazz* two days later and boarded the Old Gold Special on the first leg of the new tour. Bix, in Davenport, worked a few more jobs with Hicks while preparing to leave for Chicago and the reunion he'd dreamt of all winter. One Hicks engagement even found him behind a set of drums after the leader, who had inadvertently double-booked the evening, was forced to split his band to make both engagements. Bix borrowed Bill Greer's set, said Les Swanson, and "did a great job, really kept a steady beat. Nothing flashy or noisy, mind you. But I really have to say he did a lot better than many drummers who were active in those days. His beat was solid and rhythmic."

Time to kill. Swanson and Bix took in boxing matches and movies. There was music and conversation with Spurrier. Bix could hardly talk about anything but Whiteman, and how it would be when he saw Tram again, and "You ought to hear Mildred sing."

At last it was time. On Monday, the 7th of April, Bix paid up his Local 67 dues for the next half year, listing his address as the 44th Street Hotel, New York City. Two days later he was in Chicago. He checked into the Sherman again and settled in, excited and just a bit on edge, to wait for the arrival of the "King of Jazz."

# Chapter 21

Paul Whiteman's grand tour plans were not working out as anticipated. A dispute with Canadian immigration officials over whether the orchestra should be classified as musicians or entertainers—each able to take engagements the other could not—had caused delays which hopelessly snarled most of the itinerary. Finally, A. E. Skinner, Canadian Commissioner of Immigration, decreed the Whiteman ensemble could enter Canada only as entertainers, playing from theater stages; they could not play for dancing. Despite the protests of the "King of Jazz," Skinner's decision was final. After days of soaring tempers and coast-to-coast telephone calls, Whiteman took the only course left to him with his schedule so badly disrupted: he ordered the entire tour cancelled and headed back, nonstop, for New York.

Bix, cooling his heels at the Sherman, knew none of this. When Whiteman was late in arriving, he phoned Gillespie. "Just hang on awhile there, Bix," came the reply. "There's been some delay, but it'll be okay in a day or two. If you haven't heard anything by the weekend, give me another call."

By the middle of the following week, Whiteman had made up his mind, and the band was on its way back east, due to arrive in New York on Tuesday, April 22. When they got in, Bix was waiting.

"Bix! You old so-and-so! How's it going? You look great!" Thus Paul Whiteman's reaction upon seeing his former star cornetist for the first time in more than seven months. Bix confirmed that he felt as good as he looked.

"How about it, then? When do you want to come back? Just give me a date."

Bix, a little uncertain: "What's lined up for the rest of the spring, Paul? Can I handle it?" Whiteman ran down the schedule. With the tour as good as dead, there was still plenty to do. More recording for Columbia, the world premiere of *King of Jazz* at the beginning of May, then another season at the Ziegfeld Roof, more Old Gold broadcasts. The usual—but a lot more of it. "When we did Loew's State out there in February we were doing five shows a day. It's a lot of work, Bix, but the boys want you back. So do I."

Five shows a day. *And* recording. *And* broadcasting. Memories began to crowd back into Bix's mind, memories banished months ago in the quiet of Keeley and Grand Avenue, and in the glare of the spotlight at the Deuces.

"How about Andy? How's he doing?"

Whiteman laughed. "He's fine. Sounding more and more like his idol every day. Good in the section, too."

Involuntarily, Bix shuddered. If Secrest could blow the parts *and* turn in an ever-better imitation of him, what use was there to having Bix himself back in the band?

"Paul, Jimmy said you're going to cut the band down. Where does that leave me? What about Andy?"

Somewhere in Paul Whiteman's mind an alarm bell went off. He looked long and hard at Bix. "Look, Bix," he said, the jocularity suddenly drained from his voice. "It's your chair. I want you back, and I'll have you back any time. But you've gotta be sure you want it. You can't say yes one day and no, you're not sure, the next. It'll be tough, but you can do it. Only *you* have to believe that, too."

But doubts—nameless, persistent—were nagging at Bix Beiderbecke's mind. He was scared, and not hiding it well. "I just don't know, Paul. Give me a day or two to think about it. I'll let you know at the beginning of next week."

Full of misgivings he returned to the 44th Street Hotel. Looking back, Andy Secrest was in no doubt both about Whiteman's attitude and Bix's dilemma.

"Paul had kept him on full salary while he was out of the band, you know," he told the authors. "I'm positive Paul kept that place for him. He loved Bix. I honestly think that when Bix talked to Paul and Paul asked him if he was ready to return, Bix decided that his nerves just weren't up to the daily routine and that he didn't feel he could handle it. He didn't have the stamina. Paul had engagements that were making terrific demands on us—so many shows a day and all—and Bix wouldn't have been able to handle that kind of responsibility. But even then, Paul always said the spot was his any time he wanted it."

Bix's answer came early the following week. He wasn't ready yet, he told Whiteman. Just another few months, time to play around a bit and test himself, see if he could take the pace, build up his confidence. Whiteman agreed—but told him, with regret, that he'd now have to take him off the payroll until he actually rejoined.

Later, Bix told Esten Spurrier that "he'd told Paul to keep Andy, who did a good job, and with times getting tougher and tougher Andy might have a more difficult time getting a job than Bix. It was really a from-the-heart sacrifice, because Bix loved Paul, always said he was like a second father to him. It could have been a face-saving story, but I somehow think there was a lot of truth in it."

But there was no kidding himself. He wasn't going back—and, sometime around this time, Bix Beiderbecke's seven-month stretch as a teetotaler came to an end. Exactly when and how he began drinking again is unclear, but there is strong likelihood that it was within weeks, perhaps even days, of his interview with his former boss. Insecure, he telephoned some old friends and invited them around to the hotel. Most of them knew little of the events of the previous winter, or of Bix's brush with a potentially fatal illness. For them, Dick Turner included, Bix was back, and all too often that meant the best thing to do was to head for the nearest speakeasy.

Turner, dropping by the hotel one afternoon, found Bix pensive, full of doubt, in need of reassurance who he was, who he'd been—and who he again might be.

"We were on our way to hoist a few at a West Side speak I knew . . . when we passed the back of the Roseland building. About eight or ten of Fletcher Henderson's men were on a fire escape, smoking. Bix, looked up and waved, but got no recognition. He got all alarmed, panicky, and tore his hat off so they could better see him. The result was magic: they all nodded and beamed and babbled like so many monkeys. 'See? They all still know me,' Bix said to me. It seemed to make him happy to know that."

The Technicolor musical *King of Jazz* opened at New York's Roxy Theater on Monday, the 5th of May, with the full Whiteman orchestra onstage to provide an in-person sendoff. For the first week, George Gershwin was featured daily at the piano as soloist on *Rhapsody in Blue*. It was to be his last appearance with the band which had helped make his international reputation.

Whiteman had plenty on his mind. First the Wall Street crash, then the orchestra's long layoff in California, and now the collapse of his plans for a grand tour, had cut deep into his popularity. Popular tastes were changing before his eyes, veering toward less extravagant entertainment and smaller, less lavish, productions. New, instantly danceable groups, among them Rudy Vallee's Connecticut Yankees and Goldkette's Orange Blossoms, now achieving maturity as the precision-drilled Casa Loma Orchestra, were putting up stiff competition on the ballroom circuit and even in the recording studios.

Right after the Roxy engagement, said Bargy, Whiteman chopped his personnel to 18. "Then we really got back to work—to help Paul recover his lost reputation as a dance band."

Bix, still in a quandary about Whiteman, moved into room 605 of the 44th Street Hotel and began looking for freelance work. He took to dropping in afternoons on his next-door neighbor, a young trumpet player named Pasquale "Pat" Ciricillo, who was trying to finish a music degree at Columbia during the day and playing around town in the evenings. Ciricillo had a piano, a Wurlitzer upright he'd bought the previous autumn for $300 but seldom had a chance to use. He was leaving at the beginning of June for a summer resort job, which meant the Wurlitzer would be sitting there, unused, for more than three months. Unless—

Ciricillo's answer was yes, and a few days later Bix moved the piano next door into his own room—or, more exactly, into the bathroom. Bill Priestley, an occasional visitor during those May days, had just gone to work as a junior architect, and he recalled with an architect's precision that the bathroom of Bix's room was bigger than the bedroom, "about 20 feet long. It had been built in the days when hotel bathrooms had windows instead of mechanical ventilation, which resulted in some strange floor plans."

So the piano wound up in the bathroom. Bix, meanwhile, was beginning to pick up dates. On Friday, May 2, he joined the Dorseys and Bud Freeman for a weekend at Princeton. As always, he was the hero; his name alone appeared to evoke the old magic. It was a good feeling, if a temporary one.

He wrote to Spurrier, complaining that pickings were slim. Even so, said Esten, Bix felt he had to be "a little selective as to who he was playing with—a lot of offers from bad unknown bands, but since he was not financially desperate, many of them he fluffed off. As you know, Bix liked to play with men who were tried and tested, liked the security of an organized band. Hence this attitude. Everyone was scrambling for jobs then, so a steady, well-knit group was sort of out of the question."

Scrambling was hardly the word to describe the New York freelance music scene in mid-1930. When the crash had put the lid on the entertainment business, those musicians who could made tracks for the radio studios or for the movie lots on the Coast, where the work might be boring but the money was steady and reasonably good. But competition was keen, and a lot of trumpet men with better technical equipment than Bix Beiderbecke's were scuffling for jobs.

Friday, May 16, found Tommy Dorsey and Bix at Williams College in Massachusetts billed as the "Beiderbecke-Dorsey Orchestra" for a private house party, then again the following night for a dance at the Phi Gamma Delta fraternity house. Almost like Indiana days, Bix still comfortable in a collegiate setting. Most of the band drove back to New York Sunday, but Bix, Dorsey and the guitarist Carl Kress stayed on until Tuesday, perhaps wooed by the adulation of the undergraduate fans.

At one point, an enthusiastic Phi Gam asked how a jazz band made records. That, said a slightly tipsy Dorsey, called for a demonstration. Using a floor lamp as a microphone, they jammed softly on "Jazz Me Blues," each stepping forward to the mike when his turn came to solo.

Bix was working a lot at the bathroom piano, and Challis came around to help take down final versions of "Flashes" and "In the Dark." "Candlelights" was now ready for publication. The ideas, at least, were flowing.

Hoagy Carmichael looked in with an offer. "Hey, ol' buddy, got a date with Victor on the 21st to make a coupla sides. Wanna do it?"

Bix hesitated. Could he? If he couldn't take the pace with Whiteman, would he be able to make it in his first crack at a recording studio since "Waiting at the End of the Road"? The company was certainly reassuring: Bud Freeman, Venuti, Benny Goodman. Yes. Yes indeed, he'd do it.

Carmichael was not without misgivings. Bix had been sick; he wasn't yet altogether himself. He tired easily, sometimes appeared to lack energy. Although the drinking still seemed under control, he was clearly no longer on the wagon. But "he looked fine; I figured he was still convalescing and therefore didn't give him as much to do as I might have," Hoagy told the authors. As things turned out, Bix soloed both on Carmichael's "Rockin' Chair," originally written for Mildred Bailey, and on "Barnacle Bill, the Sailor." But he split the trumpet work with James "Bubber" Miley, just a few months out of Duke Ellington's brass section.

Though Beiderbecke's contribution to "Rockin' Chair" is brief and relatively ill at ease, he turns on the old fire for a 20-bar, up-tempo outburst on "Barnacle Bill." Some deterioration is obvious: the open tone is coarser, a reminder of Bix's increased use of the derby in his latter weeks with Whiteman, and the notes no longer tumble out so effortlessly. Where Goodman is already riding Gene Krupa's heavy four-to-the-bar with a comfort presaging their long and successful association, Bix seems stiff with it, as though hankering after the looser style of earlier days. At one point in the solo he and Krupa almost part company altogether.

But for all that the solo glows with optimism. The musicians remembered the "Barnacle Bill" session as one of high spirits, a momentary recapturing of carefree good times. Venuti, never able to resist a gag, joined the male chorus chanting "Barnacle Bill, the Sailor" on the tune's refrain—but inserting "Shithead" for "Sailor." The record was issued anyway, with Victor executive heads none the wiser. But what may have been muddy and indistinct on 1930 reproduction equipment comes across loud and clear with a modern pickup.

By now Bix had a roommate in Ray Lodwig, who had also decided to cast his lot on the New York freelance market. They decided to make it a partnership, each including the other whenever possible on whatever work he found.

There were always visitors—some just dropping up to drink and talk, others to jazz. One memorable evening's music in room 605 included Bud Freeman, Lennie Hayton—one of those let go in Whiteman's May purge —Red McKenzie and others. Mildred Bailey, a motherly arm around Bix's shoulders, his head resting on her ample bosom, sang her unexpurgated lyrics to the blues, "The Boy in the Boat."

One non-playing guest that night was John Wiggin, a Bix fan since his undergraduate days at Stanford University. He had just been named by NBC to help produce their new Camel Pleasure Hour radio series, sponsored by Camel cigarettes in a belated attempt to cash in on the successful formula pioneered by Old Gold with Whiteman and Lucky Strike with B. A. Rolfe. N.W. Ayer & Son, the advertising agency handling the account, nominated Nat Shilkret to form the orchestra. Not illogically, Shilkret's choice for arranging and general musical organization was Bill Challis.

Together, the two men set about recruiting what was, in effect, a large Whiteman-style orchestra with a nucleus of Goldkette and Whiteman alumni, including some of the May castoffs. They even went so far as to suggest going after the Rhythm Boys; but the trio was still on the Coast and doing well. Unanimous choice for hot cornet soloist was Bix Beiderbecke. "I'd always found the Goldkette outfit a group of extraordinarily talented young musicians," Shilkret explained in a letter to the authors. "They combined the then modern style of playing plus a free, improvising type of music.

"Bix . . . had the innate ability to weave wonderful results in solo spots with a given popular melody. . . . He played in a melodic vein, and had a way of turning a pop chorus into a gem which was eagerly listened to and copied by hundreds of trumpet players."

Shilkret soon found his dual obligations to Victor and the Camel series too numerous to carry, and turned the baton of the new orchestra over to Charles Previn. But he remained in close association with the show; there is even a good chance, he said, that he used Bix on some of his regular Victor recording sessions at this time, though he was unable to recall dates or titles.

Landing the Camel job left Bix giddy with excitement. It seemed that a tailor-made second chance in a Whiteman-style musical environment had been dropped into his lap—but without the extra pressures of theater dates, records and traveling. With renewed determination to stay straight and make a go of it, he took his place in the brass section between Whiteman's former lead man Charlie Margulis and Leo McConville, a New York studio musician who had worked extensively with Red Nichols and Roger Wolfe Kahn and himself developed a jazz style along markedly Bix-influenced lines.

The band featured other old friends: Tommy Dorsey, Red Mayer, Min Leibrook, Lennie Hayton, Arthur Schutt, Carl Kress—all men he knew and who respected him.

The Camel Pleasure Hour went on the air at 9:30 P.M. Wednesday, June 4, 1930, over WJZ, an NBC station in New York. Among the guest artists was Helen Kane, the "boop-boop-be-doop" girl of popular song. Hayton and Schutt did a "modern" novelty duet and Bix had a couple of spirited choruses in Challis' arrangement of "Strike Up the Band" and a reworking of his "I've Found a New Baby" score.

It was almost too good to be true. The band rehearsed a lot, something Bix had never enjoyed, and there was plenty of new material to read off virtually at sight. But he found he could cope reasonably well with it, relying on McConville to steer him through the more complicated ensemble passages.

It was a break not to be wasted. Musicians arriving at the studio on rehearsal or broadcast days would often find Bix the first man there, an hour or more early. Shilkret even recalled that the cornetist "often came to a studio the night before and slept there in order to be ready for a morning date." Exaggeration or not, the remark is true to other impressions of Bix's new-found conscientiousness.

Even Bismark and Agatha, encouraged at this turn of events, made the long journey east to visit their son during a broadcast in NBC's Studio B on Fifth Avenue. Bix, John Wiggin recalled, took special pride in introducing his parents to his friends on the show.

But on the broadcasts themselves, direct action was sometimes necessary to make sure he got through the arrangements. McConville remembered it with fondness before his death in 1968:

"Bix wasn't exactly the best at sight-reading music, you know. I remember one arrangement—forget what the name was—but it had a lot of notes in it, and Bix had four bars to play, then rest four, then play four more, and so on. He was pretty worried about it, and told me, 'I won't know when to come in. What should I do?'

"So I told him, 'You stand up, and when I give you a little kick you start playing for all you're worth.' So I cued him for his entries by kicking him. That's all he needed. He played it fine."

Bix's gratitude was immediate and lasting. He later autographed a copy of the sheet music of "In the Dark": "To Leo, one of the best personally and musically—thanks for saving my life on the Camel Hour numerous times."

McConville was running down his part on a new Challis score at rehearsal one morning when Bix eased quietly into the seat beside him and leaned over. "It's behind can number three," he said in a whisper. Puzzled, McConville glanced up at him. Then, realization. Bix, now making a show of poring attentively over his own part, had stashed a jug of gin behind one of the toilets in the men's room.

So again it had begun. Not surprising; if he had been unable to work up enough courage to face the pressure of life with Whiteman, Bix was not going to let his Camel Hour reprieve slip away. Just one shot before rehearsal. Just one before the show—insurance, to steady the nerves. That, as Dr. Rodney Long has pointed out, was all that was necessary to start the old process all over again:

> People talk about "taking the cure." There is no "cure" for alcoholism. It is not quibbling to say that a "cured" alcoholic would be able to drink moderately, but there is no treatment known which can achieve this objective. Only recovery from the disease is possible, and the recovered alcoholic is always one drink away from disaster.[15]

Or again, in the same article:

> Another early indication of the disease is the resort to alcohol on every occasion of stress and anxiety. The alcoholic fondly imagines that he can pull himself out of all his troubles with a bottle-opener. Recovered alcoholics constantly refer to that point in time when drinking was no longer a social asset but a serious liability, to the time when they first had to have "the morning eye-opener" to make them fighting fit for the day ahead.

Two days after the first Camel broadcast, Ray Lodwig and Bix turned up at the Brunswick Record Company's New York studios to do three jazz sides in company with Goodman, Jack Teagarden, Krupa, Venuti, Frank Signorelli and Leibrook. The resulting records have provoked decades of dispute among jazz scholars. One of the three titles was a pop tune, "Strut Miss Lizzie." The other two are intimately connected with Bix and his circle of musical acquaintances. All include jazz cornet solos in the Bix style, but many critics, comparing the work to Bix's efforts of two years before, have questioned his presence.

The authors played the records for Jimmy McPartland, Red Nichols, Andy Secrest and Leo McConville. All identified Bix at once, Secrest calling attention to the fact that "Loved One," one of the three titles, is a reworking of "I Like That," a Trumbauer-Hayton collaboration Bix had recorded for Okeh a year before. The cornet work on both records is similar in concept. All four musicians echoed an observation by Sylvan Kirsner, violinist in the Camel orchestra, that it "wasn't the Bix of old." The tone had lost some of its luster; ideas and execution were stiff in spots. But all agreed it was Bix.

The participating musicians themselves were quick to agree. Benny Goodman, hardly the possessor of an infallible memory, expressed some doubt, though he could suggest no alternative. Teagarden and Venuti, though equally unreliable as historians, were certain of Bix's presence on musical grounds. Venuti, on listening to the last chorus of "Strut Miss Lizzie," burst out laughing at a four-bar passage which sounds remarkably like one of his famed "Bronx cheer" effects. "Yeah—that's me on the fart chorus," he said. "Wanna see how it's done?" He demonstrated for the authors by crossing the thumb of his left hand across his index finger at the knuckle, forming a "mouthpiece," then blowing into it as one would a trumpet or cornet.

---

15. Long, Rodney, M.R.C.S., L.R.C.P. and Williams, Lincoln, M.R.C.S., L.R.C.P.: "The Clinical Problem and Management of Alcoholism," *The Practitioner,* February 1968, Vol. 200, pp. 205–214.

Perhaps even more significant, Secrest, who sat next to Bix in Whiteman's orchestra during the last days, and McConville, his sectionmate in the Camel Hour ensemble, were most certain of his identity. All agreed, with regret, that Bix had slipped badly.

Around this time Bix and Tommy Dorsey joined violinist Cass Hagan in an attempt to sell a new all-star band to bookers around New York, and even perhaps interest them in a European tour. Audiences in Britain and on the Continent had been getting the Victor, Columbia and Okeh records regularly on their own labels. They knew the names of the sidemen in such bands as Whiteman's far better than did the average American. According to "Slim Evans" Neirouter, friend from Cincinnati and Chicago days, the proposed big band actually rehearsed a few times and played one engagement, an American legion outing in Merrick, Long Island, out near where Dorsey lived.

*Variety* ran a two-sentence squib in its August 6 issue, announcing: "Bix Beiderbecke starting his own band. Formerly with Whiteman orchestra and wants Whiteman to manage him."

Neirouter said he thought Max Kaminsky, from Boston, was among the trumpets and Hymie Schertzer, later to become the lead alto mainstay of Benny Goodman's swing band, was in the sax section.

Neirouter was living at the time in a room above Jimmy Plunkett's speakeasy at 205½ West 53rd Street, named "The Trombone Club" for Dorsey, a regular and vociferous patron. Plunkett had a piano, and his speak had become New York's most popular musicians' hangout throughout the late 1920s and early 1930s. Bix, too, was a frequent Plunkett's customer at this time, said Neirouter, and the band had been largely recruited from among the regulars. Others in the personnel included Joe Sullivan at the piano, Benny Goodman's brother Harry on bass, Bud Freeman and Pee Wee Russell. "Hymie couldn't make the Merrick gig," said Slim, "so I filled in. Everyone met in the basement of a red schoolhouse. A little round baldheaded man poured beer from a five-gallon coffee pot.

"Bix and Ray Lodwig were late, but came up over a hill on the front lawn playing 'The Billboard March' with two cornets. Tunes like 'Exactly Like You' kept things moving. Lots of jamming. Then we all moved over to the sea shore club and played. Some of the boys were on the Camel Hour the next day. I doubt if they made it."

For all the apparent promise of such a group, the bookers weren't interested. The venture failed to get off the ground.

Somebody at Plunkett's came up with the idea that a jazzman's nocturnal indoor life wasn't good for the health. So, under the younger Dorsey's self-proclaimed expert tutelage, a group of the regulars was transformed one Sunday afternoon into a softball team, playing every week in Central Park. As their confidence grew, they challenged other musicians, getting an immediate rise out of the bands of Duke Ellington and Fred Waring.

Bix, who had never lost his love for baseball, shared the outfield with Red Nichols. Lew Green, guitarist in the Camel band, was the pitcher, while manager Dorsey directed traffic from the catcher's position. Infielders included Neirouter, tenor saxophonist Larry Binyon, drummer Vic Engle and Carl Kress, whom Lew Green had replaced on the Camel show.

Dorsey, said Nichols, ran the team "like a dictator. One day during practice he was batting and hit a long fly ball. I took off running after it, of course, even though I could hear him laughing as he jogged to first base. He thought I'd never get it. But somehow I did, caught it on the fly. My delight at having caught it was only exceeded by Tom's rage. He really blew a gasket at that one."

Bix enjoyed the Sunday afternoons. It seemed to some who knew him during this time that he revelled in anything which reminded him of earlier days. Room 605 was becoming a regular rendezvous for hangers-on, especially Priestley and his crowd of Princeton old grads. Bix seemed almost to invite their attentions, a chance to be the cynosure all over again, just as he had been back in Indiana. Sprawled in a chair, he would challenge one or another of his courtiers to bang out a full, two-handed chord on the piano. Then, without bothering to get up, he would pull the old trick—betting each man a dollar that he could call out all ten notes, bottom to top.

"He never lost a bet," said Priestley, "though we'd take him on every time in the hope he'd miss just one."

He was still holding his own on the Camel Hour, sometimes even delivering solos that took Challis back to the beginning with Whiteman. Vocalist Frances Williams, guesting on the July 2 show, got "so wrapped up in what Bix was playing" in his half-chorus solo after her vocal on "All Fall in Love" that she forgot the lyric and muffed her next entrance immediately afterward. Bix, seeing the singer falter, stepped coolly back to the microphone and played another chorus while she pulled herself together, "and it was even better than the one he'd played before."

But things were starting to slip. By September, his resolution to stay punctual, rested and reasonably sober had done a three-part vanishing act. He began missing rehearsals. Still, he was straight enough to land a recording date at Victor on Monday, September 8. If he could click with this one, it might be what he needed to plug his all-star big band idea. Inevitably, he made for Plunkett's to round up some sidemen. At the bar he found Pee Wee Russell, Jimmy Dorsey and Benny Goodman in animated conversation. Whom to hire? The arrangements called for two alto saxes and a tenor. Bud Freeman was already booked. Bix accepted Pee Wee's invitation to join the trio for a quick one—and thanked them by hiring all three men for the date. Each is featured on one of the three sides recorded that day. Goodman has an eight-bar solo after Bix's half-chorus on "Deep Down South," Dorsey is heard on "I'll Be a Friend with Pleasure," and Pee Wee plays on "I Don't Mind Walking in the Rain."

A week later it was back to Victor's Studio Two on West 24th Street, this time to make two more sides for Hoagy. Shortly after 12:30 P.M., Jack Teagarden strolled in, glanced at the wall clock and put his trombone case on a chair. Two of the other musicians were standing near a cluster of music stands and microphones, talking quietly. No sign of Bix. Hoagy showed up, scores to "Bessie Couldn't Help It" and his own "Georgia on My Mind" under his arm. Still no Bix.

Ten minutes to go, and recording engineer L.L. Watson came out to ask the musicians to take their places. Jimmy Dorsey, Freeman, even Bix's roommate, Ray Lodwig: all were there. All but Bix.

By chance, Teagarden glanced over at the darkened, drape-covered far corner of the studio. There, horn across knee, sat Bix, working the valves, talking inaudibly to himself. He had been there the entire time. Quietly, gently, "Big Tea" walked over, in time to hear a few half-whispered words. "C'mon now, give me a break this time. Don't let me down." Talking to his horn, as though the Bach cornet alone would decide whether he made it through the session.

Hoagy, too, recalled Bix's nervousness that day, but "when he did play he was fine, and really lifted the music." Bix stayed out of the session's third selection, a rhumba called "One Night in Havana." It had no jazz. No reason why Lodwig, with his straight mute and pronounced "nanny-goat" vibrato, couldn't handle it alone.

Bix was now missing as many Camel Hour rehearsals as he made, and sometimes he wasn't even there for the broadcasts. Sometimes he would show up just in time to go on the air without having run down any of the arrangements first. Once he arrived without a horn. McConville and Arthur Schutt, independently of each other, spoke of feeling a "torture of uncertainty" at whether Bix would make it through one more show.

If Bix couldn't take care of himself, someone would have to do it for him. Several of the men on the show, McConville, Schutt and Shilkret among them, took turns stopping by the hotel to pick him up on the way to work and making sure he was in his chair, ready to play, when the red light went on.

"He tried hard to cure his drinking habit, that I have to say," said Shilkret in a letter. "For awhile he succeeded in falling off and on the wagon. Just what made him drink I don't know. Was it loneliness, companionship or habit? Bix certainly was intelligent enough to know that drinking was not good for him.

"But when he started missing broadcasts we searched for him and usually found him at some bar or at his home, sleeping it off."

Pat Ciricillo, back in Manhattan for the beginning of the Columbia fall term, was appalled at the change in Bix. "He was in bad shape, even drinking straight alcohol with lemon juice drops in it. He told me that every time he tried to go on the wagon, friends came up and visited him with gin bottles, and that tempted him."

The breaking point, inevitable now, came toward the end of the October 8 Camel Hour broadcast. Bix had been unusually withdrawn, almost absent-minded, during the rundown and early part of the show. Now, in the final chorus of a Challis arrangement, he stood to blow one of those eight-bar slots which had helped make his reputation with Whiteman. No sound came out of his horn. Leo McConville, reading a supporting figure, looked up, alarmed, to see Bix, blank-faced and staring, helpless, horn away from mouth, fear and incomprehension in his eyes. He shook his head in a silent plea for help, and automatically Leo stood to play the rest of the solo, then ease his stricken colleague back into a chair. Afterwards, Bix was unable to say what had happened—only that everything had "gone blank." He had registered what was going on around him, but could not relate it to himself.

His world, his hopes and dreams, were shattered. Another chance gone, little more than a year after "Waiting at the End of the Road." Within a few days, Bobby Effros had taken over the third chair in the Camel Hour orchestra and Bix Beiderbecke, lonely and scared, was again on a train headed home for Davenport.

310

# Chapter 22

Bix telephoned Esten Spurrier from the Davenport station when his train got in. "Hey, how about picking me up and taking me home?" He sounded cheerful, composed.

Spurrier was taken aback. "He'd written some time earlier, maybe a month or so, that he would like to come home for the winter, but I'd discounted it as a nostalgic hour in which he wrote. Yet here he was. Far from looking like a guy who's just had a breakdown, he was as bright-eyed and bushy-tailed as I'd seen him.

"He said he'd stopped off briefly in Chicago, and was disappointed to find that some of his buddies weren't in town. But now he was home, and genuinely happy to be back, I thought."

On the way to Grand Avenue they talked about the events of the weeks just past, Bix carefully skirting any reference to his last days on the Camel Hour. "He mentioned 'Barnacle Bill'—he couldn't believe something like that would ever be pressed, felt it was done more for laughs, and said he just did a lot of blowing without inhibition. He was disappointed about the Victor date under his own name. He'd always hoped to record with a handpicked group. Thought this one was it. But with hard times and all, and all sorts of old friends and associates out of work prevailing on him to do the dates, he ended up with a sort of big muddy group, far from his fulfillment.

"He didn't say much about the drinking then. But in every letter he'd sent to me he'd always included a squib about it—how life was better without it, that he got a great satisfaction out of saying no gracefully."

Bix spent the remainder of the autumn cloistered in the big white house on Grand Avenue. He seldom ventured outside, though it is not clear whether the decision was Aggie's or his. Certainly family members did what they could to discourage callers and afford him what they called "a little peace." A few old friends, learning he was about, tried to reach him by telephone, only to be told he was resting or simply unable to come to the phone to speak. Not even Spurrier was able to break through the wall of silence. Aggie, shocked at her son's new setback, clearly felt full recuperation would only be possible through rest and near-total seclusion.

October melted red and gold into November. Bix remained indoors. Sometimes, neighbors said, he would come out to sit on the screened-in front porch, a pale, solitary figure in a maroon sweater, watching the leaves on the lawn. But no one ventured near, and ultimately he would again disappear into the house.

Winter set in cold and crisp during the first week of December, and with it a break in Bix's isolation. A few outsiders, Spurrier and Swanson among them, were allowed up at last to visit. Bix appeared happy to see them, and to Aggie's dismay accepted playing jobs alongside them for December 10 and 17 in Trave O'Hearn's band. Spurrier's presence, at least, was ground for confidence. A teetotaler and family man, he took a personal interest in Bix's welfare. "I was with him as a kind of constant deterrent —and no secrets," he said.

Back again in a secure environment, Bix seemed to have rallied. One day, out of the blue, he telephoned Spurrier. "There was a Ted Lewis picture playing downtown—*Is Everybody Happy?* or something of that ilk —and he wanted to go down to the Garden Theater to see it, but he didn't want to go alone. Asked me to go with him. Ted Lewis was a bit off the beaten path for us, but he told me Don Murray was in it, and he wasn't up to seeing it alone. Don's death had hit him very hard. We all know that Bix was replete with friendly acquaintances, that he gave of himself and his time freely. But his really deep, abiding love and friendship was sparingly given. This was brought home so forcefully to me here. His true love and affection for Don, his grief at Don's passing, was so poignant.

"We went. And for Bix it was a terrifically emotional thing—his pleasure at seeing Don on the screen, and yet the sadness that comes from the finality of death."

Then Christmas and New Year's with the usual family festivities—and much crossing of fingers on Bix's behalf for the coming year. By mid-January, he again seemed on the way to complete rejuvenation, as though repeating the events of a year before.

"Hey, Bix, y'hear who's coming through next week?" Les Swanson, excited, on the telephone. Bix chuckled.

"Try me."

"Pops. Whiteman. They're playing Danceland next Saturday night. Wanna go?"

In all probability Bix had already heard from Pops and knew in advance about the forthcoming visit. At any event, when the Old Gold Special pulled into Davenport on January 17, Bix Beiderbecke was on the platform to meet them, smiling and confident. Whiteman's delight at seeing him was obvious. They shook hands warmly, and Tram, Rank and the others greeted him like a long-lost brother. At his former employer's request, Bix promised to be in the audience at Danceland that evening— and even to bring along the Bach cornet, "just in case."

"Bix picked up my wife and me early," said Spurrier, "and we entered the back of the ballroom together. The band was just setting up, and one of the eagle-eyed Whiteman men spotted Bix at once. Helen and I almost got trampled in the stampede. It was so gratifying to see his acceptance and the genuine appreciation shown him."

"Bix! Bix, *honey!* You naughty little son of a bitch! Come to mama." Moving across the floor, tears welling in her eyes, Mildred Bailey stretched out her arms to embrace a suddenly sheepish Bix. "Oh, you mean ol' bastard, staying away so long. We've missed you so! How could you *do* this to mama?" She hugged him and cried.

"Oh, how she clucked over him," said an awed Spurrier. "Like a mother, words of love and admiration, then giving him heck in the next breath."

Whiteman, too, embraced his former star sideman. "Come on backstage after the show, Bix, and let's have a little talk," he said.

The evening began with Bix, Spurrier and friends at a table off to the side of the bandstand. Secrest was sounding good and sure, stronger and more consistent in solo than in his days sitting beside Bix. The band had just moved back to Victor and there were some new faces in the personnel, among them Nat Natoli, a friend from the Goldkette days and Walled Lake.

Shortly before intermission, Whiteman motioned to the audience for silence and stepped to the microphone. His exact words are lost to history: in 1931, "on location" recording was still a gift of the future. But Whiteman bandsmen and Davenport friends recalled a lengthy tribute to Bix's achievements as both cornetist and pianist, his extraordinary ear, and above all the personal qualities of the man Whiteman was later to laud as "the greatest gentleman I've ever known." It had been his privilege, he said, "to have this extraordinary musician in my orchestra." When Paul concluded his remarks by inviting Bix up on the bandstand to take his old place for a few tunes, Davenporter Hal Olm told the authors, the applause "was like thunder.

"It was a great moment in my life," said Olm, who had been introduced to Bix only moments before. "Whiteman had an awful time coaxing Bix up on the stand—and I'm sure it was modesty on Bix's part. They played a number—I don't remember any more what it was—but he took a solo, and I can still see the members of that great band as they turned to watch and listen to him in the purest sort of admiration."

After the show Bix came backstage to see Whiteman, with Spurrier in tow. The bandleader was jubilant—and got right to the point.

"Want to come back now, Bix? Why not give it one more try? You're sounding fine."

Bix, hesitant, avoided the big man's gaze. "Aw, I don't know, Paul. Andy's doing a great job, and—"

Whiteman stopped him short with a hand on his shoulder. "Sure, Bix, I know. But just don't forget, now or ever. That cornet chair in my band will always be there for you whenever you want to claim it. Only you can kick yourself out of it."

The rest of January and February was a slack time throughout the midwest. With the Depression taking hold and spending cut back almost to nothing, there was little regular employment for musicians. Bix did a few jobs with Hicks again at Danceland, but mostly he hung around home, socializing with Davenport friends and practicing the piano, but generally neglecting the cornet. When he dropped in at the Coliseum one January night to sit in with Cliff Mandy's band from Mason City, he took pains to apologize for his rusty embouchure.

"He was carrying his horn in a black velvet sack," tenor saxophonist Neil Whiteside recalled, dwelling on the detail. "He was very quiet, very unassuming, polite—but sort of distant. He apologized to us that his lip was weak because he hadn't been playing much.

"But when he sat in with us—for two and a half hours in all—he sounded great, though no one in the audience seemed particularly impressed."

Bix now felt he was ready for another crack at New York. Whiteman had opened on February 9 at the Granada Cafe in Chicago, and a few nights later Bix turned up to listen and say hello. Several of the musicians, Roy

Bargy among them, were surprised at the appearance of the high-spirited young man in the knit sweater.

"He looked just great—like a college kid. He was in fine shape, and we all hoped he would never again fall into bad habits," Bargy said.

Bix did not sit in that night. But he talked enthusiastically of his determination to stay on the wagon for good this time and pick up his career where he had left it. To a man, the band wished him well—and silently prayed it might be so.

Back in New York the freelance market was, if anything, even tougher. Competition was keener, jobs scarcer. Bix joined the Dorsey Brothers' big band on Saturday, March 14, for a senior hop weekend at Amherst College in Massachusetts. Drummer Johnny Morris recalled finding him "very moody and despondent" at the general situation, and reluctant to solo. But student jazz fans in the crowd soon noticed him and began clamoring for him.

"Bix wasn't anxious to play. But out of the big band we formed a small jazz group and finally succeeded in getting him to jam with us. He played all his own tunes—the recordings which had made him famous. He was just tremendous, and the crowd gave him a great ovation."

Bix, Tommy, Jimmy and the rhythm section worked through "Jazz Me Blues," "At the Jazz Band Ball" and several of the other dixieland standards, following much the same format as Bix's small-band Okeh records. But new times were bringing new stars, and for the first time, Bix felt himself overshadowed by a trumpet man who was not an imitator, but a new and original talent in the making.

Bernard "Bunny" Berigan, playing lead that night, had just come back from Europe with Jimmy and "was the trumpet player of the day," said Morris. "Tommy had brought Bix along on the date to help him make a few dollars. It was quite apparent that Bix was professionally jealous of Berigan, but on that night Bix completely captured the audience and Berigan was definitely in the background."

The Amherst college newspaper the next morning bore this out. Bix's jam group, it said, "was considered one of the best five-piece [sic] outfits in the country."

The next weeks brought occasional Dorsey dates, a bit of radio work. But most of the time Bix just hung around, dropping in on Pat Ciricillo to play the Wurlitzer upright, sometimes going by Challis' place for transcribing sessions on the piano compositions.

"Jeez, Bill, haven't you got that down yet?" Challis, scribbling on a pad of manuscript paper, looked up.

"Look, pal. You play it differently each time. It's gonna take more time that way to get down."

Challis remembered the exchange vividly in later years. "Each time he'd play a passage he'd think of some way to improve on it. That was okay, really, because most of the time they actually were improvements.

"But he didn't seem willing to accept that it took me awhile to get the thing on paper, and if he improved something, I'd have to change it. He'd get annoyed, impatient, just like a kid, with things he felt should happen in a short time and in fact took a long time."

A visit from Jack Teagarden about this time found Bix at the piano, puzzling over how to connect the melodic second strain of the final version of "In the Dark" with a recapitulation of the more chromatic first subject. The trombonist, leaning over his shoulder as Bix played, whistled a melodic fragment.

"Hey, that's nice. Whistle it again." Teagarden did, and it became the basis for a 16-bar transitional passage, transcribed several days later by Challis, neatly lacing the work together.

Teagarden and Bix were sitting around the room talking when the cornetist came up with a bizarre idea. Brother Burnie had just written from Davenport to say he had gone into the cemetary business. Bix, intrigued, proposed a bit of independent research.

"He wanted to go down to the Bellevue morgue and have a look at the stiffs," Teagarden said. "I told him, well, if I had a pint of gin first, I might be able to go. So I had my gin and off we went.

"It must be the most gruesome morgue in the world, that place. There we were, and Bix slipped the night caretaker a five-dollar bill to let us through, and in we went. By then I was doing pretty good and it didn't bother me, but after awhile Bix started to get sick. So we left."

Later, Jack got to wondering whether Bix, who had begun by then to take an increasingly fatalistic view of his drinking, might have been giving vent to a premonition of early death. He later put this question to Burnie, who characteristically dismissed it. "Nope—I was in the business and he wanted to see the best in the world. That's all there was to it." Teagarden remained unconvinced, and wondered about the incident for years afterwards.

Bix Beiderbecke's "Flashes" and "In the Dark" were copyrighted April 18 by Robbins Music Company. As usual, said Bill Challis, Bix first spent hours just contemplating what to call them. "He wanted the titles to fit the music. The results were reflections of the way he felt about the pieces."

One April afternoon Challis roused Bix out of bed with a proposal. He and Cork O'Keefe, Tom Rockwell's partner in the new Rockwell-O'Keefe booking agency, had been talking to some of the members of the Casa Loma Orchestra and discovered they planned to drop "Dub" Schoefner, their jazz trumpet man, because of his excessive drinking and unreliability. Challis suggested Bix as a replacement. A band huddle yielded a tentative yes—at least the willingness to give him a tryout.

"Bix didn't have too much love for the Casa Loma band," Challis said. "It was a real precision, polished outfit, and Bix wasn't really a section man. Give him a third part and it was a struggle—it meant he had to read.

"But I kept after him—told him that the band had a lot of arrangements he knew and had played with Whiteman, stuff I'd done like 'Dardanella.' He kept saying 'Good, good,' and shaking his head up and down."

It was a listless time for Bix. He was getting only sporadic work and his spirits were wavering. Despite reservations about the reading, he finally agreed to drive up to Connecticut with his friend to hear the Casa Lomans on a characteristic evening.

"He was all set. Got his horn, spruced up and ready. We set off, driving through the traffic up Fifth Avenue. Well, we're stopping for traffic and things, and Bix has a chance to think. I could feel the tension as he thinks, 'Where the hell am I going? What am I going for? What am I going to do? I'm gonna be stranded up there. What's this all about?'

"We got as far as Central Park, and it just wasn't appealing to him. He says, all of a sudden, 'I don't think I want to go tonight. Wait'll they come closer.' So out of the car he gets, and that was that."

Though Squirrel Ashcraft, Bill Priestley and the other cult ringleaders at Princeton had graduated in 1929, the Beiderbecke name still carried weight on the campus. Friday night, May 1, Bix appeared there for a house party weekend as nominal leader of a band which included Goodman, Freeman and Joe Sullivan. Jack Teagarden's trumpet-playing kid brother, Charlie, was also along as, in his own words a "substitute for Bix in case he couldn't make the whole job, as he had been ill. But as it turned out he felt pretty good, and we both played the entire job."

With Goodman fronting, the band kicked off the first evening, a Cottage Club houseparty, at 8:30 P.M. sharp with a relaxed, medium-tempo "Dinah." Priestley, Dick Turner and a few other old grads drove down to listen. Entering, they found the bandstand ringed by couples stamping and calling for Bix.

"To say Bix stole the show is trite but true," Turner wrote years later. "He was the lion of the prom, and the crowds screamed as they were not to again until Sinatra, and Goodman before him, hit the Paramount years later."

Even allowing for the exaggeration of enthusiasm, it is clear that Bix got a warm reception both this night and the next, a party at the Charter Club down the road. Goodman had returned to New York during the day, Saturday, to be replaced by Jimmy Dorsey. Otherwise the personnel was the same.

By now things had loosened up. The band was in high spirits and deep into the apple jack, available in near unlimited supply, when the Saturday night party broke up at midnight. Princetonian Byrnes McDonald suggested they carry on blowing at his nearby home, an invitation readily accepted.

Drummer Johnny Powell clearly remembered McDonald's "enormous mansion, with a long, winding drive leading up to it. Inside, the drinking continued, and it became much more a party than a band session. As the night wore on, the band got more lubricated. Bix, again, had taken that first drink—with the inevitable result. At one point he forsook the cornet and tried to assist Sullivan at the piano, Joe playing bass, Bix treble.

"Sober, Bix was a fine pianist. But in this potted condition, he was playing very badly—so badly that Sullivan became progressively angrier with him. Finally he got so enraged that he pulled his hair down over his face and began pounding his fists on the piano keys, demanding loudly that Bix get the hell away from there.

"This hurt Bix's feelings deeply. He got up and left."

Sometime in Sunday's early hours, somebody thought of getting back to New York. Bix was nowhere to be found. Drunk and now sleepy, the merrymakers stumbled around McDonald's house in search of the cornetist. No luck. By daybreak they had all gone, leaving Bix fast asleep deep in the leather-upholstered couch in the family's oak-panelled library.

He awoke about breakfast time with a headache and the beginnings of a cold, and feeling miserable. At McDonald's insistence he ate, then took his leave with embarrassed thanks and stumbling apology for having inconvenienced the family. After picking up the $125 due the band for the night's playing, he phoned a friend, Jack Delaney, who drove him over to

Vandeventer Avenue and the home of Doug McNamee, banjoist of the original Priestley-Ashcraft Triangle Club band and still a student.

There, after a flurry of telephone calls, Priestley and a few others turned up ready to play some jazz. Bix, hung over and sneezing, was none too enthusiastic about the idea. "He was as ashen as the underside of a toad," Dick Turner said, "and he had this pitiful hangover. It might be sacrilegious to say it this way, but he couldn't play a nickel's worth. He was completely uninspired—and no wonder."

But a few of the fans present were determined to put Bix Beiderbecke through his paces anyway. One would call out a tune, usually something Bix had recorded. Another hummed the first few bars of his cornet solo. "C'mon, Bix, play it." Bix, still dazed, tried to oblige, all the while forcing a wan smile. He would manage a bar or two, then turn to Priestley, who stood, cornet at the ready, beside his mentor. The younger man carried on, playing the solos note for note as he had learned them from the recordings.

Ultimately even this diversion lost its charm, and a group of the faithful shepherded their hero aboard a New York-bound Pennsylvania Railroad coach shortly after 4 P.M. By this time, said Turner, "Bix had turned mean, sarcastic and downright ornery. It was the only time I'd ever seen him that way. We dropped him off at the 44th Street Hotel, where he lived."

Toward evening, still sniffling, Bix dropped in on Johnny Powell over at the Belvedere to deliver the drummer's share of the job money. By then, said Powell, the cornetist's spirits had picked up. "See how I take care of you boys?" he said, tossing a wad of bills on the bed. They talked, Bix waxing suddenly "quite serious about things." The conversation formed the basis for a friendship. During the following weeks, Bix became a frequent visitor to the Belvedere.

"I was impressed by him," Powell said in recollection. "He had a fine mind and was very intelligent. We talked about serious things, and sometimes played records of the Ethel Waters type and discussed music."

But it wasn't all discussion. "Sometimes he'd arrive early and we'd go over to the Loew's New York Theater and catch the 8:30 A.M. movie. We'd sit in the balcony, with—yes, I'm afraid so—a jug of gin under the seat. Whenever someone in the film took a drink we'd join in. Some of the 'society' films featured considerable drinking, and it got to be a bit hard to stumble out of the theater at 11 A.M., drunk, into the bright sunlight and the press of crowded streets."

Bill Challis, now living briefly just over the state line in Greenwich, Connecticut, looked in Tuesday afternoon for another try at coaxing Bix along on a visit to the Casa Loma Orchestra. He'd talked to them again since the first false start, he said, and they were still interested.

Bix was dubious. Same old nagging doubts, especially the reading. Challis persisted. Finally, exasperated, Bix agreed, and they set out again, this time with O'Keefe along for moral support. All the way up to Boston, both men talked a steady stream of encouragement to a none-too-certain Bix Beiderbecke.

Members of the Casa Loma band later disagreed as to just where they were playing the night Bix, Bill and O'Keefe visited them to listen and talk. Violinist-director Mel Jenssen felt certain it was Nuttings-on-the-Charles, the big old riverside ballroom in suburban Waltham where Bix had played five years before with Goldkette. But Pat Davis, the orchestra's hot tenor sax soloist, thought it was Le Vagge's Lido Venice, on Warrenton Street downtown, around the corner from the Metropolitan Hotel, the Casa Lomans' base whenever they played the Boston area.

Billy Rauch, lead trombonist and captain of the brass section, was astonished to see Bix apparently fit and taking an interest in things again. "He looked good, and we thought that he finally had the drinking problem under control." They talked at length, Rauch describing in detail how he and Jenssen, who roomed together on the road, generally confined their drinking to their hotel room after the job. With the exception of Dub Schoefner and a few others, most of the other bandsmen did the same in order to avoid the all too obvious pitfalls of onstand drunkenness. The Casa Loma Orchestra, a cooperative, had forged a reputation for precision and elegance, professional decorum enhancing highly stylized music. As Rauch put it, booze on the bandstand just didn't fit the image.

"We told Bix we would like him to join us after the jobs for relaxing and a good time. He seemed to like the idea, and we thought we had persuaded him not to drink while playing. I understood he'd been on the wagon for a few weeks prior to coming up to Boston, and he was to replace Dub, whom we were letting go on account of liquor on the job."

Bix showed interest, and after spending the night at the Metropolitan he, Challis and O'Keefe headed back for New York. It seemed—and Bill Challis firmly believed—that Bix Beiderbecke was to be third time lucky.

Even so, there were warnings that all was not well with his health. Friday night he played a Dorsey college date in New Jersey. In the car on the way home he kept losing sensation in his legs. By the time they reached his hotel Bix was unable to move. Carl Kress and tenor saxophonist Eddie Miller spent more than 15 minutes helping restore sufficient circulation to Bix's legs to get him on his feet and on the way upstairs to bed.

The following Thursday, May 15, O'Keefe drove Bix up to Springfield, Massachusetts, for another listen to the Casa Lomans at Cook's Butterfly Ballroom. This time he was convinced, and agreed to join the band in Boston the following Friday in time to begin a string of one-nighters throughout New England.

He was happy and talkative on the way up to New Haven the next night to play a Yale University Derby Day dance with the Dorseys, and apologized at length for "putting you fellows out" with his circulation problems Friday. Again, Berigan was on the job; but this time if Bix was jealous he kept it to himself.

His good spirits almost didn't survive the evening. During a stop at a roadside diner en route back to New York, bickering between Tommy and Jimmy over a number or a tempo suddenly turned nasty. Bix stepped in to mediate—just in time to catch one of Tommy's famed roundhouse rights square on the jaw. It sent him sprawling—and ended the argument. Both brothers burst out laughing at the shock on Bix's face and rushed to help him up, the argument forgotten.

The week seemed to drag by. Bix's cold was no better. Challis phoned Wednesday to say he had a radio show Friday and wouldn't be able to follow through on his promise to drive Bix up to Boston.

"He had to go up alone. He assured me he'd be okay. It was all set, he said, and he had a good grip on himself—and I, like a fool, believed him." Challis soon had cause to regret his credulity.

Bix went by train and checked in at the Metropolitan in late morning. Both Jenssen and trombonist Pee Wee Hunt were under the impression he registered under an assumed name, but were at a loss to remember why.

Saturday morning, Rauch called a brass section rehearsal to break Bix in for a ballroom job that night at Wilbur's-on-the-Taunton, at Somerset, between Fall River and Cape Cod. The band had met several days before to discuss their new cornetist's debut and reached a private agreement: no drinking in front of the newcomer. No unnecessary talk about booze or getting drunk.

The rehearsal lasted nearly three hours, with both Rauch and trumpet sectionmates Bobby Jones and Joe Hostetter helping Bix through Gene Gifford's often technically tricky scoring. One especially difficult number was a Gifford original called "China Girl," which built to its climax through two closely-arranged ensemble choruses, the trumpets playing without a break.

But Challis had been as good as his word: the band library also included many of the arrangements he had done for Whiteman, and even a few from Goldkette days, only slightly reworked to fit the Casa Loma instrumentation. Here, at least, Bix was on home ground.

But it was tough going all the same, and afterwards he welcomed Dub Schoefner's invitation to move in with him so they could share a jug away from Rauch's schoolmasterish surveillance. For the Taunton job that night, Dub promised to bring along a suitable inaugural libation for their association. That, said Rauch, was the beginning of the end. "We were travelling in private cars. In our car were Bix, Dub, Mel, drummer Tony Briglia and myself. On the way we had a flat tire, and while Mel, Tony and I fixed it, Dub and Bix stayed in the car.

"Later we found out Dub, who worshipped Bix, had a jug, and the two of them had killed it while we fixed the tire. He did the job, but we were all terribly disappointed because of the drinking."

Sunday, said Pat Davis, it was the same all over again. "Dub really idolized Bix, you know. He played his style and loved the guy. Well, that afternoon he ordered some gin from the 'drugstore' (speakeasy) in the hotel and the two of them really had at it." By evening, neither was in any shape to play. Monday, largely at the behest of Rauch, Jenssen and several of the others, Gene Gifford took Bix aside for a chat.

"Bix was despondent. Obviously we had had our doubts. He wasn't really a section man, and we as a cooperative couldn't afford (as had Whiteman) an extra trumpet player for solo work alone. Bix said himself that his heart wasn't really inclined toward big band work.

"But the thing he kept emphasizing was his conviction by now that his was a hopeless condition, that he was apparently simply unable to reconcile his alcoholic problems."

The decision was made: Bix had to go. He took the news without surprise, packed his horn and suitcase, and caught a train back to New York.

Challis blamed himself for not having been free to watch over his friend during those four days. "I should have known. He had no self-control. If I'd gone with him and had a chance to be with him awhile it would have been okay, I'm sure of it.

"But they had some real tough drinkers in that band. And Bix—well, a couple of sniffs of gin and he was on his way. Then there goes the whole bottle. After those first few drinks the rest didn't make any difference."

Bix ran into Gifford a few weeks later in New York. The arranger began an apology—only to be cut off in mid-sentence. "It's my fault," said Bix. "Really, I'm sorry. My heart just wasn't in it. Please—" his face weary, resigned—"tell the boys I hope they'll forgive me for causing them any embarrassment."

For Bix there was to be no third time lucky. It was already far too late for that.

Vincent Bach cornet no. 620, inscribed "Bix, 1927," on the bell. The black corduroy carrying case is the one Bix used.

# Chapter 23

"Bix! Hey—you in there?"

Dick Turner knocked again on the door of room 605. He had to be there. The desk clerk downstairs hadn't seen him go out in days, and the chambermaid had heard him noodling at the piano.

"C'mon, Bix, open up. It's me."

Sound within. The creaking of bedsprings and someone shuffling to the door, turning the latch, opening it just wide enough to peer out. "Oh— yeah. Hi. C'mon in."

He'd been sleeping, but sleeping badly. Even allowing for that, Turner thought, "he looked just awful. His face had gone all puffy and pale, his eyes washed out and popped. Terrible."

Bix held out something in a glass. Turner accepted it, took a sip. Pure alcohol, with what tasted like a bit of lemon juice mixed in. Oh my God, he thought.

"He'd grown a slight fuzz on his lower lip and a tiny, Hitler-type moustache on his upper. He said it helped his embouchure. But he looked lost. His resistance was down. He said he often felt lousy."

They chatted, sitting on a corner of the bed, Turner steering Bix, whenever possible, away from himself and from the resentment showing up in his views on everything and everybody. But it kept coming back anyway. Dick pulled out all the stops: Bertie Wooster, the golf stories—always good for a laugh, only Bix's was now a wan, hollow echo of some earlier day when the Jean Goldkette band was the toast of Roseland and Bix Beiderbecke owned New York. Baseball? Another dimension. Common friends were names, no more. How about Ethel Waters? Had he heard her new record of . . .

"Y'know, Don Murray always says that she—" Bix stopped, shook his head. "No. Not says. Said. I forgot . . ." Finally, a remark about Stravinsky, and Bix brightened for a moment. He'd been working on Ciricillo's piano. Pat was taking off for Italy, wouldn't be back until August, and he'd rented the Wurlitzer out to Bix in the meantime. That, at least, was good. He'd been reading a lot of poetry, especially Byron and Keats. It seemed to give him solace.

"Been doing anything lately?" Turner found himself groping for conversation. At last, a rise. Yes—Red Nichols' jazz choruses might be kinda mechanical, but he'd been a buddy. He'd hired Bix for an all-star group doing June 10–11 up at Williams College in Massachusetts. That had been fun—even though Red had gotten sick and had to miss it, leaving Benny Goodman to front. They'd had Charlie Spivak on lead trumpet, the Dorseys, and Irving "Babe" Russin, pianist Jack Russin's kid brother, on tenor.

The job was to be on a Wednesday afternoon. But Tuesday night, Tommy Dorsey phoned Goodman to say he had a recording date at Columbia in the morning and would catch an early afternoon train to Williamstown rather than drive up with the others. Bix, hearing of this, told Benny he'd wait for Tom to finish, then keep him company on the way up.

The record date ran overtime, and by the time the two of them got over to Grand Central they discovered that the only train available would get to Williams just before midnight. No time to motor up. Just like Oklahoma and Ponca City all over again, said Bix—and it worked out pretty much the same way. They drove out to a private airstrip on Long Island, wired Benny that they were on their way, and hired a small private plane to fly them up.

It had been fun, but it left Bix tired and feeling all the more down in the dumps. People came around, sure. At all times of day and night they'd bang on the door, come trooping in to hoist a jug or shoot the breeze or pester him to play the piano. Turner, at least, came to listen and that was good. But he'd never before heard the kind of thing from Bix that he was hearing now. Always the same theme, that "Life has passed me by," and that all the musicians who came around to flatter and pay court had "stolen my stuff" for commercial gain. "What about all those guys who aren't ever around when you really need them? They wouldn't give me a quarter now."

Or, "Hell, there are only two musicians I'd go across a street to hear now. That's Louis and LaRocca."

Armstrong, undisputed king of all jazzmen, was then just hitting the peak of a success which in Bix's eyes was fully justified. Louis had stolen nobody's stuff; it was all his own. LaRocca, however, was a revealing choice. Bix's boyhood idol was already a semi-obscure, embittered figure melting into history, victim of his own inability to adapt to changing styles and conditions.

"No one else?" Dick ventured. Bix, silent, lay back on the bed and stared up at the ceiling. "Yeah, sure. Maybe Teagarden and a couple of other good guys. But who the hell cares about *me* now?"

> Every alcoholic experiences an overwhelming sense of isolation and loneliness. The encircling barrier of self-defense, building higher as one drinking bout succeeds another, produces in the end a self-imprisonment from which he cannot find release. Onlookers stand on the outside in a state of helpless bewilderment, unable to break the barrier down; he cannot get out and they cannot get in . . . there is the inability to accept frustration and the failure to complete particular objectives. Emotional sensitivity is marked and feelings of resentment are easily provoked . . .[16]

The courtiers kept coming around. "They never let him alone," Pee Wee Russell told the authors in a long, frequently bitter monologue. "They came around at all hours of the day and night. He couldn't even play the goddam piano without somebody hanging around."

Bill Priestley phoned to say Ashcraft was in town and that alone seemed

---

16. *Op. cit.*, p. 6.

excuse for a party the following Sunday. It would do Bix good, snap him out of his depression. He'd be guest of honor. Good times. Eddie Condon would be along. Joe Sullivan. All the gang.

Turner had offered them the use of his uncle's 15-room apartment at 1 West 72nd Street, the famed Dakota, a substantial edifice built in the 1880s. "It even had a moat around it, water and all. The flat was all soundproofed and the family, fortunately, was out, so we could tear the place down."

The family "music room," a showplace of overstuffed furniture, antique vases and white polar bear rugs, also boasted a Steinway grand piano. Sullivan eased in behind it while Bix, working steadily through a fresh bottle of gin, blew a few tentative notes on Dick's Beuscher trumpet. With a grimace he put the horn aside, leaving the brass playing to the ever-willing Priestley. Condon, seeing "Beiderbix" unoccupied, collared him and the two reeled off toward the servants' quarters behind the dining room, where the family's Irish cook and maid were staying. The two musicians "tried to make those two poor County Cork immigrants," said Turner, "but the girls were definitely not in the mood."

Eventually even the Steinway lost its appeal. The whole gang, a very shaky Bix in the lead, piled into three taxis and made for Challis' sister's place at West 81st and Riverside Drive. The arranger remembered their arrival well.

"There were about 17 of them in all, plus one girl. Bix brought them. He said they didn't know where to go on a Sunday afternoon and were looking for a piano. So I had to go out. I was working on arrangements for a show with Rubinoff at the time and had a score to finish, so I left them all there. When I got back there were four guys passed out on the floor, loaded. I don't know where the rest of the gang had gone."

By this time even Bill was one of those standing "on the outside in a state of helpless bewilderment." Bix seemed at times like this to be systematically destroying himself, and there was nothing Bill, or anyone, seemed to be able to do about it.

"He shouldn't have been hanging around with guys like that. Condon has started a lot of—well, he was one of the guys who used to always drink with Bix. Before Eddie got started he was bumming around New York trying to get gigs, but he was never very successful at it. Borrowed a guitar to do this or that recording date. He was always hanging around Bix—a real Bix fan, a fanatic. Laughs—that was Condon's style, everything for laughs. He figured Bix was a real character, although he himself was as much of a character as anybody, an operator.

"Bix wasn't like that. He was still a kid—naive, not childish, but a trusting sort. Trust everybody. Well-mannered, well-behaved. A very nice guy, and he was well-liked by most people. But the thing is, they made fun of his drinking. They made fun of his remarks. Good old Bix—everything was funny to them . . .

"You remember things. There was this one time—he was always getting credit for what in those days they called muggles. Smoking tea—some of his closest pals used to say it. But I remember at my place one time a guy I went to school with—a musician—just happened to be there when Bix and I were working. I said, 'This is Beiderbecke—Bix—you know Bix.' Yeah. He figured he was in good company, so he started to prod Bix. How's this and how's that, and how is the muggles? And gee—Bix laid right into him: 'I never smoked one of those in my life. I don't know where guys get that idea.'"

Even Louis Armstrong, not usually one to comment, couldn't help noticing what was happening to "that dear boy" he'd met on the *Capitol* twelve years before. "He had a lot of admirers. In fact that's what mostly killed him. He wasn't the type of lad who had his own strong mind. When he felt bad and wanted to say good night to the gang he ran with, they would always say, 'Aw, man, stay a little longer . . . and have another drink.' Poor Bix would force himself, against his will. And so he kept this up, until the gang just didn't believe him when he said, 'Fellers, I don't feel well.' When he finally did get home, he died."

Hoagy Carmichael, working at S.W. Strauss over on Fifth Avenue, came around or phoned occasionally to make sure Bix was all right. Sometimes he could be coaxed out to a film or just for a walk. All too often the trail led to Plunkett's. Bix hadn't yet shaken the cold he'd picked up during the all-night party at Princeton. Some of The Trombone Club regulars remembered seeing him alone in a corner, a bottle on the table in front of him, coughing and mumbling to himself.

"Who's that over there?" The questioner was Ruby Weinstein, a young trumpeter just establishing himself in radio and the pit bands on Broadway.

"Oh him—that's the great Bix Beiderbecke. Can't you tell?"

Such *Schadenfreude* was hardly rare. There were some days, said Red Nichols, when Bix had the Bach along, and "there were some guys who liked to get him really loaded, then stand him up against the bar and say, 'C'mon, Bix, give us a tune.' He'd try—and blow all sorts of clinkers—and they'd double over laughing at the sound of it. These same guys, many of 'em, owed their styles to him, never could come near equalling what he'd done. Now they were using him for fun."

Around mid-June came what appeared to be a turning point. Bix dropped in at Salzman's Restaurant, in the Lincoln Building at 60 East 42nd Street, to hear the band of Smith Ballew, who had done the vocals on most of the 1929 Trumbauer Okeh dates. Ballew's men knew and admired Whiteman's former star, and were concerned at the deterioration in his appearance and morale. One of them decided to do something about it. Within a few days Bix had moved out of the 44th Street Hotel for good and was staying with Rex Gavitte, Ballew's bassist, at 24–60 32nd Street in Astoria, just across the East River in Queens, while he looked around for a place of his own in the same area. He found one not far away, on the ground floor of a new building, at 43–30 46th Street, in neighboring Sunnyside.

And he met a girl. Where and how he met her is unclear, but she was with him when he picked out the apartment. He first mentioned her the night Hoagy invited him along to a mutual friend's house for dinner. Frustrated at the failure of his every attempt to snap Bix out of his depression, Carmichael jumped at a straw. "Why not bring her around some night?"

For almost the first time in the evening, Bix smiled, the secret little half-smile that came out when he liked an idea. "Sure. Any time." They set a date for mid-July.

He was hardly playing the cornet at all. The cold still hung on, and with it the shadow of his exhausting bout with pneumonia. But he was on his own now, and the fight was his, to win or lose himself. George Kraslow, rental agent for the building, watched with growing concern.

"He seldom went out, except to buy gin. He seemed to be struggling with himself and drank almost continuously. It wasn't until a few people living in the apartment house complained to me, halfheartedly I would say, about someone playing the piano around 2 A.M. that I discovered Bix was working on musical arrangements during the wee hours of the morning.

"The tenants explained that they really enjoyed the piano playing and didn't want to get anyone in trouble, but had to get up in the morning. I became friendly with him and tried to stop him drinking so heavily, but it seemed to be an obsession with him. He just couldn't stop."

Then, abruptly, sometime in mid-July, things took a turn for the better. Helen Weiss, the girl Bix had mentioned to Hoagy, was becoming an important feature of his day-to-day life. They took walks, went to restaurants and films together. The drinking began to taper off and Bix began to take an interest in his appearance for the first time in months.

He wrote to Spurrier about it, saying "that he had bought a piano, and was very seriously playing and noodling around and expected to come up with some piano compositions. Also that he thought that, at last, he had fallen in love, and his outlook and demeanor had undergone a change. Bix and I were so close that he was more confidential with me than with most friends, so I truly believe this was factual. I think this letter to me was trying to tell me he was searching for stability. We do know that he was more and more in love with what could be done on a piano. This, then, could be the reason not much is documented in his summer, 1931, activities. He was out of circulation, and if the love bug *had* bitten him, certainly time spent with a girl would keep him from his old haunts and aimless existence.

"Bix knew, always, that his danger was in the first drink and that if he could take one and refuse the next, he had conquered. In writing, he remembered this, and seemed proud to say he was able to do so. His class and pride of being rebelled against being an alcoholic. Poor man—because of his great name and personality, he just had to be tempted so often and severely in comparison to us 'little people.' But I firmly and with all honesty believe with all my heart that a new Bix was abornin' in 1931."

Bix brought Helen around to Carmichael's place at 114 East 57th for dinner. Hoagy was stunned at how good Bix looked. The girl struck him as "a bit mothery, maybe lost herself, but neat," and willing to adapt to Bix and his needs. They talked quietly as they ate—not much about music and not much about people they knew from the old days. Just things in general. Pleasant, with what seemed a total lack of the despair which had distressed Hoagy less than a month before. Carmichael waited for his moment, then took Helen aside for a quick word.

"If he ever gets sick, if anything happens, let me know. Let me know right away." Easier said than done, she said. Bix wasn't an easy one to help. But yes, she said, she'd call.

This visit is the last event in Bix Beiderbecke's life that is generally agreed upon in the accounts of his final days. As Esten Spurrier has observed, fewer people saw him at the end, thus there is less opportunity to check and corroborate already meager evidence.

Some things may never be clarified, such as the extent of his relationship with Helen Weiss. Rumor persists that they became engaged sometime in July. But all attempts to find Miss Weiss have proved fruitless. There seems little possibility now of establishing the facts.

Too, the question of whether Bix, his will to recover and get back on his feet stimulated by the attention of a woman who cared about him, attempted once again to "take the cure"—or even to dry himself out by sheer will power.

"He seemed dreamy, far away, a lot of the time," said Kraslow, who made it a point to drop in regularly to see how Bix was faring. "Sometimes, I would say about eight or nine times in all, I brought him along when I took a drive in my convertible during the hot weather. He usually talked about his previous connections with different top musicians. There were times when he wasn't entirely coherent. But even then, his love for jazz was the basic theme of any conversations I had with him, and I pretty much knew what thoughts he was trying to express.

"I never did learn the identity of the girl who was with him the day he picked out the apartment. Extremely attractive—she came once or twice afterwards, maybe more, but I just caught glimpses of her.

"He lived alone. There was only a small bed, a bureau and a piano, the grand he'd bought, in the apartment. It would have been impossible for someone to share the bed with him . . ."

Despite the coughing and sneezing, despite the moist, stifling heat of midsummer New York, he was determined to make it this time. Forget the booze, forget the past. Just compose, straighten out, find the path again, little boy lost.

He craved sleep. Just to dream, deep and cool, between crisp sheets in a fresh, soft bed, with the wind rustling the leaves in the trees along Grand Avenue; wake up to the smell of bacon crackling in the pan downstairs; sprawl on the lawn listening to the crickets and the sounds of music floating up from the river front. Images. Vera in a pinafore, smiling from the porch swing. Bargy and Hayton, smiling at him onstage at Carnegie Hall as the applause welled up. Don Murray, always laughing; Ruth, Cornelia; a thousand smiles, a thousand railway stations.

He tossed, alone and sweating with fever, coughs rumbling in his lungs. He tried to cool off nights by turning a small electric fan on the bed. Sometimes, nearly frantic for sleep, he doused his rumpled, sweaty top sheet under the cold water tap in the bathtub, then wrung it out and swathed himself in it. At last, shivering, he slept.

And silently, inevitably, the abyss opened again.

On Monday evening, the 3rd of August, the telephone rang in Red Nichols' flat at 515 West End Avenue in Manhattan. His wife Bobbi, alone, answered. It was Bix, coughing, sounding weak. He felt sick and wanted to talk. Red was out, working downtown at the Park Central Hotel, wouldn't be back for hours. But Bix sounded desperate enough for Bobbi to stand for nearly an hour in the hall, listening as he rambled on, mumbling apologies. Suddenly, inexplicably, all the old ghosts had risen to claim him, sweeping away as nothing all his attempts at rejuvenation. He

328

had failed in life, he said, failed at everything he tried. No one cared, he couldn't cope any more. For the first time in weeks, he began to maunder incoherently about Paul Whiteman. Did she think he was ready to make it yet? Did he have to wait any longer?

Bobbi stood shocked, unable to speak. Finally Bix trailed off into a long, racking cough, then quietly apologized for taking up so much time, asked her to tell Red he'd called, and hung up.

The next day Red returned the call. Bix's phone didn't answer.

Thursday, August 6th, just before lunchtime at 1934 Grand Avenue in Davenport, Charles Burnette Beiderbecke took a long-distance call from Chicago. It was Frank Trumbauer.

"Hey there, Tram, how are—"

"Never mind that, Burnie. I think you'd better get to New York. Bix is in trouble."

Burnie had heard it all before. "Yeah. Sure. Okay, Tram. I was thinking of dropping out East in a day or two anyway, and—"

"No, dammit!" In all the years he'd known Frank Trumbauer, Burnie had never once heard him swear. "Not in a day or two, man. Now. Right now! It's really serious this time. His doctor phoned Paul. I'd go myself, but I can't leave the band. Get moving right now or—you may be too late."

Burnie, shaken, told Aggie. They called Davenport station and booked two seats on the 3:40 for New York, and then Burnie went upstairs to pack. Aggie stood for a moment at the front window, staring out at the sunlight on the lawn, the walk sloping down to the street. Like yesterday, so very long ago. Oh, Bix. Not like this . . .

Eyes dry and with firm step, she mounted the stairs to get ready.

Thursday, August 6th, and the instruments on the roof of the U.S. Weather Center at 17 Battery Place registered a high of 92 degrees Fahrenheit, with 58% humidity. George Kraslow, reading in his room, started from his chair at the sound of screams coming from Bix Beiderbecke's room.

It was 9:30 P.M.

He met the superintendent in the hall. "You better get in there, George —he's in trouble."

Kraslow came running. Bix, wild-eyed and ashen, "pulled me in and pointed to the bed. His whole body was trembling violently. There were welts standing out on his arms. He kept screaming at me that there were two Mexicans hiding under the bed, with long daggers, waiting to kill him.

"I knelt, lifted the bedspread and looked under. I rose to assure him there was no one hiding there. Bix lurched toward me, mumbling something, staggered and fell deadweight in my arms. I carried him to the bed and ran across the hall to call Dr. Haberski."

Dr. John James Haberski came in and rapidly examined the still figure on the bed. "I'm sorry, George," he said, turning to face an incredulous Kraslow. "This boy is dead."

The next day's *Davenport Democrat* carried it, under the 1921 photo, as front-page news:

While his mother sped to his bedside, word was received here Thursday night of the death in New York City of Leon Bix Beiderbecke, Davenport

329

# CATHOLIC ORDERS FACE BAN IN SPAIN

## Harry Steeb, Moline Student Flyer, Hurt in Crash

## SEIZURE OF PROPERTY IS POSSIBILITY

$6,000,000 Worth of Holdings Reverts to State Under Bill.

### CHURCHMEN BLAME 'REDS'

Abolishment of Official Religion of Nation Is Also Advocated.

Madrid, Aug. 7.—

## PLANE FALLS 200 FEET AT LOCAL FIELD

Accident Occurs Soon After Take-Off in Home-made Ship.

### RECOVERY IS EXPECTED

Fracture of the Left Leg and Internal Injuries Received.

Harry Steeb, 21, Moline, a Sandburg student pilot, is in Mercy hospital in a serious condition.

## SEEK TO PIN MANY CRIMES ON WINKLER

Pal of Fred Burke in Hospital as Officers Gather To View Him.

St. Joseph, Mich., Aug. 7.—(AP)—Gus Winkler, pal of Fred Burke, notorious killer, and member of a noted murder and kidnaping gang

*DEAD IN NEW YORK*

*AFTER FIRE HAD DONE ITS WORK*

## Succumbs to Pneumonia

### U. S. CHAMBER TO PUSH PLAN TO HELP IDLE

Dies While Mother and Brother Are Speeding To Bedside.

Regard Quick Action Necessary to Forestall Dole Legislation.

### DUBUQUE COUNTY TREASURER FREE ON $10,000 BOND

### CRAMER OFF FOR ISLANDS

### PLAYS WITH OLD PISTOL, IS SHOT

## $24,000 Suit Outgrowth of Lake Tragedy

### OUR WEATHER MAN

## Want Ads

DEMOCRAT
AND EXTRA
WANT ADS
Bring Results

## Oklahoma's Oil Shutdown Move May Spread to Texas; Operators Support Murray

## RIVAL OF 'STAR'

Doherty Indicates He'll Carry War Into Newspaper Field.

## Markets at a Glance

### TOLEDO, IOWA, BANK CLOSED

### The Care Man Started This

New York City death certificate for Leon Bix Beiderbecke, signed by Dr. John J. Haberski.

Bix Beiderbecke's grave in the Beiderbecke family plot in Oakdale Cemetery in Davenport.

Paul Whiteman places a wreath on the Beiderbecke family stone in memory of Bix.

youth who became nationally known as star cornetist of Paul Whiteman's orchestra, and son of Mr. and Mrs. B. H. Beiderbecke, 1934 Grand Avenue, Davenport.

Death occurred Thursday night at 9:30 o'clock following a short illness with pneumonia. Friends of the youth telephoned Mr. and Mrs. Beiderbecke here Thursday morning that he was seriously ill. His mother, accompanied by his brother, Burnette, left for New York City Thursday afternoon at 3:40 o'clock. During the night Mr. Beiderbecke received a telegram stating that his son had died.

Due to the fact that the train bearing Mrs. Beiderbecke will not reach New York until late this afternoon, it is assumed that she is unaware of her son's death.

Altho details have not been arranged, the body will be returned here for funeral services and burial. Besides the parents and the brother, Burnette, of this city, he is survived by one sister, Mrs. Theodore Shoemaker, of Atlanta, Ga.

Dr. Haberski signed the New York City death records listing the cause of Bix Beiderbecke's death as lobar pneumonia, with edema of the brain. Privately, he ventured the opinion that death had been at least hastened, if not caused outright, by the effects of alcohol on the deceased's system.

Aggie and Burnie saw those whom they had to see: Haberski, Kraslow, and Michael J. Kimmel, director of the mortuary where the body was to be shown. Helen Weiss had apparently contacted Kimmel before the train from Davenport arrived at Grand Central. But they did not meet her, and Burnie remembered little else. "It all happened so fast . . . I'm sure that we were told that Bix wanted Miss Weiss to have his Weber grand piano. It is, however, still in our family."

All descriptions of the circumstances of Bix's death point to a hallucinatory seizure of delirium tremens. Again, as in early 1929, he had forcibly cut off his consumption of alcohol at a time when his body was harboring illness and his resistance was generally low. The seizure which killed him appears to have been an almost exact repetition of his Cleveland Hotel room ordeal.

Several doctors consulted ventured the opinion that Bix, already ill and running a high fever, may have vomited while sleeping, and inhaled a quantity of vomit. This could have brought on sudden death through drowning in his own vomit. Before the advent of modern diagnostic techniques, what is now known as inhalation pneumonia was classified with lobar pneumonia, which, strictly speaking, relates to inflammation of the lobes of the lungs.

He had seen Haberski, who doubtless realized Bix was seriously ill and telephoned Whiteman. Bix had begun drinking again—up to three milk bottles full of gin and orange juice a day. There is no known explanation for this, though it is consistent with renewed depression. By 9:30 P.M. the night of August 6, it is overwhelmingly likely that his system had simply had enough. It rebelled against the alcohol, rebelled against illness. It simply collapsed in one, final nightmare seizure.

Agatha and Burnie took the body back with them to Davenport, where Bix Beiderbecke was buried the following Tuesday after the largest funeral in the city's memory.

Radio station WOC devoted the day to Bix's records. At Oakdale Cemetery, someone carted a windup phonograph to the graveside to play "In a Mist" just once more before he was laid to rest.

But not a single jazz musician or friend of Bix's walked among the men who carried the coffin down the gravel drive in brilliant Iowa sunshine. "There was only one musician—from a wealthy family—in the lot," said Wayne Rohlf. "He was a longhair violinist and orchestra conductor named Bill Henigbaum. The rest of the pallbearers were wealthy friends of the family, some of society's upper crust. They were either selected by C.B. [Burnie] or by Bix's folks."

Of the hundreds of floral tributes spilling out of Oakdale's tiny brick chapel on to the neatly-mowed summer grass, one in particular caught the eye. It was a six-foot-high cornet, shaped entirely out of roses. It had come from Paul Whiteman.

The "King of Jazz" had been as good as his word. Bix's chair had stayed open to the end.

Sketch of proposed Bix Beiderbecke Museum.

Former Bix associates Bill Challis, Bill Krenz, Paul Mertz, Bill Rank, Doc Ryker at the Bix Beiderbecke Memorial Society bash of July 27, 1973, at Danceland in Davenport. Society President Don O'Dette with microphone at right.

# Epilogue

Bix Beiderbecke's passing cut deep into the lives of those few who had been close to him. Esten Spurrier, in the solitude and privacy of a late evening, played Bix's recording of "I'll Be a Friend with Pleasure," made a year before, and wept.

In St. Louis, Ruth Shaffner, celebrating her 25th birthday, stared in dumb incomprehension at the copy of the *Davenport Democrat* in her hands, reading the headline over and over in her mind: "Davenport Youth, famed as master of trumpet, succumbs to pneumonia." Her mind fought against it. She'd moved, after an operation the year before, and had lost contact with Bix. Perhaps, if he'd only known how to reach her . . . perhaps he'd tried, needing someone . . . "I was stunned, I couldn't talk. There aren't words to express my feeling . . . my mother, and God's help, gave me the strength to live through that day."

Larry Andrews, boyhood friend and sometime banjoist, provided a postscript and, perhaps, the first chapter in the legend. In spring, 1931, about the time Bix returned to New York for the last time, Andrews, too, left Davenport bound for northwest Iowa, a place of open, windswept farmland and small villages with still more than a little of the frontier about them.

He knew of Bix's death through the same copy of the August 7 *Democrat* which brought the news to Ruth. The day of the funeral he heard Beiderbecke records broadcast by radio station KFAB in Lincoln, Nebraska.

Andrews did not know of Helen Weiss. Her existence was known only to Carmichael, a few of Bix's other New York acquaintances, and to members of the Beiderbecke family after Aggie and Burnie returned from the East.

Until his death in 1964 after a heart attack, Andrews swore to the accuracy of the following, related in 1939 correspondence with Otis Ferguson, author of two *New Republic* articles on Bix:

"I was in the insurance business . . . and had 18 agents under me and collection agents in several towns around that area. There was a spiritualist medium who was a member of our organization who chanced to be at the collector's house one day when I called on her in Storm Lake, Iowa.

"I dodge such things myself . . . but this one told me she had something to tell me. She said there was a young fellow who had recently passed on and told me to tell 'Helen' that he couldn't understand why that had to happen now. I laughed and said, 'Well, I don't know any young fellow and right offhand I don't know any Helen to which he might refer.'

"Imagine my utter astonishment . . . when she told me this young fellow says his name is Dix—no, he shakes his head and writes the letter 'B,' and what could he mean by that? In my astonishment I said 'Bix' and she informed me that that was correct and that he also wanted to tell his folks the same message as Helen . . . this name Helen does not seem correct to me but you could probably check it out with some of the boys in New York . . .

"That incident happened shortly before Christmas (1931), and when I came down here to Davenport at Christmas I came within one of calling his folks and telling them about the incident, but finally decided against it. But I did find out that Bix had found a girl when he returned to New York that really started to put him straight, and he was contemplating matrimony with her when his death occurred . . ."

A group of Bix's Davenport friends laying a wreath on his grave to mark the anniversary of his birth, c. 1953. L to R, rear: Dr. Dave Palmer of the Bix Beiderbecke Memorial Committee, unknown, Larry Andrews, Charles "Burnie" Beiderbecke. Front, kneeling: Esten Spurrier, Chicago jazz historian John Steiner, unknown.

PHOTO COURTESY C. B. BEIDERBECKE

Co-author Evans with Ruth (left) and Estelle Shaffner in Davenport, July 11, 1973.

# Appendix A

# WHO, WHAT, WHERE & WHEN?

*A Bix Beiderbecke Diary*

*by*

Philip R. Evans,
William Dean-Myatt
& Richard M. Sudhalter

# 1903–1917

**March 10, 1903** (Tue)—Leon Bix Beiderbecke born in Davenport, Iowa.

**September 1908 thru June 1909**—Enrolled in kindergarten class at Tyler School, Grand Avenue. Teacher was Miss Alice Robinson.

**August 30, 1909** (Mon) thru June 17, 1910 (Fri)—Enrolled in first grade at Tyler School. Teacher was Miss Marguerite LeClaire.

**September 5, 1910** (Mon) thru June 23, 1911 (Fri)—Enrolled in second grade at Tyler School. Teacher was Miss Carrie Brown.

**September 4, 1911** (Mon)—Began third grade at Tyler School with Miss Myrtle Petersen. Taken ill, and did not complete school year.

**September 2, 1912** (Mon) thru June 20, 1913 (Fri)—Enrolled in third grade at Tyler School. Teacher was Miss Blythe Bennett.

**September 15, 1913** (Mon) thru June 19, 1914 (Fri)—Enrolled in fourth grade at Tyler School. Teacher was either Miss Bennett or Miss Frances Martin.

**August 31, 1914** (Mon) thru June 18, 1915 (Fri)—Enrolled in fifth grade at Tyler School. Teacher was either Miss Elsie Greenlee or Miss Rozella Brown.

**August 30, 1915** (Mon) thru June 16, 1916 (Fri)—Enrolled in sixth grade at Tyler School. Teacher was Miss Hazel Strike.

**April 20, 1916** (Thu)—Leon Bix Beiderbecke baptized a communicant member of First Presbyterian Church in Davenport.

**September 4, 1916** (Mon) thru January 1917—Enrolled in seventh grade at Tyler School. Teacher was Miss Mildred Colby.

**January 1917 thru June 22, 1917** (Fri)—Promoted to grade 8-B at Tyler School. Teacher unknown.

**September 3, 1917** (Mon)—Enrolled in grade 8-A at Tyler School. Teacher was Miss Mildred Colby. While the school year was not to be completed until June 21, 1918, the records show that Bix completed grade eight on Friday, January 25, 1918.

# 1918

**January 28, 1918** (Mon) thru June 21, 1918 (Fri)—Enrolled in Davenport High School.

**September 2** (Mon)—Enrolled in the ninth grade at Davenport High School.

**November 11** (Mon)—End of World War I.

**December ??**—Charles Burnette Beiderbecke returns from military service.

# 1919

**January**—Charles Burnette Beiderbecke purchases several recordings by popular bands including "Tiger Rag" and "Skeleton Jangle" by the Original Dixieland Jazz Band on Victor 18472. Bix borrows silver cornet from Lea Ely, neighbor and schoolmate.

**March**—Bix plays piano in school dance band organized by Erkie Albright for Friday afternoon dances at Davenport High. Others include Richard Fritz Putzier (cornet) and Bob Struve (trombone).

**June 18** (Wed)—End of school year.

**August**—Meets Louis Armstrong, playing on Streckfus Lines stern-wheeler *Capitol* with Fate Marable's band. Hears other riverboat jazz groups.

**Sept. 2** (Tue)—Bix enrolls in tenth grade at Davenport High School. Buys first cornet of his own for $35 from Fritz Putzier, who switches to C-melody saxophone.

# 1920

**May 28** (Fri)—Concert-vaudeville program given by the musical organizations of Davenport High School at the Grand Opera House, 8 P.M. Bix featured on cornet in two numbers.

**June 18** (Fri)—School year ends.

**July 10** (Sat)—Bix writes to Vera Cox in Vermont, Illinois.

**July 15** (Thu)—Bix takes Vera to party at Hillie Kohler's.

**July 16** (Fri)—Party at George Van Maur's. Bix presumably takes Vera.

**July 30** (Fri)—Neal Buckley's Novelty Orchestra appears at Linwood Park. Personnel: Bix (cornet); Putzier (C-melody sax); Struve (trombone); Buckley (piano); Harvey Berry (violin); Dick Woolsey (drums).

**July 31** (Sat)—Another job at Linwood Park.

**August 30** (Mon)—Bix enrolls in eleventh grade at Davenport High School.

**November 5** (Fri)—Buckley band appears as "Billy Greer's Melody Jazz Band" with Greer on drums at the auditorium in Sabula, Illinois.

**December 21** (Tue)—Buckley band auditions before Roy Kautz for membership in Davenport Local 67, American Federation of Musicians. Bix fails the audition, and band as a result turns down opportunity to open at Terrace Gardens restaurant.

# 1921

**January**—Bee Palmer, "The Shimmy Queen," booked into Columbia Theatre, Davenport. Accompanying band includes Leon Roppolo (clarinet) and Emmett Hardy (trumpet). The act moved to Peoria, Illinois, following this engagement.

**February**—Roppolo and Hardy return to Davenport and join Carlisle Evans' band at Coliseum from February 13 thru May 30. Personnel: Hardy (trumpet); Roppolo (clarinet); Tal Sexton (trombone); Evans (piano); Louis Black (banjo); Jack Willett (drums).

**March 23** (Wed)—Buckley's Novelty Orchestra plays at Hayne's Dancing School.

**March 26** (Sat)—Buckley's again at Hayne's.

**April 20** (Wed)—Buckley's again at Hayne's.

**May 13** (Fri)—Buckley's Novelty Orchestra plays an A.Z.K. dance at Forest Park.

**June 14** (Tue)—Buckley's Novelty Orchestra plays a dance at Forest Park.

**June 16** (Thu)—Buckley's Novelty Orchestra plays a dance at Forest Park.

**June 17** (Fri)—End of school year.

**June 18** (Sat)—Buckley's Novelty Orchestra plays a dance at Forest Park.

**June 19** (Sun)—Buckley's again at Forest Park. Emmett Hardy leaves Carlisle Evans' band at Waterloo, Iowa, and joins Albert "Doc" Wrixon's band on the Streckfus steamer *Capitol*.

**June 21** (Tue)—Bix Beiderbecke joins the band on the steamer *Majestic*. The sailing schedule calls for excursions June 21, 25, 28, and 30. Personnel: Bix (cornet); Struve (trombone); Wade Foster (violin); Al Woodyatt (clarinet); Rome Siemons (piano); Pee Wee Rank (drums).

**June 27** (Mon)—Leon Roppolo leaves Carlisle Evans. He, too, may have joined Wrixon, though this is in doubt.

**July 4** (Mon)—Independence Day celebrations aboard the *Majestic*. Bix leaves the *Majestic* band. Around this time Hardy, George Brunies, Hal Sears and others fell out with Doc Wrixon and quit his band en masse. Wrixon was forced to recruit virtually an entire new band at short notice.

**c. July 6** (Wed)—Bix joins Wrixon band on the *Capitol*. Personnel: Bix (cornet); Johnny Watson (trombone); George Byron Webb, Grant Harris, Omer Van Speybroek (clarinets and saxophones); I. V. "Bud" Shepherd (piano); A. A. "Happy" Conger (banjo); Albert "Doc" Wrixon (drums).

**c. July 16** (Sat)—Bix forced by musicians' union to leave *Capitol* band.

**c. early August**—Brunies, Roppolo, Louis Black and Paul Mares (trumpet) arrive in Chicago; once again teamed with Bee Palmer to open at the Friars' Inn as "Bee Palmer and Her Boys." Steve Brown (bass) soon replaces Arnold Loyocano.

**Aug. 5** (Fri)—The "Bix Beiderbecke Five" plays a dance at Hayne's Dancing School. Personnel also includes Fritz Putzier (C-melody sax). First engagement booked under Bix's name.

**Aug. 30** (Tue)—Ralph Miedke Society Orchestra, including Bix and Putzier, plays in the lobby of the Moline, Illinois, State Trust and Savings Bank for its grand opening. Before the engagement, Fritz and Bix have posed photographs taken at a Davenport studio. This is the familiar portrait showing Bix in a tuxedo, cornet on knee.

**mid-September**—Bix enrolls in Lake Forest Academy as a member of the Lower Middle (sophomore) class. Assigned ground floor room at northwest corner of East House dormitory. Total Lake Forest enrollment for school year 1921–22: 129 students. Total faculty: 12 instructors plus John Wayne Richards, headmaster. The Lower Middle class contained 31 students. Lake Forest lies directly on Lake Michigan, 35 miles northwest of Chicago, between Highland Park and Waukegan, Illinois.

**c. early October**—Jimmie Caldwell's "Jazz Jesters" play weekend dance at Lake Forest Academy. Bix sits in. Personnel: Don Murray (tenor sax); Jimmie Fallis (clarinet); Caldwell (piano); Chuck Cheney (banjo); Virgil Leech or Harry Gale (drums).

**Oct. 16** (Sun)—Bix plays for Orange team in intramural football game against the Black team. Score: Black 6–Orange 0. Subsequent results in the series: Orange 14–Black 0; Black 0–Orange 0; Orange 7–Black 0.

**Oct. 29** (Sat)—Cy-Bix Orchestra plays its maiden engagement, a Lake Forest campus dance. Personnel drawn from the following: E. Clinton Parker (tpt); Bix Beiderbecke (cnt); Samuel Sidney Stewart Jr., Bill Haysen, F. Wagner (saxes); M. H. Rising (tbn); M. Sargent, S. Smith (vlns); Walter Ernest "Cy" Welge (dms). Under the supervision of Prof. R. P. Koepke.

**Nov. 8** (Tue)—Bix writes to his parents asking permission to go to Chicago for Thanksgiving holidays.

**Nov. 23** (Wed)—Caldwell band plays Three-Arts Club Dance (at Northwestern?). Personnel similar to Lake Forest. Bix's presence possible.

**Nov. 24** (Thu)—Caldwell band plays at Congress Hotel, Chicago. Similar personnel. Bix may have been present.

**Nov. 25** (Fri)—Bix sits in with Caldwell group at the Black Cat Room in the basement of the Edgewater Beach Hotel, Chicago.

**Nov. 26** (Sat)—"Sid-Bix-Wally's" Orchestra plays Lake Forest campus dance. Personnel considerably reduced.

# 1922

mid-January —Bix-Wally Orchestra plays for Lake Forest "Pre-Mid" winter dance. Personnel as before.

Jan. 26 (Thu)—Caldwell group plays for a crowd of more than 2,000 at Senn High School Prom in Chicago. Bix's first official job with the band. Personnel: Bix (cornet); Murray (sax); Fallis (clarinet); Caldwell (piano); Cheney (banjo); Jean Murphy (bass); Gale (drums).

c. Feb. 7–10 (Tue-Fri)—Caldwell band plays dance at Ferry Hall Girls' School. Personnel includes Bix, Caldwell, Cheney, Gale.

Feb. 17 (Fri)—Lake Forest Midwinter Weekend begins with combined Glee Club, Mandolin Club and School Orchestra presenting the following program for students, their relatives and friends:

   1. Lake Forest, Go! . . . . . . . . . . Koepke
                 Orchestra
   2. Forsaken . . . . . . . . . . . . Koschat
              Glee Club
    What the Nightingale Sang . . . . . H. Parker
         Solo, W. P. Butler Jr.
   3. The Sheik . . . . . . . . . . . Ted Snyder
    Leave Me with a Smile . . . . . . Burtnett-Koehler
          Mandolin Club
   4. Marching . . . . . . . . . . E. Nevin
              Glee Club
    Mighty Lak' a Rose . . . . . . . . E. Nevin
          Solo, G. Flues
   5. In Old Madrid . . . . . . . . . Trottere
        Cornet solo, E. Parker
   6. Waltz of the Mountaineers . . . . . R. P. Kay
             Orchestra
   7. Tuck Me to Sleep . . . . . . . . Meyer
           Mandolin Club
    Ka-Lu-A . . . . . . . . . . . . Kern
         Mandolin Quartet
   8. Still Waters
    The Torrent . . . . . . . . . . Koepke
         Piano solo, E. Bilharz
   9. Alma Mater . . . . . . . . . . Combined Clubs

Following this, the students presented their *Academy Follies of 1922*. Bix took part in two of the ten sketches, singing "Who's Going to Love You?" and "Please Don't Send Me Posies" with a barbershop quartet, then playing the piano for Sid Stewart's performance of Rudy Wiedoft's "Saxophobia" on the C-melody saxophone. Following the "Follies," the Cy-Bix Orchestra played for what the Lake Forest yearbook, *The Caxy*, termed "an informal dance in the gym . . . Bix-Wally's lived up to their reputation by turning out wonderful music."

Feb. 18 (Sat)—Midwinter Weekend formal dance. Music supplied by pianist William T. "Bill" Grimm. Bix meets and sits in with Grimm, who invites him to further jobs.

Feb. 26 (Sat)—Bix works with Bill Grimm's "Varsity Five" at Northwestern University fraternity house.

March 10 (Fri)—Caldwell band with Bix plays for Northwestern University Senior Ball. Personnel as at Senn, plus Reggie Severance (sax).

April—Bix sits in, works occasional weekend jobs with Caldwell band, mostly at

346

the Black Cat Room in the basement of the Edgewater Beach Hotel in Chicago.

**May 6** (Sat)—Cy-Bix Orchestra plays in Gary, Indiana, rather than at Lake Forest Junior Prom. Bill Grimm contracted for Lake Forest.

**May 17** (Wed)—Bix summoned to headmaster's office but cannot be found.

**May 19** (Fri)—Bix discovered out of the dormitory at night.

**May 20** (Sat)—"Sned" Rendtorff catches Bix climbing down the dormitory fire escape after lights-out.

**May 21** (Sun)—Faculty votes, and Bix is asked to withdraw from Lake Forest.

**May 22** (Mon)—Bix leaves Lake Forest Academy.

**c. May 25** (Thu)—Bix engaged by Marty Bloom for "Orpheum Time" revue band. Rehearsals begin early the following week.

**c. June 1** (Thu)—Bix returns with his father to Davenport.

**c. June 7** (Wed)—Bix back in Chicago, joins Bill Grimm aboard Graham and Morton Lines excursion steamer *Michigan City*, offering one round trip a day from Chicago to Michigan City, Indiana, and back. Personnel: Bix (cornet); Don Murray (clarinet and saxophone); Grimm (piano); Frank Lehman (banjo); Ray Landis (drums).

**July 1** (Sat)—Bix appears at White Lake Yacht Club, White Lake, Michigan, with band led by Sid Stewart and including Davenporter Ed Meikel (piano), Piers Williams (xylophone), Ed Shears (drums). Bix plays both cornet and piano.

**July-August**—Bix continues with Grimm on the boat.

**Aug. 12** (Sat)—Bix appears with Vic Moore-Bud Hatch quartet at Delavan Lake Country Club, Delavan, Wisconsin. Personnel: Bix (cornet); Wilbur "Bud" Hatch (piano); Jules Van Gende (C-melody saxophone); Vic Moore (drums).

**Aug. 19** (Sat)—Another date at Delavan Lake.

**Aug. 26** (Sat)—Another date at Delavan Lake.

**Sept. 4** (Mon)—Labor Day. End of lake-boat season. Bix travels with Jimmy Hartwell (clarinet) to Indianapolis, thence home to Davenport.

**c. Sept. 6–7** (Wed-Thu)—Pee Wee Rank contacts Bix with offer to go to Syracuse, New York. Bix accepts.

**Sept. 21** (Thu)—The "Royal Harmonists of Indiana" open at Alhambra Ballroom, 275 James Street, Syracuse. Salary $45 per man per week. Owner: Harry E. Morton. Personnel: Bix Beiderbecke (cornet); Wayne "Doc" Hostetter (clarinet, saxophone, violin); Johnny Eberhardt (saxophone, violin); Eddie Condon (banjo); Pee Wee Rank (drums); unknown pianist plus two other unidentified instruments to make up eight-piece orchestra.

**Oct. 7** (Sat)—Royal Harmonists present their "interpretation from a famous opera."

**end of October**—close of Alhambra engagement. Bix and Hostetter arrive in New York, meet members of the Original Dixieland Jazz Band, Phil Napoleon, other musicians.

**Nov. 7–8** (Tue-Wed)—Bix returns to Chicago, visits Friars' Inn.

**Nov. 10** (Fri)—Bix works for pianist Charles "Murphy" Podalsky at Northwestern University homecoming week dance.

**Nov. 20** (Mon)—Bix returns by train to Davenport, writes to D. J. "Nick" LaRocca en route.

**December**—Bix at home in Davenport, working in the office of the East Davenport Coal and Lumber Company.

**mid-December**—Bix plays society dance with Bud Hatch somewhere just outside Chicago.

**Dec. 25** (Mon)—Bix plays high school fraternity dance with Bill Grimm in Dubuque, Iowa, at Julien Dubuque Hotel. Don Murray (clarinet and tenor saxophone) also present.

# 1923

**January—June:** Bix at home in Davenport, playing only pickup dates and sitting in occasionally with groups in the area.

**April 24–25 (Tue-Wed)**—The Benson Orchestra of Chicago plays Davenport Coliseum. Frankie Trumbauer (C-melody saxophone) in the band. Bix and Esten Spurrier present. Bix meets Trumbauer.

**May 30 (Wed)**—Bix, Spurrier, Bob Struve and Davenport clarinetist Jimmy Cannon go aboard Streckfus steamer *J.S.* to listen to the band. Cannon sits in. Band billed as Ralph Williams & His Famous Benson Orchestra.

**July 2 (Mon)**—Bix joins Dale Skinner's band at Valentino Inn, 22 East Adams Street, between State and Wabash, replacing Gene Cafferelli. Personnel: Bix (cornet); Skinner (clarinet and tenor sax); George Brunies (trombone); Kyle Pierce (piano); Chink Martin (bass); Bill Paley (drums). Bob Gillette (banjo) auditioned for but did not become a member of this band.

**July 17–18 (Tue-Wed)**—Reconstituted New Orleans Rhythm Kings record for Gennett in Richmond, Indiana, using Brunies, Martin, Pierce, Gillette, plus Paul Mares (trumpet), Roppolo (clarinet), Glenn Scoville and Don Murray (saxes) and others including Ferdinand "Jelly Roll" Morton (piano). Bix probably present to watch.

**July 20 (Fri)**—Bix leaves Skinner band, replaced by Cafferelli.

**c. July 23 (Mon)**—Bix rejoins Bill Grimm band aboard Graham & Morton lines ship *Michigan City*. Personnel: Bix (cornet); Jimmy Hartwell (clarinet & saxophone); Johnny Carsella (trombone); Grimm (piano); Frank Lehman (banjo); Harry Gale (drums). Works on this boat until end of summer season.

**Aug. 8 (Wed)** – Benny Goodman replaces Jimmy Hartwell aboard the excursion boat *Michigan City* with Grimm.

**Sept. 3 (Mon)**—Labor Day, end of the lake-boat season. Bix remains a few days around Chicago, working one or two jobs, then returns to Davenport.

**mid-September**—George "Red" Bird visits Chicago to recruit personnel for job at the Stockton Club outside Hamilton, Ohio. Returns and opens with band including Bird (trumpet); Clyde Reynolds (trombone); Jimmy Hartwell (clarinet and alto sax); Dudley Mecum (piano); Gene Huls (banjo); Ole Vangsness (tuba and bass sax); Bob Conzelman (drums).

**Oct. 1 (Mon)**—Bix awarded a card in American Federation of Musicians Davenport Local 67.

**early November**—Bix works theater job in St. Louis with drummer Charles Cotterel. Partial personnel: Frank Cotterel, Bix (cornets); Floyd O'Brien (trombone); George Johnson (tenor sax); Dick Voynow (piano); Cotterel (drums). Rest now forgotten.

**mid-November**—Bix back in Chicago looking for work. Hartwell takes over Stockton Club band, drops Huls and Reynolds. Bird resigns. Hartwell hires Bix, Bob Gillette (banjo) and Abe Cholden (tenor sax). Cholden plays a week and is replaced by George Johnson.

**December**—Bird departs. Mecum departs, replaced by Voynow. Band renamed Wolverine Orchestra.

# 1924

**Jan. 1 (Tue)**—Stockton Club engagement ends in brawl between gangster factions from Hamilton and Cincinnati.

**c. Jan. 3** (Thu)—Wolverines return to Chicago, play brief engagement at Palmer Cody's Cascades Ballroom at Sheridan and Argyle. Conzelman leaves the band; Ole Vangsness out. Bix engages Vic Moore.

**Jan. 14** (Mon)—Wolverine Orchestra opens at Doyle's Dancing Academy, Court and Central Avenue, third floor, in Cincinnati. Eddie Johnson, local drummer, fills in until Moore arrives. Al Gandee (trombone) and Wilford "Min" Leibrook (sousaphone) added. Personnel now Bix, Hartwell, Johnson, Voynow, Gillette, Leibrook, Gandee, Moore.

**Jan. 18** (Fri)—Wolverine Orchestra hired to play junior prom at Miami University, Oxford, Ohio.

**Jan. 25** (Fri)—Wolverines play at Miami University.

**Feb. 18** (Mon)—Wolverine Orchestra makes its first records for Gennett at Richmond, Indiana.

**March 31** (Mon)—Wolverine Orchestra jumps its contract at Doyle's, drives to Indianapolis, Indiana.

**April 1** (Tue)—Wolverines audition unsuccessfully for house band job at Indianapolis Athletic Club.

**April 5** (Sat)—Charlie Davis orchestra opens at Ohio Theater. Wolverines in attendance, hear "Copenhagen," Davis' new composition, for the first time, meet Davis musicians.

**c. April 10** (Thu)—Wolverines return to Hamilton, Ohio, with Davis' promise to get them work. Shortly thereafter, he wires them that they are to play Butler College prom as second band and do four days immediately thereafter in Marion, Indiana.

**April 18** (Fri)—Butler College prom. Davis orchestra plays in main ballroom, Wolverines in smaller south room and between Davis' sets as well. Davis' recollection of their reception: "This was a spectacle!" Butler campus newspaper, *The Collegian:* "greatest social event in Butler's history."

**April 19** (Sat)—Wolverines open at Luna Lite Theater, Marion, Indiana, for three nights.

**April 22** (Tue)—Wolverines play Civic Hall dance in Marion.

**April 25** (Fri)—Wolverines play Spring Dance of the Boosters' Club at Indiana University, Bloomington.

**April 26** (Sat)—Wolverines play dance at Sigma Alpha Epsilon fraternity, Indiana University.

**c. late April**—Gennett releases first Wolverines record, "Fidgety Feet" and "Jazz Me Blues" on GE 5408.

**May 2** (Fri)—Wolverines play Sphinx Club dance at Sigma Chi House, Indiana University. Bob Gillette a guest for the weekend at Delta Tau Delta house.

**May 3** (Sat)—Wolverines play formal at Kappa Sigma house, Hoagy Carmichael's fraternity at Indiana University.

**May 6** (Tue)—Wolverines in Richmond, Indiana, for their second Gennett recording session. Among the selections: Hoagy's composition "Free Wheeling," retitled "Riverboat Shuffle," and Charlie Davis' "Copenhagen."

**May 10** (Sat)—Wolverines appear at Ed Williams' music store in Bloomington, Indiana. Advertisement in *Indiana Daily Student:* "A rare treat Saturday noon hour May 10th. Wolverine Orchestra of nine musicians will play their own selections—as played to make their fox-trot records." Extra musicians referred to either an error by the reporter or possibly Hoagy Carmichael and friend sitting in.

**May 16** (Fri)—Wolverines play Delta Upsilon dance at Phi Gam House, Indiana University.

**May 17** (Sat)—Wolverines play informal dance at Sigma Chi House.

**May 23** (Fri)—Wolverines play WSGA dance in auditorium of the student building at Indiana University.

**May 29** (Thu)—Wolverines open at Rainbow Casino Gardens, 19101 Lafayette Road, Indianapolis, playing on the Rainbow Terrace as "Charlie Davis Wolverines." Staying at the Lincoln Hotel. It is probably during this engagement that drummer Vic Berton approaches them with proposal for work during rest of summer under his management and with him on drums.

**June 20** (Fri)—Wolverines record for Gennett in Richmond, Indiana, with Berton on drums.

**c. June 22** (Sun)—Garnett R. Lawrence and Otto Ray, owner-managers of Casino Gardens, contact Charlie Davis to say they have given Wolverines notice because they are not drawing crowds. "Too advanced" among the criticisms. Wolverines leave Casino Gardens this week.

**July** —The Wolverines appear to have spent this month touring and playing casuals and theater dates under the leadership of Vic Berton. Red Nichols recalled sitting in with them somewhere in Indiana while en route west to join Dick Bowen and his "Blue Streak Orchestra of New York" at Walled Lake, Michigan. Toward the end of the month they played the Gay Mill Dance Hall at Miller Beach, by Gary, Indiana. One date, at least, is certain:

**July 21–23** (Mon-Wed)—Wolverines play Palace Theater in Indianapolis as "Vic Berton Wolverine Orch., famous recorder for Gennett Records."

**Aug. 2** (Sat)—Wolverine Orchestra opens at Marquette Park Pavilion in Lake Front Park, Gary, Indiana. They remained for the entire month, and the following amounts of money were paid them by the office of the Park Commissioner:

| | |
|---|---|
| Aug. 2–4 (Sat-Mon) | $ 350.00 |
| Aug. 5–8 (Tue-Fri) | $ 400.00 |
| Aug. 13–22 (Wed-Fri) | $1500.00 |
| Aug. 23–26 (Sat-Tue) | $ 428.56 |
| Aug. 27–29 (Wed-Fri) | $ 321.44 |
| Aug. 30–Sept. 2 (Sat-Tue) | $ 428.00 |
| | $3248.00 |

There is no indication what the Wolverines did, if anything, between Aug. 8–13. The clarinetist and saxophonist Milton "Mezz" Mezzrow insisted that at some point during the summer of 1924 Bix filled in for a short time with a band he led in Indiana Harbor, not far distant, at a roadhouse called the Martinique Inn. It is possible that Bix, a frequent after-hours visitor to the Inn, also played cornet there during this missing week.

**Sept. 3** (Wed)—Wolverines set out by automobile for New York City.

**Sept. 6** (Sat)—Arrival in New York City.

**Sept. 7** (Sun)—Wolverines attend Ray Miller performance at Hippodrome Theater to hear Miff Mole (trombone) and Frank Trumbauer (C-melody sax).

**Sept. 12** (Fri)—Wolverines open at Cinderella Ballroom, 48th and Broadway, playing opposite orchestra of Willie Creager.

**Sept. 16** (Tue)—Wolverines record for Gennett at 9–11 East 37th Street studio; Ray Mayer, sound engineer. George Brunies (trombone) joins the band for this date.

**Sept. 24** (Wed)—*Variety* reviewer Abel Green hails the Wolverines as a "torrid unit" which "need doff the mythical chapeau to no one."

**Oct. 7 or 8** (Tue/Wed)—Wolverines record again for Gennett in New York.

**Oct. 10** (Fri)—Bix Beiderbecke leaves the Wolverine Orchestra.

**Oct. 11** (Sat)—The "Sioux City Six" record for Gennett with Bix, Trumbauer, Mole, and a combination of musicians from Wolverines and Ray Miller orchestras.

350

**Oct. 12** (Sun)—Bix fills in for trumpeter Harry Gluck with the New Orleans Jazz Band. Probable personnel: Bix (cornet); Sidney Arodin (clarinet); Mike Martini (trombone); Wilder Chase (piano); Tommy DeRose (drums).

**Oct. 13** (Mon)—Bix Beiderbecke leaves New York by train for Detroit.

**Oct. 14** (Tue)—Bix arrives in Detroit.

**Oct. 15** (Wed)—Bix deposits his transfer with Detroit Local 5, listing his address as c/o William and Freda Kraft, 5323 Parker Avenue. Joins Jean Goldkette Victor Recording Orchestra at Graystone Ballroom, 4237 Woodward. Personnel: Fred "Fuzzy" Farrar (trumpet); Bix (cornet); Bill Rank, Tommy Dorsey (trombones); Stanley "Doc" Ryker, Don Murray, George Williams (reeds); Sam Anflick, Charles Hammell (violins); Howard "Howdy" Quicksell (banjo); Paul Mertz (piano); "Irish" Henry (tuba); Charles Horvath (drums).

**Oct. 16** (Thu)—Goldkette orchestra broadcasts over station WWJ from the Graystone, 10–11 P.M.

**Oct. 23** (Thu)—Another broadcast over WWJ.

**Oct. 30** (Thu)—Another broadcast over WWJ.

**Nov. 6** (Thu)—Another broadcast over WWJ.

**Nov. 8** (Sat)—Bix takes brief leave of absence to return to Davenport to attend the wedding of his sister, Mary Louise, to Theodore Shoemaker at the Davenport Outing Club.

**Nov. 13** (Thu)—Regular Goldkette broadcast over WWJ.

**Nov. 20** (Thu)—Regular Goldkette broadcast over WWJ.

**Nov. 24** (Mon)—Goldkette orchestra records for Victor on portable equipment at Detroit Athletic Club. Bix plays 16-bar solo on "I Didn't Know."

**Nov. 25** (Tue)—Goldkette orchestra records again for Victor.

**Nov. 27** (Thu)—Regular Goldkette broadcast from Graystone over WWJ.

**Dec. 4** (Thu)—Regular WWJ broadcast. Program as follows: Romance; At the End of the Winding Lane; Walla Walla; After You've Gone; By the Waters of the Minnetonka; Caressing Butterfly; No One Knows What It's All About; Fox Trot Classique; No, No, Nanette; Sally Lou; Poplar Street Blues; Allah's Holiday; Mandy, Make Up Your Mind.

**Dec. 8** (Mon)—Bix Beiderbecke leaves Jean Goldkette orchestra, goes to Indianapolis.

**c. Dec. 10–12** (Wed-Fri)—Bix and Cornelia Marshall, Hoagy Carmichael and his date, spend an evening of dining and dancing at the Roof Garden of the Severin Hotel listening to Charlie Davis orchestra. Cy Milders sings "I'll See You in My Dreams."

**Dec. 17** (Wed)—Marion McKay band records in Richmond for Gennett. Bix present and solos.

**c. Dec. 18–20** (Thu-Sat)—Bix returns to Davenport.

**Dec. 28** (Sun)—Merton "Bromo" Sulser and His Iowa Collegians open brief run at Garden Theater, Davenport. Bix comes to talk about going to Iowa City.


# 1925


**Jan. 3** (Sat)—Bromo Sulser and His Iowa Collegians close their Davenport engagement.

**Jan. 16** (Fri)—Bix joins Sulser band for Lions Charity Ball at the men's gym on Iowa University campus, Iowa City. Personnel: Chet Ogden (trumpet); Bix (cornet); Lindell "Romey" Rome (trombone); Walter Long, Russ Brobile, one other (saxophones); Merton "Bromo" Sulser (violin); Cecil

Huntzinger (piano); Armand "Dick" Dickeson (drums); Arnold Olson or Einar Johnson (brass bass).

**Jan. 17** (Sat)—Sulser band appears at the Blue Goose Ballroom of the Burkley Hotel, 9 West Washington, Iowa City.

**Jan. 19** (Mon)—Bix in Detroit for opening of Detroit Automobile Show. Stops by to see Goldkette.

**Jan. 23** (Fri)—Sulser band again at Blue Goose Ballroom.

**Jan. 24** (Sat)—Sulser band again at Blue Goose Ballroom.

**Jan. 25** (Sun) – Bix arrives in Indianapolis, looks up Hoagy Carmichael.

**Jan. 26** (Mon)—Bix and His Rhythm Jugglers record in Richmond, Indiana, for Gennett. Listed on company file card as "Leon B. Beiderbecke and his Orchestra."

**Jan. 30** (Fri)—Bix back with Sulser for regular Blue Goose job.

**Feb. 2** (Mon)—Bix enrolls as "unclassified student" at University of Iowa. His program of study was:
Freshman English (3 hours)
Religion and Ethics (Philosophy) (3 hours)
Music Theory (3-hour introductory course)
Piano Lessons (may have been incorporated into Theory, accounting for one of its three hours)
Music History (Romantic Period) (2 hours)
Music History (Modern Period) (2 hours)

**Feb. 5** (Thu)—*The Daily Iowan,* campus newspaper, announces Bix has pledged Beta Theta Phi fraternity.

**Feb. 6** (Fri)—Bix plays with Jean Goldkette orchestra for University of Michigan's annual "J-Hop" in Ann Arbor.

**Feb. 7** (Sat)—Sulser band at Blue Goose as usual. It is doubtful that Bix returned in time for this engagement.

**Feb. 9** (Mon)—Bix resumes classes.

**Feb. 14** (Sat)—Sulser band at the Blue Goose. Bix probably present.

**Feb. 16** (Mon)—Bix interviewed by freshman counselor. Excerpt from his note card: "Had $400 with him when he came. Gets money from home. Asked to drop Religion and take more music. Is not registered for military training, physical education, or Freshman Lectures. Was told to do so promptly. Plays one night a week."

**Feb. 19** (Thu)—Bix involved in fight at Reichart's Cafe.

**Feb. 20** (Fri)—Bix withdraws from University of Iowa.

**March 11** (Wed)—Bix withdraws his union card from Detroit local and takes a train for New York.

**March 13** (Fri)—Bix in New York. Plays in band including Herb Weil (drums) and Spencer Clark (bass sax) at Orienta Beach Club, Orienta Point, Mamaroneck, Westchester County, New York. Sits in later same night with the California Ramblers at the Ramblers Inn.

**March 14** (Sat)—Bix moves in with Ernest Loring "Red" Nichols at the Pasadena Hotel, 60th and Broadway, New York. During the following week Bix sat in frequently with the Ramblers. Personnel: Frank Cush, Red Nichols (trumpets); Tommy Dorsey (trombone); Jimmy Dorsey, Arnold Brilhart, Fred Cusick (reeds); Irving Brodsky (piano); Tommy Felline (banjo); Adrian Rollini (bass sax, "goofus," hot fountain pen, etc.); Stanley King (drums).

**March 21** (Sat)—Bix leaves New York and returns by train to Chicago.

**March 23** (Mon)—Bix deposits his union card at Chicago Local 10, requesting permission to seek regular employment. Goes to work at the Rendez-vous Cafe, 622 West Diversey Avenue, for Charley Straight. Personnel: Gene Cafferelli, Rex Maupin (trumpets); Bix (cornet); Shorty Lentz, later Herb

Winfield (trombones); Bob Strong, Dale Skinner, Joe Gist (saxes and clarinets); Straight (piano); Elmer Brown (bass and tuba); George Menden (banjo); Don Morgan (drums). Arrangements by Skinner and Strong.

Bix's official job was not in the full band but in the relief band: Bix, Lentz, Skinner, Gist (tuba), Art Gronwall (piano), Bob Conzelman (drums).

**March 24** (Tue)—Union board of directors votes to accept Bix's application.

**May 1** (Fri)—Straight loans Bix to Jean Goldkette's Victor Orchestra to play annual Indiana University prom.

**c. mid-June**—Frankie Trumbauer (C-melody sax) contacts Bix about possible autumn engagement at the Arcadia Ballroom, St. Louis.

**July 2** (Thu)—Bix leaves Straight, withdraws his card and leaves Chicago.

**July 4** (Sat)—Bix joins Nat Natoli's band at Walled Lake, Michigan, playing every night except Monday at the Casino, owned by Albert Tollenttino. Personnel: Natoli (trumpet); Bix (cornet); Phil Applin (trombone); Jimmie Jenkins, Harry Vail, one other (saxes); Gerald Finey (piano); Bill Bailey (banjo); Ted Campbell (drums). Name of bassist forgotten.

**July 6** (Mon)—Probable date of Bix's first visit to Island Lake, eight miles up the lake shore, to hear Jean Goldkette's "Breeze Blowers" at the Blue Lantern Inn. Personnel: Ray Lodwig (leader) and Jimmy Criswell (trumpets); Bill Rank (trombone); Jimmy Dorsey, Stanley "Doc" Ryker, Don Murray (saxophones); Howard "Howdy" Quicksell (banjo); Paul Mertz, later Fred Bergin (piano); Steve Brown (bass); Chauncey Morehouse (drums).

**c. July 13–15** (Mon-Wed)—Bix leaves Walled Lake band and joins Island Lake band at $60 per week, replacing Criswell.

**c. July 17–18** (Fri-Sat)—Jimmy Dorsey leaves for the East. Within several days he is replaced by Frank Trumbauer (C-melody saxophone).

**Aug. 13–14** (Thu-Fri)—Bix leaves Island Lake for St. Louis. It is probable that this coincided with Trumbauer's departure for New York City.

**Aug. 15** (Sat)—Bix Beiderbecke transfers into St. Louis Local 2, American Federation of Musicians.

**Aug. 18** (Tue) – Karl Spaeth, tenor saxophone, transfers to St. Louis local.

**Aug. 21** (Fri)—Frank Trumbauer records two titles for Brunswick in New York with the Cotton Pickers.

**c. Aug 25–26** (Tue-Wed)—Frank Trumbauer in St. Louis.

**Sept. 8** (Tue)—Frank Trumbauer's orchestra opens at the Arcadia Ballroom, 3515–3523 Olive Street, St. Louis. Personnel: Bix (cornet); Trumbauer (C-melody sax); Charles "Pee Wee" Russell, Karl Spaeth (reeds); Irving Kordick (trombone); Louis Feldman (piano); Wayne Jacobson (banjo); Anton Casertani (bass); Edgar "Eggie" Krewinhaus (drums); Marty Livingston (vocals).

**Sept. 12** (Sat)—Ray Thurston (trombone) replaces Kordick.

**Sept. 16** (Wed)—Les Karbach band shares bill with Trumbauer. Playing opposite the Trumbauer unit on Wednesdays, Saturdays and Sundays was a jazz band called the Arcadian Serenaders. Personnel: Sterling Bose (cornet); Avery Loposer (trombone); Cliff Holman (clarinet and alto sax); Johnny Riddick (piano); Bob Marvin (banjo); Felix Guarino (drums). Marty Livingston, though principally vocalist with Trumbauer, occasionally sang with the Serenaders and recorded with them for Okeh.

**Sept. 18** (Fri)—Probable date of Ruth Shaffner's first meeting with Bix Beiderbecke.

**Sept. 20** (Sun)—First regular payday for the Trumbauer group.

**Sept. 23** (Wed)—Joe Lechner band also appears at the Arcadia.

**Sept. 30** (Wed)—Conley-Silverman dance band also appears at the Arcadia.

**Oct. 3** (Sat)—Ruth Shaffner dates Bix, celebrates her sister Estelle's birthday.

**Oct. 6** (Tue)—After the Arcadia job the band plays from midnight until 5:30 A.M. at the Racquet Club near Forest Park.

**Oct. 10** (Sat)—Bix and Ruth join Wayne Jacobson and his girl Alberta and go to "Larry's" club after the job.

**Oct. 11** (Sun)—Ted Jansen band in guest appearance at the Arcadia.

**Oct. 12** (Mon)—Trumbauer band works at the Arcadia instead of taking its regular night off, playing opposite Joe Lechner band. Bix dates Ruth afterwards.

**Oct. 14** (Wed)—Guest appearances at the Arcadia by Conley-Silverman and Les Karbach bands.

**Oct. 17** (Sat)—Shaffner sisters cook a fried chicken dinner for Bix, Feldman and Spaeth. Missouri Cotton Pickers share the bill with Trumbauer at the Arcadia. Bix, Karl and Louis date the sisters after the job.

**Oct. 20** (Tue)—Ruth and Bess Shaffner stop off at the Arcadia on their way home from a movie, later go bowling with Feldman and Bix.

**Oct. 25** (Sun)—The three Shaffner sisters eat dinner out, visit the Arcadia and are driven home at evening's end by Feldman, Pee Wee Russell and Bix.

**Oct. 31** (Sat)—A night off for the band at the Arcadia. They play instead at Tremps Hall, 4458 Delmar, from 8:30 P.M. to 1:00 A.M. opposite the Missouri Cotton Pickers. Ruth and Bix go out together afterwards.

**Nov. 4** (Wed)—Bix moves into the Coronado Hotel, room 608. In addition to its two regular bands, the Arcadia also features spots by the Missouri Cotton Pickers, Les Karbach, Joe Lechner, and the 'Frisco Ramblers. Bix dates Ruth after work.

**Nov. 5** (Thu)—Ruth spends most of the day with Bix. They have breakfast, then go to the Arcadia for rehearsal. Then dinner at the Coronado Hotel. They play indoor golf at the hotel until it is time for Bix to leave for work. After the job, Bix takes Ruth bowling.

**Nov. 6** (Fri)—Beginning of St. Louis Symphony winter weekend concert season, with Friday afternoon performances at 3 P.M. and Saturday evenings.

**Nov. 7** (Sat)—Ruth and Bix double-date with Estelle and Bud Hassler. Later, Bix and Bud go to a farewell party at Frank Trumbauer's for Karl Spaeth.

**Nov. 8** (Sun)—Karl Spaeth leaves St. Louis, replaced by Damon "Bud" Hassler, after afternoon performance. Ruth in attendance, later driven home by Russell and Feldman. Later that night Stella (Estelle), Pee Wee, Ruth and Bix go to the West End in St. Louis.

**Nov. 12** (Thu)—Ted Weems and Frank Whitaker bands for spots at the Arcadia.

**Nov. 13** (Fri)—Bix and Hassler attend St. Louis Symphony concert.

**Nov. 14** (Sat)—Snow. Bix and Ruth at the bowling alley after work, then to one of their late-night haunts. Bix plays the piano and they eat sandwiches and coffee. Another stop for a snack en route home.

**Nov. 15** (Sun)—Ruth looks in on Arcadia matinee but comes home early. Later, Estelle and Pee Wee, Sonny Lee and Melba (?), Dee Orr and his date join Bix and Ruth for a bite to eat. Frank Trumbauer joins the party for a change, and they all wind up at the Eastern Cafe, Grand and Olive, to dance and eat chop suey.

**Nov. 18** (Wed)—Arcadia "country night," with band dressed in overalls and Ruth "winning" raffled turkey. After work, Bix and Ruth, plus Pee Wee, Hassler, Dee and their dates go to Larry's Club for breakfast.

**Nov. 19** (Thu)—Bix, Pee Wee and friend named Max drop in to ask Shaffner girls to join them at one of the clubs after work. Ruth inexplicably declines.

**Nov. 20** (Fri)—St. Louis Symphony concert. Bix and Hassler attend.

**Nov. 26** (Thu)—Thanksgiving Day.

**Nov. 27** (Fri)—St. Louis Symphony concert. Bix, Hassler and Pee Wee present. Shaffner sisters receive short note from Karl Spaeth.

**Nov. 28** (Sat)—Bix dates Ruth.

Nov. 29 (Sun)—Ruth and Bix, along with most members of Trumbauer and Serenaders bands, go to party at the home of friends named Pellet. Hassler sits
in a corner writing arrangements.

Dec. 3 (Thu)—Bix dates Ruth.

Dec. 4 (Fri)—St. Louis Symphony concert. Bix, Hassler, Pee Wee present.

Dec. 11 (Fri)—Another concert. Others scheduled Dec. 18 and 25.

Dec. 12 (Sat)—Bix dates Ruth.

Dec. 20 (Sun)—Shaffner sisters visit the Arcadia. Later driven home by group of
musicians including Bix and Jacobson. Bix stops by later after evening's
work.

Dec. 23 (Wed) – Shaffner sisters celebrate Christmas holidays with Bix, Pee Wee
and friends at Joe's Club, across the street from the Arcadia, after work.

Dec. 24 (Thu)—Shaffner sisters leave for home to spend Christmas with their
family.

Dec. 31 (Thu)—Trumbauer and Serenaders bands only two attractions at Arcadia's
New Year's Eve dance. Management spices the evening with offer to
wager $1,000 with any customer that crowd attending the ballroom this
evening will be the largest anywhere in St. Louis.

# 1926

Jan. 1 (Fri)—Bix returns to Davenport for brief holiday visit with his family.

Jan. 3 (Sun)—Shaffner sisters back in St. Louis. Arcadia sponsors big Charleston
contest, the winners to be sent to the Trianon Ballroom in Chicago for
finals Feb. 8 and 9.

Jan. 7 (Thu)—Bix returns to St. Louis, dates Ruth in the evening and introduces
her to Red McKenzie, leader of the Mound City Blue Blowers.

Jan. 10 (Sun)—Bix and Sterling Bose late for work. Hassler indisposed.

Jan. 16 (Sat)—*Carbondale Free Press* of Carbondale, Illinois, carries first of a series
of articles on Frank Trumbauer in connection with forthcoming appearance there by Arcadia band.

Jan. 29 (Fri)—Trumbauer orchestra plays at Elks Club in Carbondale.

Jan. 30 (Sat)—Ruth and Bix, Pee Wee and Estelle, Hassler, Feldman and their
dates go to Larry's Club after work.

Feb. 2 (Tue)—Bix takes Ruth backstage at St. Louis Theater to meet house band
and arranger Tommy Satterfield.

Feb. 3 (Wed)—Bix and Ruth, Estelle and Pee Wee and some other friends go to
Joe's Club after work, later to the West End, where joined by Bess, Dee
Orr, Hassler, Trumbauer and others; went square dancing.

Feb. 8 (Mon)—Band's day off. Ray Thurston leaves to go on the road, replaced
temporarily by Sonny Lee.

Feb. 9 (Tue)—Ruth entertains Bix at home for dinner. Then Trumbauer orchestra
plays St. Louis University "Prom of '26" at the Statler Hotel, beginning
at 9:30 P.M.

Feb. 10 (Wed)—Bix spends the afternoon playing indoor golf. Another double date
after work with Estelle and Pee Wee, winding up at Joe's Place.

Feb. 12 (Fri)—Friday afternoon symphony concerts resume.

Feb. 15 (Mon)—Bix and Ruth go out together. About this time, Vernon Brown
takes over the trombone chair from Sonny Lee. Trumbauer suspends
Wayne Jacobson for a week or two. Bob Marvin fills in on banjo, doubling
with both bands.

Feb. 19 (Fri)—Symphony concert. Bix and Hassler present.

Feb. 22 (Mon)—Bix and Ruth go out together.

Feb. 23 (Tue)—St. Louis Local 2 accepts Bix as full member.

**Feb. 24** (Wed)—*Carbondale Free Press* runs another item on Trumbauer and his band.

**Feb. 26** (Fri)—Another Elks Club job in Carbondale.

**March 3** (Wed)—Bix and Ruth double date with Stella and Pee Wee.

**March 4** (Thu)—Bix, Pee Wee and Dick (?) have dinner with the Shaffner sisters.

**March 5** (Fri)—Symphony concert. Bix and Hassler, perhaps Pee Wee, attend.

**March 7** (Sun)—Bix moves into Chase Hotel. Date with Ruth in the evening.

**March 12** (Fri)—Final winter symphony concert.

**March 16** (Tue)—Bix takes Ruth backstage at the Loew's State Theater, introduces her to the house band.

**March 18** (Thu)—Bix and Pee Wee to dinner at Ruth's.

**March 20** (Sat)—Long telephone conversation between Bix and Ruth. Bix gets a new roommate, a drummer named Mac.

**March 22** (Mon)—Bix takes Ruth out to dinner.

**March 29** (Mon)—Bix in Detroit for the day. Band's day off. Vernon Brown leaves the Trumbauer orchestra, replaced by Sonny Lee.

**April 3** (Sat)—Bix, Trumbauer and rhythm section play for grand opening of Thiebes Music Company on 12th Street downtown (formerly Kirkland Piano Company).

**April 4** (Sun)—Easter. Ruth at the Arcadia to hear Bix, make a date for Wednesday.

**April 7** (Wed)—Bix and Ruth to Joe's Club after the job.

**April 8** (Thu)—Bix and Ruth go to Loew's State Theater to see film *The Bat*.

**April 16** (Fri)—Trumbauer orchestra plays for Indiana University Junior Prom in Bloomington.

**April 21** (Wed)—Ruth and Bix see film *Stella Dallas* at Loew's State.

**May 1** (Sat)—Bix dates Ruth.

**May 2** (Sun)—Bix dates Ruth.

**May 3** (Mon)—Arcadia closes for the summer. Bix dates Ruth.

**May 4** (Tue)—Bix dates Ruth.

**May 6** (Thu)—Bix telephones Ruth, comes to see her. They spend most of the day together, later spend time with Orr, Frank, Hassler and Jacobson. End up at Ethel's Club and take a cab home early in the morning.

**May 7** (Fri)—Bix phones about noon to say he is leaving St. Louis. Ruth and Stella meet him for farewell drink at Joe's. Bix then leaves in Dan Gaebe's car.

**May 8–11** (Sat-Tue)—Bix in Chicago, thence to Detroit.

**May 12** (Wed)—Bix deposits his union card with Detroit Local 5, listing address as Addison Hotel.

**May 13** (Thu)—Bix and Trumbauer join the Jean Goldkette Victor Recording Orchestra in Terre Haute, Indiana, to play for the Rose Polytechnic Institute Junior Prom.

**May 14** (Fri)—Goldkette orchestra at South Bend, Indiana, for Notre Dame University Senior Ball. Band broadcasts at 10 P.M. over WSBT from Palais Royale building on campus, features waltz "Sorry and Blue" written by local composers Robert and Donald Elbel.

**May 15** (Sat)—Orchestra returns to Detroit and Graystone Ballroom.

**May 21** (Fri)—Broadcast over WCX from the Graystone at 10 P.M. for one hour.

**May 22** (Sat)—Goldkette unit led by Frank Trumbauer opens at Hudson Lake, Indiana, replacing Soash and Dockstader's Indianans, who move to Lake Orein, near Detroit. Trumbauer band personnel: Fred "Fuzzy" Farrar (trumpet); Bix (cornet); Sonny Lee (trombone); Stanley "Doc" Ryker, Pee Wee Russell, Frank Trumbauer (saxes and clarinets); Irving "Itzy" Riskin (piano); Frank DiPrima (banjo); Dan Gaebe (bass); Dee Orr (drums).

**June 12** (Sat)—The Indianans, directed by Joe Dockstader and featuring Lola Trowbridge and her songs, open at the Blue Lantern Inn, Hudson Lake, and alternate nightly with the Trumbauer-led Goldkette group for the duration of the summer.

June 18 (Fri)—Bix withdraws his union card from Detroit local.

June 21 (Mon)—Trumbauer group broadcasts over WSBT, South Bend, sharing the program with the Day Trio of Lakeville, Indiana, and recitals by Miss Phyllis Stepler of Chicago. The Trumbauer-Goldkette unit played the following three-part program:

*Group One:*
> Five Foot Two, Eyes of Blue
> Dinah
> Dream of Love
> Washboard Blues (banjo solo by Frank DiPrima)
> My Gal Sal (featuring a modern arrangement)

*Group Two:*
> On the Road to Mandalay
> Singin' the Blues
> To-night's My Night with Baby
> Lulu Belle
> The Legend of Lonesome Lake (descriptive piano solo by Bix Beiderbecke)
> Jig Walk

*Group Three:*
> Drifting Apart (cornet solo by Fred Farrar)
> Hi Diddle Diddle
> Play That Thing (saxophone solo by Frank Trumbauer)
> Medley of 1920 Song Hits
> Pale Moon (special concert arrangement)
> Tiger Rag
> Good Night

June 22 (Tue)—A review of the program in the *South Bend Tribune* includes: "Bix Beiderbecke varied the program with a unique piano solo, 'The Legend of Lonesome Lake' by Eastwood Lane. Mr. Beiderbecke, who plays cornet with the band, is an accomplished pianist."

July 4 (Sun)—Band holds its own Fourth of July celebration. Trumbauer turns up in full cowboy outfit.

Aug. 6 (Fri)—*South Bend Tribune* radio page advertises a "barn dance, the season's event, square and modern dances. Two orchestras, Willcox and Jean Goldkette."

Aug. 14 (Sat)—*Tribune* radio page advertises "All-nite dance, dusk to dawn, two superb orchestras, Jean Goldkette and Indianans."

Aug. 26 (Thu)—From the *Tribune:* "So interested is Frank Trumbauer, the orchestra's director, in what WSBT's listeners think of his band that he is offering five prizes for the five best letters on the subject, 'My opinion of your orchestra.' Arrangements have been made to print in the *Tribune* the five prize-winning letters, and the prizes will be awarded at the WSBT-Blue Lantern Radio Frolic, Saturday, Sept. 4 . . ."

Aug. 29 (Sun)—From the *Tribune:* "Art Haerens' Orchestra, under the direction of Myron Walz, will replace Goldkette's orchestra on tomorrow's broadcast. The Goldkette organization is leaving the Blue Lantern due to a last-minute decision."

Aug. 30 (Mon)—Trumbauer unit leaves Hudson Lake. Bix, Tram, Farrar, Ryker, Riskin return to Detroit.

early September—Reconstituted Jean Goldkette orchestra in rehearsal in Detroit.

Sept. 12 (Sun)—Helen Willcox gives birth to a son in Cortland, New York. Bix, Murray, Riskin and others attend horse race at Lincoln Field, Crete, Illinois, just outside Chicago, and place winning bets on Helen's Babe.

**Sept. 13–14** (Mon-Tue)—Jean Goldkette Victor Orchestra leaves for the East, playing one-nighters en route. Personnel: Fred Farrar, Ray Lodwig (trumpets); Bix (cornet); Bill Rank, Spiegle Willcox (temporarily replaced by Tommy Dorsey) (trombone); "Doc" Ryker, Frank Trumbauer, Don Murray (saxes and clarinets); Riskin (piano); Howard "Howdy" Quicksell (banjo); Steve Brown (bass); Chauncey Morehouse (drums).

**Sept. 21** (Tue)—Band arrives at Hillcrest Inn, Southboro, Massachusetts, and sets up headquarters for New England tour.

**Sept. 22** (Wed)—Band does noon publicity broadcast over station WTAG in Marlboro, Massachusetts.

**Sept. 25** (Sat)—Orchestra plays first dance engagement at Lyonhurst Ballroom, opposite Mal Hallett orchestra featuring Nuncio "Toots" Mondello (alto sax). About this time, William H. "Bill" Challis arrives from Wilkes Barre, Pennsylvania, to become band's regular arranger.

**Oct. 2** (Sat)—Final dance engagement at Lyonhurst.

**Oct. 4** (Mon)—Orchestra leaves Hillcrest Inn, travels to New York.

**Oct. 5** (Tue)—Bix checks into 44th Street Hotel, 120 West 44th Street, New York.

**Oct. 6** (Wed)—Jean Goldkette orchestra opens at Roseland Ballroom playing Battle of Music opposite Fletcher Henderson orchestra.

**Oct. 7** (Thu)—Roseland management presents Bix with large wooden tooth.

**Oct. 12** (Tue)—Recording date for Goldkette orchestra at Victor, Bix's first with the band since 1924.

**Oct. 13** (Wed)—Henderson orchestra returns to Roseland for another Battle of Music with Goldkette.

**Oct. 15** (Fri)—Goldkette records for Victor.

**Oct. 17** (Sun)—Probable ending of Roseland engagement, according to *New York Times*.

**Nov. 5** (Fri)—Orchestra back in Detroit.

**Nov. 6** (Sat)—Graystone Ballroom advertises two orchestras: Goldkette's and, probably, the Orange Blossom band.

**Nov. 7** (Sun)—Goldkette Victor Orchestra offers continuous music from 4 P.M. until early hours. Orange Blossoms again probably present and alternating with Victor band.

**Nov. 8** (Mon)—Band's night off. Bix leaves for Davenport.

**Nov. 9** (Tue)—Bix acts as best man at Charles Burnette Beiderbecke's marriage to Mary Dennison Neelans in Maquoketa, Iowa, about 40 miles north of Davenport.

**Nov. 11** (Thu)—Bix returns to Detroit.

The following is a day-by-day program of events at the Graystone for the rest of November. Sometime during this period Paul Mertz replaces Irving Riskin as pianist. He in turn is replaced by Marlin Skiles between Dec. 19 (Sun) and 26 (Sun). Other personnel remained the same.

**Nov. 12–19–26** (Fri)—"Gift Night" at the Graystone Ballroom.

**Nov. 13–20–27** (Sat)—Regular dance program.

**Nov. 14–21–28** (Sun)—Program as for November 7.

**Nov. 15–22–29** (Mon)—Night off.

**Nov. 16–23–30** (Tue)—Regular dance program at 8:45 P.M., with 7:45 P.M. dance class added.

**Nov. 17–24** (Wed)—Feature Night, with novelty attractions.

**Nov. 18–25** (Thu)—Weekly radio broadcast over WJR from 10–11 P.M. direct from the ballroom.

And again for December:

**Dec. 1–8–15–22–29** (Wed)—Feature Night. These nights are typified by the program for the 29th, when the management placed large tanks of fish in the ballroom and presented fishing rods to the guests. The guest catching the largest fish received a prize.

**Dec. 2–9–16–23–30** (Thu)—Except for the 2nd, for which we can find no trace of a broadcast, the band continued weekly Thursday evening transmissions from the Graystone over WJR. Exact programs appear to have been lost. Also, beginning the 9th, the Graystone presented a weekly Waltz Night aimed at older dancers.

**Dec. 3–10–17–24–31** (Fri)—Gift Night.

**Dec. 4–11–18–25** (Sat)—Matinee added on Christmas Day only. Otherwise weekly dance programs as usual.

**Dec. 5–12–19–26** (Sun)—Matinee and evening dancing.

**Dec. 6–13–20–27** (Mon)—Band's night off.

**Dec. 7–14–21–28** (Tue)—Dancing classes at 7:45 P.M. before evening program.

**Dec. 11** (Sat)—Prior to nightly Graystone appearance, Victor band featured in special program at Detroit Athletic Club starting at 8:30 P.M. Also featured: the Revelers, popular vocal group. The program, complete, offers:

    I.  A) Adoration . . . . . . . . . . . Borowski
          B) Transcription of Indian Melodies:
             Pale Moon; Kashmiri Song; By the
             Waters of the Minnetonka . . . . . Goldkette
          C) Hurricane (Novelty for Orchestra) . . Mertz
          D) Waltz Selection of Popular Melodies
          E) Excerpts from *Rhapsody in Blue* . . Gershwin
          F) On the Road to Mandalay . . . . . Speaks-Kipling
    II.  The Revelers
    III.  American Concerto
          Lento . . . . . . . . . . . . Scott
          Andante and Presto . . . . . . . MacDowell
          (According to reviews, this was scored for orchestra and conducted by V. P. Coffey, and featured Jean Goldkette at the piano with jazz orchestra accompaniment.)
    IV.  The Revelers
    V.  Valencia; Medley of Musical Comedy Hits; Selection of Popular Airs; Original Interpretations of Modern "Blues"
    VI.  The Revelers

**Dec. 31** (Fri)—Band reported variously as playing at Graystone and Detroit Athletic Club. Goldkette, said both reports, gave "orders to toot to kill until there isn't a shake left in the most festive hoof." New Year's Eve program lasted from 8:30 P.M. until 4 A.M. It is the authors' opinion that the Victor orchestra was at the Graystone, and that the report placing it elsewhere is in error.

# 1927

**Jan. 1** (Sat)—Graystone dance programs resume at 4 P.M. Although a complete check of Detroit newspapers from Jan. 2–19 failed to yield any trace of the band's weekly broadcasts, it is the authors' opinion that these, as well as other weekly Graystone fixtures, continue through the month.

**Jan. 17** (Mon)—Band plays annual Masque Ball at Graystone.

**Jan. 18** (Tue)—Band plays annual Scarab Club Ball at Graystone.

**Jan. 19** (Wed)—Band plays for dedication of new Savarine Hotel, with special broadcast over WJR.

**Jan. 20** (Fri)—Final appearance at the Graystone. The orchestra now left for New York and its second Roseland engagement. Personnel: Farrar, Lodwig (trumpets); Bix (cornet); Rank, Willcox (trombones); Ryker, Trumbauer,

Murray (reeds); Mertz (piano); Quicksell (banjo); Brown (bass); Morehouse (drums); Challis (arranger).

Jan. 23 (Sun)—Band arrives in New York. Murray taken ill, replaced temporarily by Jimmy Dorsey.

Jan. 24 (Mon)—Goldkette band opens at Roseland opposite Fletcher Henderson.

Jan. 28 (Fri)—Recording date at Victor.

Jan. 31 (Mon)—Recording date at Victor. Dorsey leaves due to other commitments; replaced by Danny Polo (tenor sax and clarinet).

Feb. 1 (Tue)—Recording date at Victor.

Feb. 3 (Thu)—Recording date at Victor.

Feb. 4 (Fri)—Trumbauer small group records "Singin' the Blues," two other titles for Okeh.

Feb. 6 (Sun)—Goldkette orchestra closes at Roseland.

Feb. 7 (Mon)—Band opens three-day stint at Cook's Butterfly Ballroom in Springfield, Massachusetts. Bix's "Davenport Blues" copyrighted in the name of Robbins-Engel, Inc., under number E658002. Copyright subsequently renewed under R125432 (Feb. 8, 1954) by Charles Burnette Beiderbecke and Mary Louise Shoemaker.

Feb. 9 (Wed)—Band closes at Cook's Butterfly.

Feb. 11 (Fri)—Band returns to Detroit, then to Ann Arbor to play University of Michigan "J-Hop" opposite Fletcher Henderson and Guy Lombardo bands.

Feb. 12 (Sat)—Band broadcasts from the Graystone from 9–10 P.M. over WJR. Paul Mertz leaves to join Fred Waring; temporarily replaced by Marlin Skiles. Murray still ill.

Feb. 17 (Thu)—Band continues weekly WJR broadcasts, but Bix is in New York. The ledgers of Hans Bach, brother of instrument maker Vincent Bach, show that Bix picked up Bach Stradivarius model cornet number 616, medium large bore, with bell number 101, at the music store on West 48th Street. Bix also ordered an additional cornet, which was sent to him later in the month: number 620, gold-plated, with bell number 106. Also medium large bore. Cornet number 616 later became the property of Jimmy McPartland. Number 620 was for many years in the possession of Bix's sister, Mary Louise Shoemaker. Bix used a Bach number seven mouthpiece with these instruments.

Feb. 22 (Tue)—Band provides dance music for the Bohemians (Musicians Club of Detroit) program at the Grand Ballroom of the Book-Cadillac Hotel starting at 6:30 P.M. Jean Goldkette, a club member, was chairman of the ballroom music committee.

Feb. 24 (Thu)—Band continues weekly WJR broadcasts. About this time Don Murray returns, but Danny Polo remains for a short time, bringing the reed section to four and allowing Trumbauer more time to front the band. Chris Fletcher and Ernest "Red" Ingle (violins and auxiliary reeds) added temporarily.

February & March—Schedule much as before, including weekly radio broadcasts over WJR on March 3, 10, 17, 24, 31.

late March—Polo, Fletcher, Ingle depart. Eddy Sheasby (violin and arranger) placed in charge of band. Irving Riskin returns, replacing Marlin Skiles.

April 7 (Thu)—Final WJR broadcast from the Graystone, 9–10 P.M.

April 10 (Sun)—Farewell performance at the Graystone.

April 13 (Wed)—Graystone band on the road. In Dayton, Ohio, for General Motors Convention.

April 15 (Fri)—Band in Dayton at the Greystone Dance Hall, 120 West 4th Street.

April 16 (Sat)—Another date at the Greystone in Dayton.

April 17 (Sun)—Easter. Band in Columbus, Ohio, at Valley Dale Ballroom, 1590 Sunbury Road.

**April 18** (Mon)—Columbus, at Hannah Neil Charity Ball at the Neil Home. Broadcast from the Neil Home over WAIU at 11 P.M.

**April 21** (Thu)—Terre Haute, Indiana, for Rose Polytechnic Institute Junior Prom.

**April 22** (Fri)—Bloomington, for Indiana University Junior Prom.

**April 29** (Fri)—State College, Pennsylvania, for Penn State Prom.

**April 30** (Sat)—Reading, Pennsylvania, at Bach's Natatorium, 134 North 5th Street.

**May 2** (Mon)—Another date at Bach's Natatorium.

**May 4** (Wed)—Chambersburg, Pennsylvania.

**May 5** (Thu)—Allentown, Pennsylvania. Band spends day rehearsing for following day's recording date.

**May 6** (Fri)—Recording date for Victor in Camden, New Jersey. Dance at University of Pennsylvania.

**May 7–8** (Sat-Sun)—Band in Scranton, Pennsylvania.

**May 9** (Mon)—Trumbauer group with Bix records for Okeh in New York, then rejoins Goldkette band for evening job in Bridgeport, Connecticut, at the Ritz Ballroom.

**May 13** (Fri)—Trumbauer band records again for Okeh in New York, then joins Goldkette orchestra in Princeton. Scheduled to play at the Cloister Club, they wind up playing instead for the Charter Club, at 79 Prospect.

**May 14** (Sat)—Goldkette orchestra again persuaded to play for Charter Club, cancelling Cottage Club.

**May 16** (Mon)—Full band in Camden to record for Victor. To Philadelphia in the evening for a dance at Philadelphia Athletic Club opposite Roger Wolfe Kahn orchestra. Afterwards, musicians go to Longo's restaurant for spaghetti.

**May 20** (Fri)—Band in Ithaca, New York, for Cornell University Spring Day Ball.

**May 21** (Sat)—Scranton, Pennsylvania, Town Hall.

**May 22** (Sun)—Harrisburg, Pennsylvania. Rehearsed at the State Restaurant for recording date the following day.

**May 23** (Mon)—Recording date for Victor in Camden at 9:30 A.M., then to Hershey, Pennsylvania, to play at Central Park Pavilion. Spiegle Willcox, after playing on the recording date, leaves the band and is replaced by Lloyd Turner.

**May 24** (Tue)—Harrisburg, Pennsylvania.

**May 25** (Wed)—Chambersburg, Pennsylvania.

**May 26** (Thu)—Allentown, Pennsylvania.

**May 27** (Fri)—Philadelphia; advertisements state Goldkette band to appear opposite Vincent Lopez unit, but failed to say where.

**May 28** (Sat)—Day off in Scranton, Pennsylvania, en route west to Cincinnati.

**May 29** (Sun)—Jean Goldkette Victor Orchestra opens at A. J. "Toots" Marshall's Castle Farms in Cincinnati. Ingle and Fletcher rejoin for this engagement.

**June 10** (Fri)—Band due to close at Castle Farms, but advertisement in local newspaper says it is being held over by popular demand.

**June 25** (Sat)—Last newspaper announcement of band's appearance at Castle Farms.

**July 1** (Fri)—Closing night at Castle Farms. Band leaves for St. Louis.

**July 2** (Sat)—Orchestra opens at Loew's State Theater, 713–719 Washington Avenue, St. Louis. Appearing onstage with Don Albert's orchestra; Edwin Snyder and Jean Bronenkamp (tenor and soprano); Tom Terry and his "Organologue" on "I'll Always Remember You." According to the *St. Louis Star,* the feature film is *Altars of Desire* starring Mae Murray and Conway Tearle. Ruth Shaffner and Rose Meyers, coming home from work, bump into Bix in the parking lot behind the theater.

**July 8** (Fri)—Orchestra closes at Loew's State. Their movements for the next month are uncertain, though these probably include more one-nighters and an eventual return to Detroit. This is not announced in the Detroit press.

Aug. 5 (Fri)—Band's final night at the Graystone before heading east to Atlantic City.

Aug. 6 (Sat)—Bix and Bill Challis leave for Atlantic City driving car belonging to Francis "Cork" O'Keefe.

Aug. 8 (Mon)—Orchestra opens at Young's Million Dollar Pier on the boardwalk in Atlantic City, New Jersey.

c. Aug. 10–15 (Wed-Mon)—Visits from Adrian Rollini and Paul Whiteman.

Aug. 23 (Tue)—Orchestra in New York for Victor recording date at Liederkranz Hall. Vocalist Johnny Marvin also present. Band rehearses four numbers, then Victor executives Leonard Joy and Mr. Porter decide to postpone the date until Friday. Meanwhile Adrian Rollini, having secured engagement at Club New Yorker (formerly Paul Whiteman Club), 48th and Broadway, begins offering jobs to musicians. Phones Sylvester Ahola, trumpet with Peter Van Steeden, at Half Moon Hotel, Coney Island.

Aug. 24 (Wed)—Rollini and Ahola meet in front of Club. Ahola says he'll think it over.

Aug. 25 (Thu)—Trumbauer recording date for Okeh with Bix.

Aug. 26 (Fri)—Orchestra tries again to record at Victor. Again cancelled, following 9:15 A.M. telegram to Porter. No reason given.

Aug. 28 (Sun)—Bill Challis leaves band to join Paul Whiteman.

Sept. 5 (Mon)—Goldkette closes at Atlantic City. Spiegle and Helen Willcox visit the band and Spiegle sits in for a few numbers.

Sept. 8 (Thu)—Orchestra opens at Roseland. Ahola visits Rollini at Pathe Studios where Adrian, Joe Venuti, Eddie Lang and Vic Berton are recording with Annette Hanshaw. Ahola accepts the New Yorker job.

Sept. 9 (Fri)—Bix records "In a Mist" at Okeh, then goes off to New Yorker for first rehearsal with Rollini.

Sept. 12 (Mon)—Rollini band rehearses at Club New Yorker.

Sept. 13 (Tue)—Rehearsal at New Yorker.

Sept. 14 (Wed)—Rehearsal at New Yorker.

Sept. 15 (Thu)—Final Victor recording date for Goldkette Graystone orchestra. Band rehearses all morning, records "Blue River" and "Clementine" in the afternoon. Goldkette present.

Sept. 16 (Fri)—Rollini band rehearses at New Yorker, then has photograph taken at Apeda Studios. Afterwards they try out for radio broadcast. Job does not materialize.

Sept. 17 (Sat)—Tram, Bix and Lang record a trio number, "Wringin' an' Twistin'," for Okeh.

Sept. 18 (Sun)—Closing night at Roseland for Goldkette orchestra. Goldkette officially disbands.

Sept. 19 (Mon)—Rollini band rehearses at New Yorker from 11 A.M. until 5 P.M.

Sept. 20 (Tue)—Another rehearsal, same times. "These are long sessions," Ahola remarks in his diary.

Sept. 21 (Wed)—Two rehearsals: one from 11–5 as usual, then another from midnight until 5 A.M.

Sept. 22 (Thu)—Opening night at the Club New Yorker. Special permit allows club to operate from 11 P.M. until 5 A.M. for its grand opening. Gene Tunney defeats Jack Dempsey in Long Count heavyweight title match in Chicago.

Sept. 23 (Fri)—New Yorker regular hours now 11 P.M. to 3 A.M. Band knocks off at 2:45 A.M. Members of Art Landry's band in the audience. Personnel of Rollini's New Yorkers: Sylvester Ahola (trumpet); Bix (cornet); Bill Rank (trombone); Frank Trumbauer, Don Murray, Bobby Davis (reeds); Frank

Signorelli (piano); Rollini (bass sax); Eddie Lang (guitar); Joe Venuti (violin); Chauncey Morehouse (drums).

Sept. 24 (Sat)—Paul Specht among the guests at New Yorker.

Sept. 25 (Sun)—Band plays benefit at 44th Street Theater. Business picking up at the New Yorker.

Sept. 28 (Wed)—Full band minus Ahola (he was not told the time of the session and is therefore absent, though scheduled to participate) records under Trumbauer's name for Okeh. Later plays New Yorker from 7 P.M. until 9 P.M., resuming at 11:30 P.M. Eddie Lang sick most of the night. "Someone hearing band tonight, as we had to play good," Ahola notes.

Sept. 29 (Thu)—Several members of band, including Bix, Tram, and Venuti, record for Sam Lanin at Harmony studios as the Broadway Bell-Hops. After work, band stays to rehearse with dance team of Deno and Rochelle, scheduled to open at New Yorker. Rehearsal ends 4:45 A.M.

Sept. 30 (Fri)—Full band records for Okeh. Titles ultimately released in United States under Benny Meroff's name, abroad under Trumbauer's. Guests during evening at New Yorker include bandleaders Nat Shilkret and Roger Wolfe Kahn, who talks to musicians about airplanes. Band "going terrible," notes Ahola.

Oct. 3 (Mon)—Boston musicians Phil Wall and Frank Dunn visit Ahola on the job.

Oct. 4 (Tue)—Bix, Tram, Ahola and Bobby Davis see movie *Wings*.

Oct. 5 (Wed)—Bix takes Rank, Murray, Rollini, Signorelli and Morehouse up to Okeh to make first batch of dixieland titles under his own leadership. In the evening, during intermission, Ahola shows home movies to the band.

Oct. 6 (Thu)—More home movies in the back room at the New Yorker. Rehearsal after the job for Saturday, when band begins doubling with master of ceremonies Frank Fay at the Strand Theater. Note from Ahola: "I had a hand-crank Model A Kodak 16 mm movie camera, big tripod. Still have it!"

Oct. 7 (Fri)—Fifteen-minute rehearsal at work for Strand job.

Oct. 8 (Sat)—Band opens at the Strand, plays only late session at New Yorker from now on. Good business both places.

Oct. 9 (Sun)—Business bad at both Strand and New Yorker.

Oct. 10 (Mon)—Business worse at New Yorker. Lang still out sick, replaced by Howdy Quicksell (banjo). "It looks as though the place is going on the rocks," says Ahola in his diary.

Oct. 12 (Wed)—Joe Venuti misses the first show. Business worse at New Yorker.

Oct. 13 (Thu)—Rollini tells the band the Club is going to fold.

Oct. 14 (Fri)—Band finishes at the Strand.

Oct. 15 (Sat)—Band finishes at New Yorker. Rollini asks for a week to come up with further bookings. All agree.

Oct. 18 (Tue)—Ahola meets Trumbauer, but no news yet from Rollini. Musicians feel it hopeless to wait further.

c. Oct. 20 (Thu)—Bix and Trumbauer, Murray, Signorelli, Lang and Vic Berton record for Willard Robison at Pathe under name "Chicago Loopers." Studio at East 53rd Street. On this day, Sam Lanin wrote Bix a check for $25, spurring speculation that Bix may have been on the Lanin records; three sides made that day for the Plaza group. See discography for further discussion of this question.

Oct. 25 (Tue)—Bix makes second batch of dixieland titles for Okeh, this time as part of Trumbauer record date.

Oct. 26 (Wed)—Trumbauer, Rank and others record with Red Nichols at Victor. "Sugar" among the titles. Trumbauer band records same selection in the afternoon for Okeh.

Oct. 27 (Thu)—Bix and Trumbauer join Paul Whiteman's orchestra in Indianapolis at the Indiana Theater. Band personnel: Henry Busse, Charles Margulis,

Bob Mayhew (trumpets); Bix (cornet); Boyce Cullen, Wilbur Hall, Tommy Dorsey, Jack Fulton (trombones); Chester "Chet" Hazlett, Hal McLean, Frank Trumbauer, Jimmy Dorsey, Jack Mayhew, Nye Mayhew, Rupert "Rube" Crozier, Charles Strickfaden (reeds); Kurt Dieterle, Mischa Russell, Matty Malneck, Mario Perry (doubling accordion), Charles Gaylord, John Bowman (strings); Mike Pingitore (banjo); Mike Trafficante (tuba); Steve Brown (string bass); Harry Perrella, Tom Satterfield (pianos); Hal McDonald (drums).

Bing Crosby, Harry Barris, Alton Rinker (Paul Whiteman Rhythm Boys), vocalists.

Austin "Skin" Young, Jack Fulton, Charles Gaylord (Paul Whiteman Trio), vocalists.

Ferde Grofe, Tom Satterfield, Bill Challis and occasionally Matty Malneck (arrangers); John Bowman (librarian).

Oct. 28 (Fri)—End of Indiana Theater engagement.

Oct. 29 (Sat)—Whiteman opens at Ambassador Theater on Seventh Street, St. Louis. Bix re-establishes contact with Ruth Shaffner.

Nov. 4 (Fri)—Whiteman closes at Ambassador, departs for Chicago. Bix stays behind to spend two free days with Ruth.

Nov. 7 (Mon)—Whiteman opens at Chicago Theater. Bix, the Dorseys, *et al.* go to Sam Beers' "My Cellar," 222 North State Street, to jam until dawn.

Nov. 13 (Sun)—End of Chicago Theater engagement.

Nov. 14 (Mon)—Whiteman opens at Uptown Theater, Chicago.

Nov. 18 (Fri)—Copyright for "In a Mist" registered in the name of Robbins Music Corp., under E678864. Copyright renewed under R139807 on November 19, 1954, under names of C. B. Beiderbecke and Mary Louise Shoemaker. Whiteman records "Washboard Blues" for Victor with vocal and piano by the composer, Hoagy Carmichael.

Nov. 20 (Sun)—Whiteman closes at Uptown Theater.

Nov. 21 (Mon)—Orchestra opens at Tivoli Theater in Chicago.

Nov. 22 (Tue)—Whiteman records "Among My Souvenirs" for Victor. Bix not included.

Nov. 23 (Wed)—Whiteman records "Changes" for Victor. Bix featured.

Nov. 25 (Fri)—Orchestra records for Victor.

Nov. 27 (Sun)—Whiteman closes at Tivoli Theater. Tommy Dorsey leaves the band.

Nov. 29 (Tue)—Orchestra at Memorial Hall, Columbus, Ohio.

Nov. 30 (Wed)—Orchestra at Land o' Dance, Canton, Ohio.

Dec. 1 (Thu)—Whiteman presents four-hour concert and dance program at Madison Gardens, Toledo, Ohio.

Dec. 2 (Fri)—Orchestra arrives in Lansing, Michigan, for similar concert and dance program. Whiteman visits Governor Fred W. Green, accompanies him on inspection tour of new Ford automobiles. The concert, at 8:15 P.M. at Prudden Auditorium:

Rhapsody in Blue
Dancing Tambourine
Just a Memory
Under the Moon
Sometimes I'm Happy
Limehouse Blues
Wide Open Spaces
My Blue Heaven (Jack Fulton, vocal)
Falling Leaf
Tigerette
When Day Is Done (Henry Busse, trumpet)
Program also features the Rhythm Boys, with two baby pianos, slam-

ming lids, etc., plus Willy Hall doing "Pop! Goes the Weasel" on violin and "Stars and Stripes Forever" on his bicycle pump.

Dance program held later at 119th Field Artillery Armory.

Dec. 4 (Sun)—Whiteman opens at Allen Theater, Cleveland.

Dec. 11 (Sun)—Whiteman closes at Allen Theater.

Dec. 12 (Mon)—Orchestra opens at Loew's Penn Theater in Pittsburgh. Bill Rank joins the trombone section, replacing Tommy Dorsey.

Dec. 16 (Fri)—End of Loew's Penn engagement.

Dec. 19 (Mon)—Whiteman opens at the Century Theater in Baltimore.

Dec. 22 (Thu)—Princeton Triangle Club show, *Napoleon Passes,* opens at Lyric Theater, Baltimore. Bill Priestley (cornet and guitar) and Edwin "Squirrel" Ashcraft (accordion) among the performers.

Dec. 24 (Sat)—Whiteman closes at the Century.

Dec. 26 (Mon)—Orchestra appears at Coliseum Ballroom, in York, Pennsylvania, offering dance program from 8:30 P.M. to 12:30 A.M. Attendance: 2,500.

Dec. 27 (Tue)—Whiteman appears at a party held at the Ritz-Carleton Hotel in New York. Uncertain whether full band, small instrumental group, or just Whiteman himself at this appearance.

Dec. 28 (Wed)—Whiteman gives a concert at Town Hall, Scranton, Pennsylvania.

Dec. 29 (Thu)—Orchestra at the Armory in Wilkes Barre, Pennsylvania.

Dec. 30 (Fri)—Orchestra at the Kalurah Temple in Binghamton, New York. From the *Binghamton Sun* of the following morning: ". . . the program is new, with three exceptions, straight dance music, the type of music in which Whiteman excels. The three exceptions included George Gershwin's 'Rhapsody In Blue' and two similar selections. All three were well received, the 'Rhapsody In Blue' receiving the greatest ovation probably since it is so well-known.

"After a short concert program which included several vaudeville acts, Whiteman turned to the audience and said, 'now let's dance.' The dance program included a large number of the more popular song hits of the past four or five years and it was here that Whiteman demonstrated his superiority as a leader. He has colored dance music in many ways and introduced tonal novelties, but in doing so he has avoided effects which submerge the melody."

Dec. 31 (Sat)—Orchestra provides stage show for New Year's Eve festivities at Bellevue-Stratford Hotel, Philadelphia. Sam Lanin furnishes dance music.

# 1928

Jan. 4 (Wed)—Whiteman records for Victor in New York. Later takes part in new nationwide NBC radio broadcast (10:30–11:30 P.M. EST) sponsored by Dodge Brothers Automobile Company, offering a different entertainer from each section of the United States. Will Rogers emcees from West Coast. Whiteman opens with *Rhapsody in Blue.* Chicago follows with Dorothy Stone, Fred Stone and the Criss Cross Four, with Mary Cooke at the piano. Over to New Orleans for two medleys of hits sung by Al Jolson, with Dave Dreyer at the piano. Back to Whiteman, wrapping it up with "Among My Souvenirs" and "Changes," the latter presumably featuring Bix.

Jan. 5 (Thu)—Whiteman records for Victor.

Jan. 9 (Mon)—(*Billboard* for December 24, 1927, mentions a projected tour of the orchestra through New England and Pennsylvania, starting on this date. All efforts to trace this alleged tour have proven fruitless.) Bix and Trumbauer record for Okeh.

Jan. 11 (Wed)—Orchestra records for Victor.
Jan. 12 (Thu)—Orchestra records for Victor.
Jan. 14 (Sat)—Whiteman opens at the Mosque Theater, Newark, New Jersey.
Jan. 20 (Fri)—Bix and Trumbauer record for Okeh. End of Mosque Theater engagement.
Jan. 21 (Sat)—Whiteman records for Victor in Camden.
Jan. 22 (Sun)—Whiteman opens at Stanley Theater, Philadelphia.
Jan. 24 (Tue)—Orchestra records for Victor in Camden.
Jan. 26 (Thu)—Orchestra rehearses but does not record "Whispering" with Thomas "Fats" Waller at the organ in Camden.
Jan. 27 (Fri)—Orchestra records for Victor. Bix not present.
Jan. 28 (Sat)—Orchestra records for Victor in Camden under direction of Bill Challis. Bix featured. Stanley Theater engagement ends.
Jan. 29 (Sun)—Whiteman leaves Philadelphia for Allentown.
Jan. 30 (Mon)—Arrival in Allentown. Afternoon rehearsal. Evening engagement at Mealey's Auditorium. *Allentown Chronicle and News and Evening Item* notes that "Mr. Whiteman's four pianists, including two men who play on the smallest upright Chickering piano, are also on the program . . ." Program includes musical adaptation of Kipling's "On the Road to Mandalay."
Feb. 1 (Wed)—Orchestra at the Coliseum Ballroom, Harrisburg. Roy Bargy, pianist, joins the band, replacing Harry Perrella.
Feb. 2 (Thu)—Orchestra at Cathaum Theater at Penn State College.
Feb. 3 (Fri)—Dance program at Auditorium Dance Hall, Johnstown, Pennsylvania.
Feb. 4 (Sat)—Whiteman returns to New York. Perrella leaves. Nye and Jack Mayhew leave, except for one further record date. Steve Brown gives notice but remains until Whiteman can find a replacement. Whiteman's schedule not clear for next few days, but presumably plays the Paramount Theater in New York.
Feb. 7 (Tue)—Orchestra records for Victor. All Grofe scores. Bix not present.
Feb. 8 (Wed)—Orchestra records for Victor. Bix present.
Feb. 9 (Thu)—Orchestra records for Victor.
Feb. 10 (Fri)—Orchestra records for Victor. Jimmy Dorsey departs, replaced by Irving "Izzy" Friedman. Bob Mayhew replaced by Eddie Pinder. Hal McLean replaced by Roy "Red" Mayer (Maier) but stays on for some time thereafter.
Feb. 13 (Mon)—Whiteman records for Victor.
Feb. 14 (Tue)—Whiteman records for Victor.
Feb. 15 (Wed)—Whiteman records for Victor. Steve Brown leaves. Trafficante switches from tuba to string bass. Wilford "Min" Leibrook (tuba and bass sax) joins.
Feb. 16 (Thu)—Whiteman records for Victor.
Feb. 18 (Sat)—Whiteman records for Victor.
Feb. 19–26 (Sun-Sun)—Orchestra reportedly makes a tour of one-nighters through Ohio and West Virginia this week. No dates or engagements have been traced.
Feb. 27 (Mon)—Orchestra records for Victor.
Feb. 28 (Tue)—Orchestra records for Victor.
Feb. 29 (Wed)—Orchestra records for Victor.
March 1 (Thu)—Orchestra records for Victor.
March 2 (Fri)—Orchestra records for Victor.
March 3–11 (Sat-Sun)—One-nighters outside New York. No available information.
March 12 (Mon)—Whiteman returns to New York, records for Victor.
March 13 (Tue)—Whiteman records for Victor.
March 14 (Wed)—Whiteman records for Victor.

**March 15** (Thu)—Whiteman records for Victor.

**March 16** (Fri)—Whiteman records for Victor. Bix not present.

**March 17** (Sat)—Whiteman records for Victor.

**March 18–27** (Sun-Tue)—Whiteman plays one-nighters. No recording activity.

**March 28** (Wed)—Orchestra plays concert for the Woman's Pay Club in New York.

**March 30** (Fri)—A night off. Bix, Bill Priestley and Squirrel Ashcraft make the rounds of places featuring jazz bands, including a visit to the Little Club on 44th Street to hear Ben Pollack's orchestra. Priestley persuades Bix to sit in on Princeton Triangle Club band's record date the following afternoon and Bix consents. At the last moment, Whiteman calls an afternoon rehearsal and Bix has to miss the Princeton date.

**March 31** (Sat)—Whiteman opens at the Paramount. At this point, or shortly before, Lennie Hayton joins as second pianist.

**April 3** (Tue)—Trumbauer band with Bix records for Okeh.

**April 10** (Tue)—Another Trumbauer date for Okeh.

**April 17** (Tue)—Bix Beiderbecke and His Gang record for Okeh.

**April 21** (Sat)—Whiteman closes at the Paramount, records for Victor.

**April 22** (Sun)—Whiteman records for Victor.

**April 23** (Mon)—Orchestra rehearses but does not record at Victor.

**April 24** (Tue)—Orchestra records for Victor.

**April 25** (Wed)—Orchestra records for Victor. A quarrel between Whiteman and Henry Busse precipitates departure of Busse and Hal McDonald. They are replaced midway through the date by Harry "Goldie" Goldfield (trumpet) and George Marsh (drums).

**April 27** (Fri)—Whiteman opens at Loew's Metropolitan Theater in Boston. Program includes "Mississippi Mud," "Ramona" and musical reminiscences.

**May 10** (Thu)—End of Boston engagement. Band returns to New York.

**May 12** (Sat)—Whiteman records for Columbia; first date under its new contract.

**May 13** (Sun)—Records for Columbia. Bix not present.

**May 14** (Mon)—Orchestra opens at Loew's Metropolitan Theater in Brooklyn.

**May 15** (Tue)—Records for Columbia.

**May 16** (Wed)—Records for Columbia.

**May 17** (Thu)—Records for Columbia.

**May 19** (Sat)—End of Brooklyn engagement.

**May 21** (Mon)—Records for Columbia.

**May 22** (Tue)—Records for Columbia.

**May 23** (Wed)—Records for Columbia.

**May 24** (Thu)—Records for Columbia.

**May 25** (Fri)—Records for Columbia.

**May 26** (Sat)—Orchestra opens at Capitol Theater, Detroit.

**May 27** (Sun)—From a review in the *Detroit Free Press:* "Harry Barris, one of Whiteman's Rhythm Boys, was a piano player in vaudeville and never having had the opportunity to take up a memory system, was always forgetting lyrics, and filled in the gaps with 'wha-to-de-bo-do-n-do' and similar fanciful expressions. Barris appeared at the State, doing a 'single,' shortly after it opened. The audience failed to understand him, but the musicians of Detroit flocked to hear this youngster. Then Harry ran into Bing Crosby and Al Rinker. These two had been doing similar work on the west coast, and they formed a trio . . ."

**May 28** (Mon)—From the *Detroit Free Press:* "He has not lost any of his charm, none of his novelty, none of the qualities that have dubbed him the greatest jazz conductor—this Paul Whiteman. Perhaps he has lost a trifle of the rotundity which has marked him heretofore—road work is wearing on even so much a master as he, but rotundity, thank goodness, has nothing to do with his music . . . many have condemned jazz but few who have had the good fortune to hear Whiteman's interpretation of it could honestly look askance. He lends a symphonic touch which thrills and ignores the blatancy which sours . . ."

June 1 (Fri)—End of Detroit engagement.

June 2 (Sat)—Orchestra opens at Shea's Buffalo Theater, Buffalo, New York. Also featured on the program: Cy Landry (comedian), Charles Chesney and Kathryn Lewis (singers), The Swanee Sextet and the Foster Girls. Whiteman selections: "Three Shades of Blue," "My Ohio Home" and "Ramona."

June 8 (Fri)—Closing night at Shea's. Band leaves for New York.

June 9 (Sat)—A day off in New York.

June 10 (Sun)—Whiteman records for Columbia.

June 11 (Mon)—Orchestra opens at Lincoln Theater, Trenton, New Jersey, doing four shows a day: 3, 6, 8 and 10 P.M. A review in the *Trenton Evening Times* for Tuesday, June 12, remarks that "One of the disappointing features of the program was Whiteman's failure to do George Gershwin's 'Rhapsody in Blue.' " Two days later, the *Evening Times* notes with satisfaction that "Paul Whiteman and his orchestra change their program at the Lincoln Theatre today and feature Gershwin's 'Rhapsody in Blue.' "

June 15 (Fri)—End of Trenton engagement.

June 16 (Sat)—Back in New York. Day off.

June 17 (Sun)—Records for Columbia.

June 18 (Mon)—Records for Columbia.

June 19 (Tue)—Records for Columbia. In the evening, from 10 to 11 P.M., the orchestra broadcasts over station WEAF in New York. Selections include "Chiquita," "Tchaikowskiana," "The Man I Love," "La Paloma," "That's Grandma" (Rhythm Boys feature), and "My Melancholy Baby." After the program, the orchestra travels to Hastings-on-Hudson to play for Mayor Jimmy Walker's birthday party, starting at 12:01 A.M.

June 20 (Wed)—Records for Columbia.

June 23 (Sat)—Whiteman opens at Minnesota Theater, Minneapolis, playing for the Boris Petroff stage production of *Say It with Music*. Also featured: Rita Owen (comedienne and dancer), The Midnight Trio (dancers), and the dancing of the Albertina Rasch girls. Whiteman spotlights the Rhythm Boys, Jack Fulton (vocals), Willy Hall, and Harry Goldfield as a "miniature Whiteman" directing the band in a comedy sketch.

June 29 (Fri)—Closing day at the Minnesota Theater.

July 2 (Mon)—Whiteman orchestra opens at Chicago Theater, Chicago. Program, according to Louis Armstrong's recollection, includes "From Monday On" and an arrangement of Tchaikowsky's *1812 Overture*.

July 2 (Mon)—In New York, a studio orchestra presumably directed by Ben Selvin records for Columbia under Paul Whiteman's name, using arrangements by Challis and Grofe.

July 5 (Thu)—Trumbauer record date for Okeh. Bix included.

July 7 (Sat)—Bix and His Gang record for Okeh. Charles Beiderbecke present in the studio.

July 8 (Sun)—End of Chicago Theater engagement.

July 9 (Mon)—Orchestra opens at Uptown Theater in Chicago.

July 12 (Thu)—Jean Goldkette orchestra (formed at Pla-mor Ballroom, Kansas City, after breakup of Graystone unit) records "Just Imagine" for Victor. Bix's presence, once suspected on the strength of a cornet obligato to Greta Woodson's vocal, can be discounted. Vernon Brown and Dale Skinner, who participated, confirm that the player is Sterling Bose, as does Goldkette himself.

July 15 (Sun)—End of Uptown Theater engagement.

July 16 (Mon)—Whiteman opens at Tivoli Theater, Chicago. During this period Bix, Izzy Friedman and other Whiteman musicians visit Dale Skinner more than once, spend time talking and listening to records.

**July 20** (Fri)—New York: Another Selvin-led "Paul Whiteman" session for Columbia (see entry for July 2).

**July 22** (Sun)—End of Tivoli Theater engagement.

**July 23** (Mon)—Bix returns to Davenport as orchestra vacations two weeks. During this time he sits in with several groups around town, including one at the Eagles Hall which includes banjoist Herbert Ross Reaver. He visits Tony Catalano aboard the Davenport-Rock Island ferry *W. J. Quinlan.*

**c. Aug. 14–15** (Tue-Wed)—Orchestra reassembles in New York, embarks on one-nighters. Almost all contemporary reviews mention capacity crowds.

**Aug. 16** (Thu)—Sugarcreek Pavilion in Franklin, Pennsylvania.

**Aug. 17** (Fri)—Sunset Park in Johnstown, Pennsylvania.

**Aug. 18** (Sat)—Willow Grove in Philadelphia, Pennsylvania.

**Aug. 19** (Sun)—Day off.

**Aug. 20** (Mon)—Carlin's, in Baltimore.

**Aug. 21** (Tue)—Dorney Park in Allentown, Pennsylvania.

**Aug. 22** (Wed)—George F. (?) Pavilion in Johnson City, New York.

**Aug. 23** (Thu)—Lakeside in Mahanoy City, Pennsylvania.

**Aug. 24** (Fri)—Fennbrook Park in Wilkes Barre.

**Aug. 25** (Sat)—Steel Pier in Atlantic City.

**Aug. 26** (Sun)—Open en route.

**Aug. 27** (Mon)—Nutting's-on-the-Charles in Waltham, Massachusetts.

**Aug. 28** (Tue)—Bournehurst in Bourne, Massachusetts.

**Aug. 29** (Wed)—Crystal Ballroom, Riverside Park in Springfield, Massachusetts.

**Aug. 30** (Thu)—Arcadia Roof Garden in Providence, Rhode Island.

**Aug. 31** (Fri)—Shelburne Inn in Berlin, New Hampshire.

**Sept. 1** (Sat)—Palace Ballroom at Old Orchard Beach, Maine.

**Sept. 2** (Sun)—Crescent Gardens, Revere Beach, Revere, Massachusetts.

**Sept. 3** (Mon)—Orchestra returns to New York, gets day off.

**Sept. 4** (Tue)—Records for Columbia.

**Sept. 5** (Wed)—Records for Columbia.

**Sept. 6** (Thu)—Records for Columbia.

**Sept. 7** (Fri)—Orchestra opens at Loew's Metropolitan Theater in Boston.

**Sept. 14** (Fri)—End of Boston engagement. Orchestra returns immediately to New York and records for Columbia.

**Sept. 15** (Sat)—Records for Columbia.

**Sept. 16** (Sun)—Open date.

**Sept. 17** (Mon)—Records for Columbia.

**Sept. 18** (Tue)—Records for Columbia. In the evening, from 9:30 to 11:00 P.M. EDT, band participates in NBC network broadcast from Hotel Astor, New York. Program features following performers, each limited to ten minutes:

> Evelyn Herbert
> Fannie Brice
> Paul Whiteman and His Orchestra
>> ("Get Out and Get Under The Moon" and "Metropolis (A Blue Fantasie)")
>
> John Charles Thomas
> Mme. Ernestine Schumann-Heink
> Vincent Lopez and His Orchestra
> Moran and Mack
> John Parker
> Andy Sannella and His Spanish Guitar
> Ben Selvin and His Orchestra
> Atwater Kent Male Quartet
>> Announcers: Graham McNamee, Milton Cross, Louis Witten

Sept. 19 (Wed)—Records for Columbia.

Sept. 20 (Thu)—Trumbauer record date for Okeh.

Sept. 21 (Fri)—Whiteman records for Columbia. Then Bix and small group go over to Okeh for "Bix and His Gang" session.

Sept. 22 (Sat)—Whiteman plays a dance at the Coliseum in Harrisburg. Dick Turner present.

Sept. 23 (Sun)—Free day. Bix most of the day in Harrisburg with Turner.

Sept. 24 (Mon)—Whiteman at Rainbow Gardens, Erie, Pennsylvania.

Sept. 26 (Wed)—Orchestra at Market Auditorium in Wheeling, West Virginia. Opens with concert presentation of "When Day Is Done," moves on to program including "Soliloquy" and *Rhapsody in Blue*. Features Austin "Skin" Young on vocals. Latter part of the evening devoted to dancing.

Sept. 27 (Thu)—Whiteman's ledgers place him in Columbus Auditorium, Columbus, Ohio, but there is no mention of this appearance in Columbus newspapers. It all probability the orchestra returned to New York to rehearse for its autumn concert tour.

Oct. 4 (Thu)—Whiteman appears at Queen Anne Theater in Bogota, New Jersey, for "dry run" concert (see program below). Offers most of the tour selections but drops *Concerto in F* and substitutes "I Can't Give You Anything but Love," "Valse Inspiration" and "American Tune." Bix featured playing "In a Mist," supported by Hayton and Bargy. Popular request numbers included "My Melancholy Baby," "Chiquita" and "Just Like a Melody Out of the Sky."

Oct. 5 (Fri)—Records for Columbia. Afternoon Trumbauer record date for Okeh.

Oct. 6 (Sat)—Whiteman records for Columbia.

Oct. 7 (Sun)—Whiteman autumn tour begins with concert in Carnegie Hall. The program outlined below is the basic program for the tour, with one exception: for the Carnegie Hall concert, "In a Mist" is added, featuring Bix at the piano, with supporting piano accompaniment by Roy Bargy and Lennie Hayton.

### PAUL WHITEMAN PRESENTS:

I. Introduction: Yes, Jazz Is Savage . . . . . . . . . . .
(Roy Bargy comments: "The number was put together to show the development of jazz up to that time, starting with jungle drums and primitive music, a dixieland group, etc. The dixieland was played by Bix, Rank, Friedman, Marsh and probably Hayton.")

II. Sugar . . . . . . . . . . . . . . Nichols-Ager-Yellen
(This is the "Sugar" recorded by Trumbauer on Okeh. Bargy: "This was a Bill Challis arrangement and was used to show how jazz had been refined for big band. I don't recall any vocal and I think Bix was featured along with Tram.")

Gypsy . . . . . . . . . . . . . Gilbert-Malneck-Signorelli
(Vocal by Charles Gaylord. Bargy: "On the tour I improvised on the piano as the cimbalom player was not a regular member." Arrangement as recorded.)

Tiger Rag . . . . . . . . . . . . . . . . . . LaRocca
(Bargy: "Big band arrangement of this old jazz standard with solos by Bix, Tram, Izzy, Rank, etc.")

III. Concerto in F (for pianoforte and orchestra) . . . . . Gershwin
(Scored by Ferde Grofe. Roy Bargy, piano)
Allegro
Andante Con Moto
Allegro Con Brio
(Bargy remarks: "At Carnegie and on the tour Paul knew the piece well and always did a great job with the stick.")

IV. Just Like a Melody Out of the Sky . . . . . . . . Donaldson
(As recorded for Columbia. Vocal by Austin Young)
Valse Inspiration . . . . . . . . . . . . . . . . Hazlett
(Alto saxophone solo by Chester Hazlett)
My Melancholy Baby . . . . . . . . . . Norton-Burnett
(As recorded for Columbia. Vocal by Austin Young)

### INTERMISSION

V. Metropolis (A Blue Fantasie) . . . . . . . . . . . Grofe
(First public performance. Bargy comments: "Arranged and composed by Grofe using themes by Malneck and Signorelli. This was
not a 'piano and orchestra' piece like the *Concerto* or *Rhapsody in
Blue*, but there were many piano passages. When we recorded it
for Victor, Paul asked me to compose a cadenza to sort of tie two
of the movements together, which I did on a lunch break at Liederkranz Hall at the recording session. This version was played on
the tour.")

VI. Band Divertissement:
Free Air: Variations based on noises from a garage . . . Grofe
(Feature for Wilbur Hall. Bargy: "That was the full title and did
feature Willie Hall on a bicycle pump which he played with the hose
end in the palm of his left hand and pumping with his right. He
regulated the tones by pressure on his palm with remarkable results.
Ferde wrote it in the ancient style a la Bach. Willie then went into
his regular act starting with 'Pop! Goes the Weasel' on fiddle, which
he played in all positions, behind his back, over his head, between
his knees, etc. Willie had perfect pitch and used piano accompaniment and I used to change keys on him in the middle of a phrase
but never could lose him. He then played 'Nola' on trombone, very
fast, and I have never heard another trombone player do it before
or since. His finale was the bicycle pump again, 'Stars and Stripes
Forever,' and it was in this number that the guys filled the pump
with water or sometimes lamp black. He usually caught on and
turned the pump on the orchestra to the delight of the audience.
Tram sometimes did an encore with Willie for which Tram made a
pair of shoes mounted on long boards. Willie played fiddle and Tram
sax and in the routine they could lean forward almost to the floor and
keep playing.")

VII. Popular Request Numbers:
Chiquita . . . . . . . . . . . . . . . . . Gilbert-Wayne
(vocal by Jack Fulton)
American Tune . . . . . . . . . . . . . . . Henderson
(vocal by Austin Young)
(Additional comments by Bargy: "Additional numbers were played
on the tour, including the *Rhapsody* by popular demand. I know,
too, that Goldie did a specialty where he sang a song and danced the
last chorus. He also played the Busse chorus of 'When Day Is Done,'
stopping at the finish to make a speech: 'I will now attempt to play
the highest note in the world.' After a piano cadenza he played one
and then 'ghosted' the high note which was actually played by Chet
Hazlett on E-flat clarinet, B-flat above high B-flat."

Oct. 8 (Mon)—Wells Theater in Norfolk, Virginia. Program as outlined, with *Rhapsody in Blue* as an encore.
Oct. 9 (Tue)—Academy of Music in Lynchburg, Virginia. Program as outlined, but
popular request numbers as on October 4.

**Oct. 10** (Wed)—Carolina Theater in Greensboro, North Carolina. Program as outlined.

**Oct. 11** (Thu)—Campus Auditorium in Greenville, North Carolina. Program as outlined.

**Oct. 12** (Fri)—Memorial Hall in Chapel Hill, North Carolina. Program as outlined.

**Oct. 13** (Sat)—State Theater in Raleigh, North Carolina. Program as outlined.

**Oct. 14** (Sun)—War Department Theater (Fort Bragg) in Fayetteville, North Carolina. Program as outlined, except *Rhapsody in Blue* inserted in place of *Metropolis*.

**Oct. 15** (Mon)—Reynolds Memorial Auditorium, Winston-Salem, North Carolina. Program as outlined, except substitute "That's My Weakness Now," featuring Harry Goldfield, as closing number in place of "American Tune."

**Oct. 16** (Tue)—City Auditorium, Charlotte, North Carolina. Whiteman cancels afternoon performance, first of two scheduled, at last minute, then alters evening program. Band opens with "Tiger Rag," "Sugar" and "Gypsy," then into a group of such old favorites as "Japanese Sandman," "Do You Ever Think Of Me?" "Who" and "Linger Awhile," featuring the Rhythm Boys. First half closes with "My Melancholy Baby." *Concerto in F* as usual in second half, but then program ends with "Chiquita," and "Liebestraum" as encore.

**Oct. 17** (Wed)—City Auditorium, Asheville, North Carolina. Program as outlined.

**Oct. 18** (Thu)—Columbia Theater, Columbia, South Carolina. Program as outlined, with "Liebestraum" again as encore. From the *Columbia State*, October 19, 1928: "Paul Whiteman and his symphonic jazz orchestra presented in two bills at the Columbia Theater yesterday programs that were broadly catholic . . . Something there was for every taste. If the menu was not extensive, its variety comprehended nightingales' tongues as well as garlic; both much relished, though hardly by the same persons . . . Whiteman himself when conducting is a continual delight. The familiar time-wiggling knee, facile in movement as the shoulders of Gilda Gray, is in itself a 'property' good for many a grin. He pleased most when tendering the old favorites he had introduced, and it must be said that with scraps of these, cleverly patchworked together, he was fairly liberal . . ."

**Oct. 19** (Fri)—Richmond Academy, Augusta, Georgia. Program as outlined, but popular request numbers changed to "That's My Weakness Now" and "Tchaikowskiana," and "Liebestraum" again as encore.

**Oct. 20** (Sat)—New City Auditorium, Macon, Georgia. Program as outlined. Encore with "That's My Weakness Now."

**Oct. 21** (Sun)—Day off for the band.

**Oct. 22** (Mon)—Municipal Auditorium, Birmingham, Alabama. Program as outlined.

**Oct. 23** (Tue)—City Auditorium, Atlanta, Georgia. Program as outlined, except following changes: Willy Hall follows "Free Air" with "Pop! Goes the Weasel." Then orchestra plays "Thinking of Me, Thinking of You," followed by "My Melancholy Baby." "Liebestraum" added to popular requests. "That's My Weakness Now" as encore. After the concert, Bix's sister, now Mrs. Mary Louise Shoemaker, hosts a few of the musicians at a party.

**Oct. 24** (Wed)—Memorial Auditorium, Chattanooga, Tennessee. Changes in the program: After "Sugar," "Gypsy" and "Tiger Rag," add "Whispering," "Japanese Sandman," "Avalon," "Who" and "Linger Awhile." Second half substitute *Rhapsody in Blue* for the *Concerto*, add Hall playing "Pop! Goes The Weasel" after "Free Air," and add "Liebestraum" to popular request numbers. "That's My Weakness Now," added as encore, draws such applause that Whiteman adds second encore, "That's a Plenty," presumably featuring Bix.

Oct. 25 (Thu)—Ryman Auditorium, Nashville, Tennessee. Minor program changes include substitution of "Liebestraum" for "Just Like a Melody Out of the Sky" and move of the latter to the second half, plus Austin Young singing "I'm Sorry, Sally." "That's My Weakness Now," featuring Goldfield, as an encore.

Oct. 26 (Fri)—Auditorium in Memphis, Tennessee. Program as outlined. Encore with "The Sidewalks of New York" as recorded for Columbia.

Oct. 27 (Sat)—Auditorium in Jackson, Mississippi. Program as outlined.

Oct. 28 (Sun)—St. Charles Theater, New Orleans. Program as outlined. Armand Hug, Eddie Miller, Paul Mares and Monk Hazel visit Bix at the theater, as does Nick LaRocca. Whiteman adds Edwin "Snoozer" Quinn (guitar) to the band. Bix, Hug and others attend after-hours jam session at Paul Mares's home. Tram also present.

Oct. 29 (Mon)—Strand Theater, Shreveport, Louisiana. Program as outlined.

Oct. 30 (Tue)—Baton Rouge High School, Baton Rouge, Louisiana. Program as outlined.

Oct. 31 (Wed)—City Auditorium, Beaumont, Texas. Program as outlined with "Kentucky Babe" inserted before "Valse Inspiration." From the *Beaumont Enterprise*, November 1, 1928: "The audience refused to permit the program to continue until an encore to this number ("Valse Inspiration") had been given. It was the only encore permitted during the entire program." And later: "The 'King' himself met with the approval of all. His every motion expressed jazz as he was unable to keep his feet still during the rendition of the particularly jazzy selections. His characteristic smile and plump figure, which have been so emphasized in drawings and cartoons, won him the audience from the start."

Nov. 1 (Thu)—Auditorium in Houston. Program as outlined.

Nov. 2 (Fri)—Municipal Auditorium, San Antonio, Texas. Program as outlined.

Nov. 3 (Sat)—Hardin-Simmons University, Abilene, Texas. Program as outlined.

Nov. 4 (Sun)—Cotton Palace, Waco, Texas. Program as outlined, except that following *Metropolis*, Bix Beiderbecke is featured at the piano playing "In a Mist."

Nov. 5 (Mon)—Fair Park Auditorium, Dallas. Program as outlined.

Nov. 6 (Tue)—Memorial Auditorium, Wichita Falls, Texas. Program as outlined.

Nov. 7 (Wed)—City Auditorium, Amarillo, Texas. Program as outlined. Feeling the band not up to his standard of precision, Whiteman calls 3:45 P.M. rehearsal before the concert.

Nov. 8 (Thu)—Shrine Auditorium, Oklahoma City. Program as outlined. Goldfield featured on "That's My Weakness Now" as encore.

Nov. 9 (Fri)—University of Oklahoma Field House, Norman. Program as outlined.

Nov. 10 (Sat)—Convention Hall, Tulsa, Oklahoma. Program as outlined.

Nov. 11 (Sun)—Auditorium in Ponca City, Oklahoma. Band scheduled for both afternoon and evening performances, but only one program listed—as outlined, save *Rhapsody in Blue* replaces *Metropolis*. Bix takes wrong train from Tulsa, gets off, hires an airplane to fly him to Ponca City in time for afternoon performance. Sleeps through evening show and is fined by Whiteman.

Nov. 12 (Mon)—University of Kansas Auditorium, Lawrence. Program as outlined.

Nov. 13 (Tue)—Memorial Hall, Joplin, Missouri. Program as outlined.

Nov. 14 (Wed)—College Auditorium, Warrensburg, Missouri. Program as outlined.

Nov. 15 (Thu)—Ivanhoe Auditorium, Kansas City, Missouri. Program as outlined.

This was to be the second half of a three-hour concert broadcast over station KMBC, beginning at 7:00 P.M. and sponsored by the Old Gold Cigarette Company.

Nov. 16 (Fri)—Memorial Hall, Salina, Kansas. Program as outlined.

Nov. 17 (Sat)—Sheridan Coliseum, Hays, Kansas. Program as outlined.

Nov. 18 (Sun)—Auditorium in Omaha, Nebraska. Program as outlined. From the *Omaha World-Herald* of Monday, November 19: "Several hundred persons, welcoming Paul Whiteman at the Union Station Sunday afternoon on his arrival in Omaha, applauded as he took a baton and led Father Flanagan's boys' band through one of the band's favorite numbers . . ." Whiteman later gave the boys a $10 bill to buy them all sodas.

Nov. 19 (Mon)—Central High School Auditorium, Sioux City, Iowa. Program as outlined. "That's My Weakness Now" as encore.

Nov. 20 (Tue)—Sioux Falls Coliseum, Sioux Falls, South Dakota. Program as outlined. From the *Sioux Falls Argus-Leader* of the following day: "In spite of rather careless grooming, a condescending manner, and a little more noise than one had expected, the Paul Whiteman Orchestra continues to be an outstanding musical organization in the United States today . . ."

Nov. 21 (Wed)—St. Paul Auditorium, St. Paul, Minnesota. Program as outlined.

Nov. 22 (Thu)—Shrine Auditorium, Cedar Rapids, Iowa. Program as outlined.

Nov. 23 (Fri)—Clinton Theater, Clinton, Iowa. Two concerts. Afternoon performance opens with *Rhapsody in Blue*, followed by "Limehouse Blues," "Roses of Yesterday," "That's a Plenty." Second half has "Tchaikowskiana" and "Sweet Sue," and closes with "American Tune." Evening program as outlined.

Nov. 24 (Sat)—Majestic Theater, Peoria, Illinois. Program as outlined.

Nov. 25 (Sun)—Auditorium Theater, Chicago. Program as outlined.

Nov. 26 (Mon)—Purdue University Gymnasium, Lafayette, Indiana. Program as outlined, but "Limehouse Blues" added to popular request numbers.

Nov. 27 (Tue)—Pease Auditorium, Ypsilanti, Michigan. Hill Auditorium, Ann Arbor, Michigan. No information on either concert.

Nov. 28 (Wed)—Band listed for Akron, Ohio, but postponed until December 5. Possible day off after long string of concerts.

Nov. 29 (Thu)—Charleston High School Auditorium, Charleston, West Virginia. Program as outlined.

Nov. 30 (Fri)—New Music Hall, Cleveland. Program as outlined.

Dec. 1 (Sat)—Memorial Hall, Columbus, Ohio. Two performances, using basic program. Afternoon: *Rhapsody in Blue* and "Tchaikowskiana" replace *Concerto in F* and *Metropolis*. Austin Young, a native of Columbus, spotlighted on "Just Like a Melody Out of the Sky," "Diane" and "Sonny Boy" during both shows. Willy Hall augments his evening show routine with "Stars and Stripes Forever" and "Turkey in the Straw."

Dec. 2 (Sun)—Taft Auditorium, Cincinnati, Ohio. Two performances, at 3 P.M. and 8:15 P.M. Afternoon show: *Rhapsody in Blue* and "Tchaikowskiana" for *Concerto in F* and *Metropolis*. After "Yes, Jazz Is Savage," insert "Limehouse Blues," "Roses of Yesterday" and "That's a Plenty." Close with "Sweet Sue" substituted for "Chiquita."

Dec. 3 (Mon)—Arcadia Auditorium, Detroit. Program as outlined.

Dec. 4 (Tue)—Memorial Auditorium, Athens, Ohio. Program as outlined.

Dec. 5 (Wed)—Armory in Akron, Ohio. Program as outlined, except omit final two selections and insert "That's My Weakness Now" as closer.

Dec. 6 (Thu)—Massey Hall, Toronto, Canada. Program as outlined.

Dec. 7 (Fri)—Consistory Auditorium, Buffalo, New York. Program as outlined.

Dec. 8 (Sat)—Holy Family School Auditorium, Auburn, New York. Program as outlined.

Dec. 9 (Sun)—Symphony Hall, Boston. Program as outlined.

**Dec. 10** (Mon)—Orchestra returns to New York.

**Dec. 11** (Tue)—Records for Columbia.

**Dec. 12** (Wed)—Records for Columbia.

**Dec. 13** (Thu)—Records for Columbia.

**Dec. 14** (Fri)—Records for Columbia. Bix not present.

**Dec. 15** (Sat)—Washington Auditorium, Washington, D.C. Program as outlined.

**Dec. 16** (Sun)—Penn Athletic Club, Philadelphia. Program as outlined. Bix out of the orchestra temporarily on its return to New York City; hospitalized in Astoria, Long Island, with what is diagnosed as pneumonia. The schedule continues.

**Dec. 19** (Wed)—Orchestra records for Columbia. Bix still in the hospital.

**Dec. 22** (Sat)—Records for Columbia. Bix still absent. Mannie Klein and Mickey Bloom sit in for him.

**Dec. 23** (Sun)—Whiteman concert at Carnegie Hall, concluding tour. Uncertain whether Bix still absent.

**Dec. 29** (Sat)—Orchestra opens atop New Amsterdam Theater in New York in the *Ziegfeld Midnite Frolic.*

**Dec. 30** (Sun)—Whiteman opens at Palace Theater, doubling at the New Amsterdam. Bix rejoins about this time but still misses occasional evenings over next few days. Mickey Bloom sits in for him.

# 1929

**Jan. 5** (Sat)—End of Palace Theater engagement. Among items featured on closing night: medley of "Whispering," "Who," "Avalon," "Do You Ever Think of Me?" and "Japanese Sandman." Concert arrangement of "I'm Sorry, Sally" with Jack Fulton falsetto vocal. *Rhapsody in Blue,* with Bargy as solo pianist. Goldfield specialty on "That's My Weakness Now." Arrangement of "Gypsy" as recorded, save Bargy playing cimbalom solo on the piano and Tram doing Bix's cornet solo on C-melody sax in Bix's absence. Program concluded with Austin Young singing "American Tune."

**Jan. 10** (Thu)—Whiteman records for Columbia. Bix definitely present though not featured. Then, later in same session, two sides listed as "Paul Whiteman presents Bea *(sic)* Palmer with the Frank Trumbauer Orchestra." At least one title, "Singin' the Blues," features Bix in a full chorus based loosely on his 1927 Okeh record with Trumbauer. Both small-band titles here rejected for issue. (Further information in the discography section of this book.)

**Jan. 11** (Fri)—Whiteman records for Columbia. Bix not present. End of New Amsterdam Theater engagement.

**Jan. 13** (Sun)—Orchestra opens at the Music Hall, Cincinnati.

**Jan. 19** (Sat)—End of Cincinnati engagement.

**Jan. 20** (Sun)—Orchestra opens at Palace Theater in Cleveland. Among the selections: *Rhapsody in Blue,* "Gypsy" and "I'm Sorry, Sally."

**Jan. 21** (Mon)—*Cleveland Press,* reviewing Whiteman's opening night, notes that "one of his best musicians is absent." The reference is to Bix, who sometime during this week suffers a violent mental and physical breakdown in his room at the Cleveland Hotel. The combination of a weakened physical state due to pneumonia and general fatigue, and sudden cessation of consumption of alcohol during his hospitalization in New York, appears to have triggered a massive attack of delirium tremens. This seizure and its attendant physical circumstances bear unmistakable resemblance to those attending Bix's death two and a half years later.

**Jan. 25** (Fri)—From the *Cleveland Press:* "Paul Whiteman . . . hopes to have Bix Beiderbecke . . . back in time for opening of Old Gold broadcast series Feb. 5. Beiderbecke is recovering from an illness at his home in Davenport, Iowa."

**Jan. 26** (Sat)—Whiteman closes at the Palace, travels to Detroit for opening at General Motors Research Building.

**Jan. 27** (Sun)—Orchestra opens in Detroit. Whiteman obtains cornetist Andy Secrest from the Jean Goldkette organization on recommendation of Min Leibrook as temporary replacement for Bix.

**Feb. 2** (Sat)—Whiteman closes in Detroit.

**Feb. 3** (Sun)—Orchestra returns to New York. Men discover Bix has not returned to Davenport but has escaped male nurse caring for him in Cleveland and has come to New York to rejoin the band. He is found beaten up and badly slashed by unknown assailants. Whiteman sends him home to Davenport on full salary.

**Feb. 5** (Tue)—Bix, in Davenport, writes to Tom Rockwell of Okeh, promising to return soon to New York and make "some bigger and better Okeh records." Whiteman orchestra, with Secrest reading Bix's book, does first radio broadcast for Old Gold Cigarettes over WABC in New York at 9 P.M. EST. Plays 13 numbers, ending with Eddie Cantor speaking from New Amsterdam Theater and giving two-minute plug for *Whoopee*, new show in which he is appearing.

**Feb. 6** (Wed)—Whiteman reopens atop New Amsterdam Theater in *Ziegfeld Midnite Frolic*.

**Feb. 10** (Sun)—*Davenport Sunday Democrat* runs feature interview with Bix under headline, " 'Jazz Is Musical Humor,' Says Davenport Composer and Cornetist of Whiteman's Band."

**Feb. 7** (Thu), 8 (Fri) and 28 (Thu)—Whiteman records for Columbia. Bix still in Davenport. William Grant Still added as arranger and Austin Young departs, replaced by Ray Heatherton.

**March 4** (Mon)—Bix Beiderbecke rejoins orchestra in New York, replacing Eddie Pinder.

**March 5** (Tue)—Whiteman Old Gold broadcast from WABC, Ted Husing announcing. The program, as transcribed by Warren W. Scholl:

> Song of India (as recorded on Columbia 50198-D)
> Till We Meet (first performance—ballad sung by Jack Fulton)
> Old Time Medley (probably Grofe arrangement): Caresses; Say It with Music; April Showers; An Orange Grove in California; The Sheik of Araby
> Waltz Medley (probably Grofe arrangement): My Hero; Blue Danube; Pink Lady; Merry Widow; Sympathy
> Sweethearts on Parade (straight orchestral)
> China Boy (as recorded on Columbia 1945-D)
> My Suppressed Desire (The Rhythm Boys)
> Where the Shy Little Violets Grow (same)
> Liebestraum (as recorded on Columbia 50198-D)
> Give Your Little Baby Lots of Lovin' (Crosby vocal, plus eight bars by Tram on release of final chorus)
> Popular Medley: A Precious Little Thing Called Love (Rhythm Boys vocal, Bix on release) A Love Tale of Alsace-Lorraine (Fulton vocal) Glad Rag Doll (Tram intro, plus Bix-Tram chase)
> I Wanna Be Loved by You (a few hot trumpet breaks in one chorus)
> Sweet Georgia Brown (four saxes led by Tram in first chorus, hot verse, then Bix (muted) for whole next chorus, with final chorus featuring Tram in several places)

**March 7** (Thu)—Orchestra records for Columbia. Bix not present.

**March 8** (Fri)—Trumbauer recording date for Okeh. Bix and Andy Secrest participate.

**March 12** (Tue)—Orchestra broadcast for Old Gold over WABC, Ted Husing announcing. The program:

> Orientale (Grofe arrangement, as on Victor 21599)
> Louise (premiere—as recorded on Columbia 1771–D–Bing Crosby vocal)
> Old-Time Medley (Grofe arrangement):
> > Whispering; Who; Avalon; Do You Ever Think of Me?; Japanese Sandman)
> Waltz Medley:
> > What'll I Do?; Marie; Jeanine; My Angeline (with Jack Fulton vocal)
> *Lady Fingers* Medley:
> > Ga Ga; You're Perfect; You Give Me Something to Love For (Crosby vocal)
> American Tune (as on Columbia 1464-D, but Crosby takes the vocal)
> So the Bluebirds and the Blackbirds Got Together
> From Monday On (both by the Rhythm Boys)
> O Ya Ya (as recorded on Victor 21304)
> Popular Medley:
> > Doin' the Raccoon (Tram 24 bars); I Faw Down and Go Boom (Rhythm Boys vocal); My Mother's Eyes (Tram 8 bars); I'll Never Ask for More (Bix full chorus and eight bars trumpet section in final chorus)
> Avalon Town (straight orchestral with Fulton vocal)
> Singin' the Blues (four saxes doing Tram's original Okeh solo, full chorus of Bix, Rank featured in the rideout)
> Don't Hold Everything (commercial arrangement, first in a series aimed at competing with B. A. Rolfe Lucky Strike band on NBC, at insistence of Old Gold Company. Atypical arrangement for Whiteman, with Mario Perry heavily spotted on xylophone and accordion)

**March 15** (Fri)—Orchestra records for Columbia. Bix present.

**March 19** (Tue)—Another Old Gold Broadcast, as before. The program:

> Canadian Capers (novelty, in the Rolfe manner)
> Diga Diga Doo (Rhythm Boys vocal in fast, hot tempo. Rank takes release of second chorus, then Bix for full third chorus. Trumbauer for spots in final chorus)
> Old-Time Medley (Grofe arrangement):
> > Gypsy Blues; When Buddha Smiles; Sweet Lady; My Man; Dear Old Southland
> Dusky Stevedore (hot arrangement featuring Tram for full second chorus)
> Who (two vocal spots for Fulton-Gaylord-Heatherton, the Whiteman Trio)
> Hawaiian Medley:
> > 1, 2, 3, 4; Honolulu Eyes; Aloha Oe
> Parade of the Wooden Soldiers (as recorded on Victor 21304)
> I'll Get By (Bing Crosby vocal)
> Tango Medley:
> > Irresistible; La Seduction; Rose Room
> Old-Time Medley:
> > Carolina in the Morning (bits of Tram and eight bars of Bix); In the Shadows; Bambalina; California, Here I Come (hot band arrangement)
> I Kiss Your Hand, Madame (first public performance—Crosby vocal)

Hot Lips (Tram spotted early with Bix, derby-muted, in finale)
Pickin' Cotton (Rolfe-like arrangement)
**March 26** (Tue)—Another Old Gold broadcast, as before. The program:
Hymn to the Sun (Grofe arrangement, as recorded on Victor 19862)
Nola (Willy Hall featured, as recorded on Columbia 2277-D)
Negro Spiritual Medley (Grofe arrangement):
Swing Low, Sweet Chariot (Crosby vocal); Nobody Knows the Trouble I've Seen; All God's Chillun; Deep River
There's a Rainbow Round My Shoulder (Tram and Bix in parts of verse. Crosby vocal, Bix in first 16 bars of last chorus)
Punch and Judy (Rolfe-type novelty)
Blue Hawaii (first time on the air—as recorded on Columbia 1771-D. Jack Fulton vocal)
Coquette (as recorded on Columbia 1755-D. Crosby vocal)
Runnin' Wild (hot Friedman clarinet behind band in first chorus; Tram for entire second chorus; band verse; Bix, derby-muted, whole third chorus; whole band last chorus with Friedman spotted briefly. Ending not unlike "China Boy" arrangement as recorded)
Till We Meet (Jack Fulton vocal)
Everybody Loves You ("A miserable Rolfe-like arrangement"—Scholl)
Things That Were Made for Love (Crosby vocal, Tram in spots during last chorus)
Medley:
Magnolia (Bix 16 bars); I'm on the Crest of a Wave; I'd Rather Be Blue; Anything Your Heart Desires
Cradle of Love (first time on the air. Bargy piano solo in place of vocal)
Weary River (Ray Heatherton vocal)
Bo Peep (another novelty-type arrangement)
**April 1** (Mon)—Orchestra still appearing atop New Amsterdam Theater. About this time Rube Crozier departs, replaced by Bernie Daly.
**April 2** (Tue)—Regular Old Gold broadcast over WABC. The program:
Pompanola (Rolfe-like novelty tune)
(title missed)
French Medley:
Madelon; On the Boulevard; Ca C'est Paris
Medley:
Moonlight and Roses; Among My Souvenirs; My Buddy; Ramona
Diga Diga Doo (as on March 19)
I Kiss Your Hand, Madame (Ray Heatherton vocal)
South Wind (Rhythm Boys vocal, featured trumpet and two brief Tram solos)
The Song I Love (Ray Heatherton vocal, straight arrangement)
La Traviata ("Violetta" theme—tango)
China Boy (as recorded on Columbia 1945-D; Friedman, Tram and Bix spotted)
If I Had You (Ponce Sisters vocal. Tram 16 bars of last chorus)
Medley:
Sleepy Time Gal; Somebody Stole My Gal (Rank trombone chorus and Friedman clarinet in part of second chorus); Mary Lou (Tram featured); Things That Were Made for Love (Bix whole first chorus)
My Sin (straight, with Ray Heatherton vocal)
That's a Plenty (Tram, Friedman, Bix spotted)
**April 5** (Fri)—Orchestra records for Columbia. Bix featured.
**April 9** (Tue)—Another Old Gold broadcast over WABC. Program:
Valencia (straight arrangement)

Jericho (straight arrangement except for Malneck hot violin in fourth chorus)
Medley:
Pretty, Petite and Sweet (Friedman clarinet in bridge); My Angel (Heatherton vocal); Indian Love Call; Roses of Yesterday
Let's Do It (as recorded on Columbia 1701-D, but omit intro. Crosby vocal, Barris and Rinker accompanying)
I Love to Hear You Singing (heavy Grofe arrangement. Jack Fulton vocal)
Waltz Medley:
Down by the Old Mill Stream; Sweet Adeline; In the Shade of the Old Apple Tree; After the Ball
Futuristic Rhythm (Rhythm Boys vocal. Tram for bridge of first chorus. Andy and Bix trade solos near the end, first Secrest, then Bix)
Lover, Come Back to Me (basically as recorded on Columbia 1731-D, with minor changes)
Hay Straw (Rolfe-like arrangement)
Deep Night (straight, slow, good arrangement. Crosby vocal)
My Melody Man (Rhythm Boys vocal. No solos, but good hot ensemble work)
Medley:
Allah's Holiday; Tea for Two; Dardanella (as recorded on Victor 25238, including full-chorus Bix solo); I'm Always Chasing Rainbows
Honey (straight arrangement—Crosby vocal)
Sugar Is Back in Town (straight arrangement)
**April 16** (Tue)—Another Old Gold broadcast for WABC. Program:
I'm Just Wild About Harry (Bix 16 bars in last chorus)
Stars and Stripes Forever
Medley from *Spring Is Here:*
With a Song in My Heart; Why Can't I? (hot trumpet ensemble work, Tram and Margulis prominent); Yours Sincerely
Waltz Medley:
An Old Love Affair; Heart of Mine; Love, Take My Heart; Softly, as in a Morning Sunrise
Things That Were Made for Love (as on March 26)
When Day Is Done (as foxtrot, not the concert arrangement)
Hallelujah (Rhythm Boys vocal, followed by 24 bars of derby-muted Bix)
I'll Get By (Crosby vocal)
Tango Medley:
La Seduction; Rose Room; La Rosita
Medley:
Dreaming of the Day; My Heart Stood Still; Miss Annabelle Lee (Rhythm Boys vocal with eight bars of Bix); I'd Rather Be Blue (Rank spotted briefly)
Sunrise to Sunset (Heatherton vocal. Secrest and Bix eight bars apiece in last chorus)
When Summer Is Gone (Crosby vocal. Foxtrot, but concert-style arrangement)
Where the Shy Little Violets Grow (Tram first 16 bars of second chorus, Bix last eight)
Sweet Georgia Brown (as on March 5; Crosby sings)
**April 17** (Wed)—Trumbauer record date for Okeh. Bix and Secrest, cornets.
**April 23** (Tue)—Another Whiteman broadcast for Old Gold. The program:

379

March of the Musketeers (as recorded on Victor 21315. Crosby vocal)

Doin' the New Lowdown (Tram in part of second chorus, Friedman for most of third with Rank in the release; Tram in release of final chorus)

Medley:
You're the Cream in My Coffee; A Room with a View; Lover, Come Back to Me; Button Up Your Overcoat (Rhythm Boys vocal; Tram in most of opening chorus, with last chorus as recorded on Columbia 1736-D)

Waltz Medley:
My Hero; Blue Danube; Pink Lady; Merry Widow Waltz; Sympathy

Nobody's Fault but Your Own (Crosby vocal)

Every Moon's a Honeymoon (vocal by Fulton, Gaylord and Heatherton)

Doin' the Raccoon (hot arrangement, featuring Tram and Friedman)

Ma Belle (as recorded on Victor 21315. Heatherton vocal)

*Showboat* Medley:
Ol' Man River (Bix release of first chorus. Crosby vocal); Make Believe; Can't Help Lovin' That Man; Why Do I Love You?

Medley:
Caresses; Say It with Music; April Showers (Bix behind Strickfaden's baritone sax for full chorus); An Orange Grove in California; The Sheik of Araby

Sleepy Water (straight, slow arrangement. Fulton vocal)

Building a Nest for Mary (Rhythm Boys vocal. Tram in parts of one chorus)

Don't Hold Everything (as on March 12)

**April 25** (Thu)—Whiteman records for Columbia. Later plays at home of cartoonist Rube Goldberg, where New York Mayor Jimmy Walker performs ceremony marrying Phyllis Haver to William Seeman.

**April 26** (Fri)—Orchestra appears at Star Casino, New York.

**April 27** (Sat)—End of New Amsterdam Theater engagement.

**April 30** (Tue)—Trumbauer record date for Okeh. Bix, Secrest both present. In the evening, regular Whiteman Old Gold broadcast over WABC. The program:
Here Comes the Showboat

Steamboat

Popular Medley:
(It's) A Precious Little Thing Called Love (hot solos all around); A Love-Tale of Alsace-Lorraine; Glad Rag Doll (some solos)

Irving Berlin Waltz Medley:
Remember; Marie; Where Is the Song of Songs for Me?; Russian Lullaby (Fulton vocal); Coquette

Diga Diga Doo (as on March 19)

Louise (as recorded on Columbia 1771–D, but quartet vocal with Crosby)

Honey (Crosby vocal)

Oh Miss Hannah (as recorded on Columbia 1945-D, with good solos by Bix and Tram, plus Crosby vocal)

That's Living (muted cornet, probably Secrest, in release of last chorus)

She's My Girl (hot arrangement. Last chorus spots four bars apiece cornet, Rank, Tram, Bargy. Cornet probably Secrest)

Meditation from *Thais* (as recorded on Victor 21796)

Liebestraum (as recorded on Columbia 50198-D)

My Lucky Star (as recorded on Columbia 1736-D; Heatherton vocal)

Laughing Marionette (first time on the air—as recorded on Columbia 1862-D)

China Boy (as recorded on Columbia 1945-D—Friedman, Tram, Bix featured)

**May 3** (Fri)—Orchestra records for Columbia.

**May 4** (Sat)—Orchestra records for Columbia. Opens at Pavilion Royale on Long Island.

**May 7** (Tue)—Whiteman Orchestra regular broadcast for Old Gold over WABC, Ted Husing announcing. The program:

Jericho (straight arrangement, but Malneck hot violin in fourth chorus)

Canadian Capers (novelty, a la Rolfe)

Popular Medley:

That's How I Feel About You; (It's) A Precious Little Thing Called Love (Bix spotted briefly); Sleepy Time Gal; Let's Dream

Waltz Medley:

Ramona; Charmaine; Jeanine; Chiquita

Old-Time Medley:

Alexander's Ragtime Band; King Chanticleer; Everybody's Doin' It

Sunrise to Sunset (as on April 16)

Nobody's Fault but Your Own (Crosby vocal)

I Kiss Your Hand, Madame (Heatherton vocal)

Spain (instrumental)

La Veda (instrumental)

French Medley:

Madelon; On the Boulevard; Ca C'est Paris

An Eyeful of You (Bix for eight bars)

Castle in Spain (Crosby vocal)

You Wouldn't Fool Me, Would You? (Crosby vocal)

Valencia (straight arrangement, stretched out an extra chorus or two to fill out the time remaining on the program)

**May 14** (Tue)—Regularly-scheduled broadcast over WABC for Old Gold. The program:

Futuristic Rhythm (Rhythm Boys vocal, and Tram for release of first chorus)

Runnin' Wild (as on April 9)

Negro Spirituals Medley:

Swing Low, Sweet Chariot (Crosby vocal); All God's Chillun Got Wings; Deep River

Hawaiian Waltz Medley:

Blue Hawaii; Aloha Oe; Honolulu Eyes

There's a Rainbow Round My Shoulder (as on March 26)

Sittlin' and Whittlin' (song by Hoagy Carmichael. Eight bars of Rank in release of first chorus, muted Bix in release of last. Vocal by Rinker, singing like a lazy farmer)

Ma Cherie (Rolfe-like arrangement featuring Mario Perry on accordion)

The One That I Love, Loves Me (Bix for 24 of first 32-bar chorus; orchestra for verse and second chorus; Crosby for third, and Tram spotted briefly in finale)

Weary River (Fulton vocal)

Tango Medley: (titles missed)

I'm Looking for Someone to Love (straight instrumental)

Hallelujah (Rhythm Boys vocal, followed by Bix for 24 bars, derby-muted)

Avalon Town (Fulton vocal)

In the Land of Make Believe (Instrumental)

Oh Baby, Have a Heart (hot arrangement, with bits of Bix and Rank, plus Crosby vocal. Hot scored passages toward the end in style of "Oh, You Have No Idea," as recorded on Columbia 1491–D)

Good Morning, Evening and Night (straight arrangement, with vocal by Bing and quartet)

**May 15** (Wed)—Trumbauer group records for Columbia as "Mason-Dixon Orchestra." Bix not present; all cornet solo work by Andy Secrest.

**May 16** (Thu)—Whiteman records for Columbia.

**May 18** (Sat)—End of Pavilion Royale engagement.

**May 19** (Sun)—Orchestra appears at the Friar's Frolic at the Metropolitan Opera House, New York. Around this time Matty Malneck takes ill and goes home to Denver for a rest; replaced by Otto Landau. Joe Venuti (violin) and Eddie Lang (guitar) join band.

**May 21** (Tue)—Trumbauer record date for Okeh. Bix not present; all cornet solos by Secrest. In the evening, Whiteman's regular broadcast for Old Gold over WABC. Following Ted Husing's opening introduction, Whiteman says a few words about band's preparations for trip to California. Band follows by playing:

Medley:
> California, Here I Come; I Love You, California

Medley from *Spring Is Here:*
> With a Song in My Heart; Why Can't I?; Yours Sincerely

Waltz Medley:
> I'm Sorry, Dear; Evangeline; Where Are You Tonight?

Canoodle Oodle Along (Bix intro, Tram for most of second chorus, with muted trumpets in release; Rhythm Boys vocal, and hot trumpet release in last chorus. Ending as intro)

Oh, Miss Hannah (as recorded on Columbia 1945-D)

Laughing Marionette (as recorded on Columbia 1862-D)

I've Got a Feeling I'm Falling (Crosby vocal, backed by Rhythm Boys. Bix in spots, plus Tram for 16 bars final chorus)

Orange Blossom Time (as recorded on Columbia 1845–D)

Nobody's Sweetheart (as recorded on Columbia 2098-D, but solo by Bix in opening chorus)

Mean to Me (Fulton vocal on second chorus, Tram eight bars in last chorus)

Old-Time Medley:
> I Never Knew; I Can't Give You Anything but Love; Tea for Two; Lady of the Evening; Margie

Building a Nest for Mary (as on April 23)

I Love to Hear You Singing (as on April 9)

S'Posin' (as on Columbia 1862–D. Crosby vocal)

Stars and Stripes Forever (Sousa march)

**May 22** (Wed)—Trumbauer record date for Okeh. Bix not present; all cornet solos by Secrest.

**May 24** (Fri)—Orchestra sets out for California on the Old Gold Special. First stop Philadelphia, and an appearance at the Metropolitan Opera House.

**May 25** (Sat)—Orchestra broadcasts from Syria Mosque over station WJAS. Ted Husing, announcing. The program:

Diga Diga Doo (as on March 19)

Stars and Stripes Forever

Tango Medley (Grofe arrangement):
> La Seduction; Rose Room; La Rosita

Honey (Fulton vocal)

Nola (as recorded on Columbia 2277-D, with Roy Bargy, piano, and
Willy Hall, trombone)
I Kiss Your Hand, Madame (Crosby vocal)
Waltz Medley (William Grant Still arrangement):
Down by the Old Mill Stream; Sweet Adeline; In the Shade of the
Old Apple Tree; After the Ball
*Showboat* Selections (featuring Bing and the Rhythm Boys):
Ol' Man River; Make Believe; Can't Help Lovin' Dat Man; Why Do
I Love You?; Ol' Man River
Sunrise to Sunset (as on April 16, but Crosby vocal)
Hallelujah (Rhythm Boys vocal)
Mean to Me (Crosby vocal)
Rhapsody in Blue (Bargy, piano solo)

From the *Pittsburgh Post-Gazette:* "Paul Whiteman, the master of jazz
and his orchestra tonight will broadcast a special Pittsburgh concert over
WJAS from the Syria Mosque. The P. Lorillard Tobacco Company, makers
of Old Gold cigarettes, and Pickerings Furniture Company are sponsor-
ing the local concert. Whiteman is on his way west to make a sound film
and the trip was arranged so that there should be no interruption in the
regular Tuesday night Old Gold hour on the Columbia chain."

**May 26** (Sun)—Whiteman orchestra in Cleveland at station WHK studio (10:00
A.M.); moves on to Toledo for appearance at the Armory (2:00 P.M.); then
to Detroit for concert at the Olympia (8:30 P.M.). Among selections played
in Detroit: "Nola," the *Showboat* selections, "When My Dreams Come
True" (as recorded on Columbia 1822-D) and "Hallelujah." Program
ends with Bargy featured on *Rhapsody in Blue* with full orchestra.

**May 27** (Mon)—Orchestra arrives in Pennsylvania Station, Fort Wayne, Indiana,
in driving rain. From the *Fort Wayne Journal-Gazette:* The orchestra
played in the station to "an enormous crowd which parked itself around
the 'King of Jazz' and his players trying to escape the rain and hear the
music at the same time . . . The regular program was cut short, but the
seven numbers played were well worth waiting for. Moving the microphone down from the platform to the shelter of the station arcade, the
piano and the other band instruments were arranged in a small space."
The seven selections played were *Rhapsody in Blue*, "Diga Diga Doo,"
"Stars and Stripes Forever," Grofe's tango medley, "I Kiss Your Hand,
Madame" featuring Heatherton. Again, the *Journal-Gazette:* "By this
time the cherubic Whiteman was shifting from one foot to another, trying
to get a breath of air and at the same time appear at ease before the
crowd. A flashlight was taken and the high school girls were still shaking
in time with the band. A baby girl perched on an ivory-colored piano
began to direct the band, watching the 'King of Jazz' intently. A lively
jazz number featuring the violinists, trumpet players, accordion and
trombones closed the program.

"The Old Gold-Paul Whiteman party numbers approximately fifty
men. The train is outfitted luxuriously, carrying the extra diners and
observation cars."

**May 28** (Tue)—Orchestra at the Auditorium Theater, Chicago, for a benefit con-
cert at 8:30 P.M. Also regular weekly Old Gold broadcast from station
WBBM studios. The program:
Diga Diga Doo (regular routine)
Canadian Capers (Rolfe-like arrangement)
French Medley (as on April 2)
*My Dear* Waltz Medley:

A Smile, a Kiss (Fulton vocal); (When You Come to the End of) A
Perfect Day; My Dear
Hallelujah (as on May 14)
Till We Meet (Crosby vocal)
O Ya Ya (as recorded on Victor 21304)
Pickin' Cotton (Rolfe-like arrangement)
*Lady Fingers* Medley:
You're Perfect; Ga Ga; You Give Me Something to Live For (Crosby
vocal)
Popular Medley:
Doin' the Raccoon (Tram 24 bars); I Faw Down and Go Boom
(Rhythm Boys vocal); My Mother's Eyes (Tram eight bars); I'll Never
Ask for More (Bix full chorus plus eight bars trumpet section in final
chorus)
Red Hair and Freckles (Rhythm Boys vocal; Rank eight bars)
My Sin (straight arrangement; Crosby vocal)
Sugar Is Back in Town (straight)
China Boy (arrangement altered slightly, with Friedman spotted
throughout whole first chorus; "a bit hotter," says Scholl)

**May 29** (Wed)—Orchestra at Springfield, Illinois, State Arsenal. Visit from Daven-
porter Jack Teegen. Band program: Diga Diga Doo; Stars and Stripes
Forever; tango medley (as broadcast); Honey (Fulton); Nola (Bargy and
Hall); I Kiss Your Hand, Madame (Heatherton); Old Golds (Rhythm Boys);
waltz medley; *Showboat* medley (Rhythm Boys); Sunrise to Sunset (Bix,
Secrest and Heatherton); Hallelujah (as broadcast); Mean to Me (Crosby);
*Rhapsody in Blue* (Bargy); plus Hall, Hazlett, Goldfield features.

**May 30** (Thu)—Indianapolis, to play at the Memorial Day "500" race. Band, in Roy
Bargy's recollection, "towed round the track before the start of the race,
then parked on the infield near the first turn, where we watched the race.
And brother, was it hot!"

**May 31** (Fri)—St. Louis. Washington University Field House. Broadcast from
station KMOX; no details available. Bix and Ruth together; she accompanies him to the train to see him off.

**June 1** (Sat)—Kansas City, Missouri, for three-hour concert from Convention Hall,
7–10 P.M., and broadcast from radio station KMBC. No details available.

**June 2** (Sun)—Omaha, for concert at City Auditorium. Entire troupe first taken
on tour of Omaha and Council Bluffs by city officials and executives of
Mona Motor Oil Company, then to Hotel Chieftain for lunch. Concert
attended by 4,500—500 over capacity. Band plays "Tchaikowskiana,"
*Concerto in F,* plus specialties by Hall and Goldfield. Concert broadcast
by station KOIL.

Afterwards, band departs immediately for Lincoln, Nebraska, for
scheduled 6:30 P.M. concert at Burlington Station. Arrival delayed by
heavy rain en route and overflow crowd at station. A news report on this
event is quoted in full in the text. Band begins playing at 7 P.M., offering
program including "Stars and Stripes Forever," "Diga Diga Doo," tango
medley, "Honey," "Hallelujah," "I Kiss Your Hand, Madame" and "China
Boy." Band then departs for Denver after brief visit to Bix's compartment
by Esten Spurrier, Lennie Esterdahl and other musicians.

**June 3** (Mon)—Arrival in Denver at 8:30 A.M. Free day, including lunch at Placer
Inn, Idaho Springs, a tour of the city, and dinner at Whiteman family
farm. A newspaper account is quoted in the text.

**June 4** (Tue)—Band still in Denver. Rehearsal from 11 A.M. to 2 P.M. at Shirley-
Savoy Hotel. Free concert at Municipal Auditorium from 3–4:30 P.M.
Then, from 6 to 7 over radio station KLZ, the weekly Old Gold broadcast,
with program as follows:

Pompanola

Jericho (as on April 9, but Venuti in hot violin spot)

Popular Medley:

> I've Got a Feeling I'm Falling (one chorus only); To Be in Love (Fulton vocal); Please Let Me Dream; In the Land of Make Believe

Waltz Medley:

> My Hero; Blue Danube; Pink Lady; Merry Widow Waltz; Cecille

By the Waters of the Minnetonka (as recorded on Victor 21796)

I'll Get By (Crosby vocal)

Nola (as on Columbia 2277–D; Hall featured)

If I Had You (as on April 2, but with Crosby vocal)

Popular Medley:

> Titles missed, but Tram featured on second selection, Bix on third

Popular Medley:

> A Precious Little Thing Called Love (hot solos for all); A Love Tale of Alsace-Lorraine; Glad Rag Doll (Bix-Tram chase chorus)

> Sweet Georgia Brown (as on March 5, but Tram solos in first chorus, Bix solos with derby for second)

> Lover, Come Back to Me (as recorded on Columbia 1731–D, with Fulton vocal)

> Runnin' Wild (Hayton arrangement; Tram and Bix full chorus each, Bix's in a derby)

Punch and Judy (novelty)

The band now leaves for Salt Lake City at 8:30 P.M.

c. **June 5–13** (Wed-Thu)—Don Murray killed in Hollywood.

**June 5** (Wed)—Whiteman in Salt Lake City for concert at Granada Theater. Seats by invitation only, says the *Deseret News*, due to the limited seating capacity of the theater.

**June 6** (Thu)—Arrival at Los Angeles and brief stop en route north to San Francisco.

**June 7** (Fri)—Whiteman opens at Pantages Theater, San Francisco. Program includes *Rhapsody in Blue* and "I Kiss Your Hand, Madame."

**June 8** (Sat)—Second day at the Pantages. Program includes "Hallelujah," "Lover, Come Back to Me" and *Rhapsody in Blue*. Vocal selections by Rhythm Boys.

**June 11** (Tue)—Weekly broadcast for Old Gold, this time over station KYA at 5–6 P.M., Pacific Standard Time. Husing announcing. (It is worth noting that from here on, and perhaps in the previous several broadcasts as well, cornet solos attributed to Bix by Warren Scholl, who kept notes on the broadcasts, may be Andy Secrest as well. Their sounds at this point, especially given the uneven quality of long-distance radio transmission in these years, may well have been mistaken for each other's.) The program follows:

O Ya Ya (as recorded on Victor 21304)

Here Comes the Showboat ("not much of an arrangement," says Scholl)

*The Little Show* Medley:

> I've Made a Habit of You; Moanin' Low (Crosby sings verse and chorus, then modulation and full chorus by Venuti and Lang); Or What Have You?

Waltz Medley:

> Please Let Me Dream; A Smile, a Kiss; Heart of Mine; Old Fashioned Love Affair; Please Let Me Dream

Red Hair and Freckles (Rhythm Boys vocal)

Louise (as recorded on Columbia 1771–D, but Crosby sings verse alone, and is joined by Rhythm Boys on chorus)

Ploddin' Along (four-sax hot release in first chorus, then verse sung by Al Rinker with chorus backed by Lennie Hayton on celeste. Eight bars muted cornet in final chorus, followed by hot saxophone in release)

Tiger Rag (different arrangement from that recorded on Columbia 2277–D. As before, Rank in opening chorus, then Bix (derby) and Trumbauer solos)

When My Dreams Come True (as recorded on Columbia 1822-D. Lang alone accompanies vocal, rather than full orchestra)

Canoodle Oodle Along (Bix intro, then Tram for most of second chorus with muted trumpets in the release. Rhythm Boys vocal, and Secrest for bridge of final chorus. Ending as intro)

Nobody's Fault but Your Own (Crosby vocal)

S'Posin' (as recorded on Columbia 1862–D. Crosby vocal)

I Want to Meander in the Meadow (Grofe arrangement, with Fulton vocal)

There's a Rainbow Round My Shoulder (as on March 26; Tram and Bix spotted—Crosby vocal)

To Be in Love (full chorus of Venuti)

An Eyeful of You (instrumental with bit of Bix in last chorus)

Sweet Georgia Brown (as on March 5—Bix and Tram spotted)

**June 12** (Wed)—Orchestra plays for San Francisco Optimist Club Luncheon at Bellevue Hotel.

**June 13** (Thu)—End of Pantages Theater engagement.

**June 14** (Fri)—A free day.

**June 15** (Sat)—Orchestra arrives in Los Angeles at 9:30 A.M. to gala welcome led by theater impresario Alexander Pantages. Parade to Pantages Theater, where band scheduled to appear for a week prior to filming.

**June 16** (Sun)—Whiteman quoted by *Los Angeles Times* as saying of the forthcoming film: "One thing I will insist upon, and that is perfect recordings." Paul Fejos to direct.

**June 17** (Mon)—Whiteman plays for Chamber of Commerce benefit dinner at Majestic Theater.

**June 18** (Tue)—Regular Old Gold broadcast from station KMTR, Los Angeles, at 5–6 P.M., PST. The program:

Jericho (as before)

Feeling the Way I Do (Rhythm Boys vocal. Tram 16 bars in final chorus with Bix in the release)

*Music in May* Medley: (titles missed)

Pompanola

*Student Prince* Medley: two titles missed

Oh Miss Hannah (as recorded on Columbia 1945–D. Bix and Tram spotted)

You're My Silver Lining of Love (Fulton vocal, and brief Bix spot in final chorus)

(next five titles missed, though one was probably "El Choclo," a tango)

Reachin' for Someone (as recorded on Columbia 1822–D)

Oh Baby, Have a Heart (Crosby vocal, Bix briefly in the verse)

Things That Are Made for Love

China Boy (as recorded on Columbia 1945–D)

(balance of program lost)

**June 22** (Sat)—End of Pantages Theater engagement.

**June 25** (Tue)—Weekly Old Gold broadcast over KMTR. Ted Husing replaced as announcer by Harry Von Zell. The program:

Valencia (as recorded on Victor 20007)

March of the Musketeers (about as recorded on Victor 21315)

Deep Night

Futuristic Rhythm (Rhythm Boys vocal, plus eight bars of Tram in
release of first chorus)

Waltz Medley:
Song of Songs; Love, Here Is My Heart; Love Everlasting

Wedding of the Painted Doll ("very ordinary," says Scholl)

I've Made a Habit of You

Doin' the Raccoon (Tram and Friedman featured)

Broken Idol (straight arrangement by Grofe)

Tango Medley:
Pavo Real Girl; Violetta (from *La Traviata*)

Hallelujah (Bix muted, featured as before)

Nobody but You (Crosby vocal, Bix derby-muted for 16 bars in last
chorus, plus Rank release)

You're My Silver Lining of Love (as June 18)

Building a Nest for Mary (Rhythm Boys vocal; some bits of Trumbauer)

What a Day (essentially same arrangement as Trumbauer's Columbia
1861–D "Mason-Dixon Orchestra" record)

Don't Hold Everything (Rolfe-type novelty)

July 2 (Tue)—Regularly-scheduled Old Gold broadcast over KMTR. Harry Von
Zell, announcing. The program:

Hitting the Ceiling

Wildflower

Wartime Medley (probably Grofe arrangement):
Over There; You're a Grand Old Flag; Inky Dinky Parlay Voo; It's
a Long Way to Tipperary

Waltz Medley: three titles missed

My Sin (straight, with Crosby vocal)

Cigarette (concert-type arrangement)

A special feature: Rhythm Boys singing "Number Three," number
tied in with Old Gold commercial. Later published

Parade of the Wooden Soldiers ( as recorded on Victor 21304)

You Were Meant for Me (Crosby vocal)

Makin' Whoopee (essentially as Columbia 1683-D, but Bix on eight-
bar solo near the end)

I'm Bringing a Red, Red Rose (as recorded on Columbia 1683-D, but
Bargy piano solo in place of vocal)

Lady of the Morning (Fulton vocal)

Kewpie (novelty number)

Dardanella (as recorded on Victor 25238, complete with Bix solo)

Honey (Crosby vocal)

Little Coat of Tan

I'm Just Wild About Harry (as on April 16—Bix spotted)

Pickin' Cotton (Rolfe-type novelty)

July 3 (Wed)—Paul Whiteman's Rhythm Boys opened at the Montmartre Club as
separate act.

July 9 (Tue)—Regular Old Gold broadcast from KMTR. The program:

I'm Referrin' to Her 'n' Me (Rhythm Boys vocal)

Liza (Venuti & Lang featured for full chorus)

You, Just You (straight arrangement)

Singin' in the Rain (good Grofe arrangement)

Song of Siberia (verse and opening chorus sung by Bing Crosby)

Driego's Serenade (waltz instrumental)

Number Three ( hot arrangement written for and played by the band
for Old Gold cigarettes, based on current commercial slogan. Bix,
muted, in spots and good hot ensembles by the brass)

Laughing Marionette (as recorded on Columbia 1862–D)
Ma Belle (as on Victor 21315, but quartet vocal)
O Ya Ya (as on Victor 21304)
Pagan Love Song (vocal by Whiteman Trio)
I Want to Meander in the Meadow (Bargy piano solo replaces vocal)
Out Where the Moonbeams Are Born (Crosby vocal, with Bix for eight
    bars in last chorus)
Sun Is at My Window (instrumental)
Canoodle Oodle Along (quartet vocal)
Baby, Where Can You Be? (Bix in release of first chorus, Crosby sings
    second verse and chorus; last chorus hot arrangement with Bix
    spotted and Tram in the release)
Runnin' Wild (usual arrangement, Bix soloing in a derby)

July 16 (Tue)—Regular Old Gold Broadcast over KMTR. The program:
It Goes Like This (undistinguished instrumental)
Back in Your Own Backyard (quartet vocal chorus, plus bits of Bix)
Medley:
    Where Were You?; Right Out of Heaven; Yours Sincerely
Waltz Medley:
    Evangeline; Where Are You Tonight? (quartet vocal); Marie
Hollywood Revue Medley:
    Your Mother and Mine (chorus as recorded on Columbia 1845–D);
    Singin' in the Rain (quartet vocals, with solo verse by Al Rinker);
    Orange Blossom Time (as on Columbia 1845–D)
*The Little Show* Medley:
    I've Made a Habit of You (Venuti chorus); Or What Have You?
I'm Just a Vagabond Lover (Crosby vocal)
Sweetheart's Holiday (quartet vocal. Trumbauer 16 bars in final
    chorus)
Miss You (16 bars hot saxophone ensemble in last chorus)
Finding the Long Way Home (Venuti most of second chorus, with Bix
    in release. Bix and Tram together for eight bars in final chorus)
Things That Were Made for Love (as before)
Sing a Little Love Song (quartet vocal)
When We Get Together in the Moonlight (same)
Down Among the Sugar Cane (instrumental featuring Trumbauer for
    entire chorus)
To Be in Love (Venuti chorus)
I Want to Meander in the Meadow (instrumental)
Kewpie (novelty)

July 17 (Wed)—Rhythm Boys still at Montmartre Cafe; joined by Professor Moore
and his orchestra. From the *Los Angeles Times*: "Charles McArthur, co-
author with Ben Hecht of 'The Front Page,' is sitting in on the writing of
Paul Whiteman's picture for Universal. McArthur, signed by the Laemmle organization to write 'The Homicide Squad,' a sequel to 'Broadway,'
was called off his first assignment to help in preparation of the Whiteman
effort."

July 23 (Tue)—Regular broadcast for Old Gold over KMTR. The program:
Breakaway (undistinguished Rolfe-type arrangement)
What a Day (as on June 25)
The One I Love, Loves Me (as on May 14)
If You Believe in Me ("miserable," says Scholl)
I'd Do Anything for You ("miserable")
Here We Are ("even worse")
(next two titles missed)
Some Sweet Day (vocal by trio. Trumbauer eight bars in final chorus)

Give Your Little Baby Lots of Lovin' (Crosby vocal, and Trumbauer
   release in last chorus)
Just Another Day Wasted Away (Venuti spotted)
It Don't Mean a Thing without You (instrumental)
My Blue Heaven (Crosby and trio sing third chorus)
Someday You'll Realize You're Wrong (Trumbauer chorus with Bix in
   the release)
In the Garden of Tomorrow (Fulton vocal)
Love Me or Leave Me (Crosby vocal, Trumbauer and Bix spotted)
Glad Rag Doll (Bix-Tram chase chorus for 24 bars)

July 29 (Mon)—Rhythm Boys headline Orpheum Theater for one week in addition to Montmartre Cafe engagement.

July 30 (Tue)—Regular broadcast for Old Gold over KMTR. The program:
Hitting the Ceiling (instrumental)
Ca C'est Paris
Broadway Melody (Crosby vocal)
Your Mother and Mine (as recorded on Columbia 1845–D)
That's Living (eight bars of Bix in last chorus)
My Dear (waltz, with Crosby vocal)
My Lucky Star (as recorded on Columbia 1736–D, but no vocal. Tram
   spotted briefly)
Hindustan (Rhythm Boys vocal)
Punch and Judy (Rolfe-esque novelty)
Dusky Stevedore (trio vocal; Bix and Tram spotted)
Sugar Is Back in Town (straight arrangement)
Dream Memory (straight instrumental)
S'Posin' (as recorded on Columbia 1862–D, but tempo slower)
Happy Because I'm in Love
(title missed; hot instrumental with Bix for 24 bars, plus Tram and
   Rank 16 bars duet in third chorus)
Nobody's Fault but Your Own (Crosby vocal)
Every Moon Is a Honeymoon (vocal by Fulton-Gaylord-Rinker trio)
Do What You Do (Venuti & Lang spotted for full chorus)

July 31 (Wed)—Automobile accident involving Joe Venuti and Mario Perry.
Perry dies later of injuries; Venuti's bowing arm broken.

Aug. 1 (Thu)—From the *Los Angeles Examiner*: "Two members of Paul Whiteman's orchestra were injured, one of them seriously, when the automobile in which they were en route to Santa Barbara collided yesterday afternoon with a car containing two women tourists from Springfield, Ill. The accident happened on the Roosevelt Highway near Sycamore Canyon.

"The injured musicians are Mario Perry, who is said to be in critical condition from internal injuries, and Joe Cesuti [*sic*], who suffered a fractured wrist and multiple lacerations."

Aug. 3 (Sat)—Al Rinker's sister, Mildred Bailey, throws a party for Whiteman and several members of the orchestra including Bix, Tram, Venuti, Lang, Bargy, Hayton, Malneck, Bing and Friedman. She sings, and Whiteman decides to sign her to perform with the band.

Aug. 5 (Mon)—Whiteman signs Mildred Bailey.

Aug. 6 (Tue)—Regular broadcast for Old Gold over KMTR. The program:
I'd Do Anything for You
Heigh-Ho, Everybody, Heigh-Ho (entire orchestra in opening and
   closing choruses. Bix for 24 bars, derby-muted, in third chorus, with
   release by Rank)
Pagan Love Song (vocal by trio)
Wake Up, Chillun, Wake Up (Tram 16 bars and bits of Bix in the verse.

Vocal Trio. "Typical Whiteman-style number," says Scholl)

Beautiful Ohio (waltz)

My Madonna (Crosby vocal)

Garden in the Rain (vocal by trio, with Bing doing jive stuff in release)

Ain't Misbehavin' (Rolfe-type arrangement, with accordion solo by unknown musician)

Walking with Susie (up-tempo; Bing vocal in fourth chorus and Malneck hot accompaniment to melody in another)

Moanin' Low (Mildred Bailey's debut with the Whiteman Orchestra. After intro and full band verse, Trumbauer for 24 bars; then Bailey for verse and chorus, followed by modulation, brass-led ensemble for 16 bars with Bix blowing the release open before band takes it out. Roy Bargy arrangement)

If You Believe in Me ("not much": Scholl)

Little Pal (as recorded on Columbia 1877–D. Crosby vocal)

"Mary" Medley:

Mary Make Believe; Mary Lou; Building a Nest for Mary

You're My Silver Lining of Love (Crosby vocal)

Rhythm Man (Rolfe-like arrangement, but with Friedman on tenor for a chorus, Rank in the release. To fill up extra time, band repeated first two choruses)

Before end of program, Whiteman announces that a fan has just telephoned the studio to say that "Moanin' Low" was the best number he had ever heard the band perform.

**Aug. 7** (Wed)—Orchestra takes part in Hollywood Midsummer Jubilee at Hollywood Bowl, broadcast over KFWB from 8:30–10:30 P.M. Among the other attractions: Los Angeles Grand Opera Chorus, South Pasadena Legion Drum Corps, Belle Baker, Moran and Mack, Elsie Janis, Clara Bow, Olga Baclanova, Stepin Fetchit, Jack Benny, Polly Moran, Benny Rubin, the Duncan Sisters, Al Jolson, Gus Edwards' "School Days" with Fannie Brice and George Jessel, Warner Brothers' 125-piece orchestra, Nick Lucas, Ceballos and others. Same evening advertised as "Show of Shows Night" at Club Montmartre; Rhythm Boys headline the bill.

**Aug. 13** (Tue)—Regular Old Gold broadcast over station KMTR. The program:

Alabamy Bound (vocal by Crosby and trio; bits of Bix in last chorus with ending resembling that on "China Boy" arrangement)

Fiddlin' Joe (instrumental; Rank for eight bars in last chorus)

You Were Meant for Me (Crosby vocal)

Sugar Cane 'Round My Door (Bix and Rank split second chorus 16 bars each, then hot ensemble, Bix leading trumpets through release. Eight bars of Malneck in last chorus after quartet vocal)

I've Found a New Baby (Bix muted cornet for 24 of first 32 bars, then hot ensemble verse and rest of selection wiped out by station trouble)

Just Another Kiss (waltz—Crosby vocal)

*Hot Chocolate* Medley:

(title missed); Dixie Cinderella (Bix muted 24 bars; vocal quartet); (title missed; Trumbauer spotted briefly)

Where the Sweet Forget-Me-Nots Remember (eight bars of Secrest in release of last chorus)

Toymaker's Dream ("miserable," says Scholl)

Don't Wake Baby Up (Bix for entire second chorus. Accordion and xylophone featured)

Am I Blue (Bill Rank 24 bars in second chorus; Mildred Bailey sings verse and chorus; Tram eight bars release in final chorus)

Believe It or Not (straight arrangement)

Till We Meet (vocal by quartet)
My Melody Man
(title missed)
No One Can Take Your Place (Bix in release of last chorus, as on
    Trumbauer record)
Song of the West (instrumental)
Liza (Malneck and Lang for a chorus)
Waitin' for the Robert E. Lee (Rank spotted briefly)

Bix was the subject of tonight's Old Gold commercial, in a routine about
trying on different hats.

Aug. 16 (Fri)—Orchestra plays for Santa Barbara Fiesta Day, performing for street
dancers at De La Guerra plaza from 10 P.M. until early morning. From
the *Santa Barbara News-Press:* " . . . the jazz king and his musicians
donated their services to the fiesta and it may safely be said they never
worked harder in their lives."

Aug. 20 (Tue)—Regular broadcast for Old Gold over station KMTR. Program:
I'm Referrin' to Her 'n' Me (Rhythm Boys vocal)
Alabamy Snow (not same arrangement as Trumbauer recording. This
    features full Tram chorus plus accordion-xylophone chorus)
Memories of One Sweet Kiss (Crosby vocal)
Feeling the Way I Do (Rhythm Boys vocal. Tram 16 bars of final chorus
    with Bix in the release)
Waiting at the End of the Road (Crosby vocal. Arrangement as re-
    corded on Columbia 1974–D with Bix in release of last chorus)
Waltz Medley:
Sleepy Valley; Can't Forget Hawaii; Celia; Finesse
Oh Baby, Have a Heart (Crosby vocal. Bits of Bix and Rank)
Last Night, Honey (two spots of eight bars by Bix and Trumbauer.
    Vocal by quartet)
Futuristic Rhythm (Rhythm Boys vocal. Tram in release of last chorus)
I'm Just a Vagabond Lover (Crosby vocal)
Good Little, Bad Little You (Mildred Bailey vocal)
I'll Tell the World About You (instrumental)
Satisfied
"Sally" Medley:
Sally, Won't You Please Come Back?; I Wonder What's Become of
    Sally; I'm Sorry, Sally
I'll Never Ask for More (Mildred Bailey vocal; Bix, derby-muted, for
    16 bars of last chorus)
Let's Do It (as recorded, but Hayton accompanies vocal trio on celeste,
    and flute replaces baritone sax in last chorus)
Jericho (usual arrangement, with Malneck spot in fourth chorus)

Aug. 27 (Tue)—Regular broadcast for Old Gold over station KMTR. Program:
March of the Musketeers (as recorded on Victor 21315)
"I've Made A Habit of You" and "Or What Have You?" (played as
    medley)
Sweetness (Trumbauer-Friedman duet in second chorus, then Tram
    entire third chorus and Crosby in fifth. Bix spotted briefly in last
    chorus)
Medley
Honey (Crosby & trio vocal); Nobody's Fault but Your Own (Crosby
    vocal); An Eyeful of You (instrumental); Honey (reprise)
Where Is the Song of Songs for Me? (waltz, with Mildred Bailey vocal)
Do Something (Bix entire second chorus over saxophones)
Beautiful (instrumental, Grofe arrangement)
Maybe, Who Knows (Mildred Bailey vocal)

Wedding of the Painted Doll (instrumental with Malneck violin chorus)

Looking for Love (vocal by trio)

I've Got a Feeling I'm Falling (Mildred Bailey vocal)

Sweet Georgia Brown (as on March 5—Bix with derby mute)

You Wouldn't Fool Me, Would You? (Crosby and trio vocal)

Junior (Crosby vocal; Bix release, in derby, last chorus)

Avalon Town (straight arrangement)

I Wanna Be Loved by You (Bix in most of third chorus)

China Boy (as recorded; time remained, so played through again as far as Trumbauer's third-chorus solo)

**Aug. 28** (Wed)—After extensive bickering with Universal over the band's inactivity, possible effects on his popularity, and other considerations, Whiteman decides to leave Hollywood and return East until a finished script is available. Band boards Old Gold Special for return trip. Hoagy Carmichael "hitches" a ride, bunking with Bing Crosby.

**Aug. 31** (Sat)—Orchestra opens at Pavilion Royale in Valley Stream, Long Island.

**Sept. 1** (Sun)—Warren W. Scholl listens to the band at Pavilion Royale from 7:30–10:00 P.M., noting that Bix did not take part but remained at a table off to the side for the entire evening.

**Sept. 3** (Tue)—Weekly broadcast for Old Golds, this time again over WABC from 9–10 P.M., EST. Harry Von Zell announced the program:

Valencia (as recorded on Victor 20007)

O Ya Ya (as recorded on Victor 21304)

When You're Counting the Stars Alone (as recorded on Columbia 1993-D, but with solos by Trumbauer and Bix)

Same Old Moon (Ponce Sisters vocal)

Singin' in the Rain (instrumental)

Merry Widow Waltz

Dancing Dominoes (instrumental)

Moanin' Low (Mildred Bailey vocal on Bargy's arrangement)

Butterflies Kiss Buttercups Goodnight (Ponce Sisters vocal)

Broadway Melody (Crosby vocal)

Heigh-Ho, Everybody, Heigh-Ho (Bix, muted, for 24 bars of third chorus)

I'd Do Anything for You

I'm Doing What I'm Doing for Love (Crosby vocal, with Trumbauer in 16 bars of last chorus)

If You Believe in Me (Mildred Bailey vocal, accompanied by the Rhythm Boys)

Huggable, Kissable You (Crosby vocal, with Friedman on clarinet in last chorus)

Scotchie (instrumental)

What a Day (as recorded by Trumbauer on Columbia 1861-D, by the "Mason-Dixon Orchestra")

Breakaway (Rhythm Boys vocal)

**Sept. 6** (Fri)—Whiteman records for Columbia in New York.

**Sept. 10** (Tue)—Bix's last appearance on a Paul Whiteman Old Gold radio broadcast. The program:

Swanee (instrumental)

Alabamy Bound (Crosby and trio vocal. Bits of Bix in last chorus)

St. Louis Blues (Mildred Bailey vocal)

Love, Your Magic Spell Is Everywhere (Crosby vocal)

Red Hair and Freckles (Ponce Sisters vocal, with Crosby release. Malneck takes verse on violin; next chorus eight bars of Rank, and Trumbauer in release of last chorus)

Victor Herbert Medley:
> Angelus; Kiss Me Again; Kiss in the Dark; Ah, Sweet Mystery of Life (Fulton vocal)
> Back in Your Own Backyard (Ponce Sisters vocal)
> After You've Gone (Mildred Bailey vocal)
> El Choclo (instrumental)
> Song of Siberia (Crosby vocal)
> Bugle Call Rag (Trumbauer and Friedman choruses, with Bix in final chorus)
> Nobody's Sweetheart (as recorded on Columbia 2098–D, but Bix takes opening solo)
> Sweetness (as on August 27)
> Wake Up, Chillun, Wake Up (vocal by Whiteman's "New Trio"; Trumbauer 16 bars, Bix briefly in the verse)
> Laughing Marionette (as recorded on Columbia 1862–D)
> National Emblem March

**Sept. 13** (Fri)—Whiteman records for Columbia. First selection of the day is remake of "Waiting at the End of the Road"; this is Bix's last issued solo with the Whiteman orchestra, eight bars in the final chorus. He is then able to complete only one take of the following selection, "When You're Counting the Stars Alone," before being taken ill. He then leaves the studio.

**Sept. 14** (Sat)—Bix remains in his room at the 44th Street Hotel all day.

**Sept. 15** (Sun)—Whiteman and Kurt Dieterle accompany Bix to Grand Central Station, where Bix boards a train home to Davenport for an extended rest on full salary.

**Sept. 16** (Mon) **to Oct. 13** (Sun)—Bix at home in Davenport.

**Oct. 14** (Mon)—Bix Beiderbecke admitted as a patient to Keeley Institute, Dwight, Illinois.

**Nov. 18** (Mon)—Bix checks himself out of Keeley Institute and returns to Davenport.

**c. early December**—Esten Spurrier brings Bix into the Jimmy Hicks orchestra playing at Danceland Ballroom, Fourth Street and Scott, and other locations around town. Personnel: Hicks (trumpet and leader); Spurrier and Bix (cornets); Bob Struve (trombone); Leo Bahr (alto sax); Nate Marblestone (tenor sax); Louis Bruhn (piano); "Penny" Penningter (sousaphone); Earl Bruckman (drums).

**Dec. 18** (Wed)—Bix appears with Hicks band at Danceland. Advertised as "featured trumpet with Paul Whiteman."

**Dec. 21** (Sat)—Hicks band again at Danceland.

**Dec. 23** (Mon)—Trave O'Hearn and his 11-piece dance orchestra play Kappa Delta dance at Hotel Blackhawk. Attendance 500. Partial personnel: Ed Sidebotham (trumpet); Bix (cornet); O'Hearn (alto sax); Frank Skinner (trombone); Les Swanson (piano); Larry Andrews (banjo); Glenn Sears (drums).

**Dec. 25** (Wed)—Christmas. Hicks band does not play at Danceland.

**Dec. 27** (Fri)—O'Hearn band, booked by Larry Andrews, plays for Frigidaire employee Christmas dance at Hotel Blackhawk. Personnel probably as before, but with Harry Rathjens (trumpet) replacing Sidebotham.

**Dec. 28** (Sat)—Hicks band again at Danceland.

**Dec. 29** (Sun)—*Davenport Sunday Democrat* advertises Danceland: "Don't fail to hear Bix" plus added attraction, Tony's Iowans.

**Dec. 31** (Tue)—New Year's Eve dance at Elks Club 980, Rock Island, Illinois, lasting until 4 A.M. Personnel: O'Hearn, Rathjens, Bix, Andrews, Art Kurth (piano); Mervin "Pee Wee" Rank (drums).

# 1930

**Jan. 1** (Wed)—Advertisement for Danceland: "Come Out To Hear Bix."

**Jan. 4** (Sat)—Hicks band at Danceland.

**Jan. 5** (Sun)—*Sunday Democrat* advertisement: "Featuring Bix Beiderbecke—hottest trumpet player in the country" with Hicks at Danceland. Gentlemen admitted for 50¢, ladies for 25¢. After this, according to Esten Spurrier, Bix "put his foot down" and insisted that his name no longer be used in the Hicks advertising.

**Jan. 8** (Wed)—Advertisement: "Jimmy Hicks with added attraction."

**Jan. 11** (Sat)—Hicks band at Danceland. Bix present.

**Jan. 12** (Sun)—Hicks band at Danceland. Bix present.

**Jan. 15** (Wed)—Hicks band at Danceland. Bix present.

**Jan. 18** (Sat)—Hicks band at Danceland. Bix present.

**Jan. 19** (Sun)—Advertisement: "Hear America's foremost trumpet player." No name mentioned.

**January**—Bix continues with Hicks band.

**c. Feb. 2–4** (Sun-Tue)—Bix travels to Chicago, sits in with Wingy Manone at "My Cellar" (Three Deuces) speakeasy. Continues to New York. Visits Bill Challis. Talks to Jimmy Gillespie at Whiteman office, learns of projected tour of United States, Canada and Europe. Arranges to rejoin in Chicago when Whiteman comes through en route east.

**c. Feb. 10–12** (Mon-Wed)—Bix back in Chicago, sits in with Ted Weems at Granada Cafe. Rehearses with band Joe Haymes plans to take to Tulsa for March 9 job at Mayo Hotel.

**Feb. 14** (Fri)—Bix back in Davenport. St. Valentine's Day dance at Elks' Club, Rock Island. Probable personnel: Harry Rathjens, Ken Dick (trumpets); Bix (cornet); Jess Thordsen (trombone); Johnny Eberhardt (saxophone); Buck Sarinson (saxophone); Art Kurth (piano); others. Band under Rathjens' name.

**March 1** (Sat)—Bix appears with Bob Tyldesley's Kentucky Reveillers at Roof Garden of the LeClaire Hotel, in Moline, Illinois. Dancing from 9 P.M. to 2:30 A.M. Partial personnel: Bix (cornet); Irv Dornacher (tenor sax); Archie Long (sousaphone and librarian); Ray Long (drums); six others. Tyldesley, also a drummer, fronted.

**March 2** (Sun)—Bix with Tyldesley at the Roof Garden from 9 P.M. to 1 A.M.

**March 3** (Mon)—Band's day off.

**March 4** (Tue)—Bix with Tyldesley at the Roof Garden, 9–1.

**March 5** (Wed)—Bix with Tyldesley at the Roof Garden, 9–1.

**March 6** (Thu)—Bix with Tyldesley at the Roof Garden; sends note to Wayne Rohlf, working at the Capitol Orpheum Theater in Davenport, to come "after the show and work in my place. I'm sick." Rohlf, thinking the note a gag, disregards it.

**March 7** (Fri)—Bix with Tyldesley at the Roof Garden, 9–1.

**March 8** (Sat)—Bix's last evening with Tyldesley at the Roof Garden, playing from 9 P.M. to 2:30 A.M.

**March 17** (Mon)—Jimmy Hicks, double-booked for the evening, splits his band into two units to fulfil both engagements. Bix borrows Bill Greer's drums and works with Hicks unit at Fraternal Hall in Rock Island. Personnel: Esten Spurrier (cornet); Bob Struve (trombone); Ed Anderson (clarinet and saxophone); Les Swanson (piano); Bix (drums).

**March 18** (Tue)—Bix writes to Ruth Shaffner in St. Louis.

**March 21** (Fri)—Les Swanson visits Bix at Beiderbecke home, taking turns on the grand piano in the parlor. Says Swanson: "I recall we both did 'In a Mist,' and of course my version sounded like another number compared with his interpretation."

**March 27** (Thu)—Swanson: "Bix was my guest in a ringside seat at the Moline Field House, where the Moline Elks presented a boxing show. I had been assigned to write the story . . . as a reporter for the *Davenport Times*. I had heard Bix mention that he was a boxing fan so I invited him along as my guest."

**March 30** (Sun)—Swanson: "Bix returned the favor by inviting me to see a show with him at the Garden Theater in Davenport. It was *Chasing Rainbows* with Charles King, Bessie Love and Jack Benny. Following that we went to Danceland, where Al "Krazy" Katz and his kittens were holding forth. Bix renewed his acquaintance with some of the boys in Katz's band, but did not sit in as I recall."

**April 4** (Fri)—Bix and Swanson see *Pointed Heels* with Helen Kane and William Powell, at the Garden. Canadian officials, meanwhile, bar Whiteman orchestra from entering Canada except as entertainers who can perform from theater stages but not play for dancing.

**April 8–9** (Tue-Wed)—Bix goes to Chicago to await Whiteman. Checks into Sherman Hotel.

**April 15** (Tue)—Whiteman troupe stuck in Seattle as a consequence of Canadian decision. Whiteman announces: "I will make the city of Vancouver an offer: since I can't play for hire I will play dance music for any charity or Saturday night dance and won't take a dime for it either." A. E. Skinner, Commissioner of Immigration, adamant in his ban. Whiteman's tour schedule so badly disrupted that he cancels entire itinerary and returns to New York nonstop.

**April 22** (Tue)—Whiteman orchestra arrives back in New York.

**April 23** (Wed)—Bix in New York; takes room 605 at the 44th Street Hotel, 120 West 44th Street.

**c. April 24–25** (Thu-Fri)—Speaks to Whiteman and is unable to decide whether he has the stability and endurance to rejoin the band. Within the next week, he tells Whiteman he is "not ready yet," urges him to retain Andy Secrest.

**May 2–3** (Fri-Sat)—Bix joins group led by Tommy and Jimmy Dorsey playing house parties at Princeton University for the Colonial Club, Ivy Club and Tiger Inn, which holds its affair jointly with Colonial Club. Bud Freeman is also a member of this pickup band.

**May 5** (Mon)—Universal Technicolor musical film *King of Jazz* opens at the Roxy Theater, New York. Whiteman orchestra headlines the stage show, and George Gershwin performs *Rhapsody in Blue* daily with them for the first week. Following this engagement, Whiteman reduces his orchestra to 18 men. Among those given notice: Charles Margulis (trumpet), Boyce Cullen (trombone), Lennie Hayton (piano).

**May 16** (Fri)—Bix and Tommy Dorsey travel to Williams College, Williamstown, Massachusetts, to play a private house party.

**May 17** (Sat)—Billed as the "Beiderbecke-Dorsey Orchestra," this pickup group plays a dance at Phi Gamma Delta fraternity house, Williams College.

**May 18–19** (Sun-Mon)—Other band members return to New York, but Bix, Dorsey and guitarist Carl Kress stay over at the fraternity house.

**May 21** (Wed)—Bix records two titles with Hoagy Carmichael's orchestra for Victor.

**c. May 22–25** (Thu-Sun)—Formation of orchestra for Camel Pleasure Hour weekly radio show on NBC.

**June 4** (Wed)—Camel Pleasure Hour goes on the air, 9:30–10:30 P.M., over station

WJZ. John Young, announcer; John Wiggin, producer; Charles Previn, director; and Gordon White, assistant director. Contractor is Nat Shilkret. Personnel:

Charles Margulis, Leo McConville (trumpets); Bix Beiderbecke (cornet); George Chafflin, Tommy Dorsey (trombones); Louis Martin, Red Mayer, three others (reeds); Aaron Gershunoff, Sam Feinsmith, Ross Gorman, two others (woodwinds, bagpipes); Murray Kellner, Jascha Bron, Samuel Silverman, George Green, Joseph Raymond, Samuel Kerman, Sylvan Kirsner, three others (violins); two unknown (cellos); Charles Magnante (accordion); Min Leibrook (tuba); Eddie Brader (bass); Carl Kress (guitar; later replaced by Lew Green); Sidney "Happy" Reiss (drums); Joseph Green (bells); unknown (cymbals); Lennie Hayton and Arthur Schutt (pianos).

Vocals by the Ken Christie Male Quartet; Mary McCoy (soprano); Billy Hughes (baritone; sometimes known as "Billy Hillpot"); Reinald Warrenrath (baritone); Willard Robison (featured variety artist).

Helen Kane (vocals and comedienne) also featured on first broadcast.

**June 6** (Fri)—Bix records for Brunswick with Irving Mills and His Hotsy-Totsy Gang. See both text and discography for further discussion of this controversial date.

**June 11** (Wed)—Camel Pleasure Hour broadcast, featuring Mary McCoy, Billy Hughes, Reinald Warrenrath, and the comedy skits of "Doc" Rockwell.

**June 16** (Mon)—Yale University Senior Prom, with Eddie Wittstein band playing. All attempts to investigate rumors Bix played this engagement have proved fruitless.

**June 18** (Wed)—Camel Pleasure Hour broadcast, featuring McCoy, Warrenrath and Willard Robison's Deep River Orchestra.

**June 25** (Wed)—Camel Pleasure Hour broadcast, featuring McCoy, Warrenrath, Rockwell and Robison.

**July 2** (Wed)—Camel Pleasure Hour broadcast, featuring Frances Williams singing "All Fall in Love." Bix takes an extended solo (see text).

**July 9** (Wed)—Camel Pleasure Hour broadcast, featuring Mary McCoy.

**July 16** (Wed)—Camel Pleasure Hour broadcast, featuring McCoy, Hughes, Rockwell and Robison.

**July 23** (Wed)—Camel Pleasure Hour broadcast, featuring McCoy, Hughes and quartet.

**July 30** (Wed)—Camel Pleasure Hour broadcast, featuring McCoy, Hughes, Warrenrath and guest star Nancy Carroll.

**Aug. 6** (Wed)—*Variety* notes: "Bix Beiderbecke starting his own band. Formerly with Whiteman orchestra and wants Whiteman to manage him." See text for fuller discussion of this episode.

**Aug. 6** (Wed)—Camel Pleasure Hour Broadcast, featuring McCoy, Hughes, Warrenrath.

**Aug. 13** (Wed)—Camel Pleasure Hour broadcast. In the following list of selections there is no indication which of them, if any, featured Bix Beiderbecke. We have singled out likely possibilities only.

> In the Good Old Sun-Sun Shine (orchestra)
> I Don't Mind Walking in the Rain (Bix?)
> San Toy (Glee Club—18 voices)
> I'm Yours (McCoy and Hughes)
> Okay, Baby (Bix?)
> Smilin' Through (Warrenrath)
> Here Comes Emily Brown (orchestra; Bix?)
> Musical Comedy Medley:
>     The Girl Friend; My Heart Stood Still
> The Blue Moon (glee club)

You May Not Like It (orchestra)
St. Louis Blues (Robison solo)
I Don't Mind Walking in the Rain (orchestra)
Spanish Shawl (Lennie Hayton and Arthur Schutt)
I'se Got Religion (male quartet)

**Aug. 20** (Wed)—Camel Pleasure Hour broadcast, featuring McCoy, Warrenrath, Hughes, Robison's orchestra.

**Aug. 27** (Wed)—Camel Pleasure Hour broadcast, featuring Warrenrath.

**Aug. 29** (Fri)—Registration of copyright of "Candlelights" in the name of Robbins Music Corp., under E17508. Copyright renewed under R198321 (August 30, 1957), by C. B. Beiderbecke, Mary Louise Shoemaker and William H. Challis.

**Sept. 3** (Wed)—Camel Pleasure Hour broadcast, featuring McCoy, Hughes, Warrenrath, Robison, male chorus, pianists Hayton & Schutt.

**Sept. 8** (Mon)—Bix Beiderbecke and his orchestra do three titles for Victor.

**Sept. 10** (Wed)—Camel Pleasure Hour broadcast, featuring McCoy, Warrenrath, Hughes, Robison, male chorus, Schutt & Hayton.

**Sept. 15** (Mon)—Bix Beiderbecke records with Hoagy Carmichael and his orchestra for Victor.

**Sept. 17** (Wed)—Camel Pleasure Hour broadcast, featuring McCoy, Warrenrath, Hughes, Robison, male chorus, Hayton & Schutt, plus Irene Bordoni.

**Sept. 24** (Wed)—Camel Pleasure Hour broadcast, featuring McCoy, Warrenrath, Hughes, Robison, male chorus, Hayton & Schutt.

**Oct. 1** (Wed)—Camel Pleasure Hour broadcast, featuring McCoy, Warrenrath, Hughes, Robison, male chorus, Hayton & Schutt, and added attraction the Ponce Sisters.

**Oct. 8** (Wed)—Camel Pleasure Hour broadcast, with usual cast. It is on this broadcast that Bix blacks out in the middle of a solo. He returns to Davenport within two or three days, and his place in the orchestra is taken by Robert "Bobby" Effros.

**Nov. 7** (Fri)—Dorsey Brothers orchestra at Princeton University dance. Some reports have placed Bix in this band, but on the evidence available this appears unlikely.

**Nov. 12** (Wed)—Report in British music journal *Melody Maker* that Bix has left New York for Davenport. This report appears to be belated.

**Dec. 10** (Wed)—Bix plays with Trave O'Hearn band for dance at Eagles Hall in Moline, Illinois. Partial personnel: Esten Spurrier, Bix (cornets); O'Hearn (saxophone); Les Swanson (piano).

**Dec. 17** (Wed)—Another Eagles dance with O'Hearn in Moline. Personnel as before, but add Francis Ellsworth (tenor sax).

**Dec. 31** (Wed)—Bix works New Year's Eve party with local band. Details unknown.

# 1931

**Jan. 17** (Sat)—Paul Whiteman orchestra appears for one night at Danceland, in the Davenport Eagles Building. Bix sits in. Whiteman offers him his chair back again, but Bix again declines.

**c. Jan. 20** (Tue)—Bix sits in with Cliff Mandy's band at Davenport Coliseum. Personnel (partial): Mandy (piano); John Schultz (alto sax); Neil Whiteside (tenor sax); unknown saxophone, two trumpets; Vic Servoss (trombone); Fred Morgan (bass); Duke McGurk (drums).

**Feb. 9** (Mon)—Whiteman opens at Granada Cafe, Chicago.

**c. Feb. 13–15** (Fri-Sun)—Bix visits Whiteman musicians at the Granada.

**c. late February** —Bix returns to New York, moves back into 44th Street Hotel.

**March 14** (Sat)—Dorsey Brothers orchestra plays Amherst College Senior Hop in Amherst, Massachusetts. Date booked by Art Michaud. Personnel: Bunny Berigan, Bill Moore (trumpets); Bix (cornet); Tommy Dorsey, Glenn Miller (trombones); Jimmy Dorsey, three others (reeds); Arthur Schutt (piano); Carl Kress (guitar); Johnny Morris (drums); unknown (bass).

**April 16** (Thu)—"Sunny" Clapp and his Band o' Sunshine record two takes of "Come Easy, Go Easy Love" for Victor in New York. Neither was issued, the titles being remade July 1 with a different personnel. Despite persistent rumors of Bix's presence, the authors were unable to place him on the first Clapp session.

**April 18** (Sat)—Copyright registration for "Flashes" (E22489) and "In the Dark" (E22490) by Robbins Music Corp. Renewed April 21, 1958, under R213591 and R213592 respectively, by C. B. Beiderbecke and Mary Louise Shoemaker.

**May 1** (Fri)—Bix leads group fronted by Benny Goodman, playing for house party at Princeton University Cottage Club. Personnel: Bix (cornet); Charlie Teagarden (trumpet); Will Bradley (trombone); Benny Goodman (clarinet); John Geller, Bud Freeman (saxophones); Joe Sullivan (piano); Bill Challoner (guitar); Johnny Powell (drums).

**May 2** (Sat)—Another job for same band at the Charter Club, with Jimmy Dorsey (clarinet and alto sax) replacing Goodman. Following the job, the band moved to the home of Byrnes McDonald.

**May 3** (Sun)—Bix returns in the afternoon to New York.

**c. May 5** (Tue)—Bix, Bill Challis and Cork O'Keefe visit the Casa Loma Orchestra at the Metropolitan Hotel in Boston.

**May 7** (Thu)—Casa Loma plays at Amherst College.

**May 8** (Fri)—Dorsey Brothers orchestra plays college date at Princeton. Personnel: Bunny Berigan (trumpet); Bix (cornet); Tommy Dorsey (trombone); Jimmy Dorsey, Artie Shaw, Eddie Miller (reeds); Carl Kress (guitar); Terry Shand (piano); Min Leibrook (bass sax); Ray Bauduc or Gene Krupa (drums). Bix experiences circulation trouble during the ride home, must be helped to his room.

**May 14** (Thu)—Bix and O'Keefe visit Casa Loma at Cook's Butterfly Ballroom, Springfield, Massachusetts.

**May 15** (Fri)—Dorsey Brothers orchestra plays Derby Day festivities at Beta Theta Phi house, Yale, from 9 P.M. to 4 A.M. Personnel: Berigan; Bix; T. Dorsey; J. Dorsey; Shaw, Miller; Jules Bauduc (banjo); Leibrook; Lennie Hayton (piano); Bauduc or Krupa (drums).

**May 22** (Fri)—Bix joins the Casa Loma Orchestra at the Metropolitan Hotel in Boston. Personnel: Bobby Jones, Dub Schoefner, Joe Hostetter (trumpets); Billy Rauch, Walter "Pee Wee" Hunt (trombones); Spike (Glen Gray) Knoblauch, Ray Eberle (alto saxes); Pat Davis (tenor sax); Howard "Joe Horse" Hall (piano); Gene Gifford (guitar, banjo and arranger); Stan Dennis (bass); Tony Briglia (drums); Mel Jenssen (violin and conductor); Jack Richman (vocals).

**May 23** (Sat)—Casa Loma plays at Wilbur's-on-the-Taunton ballroom, Taunton, Massachusetts.

**May 24** (Sun)—Bix remains in his hotel room all day.

**May 25** (Mon)—Bix leaves the orchestra, returns to New York.

**June 10** (Wed)—Benny Goodman group travels to Williams College in Williamstown, Massachusetts for two days of engagements, beginning with 4 P.M. party at Phi Gamma Delta fraternity house. Bix and Tommy Dorsey fly up. Personnel: Charlie Spivak (trumpet); Bix (cornet); Dorsey (trombone); Irving "Babe" Russin (tenor sax); at least one other saxophone; Goodman (alto sax and clarinet); Irving Brodsky (piano); guitar, bass, drums forgotten.

**June 11** (Thu)—Goodman group plays Sophomore Prom at Williams from 10 P.M. until 5 A.M. in Lasell Gymnasium.

**June 14** (Sun)—Party at Dick Turner's uncle's apartment, 1 West 72nd Street, New York, eventually moving on to Bill Challis' sister's place, West 81st and Riverside Drive. Among those present: Bix, Bill Priestley, Squirrel Ashcraft, Turner, Eddie Condon.

**June 15** (Mon)—Some reports place Bix and Tommy Dorsey with a band led by singer Smith Ballew for a Princeton University sophomore prom, 10 P.M. to 5 A.M. The authors are unable to corroborate this. But it is known that sometime during this or the following week Bix sits in with Ballew's band at Salzman's Restaurant.

**c. June 22–25** (Mon-Thu)—Bix moves out of 44th Street Hotel and in with Ballew's bassist, Rex Gavitte, at 24–60 32nd Street, Astoria, Queens. At about this time he spends an evening with Hoagy Carmichael at a friend's house and mentions that he has just met a girl who interests him.

**c. end of June or early July**—Bix moves into ground floor of new apartment building at 43–30 46th Street, Sunnyside, Queens.

**c. July 14–15** (Tue-Wed)—Bix and Helen Weiss, his new girl, visit Hoagy Carmichael's apartment at 114 East 57th Street. According to Hoagy, Bix "was looking good." Carmichael warns her to "call me if anything happens."

**Aug. 3** (Mon)—Bix telephones Red Nichols in state of despondency, speaks to Red's wife Bobbi.

**Aug. 4** (Tue)—Bix ill, treated by Dr. John J. Haberski, a resident of his building.

**Aug. 6** (Thu)—Bix Beiderbecke dies at 9:30 P.M. in his apartment. Cause of death: lobar pneumonia, with edema of the brain. From the account of his death given by George Kraslow, rental agent for the building, and by Haberski himself, it is easily inferred that Bix died in a seizure of delirium tremens. Earlier in the day, his family in Davenport received a telephone call from Frank Trumbauer, then appearing with the Whiteman orchestra at the Edgewater Beach Hotel in Chicago. Trumbauer had received a call from New York earlier, from which it was apparent that Beiderbecke was gravely ill. Trumbauer urged Charles Beiderbecke, to whom he spoke, to go to New York at once. Both Burnie and Agatha Beiderbecke left on a 3:40 P.M. train for New York, but Bix died while they were still en route.

**Aug. 11** (Tue)—Bix Beiderbecke buried at Oakdale Cemetery, Davenport. Pallbearers: George Von Maur, Louis Best, Karl Vollmer Jr., William Henigbaum Jr. and Dr. John Wormley.

# Appendix B

# BIX BEIDERBECKE ON RECORD

*A Comprehensive Discography*

*by*

Philip R. Evans
& William Dean-Myatt

*Musical Notations of Excerpts from*
*Bix Beiderbecke's Most Famous Cornet Improvisations*
*by Richard M. Sudhalter*

# ABBREVIATIONS OF RECORD LABELS

|     | Banner |
| Bm | Biltmore |
| Br | Brunswick |
| BRS | British Rhythm Society |
| Bwy | Broadway (LP) |
| Cl | Clarion |
| Col | Columbia |
| Cx | Claxtonola |
|     | Davon |
|     | Decatur |
| Dec | Decca |
|     | Diva |
|     | Domino |
| EBW | Edison Bell Winner |
| El | Electrola |
| Gnt | Gennett |
| Gr | Gramophon |
| Har | Harmony |
| HJCA | Hot Jazz Clubs of America |
| HMV | His Masters Voice |
| HRS | Hot Record Society |
|     | Imperial |
| Jcl | Jazz Classics |
|     | Jewel |
|     | Kismet |
| LO | London (LP) |
|     | Lucky |
| MT | Melotone |
| NAT | Natchez |
| Od | Odeon |
| OK | Okeh |
|     | Oriole |
| PA | Pathe Actuelle |
| Par | Parlophon(e) |
| Per | Perfect |
|     | Poydras |
| RCA | Radio Corporation of America |
|     | Raretone Reeditions Hot |
| Re | Regal |
| Res | Reissue |
| RIV | Riverside (LP) |
|     | Sentry |
| Ses | Session |
|     | Special Editions |
|     | Starr |
| Tem | Tempo |
| Tpl | Temple |
| UHCA | United Hot Clubs of America |
| VdP | Voce del Padrone |
| Vic | Victor |
| Vic "x" | Victor "X" |
| VJR | Vintage Jazz Reissues |
| Voc | Vocalion |
| VT | Velvetone |

# COUNTRIES OF ISSUE

| Am | America |
| Arg | Argentina |
| Au | Australia |
|     | Brazil |
| C | Canada |
| Ch | Chile |
| Cz | Czechoslovakia |
| E | England |
| Fin | Finland |
| Fr | France |
| G | Germany |
| H | Holland |
| In | India |
| Ir | Irish |
| It | Italy |
| N | Norway |
| Sp | Spain |
| Ss | Switzerland |
| Sw | Sweden |

## NOTE:

Victor matrix numbers beginning with the prefix BVE are 10-inch (25 cm.) records; those prefixed CVE are 12-inch (30 cm.). Columbia matrix numbers beginning W–98000 et seq. are 12-inch (30 cm.) records.

# ABBREVIATIONS OF INSTRUMENTS

| | |
|---|---|
| as | Alto Saxophone |
| bar | Baritone Saxophone |
| bb | Brass Bass (Tuba or Sousaphone) |
| bcl | Bass Clarinet |
| bj | Banjo |
| bsn | Bassoon |
| bsx | Bass Saxophone |
| c | Cornet |
| cel | Celeste |
| | Cimbalom |
| cl | Clarinet |
| C-m | C-Melody Saxophone |
| d | Drums |
| Ebcl | E Flat Clarinet |
| EngHorn | English Horn |
| f | Flute |
| g | Guitar |
| | Heckelphone |
| | Kazoo |
| o | Oboe |
| p | Piano |
| p-ac | Piano Accordion |
| perc | Percussion |
| pic | Piccolo |
| p-o | Pipe Organ |
| sb | String Bass |
| | Slide Whistle |
| ss | Soprano Saxophone |
| stg | Steel (Hawaiian) Guitar |
| t | Trumpet |
| tb | Trombone |
| ts | Tenor Saxophone |
| va | Viola |
| vn | Violin |

NOTE: Issue numbers in Roman type are master pressings.
Those in italics are dubs.

**1924:**

| | | |
|---|---|---|
| *Feb 18 (Mon)* | | **WOLVERINE ORCHESTRA**<br>*Starr Piano Co. Gennett Studios*<br>*Richmond, Indiana*<br>Bix Beiderbecke (c); Jimmy Hartwell (cl); Al Gandee (tb); George Johnson (ts); Dick Voynow (p); Bob Gillette (bj); Min Leibrook (bb); Vic Moore (d). |
| | 11751 | **Fidgety Feet** (LaRocca-Shields)<br>*Instrumental* |
| | 11751 | Rejected. |
| | 11751–A | Mastered: Gnt 5408; *HRS 22; BrE 02204; HJCA HC–120; Tpl 546; DecE BM–02204; DecCz BM–02204.* |
| | 11751–B | Rejected. |
| | 11751–C | Rejected. |
| | 11752 | **Lazy Daddy** (LaRocca-Shields-Ragas)<br>*Instrumental* |
| | 11752 | Rejected. |
| | 11752–A | Rejected. |
| | 11752–B | Rejected. |
| | 11753 | **Sensation Rag** (ODJB)<br>*Instrumental* |
| | 11753 | Rejected. |
| | 11753–A | Rejected. |
| | 11754 | **Jazz Me Blues** (Delaney)<br>*Instrumental* |
| | 11754 | Rejected. |
| | 11754–A | Mastered: Gnt 5408; *HRS 25; BrE 02203; HJCA HC–120; Tpl 546; DecE BM–02203; DecCz BM–02203.* |

| | | |
|---|---|---|
| *May 6 (Tue)* | | **WOLVERINE ORCHESTRA**<br>*Starr Piano Co. Gennett Studios*<br>*Richmond, Indiana*<br>Bix Beiderbecke (c); Jimmy Hartwell (cl); George Johnson (ts); Dick Voynow (p); Bob Gillette (bj); Min Leibrook (bb); Vic Moore (d). |
| | 11852 | **Oh Baby** (Donaldson-deSylva)<br>*Instrumental* |
| | 11852 | Mastered: Gnt 5453; Cx 40336; *HRS 25; Tpl 554; BrE 02501; DecE BM–02501; DecCz BM–02501.* |
| | 11852–A | Rejected. |
| | 11852–B | Rejected.<br>*Gillette switches to guitar.* |
| | 11853 | **Copenhagen** (Davis-Melrose)<br>*Instrumental* |
| | 11853 | Mastered: Gnt 5453; Cx 40336; *Tpl 554; UHCA 46; BrE 02205; DecE BM–02205; DecCz BM–02205.* |
| | 11853–A | Rejected. |
| | 11853–B | Rejected.<br>*Gillette again on banjo.* |
| | 11854 | **Riverboat Shuffle** (Carmichael-Voynow-Mills)<br>*Instrumental* |
| | 11854 | Rejected. |
| | 11854–A | Rejected. |
| | 11854–B | Rejected. |
| | 11854–C | Mastered: Gnt 5454; Cx 40339; *VJR 19; HRS 9; HRS *; TemE R–44; Tpl 536.* |
| | 11855 | **Susie (of the Islands)** (Naset-Kahn)<br>*Instrumental* |
| | 11855 | Rejected. |
| | 11855–A | Mastered: Gnt 5454; Cx 40339; *TemE R–44; Tpl 536; VJR 19.* |

**1924:**

| | |
|---|---|
| 11855–B | Mastered: Gnt 5454. |
| **11856** | **Royal Garden Blues** (Williams-Williams) |
| | *Instrumental* |
| 11856 | Rejected. |

Note: July 1938 issue of HRS * has no catalogue number. All Claxtonola issues as by "The Jazz Harmonists." Only three copies are known to exist of the 'B' master of "Susie."

*Jun 20 (Fri)*   WOLVERINE ORCHESTRA
*Starr Piano Co. Gennett Studios*
*Richmond, Indiana*
Bix Beiderbecke (c); Jimmy Hartwell (cl); George Johnson (ts); Dick Voynow (p); Bob Gillette (bj); Min Leibrook (bb); Vic Berton (d).

| | |
|---|---|
| **11930** | **I Need Some Pettin'** (King-Fio Rito-Kahn) |
| | *Instrumental* |
| 11930 | Rejected. |
| 11930–A | Rejected. |
| 11930–B | Mastered: Gnt 20062; *Re-editions Hot R–1001.* |
| **11931** | **Royal Garden Blues** (Williams-Williams) |
| | *Instrumental* |
| 11931 | Rejected. |
| 11931–A | Rejected. |
| 11931–B | Rejected. |
| 11931–C | Mastered: Gnt 20062; *HRS 26; BrE 02204; Tpl 524; DecE BM–02204; DecCz BM–02204.* |
| **11932** | **Tiger Rag** (La Rocca) |
| | *Instrumental* |
| 11932 | Mastered (Cracked): *BrE 02205; DecE BM–02205; DecCz BM–02205; HRS 24; Tpl 524; PolJap 15387.* |
| | Mastered (Uncracked): all LP issues - *Riv LP–1050; Riv 12–123; Triton 101/2; LoE AL–3543; LoGe AL–3543.* |

Note: Although two different pressings of "Tiger Rag" exist, only one take was made. Early copies of Delauney's "Hot Discography" refer to an unissued master of "China Boy." This does not exist and is in fact a mistake on the part of Vic Moore. The originally-used test belonged to Edwin "Squirrel" Ashcraft and was dropped and cracked by him while he was taking it to the Brunswick Studios; in view of its extreme rarity it was decided that it be used nevertheless. The uncracked test used for the LP issues comes from the collection of J. Robert Mantler.

*Sept 16 (Tue)*   WOLVERINE ORCHESTRA
*Starr Piano Co. Gennett Studios*
*New York City*
Bix Beiderbecke (c); George Brunies (tb); Jimmy Hartwell (cl); George Johnson (ts); Dick Voynow (p); Bob Gillette (bj); Min Leibrook (bb); Vic Moore (d).

| | |
|---|---|
| **9079** | **Sensation** (Edwards) |
| | *Instrumental* |
| 9079 | Mastered: Gnt 5542; Cx 40375; StarrCan 9598; 9595; *HRS 23; VJR 8; TemE R–45; Poydras MJC–13.* |
| 9079–A | Rejected. |
| 9079–B | Rejected. |
| | *Brunies plays kazoo solo on "Lazy Daddy"* |
| **9080** | **Lazy Daddy** (LaRocca-Shields-Ragas) |
| | *Instrumental* |
| 9080 | Rejected. |
| 9080–A | Mastered: Gnt 5542; StarrCan 9598; 9595; *HRS 9; HRS *; BRS 8.* |
| 9080–B | Mastered: Gnt 5542; Cx 40375; *TemE R–45; VJR 8; Poydras MJC–13.* |

Note: July 1938 issue of HRS * does not bear a catalogue number. All Claxtonola issues as by "The Jazz Harmonists."

Oct 8 (Wed)     **WOLVERINE ORCHESTRA**
*Starr Piano Co. Gennett Studios*
*New York City*
Bix Beiderbecke (c); Jimmy Hartwell (cl); George Johnson (ts); Dick Voynow (p); Bob Gillette (bj); Min Leibrook (bb); Vic Moore (d).

| | |
|---|---|
| **9115** | **Tia Juana** (Rodemich-Conley) |
| | *Instrumental* |
| 9115 | Rejected. |
| 9115–A | Rejected. |
| 9115–B | Mastered: Gnt 5565; *HRS 26; Tpl 552.* |
| **9116** | **Big Boy** (Ager-Yellen) |
| | *Instrumental* |
| 9116 | Mastered: Gnt 5565; *HRS 24; Tpl 552; BrE 02203; DecE BM–02203; DecCz BM–02203.* |
| 9116–A | Rejected. |

*Beiderbecke plays piano solo on "Big Boy."*

Oct. 11 (Sat)     **SIOUX CITY SIX**
*Starr Piano Co. Gennett Studios*
*New York City*
Bix Beiderbecke (c); Miff Mole (tb); Frank Trumbauer (C-Mel); Rube Bloom (p); Min Leibrook (bb); Vic Moore (d).

| | |
|---|---|
| **9119** | **Flock o' Blues** (Bloom) |
| | *Instrumental* |
| 9119 | Rejected. |
| 9119–A | Mastered: Gnt 5569; *Ses 7; Res 7; BrE 02207; DecE BM–02207; DecCz BM–02207.* |
| 9119–B | Rejected. |
| **9120** | **I'm Glad** (Trumbauer) |
| | *Instrumental* |
| 9120 | Rejected. |
| 9120–A | Rejected. |
| 9120–B | Rejected. |
| 9120–C | Mastered: Gnt 5569; *Ses 7; Res 7; BrE 02207; DecCz BM–02207; DecCz BM–02207.* |

Note: Gennett file card lists "under the direction of Frank Trumbauer."

Nov 24 (Mon)     **JEAN GOLDKETTE AND HIS ORCHESTRA**
*Victor Record Co. portable equipment at Detroit Athletic Club*
*Detroit, Michigan*
*Eddie King, Recording Director*
Fred "Fuzzy" Farrar, Tex Brusstar (t); Bix Beiderbecke (c); Bill Rank, Tommy Dorsey (tb); Stanley "Doc" Ryker, Don Murray, George Williams (saxes); Paul Mertz (p); Howdy Quicksell (bj); Irish Henry (bb); Joe Venuti (vn); Charles Horvath (d).

| | |
|---|---|
| **BVE 31206** | **I Didn't Know** (Williams-Jones—Stock Orchestration) |
| | *Instrumental* |
| BVE 31206–1 | Destroyed. |
| BVE 31206–2 | *Vic LPM–2323(LP)* |
| BVE 31206–3 | Destroyed. |
| BVE 31206–4 | Hold conditional. Never issued. |
| BVE 31206–5 | Hold 30 days. Never issued. |
| | Soloists: Bix (16), Venuti (16). |
| | *Bix does not appear on the other titles from this session.* |
| BVE 31207 | I Want to See My Tennessee (Yellen-Ager) |
| BVE 31208 | Remember (Berlin) |

Nov 25 (Tue)     **JEAN GOLDKETTE AND HIS ORCHESTRA**
*Victor Record Co. portable equipment at Detroit Athletic Club*
*Detroit, Michigan*
*Eddie King, Recording Director*
Fred Farrar, Tex Brusstar (t); Bix Beiderbecke (c); Bill Rank, Tommy Dorsey (tb); Doc Ryker, Don Murray, George Williams

|  |  |
|---|---|
|  | (saxes); Joe Venuti, _____ Gorner (vn); Paul Mertz (p); Howdy Quicksell (bj); Irish Henry (bb); Charles Horvath (d). |
| BVE 31212 | **Adoration** (Borowski—arr. George Crozier) |
|  | *Instrumental* |
| BVE 31212–1 | Hold conditional. Never issued. |
| BVE 31212–2 | Destroyed. |
| BVE 31212–3 | Destroyed. |
| BVE 31212–4 | Hold conditional. Never issued. |
|  | *Bix does not appear on the other titles from this session.* |
| BVE 31209 | Play Me Slow (Hagan-O'Flynn) |
| BVE 31210 | Honest and Truly (Fred Rose) |
| BVE 31211 | What's the Use of Dreaming |

*Dec 17 (Wed)*      **MARION MCKAY AND HIS ORCHESTRA**
*Starr Piano Co.*
*Gennett Studios*
*Richmond, Indiana*
Bix Beiderbecke (c); unknown t; tb; saxes; p; bj; bb; Jack Tillson (d).

|  |  |
|---|---|
| **12108** | **Honest and Truly** (Rose) |
|  | *Instrumental* |
| 12108–B | Mastered: Gnt 3045; Gnt 5615; EBW 4198. |
| **12109** | **Doo Wacka Doo** (Gaskill-Donaldson-Horther) |
|  | *Instrumental* |
| 12109 | Mastered: Gnt 3045; Gnt 5615. |
|  | Soloist: Bix (16) |
|  | Note: EBW 4198 as "The Pavilion Players." Only one trumpet can be heard, reading the arrangement, on 12108–B. Bix appears *only* on "Doo Wacka Doo." |

**1925:**

*Jan 26 (Mon)*      **BIX BEIDERBECKE AND HIS RHYTHM JUGGLERS**
*Starr Piano Co. Gennett Studios*
*Richmond, Indiana*
Bix Beiderbecke (c); Don Murray (cl); Tommy Dorsey (tb); Paul Mertz (p); Tommy Gargano (d); Howdy Quicksell (bj) on last two titles only.

|  |  |
|---|---|
| **12140** | **Toddlin' Blues** (LaRocca-Shields) |
|  | *Instrumental* |
| 12140 | Mastered: Gnt 5654; *HRS 23; Ses 6; Res 6; BrE 02501; DecE BM–02501; DecCz BM–02501.* |
| 12140–A | Rejected. "Pop dent." |
| 12140–B | Rejected. "Destroyed." |
| 12140–C | Rejected. "Lined out." |
| **12141** | **Davenport Blues** (Beiderbecke) |
|  | *Instrumental* |
| 12141 | Mastered: Gnt 5654; *HRS 22; Ses 6; Res 6; BrE 02206; DecE BM–02206; DecCz BM–02206.* |
| 12141–A | Rejected. "Pop dent." |
| 12141–B | Rejected. "Pop dent." |
| **12142** | **Magic Blues** (Unknown) |
|  | *Instrumental* |
| 12142 | Rejected. "Starting to pop. Line defect. Center pop." |
| 12142–A | Rejected. "3 pops big. Several small." |
| 12142–B | Rejected. "Best. Slight Line Defects. Slight pops" |
| **12143** | **No One Knows What It's All About** (Rose-Woods) |
|  | *Instrumental* |
| 12143 | Rejected. "Don't use." |
| 12143–A | Rejected. "Best." |
| 12143–B | Rejected. (No reason noted.) |
|  | Note: Gennett recording file card lists session as by "Leon B. Beiderbecke and his Orchestra." |
|  | Note: Stories have persisted throughout the years to the effect that Bix accompanied Red Nichols to a recording date and took part during the time in March, 1925, when the two were staying together at the Pasadena Hotel in New York. To this end, |

we offer a listing of all recordings known involving Red Nichols between Wednesday, March 11, 1925, and Monday, March 16. The authors invite further information from readers about these sessions.

*March 11 (Wed)*  JENE BAILEY AND HIS ORCHESTRA
(Sam Lanin and His Orchestra)
*Starr Piano Co. Gennett Studios*
*New York City*

9400    All Aboard for Heaven    GE 5681; GE 3013
9401    Moonlight and Roses      GE 5681

*March 12 (Thu)*  SAM LANIN AND HIS ORCHESTRA
*Pathe Record Co.*
*E. 53rd St. Studio*
*New York City*

105905   All Aboard for Heaven    PER 14400
105906   Don't Bring Lulu         PER 14415

*March 13 (Fri)*  THE MELODY SHEIKS
*Okeh Record Co.*
*New York City*

73236    All Aboard for Heaven    OK 40341
73237    Lady of the Nile         OK 40341

*March 15 (Sun)*  MIKE SPECIALE AND HIS ORCHESTRA
*Pathe Record Co.*
*E. 53rd St. Studio*
*New York City*

105910   Breakin' the Leg         PER 14405
105911   So Am I                  PER 14402
105912   We're Back Together      PER 14406
           Again

*March 16 (Mon)*  THE GOOFUS FIVE
*Okeh Record Co.*
*New York*
Red Nichols (c); Bobby Davis (cl/as/ss); Adrian Rollini (bsx/gfs); Irving Brodsky (p); Tommy Felline (bj); Stan King (d/kazoo). Vocal by Ernest Hare

73238–B  I Had Someone Else Before
           I Had You              OK 40340; Od 03036
73239–B  I Like You Best of       OK 40340; Od 03036
           All

*Oct 12 (Tue)*  JEAN GOLDKETTE AND HIS ORCHESTRA
*Victor Record Co.*
*New York City*
*Eddie King, Recording Director*
Time: 1:30 P.M. – 5:25 P.M.
Fred Farrar, Ray Lodwig (t); Bix Beiderbecke (c); Bill Rank, Newell "Spiegle" Willcox (tb); Doc Ryker, Frank Trumbauer, Don Murray (reeds); Irving Riskin (p); Howdy Quicksell (bj); Eddie Lang (g); Joe Venuti (vn); Steve Brown (sb); Chauncey Morehouse (d).

**BVE 36813**   **Idolizing** (Messenheimer-Abrahamson-West—arr. Bill Challis)
*Vocal: Frank Bessinger*
Released: Feb 4, 1927
Sales: 123,770

BVE 36813–1   Hold 30 days. *Issued NAT WEP–804.*
BVE 36813–2   Mastered: Vic 20270; HMVAu EA–152.
BVE 36813–3   Destroyed.
BVE 36813–4   Destroyed.
Soloists: Bix (16); Lang (32 obligato); Farrar (8); Venuti (8).

| BVE 36814 | I'd Rather Be the Girl in Your Arms (Thompson-Archer—arr. Bill Challis) |
| --- | --- |
| | *Vocal: Frank Magine; Joe Griffith; Frank Marvin.* |
| BVE 36814–1 | Destroyed. |
| BVE 36814–2 | Destroyed. |
| BVE 36814–3 | Destroyed. |
| BVE 36814–4 | Destroyed. |
| **BVE 36815** | **Hush-A-Bye** (Waltz) (Galvin-Spencer—arr. Bill Challis) |
| | *Vocal: Frank Bessinger* |
| | Released: Feb 4, 1927 |
| | Sales: 123,770 |
| BVE 36815–1 | Hold 30 days. Never Issued. |
| BVE 36815–2 | Mastered. Vic 20270; HMVAu EA–151. |
| BVE 36815–3 | Destroyed. |
| BVE 36815–4 | Destroyed. |

Oct 15 (Fri)

**JEAN GOLDKETTE AND HIS ORCHESTRA**
*Victor Record Co.*
*New York City*
*Eddie King, Recording Director*
*Time: 10:00 A.M. – 2:30 P.M.*
*        3:00 P.M. – 5:20 P.M.*
Fred Farrar, Ray Lodwig (t); Bix Beiderbecke (c); Bill Rank, Spiegle Willcox (tb); Doc Ryker, Frank Trumbauer, Don Murray (reeds); Irving Riskin (p); Howdy Quicksell (bj); Joe Venuti (vn); Steve Brown (sb); Chauncey Morehouse (d); Eddie Lang (g) on 36829 and 36814 only.

| **BVE 36829** | **Sunday** (Miller-Cohn-Stein-Kreuger—arr. Bill Challis) |
| --- | --- |
| | *Vocal: Keller Sisters and Lynch.* |
| | Released: Dec 3, 1926 |
| | Sales: 137,856 |
| BVE 36829–1 | Destroyed. |
| BVE 36829–2 | Hold 30 days. Issued *Vic LPM–2323*. |
| BVE 36829–3 | Mastered. Vic 20273; VicC 20273; HMVAu EA–174; GrFr K–5095; ElGe EG–357; HMVSw X–2656 |
| BVE 36829–4 | Destroyed. |
| | Soloists: Rank (16); Rank & Venuti (8); Lang (8); Murray (8). |

| **BVE 36830** | **Cover Me Up with Sunshine** (Dixon-Henderson—arr. Eddy Sheasby (?) |
| --- | --- |
| | *Vocal: Frank Bessinger* |
| | Released: May 20, 1927 |
| | Sales: 38,869 |
| BVE 36830–1 | Hold 30 days. Never issued. |
| BVE 36830–2 | Mastered. Vic 20588. |
| BVE 36830–3 | Destroyed. |
| BVE 36830–4 | Destroyed. |
| | Soloists: Willcox & Venuti (8). |

**1926:**

**BVE 36814**    **I'd Rather Be the Girl in Your Arms** (Thompson-Archer—arr. Bill Challis)
*Vocal: Frank Bessinger*
Released: Dec 3, 1926
Sales: 137,856
BVE 36814–5   Destroyed.
BVE 36814–6   Hold conditional. Never issued.
BVE 36814–7   Destroyed.
BVE 36814–8   Mastered. Vic 20273; VicC 20273; HMVAu EA–194; GrFr K–5095; ElGe EG–357.
      Soloists: Venuti (2 + 16); Willcox (8); Venuti (8); Trumbauer (8).

**BVE 36831**    **Just One More Kiss** (Owens-Montgomery—arr. Eddy Sheasby)
*Vocal: Al Lynch*
Released: Nov 4, 1926
Sales: 24,815
BVE 36831–1   Destroyed.
BVE 36831–2   Hold 30 days. Issued *Raretone RTR 24008(LP)*.
BVE 36831–3   Destroyed.
BVE 36831–4   Mastered. Vic 20300.
      *Titles given in exact order of recording.*

**1927:**

*Jan 28 (Fri)*

JEAN GOLDKETTE AND HIS ORCHESTRA
*Victor Record Co.*
*New York City*
*Leroy Shield, Recording Director*
*Time: 9:30 A.M. – 1:40 P.M.*
Fred Farrar, Ray Lodwig (t); Bix Beiderbecke (c); Bill Rank, Spiegle Willcox (tb); Doc Ryker, Frank Trumbauer, Jimmy Dorsey (saxes); Paul Mertz (p); Howdy Quicksell (bj); Joe Venuti (vn); Steve Brown (sb); Chauncey Morehouse (d).

**BVE 37579**    **Proud of a Baby Like You** (Schoenberg-Stevens-Helmick—arr. Bill Challis)
*Vocal: Keller Sisters and Lynch*
Released: Feb 8, 1927
Sales: 9,353
BVE 37579–1   Hold 30 days. Issued Vic "X" LVA–3017; Vic "X" EVA–9.
BVE 37579–2   Destroyed.
BVE 37579–3   Destroyed.
BVE 37579–4   Mastered. Vic 20469.
      Soloists: Farrar (4); Bix (16).

**BVE 37580**    **I'm Looking Over a Four Leaf Clover** (Dixon-Woods—arr. Bill Challis)
*Vocal: Billy Murray*
Released: March 11, 1927
Sales: 109,810
BVE 37580–1   Hold conditional. Issued *Bwy 102 (LP)*.

| | |
|---|---|
| BVE 37580–2 | Destroyed. |
| BVE 37580–3 | Destroyed. |
| BVE 37580–4 | Mastered. Vic 20466; HMVAu EA–163. |

Soloists: Venuti (16); Trumbauer? (8); Venuti (8); Dorsey (2); Bix (32 in ensemble, with break).

*Jan 31 (Mon)*

**JEAN GOLDKETTE AND HIS ORCHESTRA**
*Victor Record Co.*
*New York City*
*Nat Shilkret, Recording Director*
*Time: 1:45 P.M. – 5:20 P.M.*
Fred Farrar, Ray Lodwig (t); Bix Beiderbecke (c); Bill Rank, Spiegle Willcox (tb); Doc Ryker, Frank Trumbauer, Jimmy Dorsey (reeds); Paul Mertz (p); Howdy Quicksell (bj); Joe Venuti (vn); Steve Brown (sb); Chauncey Morehouse (d).

**BVE 37583**    **I'm Gonna Meet My Sweetie Now** (Davis-Greer—arr. Challis)
*Instrumental*
Released: (-2) Dec 8, 1927
Sales: 179,929
Released (-3) July 1, 1936

| | |
|---|---|
| BVE 37583–1 | Destroyed |
| BVE 37583–2 | Vic 20675; VicC 20675; HMV B–5363; VicJ 20675. |
| BVE 37583–3 | Hold 30 days. Issued Vic 25354. |

Soloists: Trumbauer (16); Rank (8); Dorsey (16 baritone); Venuti (16); Willcox (8); Venuti (8); Bix (16 in ensemble); Dorsey (8 clarinet).

**BVE 37584**    **Hoosier Sweetheart** (Goodwin-Ash-Baskette—arr. Challis)
*Vocal: Ray Muerer*
Released: March 18, 1927
Sales: 110,995

| | |
|---|---|
| BVE 37584–1 | Hold conditional. Never issued. |
| BVE 37584–2 | Mastered: Vic 20471; ElGe EG–455; HMVAu EA–157. |
| BVE 37584–3 | Destroyed. |
| BVE 37584–4 | Destroyed. |

Soloists: Bix (4 + 2); Trumbauer (16 + 8); Rank (8).

*Feb 1 (Tue)*

**JEAN GOLDKETTE AND HIS ORCHESTRA**
*Victor Record Co.*
*New York City*
*Nat Shilkret, Recording Director*
*Time: 1:45 P.M. – 5:00 P.M.*
Fred Farrar, Ray Lodwig (t); Bix Beiderbecke (c); Bill Rank, Spiegle Willcox (tb); Doc Ryker, Frank Trumbauer, Danny Polo (reeds); Paul Mertz (p); Howdy Quicksell (bj); Joe Venuti, Eddy Sheasby (vn); Steve Brown (sb); Chauncey Morehouse (d); Eddie Lang (g) on 37586 only.

**BVE 37586**    **Look at the World and Smile** (Caldwell-Hubbell—arr. Sheasby)
*Instrumental*
Released: March 18, 1927
Sales: 64,748

| | |
|---|---|
| BVE 37586–1 | Destroyed. Issued *Bwy 102 (LP)*—from test pressing. |
| BVE 37586–2 | Mastered. Vic 20472. |
| BVE 37586–3 | Hold 30 days. Issued *Bwy 102 (LP)*. |
| BVE 37586–4 | Destroyed. |

Soloists: Willcox (16 + 8); Venuti & Lang (16); Bix (16 in ensemble).

**BVE 37587**

**My Pretty Girl** (Fulcher—arr. Murray-Riskin-Challis-Dorsey from stock)
*Instrumental*
Released: May 20, 1927
Sales(-1): 38,869

BVE 37587–1    Mastered: Vic 20588; *Vic 25283; VicArg 25283;* HMV B–5324; *HMV B–9237; Jazz Classic 531;* HMVIn B–5324; *HMVIn B9237;* HMVAu EA–3617; GrFr K–5212; *ElGe EG–3856; HMVAu EA–1706.*

BVE 37587–2    Hold 30 days. Issued Vic "X" LVA–3017.

Soloists: Polo (32); Trumbauer (2 break); Rank (2 break); Venuti (8 + 8); Trumbauer (8).

Note: The original stock arrangement of "My Pretty Girl" was reworked by Don Murray. Bill Challis added additional instrumentation and Irving Riskin took Bix's chorus on the Murray arrangement and turned it into a three-trumpet chorus. Finally, Jimmy Dorsey did the ending, Bix faking harmony with a trombone lead.

**BVE 37588**

**Stampede** (Henderson—arr. Don Redman)
*Instrumental*
BVE 37588–1    Hold conditional. Never issued.
BVE 37588–2    Hold Conditional. Never issued.
Soloists: Bix, Trumbauer, Rank, Bix.

*Feb 3 (Thu)*

JEAN GOLDKETTE AND HIS ORCHESTRA
*Victor Record Co.*
*New York City*
*Nat Shilkret, Recording Director*
*Time: 1:45 P.M. – 5:00 P.M.*
Fred Farrar, Ray Lodwig (t); Bix Beiderbecke (c); Bill Rank, Spiegle Willcox (tb); Doc Ryker, Frank Trumbauer, Danny Polo (reeds), Paul Mertz (p); Howdy Quicksell (bj); Eddie Lang (g); Joe Venuti (vn); Steve Brown (sb); Chauncey Morehouse (d).

**BVE 37738**

**A Lane in Spain** (Lewis-Lombardo—arr. Challis)
*Vocal: The Revelers—Charles Harrison (1st tenor), Lewis James (2nd tenor), Elliot Shaw (baritone), Wilfred Glenn (bass).*
Released: April 8, 1927
Sales: 70,349

BVE 37738–1    Hold 30 days. Never issued. Test pressing known to exist.
BVE 37738–2    Destroyed.
BVE 37738–3    Mastered: Vic 20491; VicC 20491; HMVAu EA–195.
Soloists: Lang (4); Venuti (16); Farrar (8).

**BVE 37599**    **Sunny Disposish** (Gershwin-Charig—arr. Murray)

**1927:**

*Vocal: The Revelers*
Released: April 29, 1927
Sales: 31,328

BVE 37599–1  Destroyed.
BVE 37599–2  Hold 30 days. Issued RCA LPV 545 (LP).
BVE 37599–3  Mastered: Vic 20493; HMV B–5289; HMVAu EA–170.
Soloists: Polo (8 + 8 in ensemble)
Note: Guitar plays through vocal break "...I'm on my way..." in (–3), but breaks off clean in (–2). Only discernible difference.

*Feb 4 (Fri)*    **FRANK TRUMBAUER AND HIS ORCHESTRA**
*Okeh Record Co.*
*New York City*
Bix Beiderbecke (c); Frank Trumbauer (C-m); Jimmy Dorsey (cl/as); Bill Rank (tb); Paul Mertz (p); Eddie Lang (g); Chauncey Morehouse (d).

W 80391    **Trumbology** (Trumbauer—arr. Paul Mertz)
*Instrumental*
W 80391–A  Rejected.
W 80391–B  Rejected.
W 80391–C  Mastered: OK 40871; ParE R–3419; ParE R–2465; OdFr 165171; OdGe A–189128; ParSs PZ–11245; Col 36280.
*Doc Ryker (as) added for 80392 and 80393*

W 80392    **Clarinet Marmalade** (Shields-Ragas)
*Instrumental*
W 80392–A  Mastered: OK 40772; VOC 4412; Voc 3010; ParE R–3323; ParE R–2304; ParAu A–7534; OdArg 193001; OdArg 194718; OdG A–189019; OdG A–286089; *Col 37804;* OdFr 165093
W 80392–B  Rejected.
W 80392–C  Rejected.

W 80393    **Singin' the Blues** (Robinson-Conrad)
*Instrumental*
W 80393–A  Rejected.
W 80393–B  Mastered: OK 40772; Br 7703; ParE R–3323; ParE R–1838; ParAu A–6235; ParIt B–27597; ParIt TT–9073; OdFr 165093; OdArg 295124; OdG A189019; OdG A–286085; OdIt A–2409; ParSs PZ–11230; *LuckyJ 60175; Col 37804.*
W 80393–C  Rejected.

*May 6 (Fri)*    **JEAN GOLDKETTE AND HIS ORCHESTRA**
*Victor Record Co.*
*Camden, New Jersey (studio 3)*
*Eddy Sheasby, Recording Director*
*Time: 11:30 A.M. - 5:00 P.M.*
Fred Farrar, Ray Lodwig (t); Bix Beiderbecke (c); Bill Rank, Spiegle Willcox (tb); Doc Ryker, Frank Trumbauer, Don Murray (reeds); Irving Riskin (p); Howdy Quicksell (bj); Steve Brown (bs); Chauncey Morehouse (d).

BVE 38607    **Slow River** (Myers-Schwab—arr. Challis)
*Instrumental*
*Released: (–4) Oct 28, 1927 (–2) July 1, 1936*
BVE 38607–1  Destroyed.
BVE 38607–2  Hold indefinitely. Issued Vic 25354.
BVE 38607–3  Destroyed.
BVE 38607–4  Mastered: Vic 20926; VicJ 20926; HMV B–5397.
Soloists: Bix (8); Trumbauer (16 + 6); Bix (16 in ensembles); Willcox (8); Bix (6 in ensemble).

| | |
|---|---|
| *May 9 (Mon)* | FRANK TRUMBAUER AND HIS ORCHESTRA<br>*Okeh Record Co.*<br>*New York City*<br>Bix Beiderbecke (c); Bill Rank (tb); Frank Trumbauer (C-m)<br>Don Murray (cl/ts); Doc Ryker (as); Irving Riskin (p); Eddie<br>Lang (g); Chauncey Morehouse (d). |
| W 81071 | **Ostrich Walk** (LaRocca-Shields—arr. Challis)<br>*Instrumental* |
| W 81071–A | Rejected. |
| W 81071–B | Mastered: OK 40822; UHCA 29/30; ParE R–3349; ParE R–<br>2492; ParAu A–7555; ParG B–12501; OdFr 165126; OdArg<br>193015; OdArg 194718; OdG A–189048; ParSs PZ–11221; OdIt<br>A–2414; ParAm PNY–3349; ColGe C–6179; *Col 37805.* |
| W 81072 | **Riverboat Shuffle** (Carmichael-Voynow-Mills—arr. Challis)<br>*Instrumental* |
| W 81072–A | Rejected. |
| W 81072–B | Mastered: OK 40822; UHCA 29/30; ParE R–3349; ParE R–<br>2492; ParAu A–7555; ParG B–12501; OdFr 165126; OdArg<br>193015; OdArg 194786; ParSs PZ–11221; OdIt A–2409; ParAm<br>PNY–3349; *Col 37805;* OdG A189048. |
| *May 13 (Fri)* | FRANK TRUMBAUER AND HIS ORCHESTRA<br>*Okeh Record Co.*<br>*New York City*<br>Bix Beiderbecke (c); Bill Rank (tb); Frank Trumbauer (C-m);<br>Don Murray (clt/bar); Doc Ryker (as); Irving Riskin (p); Eddie<br>Lang (g); Chauncey Morehouse (d). |
| W 81083 | **I'm Coming Virginia** (Heywood—arr. Riskin)<br>*Instrumental* |
| W 81083–A | Rejected. |
| W 81083–B | Mastered: OK 40843; Br 7703; Col 36280; ColC C–6179; ParE<br>R–2687; ParE R–3361; OdIt A–2354; ColJ M–435; ParG A–4923;<br>OdFr 165134; OdArg 193050; *LuckyJ 60190;* ParSs PZ–11257;<br>OdG A–189060. |
| W 81084 | **Way Down Yonder in New Orleans** (Creamer-Layton—arr.<br>Murray)<br>*Instrumental* |
| W 81084–A | Rejected. |
| W 81084–B | Mastered: OK 40843; Voc 3010; Voc 4412; *Col 37806;* ParE<br>R–2687; ParE R–3361; OdFr 165134; OdIt A–2354; OdArg<br>193050; OdArg 194865; ParG A–4923; OdG A–189060; ParSs<br>PZ–11257; Col 39581. |
| *Same session:* | TRAM, BIX and LANG<br>Frank Trumbauer (C-m); Bix Beiderbecke (p/c); Eddie Lang<br>(g). |
| W 81085 | **For No Reason at All in C** (Meyer-Lewis-Young)<br>*Instrumental* |
| W 81085–A | Rejected |
| W 81085–B | Mastered: OK 40871; ParAu A–7459; ParE R–3419; ParE R–<br>2532; OdIt A–2338; OdFr 165171; OdG A–189128; Col 35667. |
| *May 16 (Mon)* | JEAN GOLDKETTE AND HIS ORCHESTRA<br>*Victor Record Co.*<br>*Camden, New Jersey (studio 3)*<br>*Time: 10.00 A.M. –12:00 P.M.*<br>Fred Farrar, Ray Lodwig (t); Bix Beiderbecke (c); Bill Rank,<br>Spiegle Willcox (tb); Doc Ryker, Frank Trumbauer, Don Mur-<br>ray (reeds); Irving Riskin (p); Howdy Quicksell (bj); Eddie Lang<br>(g); Steve Brown (sb); Joe Venuti (vn); Chauncey Morehouse<br>(d). |
| BVE 38263 | **Lily** (MacDonald-Warren-Broones—arr. Eddy Sheasby)<br>*Instrumental* |
| BVE 38263–1 | Destroyed. |
| BVE 38263–2 | Destroyed. |
| BVE 38263–3 | Destroyed. |
| BVE 38263–4 | Destroyed. |

Soloists: Unknown
*Bix does not appear on the other title from this session.*

BVE 38264     In My Merry Oldsmobile (Waltz)

*May 23 (Mon)*     **JEAN GOLDKETTE AND HIS ORCHESTRA**
*Victor Record Co.*
*Camden, New Jersey (studio 3)*
*Eddy Sheasby, Recording Director*
*Time: 9:30 A.M. – 12:00 P.M.*
Fred Farrar, Ray Lodwig (t); Bix Beiderbecke (c); Bill Rank,
Spiegle Willcox (tb); Doc Ryker, Frank Trumbauer, Don Murray (reeds); Irving Riskin (p); Howdy Quicksell (bj); Steve Brown
(sb); Eddy Sheasby (vn); Chauncey Morehouse (d).

**BVE 38267**     **Play It Red** (Harris—arr. Eddy Sheasby)
*Instrumental*
BVE 38267–1     Destroyed.
BVE–38267–2     Destroyed.
BVE 38267–3     Hold conditional. Never issued.
*Sheasby does not play on 38268.*

**BVE 38268**     **In My Merry Oldsmobile** (Fox Trot) (Edwards-Edwards—arr.
Challis)
*Vocal: Ray Lodwig; Howdy Quicksell; Doc Ryker.*
BVE 38268–1     Mastered: Victor Special; *Bm 1012.*
BVE 38268–2     Hold indefinitely. Issued *BWY 102 (LP); RCA 741093 (LP).*
BVE 38268–3     Destroyed.
Soloists: Bix (32 in ensemble).

Note: Victor Special recording of "In My Merry Oldsmobile"
commissioned by General Motors, Inc. for their 1927 Detroit
Convention. In 1936, Warren Scholl put together the Bix Beiderbecke Memorial Album for Victor Records and inquired
whether the masters of "Stampede," "Lily," and "Play It Red"
were still available. Although extensive searches were carried
out, no trace of them was found.

*Aug 25 (Thu)*     **FRANK TRUMBAUER AND HIS ORCHESTRA**
*Okeh Record Co.*
*New York City*
Bix Beiderbecke (c); Bill Rank (tb); Frank Trumbauer (C-m);
Doc Ryker (as); Don Murray (cl/bar); Adrian Rollini (bsx); Irving
Riskin (p); Eddie Lang (g); Chauncey Morehouse (d).

**W 81273**     **Three Blind Mice** (Morehouse—arr. Trumbauer-Challis)
*Instrumental*
W 81273–A     Rejected.
W 81273–B     Rejected.
W 81273–C     Mastered: OK 40903; ParE R–105; OdE PO–56; OdArg 193090;
OdFr 165223; OdG A189076.

**W 81274**     **Blue River** (Bryan-Meyer)
*Vocal: Seger Ellis*
W 81274–A     Rejected.
W 81274–B     Mastered: OK 40879; ParE R–3440; ParG A–4904; OdG O–
4031; OdFr 165173; ParAu A–2335; OdArg 193090.
W 81274–C     Rejected.
**W 81275**     **There's a Cradle in Caroline** (Young-Ahlert)
*Vocal: Seger Ellis*

| | |
|---|---|
| W 81275–A | Rejected. |
| W 81275–B | Rejected. |
| W 81275–C | Rejected. |
| W 81275–D | Mastered: OK 40879; ParE R–3340; ParG A–4904; ParAu A–2335; OdG O–4031; OdFr 165173; OdArg 193101. |

*Sept 9 (Fri)*

**BIX BEIDERBECKE**
*Okeh Record Co.*
*New York City*
Bix Beiderbecke (p).

**W 81426** — **In a Mist** (Beiderbecke)
*Instrumental*

| W 81426–A | Rejected. |
|---|---|
| W 81426–B | Mastered: OK 40916; Voc 3150; OK 3150; ParAu A–6236; ParE R–1838; ParE R–3504; OdIt A–2334; *Jolly Roger 5010;* OdArg 295124; OdCh 295118; OdG A–286085; *Tpl 553; HJCA 601;* Col A–1080; OdSs B–35633; ParFr 85781; OdSp 250531. |

Note: Some foreign issues bear the title "Bixology."

*Sept 15 (Thu)*

**JEAN GOLDKETTE AND HIS ORCHESTRA**
*Victor Record Co.*
*Leiderkranz Hall*
*New York City*
*LeRoy Shield, Recording Director*
*Time: 1:45 P.M. – 5:00 P.M.*
Fred Farrar, Ray Lodwig (t); Bix Beiderbecke (c); Bill Rank, Lloyd Turner (tb); Doc Ryker, Frank Trumbauer, Don Murray (reeds); Irving Riskin (p); Howdy Quicksell (bj); Eddie Lang (g); Joe Venuti (vn); Steve Brown (sb); Chauncey Morehouse (d).

**BVE 40211** — **Blue River** (Bryan-Meyer—arr. Challis)
*Vocal: Lewis James*
Released: Nov 11, 1927
Sales: 73,487

| BVE 40211–1 | Destroyed. |
|---|---|
| BVE 40211–2 | Hold conditional. Never issued. |
| BVE 40211–3 | Mastered. Vic 20981; HMVAu EA–260. |

Solists: Bix (8 in ensemble); Murray (16 + 8 tenor); Trumbauer (8).

**BVE 40212** — **Clementine** (from New Orleans) (Creamer-Layton—arr. Murray-Quicksell-Trumbauer from stock)
*Instrumental*
Released: Nov 18, 1927
Sales: 45,629

| BVE 40212–1 | Destroyed. |
|---|---|
| BVE 40212–2 | Mastered: Vic 20994; *Vic 25283; VicArg 25283; Jazz Classics 531;* HMV B–5402; *HMV B–9237; HMVIn B–9237; ElG EG–3856;* HMVAu EA–3617; *HMVAu EA–1706.* |
| BVE 40212–3 | Hold conditional. Never issued. |

Soloists: Bix (16 in ensemble); Rank (8); Bix (8 in ensemble); Lang (2 + 2 breaks); Bix (16); Venuti (8); Bix (8).
Note: File card lists a second violin for this session; it is not audible. Some foreign issues of 40212 have an apparent "take 1" in the runoff groove. This is not a genuine take, but a speeded-up take 2.

*Sept 17 (Sat)*

**TRAM, BIX AND LANG**
*Okeh Record Co.*
*New York City*
Frank Trumbauer (C-m); Bix Beiderbecke (p/c); Eddie Lang (g).

**W 81450** — **Wringin' an' Twistin'** (Trumbauer-Waller)
*Instrumental*

| W 81450–A | Mastered: OK 40916; Voc 3150; OK 3150; OdIt A–2338; OdArg 193104; ParE R–2532; ParE R3504; *Col 37806.* |
|---|---|
| W 81450–B | Rejected. |
| W 81450–C | Rejected. |

1927:

<table>
<tr><td>Sept 28 (Wed)</td><td colspan="2">FRANK TRUMBAUER AND HIS ORCHESTRA<br>Okeh Record Co.<br>New York City<br>Bix Beiderbecke (c); Bill Rank (tb); Don Murray (cl); Frank Trumbauer (C-m); Bobby Davis (as); Adrian Rollini (bsx); Frank Signorelli (p); Eddie Lang (g); Joe Venuti (vn); Chauncey Morehouse (d).</td></tr>
</table>

| | |
|---|---|
| **W 81488** | **Humpty Dumpty** (Livingston—arr. Livingston)<br>*Instrumental* |
| W 81488–A | Mastered: OK 40926; ParE R–3464; OdG A–189075; ParIt TT–9073. |
| W 81488–B | Rejected. |
| W 81488–C | Rejected. |
| **W 81489** | **Krazy Kat** (Morehouse-Trumbauer—arr. Murray)<br>*Instrumental* |
| W 81489–A | Rejected. |
| W 81489–B | Mastered: OK 40903; ParE R–105; OdE PO–56; OdFr 165223; OdG A–189076; OdArg 193101. |
| **W 81490** | **The Baltimore** (McHugh)<br>*Instrumental* |
| W 81490–A | Rejected. |
| W 81490–B | Mastered: OK 40926; ParE R–3464; OdG A–189075. |

Sept 29 (Thu)  BROADWAY BELL-HOPS
*Harmony Record Co.*
*New York City*
*Sam Lanin, Recording Director*
Bix Beiderbecke (c); Herman "Hymie" Farberman (t); Bill Rank (tb); Don Murray (cl); Frank Trumbauer (C-m); Bobby Davis (as); Frank Signorelli (p); John Cali (bj); Joe Tarto (bb); Joe Venuti (vn); Vic Berton, Sam Lanin (percussion).

| | |
|---|---|
| **144809** | **There Ain't No Land Like Dixieland to Me** (Donaldson)<br>*Vocal: Irving Kaufman* |
| 144809–1 | Second choice. Unissued. |
| 144809–2 | Mastered: Har 504–H; Vel 1504–V; Diva 2504–D; *Davon 104; Tpl 547.* |
| **144810** | **There's a Cradle in Caroline** (Ahlert-Lewis-Young)<br>*Vocal: Irving Kaufman* |
| 144810–1 | Second choice. Unissued. |
| 144810–2 | Mastered: Har 504–H; Vel 1504–V; Diva 2504–D; *Davon 104; Tpl 547.*<br>*Beiderbecke and Rank replaced by Manny Klein (t) and Chuck Campbell (tb).* |
| 144811 | Rainbow of Love (Squires-Perry)<br>Har 508–H<br>Note: All sides accoustically recorded, hence no 'W' prefix. |

Sept 30 (Fri)  FRANK TRUMBAUER AND HIS ORCHESTRA
*Okeh Record Co.*
*New York City*
Sylvester Ahola (t); Bix Beiderbecke (c); Bill Rank (tb); Bobby Davis, Frank Trumbauer, Don Murray (reeds); Adrian Rollini (bsx); Frank Signorelli (p); Eddie Lang (bj); Joe Venuti (vn); Chauncey Morehouse (d).

| | |
|---|---|
| **W 81499** | **Just an Hour of Love** (Trent-deRose-Von Tilzer)<br>*Vocal: Irving Kaufman* |
| W 81499–A | Mastered: OK 40912; OdFr A–189070; ParE R–3463; ParG A–4912. |
| W 81499–B | Rejected. |
| **W 81500** | **I'm Wonderin' Who** (Trent-deRose-Von Tilzer)<br>*Vocal: Irving Kaufman* |
| W 81500–A | Mastered: OK 40912; OdFr A–189070; ParE R–3463; ParG A–4912. |
| W 81500–B | Rejected.<br>Note: OK 40912 and OdFr A–189070 as "Benny Meroff and His Orchestra"; other issues as "Frankie Trumbauer's Augmented Orchestra." |

418

1927:

<table>
<tr><td>Oct 5 (Wed)</td><td></td><td>BIX BEIDERBECKE AND HIS GANG<br>Okeh Record Co.<br>New York City<br>Bix Beiderbecke (c); Bill Rank (tb); Don Murray (cl); Adrian<br>Rollini (bsx); Frank Signorelli (p); Chauncey Morehouse (d).</td></tr>
<tr><td></td><td>W 81518</td><td>At the Jazz Band Ball (LaRocca-Shields)<br>Instrumental</td></tr>
<tr><td></td><td>W 81518–A</td><td>Rejected.</td></tr>
<tr><td></td><td>W 81518–B</td><td>Mastered: OK 40923; Voc 3042; Col 36156; Col 20446; ColJ<br>S–10003; Par E R–3645; ParE R–2711; ParG A–4917; ParIt B–<br>71141; OdArg 193139; OdArg 295118; OdArg 298142; OdG<br>A–189068; OdG 028098; OdCh 295118; ParG R–3645; ParSs<br>R–2711.</td></tr>
<tr><td></td><td>W 81518–C</td><td>Rejected.</td></tr>
<tr><td></td><td>W 81519</td><td>Royal Garden Blues (Williams-Williams)<br>Instrumental</td></tr>
<tr><td></td><td>W 81519–A</td><td>Rejected.</td></tr>
<tr><td></td><td>W 81519–B</td><td>Mastered: OK 8544; Col 35664; ColAu DO–2245; ParE R–3645;<br>ParE R–2580; ParFin DPY–1069; ParSs PZ–11157; OdArg<br>295090: OdIt A–2341; OdG A–286083; ColJ EM–103.</td></tr>
<tr><td></td><td>W 81520</td><td>Jazz Me Blues (Delaney)<br>Instrumental</td></tr>
<tr><td></td><td>W 81520–A</td><td>Mastered: OK 40923; Voc 3042; Col 36156; ParE R–127; ParE<br>R–2580; ParG A–4917; ParE PO–57; ParSs PZ–11157; OdArg<br>193139; OdArg 295090; OdIt A–2341; ParG A–189068; OdG<br>A–286083; OdG 028098; ColJ EM–103; ColJ PL–5020.</td></tr>
<tr><td></td><td>W 81520–B</td><td>Rejected.</td></tr>
<tr><td></td><td>W 81520–C</td><td>Rejected.<br>Note: OK 8544 & ColAu DO–2245 as by "The New Orleans<br>Lucky Seven."</td></tr>
<tr><td>c. Oct 20 (Thu)</td><td></td><td>WILLARD ROBISON AND HIS ORCHESTRA<br>(The Chicago Loopers)<br>Pathe Record Co.<br>New York City<br>Bix Beiderbecke (c); Frank Trumbauer (C-m); Don Murray (cl);<br>Frank Signorelli (p); Eddie Lang (bj); Vic Berton (d).</td></tr>
<tr><td></td><td>See note</td><td>I'm More Than Satisfied (Klages-Waller)<br>Vocal: Deep River Quintet</td></tr>
<tr><td></td><td>–1</td><td>Mastered: Per 14905.</td></tr>
<tr><td></td><td>–2</td><td>Mastered: Per 14905; PA 36724.</td></tr>
<tr><td></td><td>–3</td><td>Take never discovered.</td></tr>
<tr><td></td><td>–4</td><td>Take never discovered.</td></tr>
<tr><td></td><td>–5</td><td>Mastered: Per 14905.</td></tr>
<tr><td></td><td>See note</td><td>Clorinda (Heywood)<br>Vocal: Deep River Quintet</td></tr>
<tr><td></td><td>–1</td><td>Mastered: Per 14910.</td></tr>
<tr><td></td><td>–2</td><td>Mastered: Per 14910; PA 36729.</td></tr>
<tr><td></td><td>–3</td><td>Take never discovered.</td></tr>
<tr><td></td><td>–4</td><td>Mastered: Per 14910; PA 36729.</td></tr>
<tr><td></td><td>–5</td><td>Mastered: Per 14910.</td></tr>
<tr><td></td><td>See note</td><td>Three Blind Mice (Morehouse)<br>Instrumental</td></tr>
<tr><td></td><td>–1</td><td>Mastered: Per 14910; PA 36729; HRS 1.</td></tr>
<tr><td></td><td>–2</td><td>Mastered: Per 14910; Tpl 553; HRS 1.</td></tr>
<tr><td></td><td>–3</td><td>Mastered: Per 14910.</td></tr>
</table>

Note: Per 14910 and PA 36729 as "The Chicago Loopers." The master numbers assigned for this session were 107854/55/56, but it is not known to which titles they applied. Nor is the exact recording date known, though it fell between Oct. 20–26 at Pathe's E. 53rd St. studio. Numbers found in the runoff grooves of these records are normally quoted as "take numbers," though they are not true takes. Two versions of each selection were issued, and the following key to their runoff numbers will enable collectors to differentiate between them:
"I'm More Than Satisfied"—no. 1 is unique, but 2 & 5 are the same.

"Clorinda"—nos. 1 & 4 are the same, and nos. 2 & 5 are the same.
"Three Blind Mice"—nos. 1 & 3 are the same, but no. 2 is unique.

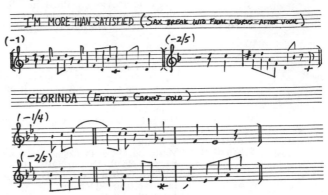

| Oct. 20 (Thu) | | SAM LANIN AND HIS ORCHESTRA |
| | | Probably includes: Herman "Hymie" Farberman, Red Nichols (t); Chuck Campbell (tb); Larry Abbott, Norman Yorke, Fred Morrow (reeds); Murray Kellner (vn); Joe Tarto (bb); Vic Berton (d). unknown bj, p. |
| | 7557 | There Must Be Somebody Else (Gottler-Clare-Pinkard) |
| | | *vocal: Harold "Scrappy" Lambert* |
| | 7557–2 | Issued: Re 8420; Domino 4043; Banner 6104 (mx reassigned as 1145–2); Jewel 5129 (as banner, but labelled Yankee Ten Dance Orch.). |
| | 7558 | Sugar (Ager-Yellen-Nichols) |
| | 7558–1 | Issued: Regal 8420; Oriole 1064 (Yankee Ten Dance Orch.); Domino 4043; Imperial 1860. |
| | 7559 | Where Is My Meyer? (Gilbert-Profes) |
| | 7559–? | Jewel 5126 (mx reassigned as 1137–2); Broadway 1113 (as by The Badgers); EBW 4856 (The Plaza Band). |

Note: These titles are included because of a check made out by Sam Lanin to Bix Beiderbecke and dated Oct. 20, 1927. This has spurred speculation that Bix may have taken part in the above date. The authors have heard 7557 and 7558; Bix is not in evidence, and only two trumpets/cornets can be heard, one of them probably Nichols. While it is possible that the check may have been in payment for the Broadway Bell-hops session of Sept. 29, there remains the possibility that this Lanin date was the one to which Red Nichols referred when he spoke of taking part in a recording session with Bix. We have included what information was available on this session for the reader's reference.

| W 81569–A | Mastered: OK 41001; Voc 3149; ParE R–3503; ParE R–2711; ParIt B–71141; OdFr 165322; OdArg 295118; OdArg 208142; OdG A–189134; OdG 028181; Col 20446; *Bm 1097*; HJCA 84; ParG R–3503; ParSs R–2711. |
| W 81569–B | Rejected. |

Note: OK 8544 & ColAu DO–2245 issued as by "New Orleans Lucky Seven."

| Oct. 25 (Tue) | | BIX BEIDERBECKE AND HIS GANG |
| | | *Okeh Record Co.* |
| | | *New York City* |
| | | Bix Beiderbecke (c); Bill Rank (tb); Don Murray (cl); Adrian Rollini (bsx); Frank Signorelli (p); Chauncey Morehouse (d). |
| | W 81568 | **Goose Pimples** (Trent-Henderson) |
| | | *Instrumental* |

| W 81568–A | Rejected |
| W 81568–B | OK 8544; Col 35664; CoAu DO–2245; ParE R–127; ParE R–2465; ParE PO–57; ParSs PZ–11245; OdIt A–2407; |
| **W 81569** | **Sorry** (Quicksell—arr. Quicksell) *Instrumental* |

*Same session*

**FRANK TRUMBAUER AND HIS ORCHESTRA**
Bix Beiderbecke (c); Bill Rank (tb); Frank Trumbauer (C-m); Don Murray (cl/ts); Charles "Pee Wee" Russell (cl/ts); Adrian Rollini (bsx); Frank Signorelli (p); Eddie Lang (g); Joe Venuti (vn); Chauncey Morehouse (d).

| **W 81570** | **Cryin' All Day** (Trumbauer-Morehouse) *Instrumental* |
| W 81570–A | Rejected. |
| W 81570–B | Rejected. |
| W 81570–C | Mastered: OK 40966; Col 35956; ParE R–2176; ParAu A–6449; OdArg 193217; OdFr 165291; *OdFr 279713;* OdG A–189125; *HJCA 601.* |

| **W 81571** | **A Good Man Is Hard to Find** (Green) *Instrumental* |
| W 81571–A | Rejected. |
| W 81571–B | Mastered: OK 40966; Col 35956; ParE R–3489; OdFr 165291; OdArg 193217; OdG A–189125; *HJCA 601.* |

*Same session*

**BIX BEIDERBECKE AND HIS GANG**
(Personnel as for 81568 & 81569)

| **W 81572** | **Since My Best Girl Turned Me Down** (Lodwig-Quicksell—arr. Quicksell) *Instrumental* |
| W 81572–A | Rejected. |
| W 81572–B | Mastered: OK 41001; Voc 3149; ParE R–3503; ParE R–2054; ParAu A–6236; OdFr 165322; OdIt A–2407; OdG A189134; OdG A–286091; OdG 028181; *Bm 1097; HJCA HC–84;* OdAm ONY–286091; ParSs PZ–11234. |

Note: The Quicksell "arrangement" of 81572 is an "edited down" version of a routine done for the Goldkette Band.

*Oct 26 (Wed)*

**FRANK TRUMBAUER AND HIS ORCHESTRA**
*Okeh Record Co.*
*New York City*
Bix Beiderbecke (c); unknown (t); Bill Rank (tb); Frank Trumbauer, Don Murray, Bobby Davis (reeds); Adrian Rollini (bsx); Eddie Lang (g); Joe Venuti (vn); Frank Signorelli (p); Chauncey Morehouse (d).

| **W 81575** | **Sugar** (Yellen-Ager-Crum-Nichols) *Vocal: Ed Macy, John Ryan.* |
| W 81575–A | Rejected. |
| W 81575–B | Mastered: OK 40938; ParE R–3489; OdArg 193134; OdG A–189092. |
| W 81575–C | Rejected. |
| **W 81576** | **Do You Mean It?** (Baker-Silvers-Lyman) *Vocal: Les Reis* |
| W 81576–A | Rejected. |
| W 81576–B | Rejected. |
| W 81576–C | Rejected. |

Note: OK 40938; OdArg 193134; OdG A–189092 as by "Russell Gray and His Orchestra."

*Nov 18 (Fri)*

**PAUL WHITEMAN AND HIS ORCHESTRA**
*Victor Record Co.*
*Chicago, Ill.*
*LeRoy Shield (?), recording director*
*Time: 9:00 A.M.—12:15 P.M.*
Bix Beiderbecke (c); Tommy Dorsey, Boyce Cullen (tb); Jimmy Dorsey (cl/as); Charles Strickfaden (bar); Chester "Chet" Hazlett (bcl); Mischa Russell, Kurt Dieterle (vn); Matty Malneck (vl); Hoagy Carmichael (p); Wilbur Hall (g); Steve Brown (sb); Harold McDonald (d/vib).

CVE 40901 **Washboard Blues** (Carmichael-Callahan—arr. Challis)
*Vocal: Hoagy Carmichael*
Released: Jan 13, 1928
Sales: 120,676

CVE 40901–1 Mastered: Vic 35877; Vic 36186; VicC 35877.
CVE 40901–2 Destroyed.
CVE 40901–3 Destroyed.
CVE 40901–4 Hold conditional. Issued RCA 741093 (LP).
CVE 40901–5 Destroyed.

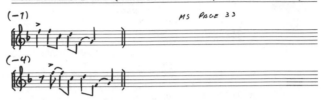

*Nov 22 (Tue)* Bix Beiderbecke does not appear on the following recording by
Paul Whiteman and His Orchestra:

CVE 40934 Among My Souvenirs (Nicholls-Leslie—arr. Satterfield)

*Nov 23 (Wed)* PAUL WHITEMAN AND HIS ORCHESTRA
*Victor Record Co.*
*Chicago, Ill.*
*Time: 9:30 A.M. – 11:45 A.M.*
Henry Busse, Charles Margulis (t); Bix Beiderbecke (c); Wilbur
Hall, Tommy Dorsey (tb); Jimmy Dorsey, Nye Mayhew, Charles
Strickfaden (bar/as); Chet Hazlett, Hal McLean (as); Kurt Die-
terle; Mischa Russell, Matty Malneck, Mario Perry (vn); Harry
Perella (p); Steve Brown (sb); Mike Trafficante (bb); Mike Pin-
gitore (bj); Hal McDonald (d).

BVE 40937 **Changes** (Donaldson—arr. Challis)
*Vocal: Bing Crosby—backed by John Fulton, Charles Gaylord,
Austin Young (1st part)—Harry Barris, Al Rinker (middle
part).*
Released: (–3) Jan 20, 1928
Released: (–2) July 30, 1936

BVE 40937–1 Destroyed.
BVE 40937–2 Hold indefinitely. Issued: Vic 25370.
BVE 40937–3 Mastered: Vic 21103; VicC 21103; HMV B–5461; HMV B–8913;
HMVIn N–4475; *Bm 1032;* ElG EG–690; VdP GW–1795;
HMVSs JK–2809; GrF K–5368.
BVE 40937–4 Destroyed.
BVE 40937–5 Destroyed.
Soloists: Bix (16)

*Nov 25 (Fri)* PAUL WHITEMAN AND HIS ORCHESTRA
*Victor Record Co.*
*Chicago, Ill.*
*Time: 9:30 A.M. – 12:00 P.M.*
Charles Margulis, Henry Busse (t); Bix Beiderbecke (c); Tommy
Dorsey (tb/t); Wilbur Hall (tb/bj); Jimmy Dorsey, Hal McLean,
Chet Hazlett (cl/as); Charles Strickfaden (ts); Frank Trumbauer
(C-m); Kurt Dieterle, Mischa Russell, Matty Malneck, Mario

Perry (vn); Harry Perrella (p); Mike Pingitore (bj); Mike Trafficante (bb); Steve Brown (sb); Hal McDonald (d).

**BVE 40945** **(What Are You Waiting For) Mary** (Donaldson—arr. Malneck)
*Vocal: Bing Crosby*
Released: (–2) Jan 20, 1928
Released: (–4) Nov 17, 1939

BVE 40945–1 Destroyed.
BVE 40945–2 Mastered: Vic 21103; HMV B–5461; HMVAu EA–291; GrF K–
5368; ElG EG–771; *BM 1032*; VicC 21103.
BVE 40945–3 Destroyed.
BVE 40945–4 Hold indefinitely. Issued: Vic 26415; HMVAu EA–2764.
Soloists: Busse (32); Bix (8); Trumbauer (2 + 2).

*Jan 4 (Wed)*

**PAUL WHITEMAN AND HIS ORCHESTRA**
*Victor Record Co*
*New York City*
*Nat Shilkret, Recording Director*
Charles Margulis, Henry Busse (t); Bix Beiderbecke (c); Wilbur
Hall, Bill Rank (tb); Chet Hazlett (bcl/B♭ss/as/E♭ss); Frank
Trumbauer (B♭ss/C-m); Hal McLean (oboe/as/B♭ss); Rupert
"Rube" Crozier (cl/as/ts/B♭ss); Jack or Nye Mayhew (B♭ss/as);
Kurt Dieterle, Mischa Russell, Matty Malneck, Mario Perry,
Charles Gaylord (vn); Harry Perrella, Tom Satterfield (p); Mike
Pingitore (bj); Mike Trafficante (bb); Steve Brown (sb); Hal Mc-
Donald (d); Wilbur Hall also doubles on guitar.

**BVE 41293** **Ramona** (Gilbert-Wayne—arr. Ferde Grofe)
*Vocal: Austin Young*
Released: March 16, 1928

BVE 41293–1 Destroyed.
BVE 41293–2 Hold indefinitely. Never issued.
BVE 41293–3 Mastered: Vic 21214; Vic 25436; HMV B5476; VicJ 21214; ElG
EG–824.

*Same session*

Charles Margulis, Henry Busse (t); Bix Beiderbecke (c); Wilbur
Hall, Bill Rank (tb); Chet Hazlett (bcl/cl/as); Hal McLean
(as/cl); Jimmy Dorsey (cl/as); Charles Strickfaden (bar/ts); Rube
Crozier (cl/as); Kurt Dieterle (vn); Harry Perrella (p); Mike
Pingitore (bj); Mike Trafficante (bb); Steve Brown (sb); Hal Mc-
Donald (d).

**BVE 41294** **Smile** (Heywood—arr. Challis)
*Vocal: Gaylord, Fulton, Rinker.*
BVE 41294–1 Hold conditional. Issued: *Bwy 102 (LP)*; *RCA 741093 (LP)*.
BVE 41294–2 Destroyed.
BVE 41294–3 Destroyed.
Note: This title was remade on Jan. 24, 1928. Music notation for
all three extant takes will be found under that session.

*Same session*

Charles Margulis, Henry Busse (t); Bix Beiderbecke (c); Wilbur
Hall, Bill Rank (tb); Chet Hazlett, Hal McLean (as); Jimmy Dorsey (as/cl); Charles Strickfaden (ts); Frank Trumbauer (C-m);
Kurt Dieterle, Mischa Russell, Matty Malneck (vn); Harry Perrella (p); Mike Pingitore (bj); Mike Trafficante (bb); Steve Brown
(sb); Hal McDonald (d).

**BVE 41295** **Lonely Melody** (Coslow-Meroff-Dyson—arr. Challis)
*Instrumental*
Released: (–1) Mar 16, 1928
Released: (–3) July 30, 1936

BVE 41295–1 Mastered: Vic 21214; VicC 21214; VicJ 21214; VicArg 21214; *Bm 1017;* HMV B–5516; HMVAu EA–371.
BVE 41295–2 Destroyed.
BVE 41295–3 Hold indefinitely. Issued: Vic 25366.
Soloists: Bix (16 + 8).

Jan 5 *(Thu)*  **PAUL WHITEMAN AND HIS ORCHESTRA**
*Victor Record Co.*
*New York City*
*LeRoy Shield, recording director*
*Time: 9:30 A.M.—1:00 P.M.*
Charles Margulis, Henry Busse (t); Bix Beiderbecke (c); Boyce Cullen, Wilbur Hall, Bill Rank, Jack Fulton (tb); Chet Hazlett; Hal McLean, Jimmy Dorsey, Frank Trumbauer, Rube Crozier, Charles Strickfaden (reeds); Kurt Dieterle, Mischa Russell, Matty Malneck, Mario Perry, John Bowman, Charles Gaylord (vn); Harry Perrella (p); Steve Brown (sb); Mike Trafficante (bb); Mike Pingitore (bj); Hal McDonald (d).

**BVE 41296**  **O Ya Ya** (Klages-de Markoff—arr. Domenico Savino)
*Instrumental*
Released: Apr 27, 1928
BVE 41296–1 Hold conditional. Never issued.
BVE 41296–2 Mastered: Vic 21304; HMV B–5488.
BVE 41296–3 Hold conditional. Never issued.

*Same session*  Charles Margulis, Henry Busse, (t); Bix Beiderbecke (c); Boyce Cullen, Wilbur Hall, Bill Rank, Jack Fulton (tb); Chet Hazlett (Ebcl/Bbcl/Bbss/); Hal McLean (o/f/as); Rube Crozier (f/as/-pic/); Charles Strickfaden (ts/o/cl); Kurt Dieterle, Mischa Russell, Mario Perry (vn); Matty Malneck (vl); Harry Perrella, Ferde Grofe (p); Steve Brown (sb); Mike Pingitore (bj); Mike Trafficante (bb); Hal McDonald (d).

**BVE 41297**  **Dolly Dimples** (Alter—arr. Ferde Grofe)
*Instrumental*
Released: Apr 27, 1928
Sales: 36,990
BVE 41197–1 Hold indefinitely. Never issued.
BVE 41297–2 Destroyed.
BVE 41297–3 Destroyed.
BVE 41297–4 Mastered: Vic 21301; HMV B–5492.

Jan 9 *(Mon)*  **FRANK TRUMBAUER AND HIS ORCHESTRA**
*Okeh Record Co.*
*New York City*
Bix Beiderbecke (c); Bill Rank (tb); Frank Trumbauer (C-m); Jimmy Dorsey (cl/as); Charles Strickfaden (as); Min Leibrook (bsx); Tommy Satterfield (p), Matty Malneck (vn); Eddie Lang (g); Hal McDonald (d).

**W 400002**  **Two Letters from Dixie**
*Instrumental*
W 400002 Rejected.
**W 400003**  **There'll Come a Time** (Manone-Mole)
*Instrumental*
W 400003–B Mastered: OK 40979; ParE R–3526; ParE R–2097; ParAu A–6311; ParAu A–7692; ParE DP–255; OdFr 165330; OdArg 193128; OdIt A–2399; OdG A–189143; OdN ND–5040S; ParSs R–2097.
*add Charles Margulis (t)*

**1928:**

**W 400004** **Jubilee** (Robison)
*Instrumental*
Released: June 15, 1928
Sales: 3,000
W 400004–C Mastered: OK 41044; ParE R–161; ParE R–2054; OdFr 165539; OdG A–189203; OdG A–286091; OdAm ONY–286091; ParSs PZ–11234.
Note: Helene F. Chmura of Columbia Records was unable to locate any information on this session, particularly in regard to the number of "takes" made and their designations. We have included "Two Letters from Dixie" on the strength of Warren Scholl's insistence that Trumbauer listed this title in his diary as having been recorded.

*Jan 11 (Wed)* PAUL WHITEMAN AND HIS ORCHESTRA
*Victor Record Co.*
*Liederkranz Hall, NYC*
*Nat Shilkret, Recording Director*
*Time: 9:30 A.M.—1:45 P.M.*
Charles Margulis, Henry Busse, Bix Beiderbecke, Bob Mayhew (t/c); Boyce Cullen, Wilbur Hall, Bill Rank, Jack Fulton (tb); Chet Hazlett (bcl/cl/ss/Ebcl); Hal McLean (cl/o/ss/f/as); Frank Trumbauer (C-m/cl/as); Jimmy Dorsey (as/cl); Charles Strickfaden (cl/ts/ss/o); Kurt Dieterle, Mischa Russell, Mario Perry, Matty Malneck (vn); Harry Perrella (p); Mike Trafficante (bb); Mike Pingitore (bj); Tommy Satterfield (cel); Hal McDonald, one unknown (d).
**BVE 27268** **Parade of the Wooden Soldiers** (Jessell—arr. Grofe)
*Instrumental*
Released: Apr 27, 1928
BVE 27268–9 Hold indefinitely. Never issued.
BVE 27268–10 Destroyed.
BVE 27268–11 Mastered: Vic 21304; HMV B–5488.
BVE 27268–12 Destroyed.

*Same session* Henry Busse, Charles Margulis (t); Bix Beiderbecke (c); Boyce Cullen, Bill Rank, Wilbur Hall, Jack Fulton (tb); Chet Hazlett (as/bcl/cl); Hal McLean (as/cl); Charles Strickfaden (ts/cl); Jimmy Dorsey (bar/cl); Frank Trumbauer (C-m); Kurt Dieterle, Mischa Russell, Mario Perry, Matty Malneck, John Bowman (vn); Harry Perrella (p); Steve Brown (sb); Mike Trafficante (bb); Mike Pingitore (bj); Hal McDonald (d).
**BVE 41607** **Ol' Man River** (Hammerstein-Kern—arr. Challis)
*Vocal: Bing Crosby*
Released: Mar 9, 1928
BVE 41607–1 Destroyed.
BVE 41607–2 Mastered: Vic 21218; Vic 25249; VicArg 21218; VicArg 25249; VicJ 21218; VicJ JA–766; *Tpl 4008; Sentry 4008;* HMV B–5471; HMV B–8929; HMV BD–5066; HMVIn B–8929; HMVIn BD–5066; HMVIr IM–129; GrIt R–4697; GrFr K–5448; ElG EG–838; HMVSs JK–2822.
BVE 41607–3 Hold indefinitely. Never issued.
Soloists: Bix (2); Trumbauer (16).

*Jan 12 (Thu)* PAUL WHITEMAN AND HIS ORCHESTRA
*Victor Record Co.*
*Liederkranz Hall, NYC*
*Leonard Joy, Recording Director*
*Time: 10:00 A.M.—1:20 P.M.*
Bix Beiderbecke (c); Charles Margulis (t); Bill Rank (tb); Jimmy Dorsey (c/cl); Frank Trumbauer (C-m); Min Leibrook (bsx); Bill Challis (p); Matty Malneck (vn); Carl Kress (g); Hal McDonald (d).
**BVE 30172** **San** (McPhail-Michaels—arr. Challis)
*Instrumental*
Released: (–6) June 2, 1933
Released: (–7) July 30, 1936
BVE 30172–6 Mastered: Vic 24078; HMV B–5581; *Bm 1031;* VicJ 24078.
BVE 30172–7 Hold indefinitely. Issued: Vic 25367.
BVE 30172–8 Destroyed.

1928:

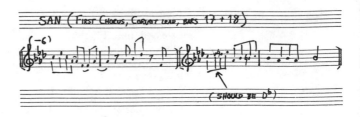

Jan 20 (Fri)      **FRANK TRUMBAUER AND HIS ORCHESTRA**
*Okeh Record Co.*
*New York City*
Bix Beiderbecke, Charles Margulis (c); Bill Rank (tb); Frank Trumbauer (C-m); Jimmy Dorsey (cl/as); Charles Strickfaden (as); Min Leibrook (bsx); Tommy Satterfield (p); Eddie Lang (g); Matty Malneck (vn); Hal McDonald (d).

**W 400033**      **From Monday On** (Barris-Crosby)
*Vocal: Bing Crosby*
W 400033      Rejected.
**W 400034**      **Mississippi Mud** (Barris)
*Vocal: Bing Crosby; Frank Trumbauer.*
W 400034–A      Mastered: OK 40979; ParE R–2097; ParE R–3526; OdE DP–255; ParAu A–6311; *Bm 1029;* OdFr 165330; OdArg 193128; OdG O–31816; OdG A–189143; OdIt A–2399; ParAu A–7692; ParSs R–2097; OdN ND–5040–S.
Note: No information on file as to "takes" made and rejected.

Jan 21 (Sat)      **PAUL WHITEMAN AND HIS ORCHESTRA**
*Victor Record Co.*
*Church Studio*
*Camden, New Jersey*
*Time: 9:30 A.M.—12:30 P.M.*
Charles Margulis, Henry Busse, Bob Mayhew, Bix Beiderbecke (t/c); Boyce Cullen, Wilbur Hall, Bill Rank, Jack Fulton (tb); Jimmy Dorsey, Jack Mayhew (cl/as); Chet Hazlett (cl/bcl/as); Hal McLean (Ebcl/as); Charles Strickfaden (cl/bar); Nye Mayhew (bar); Rube Crozier (bsn/as); Frank Trumbauer (bsn/C-m/as); Kurt Dieterle, Mischa Russell, Mario Perry, Matty Malneck, Charles Gaylord (vn); Harry Perrella, Tommy Satterfield (p); Mike Trafficante (bb), Mike Pingitore (bj); Steve Brown (sb); Hal McDonald (d).

**CVE 41635**      **Together** (de Sylva-Henderson-Brown—arr. Grofe)
*Vocal: Jack Fulton*
Released: Mar 9, 1928
Sales: 60,779
CVE 41635–1      Destroyed.
CVE 41635–2      Destroyed.
CVE 41635–3      Mastered: Vic 35883; HMV C–1472.

Jan 24 (Tue)      **PAUL WHITEMAN AND HIS ORCHESTRA**
*Victor Record Co.*
*Church Studio*
*Camden, New Jersey*
*Time: 9:30 A.M.—11:50 A.M.*
Charles Margulis, Henry Busse, Bob Mayhew, Bix Beiderbecke (t/c); Boyce Cullen, Bill Rank, Wilbur Hall, Jack Fulton (tb); Chet Hazlett (as/cl/bcl); Jimmy Dorsey (as/cl); Frank Trumbauer (as/C-m); Jack Mayhew (as); Nye Mayhew (bar); Hal McLean (o/as/cl); Charles Strickfaden (cl/ts); Rube Crozier (cl/f); Kurt Dieterle, Mischa Russell, John Bowman, Mario Perry (vn); Matty Malneck (vl); Harry Perrella (p); Mike Trafficante (bb); Mike Pingitore (bj); Steve Brown (sb); Hal McDonald (d).

**1928:**

|  |  |
|---|---|
| **CVE 41465** | **My Heart Stood Still** (Rodgers-Hart—arr. Challis)<br>*Vocal: Jack Fulton, Charles Gaylord, Austin Young, Al Rinker.*<br>Released: Mar 9, 1928<br>Sales: 60,779 |
| CVE 41465–1 | Hold conditional. Never issued. |
| CVE 41465–2 | Hold conditional. Never issued. |
| CVE 41465–3 | Mastered: Vic 35883.<br>Soloists: Trumbauer (32). |
| *Same session* | Charles Margulis, Henry Busse, Bob Mayhew, Bix Beiderbecke (t/c); Boyce Cullen, Bill Rank, Wilbur Hall, Jack Fulton (tb); Chet Hazlett (bcl/as/cl); Hal McLean (cl/as); Jimmy Dorsey (cl/as); Jack Mayhew (as); Rube Crozier (cl/as); Frank Trumbauer (C-m/as); Nye Mayhew (bar); Charles Strickfaden (bar/ts); Harry Perrella (p); Mike Trafficante (bb); Mike Pingitore (bj); Steve Brown (sb); Hal McDonald (d). |
| **BVE 41294** | **Smile** (Heywood—arr. Challis)<br>*Vocal: Jack Fulton, Charles Gaylord; Austin Young, Al Rinker*<br>Released: Mar 16, 1928<br>Sales: 45,089 |
| BVE 41294–4 | Hold indefinitely. Issued *Bwy 102; RCA 741093 (LP).* |
| BVE 41294–5 | Mastered: Vic 21228; HMV B–5465; HMVSp AE–2189; *Bm 1017.* |
| BVE 41294–6 | Destroyed.<br>Soloists: Rank (16); Dorsey (4); Bix (4). |

|  |  |
|---|---|
| *Jan 26 (Thu)* | PAUL WHITEMAN AND HIS ORCHESTRA<br>Note: Whiteman Orchestra, with Fats Waller on organ, rehearsed "Whispering" at the Victor Studios, Camden, N.J.—but did not record. |
| *Jan 27 (Fri)* | Bix Beiderbecke does not appear on the following recording by Paul Whiteman and His Orchestra. |
| **BVE 41470** | **Make Believe** (Hammerstein-Kern—arr. Grofe)<br>Vic 21218 |
| *Jan 28 (Sat)* | PAUL WHITEMAN AND HIS ORCHESTRA<br>*Victor Record Co.*<br>*Studio 3*<br>*Camden, New Jersey*<br>*Bill Challis, Recording Director*<br>*Time: 9:30 A.M. – 11:25 A.M.*<br>Charles Margulis, Henry Busse (t); Bix Beiderbecke (c); Boyce Cullen, Wilbur Hall, Bill Rank (tb); Chet Hazlett (bcl/as/ss); Jimmy Dorsey (cl/as); Rube Crozier (cl); Hal McLean (o/cl/as); Charles Strickfaden (o/cl/ts); Frank Trumbauer (cl/C-m); Kurt Dieterle, Mischa Russell, Mario Perry, Charles Gaylord (vn); Steve Brown (sb); Mike Trafficante (bb); Mike Pingitore (bj); Hal McDonald (d); Bill Challis (p) on takes 1 & 2, Ferde Grofe (p) on takes 3 & 4. |
| **BVE 41471** | **Back in Your Own Backyard** (Jolson-Rose-Dreyer—arr. Challis)<br>*Instrumental*<br>Released: (–3) Mar 23, 1928<br>Sales: 88,866<br>Released: (–4) Dec 12, 1941 |
| BVE 41471–1 | Destroyed. |
| BVE 41471–2 | Destroyed. |
| BVE 41471–3 | Mastered: Vic 21240; VicC 21240; VicJ 21240; HMV B–5564; |

HMVIn B–5564; GrFr K–5606; ElG EG–1161.
BVE 41471–4  Hold indefinitely. Issued: Vic 27689.
Soloists: Bix (4); Dorsey (1 + 8); Bix (8).

Feb 7 (Tue)  Bix Beiderbecke does not appear on the following recordings by Paul Whiteman and His Orchestra:
BVE 24390  Japanese Sandman (Egan-Whiting—arr. Grofe)
Vic 21731
BVE 24393  Whispering (Schonberger-Coburn-Rose—arr. Grofe)
Rejected
BVE 41680  Poor Butterfly (Hubbell-Golden-Burnside—arr. Grofe)
Vic 24078
BVE 24391  Avalon (Jolson-Rose—arr. Grofe)
Rejected
Note: Titles in exact order of recording.

Feb 8 (Wed)  **PAUL WHITEMAN AND HIS ORCHESTRA**
*Victor Record Co.*
*Liederkranz Hall, NYC*
*Time: 10:00 A.M. – 12:05 P.M.*
Charles Margulis, Henry Busse (t); Bix Beiderbecke (c); Boyce Cullen, Wilbur Hall, Bill Rank (tb); Chet Hazlett (cl/as); Rube Crozier (cl/ts); Jimmy Dorsey, Hal McLean (as/cl); Frank Trumbauer (C-m); Charles Strickfaden (bar/cl); Kurt Dieterle, Mischa Russell, Mario Perry, Matty Malneck, Charles Gaylord (vn); Roy Bargy (p); Steve Brown (sb); Mike Trafficante (bb); Mike Pingitore (bj); Hal McDonald (d). Henry Busse—assistant session director.
BVE 41681  **There Ain't No Sweet Man That's Worth the Salt of My Tears** (Fisher—arr. Satterfield)
*Vocal: Bing Crosby, with Jack Fulton, Austin Young, Charles Gaylord, Al Rinker, Harry Barris.*
Released: (–3) July 20, 1928
Released: (–2) Sep 22, 1937
BVE 41681–1  Destroyed.
BVE 41681–2  Hold indefinitely. Issued: Vic 25675; HMV B–8929; HMVIn B–8929; HMVSs JK–2822.
BVE 41681–3  Mastered: Vic 21464; *Bm 1031;* HMV B–5515; HMVIn B–5515.
Soloists: Bix (8 + 32 ensemble lead); Trumbauer (16); Bix (8 + 8 ensemble lead)

Same session  *Time: 1:00 P.M. – 3:00 P.M.*
Charles Margulis, Henry Busse (t); Bob Mayhew, Bix Beiderbecke (c); Boyce Cullen, Wilbur Hall, Bill Rank, Jack Fulton (tb); Chet Hazlett (cl/as); Rube Crozier (cl/ts); Jimmy Dorsey, Hal McLean (as/cl); Frank Trumbauer (C-m); Charles Strickfaden (bar/ts); Jack Mayhew (as); Nye Mayhew (bar); Kurt Dieterle,

**1928:**

Mischa Russell, Matty Malneck, Mario Perry (vn); Roy Bargy (p); Mike Pingitore (bj); Mike Trafficante (bb); Hal McDonald (d).

CVE 41682    **A Shady Tree** (Donaldson—arr. Grofe)
*Vocal: Jack Fulton, recitation by Austin Young.*
CVE 41682–1    Destroyed.
CVE 41682–2    Hold conditional. Never issued.
CVE 41682–3    Destroyed.
CVE 41682–4    Destroyed.
Note: Title remade Feb 15, 1928.
Note: The Victor files for this session have the following, which we quote verbatim: "Note: – Rehearsal from 3:30 to 4:20 (made 3 tests). Mr. Whiteman decided men were tired, did not make selections. Men present were: 4 violins, st b, 4 trumpets, 4 trombones, 8 saxes, tuba, piano, trapman. Name of selection: Midnight Reflections."

*Feb 9 (Thu)*

PAUL WHITEMAN AND HIS ORCHESTRA
*Victor Record Co.*
*Liederkranz Hall, NYC*
*Time: 10:00 A.M. – 12:20 P.M.*
*1:20 P.M. – 3:00 P.M.*
Henry Busse, Bix Beiderbecke, Charles Margulis (t/c); Bill Rank, Wilbur Hall, Boyce Cullen (tb); Chet Hazlett (as/bcl); Jimmy Dorsey, Hal McLean (as/cl); Frank Trumbauer (C-m); Charles Strickfaden (bar/ts); Matty Malneck, Mischa Russell, Kurt Dieterle (vn); Roy Bargy (p); Steve Brown (sb); Mike Trafficante (bb); Mike Pingitore (bj); Hal McDonald (d).

BVE 41683    **Dardanella** (Bernard-Black-Fisher—arr. Challis)
*Instrumental*
Released: Jan 29, 1936
BVE 41683–1    Destroyed.
BVE 41683–2    Mastered: Vic 25238; VicJ 25238; VicJ A–1281; VicJ JA–677; HMVSs JK–2810; HMV B–8931.
BVE 41683–3    Destroyed.
Soloists: Bix (32); Trumbauer (8 + 4)
Bix Beiderbecke does not appear on the additional selections from this session:
BVE 26377    Oriental (Granados—arr: Grofe)
Vic 21599
BVE 30176    Meditation from "Thaïs" (Massenet—arr. Grofe)
Vic 21796
BVE 30177    By the Waters of the Minnetonka (Cavanars-Lieurance—arr. Grofe)
Vic 21796

*Feb 10 (Fri)*

PAUL WHITEMAN AND HIS ORCHESTRA
*Victor Record Co.*
*Liederkranz Hall, NYC*
*Time: 10:00 A.M. – 12:00 P.M.*
Charles Margulis, Henry Busse (t); Bix Beiderbecke (c); Boyce Cullen, Bill Rank, Wilbur Hall (tb); Red Mayer (ts/cl); Charles Strickfaden (ts/bar); Chet Hazlett (bcl/as); Hal McLean (cl/as); Frank Trumbauer (as); Kurt Dieterle, Mischa Russell, Matty Malneck (vn); Roy Bargy (p); Steve Brown (sb); Mike Trafficante (bb); Mike Pingitore (bj); Hal McDonald (d).

BVE 41684    **Love Nest** (Harbach-Hirsch—arr. Challis)
*Vocal: "Humming" by Jack Fulton, Charles Gaylord, Austin Young.*
Released: Dec 1, 1932
BVE 41684–1    Destroyed.
BVE 41684–2    Mastered: Vic 24105.
BVE 41684–3    Destroyed.
Soloists: Bix (8).
Note: At this point, the name of Roy J. "Red" Mayer appears in the Whiteman saxophone section. He appears to have subsequently altered the spelling of his surname to "Maier," but because his signature on the 1928 Whiteman payroll sheet reproduced in this volume clearly reads "Mayer," the authors have retained that spelling throughout the listing.

1928:

| | |
|---|---|
| Feb 13 (Mon) | **PAUL WHITEMAN AND HIS ORCHESTRA**<br>*Victor Record Co.*<br>*Liederkranz Hall, NYC*<br>*Time: 1:15 P.M. – 4:00 P.M.*<br>Charles Margulis (t); Bix Beiderbecke (c); Boyce Cullen, Bill Rank (tb); Chet Hazlett (cl/as/Ebcl); Charles Strickfaden (cl/bar); Frank Trumbauer (cl/ss/as); Irving Friedman (ts/cl/as); Kurt Dieterle, Mischa Russell, Matty Malneck, Mario Perry, Charles Gaylord (vn); Roy Bargy (p); Mike Pingitore (bj); Mike Trafficante (bb); Wilbur Hall (g); Hal McDonald (d). |
| **BVE 41688** | **Sunshine** (Berlin—arr. Grofe)<br>*Vocal: Bing Crosby, Jack Fulton, Austin Young, Charles Gaylord, Al Rinker.*<br>Released: Mar 23, 1928<br>Sales: 88,866 |
| BVE 41688–1 | Destroyed. |
| BVE 41688–2 | Hold conditional. Never issued. |
| BVE 41688–3 | Mastered: Vic 21240; VicJ 21240; HMVSp AE–2236; VicC 21240. |
| Same session | Charles Margulis (t); Bix Beiderbecke, Jimmy Dorsey (c); Bill Rank (tb); Chet Hazlett, Rube Crozier, Red Mayer, Charles Strickfaden (reeds); Kurt Dieterle, Mischa Russell, Matty Malneck (vn); Harry Barris (p); Steve Brown (sb); Mike Trafficante (bb); Mike Pingitore (bj); Hal McDonald (d). |
| **BVE 41689** | **From Monday On** (Barris-Crosby—arr: Matty Malneck)<br>*Vocal: Bing Crosby, Charles Gaylord, Austin Young, Jack Fulton, Al Rinker*<br>Released: Dec 12, 1941 |
| BVE 41689–1 | Destroyed. |
| BVE 41689–2 | Destroyed. |
| BVE 41689–3 | Mastered: Vic 27688; HMVAu EA–3235; Vic 27–0136.<br>Soloists: Bix (32); Bix (ensemble lead to end).<br>Note: Two more issued takes of BVE–41689 were made on Feb. 28, 1928; musical comparison of the three follows that session. Bix Beiderbecke does not appear on the additional selections from this session: |
| CVE 41687 | Midnight Reflections (Signorelli—arr. Malneck)<br>Vic 35992 |
| BVE 27432 | Wonderful One (Whiteman-Grofe-Neilan-Terriss—arr. Grofe)<br>Vic 24105 |
| Feb 14 (Tue) | **PAUL WHITEMAN AND HIS ORCHESTRA**<br>*Victor Record Co.*<br>*Liederkranz Hall, NYC*<br>*Time: 9:30 A.M. – 12:00 P.M.*<br>Charles Margulis, Henry Busse, Eddie Pinder (t); Bix Beiderbecke (c); Boyce Cullen, Wilbur Hall, Bill Rank, Jack Fulton (tb); Chet Hazlett, Irving Friedman, Rube Crozier, Red Mayer, Charles Strickfaden, Frank Trumbauer, two others—possibly Nye and Jack Mayhew (reeds); Kurt Dieterle, Mischa Russell, Mario Perry, Matty Malneck, Charles Gaylord, John Bowman (vn); Roy Bargy (p); Steve Brown (sb); Mike Trafficante (bb); Hal McDonald, one other (d); Herman Hand, assistant recording director. |
| **CVE 41690** | **Grand Fantasia from Wagneriana** (Wagner—arr. Herman Hand)<br>*Part One Instrumental*<br>Released: Feb 23, 1928 |
| CVE 41690–1 | Hold indefinitely. Never issued. |
| CVE 41690–2 | Mastered: Vic 36065. |
| CVE 41690–3 | Hold conditional. Never issued. |
| CVE 41690–4 | Hold conditional. Never issued. |
| **CVE 41691** | **Grand Fantasia from Wagneriana** (Wagner—arr. Hand)<br>*Part Two Instrumental*<br>Released: Feb 23, 1928 |
| CVE 41691–1 | Hold conditional. Never issued. |
| CVE 41691–2 | Hold conditional. Never issued. |

| | |
|---|---|
| CVE 41691–3 | Hold indefinitely. Never issued. |
| CVE 41691–4 | Mastered: Vic 36065. |

*Feb 15 (Wed)*    **PAUL WHITEMAN AND HIS ORCHESTRA**
*Victor Record Co.*
*New York City*
Charles Margulis, Henry Busse, Eddie Pinder (t); Bix Beider-becke (c); Boyce Cullen, Wilbur Hall, Bill Rank (tb); Chet Haz-lett (cl/as); Rube Crozier (cl/ts); Irving Friedman (cl/ts); Red Mayer (cl/as); Frank Trumbauer (C-m); Charles Strickfaden (bar/ts); Kurt Dieterle, Mischa Russell, Mario Perry, Matty Mal-neck (vn); Roy Bargy (p); Mike Pingitore (bj); Mike Trafficante (bb); Hal McDonald (d).

**CVE 41682**    **A Shady Tree** (Donaldson—arr. Grofe)
*Vocal: Jack Fulton. Recitation: Austin Young.*

| | |
|---|---|
| CVE 41682–5 | Mastered. Never issued. |
| CVE 41682–6 | Destroyed. |

Note: Despite years of rumor Bix does *not* solo on "A Shady Tree." Listening to take -5, we can clearly identify Henry Busse.
Bix Beiderbecke does not appear on the additional recordings from this session:

| | |
|---|---|
| BVE 24391 | Avalon (Jolson-Rose—arr. Grofe) |
| | Vic 25238 |
| BVE 24393 | Whispering (Schonberger-Coburn-Ross—arr. Grofe) |
| | Vic 21731 |
| BVE 27431 | Underneath the Mellow Moon (Hall—arr. Grofe) |
| | Vic 25436 |

*Feb 16 (Thur)*    **PAUL WHITEMAN AND HIS ORCHESTRA**
*Victor Record Co.*
*New York City*
*Time: 10:15 A.M. – 12:45 P.M.*
*2:40 P.M. – 4:00 P.M.*
*Ferde Grofe, Recording Director*
*Paul Whiteman, Assisting*
Charles Margulis, Henry Busse, Eddie Pinder (t); Bix Beider-becke (c); Boyce Cullen, Wilbur Hall, Bill Rank, Jack Fulton (tb); Chet Hazlett, Frank Trumbauer, Irving Friedman, Red Mayer, Charles Strickfaden (reeds); Rube Crozier, Kurt Die-terle, Mischa Russell, Matty Malneck, Mario Perry, Charles Gaylord, John Bowman (vn); Roy Bargy (p); Mike Pingitore (bj); Mike Trafficante (sb); Min Leibrook (bsx); Hal McDonald (d).

**CVE 41692**    **Three Shades of Blue** (Grofe—arr. Grofe)
*Part One—Indigo—Instrumental*
Released: Dec 28, 1928

| | |
|---|---|
| CVE 41692–1 | Hold indefinitely. Never issued. |
| CVE 41692–2 | Destroyed. |
| CVE 41692–3 | Mastered: Vic 35952. |
| CVE 41692–4 | Destroyed. |

*Same session*    The instrumentation for the next section was reduced to three trumpets and five saxes. But we do not know which musicians were omitted; in all probability Bix is not present.

**CVE 41693**    Three Shades of Blue (Grofe—arr. Grofe)
*Part Two—Alice Blue and Heliotrope—Instrumental*
Released: Dec 28, 1928

| | |
|---|---|
| CVE 41693–1 | Hold indefinitely. Never issued. |
| CVE 41693–2 | Mastered: Vic 35952. |
| CVE 41693–3 | Destroyed. |
| CVE 41693–4 | Destroyed. |

*Feb 18 (Sat)*    **PAUL WHITEMAN AND HIS ORCHESTRA**
*Victor Record Co.*
*Liederkranz Hall, NYC*
*Time: 11:30 A.M. – 12:40 P.M.*
Bix Beiderbecke (c); Eddie Pinder (t); Bill Rank (tb); Chet Haz-lett, Frank Trumbauer (as); Irving Friedman (cl); Charles Strick-

faden (ts); Roy Bargy (p); Min Leibrook (bb); Mike Pingitore (bj); Mike Trafficante (sb); Hal McDonald (d).

BVE 41696    **Mississippi Mud** (Barris—arr. Satterfield)
*Vocal: Irene Taylor backed by Bing Crosby, Harry Barris, Al Rinker, Jack Fulton, Charles Gaylord, Austin Young.*
Released: (–3) Apr 13, 1928
Released: (–2) July 30, 1936

BVE 41696–1    Destroyed.
BVE 41696–2    Hold indefinitely. Issued: Vic 25366; HMVAu EA–2764; *Bm 1029.*
BVE 41696–3    Mastered: Vic 21274; VicJ 21274; HMVAu EA–429; VicC 21274.
BVE 41696–4    Destroyed.
Soloists: Bix (22 in ensemble lead); Friedman (22); Trumbauer (2).

Bix Beiderbecke does not appear on the other selection from this session:

CVE 41695    Caprice Futuristic (Malneck—arr Grofe)
Vic 36044

*Feb 27 (Mon)*    **PAUL WHITEMAN AND HIS ORCHESTRA**
*Victor Record Co.*
*Liederkranz Hall, NYC*
*Time: 12:00 P.M. – 3:15 P.M.*
Charles Margulis, Henry Busse, Eddie Pinder (t); Bix Beiderbecke (c); Boyce Cullen, Wilbur Hall, Bill Rank, Jack Fulton (tb); Chet Hazlett (cl/as); Irving Friedman (cl/ts); Red Mayer (bsn/as/EngHorn); Frank Trumbauer (bsn/as); Rube Crozier (f/bsn); Charles Strickfaden (Heckelphone/o/cl/ss); Kurt Dieterle, Mischa Russell, Matty Malneck, Mario Perry (vn); Roy Bargy (p); Mike Pingitore (bj); Mike Trafficante (sb); Min Leibrook (bb); Hal McDonald (d); Ferde Grofe, assistant director.

CVE 43116    **Chloe** (Kahn-Moret—arr. Grofe)
*Vocal: Austin Young*
Released: June 29, 1928

CVE 43116–1    Destroyed.
CVE 43116–2    Hold conditional. Never issued.
CVE 43116–3    Mastered: Vic 35921; HMV C–1548.
CVE 43116–4    Hold indefinitely. Never issued.

*Feb 28 (Tue)*    **PAUL WHITEMAN AND HIS ORCHESTRA**
*Victor Co.*
*New York City*
*Tommy Satterfield, Recording Director*
*Ferde Grofe, Assistant Director*
*Time: 11:00 A.M. – 2:30 P.M.*
    *2:30 P.M. – 3:45 P.M.*
Charles Margulis (t); Bix Beiderbecke (c); Boyce Cullen, Bill Rank (tb); Chet Hazlett; Red Mayer, Irving Friedman, Frank Trumbauer, Rube Crozier, Charles Strickfaden (reeds); Kurt Dieterle, Mischa Russell, Matty Malneck, Mario Perry (vn); Roy Bargy (p); Min Leibrook (bb); Mike Pingitore (bj); Mike Trafficante (sb); Hal McDonald (d).

CVE 43117    **High Water** (Brennan-McCardy—arr. Satterfield)
*Vocal: Bing Crosby*

**1928:**

Released: Nov 29, 1929
Sales: 4,904

CVE 43117–1  Destroyed.
CVE 43117–2  Hold indefinitely. Never issued.
CVE 43117–3  Mastered: Vic 35992; HMV C–1607.
CVE 43117–4  Destroyed.

*Same session*  Charles Margulis (t); Bix Beiderbecke (c); Bill Rank (tb); Chet Hazlett, Red Mayer, Frank Trumbauer, Irving Friedman, Charles Strickfaden (reeds); Kurt Dieterle, Mischa Russell, Matty Malneck (vn); Harry Barris (p); Min Leibrook (bsx/bb); Mike Pingitore (bj); Hal McDonald (d).

BVE 41689  **From Monday On** (Barris-Crosby—arr: Malneck)
*Vocal: Bing Crosby, Al Rinker, Charles Gaylord, Austin Young, Jack Fulton.*
Released: (–4) July 30, 1936
Released: (–6) Apr 13, 1928

BVE 41689–4  Hold indefinitely. Issued: Vic 25368.
BVE 41689–5  Destroyed.
BVE 41689–6  Mastered: Vic 21274; VicJ 21274; VicC 21274; HMV B–5492; HMVIn B–5492; *Bm 1017.*
Soloists: as before.

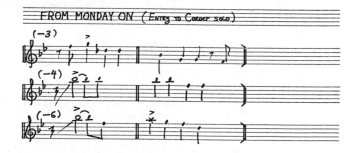

Note: The final chorus of Malneck's arrangement calls for a "hot" cornet trio, led by Bix. Though Jimmy Dorsey was out of the band by the Feb. 13 session, it is safe to assume that he "doubled" for that occasion. This is clearly not the case on Feb. 28, when the Victor file card and Whiteman's own ledgers list only two cornets, Bix and Margulis, though a third part is clearly audible during the trio. A check of the arrangement and parts at Williams College yields the answer: the third voice was written into Bill Rank's trombone part for the Feb. 28 date.

*Same session*  Charles Margulis, Henry Busse, Eddie Pinder (t); Bix Beiderbecke (c); Boyce Cullen, Wilbur Hall, Bill Rank, Jack Fulton (tb); Chet Hazlett (as/bcl/Ebcl); Irving Friedman (as/cl); Red Mayer (ts/cl); Rube Crozier (as/cl/bsx/ss/bsn); Frank Trumbauer (as/cl); Charles Strickfaden (ts/bar/EngHorn); Kurt Dieterle, Mischa Russell, Matty Malneck; Mario Perry (vn); Roy Bargy (p); Mike Pingitore (bj); Mike Trafficante (sb); Min Leibrook (bb); Hal McDonald (d).

BVE 43118  **Sugar** (Pinkard—arr. Challis)
*Instrumental.*
Released: (–2) July 20, 1928
Released: (–1) July 30, 1936

BVE 43118–1  Hold indefinitely. Issued: Vic 25368; HMV B–8931; HMVSs JK–2810.
BVE 43118–2  Mastered: Vic 21464.
BVE 43118–3  Destroyed.
BVE 43118–4  Destroyed.
Soloists: Bix (16); Rank (8); Bix (8); Trumbauer (8); Bix (8).

1928:

Feb 29 (Wed)

PAUL WHITEMAN AND HIS ORCHESTRA
*Victor Record Co.*
*Liederkranz Hall, NYC*
*Time: 9:30 A.M. – 12:00 P.M.*
Charles Margulis, Henry Busse, Eddie Pinder (t); Bix Beider-
becke (c); Boyce Cullen, Wilbur Hall, Bill Rank, Jack Fulton (tb);
Chet Hazlett (ss/cl); Red Mayer (ss/cl/as); Rube Crozier (ss/bar/
as/English Horn); Charles Strickfaden (bar/cl); Kurt Dieterle,
Mischa Russell, Matty Malneck, Mario Perry, Charles Gaylord
(vn); Roy Bargy (p); Mike Pingitore (bj); Mike Trafficante (sb);
Min Leibrook (bb); Hal McDonald (d).

CVE 43119    **Sea Burial** (Lane—arr. Grofe)
*Instrumental*
Released: Dec 18, 1931
Sales: 4,397

CVE 43119–1    Mastered: Vic 36044.
CVE 43119–2    Destroyed.
CVE 43119–3    Hold indefinitely. Never issued.

Same session

Charles Margulis, Henry Busse (t); Bix Beiderbecke (c); Boyce
Cullen, Wilbur Hall, Bill Rank (tb); Chet Hazlett, Frank Trumbauer (as); Irving Friedman (as/ts); Red Mayer (ts); Charles
Strickfaden (ts/bar); Kurt Dieterle, Mischa Russell, Matty Malneck (vn); Roy Bargy (p); Mike Pingitore (bj); Mike Trafficante
(sb); Min Leibrook (bb); Hal McDonald (d).

BVE 43120    **When You're With Somebody Else** (Etting-Gilbert—arr. Chal-
lis)
*Instrumental*
Released: (–1) May 25, 1928
Sales: 33,589
Released: (–2) Dec 12, 1941

BVE 43120–1    Mastered: Vic 21365; HMV B–5497; VicJ 21365; HMVAu EA–
346.
BVE 43120–2    Hold conditional. Vic 27689.
BVE 43120–3    Destroyed.
Soloists: Bix (2); Trumbauer (8).
Note: the only audible difference between takes –1 and –2 of
this selection is in Bix's phrasing of his two-bar written solo
during the verse. On –1, he slurs the figure; on –2, he tongues
it, and brings it out more as a solo.

Mar 1 (Thu)

PAUL WHITEMAN AND HIS ORCHESTRA
*Victor Record Co.*
*New York City*
*Time: 10:15 A.M. – 12:00 P.M.*
     *2:00 P.M. – 5:30 P.M.*
Charles Margulis, Eddie Pinder (t); Bix Beiderbecke (c); Boyce
Cullen, Wilbur Hall (tb); Chet Hazlett (cl/as); Irving Friedman
(as); Rube Crozier (cl/f); Frank Trumbauer (cl/as/bsn); Red
Mayer (o/ts/cl); Charles Strickfaden (o/f/as); Kurt Dieterle,
Mischa Russell, Mario Perry, Matty Malneck (vn); Roy Bargy (p);
Mike Pingitore (bj); Mike Trafficante (sb); Min Leibrook (bb);
Hal McDonald (d).

CVE 43123    **Selections from "Show Boat"** (Hammerstein-Kern—arr. Satterfield)

434

Vocal: Mixed Chorus—Olive Kline, D. Baker, V. Hold, R. Rogers (sopranos); E. Baker, H. Clark, E. Indermauer (altos); Lambert Murphy, Harrison, James, Hause (tenors); Glenn, Shaw, Croxtown, Kinsly (basses).
Medley: "Why Do I Love You?" (Kline, solo) "Can't Help Lovin' Dat Man" (Chorus) "You Are Love" (Murphy, solo) "Make Believe" (Kline & Murphy duet with Chorus)
Released: Apr 20, 1928

CVE 43123–1 Destroyed.
CVE 43123–2 Mastered: Vic 35912; VicC 35912; VicArg 35912; HMV C–1505; HMVIn C–1505; GrFr L–657; GrIt R–4697; ElGe EH–225.
CVE 43123–3 Destroyed.
CVE 43123–4 Hold indefinitely. Issued: NAT WEP–804 (exc).
Soloists: Bix (12).

Bix Beiderbecke does not appear on the other selections from this session:

CVE 43122 Ol' Man River (Hammerstein-Kern—arr. Satterfield)
Vic 35912
CVE 30181 Suite of Serenades (Part 1) (Herbert—arr. Grofe)
Vic 35926
BVE 43121 Assigned to The Rhythm Boys

*Mar 2 (Fri)*

PAUL WHITEMAN AND HIS ORCHESTRA
*Victor Record Co.*
*New York City*
*Domenico Savino, Recording Director*
*Paul Whiteman, Assistant Director*
*Time: 10:30 A.M. – 12:10 P.M.*
*1:15 P.M. – 3:50 P.M.*
Henry Busse, Charles Margulis, Eddie Pinder (t); Bix Beiderbecke (c); Boyce Cullen, Wilbur Hall, Bill Rank, Jack Fulton (tb); Chet Hazlett, Charles Strickfaden, Rube Crozier, Frank Trumbauer (as); Red Mayer (ts); Irving Friedman (bar); Kurt Dieterle, Mischa Russell, Matty Malneck, Mario Perry (vn); Roy Bargy, Tommy Satterfield (p); Mike Pingitore (bj); Mike Trafficante (sb); Min Leibrook (bb); Hal McDonald (d).

**CVE 43124** **A Study in Blue** (Savino—arr. Domenico Savino)
*Instrumental*
Released: Oct 21, 1932
CVE 43124–1 Destroyed.
CVE 43124–2 Hold indefinitely. Never issued.
CVE 43124–3 Mastered: Vic 36067.
*Omit Domenico Savino from rest of the session, Paul Whiteman is now the recording director.*

*Same session*

Charles Margulis, Henry Busse, Eddie Pinder (t); Bix Beiderbecke (c); Boyce Cullen, Wilbur Hall, Bill Rank (tb); Chet Hazlett (bcl/as); Irving Friedman, Rube Crozier (cl/as); Red Mayer (cl/ts); Charles Strickfaden (ts); Kurt Dieterle, Mischa Russell, Matty Malneck (vn); Roy Bargy (p); Mike Trafficante (sb); Min Leibrook (bb); Hal McDonald (d).

**BVE 43125** **Coquette** (Kahn-Lombardo—arr. Challis)
*Instrumental*
Released: (–1) Apr 27, 1928
Sales: 36,990
Released: (–2) Sept 22, 1937
BVE 43125–1 Mastered: Vic 21301; VicC 21301; VicJ 21301; HMV B–5564; HMVIn B–5564; GrFr K–5606; ElG EG–1161.

BVE 43125–2   Destroyed.
BVE 43125–3   Hold indefinitely. Issued: Vic 25675.
Soloists: Bix (16 as leader of brass trio); Rank (8).

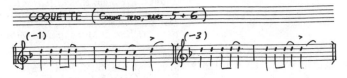

Bix Beiderbecke does not appear on the other recording from this session:
CVE 30180   Suite of Serenades (Herbert—arr. Grofe)
(Part Two) Vic 35926

*March 12 (Mon)*   PAUL WHITEMAN AND HIS ORCHESTRA
*Victor Record Co. Liederkranz Hall, NYC*
*Tommy Satterfield, Assistant Director*
*Time: 9:30 A.M. – 12:00 P.M.*
*2:00 P.M. – 3:00 P.M.*
Charles Margulis, Eddie Pinder (t); Bix Beiderbecke (c); Boyce Cullen, Bill Rank (tb); Chet Hazlett, Red Mayer (as); Rube Crozier, Charles Strickfaden (ts); Irving Friedman (cl); Frank Trumbauer (C-m); Roy Bargy (p); Mike Pingitore (bj); Mike Trafficante (sb); Min Leibrook (bb); Hal McDonald (d).
**BVE 43138**   **When** (Razaf-Schafer-Johnson—arr. Satterfield)
*Vocal: Jack Fulton, Charles Gaylord, Austin Young, Al Rinker, Harry Barris.*
Released: (–2) May 18, 1928
Sales: 32,760
BVE 43138–1   Destroyed.
BVE 43138–2   Mastered: Vic 21338; *Vic 25367*, VicJ 21338; HMV B–5493; GrFr K–5606.
BVE 43138–3   Hold indefinitely. Issued: Vic 21338.
Soloists: Friedman (8); Trumbauer (8); Bix (6 + 6).

Note: We presume the release date and sales of take –2 of "When" also apply to take –3.
Bix Beiderbecke does not appear on the other selections from this session:
BVE 43139   Down in Old Havana Town (Caesar-Friend—arr. Grofe)
Vic 27687
BVE 43140   I'm Wingin' Home (Russell-Tobias—arr. Satterfield)
Vic 21365

*March 13 (Tue)*   PAUL WHITEMAN AND HIS ORCHESTRA
*Victor Record Co.*
*New York City*
*Ferde Grofe, Assistant Recording Director*
*Time: 9:30 A.M. – 1:00 P.M.*
*2:30 P.M. – 4:00 P.M.*
Charles Margulis, Henry Busse, Eddie Pinder (t); Bix Beiderbecke (c); Boyce Cullen, Wilbur Hall, Bill Rank, Jack Fulton (tb); Chet Hazlett, Irving Friedman, Rube Crozier, Red Mayer,

Frank Trumbauer, Charles Strickfaden (reeds); Kurt Dieterle, Mischa Russell, Matty Malneck, Mario Perry (vn); Roy Bargy (p); Mike Pingitore (bj); Mike Trafficante (sb); Min Leibrook (bb); Hal McDonald (d).

**CVE 43141**    **Metropolis** (Grofe—arr. Grofe)
*Part One Instrumental*
Released: Oct 26, 1928

CVE 43141–1    Destroyed.
CVE 43141–2    Destroyed.
CVE 43141–3    Hold indefinitely. Never issued.
CVE 43141–4    Mastered: Vic 35933; VicC 35933; VicJ 35933; VicArg 35933; HMVAu EB–31.

**CVE 43142**    **Metropolis** (Grofe—arr. Grofe)
*Part Two Instrumental*
Released: Oct 26, 1928

CVE 43142–1    Destroyed.
CVE 43142–2    Destroyed.
CVE 43142–3    Hold indefinitely. Never issued.
CVE 43142–4    Mastered: Vic 35933; VicC 35933; VicJ 35933; VicArg 35933; HMVAu EB–31.
    Note: File card lists this piece as "Fantasia in E-Flat." See sessions of March 14 and 17 for additional information on "Metropolis."

*March 14 (Wed)*    PAUL WHITEMAN AND HIS ORCHESTRA
*Victor Record Co.*
*Leiderkranz Hall, NYC*
*Time: 9:30 A.M. – 12:00 P.M.*
Charles Margulis, Henry Busse, Eddie Pinder (t); Bix Beiderbecke (c); Boyce Cullen, Wilbur Hall, Bill Rank, Jack Fulton (tb); Chet Hazlett, Irving Friedman, Rube Crozier, Red Mayer, Frank Trumbauer, Charles Strickfaden (reeds); Kurt Dieterle, Mischa Russell, Matty Malneck, Mario Perry (vn); Roy Bargy (p); Mike Pingitore (bj); Mike Trafficante (sb); Min Leibrook (bb); Hal McDonald (d).

**CVE 43143**    **Metropolis** (Grofe—arr. Grofe)
*Part Three—"Incidental Singing"*
Released: Oct 26, 1928
*Vocal: Bing Crosby, Jack Fulton, Charles Gaylord, Al Rinker, Austin Young, Boyce Cullen.*

CVE 43143–1    Destroyed.
CVE 43143–2    Destroyed.
CVE 43143–3    Hold indefinitely. Never issued
CVE 43143–4    Mastered: Vic 35934; VicC 35934; VicJ 35934; VicArg 35934; HMVAu EB–32.
    Bix Beiderbecke does not appear on the other selection from this session:

**BVE 43144**    Ma Belle (Grey-Friml—arr. Grofe)
Vic 21315

*March 15 (Thu)*    PAUL WHITEMAN AND HIS ORCHESTRA
*Victor Record Co.*
*Liederkranz Hall, NYC*
*Time: 9:30 A.M. – 12:00 P.M.*
Charles Margulis, Eddie Pinder (t); Bix Beiderbecke (c); Boyce Cullen, Wilbur Hall (tb); Chet Hazlett, Rube Crozier (as); Irving Friedman, Red Mayer (cl/ts); Charles Strickfaden (ts/bar); Kurt Dieterle, Mischa Russell, Matty Malneck (vn); Roy Bargy (p); Mike Pingitore (bj); Mike Trafficante (sb); Min Leibrook (bb); Hal McDonald (d).

**BVE 43145**    **Lovable** (Holmes-Simons-Whiting—arr. Challis)
*Vocal: Bing Crosby*
Released: (USA) Dec 12, 1941

BVE 43145–1    Mastered: HMV B–5509; *Vic 27685; HMVAu EA–3235;* HMVIt AE–2302.
BVE 43145–2    Destroyed.
BVE 43145–3    Destroyed.

Soloists: Friedman (32 ts); Bix (8).

Note: "Lovable" was issued in Great Britain in 1928, but not in the USA until 1941. A test pressing bears the legend, "Not fit to use. Surface noise too bad." The US issue carries a "2R" in the runoff groove, but this does not signify an alternate take. The issue is, in fact, dubbed from HMV B–5509.

Bix Beiderbecke does not appear on the following selection from this session, recorded between 1:00 P.M. and 2:20 P.M.. Band then rehearsed until 4:15 P.M..

BVE 43146    When You're in Love (Blaufass-Donaldson—arr. Satterfield) Vic 21325

*March 16 (Fri)*    **PAUL WHITEMAN AND HIS ORCHESTRA**
Bix Beiderbecke does not appear on the following recordings from this session:

BVE 43147    Little Log Cabin of Dreams (Hanley-Dowling—arr. Challis) Vic 21325

BVE 43148    March of the Musketeers (Frey-Friml—arr. Satterfield) Vic 21315

*March 17 (Sat)*    **PAUL WHITEMAN AND HIS ORCHESTRA**
*Victor Record Co.*
*Liederkranz Hall, NYC*
*Ferde Grofe, Recording Director*
*Paul Whiteman, Assistant Director*
Charles Margulis, Henry Busse, Eddie Pinder (t); Bix Beiderbecke (c); Boyce Cullen, Wilbur Hall, Bill Rank, Jack Fulton (tb); Chet Hazlett, Irving Friedman, Rube Crozier, Red Mayer, Frank Trumbauer, Charles Strickfaden (reeds); Kurt Dieterle, Mischa Russell, Matty Malneck, Mario Perry, Charles Gaylord (vn); Roy Bargy (p); Mike Pingitore (bj); Min Leibrook (bb); Mike Trafficante (sb); Hal McDonald (d).

CVE 43149    **Metropolis** (Grofe—arr. Grofe)
*Part Four Instrumental*
Released: Oct 26, 1928

CVE 43149–1    Destroyed.
CVE 43149–2    Hold indefinitely. Never issued.
CVE 43149–3    Mastered: Vic 35934; VicC 35934; VicJ 35934; VicArg 35934; HMVAu EB–32.

*April 3 (Tue)*    **FRANK TRUMBAUER AND HIS ORCHESTRA**
*Okeh Record Co.*
*New York City*
Bix Beiderbecke (c); Charles Margulis (t); Bill Rank (tb); Irving Friedman (cl/as); Frank Trumbauer (C-m); Charles Strickfaden (as); Min Leibrook (bsx); Matty Malneck (vn); Lennie Hayton (p); Eddie Lang (g); Hal McDonald (d).

W 400188    **Our Bungalow of Dreams** (Malie-Newman-Verges)
*Vocal: "Noel Taylor"*

W 400188–A    Mastered: OK 41019; ParE R–142; ParG A–4543; *Tpl 542;* OdG 04074; OdG A–189148; OdArg 193172; OdFr 165362.
W 400188–B    Rejected.
W 400188–C    Rejected.

W 400189    **Lila** (Gottler-Tobias-Pinkard)
*Vocal: "Noel Taylor"*

W 400189–A    Rejected.
W 400189–B    Mastered: OK 41019; ParE R–141; ParG A–4543; *Tpl 542;* OdG 04074; OdG A–189148; OdArg 193172; OdFr 165362.

Note: The name "Noel Taylor" appears to have been used by Okeh to disguise several singers for a variety of reasons. The identity of this particular "Taylor" remains a mystery.

*April 10 (Tue)*    **FRANK TRUMBAUER AND HIS ORCHESTRA**
*Okeh Record Co.*
*New York City*
Bix Beiderbecke (c); Charles Margulis (t); Bill Rank (tb); Irving Friedman (cl/as); Frank Trumbauer (C-m); Charles Strickfaden

(as); Min Leibrook (bsx); Matty Malneck (vn); Lennie Hayton (p); Eddie Lang (g); Hal McDonald (d).

**W 400603**    **Borneo** (Donaldson—arr. Challis)
*Vocal: Harold "Scrappy" Lambert.*
Released: June 5, 1928
Sales: 3,000

W 400603–A    Rejected.
W 400603–B    Mastered: OK 41039; ParE R–203; OdArg 193190; OdFr 165360; OdG A–189159; ColArg 20674.
W 400603–C    Rejected.

**W 400604**    **My Pet** (Yellen-Ager—arr. Challis)
*Vocal: Harold "Scrappy" Lambert.*
Released: June 5, 1928
Sales: 3,000

W 400604–A    Rejected.
W 400604–B    Rejected.
W 400604–C    Mastered: OK 41039; ParE R–141; OdArg 193190; OdFr 165360; OdG A–189159.
Note: ParE R–203 by "The Goofus Five and Their Orchestra."

*April 17 (Tue)*      **BIX BEIDERBECKE AND HIS GANG**
*Okeh Record Co.*
*New York City*
Bix Beiderbecke (c); Irving Friedman (cl); Bill Rank (tb); Roy Bargy (p); Min Leibrook (bsx); Stan King (d).

**W 400616**    **Somebody Stole My Gal** (Wood)
*Instrumental*
Released: May 25, 1928
Sales: 2,400

W 400616–A    Rejected.
W 400616–B    Mastered: OK 41030; Br8242; ParE R–161; OdArg 193191; Special Edition 5013–S; ColArg 20304; OdG A–189169; OdArg 194491.
W 400616–C    Rejected.

**W 400617**    **Thou Swell** (Rodgers-Hart)
*Instrumental*
Released: May 25, 1928
Sales: 2,400

W 400617–A    Rejected.
W 400617–B    Rejected.
W 400617–C    Mastered: OK 41030; ParE R–451; ParE R–2355; OdArg 193191; OdArg 194491; OdFr 165358; OdG A–189169; Col 35665.

*April 21 (Sat)*      **PAUL WHITEMAN AND HIS ORCHESTRA**
*Victor Record Co.*
*Liederkranz Hall, NYC*
*Ferde Grofe, Recording Director*
*Time: 10:00 A.M. – 1:25 P.M.*
       *2:25 P.M. – 4:00 P.M.*
Charles Margulis, Henry Busse, Eddie Pinder (t); Bix Beiderbecke (c); Boyce Cullen, Bill Rank, Wilbur Hall, Jack Fulton (tb); Chet Hazlett, Frank Trumbauer, Irving Friedman, Red Mayer, Rube Crozier, Charles Strickfaden (reeds); Mischa Russell, Kurt Dieterle, Mario Perry, Matty Malneck, John Bowman, Charles Gaylord (vn); Min Leibrook (bb); Mike Trafficante (sb); Hal McDonald (d).

**BVE 43659**    **In My Bouquet of Memories** (Lewis-Young-Akst——arr. Satterfield)
*Vocal: Austin Young, Charles Gaylord, Al Rinker, Jack Fulton.*
Released: Jun 15, 1928
Sales: 96,448

BVE 43659–1    Mastered: Vic 21388; HMV B–5510; ElG EG–1000.
BVE 43659–2    Destroyed.
BVE 43659–3    Hold conditional. Never issued.
BVE 43659–4    Hold indefinitely. Never issued.

**1928:**

*Same session* Charles Margulis, Henry Busse, Eddie Pinder (t); Bix Beiderbecke (c); Boyce Cullen, Wilbur Hall, Bill Rank, Jack Fulton (tb); Chet Hazlett (cl/as); Irving Friedman (ts/cl); Rube Crozier (cl/as/f); Red Mayer (o/ts/cl/as/English Horn); Frank Trumbauer (cl/ts); Charles Strickfaden (bar/ts/o); Matty Malneck, Mario Perry, Mischa Russell, John Bowman, Charles Gaylord, Kurt Dieterle (vn); Roy Bargy, Lennie Hayton (p); Mike Pingitore (bj); Mike Trafficante (sb); Min Leibrook (bb); Hal McDonald (d).

BVE 43660 **I'm Afraid of You** (Davis-Daly-Gottler—arr. Satterfield)
*Vocal: Bing Crosby*
Released: (–4) Jun 8, 1928
Released: (–3) Dec 12, 1941
BVE 43660–1 Destroyed.
BVE 43660–2 Destroyed.
BVE 43660–3 Hold indefinitely. Issued: Vic 27685.
BVE 43660–4 Mastered: Vic 21389; HMV B–5541; HMVAu EA–373; ElG EG–979.

*Same session* Henry Busse, Charles Margulis, Eddie Pinder (t); Bix Beiderbecke (c); Boyce Cullen, Bill Rank, Wilbur Hall, Jack Fulton (tb); Chet Hazlett (as/cl); Irving Friedman (ts); Red Mayer (ts/cl/as); Rube Crozier (ts/cl/f); Frank Trumbauer (as); Charles Strickfaden (bar/o); Kurt Dieterle, Mischa Russell, Matty Malneck, Mario Perry, John Bowman, Charles Gaylord (vn); Roy Bargy, Lennie Hayton (p); Mike Pingitore (bj); Mike Trafficante (sb); Min Leibrook (bb); Hal McDonald (d).

BVE 43661 **My Angel** (Pollock-Rapee—arr. Satterfield)
*Vocal: Jack Fulton, Charles Gaylord, Al Rinker.*
Released: Jun 15, 1928
Sales: 96,448
BVE 43661–1 Mastered: Vic 21388; HMV B–5510; ElG EG–1000.
BVE 43661–2 Hold indefinitely. Never issued.
BVE 43661–3 Hold conditional. Never issued.

*April 22 (Sun)* **PAUL WHITEMAN AND HIS ORCHESTRA**
*Victor Record Co.*
*New York City*
*Ferde Grofe, Assistant Director*
*Time: 10:00 A.M. – 12:05 P.M.*
*1:05 P.M. – 3:00 P.M.*
Henry Busse, Eddie Pinder, Bix Beiderbecke, Charles Margulis (t/c); Boyce Cullen, Bill Rank, Wilbur Hall, Jack Fulton (tb); Chet Hazlett (as); Rube Crozier (as); Red Mayer (ts); Irving Friedman (cl/ts); Frank Trumbauer (C-m); Charles Strickfaden (bar/ts); Mischa Russell, Kurt Dieterle, Matty Malneck, Mario Perry, John Bowman, Charles Gaylord (vn); Roy Bargy, Lennie Hayton, Ferde Grofe (p); Mike Pingitore (bj); Mike Trafficante (sb); Min Leibrook (bb/bsx); Hal McDonald (d).

BVE 43662 **My Pet** (Yellen-Ager—arr. Challis)
*Vocal: Bing Crosby, Al Rinker, Austin Young, Charles Gaylord.*
Released: (–2) Jun 8, 1928
Released: (–1) Dec 12, 1941
BVE 43662–1 Hold indefinitely. Issued: Vic 27686.
BVE 43662–2 Mastered: Vic 21389; HMV B–5504; HMVIn B–5504; HMVAu EA–373; ElG EG–979.
BVE 43662–3 Hold conditional. Issued: *Bwy 102.*
Soloists: Bix (8 intro); Bix (16 ensemble lead in verse); Bix (16 ensemble lead); Trumbauer (8).

440

*Same session*

Charles Margulis, Henry Busse, Eddie Pinder (t); Bix Beiderbecke (c); Boyce Cullen, Bill Rank, Wilbur Hall, Jack Fulton (tb);
Chet Hazlett (bcl/cl/as); Irving Friedman (cl/ts); Red Mayer
(cl/as/English Horn); Rube Crozier (f/ts/cl); Frank Trumbauer
(C-m/as); Charles Strickfaden (cl/ts/o); Mischa Russell, Kurt
Dieterle, Mario Perry, Matty Malneck, John Bowman, Charles
Gaylord (vn); Roy Bargy, Lennie Hayton (p); Mike Pingitore
(bj); Mike Trafficante (sb); Min Leibrook (bb/bsx); Hal McDonald (d).

**BVE 43663**   **It Was the Dawn of Love** (Coots—arr. Satterfield)
*Vocal: Bing Crosby, Charles Gaylord, Austin Young, Al Rinker.*
Released: July 13, 1928
Sales: 31,119

BVE 43663–1   Hold conditional Issued: *Bwy 102 (LP).*
BVE 43663–2   Mastered: Vic 21453; HMV B–5522; GrIt R–14001; ElG EG–
932; HMVAu EA–381.
BVE 43663–3   Hold indefinitely. Issued: *Bwy 102 (LP).*

*Same session*

Charles Margulis, Henry Busse, Eddie Pinder (t); Bix Beider-
becke (c); Boyce Cullen, Bill Rank, Wilbur Hall, Jack Fulton (tb);
Chet Hazlett (cl/as); Irving Friedman (ts/cl); Red Mayer (cl);
Rube Crozier (f); Frank Trumbauer (as/C-m); Charles Strick-
faden (ts); Mischa Russell, Kurt Dieterle, Matty Malneck, Mario
Perry, John Bowman, Charles Gaylord (vn); Lennie Hayton,
Roy Bargy (p); Mike Pingitore (bj); Min Leibrook (bb); Mike
Trafficante (sb); Hal McDonald (d).

**BVE 43664**   **Dancing Shadows** (Golden—arr. Satterfield)
*Vocal: "Humming" by Bing Crosby, Al Rinker, Charles Gay-
lord, Austin Young.*
Released: June 22, 1928
Sales: 36,491

BVE 43664–1   Mastered: Vic 21341; Vic 27687; HMV B–5511, HMVAu EA–
367.
BVE 43664–2   Destroyed.

BVE 43664–3    Hold indefinitely. Never issued.
Soloists: Trumbauer (8 + 7); Rank (8 + 8)

*Same session*    Charles Margulis, Henry Busse, Eddie Pinder (t); Bix Beider-
becke (c); Boyce Cullen, Bill Rank, Wilbur Hall, Jack Fulton (tb);
Chet Hazlett (as/Ebcl); Irving Friedman (ts/cl); Red Mayer (ts);
Rube Crozier, Frank Trumbauer (as); Charles Strickfaden
(ts/bar); Mischa Russell, Kurt Dieterle, Matty Malneck, Mario
Perry, John Bowman, Charles Gaylord (vn); Mike Pingitore (bj);
Min Leibrook (bb); Mike Trafficante (sb); Hal McDonald (d).

**BVE 43665**    **Forget-Me-Not** (MacBeth—arr. Challis)
*Vocal: Jack Fulton.*
Released: Dec 12, 1941

BVE 43665–1    Destroyed.
BVE 43665–2    Hold indefinitely. Issued: Vic 27686.
BVE 43665–3    Mastered. Issued RCA 741093 (LP).
Soloists: Bix (16 lead in verse); Bix (16).

April 23 (Mon)    **PAUL WHITEMAN AND HIS ORCHESTRA**
*Victor Record Co.*
*Liederkranz Hall, NYC*
*Ferde Grofe, Recording Director (1st title)*
*Bill Challis, Recording Director (2nd title)*
*Time: 10:00 A.M. – 12:05 P.M.*
*1:05 P.M. – 4:00 P.M.*
Charles Margulis, Henry Busse, Eddie Pinder (t); Bix Beider-
becke (c); Boyce Cullen, Bill Rank, Wilbur Hall, Jack Fulton (tb);
Chet Hazlett, Irving Friedman, Red Mayer, Rube Crozier,
Frank Trumbauer (as); Charles Strickfaden (ts); Mischa Russell,
Kurt Dieterle, Matty Malneck, Mario Perry, John Bowman,
Charles Gaylord (vn); Roy Bargy (p); Lennie Hayton (p/cel);
Mike Pingitore (bj); Mike Trafficante (sb); Min Leibrook (bb);
Hal McDonald (d).

**BVE 43666**    **Dixie Dawn** (Trent-deRose—arr. Grofe)
*Vocal: Austin Young*
Released: July 6, 1928
Sales: 33,462

BVE 43666–1    Hold conditional. Never issued.
BVE 43666–2    Hold indefinitely. Never issued.
BVE 43666–3    Mastered: Vic 21438; HMV B–5515; ElG EG–933.
BVE 43666–4    Destroyed.

*Same session*    Charles Margulis, Henry Busse, Eddie Pinder (t); Bix Beider-
becke (c); Boyce Cullen, Wilbur Hall, Bill Rank, Jack Fulton (tb);
Chet Hazlett (as); Irving Friedman (ts/cl); Red Mayer (ts); Rube
Crozier (as); Frank Trumbauer (as/C-m); Charles Strickfaden
(bar); Mischa Russell, Kurt Dieterle, Matty Malneck, Mario
Perry, John Bowman, Charles Gaylord (vn); Roy Bargy, Lennie
Hayton (p); Mike Pingitore (bj); Mike Trafficante (sb); Min Lei-
brook (bb); Hal McDonald (d).

**BVE 43667**    **Louisiana** (Razaf-Schafer-Johnson—arr. Challis)
*Vocal: Bing Crosby, with Jack Fulton, Austin Young, Charles
Gaylord.*
Released: (–1) July 6, 1928
Sales: 33,462
Released: (–3) July 30, 1936

BVE 43667–1    Mastered: Vic 21438; VicC 21438; *Bm 1030;* HMV B–5522;
HMVAu EA–386; HMVIn N–4475; VdPIt GW–1759; ElG EG–
933; HMVSs JK–2809.

**1928:**

BVE 43667–2   Destroyed.
BVE 43667–3   Hold conditional. Issued: Vic 25369; HMV B–8913.
                Soloists: Friedman (16 in ensemble); Bix (16).

LOUISIANA (CORNET SOLO, BARS 15 + 16)

Note: Both sides cut during afternoon session. Morning devoted to rehearsal and cutting tests of "Blue Danube Waltz," scrapped at Whiteman's order.

*April 24 (Tue)*

PAUL WHITEMAN AND HIS ORCHESTRA
*Victor Record Co. Liederkranz Hall, NYC*
*10:00 A.M.—11:45 A.M.*
*1:00 P.M.—2:30 P.M.*
Henry Busse, Charles Margulis, Eddie Pinder (t); Bix Beiderbecke (c); Boyce Cullen, Wilbur Hall, Bill Rank, Jack Fulton (tb); Chet Hazlett (bcl/as/cl); Irving Friedman (ts); Red Mayer (cl/as/o); Rube Crozier (cl/as/bsn/ts); Frank Trumbauer (as/bsn); Charles Strickfaden (o/ts); Mischa Russell, Kurt Dieterle, Matty Malneck, Mario Perry, John Bowman, Charles Gaylord (vn); Mike Pingitore (bj); Min Leibrook (bb); Mike Trafficante (sb); Roy Bargy, Lennie Hayton (p); Hal McDonald (d).

BVE 43668     **Grieving** (Axtell—arr. Satterfield)
*Vocal: Jack Fulton, Bing Crosby, Charles Gaylord, Al Rinker.*
Released: Oct 26, 1928
Sales: 35,730

BVE 43668–1   Destroyed.
BVE 43668–2   Mastered: Vic 21678; HMV B–5541.
BVE 43668–3   Hold indefinitely. Never issued.
                Note: The band broke for lunch after recording this selection.

Henry Busse, Charles Margulis, Eddie Pinder (t); Bix Beiderbecke (c); Boyce Cullen, Wilbur Hall, Bill Rank, Jack Fulton (tb); Chet Hazlett (ss/as/); Irving Friedman (ts); Rube Crozier (ts/as); Red Mayer (as); Frank Trumbauer (as/C-m); Charles Strickfaden (ss/ts); Kurt Dieterle, Mischa Russell, Matty Malneck, Mario Perry, John Bowman, Charles Gaylord (vn); Mike Pingitore (bj); Min Leibrook (bb); Mike Trafficante (sb); Roy Bargy, Lennie Hayton (p); Hal McDonald (d).

BVE 43669     **Do I Hear You Saying** (Rodgers-Hart—arr. Satterfield)
*Vocal: Bing Crosby, Al Rinker, Charles Gaylord.*
Released: June 29, 1928
Sales: 46,282

BVE 43669–1   Destroyed.
BVE 43669–2   Mastered: Vic 21398; ElGe EG929.
BVE 43669–3   Hold indefinitely. Never issued.
                Soloists: Trumbauer (32)
                Note: At this point, a quarrel developed between Whiteman and Henry Busse, culminating in his firing both him and Hal McDonald on the spot. Whiteman then postponed the remainder of this session until the following morning. It is not entirely certain whether Busse's and McDonald's replacements, Harry "Goldie" Goldfield and George Marsh, actually played the last selection, but they were in the band two days later for an opening in Boston. The authors have assumed that they took their places on April 25.

*April 25 (Wed)*

PAUL WHITEMAN AND HIS ORCHESTRA
*Victor Record Co. Liederkranz Hall, NYC*
*Time: 10:00—11:30 A.M.*
Charles Margulis, Harry Goldfield, Eddie Pinder (t); Bix Beiderbecke (c); Boyce Cullen, Bill Rank, Wilbur Hall, Jack Fulton (tb);

1928:

|  | Chet Hazlett (bcl/cl/as); Irving Friedman (ts); Rube Crozier (cl/f/ts); Red Mayer (as/cl/bar); Frank Trumbauer (as/C-m); Charles Strickfaden (reeds); Kurt Dieterle, Mischa Russell, Matty Malneck, Mario Perry, John Bowman, Charles Gaylord (vn); Mike Pingitore (bj); Min Leibrook (bb); Mike Trafficante (sb); Roy Bargy, Lennie Hayton (p); George Marsh (d). |

**BVE 43760**     **You Took Advantage of Me** (Rodgers-Hart—arr. Satterfield)
*Vocal: Bing Crosby, with Austin Young, Jack Fulton, Charles Gaylord.*
Released: June 29, 1928
Sales: 46,282

BVE 43760–1     Mastered: Vic 21398; Vic 25369; *Blt 1030*; HMVAu EA–816; ElGe EG–929; Collector's Item No. 2.
BVE 43760–2     Destroyed.
BVE 43760–3     Hold indefinitely. Never issued.
Note: Sometimes a "2" will appear in the runoff grooves, particularly on foreign issues. This is a speeded-up version of take –1, not the issue of take –2.
Soloists: Bix & Trumbauer (32 duet)

*May 12 (Sat)*     PAUL WHITEMAN AND HIS ORCHESTRA
*Columbia Record Co.*
*New York City*
Charles Margulis, Harry Goldfield, Eddie Pinder (t); Bix Beiderbecke (c); Boyce Cullen, Bill Rank, Wilbur Hall, Jack Fulton (tb); Chet Hazlett (cl/as/Ebcl/bcl); Irving Friedman (cl/ts/as); Rube Crozier (English Horn/bsn/as/cl); Red Mayer (f/o/as/ts/bsn); Frank Trumbauer (cl/bsn/C-m); Charles Strickfaden (cl/as/bar/English Horn); Kurt Dieterle, Mischa Russell, Matty Malneck (vn); Roy Bargy, Lennie Hayton (p); Mike Pingitore (bj); Mike Trafficante (sb); Min Leibrook (bb); Wilbur Hall (g); George Marsh (d); unidentified (slide whistle).

**W 98533**     **La Paloma (The Dove)** (Yradier-Kautner—arr. Grofe)
*Instrumental*
W 98533–1     Rejected.
W 98533–2     Rejected.
W 98533–3     Rejected.

*Same session*     Charles Margulis, Harry Goldfield, Eddie Pinder (t); Bix Beiderbecke (c); Boyce Cullen, Wilbur Hall, Bill Rank, Jack Fulton (tb); Chet Hazlett (Ebcl/cl/as); Irving Friedman (cl/bar/as); Rube Crozier (as/ss/English Horn/bsn/cl); Red Mayer (as/bsn/o); Frank Trumbauer (C-m/as); Charles Strickfaden (cl/ss/o/bar/as); Kurt Dieterle, Mischa Russell, Matty Malneck; Charles Gaylord (vn); Roy Bargy, Lennie Hayton (p); Mike Pingitore (bj); Mike Trafficante (sb); Min Leibrook (bb); George Marsh (d).

**W 98534**     **La Golondrina** (Serradell—arr. Grofe)
*Instrumental*
W 98534–1     Rejected.
W 98534–2     Second choice. Unissued.
W 98534–3     Mastered: Col 50070–D; ColE 9459; ColAu 07501.

*Same session*     Bix Beiderbecke does not appear on the remaining selection from this session:
W 98535     My Hero (Stange-Strauss—arr. Satterfield)
Col 50069–D

*May 13 (Sun)*     PAUL WHITEMAN AND HIS ORCHESTRA
*Columbia Record Co.*
*New York City*
Bix Beiderbecke does not appear on any recordings from this session:
W 98536     The Merry Widow (Lehar—arr. Satterfield)
Col 50069–D
W 146249     Last Night I Dreamed You Kissed Me (Lombardo-Kahn—arr. Satterfield)
Col rejected

**1928:**

<table>
<tr><td>W 146250</td><td>Evening Star (Turk-Ahlert—arr Satterfield)<br>Col rejected</td></tr>
</table>

*May 15 (Tue)*

**PAUL WHITEMAN AND HIS ORCHESTRA**
*Columbia Record Co.*
*New York City*
Charles Margulis, Harry Goldfield, Eddie Pinder (t); Bix Beider-becke (c); Boyce Cullen, Wilbur Hall, Bill Rank, Jack Fulton (tb); Chet Hazlett (bcl/as); Irving Friedman, Rube Crozier (cl/ts); Red Mayer (cl/as); Frank Trumbauer (as); Charles Strickfaden (ts/cl); Kurt Dieterle, Mischa Russell, Matty Malneck, Charles Gaylord (vn); Roy Bargy (p); Lennie Hayton (cel); Mike Pingitore (bj); Mike Trafficante (sb); Min Leibrook (bb); George Marsh (d).

W 98537 · **My Melancholy Baby** (Burnett-Norton—arr. Satterfield)
*Vocal: Austin Young*

W 98537–1 · Rejected.
W 98537–2 · Second choice. Unissued.
W 98537–3 · Rejected.
W 98537–4 · Mastered: Col 50068–D; ColE 9578; ColAu 07053.
Soloists: Bix (32 obligato to vocal).

*May 16 (Wed)*

**PAUL WHITEMAN AND HIS ORCHESTRA**
*Columbia Record Co.*
*New York City*
Charles Margulis, Harry Goldfield, Eddie Pinder (t); Bix Beider-becke (c); Boyce Cullen, Wilbur Hall, Bill Rank, Jack Fulton (tb); Chet Hazlett (bcl/cl/as/Ebcl); Irving Friedman (cl/as); Rube Crozier (ss/bsn); Red Mayer (ss/Eng Horn/as); Frank Trum-bauer (C-m/bsn); Charles Strickfaden (ss/o/cl); Kurt Dieterle, Mischa Russell, Matty Malneck, Charles Gaylord (vn); Roy Bargy, Lennie Hayton (p); Mike Pingitore (bj); Mike Trafficante (sb); Min Leibrook (bb); George Marsh (d).

W 98538 · **The Man I Love** (G. & I. Gershwin—arr. Grofe)
*Vocal: Vaughn de Leath*

W 98538–1 · Rejected.
W 98538–2 · Mastered: Col 50068–D.
W 98538–3 · Rejected.
W 98538–4 · Second choice. "Not to be used." Issued: Col 50068–D; CoAu 07053.
Soloists: Trumbauer (16).

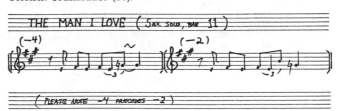

*May 17 (Thu)*

**PAUL WHITEMAN AND HIS ORCHESTRA**
*Columbia Record Co.*
*New York City*
Charles Margulis, Harry Goldfield, Eddie Pinder (t); Bix Beider-becke (c); Boyce Cullen, Bill Rank, Wilbur Hall (tb); Chet Haz-lett (cl/as); Irving Friedman (as/cl/ts); Rube Crozier (f/bsn); Charles Strickfaden (bar/ts/cl); Kurt Dieterle, Mischa Rus-sell, Matty Malneck (vn); Roy Bargy (p); Mike Pingitore (bj); Mike Trafficante (sb); Min Leibrook (bb); George Marsh (d).

W 146291 · **C-O-N-S-T-A-N-T-I-N-O-P-L-E** (de Sylva-Brown-Henderson— arr. Satterfield)

1928:

|  |  |
|---|---|
|  | Vocal: Austin Young, Jack Fulton, Charles Gaylord, Al Rinker, Harry Barris. |
|  | Released: June 20, 1928 |
|  | Sales: 30,000 |
| W 146291–1 | Rejected. |
| W 146291–2 | Mastered: Col 1402–D; ColE 4951; ColAu 07002; ColG C–4951. |
| W 146291–3 | Second choice. Issued: Col 1402–D. |

*May 21 (Mon)*    **PAUL WHITEMAN AND HIS ORCHESTRA**
*Columbia Record Co.*
*New York City*
Charles Margulis, Harry Goldfield, Eddie Pinder (t); Bix Beiderbecke (c); Boyce Cullen, Bill Rank, Wilbur Hall (tb); Chet Hazlett (cl/as/Ebcl/bcl); Irving Friedman (cl/ts/as); Rube Crozier (EngHorn/bsn/as/cl); Red Mayer (f/o/as/ts/bsn); Frank Trumbauer (cl/bsn/C-m); Charles Strickfaden (cl/bar/as/EngHorn); Kurt Dieterle, Mischa Russell, Matty Malneck (vn); Roy Bargy, Lennie Hayton (p); Mike Pingitore (bj); Mike Trafficante (sb); Min Leibrook (bb); George Marsh (d); unknown (g); unknown (slide whistle).

**W 98533**    **La Paloma (The Dove)** (Yradier-Kautner—arr. Grofe)
*Instrumental*

| W 98533–4 | Rejected. |
|---|---|
| W 98533–5 | Rejected. |
| W 98533–6 | Mastered: Col 50070–D; ColE 9459; ColAu 07501. |

*Same session*    Charles Margulis, Harry Goldfield (t); Bix Beiderbecke (c); Boyce Cullen, Wilbur Hall, Bill Rank (tb); Chet Hazlett (as/bcl); Irving Friedman (ts/cl); Rube Crozier (as/bsn); Red Mayer (ts/bar/cl); Frank Trumbauer (C-m/bsn); Charles Strickfaden (ts/bar/EngHorn); Kurt Dieterle, Matty Malneck, Mischa Russell, Mario Perry (vn); Roy Bargy (p); Mike Pingitore (bj); Mike Trafficante (sb); Min Leibrook (bb); George Marsh (d).

**W 146316**    **'Tain't So, Honey, 'Tain't So** (Robison—arr. Challis)
*Vocal: Bing Crosby*

| W 146316–1 | Rejected. |
|---|---|
| W 146316–2 | Rejected. |
| W 146316–3 | Rejected. |
| W 146316–4 | Rejected. |
|  | Bix Beiderbecke does not appear on the other selections from this session: |
| W 146249 | Last Night I Dreamed You Kissed Me (Lombardo-Kahn—arr. Satterfield) |
|  | Col 1401–D |
| W 146250 | Evening Star (Turk-Ahlert—arr. Satterfield) |
|  | Col 1401–D |

*May 22 (Tue)*    **PAUL WHITEMAN AND HIS ORCHESTRA**
*Columbia Record Co.*
*New York City*
Harry Goldfield, Charles Margulis (t); Bix Beiderbecke (c); Boyce Cullen, Bill Rank, Wilbur Hall (tb); Chet Hazlett, Rube Crozier, Frank Trumbauer (as); Irving Friedman (ts/cl); Red Mayer (ts); Charles Strickfaden (ts/bar); Kurt Dieterle, Mischa Russell, Matty Malneck, Mario Perry (vn); Roy Bargy (p); Mike Pingitore (bj); Mike Trafficante (sb); Min Leibrook (bb/bsx); George Marsh (d).

**W 146317**    **Is It Gonna Be Long** (Cowan-Abbot-Whiting—arr. Challis)
*Instrumental*
Released: Aug 30, 1928
Sales: 21,125

| W 146317–1 | Rejected. |
|---|---|
| W 146317–2 | Second choice. Unissued. |
| W 146317–3 | Mastered: Col 1496–D; ColE 4956; ColArg A–8002; ColG C–4956; ColAu 07004. |
| W 146317–4 | Rejected. |
|  | Soloists: Bix (4); Friedman (16 & 8). |

1928:

| | |
|---|---|
| *Same session* | Harry Goldfield, Charles Margulis, Eddie Pinder (t); Bix Beiderbecke (c); Boyce Cullen, Bill Rank, Wilbur Hall (tb); Chet Hazlett (bcl/Ebcl); Irving Friedman (cl); Rube Crozier (f/bsn/as/cl); Red Mayer (o/bsn/cl); Frank Trumbauer (as/bsn); Charles Strickfaden (o/cl/bar); Kurt Dieterle, Mischa Russell, Matty Malneck, Mario Perry, John Bowman, Charles Gaylord (vn); Roy Bargy, Lennie Hayton (p); Mike Pingitore (bj); Mike Trafficante (sb); Min Leibrook (bb); George Marsh (d). |
| **W 146318** | **Japanese Mammy** (Donaldson-Kahn—arr. Grofe ?) |
| | *Vocal: Quintet (or Austin Young and members of trio)* |
| W 146318–1 | Rejected. |
| W 146318–2 | Rejected. |
| W 146318–3 | Rejected. |
| W 146318–4 | Rejected. |

| | |
|---|---|
| *Same session* | Harry Goldfield, Charles Margulis, Eddie Pinder (t); Bix Beiderbecke (c); Boyce Cullen, Wilbur Hall, Bill Rank, Jack Fulton (tb); Chet Hazlett (as/cl); Irving Friedman, Rube Crozier (ts/cl); Red Mayer (as); Frank Trumbauer (as/C-m); Charles Strickfaden (ts); Mischa Russell, Kurt Dieterle, Matty Malneck, Mario Perry (vn); Roy Bargy (p); Mike Pingitore (bj); Mike Trafficante (sb); Min Leibrook (bb); George Marsh (d). |
| **W 146320** | **I'd Rather Cry Over You** (Dougherty-Ponce—arr. Challis) |
| | *Vocal: Bing Crosby, Harry Barris, Al Rinker, Jack Fulton, Charles Gaylord, Austin Young (or Charles Gaylord and members of miscellaneous trio)* |
| W 146320–1 | Rejected. |
| W 146320–2 | Rejected. |
| W 146320–3 | Rejected. |

| | |
|---|---|
| *Same session* | Bix Beiderbecke does not appear on the remaining selection from this session: |
| W 146319 | Get Out and Get Under the Moon (Tobias-Shay-Jerome—arr. Satterfield) |
| | Col 1402–D |
| | Note: The most likely explanation for two different sets of vocalists being credited for masters 146318 & 146320 is that different vocal teams were tried on different takes. Unfortunately, the files do not show details. |

| | |
|---|---|
| *May 23 (Wed)* | PAUL WHITEMAN AND HIS ORCHESTRA |
| | *Columbia Record Co.* |
| | *New York City* |
| | Charles Margulis, Harry Goldfield (t); Bix Beiderbecke (c); Boyce Cullen, Wilbur Hall, Bill Rank (tb); Chet Hazlett (as/bcl); Irving Friedman (ts/cl); Rube Crozier (as/bsn); Red Mayer (ts/bar/cl); Frank Trumbauer (C-m/bsn); Charles Strickfaden (ts/bar/EngHorn); Kurt Dieterle, Matty Malneck, Mischa Russell, Mario Perry (vn); Roy Bargy (p); Mike Pingitore (bj); Mike Trafficante (sb); Min Leibrook (bb); George Marsh (d). |
| **W 146316** | **'Tain't So, Honey, 'Tain't So** (Robison—arr. Challis) |
| | *Vocal: Bing Crosby* |
| W 146316–5 | Rejected. |
| W 146316–6 | Rejected. |
| W 146316–7 | Rejected. |

| | |
|---|---|
| *Same session* | Charles Margulis, Harry Goldfield, Eddie Pinder (t); Bix Beiderbecke (c); Boyce Cullen, Wilbur Hall, Bill Rank (tb); Chet Hazlett (as); Rube Crozier *or* Red Mayer (as); Irving Friedman (cl/ts); Frank Trumbauer (as/C-m); Charles Strickfaden (bar/ts); Kurt Dieterle, Mischa Russell, Matty Malneck, Mario Perry (vn); Roy Bargy (p); Mike Pingitore (bj); Mike Trafficante (sb); Min Leibrook (bsx); George Marsh (d). |
| **W 146327** | **Oh! You Have No Idea** (Ponce-Dougherty—arr. Challis) |
| | *Instrumental* |
| | Released: Aug 30, 1928 |
| | Sales: 21,525 |

W 146327–1    Rejected.
W 146327–2    Mastered: Col 1491–D; ColE 4956; ColG C–4956; ColAu 07005; ColJ J–540.
W 146327–3    Rejected.
W 146327–4    Second choice. Unissued.
    Soloists: Bix (16 + 8 brass lead); Leibrook (8); Friedman (4 + 4 + 8 + 4); Trumbauer (8).

*Same session*    Bix Beiderbecke does not appear on the other selections from this session:
W 146326    In the Evening (Hanley-Dowling—arr. Satterfield)
    Col rejected
W 146328    Mother Goose Parade (Bibi-Breau-Sturn—arr. Grofe)
    Col 1478–D

*May 24 (Thu)*    **PAUL WHITEMAN AND HIS ORCHESTRA**
    *Columbia Record Co.*
    *New York City*
    Charles Margulis, Harry Goldfield (t); Bix Beiderbecke (c); Boyce Cullen, Bill Rank (tb); Chet Hazlett (bcl/cl/ss); Red Mayer (o/cl/ss); Frank Trumbauer (bsn/cl/C-m); Charles Strickfaden (o/ss); Kurt Dieterle, Mischa Russell, Matty Malneck, Mario Perry (vn); Roy Bargy (p); Mike Pingitore (bj); Mike Trafficante (sb); Min Leibrook (bb); George Marsh (d).

**W 146329**    **Blue Night** (Rollins-Mahoney—arr. Satterfield)
    *Vocal: Jack Fulton*
W 146329–1    Rejected.
W 146329–2    Second choice. Unissued.
W 146329–3    Mastered: Col 1553–D; ColE 5204; ColG C–5204.
W 146329–4    Rejected.

*May 25 (Fri)*    **PAUL WHITEMAN AND HIS ORCHESTRA**
    *Columbia Record Co.*
    *New York City*
    Charles Margulis, Harry Goldfield (t); Bix Beiderbecke (c); Boyce Cullen, Wilbur Hall, Bill Rank (tb); Chet Hazlett, Red Mayer (as); Rube Crozier (ts); Frank Trumbauer (C-m); Kurt Dieterle, Mischa Russell, Matty Malneck, Mario Perry (vn); Roy Bargy (p); Mike Pingitore (bj); Mike Trafficante (sb); Min Leibrook (bb); George Marsh (d).

**W 146334**    **Felix the Cat** (Kortlander-Wendling—arr. Satterfield)
    *Vocal: Austin Young*
    Released: Aug. 20, 1928
    Sales: 20,500
W 146334–1    Rejected.
W 146334–2    Rejected.
W 146334–3    Second choice. Unissued.
W 146334–4    Mastered: Col 1478–D; ColE 5040; ColG C–5040; ColArg A8006; ColAu 07008; ColJ J–541; ReSp 5040.
    Soloists: Bix (8 + 6); Trumbauer (14).

*Same session*    Charles Margulis, Harry Goldfield, Eddie Pinder (t); Bix Beiderbecke (c); Boyce Cullen, Wilbur Hall, Bill Rank, Jack Fulton (tb); Chet Hazlett (cl); Irving Friedman (cl/as); Rube Crozier (cl/bsn/ss); Red Mayer (cl/o/bsn/as/EngHorn); Frank Trumbauer (as); Charles Strickfaden (cl/o/as/ss); Mischa Russell, Kurt Dieterle, Matty Malneck, Mario Perry (vn); Mike Pingitore (bj); Mike Trafficante (sb); Min Leibrook (bb); Roy Bargy, Lennie Hayton (p); George Marsh (d); Wilbur Hall doubles on guitar.

**W 146335**    **Chiquita** (Gilbert-Wayne—arr. Grofe)—Waltz
    *Vocal: Jack Fulton*
W 146335–1    Rejected.
W 146335–2    Rejected.
W 146335–3    Rejected.
W 146335–4    Rejected.

1928:

| | |
|---|---|
| *June 10 (Sun)* | PAUL WHITEMAN AND HIS ORCHESTRA |

*Columbia Record Co.*
*New York City*
Charles Margulis, Harry Goldfield (t); Bix Beiderbecke (c); Boyce Cullen, Wilbur Hall, Bill Rank (tb); Chet Hazlett (as/bcl); Irving Friedman (ts/cl); Rube Crozier (as/bsn); Red Mayer (ts/bar/cl); Frank Trumbauer (C-m/bsn); Charles Strickfaden (ts/bar/EngHorn); Matty Malneck, Mischa Russell, Kurt Dieterle, Mario Perry (vn); Roy Bargy (p); Mike Pingitore (bj); Mike Trafficante (sb); Min Leibrook (bb); George Marsh (d).

**W 146316**    'Tain't So, Honey, 'Tain't So (Robison—arr. Challis)
*Vocal: Bing Crosby*
Released: July 20, 1928
Sales: 29,650

W 146316-8    Second choice. Unissued.
W 146316-9    Mastered: Col 1444-D; ColE 4981; ColG C-4981; ColAu 07003; ColJ J-533; ColArg A-8230.
W 146316-10    Rejected.
Soloists: Bix (8 muted); Bix (16 verse open); Trumbauer (16).

*Same session*    Charles Margulis, Harry Goldfield, Eddie Pinder (t); Bix Beiderbecke (c); Boyce Cullen, Bill Rank, Wilbur Hall (tb); Chet Hazlett (bcl/Ebcl); Irving Friedman (f/bsn/as/cl); Rube Crozier (f/bsn/as/cl); Red Mayer (o/bsn/cl); Frank Trumbauer (as/bsn); Charles Strickfaden (o/cl/bar); Kurt Dieterle, Mario Perry, Matty Malneck, John Bowman, Charles Gaylord (vn); Roy Bargy, Lennie Hayton (p); Mike Pingitore (bj); Mike Trafficante (sb); Min Leibrook (bb); George Marsh (d).

**W 146318**    Japanese Mammy (Donaldson-Kahn—arr. Grofe)
*Vocal: (filecard) Quintet, or (ledger) Austin Young and miscellaneous trio.*
Released: Feb. 15, 1929
Sales: 13,700

W 146318-5    Rejected.
W 146318-6    Mastered: Col 1701-D.
W 146318-7    Second choice. Unissued.

*Same session*    Charles Margulis, Harry Goldfield, Eddie Pinder (t); Bix Beiderbecke (c); Boyce Cullen, Wilbur Hall, Bill Rank, Jack Fulton (tb); Chet Hazlett (as/cl); Irving Friedman, Rube Crozier (ts/cl); Red Mayer (as); Frank Trumbauer (as/C-m); Charles Strickfaden (ts); Matty Malneck, Mischa Russell, Kurt Dieterle, Mario Perry (vn); Roy Bargy (p); Mike Pingitore (bj); Mike Trafficante (sb); Min Leibrook (bb); George Marsh (d).

**W 146320**    I'd Rather Cry Over You (Doughtery-Ponce—arr. Challis)
*Vocal: Bing Crosby, with Charles Gaylord, Jack Fulton and Austin Young.*
Released: Aug 30, 1928
Sales: 21,125

W 146320-4    Rejected.
W 146320-5    Mastered: Col 1496-D; ColE 4980; ColArg A-8002; ColG C-4980; ColAu 07005; ColJ J-539.
W 146320-6    Rejected.
W 146320-7    Second choice. Unissued.
Soloists: Bix (4); Trumbauer (8).

*Same session*    Charles Margulis, Harry Goldfield, Eddie Pinder (t); Bix Beiderbecke (c); Boyce Cullen, Wilbur Hall, Bill Rank, Jack Fulton (tb); Chet Hazlett (cl); Irving Friedman (cl/as); Rube Crozier (cl/bsn/ss); Red Mayer (cl/o/bsn/EngHorn); Frank Trumbauer (as); Charles Strickfaden (cl/o/as/ss); Mischa Russell, Kurt Dieterle, Matty Malneck, Mario Perry (vn); Roy Bargy, Lennie Hayton (p); Mike Pingitore (bj); Mike Trafficante (sb); Min Leibrook (bb); George Marsh (perc); Wilbur Hall doubles on g.

**W 146335**    Chiquita (Gilbert-Wayne—arr. Grofe)—Waltz
*Vocal: Jack Fulton*

**1928:**

<table>
<tr><td></td><td>Released: July 20, 1928<br>Sales: 30,000</td></tr>
<tr><td>W 146335–5</td><td>Rejected.</td></tr>
<tr><td>W 146335–6</td><td>Mastered: Col 1448–D; ColE 4981; ColG C–4981.</td></tr>
<tr><td>W 146335–7</td><td>Second choice. Unissued.</td></tr>
</table>

*Same session*  Bix Beiderbecke does not appear on the other selection from this session:

W 146326  In the Evening (Hanley-Dowling—arr. Satterfield)
Col 1484–D

*June 17 (Sun)*  PAUL WHITEMAN AND HIS ORCHESTRA
*Columbia Record Co.*
*New York City*
Charles Margulis, Harry Goldfield (t); Eddie Pinder *or* Bix Beiderbecke (c); Boyce Cullen, Wilbur Hall, Bill Rank, Jack Fulton (tb); Chet Hazlett (bcl/as/cl/Ebcl); Irving Friedman (cl); Rube Crozier (EngHorn/f/cl); Red Mayer (o/pic/cl); Frank Trumbauer (cl/bsn); Charles Strickfaden (o/bar/cl); Kurt Dieterle, Mischa Russell, Matty Malneck (vn); Lennie Hayton, Roy Bargy (p); Mike Pingitore (bj); Mike Trafficante (sb); George Marsh (d).

W 146541  **I'm on a Crest of a Wave** (Brown-Henderson-de Sylva—arr. Grofe)
*Vocal: Bing Crosby, Jack Fulton, Austin Young, Charles Gaylord.*
Released Aug 10, 1928
Sales: 24,275

<table>
<tr><td>W 146541–1</td><td>Rejected.</td></tr>
<tr><td>W 146541–2</td><td>Rejected.</td></tr>
<tr><td>W 146541–3</td><td>Mastered: Col 1465–D; ColE 5241; ColAu 07012.</td></tr>
<tr><td>W 146541–4</td><td>Rejected.</td></tr>
<tr><td>W 146541–5</td><td>Second choice. Unissued.</td></tr>
</table>

*Same session*  Bix Beiderbecke, Charles Margulis (c); Boyce Cullen, Bill Rank (tb); Chet Hazlett (as); Irving Friedman (cl/ts); Frank Trumbauer (as/C-m); Charles Strickfaden (bar/ts); Matty Malneck, Kurt Dieterle, Mario Perry, Mischa Russell (vn); Roy Bargy (p); Mike Pingitore (bj); Mike Trafficante (sb); Min Leibrook (bb); George Marsh (d).

W 146442  **That's My Weakness Now** (Green-Stept—arr. Satterfield)
*Vocal: Bing Crosby, Harry Barris, Al Rinker.*
Released: July 20, 1928
Sales: 29,650

<table>
<tr><td>W 146442–1</td><td>Rejected.</td></tr>
<tr><td>W 146442–2</td><td>Rejected.</td></tr>
<tr><td>W 146442–3</td><td>Mastered: Col 1444–D; ColE 5006; ColG C–5006; ColAu 07008;<br>ColArg A–8230; ColJ J–533.</td></tr>
<tr><td>W 146442–4</td><td>Second choice. Unissued.</td></tr>
</table>
Soloists: Bix (2 + 2 intro); Rank (4); Bix (2); Trumbauer (4); Bix (2); Trumbauer (4); Friedman (1 + 1 + 1); Bix (1 + 1 + 1); Rank (8); Trumbauer (1 + 1 + 1).

*Same session*  Charles Margulis, Harry Goldfield (t); Bix Beiderbecke (c); Boyce Cullen, Bill Rank (tb); Chet Hazlett (as); Irving Friedman, Charles Strickfaden (ts); Frank Trumbauer (C-m/as); Matty Malneck, Kurt Dieterle, Mario Perry, Mischa Russell (vn); Roy Bargy (p); Mike Pingitore (bj); Mike Trafficante (sb); Min Leibrook (bb); George Marsh (d).

W 146543  **Georgie Porgie** (Mayerl-Paul—arr. Challis)
*Vocal: Bing Crosby, Harry Barris, Al Rinker.*
Released: Aug 30, 1928
Sales: 21,525

<table>
<tr><td>W 146543–1</td><td>Rejected.</td></tr>
<tr><td>W 146543–2</td><td>Rejected.</td></tr>
<tr><td>W 146543–3</td><td>Mastered: Col 1491–D; ColE 5040; ColG C–5040; ColAu 07011;<br>ColJ J–533; ReSp 5040.</td></tr>
</table>
Soloists: Trumbauer (8); Bix (4).

1928:

| | |
|---|---|
| *Same session* | Bix Beiderbecke does not appear on the other selections from this session: |
| W 146544 | If You Don't Love Me (Ager-Yellen—arr. Satterfield)<br>Col rejected |
| W 146545 | Just Like a Melody Out of the Sky (Donaldson—arr. Satterfield)<br>Col 1441–D |
| W 146546 | Lonesome in the Moonlight (Baer-Russell—arr. Grofe)<br>Col 1448–D |

*June 18 (Mon)*   **PAUL WHITEMAN AND HIS ORCHESTRA**
*Columbia Record Co.*
*New York City*
Charles Margulis, Eddie Pinder (t); Bix Beiderbecke (c); Wilbur Hall, Bill Rank (tb); Chet Hazlett, Frank Trumbauer (as); Irving Friedman (ts); Charles Strickfaden (bar); Kurt Dieterle, Mischa Russell, Matty Malneck (vn); Roy Bargy (p); Mike Pingitore (bj); Mike Trafficante (sb); Min Leibrook (bb); George Marsh (d).

W 146549   **Because My Baby Don't Mean "Maybe" Now** (Donaldson—arr. Challis)
*Vocal: Bing Crosby, with Jack Fulton, Charles Gaylord, Austin Young.*
Released: July 20, 1928
Sales: 36,000
W 146549–1   Second choice. Unissued.
W 146549–2   Mastered: Col 1441–D; ColE 5007; ColG C–5007; ColAu 07007; ColJ J–532; ColArg A–8010.
W 146549–3   Rejected.
Soloists: Bix (16 + 8)

*Same session*   Charles Margulis, Harry Goldfield (t); Bix Beiderbecke (c); Wilbur Hall, Bill Rank (tb); Chet Hazlett, Frank Trumbauer (as); Irving Friedman (ts); Charles Strickfaden (bar); Kurt Dieterle, Mischa Russell, Matty Malneck (vn); Roy Bargy (p); Mike Pingitore (bj); Mike Trafficante (sb); Min Leibrook (bb); George Marsh (d).

W 146550   **Out o' Town Gal** (Donaldson—arr. Challis)
*Vocal: Bing Crosby, Harry Barris, Al Rinker.*
Released: Sept 10, 1928
Sales: 19,950
W 146550–1   Rejected.
W 146550–2   Second choice. Unissued.
W 146550–3   Mastered: Col 1505–D; ColE 5039; ColG C–5039; ColArg A–8011; ColJ J–542; ColAu 07011.
W 146550–4   Rejected.
Soloists: Bix (8).

*Same session*   Bix Beiderbecke does not appear on the other selections from this session:
W 146547   Just a Little Bit of Driftwood (Davis-Davis-Lyman—arr. Grofe)
Col 1505–D
W 146548   Sorry for Me (DeSylva-Brown-Henderson)
Col rejected

*June 19 (Tue)*   **PAUL WHITEMAN AND HIS ORCHESTRA**
*Columbia Record Co.*
*New York City*
Charles Margulis, Harry Goldfield, Eddie Pinder (t); Bix Beiderbecke (c); Boyce Cullen, Wilbur Hall, Bill Rank, Jack Fulton (tb); Chet Hazlett (as/cl/Ebcl); Irving Friedman (ts/cl/as); Rube Crozier (f/bsn/ss/cl); Red Mayer (pic/f/ss/cl); Frank Trumbauer (bsn/as/C-m); Charles Strickfaden (bar/as/Hecklephone); Kurt Dieterle, Mischa Russell, Matty Malneck, John Bowman, Charles Gaylord, Mario Perry (vn); Roy Bargy, Lennie Hayton (p); Mike Pingitore (bj); Mike Trafficante (sb); Min Leibrook (bb); George Marsh (d).

W 146551   **American Tune** (de Sylva-Brown-Henderson—arr. Grofe)
*Vocal: Austin Young*

Released: Aug 10, 1928
Sales: 24,275

W 146551–1 Rejected.
W 146551–2 Mastered: Col 1464–D; ColE 5242.
W 146551–3 Second choice. Unissued.
W 146551–4 Rejected.
W 146551–5 Rejected.

*June 20 (Wed)* **PAUL WHITEMAN AND HIS ORCHESTRA**
*Columbia Record Co.*
*New York City*
Charles Margulis, Harry Goldfield, Eddie Pinder (t); Bix Beider-
becke (c); Boyce Cullen, Wilbur Hall, Bill Rank, Jack Fulton (tb);
Chet Hazlett, Irving Friedman, Rube Crozier, Red Mayer,
Frank Trumbauer, Charles Strickfaden (reeds); Kurt Dieterle,
Mischa Russell, Matty Malneck, Mario Perry, Charles Gaylord,
John Bowman (vn); Roy Bargy, Lennie Hayton (p); Mike Pin-
gitore (bj); Mike Trafficante (sb); Min Leibrook (bb); George
Marsh (perc).

**W 98556** **Tchaikowskiana** (Fantasy on Tchaikowsky Themes) (arr. Her-
man Hand)
*Part One Instrumental*
W 98556–1 Rejected.
W 98556–2 Rejected.
W 98556–3 Mastered: Col 50113–D; ColE 9470; ColG C–9470.
W 98556–4 Second choice. Unissued
**W 98557** **Tchaikowskiana** (Fantasy of Tchaikowsky Themes) (arr. Hand)
*Part Two Instrumental*
W 98557–1 Rejected.
W 98557–2 Second choice. Unissued.
W 98557–3 Rejected.
W 98557–4 Mastered: Col 50113–D; ColE 9470; ColG C–9470.

*July 2 (Mon)* **PAUL WHITEMAN AND HIS ORCHESTRA**
*Columbia Record Co.*
*New York City*
Beiderbecke does not appear on the following recordings from
this session:
W 146610 Pickin' Cotton (de Sylva-Brown-Henderson—arr. Challis)
Col 1464–D
W 146611 What D'Ya Say? (de Sylva-Brown-Henderson—arr. Grofe)
Col 1465–D
Note: Despite label and ledger credits, these titles are not by
the Whiteman orchestra. They are from a session organized by
the Columbia A & R man, Ben Selvin.

*July 5 (Thu)* **FRANK TRUMBAUER AND HIS ORCHESTRA**
*Okeh Record Co.*
*Chicago, Ill.*
Bix Beiderbecke (c); Bill Rank (tb); Irving Friedman (cl/as);
Frank Trumbauer (C-m/as); Charles Strickfaden (bar); Min Lei-
brook (bsx); Roy Bargy *or* Lennie Hayton (p); George Rose (g);
Harry Gale (d).

**W 400989** **Bless You Sister** (Dubin-Robinson)
*Vocal: Frank Trumbauer, Dee Orr, two others.*
Released: Sept. 25, 1928
Sales: 3,475
W 400989–A Rejected.
W 400989–B Rejected.
W 400989–C Mastered: OK 41100; ParE R–1882; ParAu A–3992; ParFr
22006; ParIt B–25797; ParIt TT–9073; OdArg 193236; OdFr
165488; OdG A–189190; ParFr 25293.
W 400989–D Rejected.
**W 400990** **Dusky Stevedore** (Johnson)
*Vocal: Frank Trumbauer, Dee Orr, two others.*
Released: Sept. 25, 1928
Sales: 3,475

**1928:**

| | |
|---|---|
| W 400990–A | Rejected. |
| W 400990–B | Mastered: OK 41100; ParE R–265; ParFr 22006; OdG A–189190; OdG A–221111; OdFr 165488; OdArg 193236; ParIt B–27597. |
| W 400990–C | Rejected. |
| W 400990–D | Rejected. |

*July 7 (Thu)*

BIX BEIDERBECKE AND HIS GANG
*Okeh Record Co.*
*Chicago, Ill.*
Bix Beiderbecke (c); Bill Rank (tb); Irving Friedman (cl); Min Leibrook (bsx); Roy Bargy (p); Harry Gale (d).

**W 400994**  Ol' Man River (Kern)
*Instrumental*
Released: Sept. 5, 1928
Sales: 2,900

W 400994–A  Mastered: OK 41088; UHCA 25/26; OdFr 193328; OdCh 193328; ParE R–2328; KismetAu K–722; ParSs PZ–11252; Col 35666; ParAu A–2776; OdSp 182555; OdG A–189180.

W 400994–B  Rejected.

W 400994–C  Rejected.

**W 400995**  Wa Da Da (Everybody's Doin' It Now) (Barris-Cavanaugh)
*Instrumental*
Released: Sept. 5, 1928
Sales: 2,900

W 400995–A  Mastered: OK 41088; UHCA 25/26; OdArg 193337; OdArg 194756; ParAu A–7618; OdG A–189190; ParE R 2286; Col 35666; OdSp 182555; ParSs PZ–11252.

W 400995–B  Rejected.

W 400995–C  Rejected.
Note: KismetAu as "Adrian Rollini and his Orchestra"!

*July 20 (Fri)*

PAUL WHITEMAN AND HIS ORCHESTRA
*Columbia Record Co.*
*New York City*
Bix Beiderbecke does not appear on the following recordings from this session:

W 146634  Sorry for Me (DeSylva-Brown-Henderson)
Col rejected

W 146635  If You Don't Love Me (Ager-Yellen—arr. Challis?)
Col 1484–D
Note: Despite label and ledger credits, these are not by the Whiteman orchestra. It is actually a second session organized by the Columbia A & R man, Ben Selvin.

*Sept 4 (Tue)*

PAUL WHITEMAN AND HIS ORCHESTRA
*Columbia Record Co.*
*New York City*
Charles Margulis, Eddie Pinder (t); Bix Beiderbecke (c); Boyce Cullen, Wilbur Hall, Bill Rank (tb); Chet Hazlett (cl/as); Irving Friedman (cl/ts/bar/as): Red Mayer (bar/as); Frank Trumbauer (as); Charles Strickfaden (bar/ts); Kurt Dieterle, Mischa Russell, Matty Malneck, John Bowman (vn); Roy Bargy (p); Mike Pingitore (bj); Mike Trafficante (sb); Min Leibrook (bb); George Marsh (d); Lennie Hayton (cel).

**W 146945**  In the Good Old Summertime (no composer credits—arr. Challis)
(Waltz Medley: "In the Good Old Summertime," "Little Annie Rooney," "Comrades," "Rosie O'Grady," "Yip I Addy I Ay")
*Vocal: Miscellaneous Quartet*

W 146945–1  Rejected.

W 146945–2  Rejected.

W 146945–3  Rejected.

W 146945–4  Rejected.

*Same session*

Charles Margulis, Bix Beiderbecke (c); Bill Rank, Wilbur Hall (tb); Chet Hazlett (as/cl); Red Mayer (ts); Frank Trumbauer (as);

1928:

Charles Strickfaden (bar); Kurt Dieterle, Mischa Russell, Matty
Malneck, John Bowman (vn); Roy Bargy (p); Lennie Hayton
(cel); Mike Pingitore (bj); Mike Trafficante (sb); Min Leibrook
(bb); George Marsh (d).

W 146946    **The Sidewalks of New York** (Blake-Lawler—arr. Challis)
*Vocal: "Miscellaneous Quartet"*

W 146946-1    Rejected.
W 146946-2    Rejected.
W 146946-3    Rejected.
W 146946-4    Rejected.

*Same session*    Charles Margulis, Harry Goldfield, Bix Beiderbecke, Eddie
Pinder (t/c); Boyce Cullen, Wilbur Hall, Bill Rank, Jack Fulton
(tb); Chet Hazlett, Irving Friedman, Rube Crozier, Red Mayer,
Frank Trumbauer, Charles Strickfaden (reeds); Kurt Dieterle,
Mischa Russell, Matty Malneck, John Bowman (vn); Roy Bargy
(p); Lennie Hayton (cel); Mike Pingitore (bj); Mike Trafficante
(sb); Min Leibrook (bb); George Marsh (d)

W 146947    **Roses of Yesterday** (Berlin—arr. Grofe)
*Vocal: Austin Young*

W 146947-1    Rejected.
W 146947-2    Second choice. Unissued.
W 146947-3    Mastered: Col 1553-D; ColE 5161.
W 146947-4    Rejected.

*Sept 5 (Wed)*    **PAUL WHITEMAN AND HIS ORCHESTRA**
*Columbia Record Co.*
*New York City*
Charles Margulis, Harry Goldfield, Eddie Pinder (t); Bix Beider-
becke (c); Boyce Cullen, Wilbur Hall, Bill Rank, Jack Fulton (tb);
Chet Hazlett, Irving Friedman, Rube Crozier, Red Mayer,
Frank Trumbauer, Charles Strickfaden (reeds); Kurt Dieterle,
Mischa Russell, Matty Malneck, Mario Perry, John Bowman,
Charles Gaylord (vn); Roy Bargy (p); Mike Pingitore (bj); Mike
Trafficante (sb); Min Leibrook (bb); George Marsh (d).

W 98568    **Concerto in F** (Gershwin—arr. Grofe)
*Part One: First Movement—Allegro—Commencement*
*Instrumental*

W 98568-1    Rejected.
W 98568-2    Second choice. Unissued.
W 98568-3    First choice. Unissued.
W 98568-4    Rejected.

*Sept 6 (Thu)*    **PAUL WHITEMAN AND HIS ORCHESTRA**
*Columbia Record Co.*
*New York City*
Charles Margulis, Harry Goldfield, Eddie Pinder (t); Bix Beiderbecke (c); Boyce Cullen, Wilbur Hall, Bill Rank, Jack Fulton (tb);
Chet Hazlett, Irving Friedman, Rube Crozier, Frank Trumbauer, Charles Strickfaden (reeds); Kurt Dieterle, Mischa Russell, Matty Malneck, Mario Perry, John Bowman, Charles Gaylord (vn); Roy Bargy (p); Mike Pingitore (bj); Mike Trafficante
(sb); Min Leibrook (bb); George Marsh (perc).

W 98569    **Concerto in F** (Gershwin—arr. Grofe)
*Part Two: First Movement—Allegro—Continuation*
*Instrumental*

W 98569-1    Second choice. Unissued.
W 98569-2    First choice. Unissued.
W 98569-3    Rejected.
W 98569-4    Rejected.

W 98570    **Concerto in F** (Gershwin—arr. Grofe)
*Part Three: First Movement—Allegro—Completion*
*Instrumental*

W 98570-1    Rejected.
W 98570-2    Rejected.
W 98570-3    Rejected.
W 98570-4    Rejected.

**1928:**

*Sept 14 (Fri)*

PAUL WHITEMAN AND HIS ORCHESTRA
*Columbia Record Co.*
*New York City*
Charles Margulis, Eddie Pinder (t); Bix Beiderbecke (c); Boyce
Cullen, Wilbur Hall, Bill Rank (tb); Chet Hazlett (cl/as); Irving
Friedman (cl/ts/bar/as); Red Mayer (bar/as); Frank Trumbauer
(as); Charles Strickfaden (bar/ts); Kurt Dieterle, Mischa Russell,
Matty Malneck, John Bowman (vn); Roy Bargy (p); Lennie Hay-
ton (cel); Mike Pingitore (bj); Mike Trafficante (sb); Min Lei-
brook (bb); George Marsh (d).

W 146945 **In the Good Old Summertime** (no composer credits—arr. Chal-
lis)
(Waltz Medley: "In the Good Old Summertime," "Little Annie
Rooney," "Comrades," "Rosie O'Grady," "Yip I Addy I Ay")
*Vocal: Miscellaneous Quartet*
Released: Oct. 20, 1928
Sales: 17,000

W 146945–5 Mastered: Col 1558–D.
W 146945–6 Second choice. Unissued.
W 146945–7 Rejected.

*Same session*

Charles Margulis, Bix Beiderbecke (t/c); Bill Rank, Wilbur Hall
(tb); Chet Hazlett (as/cl); Red Mayer (ts); Frank Trumbauer (as);
Charles Strickfaden (bar); Kurt Dieterle, Mischa Russell, Matty
Malneck, John Bowman (vn); Roy Bargy (p); Lennie Hayton
(cel); Mike Pingitore (bj); Mike Trafficante (sb); Min Leibrook
(bb); George Marsh (d).

W 146946 **The Sidewalks of New York** (Blake-Lawler—arr. Challis)
*Vocal: Miscellaneous Quartet*
Released: Oct 20, 1928
Sales: 17,000

W 146946–5 Rejected.
W 146946–6 Mastered: Col 1558–D.
W 146946–7 Second choice. Unissued.

*Sept. 15 (Sat)*

PAUL WHITEMAN AND HIS ORCHESTRA
*Columbia Record Co.*
*New York City*
*William Dailey, Recording Director*
Charles Margulis, Harry Goldfield, Eddie Pinder (t); Bix Beider-
becke (c); Boyce Cullen, Wilbur Hall, Bill Rank, Jack Fulton (tb);
Chet Hazlett, Irving Friedman, Rube Crozier, Red Mayer,
Frank Trumbauer, Charles Strickfaden (reeds); Roy Bargy (p);
Kurt Dieterle, Mischa Russell, Matty Malneck, John Bowman,
Charles Gaylord, Mario Perry (vn); Mike Pingitore (bj); Mike
Trafficante (sb); Min Leibrook (bb); George Marsh (perc).

W 98568 **Concerto in F** (Gershwin—arr. Grofe)
*Part One: First Movement—Allegro—Commencement*
*Instrumental*

W 98568–5 Second choice. Unissued.
W 98568–6 Rejected.
W 98568–7 Rejected.
W 98568–8 Mastered: Col 50139–D; Col 7170–M; Col ML 7315; ColE 9665;
ColIt GQX–10968; Col–A1157; ColAu 07506.

*Same session*
W 98569 **Concerto in F** (Gershwin—arr. Grofe)
*Part Two: First Movement—Allegro—Continuation*
*Instrumental*

W 98569–5 Mastered: Col 50139–D; Col 7170–M; Col ML 7315; ColE 9665;
ColIt GQX–10968; Col A–1157; ColAu 07506.
W 98569–6 Rejected.
W 98569–7 Rejected.
W 98569–8 Rejected.

*Same session*
W 98570 **Concerto in F** (Gershwin—arr. Grofe)

|  | Part Three: First Movement—Allegro—Completion |
|---|---|
|  | *Instrumental* |
| W 98570–5 | Mastered: Col 50140–D; Col 7171–M; Col ML 7316; ColE 9666; ColIt GQX–10969; Col A–1158; ColAu 07507. |
| W 98570–6 | Second choice. Unissued. |
| W 98570–7 | Rejected. |

*Same session*

**W 98576**      **Concerto in F** (Gershwin—arr. Grofe)
*Part Four: Second Movement—Andante Con Moto—First Half*
*Instrumental*

| W 98576–1 | Rejected. |
|---|---|
| W 98576–2 | Mastered: Col 50140–D; Col 7171–M; Col ML 7316; ColE 9666; ColIt GQX–10969; Col A–1158; ColAu 07507. |
| W 98576–3 | Rejected. |
| W 98576–4 | Rejected. |

Note: George Gershwin composed the Concerto in 1925. His original intention was to entitle it "A New York Concerto." He broke it down into three basic movements: 1) Employment of the Charleston rhythm; 2) A poetic atmosphere referred to as "The American Blues"; 3) Final movement refers to the style of the first and yet introduces new material, all in a briskly rhythmic combination. The listener may notice that various parts of this recording vary from later versions by other orchestras. This is due to the fact that Grofe arranged the Concerto especially for the Whiteman orchestra. This performance of the complete Concerto has just been issued abroad in its entirety on a long-playing record.

*Sept 17 (Mon)*      **PAUL WHITEMAN AND HIS ORCHESTRA**
*Columbia Record Co.*
*New York City*
*William Dailey, Recording Director*
Charles Margulis, Harry Goldfield, Eddie Pinder (t); Bix Beiderbecke (c); Boyce Cullen, Wilbur Hall, Bill Rank, Jack Fulton (tb); Chet Hazlett (cl/as/Ebcl); Irving Friedman (cl/as); Rube Crozier (bsn); Red Mayer (cl/o/ss); Frank Trumbauer (cl/bsn/as); Charles Strickfaden (bar/cl/o); Kurt Dieterle, Mischa Russell, Matty Malneck (vn); Roy Bargy (p); Lennie Hayton (cel); Mike Pingitore (bj); Mike Trafficante (sb); Min Leibrook (bb); George Marsh (d);

**W 98577**      **Jeannine, I Dream of Lilac Time** (Gilbert-Shilkret—arr. Grofe)
*Vocal: Jack Fulton*

| W 98577–1 | Second choice. Unissued. |
|---|---|
| W 98577–2 | Rejected. |
| W 98577–3 | Mastered: Col 50095–D; ColE 9578. |

*Same session*      Charles Margulis, Harry Goldfield, Eddie Pinder (t); Bix Beiderbecke (c); Boyce Cullen, Wilbur Hall, Bill Rank, Jack Fulton (tb); Chet Hazlett, Irving Friedman, Rube Crozier, Red Mayer, Frank Trumbauer, Charles Strickfaden (reeds); Kurt Dieterle, Mischa Russell, Matty Malneck, Mario Perry, John Bowman, Charles Gaylord (vn); Roy Bargy (p); Mike Pingitore (bj); Mike Trafficante (sb); Min Leibrook (bb); George Marsh (d).

**W 98578**      **Concerto in F** (Gershwin—arr. Grofe)
*Part Five: Second Movement—Andante Con Moto—Completion*
*Instrumental*

| W 98578–1 | Rejected. |
|---|---|
| W 98578–2 | Rejected. |
| W 98578–3 | Second choice. Unissued. |
| W 98578–4 | Mastered: Col 50141–D; Col 7172–M; Col ML7317; ColE 9667; ColIt GQX–10970; Col A–1159; ColAu 07508. |

**W 98575**      **Concerto in F** (Gershwin—arr. Ferde Grofe)
*Part Six: Finale—Allegro Con Brio*
*Instrumental*

| W 98575–1 | Rejected. |
|---|---|
| W 98575–2 | Rejected. |

**1928:**

W 98575–3     Mastered: ColE 9667; ColIt GQX–10970; Col 7172–M.
Note: William Dailey directed all recordings of "Concerto in F." Part Six (98575–3) was later recalled and remade Oct. 5, 1928.

*Sept. 18 (Tue)*     PAUL WHITEMAN AND HIS ORCHESTRA
*Columbia Record Co.*
*New York City*
Charles Margulis, Harry Goldfield, Bix Beiderbecke, Eddie Pinder (t/c); Boyce Cullen, Wilbur Hall, Bill Rank, Jack Fulton (tb); Chet Hazlett (bcl/ss/as); Irving Friedman (cl/ts); Rube Crozier (bsn/ss/f/as); Red Mayer (bsn/ss/f/as); Frank Trumbauer (cl/C-m/bsn); Charles Strickfaden (cl/o/ss/ts/as); Kurt Dieterle, Mischa Russell, Matty Malneck, Mario Perry, John Bowman, Charles Gaylord (vn); Mike Pingitore (bj); Min Leibrook (bb); Mike Trafficante (sb); Roy Bargy, Lennie Hayton (p); George Marsh (perc). Unknown cimbalom player. Perry plays accordion.

W 98579     **Gypsy** (Malneck-Signorelli-Gilbert—arr. Grofe)
*Vocal: Austin Young*
W 98579–1     Rejected.
W 98579–2     Rejected.
W 98579–3     Rejected.
W 98579–4     Second choice. Unissued.
W 98579–5     Mastered: Col 50095–D.

*Same session:*     Charles Margulis, Harry Goldfield, Bix Beiderbecke, Eddie Pinder (t/c); Boyce Cullen, Bill Rank, Wilbur Hall, Jack Fulton (tb); Chet Hazlett (bcl); Irving Friedman (cl/o); Red Mayer (f/bsn); Frank Trumbauer (bsn/cl); Charles Strickfaden (o/bar); Kurt Dieterle, Mischa Russell, Matty Malneck, Mario Perry (vn); Roy Bargy (p); Lennie Hayton (cel); Mike Pingitore (bj); Mike Trafficante (sb); Min Leibrook (bb); George Marsh (d).

W 98584     **Sweet Sue** (Harris-Young—arr. Challis)
*Vocal: Jack Fulton*
W 98584–1     Mastered: Col 50103–D; ColE 9572; ColAu 07509; *Col 35667;* Col A–405.
W 98584–2     Rejected.
W 98584–3     Rejected.
W 98584–4     Rejected.
Soloists: Bix (32).
Note: Col 35667 is an edited 10-inch version of the original 12-inch recording.

*Sept 19 (Wed)*     PAUL WHITEMAN AND HIS ORCHESTRA
*Columbia Record Co.*
*New York City*
Charles Margulis, Harry Goldfield, Eddie Pinder (t); Bix Beiderbecke (c); Boyce Cullen, Wilbur Hall, Bill Rank, Jack Fulton (tb); Chet Hazlett (bcl/as); Irving Friedman (ts); Rube Crozier (bsn/as); Red Mayer (bsn/bar); Frank Trumbauer (bsn/as); Charles Strickfaden (as/bar); Kurt Dieterle, Mischa Russell, Mario Perry, Matty Malneck (vn); Roy Bargy (p); Lennie Hayton (cel); Mike Pingitore (bj); Min Leibrook (bb); Mike Trafficante (sb); George Marsh (d); Eddie King (sleigh bells/p-o); unknown (harp).

W 98586     **Christmas Melodies** ("O Holy Night," "Adeste Fideles") (trad —arr. Grofe)
*Vocal: "Humming" by Miscellaneous Quartet*
W 98586–1     Rejected.
W 98586–2     Rejected.
W 98586–3     Mastered: Col 50098–D; ColE 9561; ColAu 07511.

*Same session*     Bix Beiderbecke does not appear on the other selection from this session:
W 98585     Silent Night, Holy Night (Gruber—arr. Challis)
Col 50098–D

**1928:**

| | |
|---|---|
| *Sept 20 (Thu)* | **FRANK TRUMBAUER AND HIS ORCHESTRA**<br>*Okeh Record Co.*<br>*New York City*<br>Bix Beiderbecke (c); Bill Rank (tb); Irving Friedman (cl/as); Frank Trumbauer (C-m/as); Charles Strickfaden (as); Min Leibrook (bsx); Roy Bargy (p); Eddie Lang (g); Chauncey Morehouse (d). |

**W 401133**      **Take Your Tomorrow** (Razaf-Johnson)
*Vocal: Frank Trumbauer, one other (perhaps Austin Young.)*
Released: Dec. 15, 1928
Sales: 3,325

W 401133–A    Rejected.
W 401133–B    Mastered: OK 41145; ParE R–265; ParE R–2564; ParAu A–7534; ColH DCH–339; OdArg 193297; OdG A–189210; OdG 031816; OdFr 165526; *Col 37807;* ColSs DZ–997; OdSp 182473.

W 401133–C    Rejected.
**W 401134**      **Love Affairs** (Dubin-Robinson)
*Vocal: Austin Young*
Released: Dec 15, 1928
Sales: 3,325

W 401134–A    Rejected.
W 401134–B    Rejected.
W 401134–C    Mastered: OK 41145; *Bm 1103;* OdG A–189210; OdArg 193288; OdFr 165526; OdSp 182473.

**W 401135**      **Sentimental Baby** (Palmer)
*Vocal: Austin Young.*

W 401135–A    Rejected.
W 401135–B    Rejected.
W 401135–C    Rejected.
W 401135–D    Rejected.

| | |
|---|---|
| *Sept 21 (Fri)* | **PAUL WHITEMAN AND HIS ORCHESTRA**<br>*Columbia Record Co.*<br>*New York City*<br>Charles Margulis, Harry Goldfield, Eddie Pinder (t); Bix Beiderbecke (c); Boyce Cullen, Wilbur Hall, Bill Rank, Jack Fulton (tb); Chet Hazlett (bcl/as/cl); Irving Friedman (cl/ts); Rube Crozier (o/bsn/f); Red Mayer (EngHorn/bsn/pic); Frank Trumbauer (bsn/ss/C-m/as/cl); Charles Strickfaden (o/ss/as/bar); Kurt Dieterle, Mischa Russell, Matty Malneck, Mario Perry, John Bowman, Charles Gaylord (vn); Roy Bargy (p); Lennie Hayton (cel); Mike Pingitore (bj); Min Leibrook (bb); Mike Trafficante (sb); George Marsh (d). |

**W 98589**      **I Can't Give You Anything but Love** (McHugh-Fields—arr. Grofe)
*Vocal: Jack Fulton*

W 98589–1    Rejected.
W 98589–2    Rejected.
W 98589–3    Mastered: Col 50103–D ColE 9572.
W 98589–4    Second choice. Unissued.
     Soloists: Trumbauer (8).

| | |
|---|---|
| *Same session* | Charles Margulis, Harry Goldfield (t); Eddie Pinder *or* Bix Beiderbecke (c); Boyce Cullen, Bill Rank, Wilbur Hall (tb); Chet Hazlett, Frank Trumbauer (as); Irving Friedman, Red Mayer (ts); Charles Strickfaden (bar); Kurt Dieterle, Mischa Russell, Matty Malneck, Mario Perry (vn); Roy Bargy (p); Lennie Hayton (cel); Mike Pingitore (bj); Mike Trafficante (bb); Min Leibrook (bb); George Marsh (d). |

**W 147032**      **Where Is the Song of Songs for Me** (Berlin—arr. Challis)
*Vocal: Jack Fulton*

W 147032–1    Rejected.
W 147032–2    Rejected.
W 147032–3    Rejected.
W 147032–4    Rejected.

1928:

<table>
<tr><td>*Sept 21 (Fri)*</td><td></td><td>BIX BEIDERBECKE AND HIS GANG<br>*Okeh Record Co.*<br>*New York City*<br>Bix Beiderbecke (c); Bill Rank (tb); Irving Friedman (cl); Min<br>Leibrook (bsx); Roy Bargy (p); Lennie Hayton (d/p/organ).</td></tr>
<tr><td></td><td>**W 401138**</td><td>**Rhythm King** (Hoover)<br>*Instrumental*<br>Released: Feb 5, 1929<br>Sales: 2,225</td></tr>
<tr><td></td><td>W 401138–A</td><td>Rejected.</td></tr>
<tr><td></td><td>W 401138–B</td><td>Mastered: OK 41173; Br8242; ParAu A–7600;ParE R–2269;<br>ParFin DPY–1021; ParSs PZ–11252;OdArg 193328; OdCH<br>193328; HJCA HC–601; OdG A–189236; Col 35665; *ColJ EM–<br>103.*</td></tr>
<tr><td></td><td>W 401138–C</td><td>Rejected.</td></tr>
<tr><td></td><td>**W 401139**</td><td>**Louisiana** (Razaf-Schafer-Johnson)<br>*Instrumental*<br>Released: Feb 5, 1928<br>Sales: 2,225</td></tr>
<tr><td></td><td>W 401139–A</td><td>Mastered: OK 41173; ParE R–298; ParE R–2833; ParIt B–<br>71142; ParSs PZ–11129; OdArg 193297; OdArg 194756; OdG<br>A–189236; Col 35665; ColSw DS–1392.</td></tr>
<tr><td></td><td>W 401139–B</td><td>Rejected.</td></tr>
<tr><td></td><td>W 401139–C</td><td>Rejected.</td></tr>
<tr><td></td><td>**W 401140**</td><td>**Margie** (Davis-Conrad-Robinson)<br>*Instrumental*</td></tr>
<tr><td></td><td>W 401140–A</td><td>Mastered: ParE R–2833; ParIt B–71142; ParSs PZ–11129; Special<br>Edition 5013–S; ColArg 20304; ColSw DS–1392; ColJ EM–106.<br>Note: Some uncertainty surrounds the exact personnel of "Lou-<br>isiana." During the piano solo, Hayton is heard adding a third,<br>treble hand to Bargy's two; but a cymbal is clearly audible while<br>this is going on. It is the authors' opinion that one of the other<br>musicians on the date supplied the cymbal effects, handing the<br>drumming chores back to Hayton in the bass sax break begin-<br>ning Rank's trombone solo.</td></tr>
<tr><td>*Oct 5 (Fri)*</td><td></td><td>PAUL WHITEMAN AND HIS ORCHESTRA<br>*Columbia Record Co.*<br>*New York City*<br>*William Dailey, Recording Director*<br>Charles Margulis, Harry Goldfield, Bix Beiderbecke, Eddie<br>Pinder (t/c); Boyce Cullen, Wilbur Hall, Bill Rank, Jack Fulton<br>(tb); Chet Hazlett, Irving Friedman, Rube Crozier, Red Mayer,<br>Frank Trumbauer, Charles Strickfaden (reeds); Kurt Dieterle,<br>Mischa Russell, Matty Malneck, John Bowman, Charles Gay-<br>lord, Mario Perry (vn); Roy Bargy (p); Mike Pingitore (bj); Mike<br>Trafficante (sb); Min Leibrook (bb); George Marsh (perc).</td></tr>
<tr><td></td><td>**W 98575**</td><td>**Concerto in F** (Gerhswin—arr. Grofe)<br>*Part Six: Finale—Allegro Con Brio*<br>*Instrumental*</td></tr>
<tr><td></td><td>W 98575–4</td><td>Rejected.</td></tr>
<tr><td></td><td>W 98575–5</td><td>Second choice. Unissued.</td></tr>
<tr><td></td><td>W 98575–6</td><td>Rejected.</td></tr>
<tr><td></td><td>W 98575–7</td><td>Mastered: Col 50141–D; Col 7172–M; Col ML 7317; ColIl GQX<br>10970; ColAu 07508; ColE 9667; Col A–1159.</td></tr>
<tr><td>*Oct 5 (Fri)*</td><td></td><td>FRANK TRUMBAUER AND HIS ORCHESTRA<br>*Okeh Record Co.*<br>*New York City*<br>Bix Beiderbecke (c); Charles Margulis (t); Bill Rank (tb); Irving<br>Friedman (cl/as); Frank Trumbauer (C-m/as); Charles Strick-<br>faden (as); Eddie Lang (g); Roy Bargy (p); unknown (d); Rube<br>Crozier (bsn) on last three titles.</td></tr>
<tr><td></td><td>**W 401195**</td><td>**The Love Nest** (Harbach-Hirsch)<br>*Vocal: Charles Gaylord.*</td></tr>
<tr><td></td><td>W 401195–A</td><td>Rejected.</td></tr>
<tr><td></td><td>W 401195–B</td><td>Mastered: ParE R–2645; *Decatur 501.*</td></tr>
</table>

1928:

| | |
|---|---|
| **W 401196** | **The Japanese Sandman** (Egan-Whiting) |
| | *Vocal: Frank Trumbauer.* |
| W 401196–A | Rejected. |
| W 401196–B | Rejected. |
| W 401196–C | Mastered: ParE R–2176; ParAu A–6449; *Bm 1103.* |
| W 401196–D | Rejected. |
| **W 401197** | **High Up on a Hilltop** (Baer-Whiting-Campbell) |
| | *Vocal: Charles Gaylord* |
| | Released: Nov 15, 1928 |
| | Sales: 3,325 |
| W 401197–A | Mastered: OK 41128; ParE R–2644; ParG A–4573; ParAu A– 2682; OdArg 193254; OdG A–189241. |
| W 401197–B | Rejected. |
| **W 401198** | **Sentimental Baby** (Palmer) |
| | *Vocal: Charles Gaylord (–A) or Frank Trumbauer (–B and –C)* |
| | Released: Nov 15, 1928 |
| | Sales: 3,325 |
| W 401198–A | Mastered: OK 41128; ParE R–298; ParG A–4573; *Decatur 501;* OdG A–189241; OdArg 193254. |
| W 401198–B | Rejected. |
| W 401198–C | Rejected. |

Note: Roy Bargy, pianist on this date, has questioned the presence of George Marsh, insisting that "George was not on any of the (jazz) recordings . . . he wasn't a jazz drummer . . ." so the identity of the drummer on this date remains in doubt.

| | |
|---|---|
| *Oct 6 (Sat)* | **PAUL WHITEMAN AND HIS ORCHESTRA** |
| | *Columbia Record Co.* |
| | *New York City* |
| | Charles Margulis, Harry Goldfield (t); Eddie Pinder *or* Bix Beiderbecke (c); Boyce Cullen, Bill Rank, Wilbur Hall (tb); Chet Hazlett, Frank Trumbauer (as); Irving Friedman, Red Mayer (ts); Charles Strickfaden (bar); Kurt Dieterle, Mischa Russell, Matty Malneck, Charles Gaylord (vn); Roy Bargy (p); Lennie Hayton (cel); Mike Pingitore (bj); Min Leibrook (bb); Mike Trafficante (sb); George Marsh (d). |
| **W 147032** | **Where Is the Song of Songs for Me** (Berlin—arr. Challis) |
| | *Vocal: Jack Fulton* |
| | Released: Dec 20, 1928 |
| | Sales: 13,700 |
| W 147032–5 | Rejected. |
| W 147032–6 | Second choice. Unissued. |
| W 147032–7 | Rejected. |
| W 147032–8 | Mastered: Col 1630–D; ColE 5204; ColG C–5204. |

| | |
|---|---|
| *Dec 11 (Tue)* | **PAUL WHITEMAN AND HIS ORCHESTRA** |
| | *Columbia Record Co.* |
| | *New York City* |
| | Charles Margulis, Harry Goldfield, Eddie Pinder (t); Bix Beiderbecke (c); Boyce Cullen, Wilbur Hall, Bill Rank, Jack Fulton (tb); Chet Hazlett (as/Ebcl); Irving Friedman (ts/cl/as); Rube Crozier (bsn/o/cl); Red Mayer (o/bar/cl/bsn); Frank Trumbauer (C-m/bsn/as/cl); Charles Strickfaden (bar/o/cl); Kurt Dieterle, Mischa Russell, Matty Malneck, John Bowman (vn); Roy Bargy, Lennie Hayton (p); Mike Pingitore (bj); Mike Trafficante (sb); Min Leibrook (bb); George Marsh (perc). |
| **W 147540** | **Makin' Whoopee** (Donaldson-Kahn—arr. Grofe) |
| | *Vocal: Bing Crosby, with Jack Fulton, Charles Gaylord, Austin Young.* |
| W 147540–1 | Rejected. |
| W 147540–2 | Rejected. |
| W 147540–3 | Rejected. |
| W 147540–4 | Rejected. |

| | |
|---|---|
| *Same session* | Bix Beiderbecke does not appear on the remaining selection from this session: |

**1928:**

W 147539  I've Got a Feeling I'm Falling (Rose-Link-Waller—arr. ?)
       Col rejected

*Dec 12 (Wed)*   **PAUL WHITEMAN AND HIS ORCHESTRA**
       *Columbia Record Co.*
       *New York City*
       Charles Margulis, Harry Goldfield, Eddie Pinder (t); Bix Beiderbecke (c); Boyce Cullen, Wilbur Hall, Bill Rank, Jack Fulton (tb); Chet Hazlett (as/cl); Irving Friedman (ts/cl); Rube Crozier (as/bsn); Red Mayer (bar/bsn); Frank Trumbauer (C-m/cl); Charles Strickfaden (as/EngHorn); Kurt Dieterle, Mischa Russell, Matty Malneck, Charles Gaylord (vn); Roy Bargy, Lennie Hayton (p); Mike Pingitore (bj); Mike Trafficante (sb); Min Leibrook (bb); George Marsh (d).

W 147534  **I'm Bringing a Red Red Rose** (Donaldson-Kahn—arr. Grofe)
       *Vocal: Jack Fulton*
W 147534–1  Rejected.
W 147534–2  Rejected.
W 147534–3  Rejected.
W 147534–4  Rejected.

*Same session*   Bix Beiderbecke does not appear on the remaining selection from this session:
W 147535  Sweet Dreams (Yellen-Ager—arr. ?)
       Col rejected

*Dec 13 (Thu)*   **PAUL WHITEMAN AND HIS ORCHESTRA**
       *Columbia Record Co.*
       *New York City*
       Charles Margulis, Harry Goldfield, Bix Beiderbecke, Eddie Pinder (t/c); Boyce Cullen, Wilbur Hall, Bill Rank, Jack Fulton (tb); Chet Hazlett (Ebcl/Bbcl/as); Irving Friedman (ts/cl); Rube Crozier (cl/f/bsn); Red Mayer (cl/f/ss/ts); Frank Trumbauer (as); Charles Strickfaden (bar/ss); Kurt Dieterle, Mischa Russell, Matty Malneck (vn); Roy Bargy (p); Mike Pingitore (bj); Mike Trafficante (sb); Min Leibrook (bb); George Marsh (d).

W 98610  **Liebestraum** (Liszt—arr. Bargy)
       *Instrumental*
W 98610–1  Rejected.
W 98610–2  Mastered: Col 50198-D; ColE 9798; ColG C–9798; ColAu 07510.
W 98610–3  Second choice. Unissued.
W 98610–4  Rejected.

*Dec 14 (Fri)*   **PAUL WHITEMAN AND HIS ORCHESTRA**
       *Columbia Record Co.*
       *New York City*
       Bix Beiderbecke does not appear on the following recordings from this session:
W 147536  Let's Do It, Let's Fall in Love (Porter—arr. Challis)
       Col rejected
W 147537  How About Me (Berlin—arr. Challis)
       Col rejected

*Dec 19 (Wed)*   **PAUL WHITEMAN AND HIS ORCHESTRA**
       *Columbia Record Co.*
       *New York City*
       Bix Beiderbecke does not appear on the following recordings from this session:
W 147534  I'm Bringing a Red, Red Rose (Donaldson-Kahn—arr. Grofe)
       Col 1683-D
W 147537  How About Me (Berlin—arr. Challis)
       Col rejected
W 147539  I've Got a Feeling I'm Falling (Rose-Link-Waller—arr. ?)
       Col rejected

**1928:**

| | |
|---|---|
| *Dec 22 (Sat)* | **PAUL WHITEMAN AND HIS ORCHESTRA**<br>*Columbia Record Co.*<br>*New York City*<br>Bix Beiderbecke does not appear on the following recordings from this session: |
| W 147540 | Makin' Whoopee (Donaldson-Kahn—arr. Grofe)<br>Col 1683–D |
| W 147536 | Let's Do It, Let's Fall in Love (Porter—arr. Challis)<br>Col 1701–D |

**1929:**

| | |
|---|---|
| *Jan 10 (Thu)* | **PAUL WHITEMAN AND HIS ORCHESTRA**<br>*Columbia Record Co.*<br>*New York City*<br>Charles Margulis, Harry Goldfield, Eddie Pinder (t); Bix Beiderbecke (c); Boyce Cullen, Wilbur Hall, Bill Rank, Jack Fulton (tb); Chet Hazlett (Ebcl/cl/bcl); Irving Friedman (ts/cl); Rube Crozier (as/f/ss); Red Mayer (ss/bsn/bar/f/EngHorn); Frank Trumbauer (as/bsn/cl); Charles Strickfaden (ss/o/co); Kurt Dieterle, Mischa Russell, Matty Malneck, John Bowman, Charles Gaylord, Mario Perry (vn); Roy Bargy (p); Lennie Hayton (cel); Mike Pingitore (bj); Mike Trafficante (sb); Min Leibrook (bb); George Marsh (d); |
| **W 147750** | **Chinese Lullaby** (Bowers—arr. Grofe)<br>*Instrumental* |
| W 147750–1 | Rejected. |
| W 147750–2 | Mastered: Col 2656–D; ColAu 07020. |
| W 147750–3 | Rejected. |
| W 147750–4 | Second choice. Unissued. |
| *Same session* | Bix Beiderbecke does not appear on the next selection from this session: |
| W 147749 | Cradle of Love (Wayne-Gilbert—arr. Challis)<br>Col 1723–D |
| *Same session* | The next two titles are listed on the file cards as:<br>**PAUL WHITEMAN PRESENTS BEE PALMER WITH THE FRANK TRUMBAUER ORCHESTRA**<br>Bix Beiderbecke (c); Bill Rank (tb); Irving Friedman (cl/as); Frank Trumbauer (C-m/as); Charles Strickfaden (as); Roy Bargy (p); Edward McIntosh "Snoozer" Quinn (g); George Marsh (d). |
| **W 147770** | **Don't Leave Me, Daddy** (Verges—arr. Challis)<br>*Vocal: Bee Palmer* |
| W 147770–1 | Rejected. |
| W 147770–2 | Rejected. |
| W 147770–3 | Rejected. |
| **W 147771** | **Singin' the Blues** (Conrad-Robinson—arr. Challis)<br>*Vocal: Bee Palmer* |
| W 147771–1 | Rejected. |
| W 147771–2 | Rejected. |
| W 147771–3 | Rejected. |

Note: Roy Bargy was of the opinion that Lennie Hayton, not he, was the pianist on these titles. No information is available about the first selection, but apparently Bill Challis scored both with a kind of "concerto grosso" effect in mind: the smaller unit as featured band, but using the full Whiteman ensemble in key parts, especially on the rideouts. We can offer some definite information on "Singin' the Blues," based partly on the recollections of participating musicians. After a four-bar intro by Bix, Trumbauer and the two other reeds play a scored version of his 1927 Okeh solo; Bee Palmer sings one chorus, followed by Bix, doing 32 bars roughly based on his own solo on the original record. The last chorus brings the orchestra into play, spotlighting four trombones, with Bix coming up over the ensemble to ride out the last eight bars.

**1929:**

| | |
|---|---|
| *Jan 11 (Fri)* | **PAUL WHITEMAN AND HIS ORCHESTRA** |
| | Bix Beiderbecke does not appear on this recording session. |
| W 147537 | How About Me (Berlin—arr. Challis) |
| | Col 1723–D |
| W 147751 | My Angeline (Gilbert-Wayne—arr. Grofe) |
| | Col rejected |

| | |
|---|---|
| *Feb 7 (Thu)* | **PAUL WHITEMAN AND HIS ORCHESTRA** |
| | Bix Beiderbecke does not appear on this recording session: |
| W 147925 | Lover, Come Back to Me (Romberg-Hammerstein—arr. Grofe) |
| | Col 1731–D |
| W 147943 | Marianna (Romberg-Hammerstein—arr. Grofe) |
| | Col 1731–D |

| | |
|---|---|
| *Feb 8 (Fri)* | **PAUL WHITEMAN AND HIS ORCHESTRA** |
| | Bix Beiderbecke does not appear on this recording session. |
| W 147926 | Button Up Your Overcoat (de Sylva-Brown-Henderson—arr. Grofe) |
| | Col 1736–D |
| W 147950 | My Lucky Star (de Sylva-Brown-Henderson—arr. Grofe) |
| | Col 1736–D |

| | |
|---|---|
| *Feb 28 (Thu)* | **PAUL WHITEMAN AND HIS ORCHESTRA** |
| | Bix Beiderbecke does not appear on this recording session: |
| W 148013 | Coquette (Berlin—arr. William Grant Still) |
| | Col 1755–D |
| W 147751 | My Angeline (Gilbert-Wayne—arr. Grofe) |
| | Col rejected |

| | |
|---|---|
| *March 7 (Thu)* | **PAUL WHITEMAN AND HIS ORCHESTRA** |
| | Bix Beiderbecke does not appear on this recording session: |
| W 147751 | My Angeline (Gilbert-Wayne—arr. Grofe) |
| | Col 1755–D |
| W 148028 | Nola (Arndt—arr. Bargy) |
| | Col 2277–D |

| | |
|---|---|
| *March 8 (Fri)* | **FRANK TRUMBAUER AND HIS ORCHESTRA** |
| | *Okeh Record Co.* |
| | *New York City* |
| | Bix Beiderbecke, Andy Secrest (c); Bill Rank (tb); Irving Friedman (cl/ts); Frank Trumbauer (C-m/as); Charles Strickfaden (as); Min Leibrook (bsx); Lennie Hayton (p); Matty Malneck (vn); Eddie Lang (g); Stan King (d). |
| **W 401703** | **Futuristic Rhythm** (McHugh—arr. Malneck) |
| | *Vocal: Frank Trumbauer* |
| | Released: Apr 15, 1929 |
| | Sales: 3,775 |
| W 401703–A | Rejected |
| W 401703–B | Mastered: OK 41209; ParE R–2625; OdArg 193308; OdFr 165684; ParIt B–27002; ParFr 22422. |
| W 401703–C | Rejected. |
| W 401703–D | Rejected. |
| | Soloists: Bix (16 + 8); Rank (8). |
| **W 401704** | **Raisin' the Roof** (McHugh—arr. Malneck) |
| | *Instrumental* |
| | Released: Apr 15, 1929 |
| | Sales: 3,775 |
| W 401704–A | Rejected. |
| W 401704–B | Rejected. |
| W 401704–C | Rejected. |
| W 401704–D | Mastered: OK 41209; ParE R–2644; OdArg 193308; OdFr 165684; ParIt B–27002. |
| | Soloists: Bix (8 + 8). |
| | Note: On all subsequent sessions involving both Bix and Andy Secrest, the authors have made solo identifications based on exhaustive listening to the recordings, comparisons to other examples of the styles of both, and corroborative identifications |

by participating musicians. In most cases, this mating of techniques produced a consensus. In those few cases where disagreement persists, mention is made of this.

*March 15 (Fri)*

**PAUL WHITEMAN AND HIS ORCHESTRA**
*Columbia Record Co.*
*New York City*
Charles Margulis, Harry Goldfield (t); Andy Secrest, Bix Beiderbecke (c); Boyce Cullen, Wilbur Hall, Bill Rank, Jack Fulton (tb); Chet Hazlett (cl/bcl/as); Irving Friedman (cl/bar); Rube Crozier (bsn/f/as); Red Mayer (bsn/as/bar/f); Frank Trumbauer (cl/bsn/as); Charles Strickfaden (EngHorn/cl/bar); Kurt Dieterle, Mischa Russell, Matty Malneck, Charles Gaylord (vn); Roy Bargy (p) Lennie Hayton (cel); Mike Pingitore (bj); Mike Trafficante (sb); Min Leibrook (bb); George Marsh (perc); unknown (stg).

W 148085     **Blue Hawaii** (Baer-Caesar-Schuster—arr. Grofe)
*Vocal: Charles Gaylord, Jack Fulton.*
Released: Apr 26, 1929
Sales: 15,295
W 148085–1    Rejected.
W 148085–2    Second choice. Unissued.
W 148085–3    Rejected.
W 148085–4    Mastered: Col 1771–D; ColAu 07021; ColE 5456; ColG C–5456.

*Same session*

Bix Beiderbecke does not appear on the other selection from this session:
W 148086     Louise (Robin-Whiting—arr. Bargy)
Col 1771–D

*April 5 (Fri)*

**PAUL WHITEMAN AND HIS ORCHESTRA**
*Columbia Record Co.*
*New York City*
Charles Margulis, Harry Goldfield (t); Andy Secrest, Bix Beiderbecke (c); Boyce Cullen, Bill Rank, Wilbur Hall (tb); Chet Hazlett (as); Irving Friedman (cl/ts); Bernie Daly (cl/ss); Red Mayer (cl/ts); Frank Trumbauer (as/cl); Charles Strickfaden (bar/as/ss); Kurt Dieterle, Mischa Russell, Matty Malneck (vn); Roy Bargy (p); Mike Pingitore (bj); Mike Trafficante (sb); Min Leibrook (bb); George Marsh (d).

W 148183     **I'm in Seventh Heaven** (de Sylva-Brown-Henderson—arr. Challis)
*Vocal: Bing Crosby, Al Rinker, Harry Barris.*
Released: Aug 2, 1929
Sales: 12,000
W 148183–1    Rejected.
W 148183–2    Rejected.
W 148183–3    Mastered: Col 1877–D; ColAu 07021; ColJ J–749; ColE 5544; ColG C–5544; ColArg A–8208.
W 148183–4    Second choice. Unissued.
Soloists: Bix (16 + 8).

*Same session*

Charles Margulis, Harry Goldfield (t); Andy Secrest, Bix Beiderbecke (c); Boyce Cullen, Wilbur Hall, Bill Rank, Jack Fulton (tb); Chet Hazlett (as/bcl/cl/Ebcl); Irving Friedman (cl); Bernie Daly (as/cl); Red Mayer (cl/as/o); Frank Trumbauer (cl); Charles Strickfaden (bar/cl); Kurt Dieterle, Mischa Russell, John Bowman, Charles Gaylord (vn); Roy Bargy (p); Lennie Hayton (cel); Mike Pingitore (bj); Mike Trafficante (sb); Min Leibrook (bb); George Marsh (perc).

W 148184     **Little Pal** (de Sylva-Brown-Henderson—arr. Grofe)
*Vocal: Bing Crosby*
W 148184–1    Rejected.
W 148184–2    Rejected.
W 148184–3    Rejected.
W 148184–4    Rejected.

| | |
|---|---|
| *April 17 (Wed)* | **FRANK TRUMBAUER AND HIS ORCHESTRA**<br>*Okeh Record Co.*<br>*New York City*<br>Bix Beiderbecke, Andy Secrest (c); Bill Rank (tb); Irving Friedman (cl/ts); Frank Trumbauer (C-m/as); Charles Strickfaden (as); Min Leibrook (bsx); Roy Bargy (p); Matty Malneck (vn); Eddie Lang (g); Stan King (d). |
| W 401809 | **Louise** (Robin-Whiting—arr. Malneck)<br>*Vocal: Smith Ballew*<br>Released: May 25, 1929<br>Sales: 3,475 |
| W 401809–A | Rejected. |
| W 401809–B | Mastered: OK 41231; ParAm PNY–41231; ParE E–6208; ParG A–4948; ParIt B–27029; OdBrazil 1594; ParFr 22389; OdFr 165736; OdArg 193316; OdG A–189282; OdAm ONY–41231; OdG A–189287. |
| W 401809–C | Rejected.<br>Soloists: Bix (8); last chorus—Secrest (lead), Bix (4 obligato). |
| W 401810 | **Wait Till You See "Ma Cherie"** (Robin-Whiting—arr. Malneck)<br>*Vocal: Smith Ballew*<br>Released: May 25, 1929<br>Sales: 3,475 |
| W 401810–A | Rejected. |
| W 401810–B | Rejected. |
| W 401810–C | Mastered: OK 41231; ParAm PNY–41231; ParE R–398; OdAm ONY–41231; ParIt B–27029; OdFr 165736; OdArg 193316; OdG A–189282; OdG A–189287; OdBrazil 1594; ParFr 22389; ParJ E–5081.<br>Soloists: Bix (4 + 4). |
| W 401811 | **Baby Won't You Please Come Home** (Warfield-Williams—arr. Malneck)<br>*Vocal: Frank Trumbauer.*<br>Released: Sept 25, 1929<br>Sales: 2,700 |
| W 401811–A | Rejected. |
| W 401811–B | Rejected. |
| W 401811–C | Mastered: OK 41286; OdAm ONY–41286; OdFr 165843; OdIt A–2336; ParFr 22523; ParE R–1978; OdE OR–1978; ColH DCH–339; OdG A–286087; OdG 025412; Har 1422–H; Cl 5469–C; VT 2529–V; *Col 37807;* ColSs DZ–2997; ParAm PNY–41286.<br>Soloists: Secrest (16 verse); Bix (first "fill"); Secrest (other "fills"); Bix (16); Secrest (lead last chorus); Bix (muted obligato).<br>Note: Har 1422–H, Cl 5469–c, VT 2529–V as "Tennessee Music Men"; OdAm ONY–41231 as "Eddie Gordon's Band"; ParE E–6208 as "Will Perry's Orchestra"; ParAm PNY–41231 as "Joe Curran's Band." |
| *April 25 (Thu)* | **PAUL WHITEMAN AND HIS ORCHESTRA**<br>*Columbia Record Co.*<br>*New York City*<br>Charles Margulis, Harry Goldfield (t); Andy Secrest, Bix Beiderbecke (c); Boyce Cullen, Wilbur Hall, Bill Rank, Jack Fulton (tb); Chet Hazlett (as/bcl/cl/Ebcl); Irving Friedman (cl); Bernie Daly (as/cl); Red Mayer (cl/as/o); Frank Trumbauer (cl); Charles Strickfaden (bar/cl); Kurt Dieterle, Mischa Russell, John Bowman, Charles Gaylord (vn); Roy Bargy (p); Mike Pingitore (bj); Mike Trafficante (sb); Min Leibrook (bb); Lennie Hayton (cel); George Marsh (perc). |
| W 148184 | **Little Pal** (de Sylva-Brown-Henderson—arr. Grofe)<br>*Vocal: Bing Crosby*<br>Released: Aug 2, 1929<br>Sales: 12,000 |
| W 148184–5 | Rejected. |
| W 148184–6 | Rejected. |
| W 148184–7 | Second choice. Unissued |

1929:

W 148184–8      Mastered: Col 1877–D; ColE 5544; ColAu 07023; ColG C–5544; ColArg A–8208.

*Same session*      Charles Margulis, Harry Goldfield (t); Andy Secrest, Bix Beiderbecke (c); Boyce Cullen, Bill Rank, Wilbur Hall, Jack Fulton (tb); Chet Hazlett, Bernie Daly, Irving Friedman, Frank Trumbauer, Charles Strickfaden, Red Mayer (reeds); Kurt Dieterle, Mischa Russell, John Bowman (vn); Roy Bargy (p); Mike Pingitore (bj); Mike Trafficante (sb); Min Leibrook (bb); George Marsh (d).

W 98653      **Song of India** (Rimsky-Korsakov—arr. Bargy)
*Instrumental*
W 98653–1      Rejected.
W 98653–2      Rejected.
W 98653–3      Second choice. Unissued.
W 98653–4      Mastered: Col 50198–D; ColE 9798; ColG C–9798; ColAu 07510.

*April 30 (Thu)*      FRANK TRUMBAUER AND HIS ORCHESTRA
*Okeh Record Co.*
*New York City*
Bix Beiderbecke, Andy Secrest (c); Bill Rank (tb); Irving Friedman (cl/ts); Frank Trumbauer (C-m/as) Charles Strickfaden (as/o); Min Leibrook (bsx); Lennie Hayton (p); Eddie Lang (g); Stan King (d); Mischa Russell, Kurt Dieterle, Matty Malneck (vn).

W 401840      **No One Can Take Your Place** (Gilbert-Malneck-Signorelli—arr. Malneck)
*Vocal: Smith Ballew*
W 401840–A      Rejected.
W 401840–B      Mastered: ParE R–420; ParFr 22430; OdG A–189259.
Soloists: Bix (8).
*Add Charles Margulis (t); omit Russell, Dieterle, Malneck (vn).*

W 401841      **I Like That** (Hayton-Trumbauer-Kohler—arr. Lennie Hayton)
*Instrumental*
Released: Sept 25, 1929
Sales: 2,700
W 401841–A      Rejected.
W 401841–B      Rejected.
W 401841–C      Mastered: OK 41286; OdAm ONY–41286; ParE R–714; OdFr 165843; ParFr 22523; OdIt A–2318; OdG A–286019; ParAm PNY–41286; OdIt DSEQ–552.
Soloists: Bix (8 open); Bix (16 + 8 in derby).
Note: The authors have assigned to Bix all three solo spots on "I Like That" for a variety of reasons. The composition is the same as "Loved One," as recorded for Brunswick on June 6, 1930; the phrasing and tone of the first solo passage in both cases leave little doubt as to Bix's identity. On "I Like That," the two remaining solo spots, separated by eight bars of Friedman's clarinet, appear to display two differing tone qualities; the first bears strong similarities to Bix's approach in his eight bars on "No One Can Take Your Place," made the same day. In the second, it is possible that Bix intended to end his chorus with a burst of the kind of fiery playing which climaxed "Goose Pimples" and "Riverboat Shuffle" two years before. Again, as is clear on "Futuristic Rhythm," his slightly rusty embouchure undermines his efforts; he plays the octave jumps sharp, betraying reliance on mouthpiece pressure to achieve control. None of the three solos contains characteristics normally associated with Andy Secrest, but his tone and attack are recognizable at once in the lead-in phrase to the final ensemble chorus.

*May 3 (Fri)*      PAUL WHITEMAN AND HIS ORCHESTRA
*Columbia Record Co.*
*New York City*
Charles Margulis, Harry Goldfield (t); Andy Secrest, Bix Beiderbecke (c); Boyce Cullen, Wilbur Hall, Bill Rank, Jack Fulton (tb); Chet Hazlett (cl/as), Irving Friedman, Red Mayer (ts); Bernie

466

**1929:**

Daly, Frank Trumbauer (as); Charles Strickfaden (o/as/bar); Kurt Dieterle, Mischa Russell, John Bowman, Charles Gaylord (vn); Roy Bargy (p); Lennie Hayton (cel); Mike Pingitore (bj); Mike Trafficante (sb); Min Leibrook (bb); George Marsh (d).

W 148407      **When My Dreams Come True** (Berlin—arr. Bargy)
*Vocal: Jack Fulton*
Released: June 7, 1929
Sales: 13,825

W 148407–1      Rejected.
W 148407–2      Rejected.
W 148407–3      Second choice. Unissued.
W 148407–4      Mastered: Col 1822–D; ColE 5484; ColAu 07024; ColJ J–711. Soloists: Secrest (8); Trumbauer (8).

*Same session*      Charles Margulis, Harry Goldfield (t); Andy Secrest, Bix Beiderbecke (c); Boyce Cullen, Wilbur Hall, Bill Rank, Jack Fulton (tb); Chet Hazlett (cl/as); Irving Friedman, Red Mayer (ts); Bernie Daly, Charles Strickfaden (C-m/as); Frank Trumbauer (C-m/as); Kurt Dieterle, Mischa Russell, John Bowman, Charles Gaylord (vn); Roy Bargy (p); Mike Pingitore (bj); Mike Trafficante (sb); Min Leibrook (bb); George Marsh (d).

W 148408      **Reachin' for Someone** (Donaldson-Leslie—arr. Challis)
*Vocal: Bing Crosby*
Released: June 7, 1929
Sales: 13,825

W 148408–1      Rejected.
W 148408–2      Rejected.
W 148408–3      Rejected.
W 148408–4      Mastered: Col 1822–D; ColE 5484; ColAu 07024; ColJ J–711. Soloists: Trumbauer (16 + 8); Bix (8).

*Same session*      Bix Beiderbecke, Charles Margulis, Andy Secrest (t/c); Bill Rank (tb); Chet Hazlett, Frank Trumbauer, Bernie Daly (as); Charles Strickfaden (ts); Irving Friedman (ts/cl); Kurt Dieterle, Mischa Russell (vn); Roy Bargy (p); Mike Pingitore (bj); Mike Trafficante (sb); Min Leibrook (bb); George Marsh (d).

W 148409      **China Boy** (Winfree-Boutelje—arr. Hayton)
*Instrumental*
Released: Oct 4, 1929
Sales: 11,000

W 148409–1      Second choice. Unissued.
W 148409–2      Rejected.
W 148409–3      Rejected.
W 148409–4      Mastered: Col 1945–D; ColE DC–177; *Tpl 529;* ColJ J–1518; ColAu 07025; ColArg A–8278. Soloists: Friedman (16 + 8); Trumbauer (16 + 4); Secrest (4); Bix (16).

*May 4 (Sat)*      **PAUL WHITEMAN AND HIS ORCHESTRA**
*Columbia Record Co.*
*New York City*
Charles Margulis, Harry Goldfield (t); Andy Secrest, Bix Beiderbecke (c); Boyce Cullen, Wilbur Hall, Bill Rank, Jack Fulton (tb); Chet Hazlett (cl/as); Irving Friedman (cl/ts); Bernie Daly (cl/as); Red Mayer (bsn/as/ts); Frank Trumbauer (as); Charles Strickfaden (bar/EngHorn); Kurt Dieterle, Mischa Russell, John Bowman, Charles Gaylord (vn); Roy Bargy (p); Lennie Hayton (cel); Mike Pingitore (bj); Mike Trafficante (sb); Min Leibrook (bb); George Marsh (d).

W 148421      **Oh! Miss Hannah** (Deppen-Hollingsworth—arr. Challis)
*Vocal: Bing Crosby*
Released: Oct 4, 1929
Sales: 11,000

W 148421–1      Rejected.
W 148421–2      Second choice. Unissued.
W 148421–3      Rejected.
W 148421 4      Mastered: Col 1945–D; ColE DC–176; *Tpl 529;* ColAu 07025;

1929:

ColJ J–1518; ColArg A–8278.
Soloists: Trumbauer (16); Bix (16).

*Same session* Charles Margulis, Harry Goldfield (t); Andy Secrest, Bix Beiderbecke (c); Boyce Cullen, Bill Rank, Wilbur Hall, Jack Fulton (tb); Chet Hazlett (as/Ebcl); Irving Friedman (cl/ts); Bernie Daly (ts); Red Mayer (as/cl); Frank Trumbauer (as); Charles Strickfaden (bar); Kurt Dieterle, Mischa Russell, John Bowman, Charles Gaylord (vn); Roy Bargy (p); Lennie Hayton (cel); Mike Pingitore (bj); Mike Trafficante (sb); Min Leibrook (bb); George Marsh (d).

**W 148422** **Your Mother and Mine** (Goodwin-Edwards—arr. Bargy)
*Vocal: Bing Crosby, Al Rinker, Harry Barris*
W 148422–1 Rejected.
W 148422–2 Rejected.
W 148422–3 Rejected.
W 148422–4 Rejected.

*Same session* Charles Margulis, Harry Goldfield (t); Andy Secrest, Bix Beiderbecke (c); Boyce Cullen, Wilbur Hall, Bill Rank, Jack Fulton (tb); Chet Hazlett (as/cl/Ebcl); Irving Friedman (as/cl); Bernie Daly (bar/f/cl); Red Mayer (bsn/o/as); Frank Trumbauer (bsn/as); Charles Strickfaden (bar/cl); Kurt Dieterle, Mischa Russell, John Bowman, Charles Gaylord (vn); Roy Bargy (p); Lennie Hayton (cel); Mike Pingitore (bj); Mike Trafficante (sb); Min Leibrook (bb); George Marsh (d).

**W 148423** **Orange Blossom Time** (Goodwin-Edwards—arr. Grofe)
*Vocal: Bing Crosby*
Released: June 28, 1929
Sales: 13,800
W 148423–1 Rejected.
W 148423–2 Rejected.
W 148423–3 Second choice. Unissued.
W 148423–4 Mastered: Col 1845–D; ColE 5560; ColAu 07026.

*May 15 (Wed)* MASON-DIXON ORCHESTRA
(Frank Trumbauer Orchestra)
*Columbia Record Co.*
*New York City*
Bix Beiderbecke does not appear on this session.
Charles Margulis, Harry Goldfield (t); Andy Secrest (c); Bill Rank (tb); Irving Friedman (cl/as); Frank Trumbauer (C-m); Charles Strickfaden (as/bar); Min Leibrook (bsx); Lennie Hayton (p); Snoozer Quinn (g); George Marsh (d).

**W 148537** What a Day! (Woods—arr. Hayton)
Col 1861–D
**W 148538** Alabamy Snow (Rose-David—arr. ?)
Col 1861–D
Note: This is the first Trumbauer date without Bix. From now on, all "hot" cornet work on Trumbauer sessions is by Andy Secrest. There are no exceptions.

*May 16 (Thu)* PAUL WHITEMAN AND HIS ORCHESTRA
*Columbia Record Co.*
*New York City*
Charles Margulis, Harry Goldfield (t); Andy Secrest, Bix Beiderbecke (c); Boyce Cullen, Bill Rank, Wilbur Hall, Jack Fulton (tb); Chet Hazlett (as/Ebcl); Irving Friedman (cl/ts); Bernie Daly (ts); Red Mayer (as/cl); Charles Strickfaden (bar); Kurt Dieterle, Mischa Russell, John Bowman, Charles Gaylord (vn); Roy Bargy (p); Lennie Hayton (cel); Mike Pingitore (bj); Mike Trafficante (sb); Min Leibrook (bb); George Marsh (d).

**W 148422** **Your Mother and Mine** (Goodwin-Edwards—arr. Bargy)
*Vocal: Bing Crosby, Harry Barris, Al Rinker.*
Released: June 28, 1929
Sales: 13,800
W 148422–5 Rejected.
W 148422–6 Rejected.

468

1929:

<table>
<tr><td>W 148422–7</td><td>Second choice. Unissued.</td></tr>
<tr><td>W 148422–8</td><td>Mastered: Col 1845–D; ColE 5560; ColAu 07026.</td></tr>
</table>

*Same session*

Bix Beiderbecke does not appear on the other selections from this Paul Whiteman session:

W 148544    S'posin' (Denniker-Razaf—arr. Bargy)
Col 1862–D

W 148545    Laughing Marionette (?—arr. Bargy)
Col 1862–D

*May 21 (Tue)*

**FRANK TRUMBAUER AND HIS ORCHESTRA**
*Okeh Record Co.*
*New York City*
Bix Beiderbecke does not appear on this session.

W 401952    Nobody but You (Goodwin-Edwards)
OK 41252

W 401953    I've Got a Feelin' for You (Trent-Ahlert)
OK 41252

*Sept 6 (Fri)*

**PAUL WHITEMAN AND HIS ORCHESTRA**
*Columbia Record Co.*
*New York City*
Charles Margulis, Harry Goldfield (t); Andy Secrest, Bix Beiderbecke (c); Boyce Cullen, Wilbur Hall, Bill Rank, Jack Fulton (tb); Chet Hazlett, Bernie Daly, Red Mayer, Irving Friedman, Frank Trumbauer, Charles Strickfaden (reeds); Kurt Dieterle, Mischa Russell, Matty Malneck. Otto Landau (vn); Roy Bargy (p); Lennie Hayton (cel); Mike Pingitore (bj); Mike Trafficante (sb); Eddie Lang (g); Min Leibrook (bb); George Marsh (d).

**W 148985**    **At Twilight** (Tracy-Pinkard—arr Grofe)
*Vocal: Bing Crosby, Al Rinker, Jack Fulton.*
Released: Nov 15, 1929
Sales: 12,025

W 148985–1    Rejected.
W 148985–2    Second choice. Unissued.
W 148985–3    Mastered: Col 1993–D; ColE 5655; ColAu 07028; ColG C–5655.
W 148985–4    Rejected.
**W 148986**    **Waiting at the End of the Road** (Berlin—arr. Grofe)
*Vocal: Bing Crosby*

W 148986–1    Rejected.
W 148986–2    Rejected.
W 148986–3    Rejected.
W 148986–4    Rejected.

*Sept 13 (Fri)*

**PAUL WHITEMAN AND HIS ORCHESTRA**
*Columbia Record Co.*
*New York City*
Charles Margulis, Harry Goldfield (t); Andy Secrest, Bix Beiderbecke (c); Boyce Cullen, Wilbur Hall, Bill Rank, Jack Fulton (tb); Chet Hazlett, Bernie Daly, Red Mayer, Frank Trumbauer, Irving Friedman, Charles Strickfaden (reeds); Kurt Dieterle, Mischa Russell, Matty Malneck, Otto Landau (vn); Roy Bargy (p); Lennie Hayton (cel); Mike Pingitore (bj); Mike Trafficante (sb); Min Leibrook (bb); George Marsh (d).

**W 148986**    **Waiting at the End of the Road** (Berlin—arr. Grofe)
*Vocal: Bing Crosby*
Released: Oct 25, 1929
Sales: 15,025

W 148986–5    Rejected.
W 148986–6    Rejected.
W 148986–7    Second choice. Unissued
W 148986–8    Mastered: Col 1974–D; ColE 5675; ColAu 07032; ColG C–5675.
Soloists: Bix (8)

*Same session*

Charles Margulis, Harry Goldfield (t); Andy Secrest, Bix Beiderbecke (c); Boyce Cullen, Wilbur Hall, Bill Rank, Jack Fulton (tb); Chet Hazlett, Bernie Daly, Red Mayer, Frank Trumbauer, Irving Friedman, Charles Strickfaden (reeds); Kurt Dieterle, Mischa Russell, Matty Malneck, Otto Landau (vn); Roy Bargy (p);

**1929:**

Lennie Hayton (cel); Mike Pingitore (bj); Eddie Lang (g); Mike Trafficante (sb); Min Leibrook (bb); George Marsh (d).

W 149005     **When You're Counting the Stars Alone** (Russell-Rose-Murray—arr. Challis)
*Vocal: Bing Crosby, Al Rinker, Jack Fulton.*

W 149005–1     Rejected.
Note: At this point, Bix was unable to continue and left the studio. Subsequent cornet solos are by Andy Secrest, whose part bears the pencilled notation: "Get ready for solo," then "Jump to other part."

W 149005–2     Rejected.
W 149005–3     Mastered: Col 1993–D; ColE 5675.

*Same session*     Bix Beiderbecke does not appear on the other selection from this session:

W 149006     Love Me (Aivaz-Morse—arr. Grofe)
Col 1974–D

**1930:**

*May 21 (Wed)*     HOAGY CARMICHAEL AND HIS ORCHESTRA
*Victor Record Co.*
*Liederkranz Hall, NYC*
*Time: 9:30 A.M.–1:30 P.M.*
Bix Beiderbecke (c); James "Bubber" Miley (t); Tommy Dorsey (tb); Benny Goodman (cl); Arnold Brilhart (as); Lawrence "Bud" Freeman (ts); Irving Brodsky (p); Eddie Lang (g); Joe Venuti (vn); Harry Goodman (bb); Gene Krupa (d); Hoagy Carmichael (p-o on BVE 59800 only).

BVE 59800     **Rockin' Chair** (Carmichael—arr. Carmichael)
*Vocal: Hoagy Carmichael, Irving Brodsky.*
Released: July 18, 1930

BVE 59800–1     Hold 30 days. Unissued.
BVE 59800–2     Mastered: Vic 25494; *HJCA HC–100;* HMV B–4897; HMV B–6288; HMV B–8549; HMVAu EA–1200; HMVAu EA–8549; VicArg 25494; Vic 38139–V; VicArg 38139; *VicArg 1AC–0018.*
Soloists: Miley (16 + 8); Bix (10); others as indicated in personnel listing.

BVE 62301     **Barnacle Bill, the Sailor** (Luther-Robison—arr. Carmichael)
*Vocal: Carson Robison, Hoagy Carmichael*
Released: July 18, 1930

BVE 62301–1     Mastered: Vic 38139–V; Vic 25371; *Jcl 532;* VicArg 25371; VicArg 38139; *VicArg 1AC–0018.*
BVE 62301–2     Hold conditional. Unissued.
Note: Despite the gap, the masters of this session are consecutive. The Victor files give the vocalists on BVE 62301 as "Carson Robison, plus guitar."
Soloists: Bix, Goodman, Freeman

*June 6 (Fri)*     IRVING MILLS AND HIS HOTSY TOTSY GANG
*Brunswick Record Co.*
*New York City*
Bix Beiderbecke (c); Ray Lodwig (t); Jack Teagarden (tb); Benny Goodman (cl/as); unknown (ts); Joe Venuti, Matty Malneck (vn); Min Leibrook (bsx); Frank Signorelli (p); Gene Krupa (d).

E 32948     **Loved One** (Trumbauer-Hayton-Mills)
*Instrumental*

E 32948–A     Mastered: Mt M–12051; Voc 15860; Br X–15860.
E 32948–B     Issued: Mt M–12051.

**1930:**

| | |
|---|---|
| E 32949 | **Deep Harlem** (Mills-Signorelli-Malneck) |
| | *Instrumental* |
| E 32949–A | Mastered: Br 4983; BrE 02821; BrFr A–50091. |
| E 32949–B | Rejected. |
| E 32950 | **Strut Miss Lizzie** (Creamer-Layton) |
| | *Vocal: Dick Robertson.* |
| E 32950–A | Rejected. |
| E 32950–B | Mastered: Br 4983; BrE 02821; BrFr A–50091. |
| | Note: Vocalion M–12051 & Vocalion 15860 by "Jack Winn's (or Wynn's) Dallas Dandies." |

*Sept 8 (Mon)*

BIX BEIDERBECKE AND HIS ORCHESTRA
*Victor Record Co. Studio 2, 24th Street*
*New York City*
*L.L. Watson, Recording Director*
*Time: 10:00 A.M.–1:30 P.M.*
*        2:30 P.M.–4:30 P.M.*
Bix Beiderbecke (c); Ray Lodwig (t); Boyce Cullen (tb); Benny Goodman, Jimmy Dorsey, Charles "Pee Wee" Russell (cl/as); Bud Freeman (ts); Min Leibrook (bsx); Irving Brodsky (p); Eddie Lang (g); Joe Venuti (vn); Gene Krupa (d).

| | |
|---|---|
| BVE 63630 | **Deep Down South** (Collins-Green) |
| | *Vocal: Wes Vaughan* |
| | Released: Dec 12, 1930 |
| | Sales: 5,865 |
| BVE 63630–1 | Hold 30 days. Issued: *NAT WEP–804*; RCA 731131; other LPs. |
| BVE 63630–2 | Mastered: Vic 23018; Vic 25370; HMV B–8419; GrFr K–6238. |

| | |
|---|---|
| BVE 63631 | **I Don't Mind Walkin' in the Rain** (Rich-Hoffman) |
| | *Vocal: Wes Vaughan* |
| | Released: Oct 24, 1930 |
| | Sales: 16,683 |
| BVE 63631–1 | Mastered: Vic 23008. |
| BVE 63631–2 | Hold 30 days. Unissued. |

*Same session*

Note: At this point the band took a lunch break. Venuti and Lang left for another engagement and did not return; Leibrook arrived at 3:35 PM, and played string bass.

| | |
|---|---|
| BVE 63632 | **I'll Be a Friend "With Pleasure"** (Pinkard) |
| | *Vocal: Wes Vaughan* |
| | Released: (–3) Oct 24, 1930 |
| | Sales: 16,683 |
| | Released: (–2) Oct 31, 1930 |
| BVE 63632–1 | Hold conditional. Unissued. Test pressing believed to exist. |
| BVE 63632–2 | Hold 30 days. Issued: Vic 23008. |
| BVE 63632–3 | Mastered: Vic 23008; Vic 26415; HMV B–4889; HMV B–8419. |

**1930:**

*Sept 15 (Mon)*    HOAGY CARMICHAEL AND HIS ORCHESTRA
*Victor Record Co. Studio 2, 24th Street*
*New York City*
*L.L. Watson, Recording Director*
*Time: 1:15 P.M.–5:10 P.M.*
Bix Beiderbecke (c); Ray Lodwig (t); Jack Teagarden, Boyce
Cullen (tb); Jimmy Dorsey (cl/as); Bud Freeman (ts); Pee Wee
Russell (as); Min Leibrook (bsx); Irving Brodsky (p); Joe Venuti
(v); Eddie Lang (g); Chauncey Morehouse (d).

**BVE 63653**    **Georgia on My Mind** (Carmichael-Gorrell—arr. Carmichael)
*Vocal: Hoagy Carmichael.*
Released: Nov 14, 1930
Sales: 3,641

BVE 63653–1    Mastered: Vic 23013; Vic 25494; HMV B–4885; HMV B–6133;
HMV B–8549; *HJCA HC–100;* VicArg 25494; GrFr K–6525;
HMVAu EA–8549; HMVAu EA–1200.

BVE 63653–2    Hold 30 days. Unissued.

**BVE 63655**    **Bessie Couldn't Help It** (Warner-Richmond-Bayha—arr. Car-
michael)
*Vocal: Hoagy Carmichael.*
Released: (–1)Dec 31, 1931
Sales: 3,423
Released: (–2)July 30, 1936

BVE 63655–1    Mastered: Vic 22864.

BVE 63655–2    Hold 30 days. Issued: Vic 25371; *Jcl 532.*

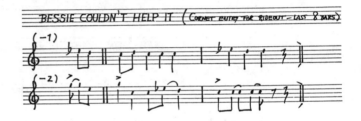

Bix Beiderbecke does not appear on the other selection from
this session:

BVE 63654    One Night in Havana (Carmichael-Porter—arr. Carmichael)
Vic 23013

# Appendix C

# ... AND A WORD ABOUT THAT ELUSIVE THIRD VALVE

One of the little understood yet often written-about facets of Bix Beiderbecke's music has been his unorthodox fingering of the cornet. Yet an understanding of its logic, and its connection with Bix's acute musical ear, helps explain the individuality of sound and intonation which sets Beiderbecke's playing apart at once from even his most faithful of imitators.

The B♭ cornet, as all cup mouthpiece brass instruments, is based on the principle that a piece of metal tubing of a specific length, whether straight or curled, will produce a tone of fixed pitch when a column of vibrating air is passed through it. A tube about 53 inches long produces a basic B♭. A combination of increased muscular tension and intensification of the air column will allow the player, without use of valves, pistons or slides, to produce an ascending series of pitches based on the physical principle of the overtone series.

A player with a strong set of lip muscles should be able to produce the following notes, beginning on the instrument's written low C, sounding B♭ in the case of a cornet or trumpet:

Somewhere in the evolution of brass instruments, two methods were evolved for producing the notes which lay between these "open" tones. Both involved lengthening the amount of tubing through which the vibrating air column blown by the player had to travel before reaching the bell, or sounding end, of the instrument.

In one, the far curve of the instrument was fitted with a sleeved slide which could be extended with the hand. This idea led to the slide trombone, and the less often used slide cornet and trumpet.

The other, which appeared in several variants, involved fitting the 53 inches with a series of carefully-measured extensions; by pushing a button or depressing a piston, the player could open a "door" into one of these extensions, redirecting the air column through a detour which dropped the overall pitch a half-step, whole-step or other fixed interval.

Eventually a series of three valves became conventional. One, the middle of the three, dropped the pitch half a step; this meant C could be lowered to B, G to G♭, E to E♭, all the way to the top. The first valve, that closest to the player, dropped the tone a full step, the third a step and a half, or the total of the first and second together.

Through this system, the player was able to sound an entire chromatic scale, from concert E (written F-sharp) below the treble staff to as high above it as the performer was capable of playing.

Because each overtone could be altered in this way, and because the "open" tones were closer together the higher they went, there was bound to be some overlap; that is, from the middle register of the instrument upwards, it is possible to produce the same note with a number of different fingerings.

The cornet's written E, concert pitch D, provides a useful example. It can be played (a) open, as part of the instrument's natural harmonic series, (b) with first and second valves, as the third step in the descent from the open written G above, (c) with third valve alone, as the mathematical equivalent of valves one and two, and (d) with all three valves, as the final stop in the descent from the "false" written $B^b$ of the open series above.

Enter Bix Beiderbecke. In learning to play his cornet as a Davenport schoolboy, he had no way of knowing that schooled brass players had long since arrived at a series of "approved" fingerings—those calculated to keep the cornet or trumpet closest to uniformity of intonation. Had he studied, he would have been told that a trained player almost *always* used his first and second valves to produce written A in the staff, adjusting intonation exactly through use of extension slides fitted to the first and third valves. He would have found out that symphonically-trained trumpeters avoid the third-valve-alone fingering because it is usually flat, and cannot be brought as easily into exact tune as the first and second.

Bix knew none of this. He pressed down a valve and got a note. Because he thought of his instrument as being in piano, or "concert" pitch, he was totally unaware of the implications of the overtone series. This also led him, in exploring his horn's second octave, to first try a straight repetition of the fingerings he had used to produce the same notes an octave below. Therefore if concert C below the treble staff was played one and three, it stood to reason that the same note, an octave higher, might also be played this way.

By the time he began to play in public, Bix had worked out a fingering system which appeared to other brass players to be no system at all. Sometimes he'd use his second valve to play a written B, as they did, but sometimes, depending on the passage and the key, he would use one and three and "lip" the note into tune. Sometimes fourth-line D came out with just valve one, sometimes with one and three.

The arbiter, it developed, was Bix's ear. He had perfect pitch, the ability not only to identify or reproduce a given tone without aid of an instrument, but to relate pitch to key, harmony and timbre in ways beyond the hearing of normal persons. To use a basic example, although the piano and other "equal-tempered" instruments make no distinction between C-sharp and D-flat and their respective scales, they are nonetheless different. Listeners "feel" this as the difference between the "bright" quality of pieces written in C-sharp and the "dark" or "mellow" sound of those in $D^b$. Improvising jazzmen often explain it by saying that they "think differently" in the two keys. This way, they are distinguishing between what they perceive as two different ends of the same tonal unit, the "sharp side" and "flat side" of the note.

One of Bix's ways of expressing his perception of this difference was his automatic, instinctive use of different fingerings in different keys. This, coupled with a natural tendency to look for fingerings which were comfortable to play and presented no major technical obstacles, resulted in an approach which often allowed him to bring off with ease passages which might have daunted technically more polished players.

Bix's records themselves hold the key. To the ear of a trumpeter or cornetist, notes fingered in different ways *ring* differently. Passage between them sounds different, "breaking" from one open tone's series into that of another. The following passage, bar three of Bix's solo on take 3 of "Back in Your Own Back Yard," produces a different effect when played with "legitimate" fingerings

from that achieved by Bix with what appear to be these fingerings:

In the "legit" approach, movement between the F and G is smooth, silent, whereas Bix's way there is a telltale "pop" as the first-valve F (descended from the open G) bursts into the first-and-third-valve G (descended from the C above, two ledger lines above the staff).

Sometimes, Bix's unorthodox fingerings allowed him to execute passages which would have been difficult or at least less effective played the "right" way. In the fifth and sixth bars of his solo on Trumbauer's Okeh recording of "Just an Hour of Love with You," he plays:

Had he used the more conventional

he would have had to do all the note-changing with his lip muscles, robbing him of the percussive impact afforded by the valve change.

Bix's solo on "Tain't So, Honey, Tain't So," with Whiteman, affords an ideal

477

example of his uncanny ear in action. It is a haunting piece of work, full of tonal depth and implication. Much of its effectiveness lies in its intonation, lending to Bix's horn a vocal quality which might well have been lacking had the passage been executed with "legit" fingerings. Bix's fingerings are written atop each note, the conventional ones below.

# Index

Compiled by *Mary Rust*

In this Index, which is divided into three sections (The People, The Places and The Tunes), illustrations are indicated by *italicized* page numbers in the first section; popular names of symphonic and other more serious works (e.g., the "New World" Symphony) are given in the third section under those names, and places where Bix played are shown under the name of the building, not the city in which it was located. In the first section, Bix himself is shown only where he is labeled as the leader of a band in the text.

# THE PEOPLE

458, 459, 460, 462, 464, 465, 466, 467, 468

Brader, Ed (sb) 396

Bradley, Will (tb) 398

Breeze Blowers, The 139, 353

Brice, Fannie (v) 369, 390

Briglia, Tony (d) 319, 398

Brilhart, Arnold (as) 352, 470

Broadway Bell-Hops, The 363, 418

Brobile, Russ (as?) *131*, 351

Brodsky, Irving (p, arr and v) 352, 399, 409, 470, 471, 472

Bron, Jascha (vn) 396

Bronenkamp, Jean 361

Brown, Carrie 343

Brown, Elmer (sb and tuba) 353

Brown, Jess 93

Brown, Rozella 343

Brown, Steve (sb and tuba) 63, 139, *164*, 166, 171, 172, 174, *175, 178, 179,* 180, *182,* 186, 188, 189, *190,* 193, *198,* 231, 232, 235, 236, *252,* 267, 345, 353, 358, 360, 364, 366, 409, 410, 411, 412, 413, 414, 415, 416, 417, 421, 422, 423, 424, 425, 426, 427, 428, 429, 430

Brown, Vernon (tb) 140, 146, 149, 152, 157, 159, 161, 355, 356, 368

Brownlee, Norman (p and ldr) 49

Bruce, Bob (t) 233

Bruckman, Earl (d) 47, 393

Bruhn, Louis (p) 393

Brunies, George (tb and kazoo) 51, 63, 83, 87, 88, 103, 345, 348, 350, 406

Brusstar, Tex (t) 127, 407

Bryan, William Jennings 99

Buckley, Neal (p and ldr) *44,* 45, 47, 48, 344

Buckley's Novelty Orchestra 48, 51, 291

Bump, Jerry (tb) *156*

Burtnett, Earl (ldr) 46

Busse, Henry (t) 126, 230, 231, 232, 239, *252,* 363, 364, 367, 371, 422, 423, 424, 425, 426, 427, 428, 429, 430, 431, 432, 433, 434, 435, 436, 437, 438, 439, 440, 441, 442, 443

Cafferelli, Gene (t) 87, 88, 136, 139, 348, 352

Caldwell, Jimmy (p) 67, 68, 69, 72, 345, 346

Caldwell's Jazz Jesters 68

Cali, John (bj) 418

California Ramblers, The 118, 133, 134, 137, 208, 211, 220

Callahan, "Red" 71, 72

Campbell, "Chuck" (tb) 418, 420

Campbell, Ted (d) 353

Candullo, Joe (vn and ldr) 134

Cannon, Jimmy (cl and as) 348

Cantor, Eddie (v) 186, 376

Carle, Frankie (p) 194

Carmichael, Hoagland "Hoagy" (c, p, p-o, arr and v) 72, 82, 83, 100, 103, 106, 109, 119, 127, 128, 130, 132, 201, 206, 228, 230, 231, 233, 283, 284, 285, 286, 304, 309, 310, 326, 327, 337, 349, 351, 352, 364, 381, 392, 395, 397, 399, 421, 422, 470, 472

Carroll, Nancy (actress) 396

Carsella, Johnny (tb) 348

Carter, Benny (cl and as) 185

Carter, Don (d) 230

Casa Loma Orchestra 189, 222, 303, 315, 318, 319, 398

Casertani, Anton "John" (sb) 145, 147, 353

Catalano, Tony (t) 47, 86, 250, 369

Ceballos 390

Chafflin, George (tb) 396

Challis, William H. "Bill" (as, p and arr) 156, *164, 175,* 176, 180, 181, 184, 185, 187, 188, 189, 192, 193, 196, 199, 200, 203, 206, 207, 208, 211, 212, 215, 223, 226, 230, 231, 232, 233, 234, 235, 236, 238, 239, 243, 251, *252,* 263, 266, 267, 270, *275,* 289, 296, 297, 304, 305, 306, 309, 310, 314, 315, 318, 319, 320, 325, *336,* 358, 360, 362, 364, 366, 368, 370, 394, 397, 398, 399, 410, 411, 412, 413, 414, 415, 416, 417, 422, 423, 425, 427, 429, 433, 434, 435, 437, 438, 439, 440, 442, 446, 447, 449, 450, 451, 452, 453, 454, 455, 457, 458, 460, 461, 462, 463, 464, 467, 470

Challoner, Bill (g) 398

Chaplin, Charlie (actor) 283

486

Powell, William (actor) 395
Previn, Charles (dir) 305, 396
Priestley, Bill (c and g) 233, 303, 309, 316, 317, 324, 325, 365, 367, 399
Princeton Triangle Club Jazz Band, The 233
Putzier, Richard "Fritz" (c) 38, 39, 40, 42, *44*, 45, 46, 47, 48, 51, *58*, 59, 68, 122, 278, 283, 286, 292, 293, 295, 343, 344, 345

Quartell, Frankie (t) 152
Quicksell, Howard "Howdy" (bj) 130, *131*, 132, 138, 139, *164*, 172, 173, *175*, *177*, *178*, *179*, *182*, 189, *190*, 192, 196, *198*, 201, 212, *213*, 219, 351, 353, 358, 360, 363, 407, 408, 409, 410, 411, 412, 413, 414, 415, 416, 417, 421
Quinn, Edward "Snoozer" (g) 263, 373, 462, 468
Quodbach, Al 297, 298

Rachmaninoff, Sergei 256
Rank, Bill (tb) 117, 127, 138, 139, *164*, 166, 171, 173, *175*, *178*, *179*, 180, *182*, 184, 188, 189, 192, 193, 194, 196, *197*, *198*, 202, 208, 209, 210, 212, *214*, 215, 216, 217, *218*, 220, *221*, 232, 235, 239, 240, 249, *252*, 256, *261*, 263, 264, *275*, *277*, 278, 283, 285, 312, *336*, 351, 353, 358, 359, 362, 363, 365, 370, 377, 378, 379, 380, 381, 382, 384, 386, 387, 389, 390, 391, 392, 407, 409, 410, 411, 412, 413, 414, 415, 416, 417, 418, 419, 420, 421, 423, 424, 425, 426, 427, 428, 429, 430, 431, 432, 433, 434, 435, 436, 437, 438, 439, 440, 441, 442, 443, 444, 445, 446, 447, 448, 449, 450, 451, 452, 453, 454, 455, 456, 457, 458, 459, 460, 461, 462, 463, 464, 465, 466, 467, 468, 469
Rank, Mervin "Pee Wee" (d) 81, 344, 347, 393
Rasch, Albertina, Girls (dancers) 368
Rathjens, Harry (t) 294, 393, 394
Rauch, Billy (tb) 318, 319, 398
Ravel, Maurice 237
Ray, Otto 350

Raymond, Joe (vn) 396
Reagan, George 94
Reaver, Herbert Ross (bj) 250, 369
Redman, Don (cl, as, arr and ldr) 183, 185, 193, 201, 234, 413
Reis, Les (v) 421
Reiss, Sidney "Happy" (d) 396
Renard, Jacques (ldr) 216
Rendtorff, Edmund J. "Sned" 62, 71, 72, *73*, 75, 347
Revelers, The (v) 359, 413, 414
Reynolds, Clyde (tb) 93, 94, 348
Rhythm Boys, The (v) 235, 237, 283, 284, 295, 305, 364, 368, 372, 376, 377, 378, 379, 380, 381, 382, 383, 384, 385, 386, 387, 388, 389, 390, 391, 392, 435
Rhythm Jugglers, The 132
Richards, John Wayne 61, 65, 72, *73*, 74, 75, 78, 345
Richman, Jack (v) 398
Riddick, Johnny (p) 353
Rinker, Al (p and v) 231, *244*, 251, *252*, *275*, 284, 285, 286, 364, 367, 379, 381, 386, 388, 389, 422, 423, 427, 428, 430, 432, 433, 436, 437, 439, 440, 441, 443, 446, 447, 450, 451, 464, 468, 469, 470
Rinker, Mildred—see Bailey, Mildred
Rising, Morris (tb) 74, 345
Riskin, Irving "Itzy" (p and arr) *164*, 166, 167, 168, 169, 171, 172, 174, *175*, *178*, *179*, 180, 185, 186, 187, 188, 189, 193, *197*, *198*, 200, 201, 202, 204, 271, 356, 357, 358, 360, 409, 410, 413, 414, 415, 416, 417
Robertson, Dick (v) 471
Robinson, Alice 24, 25, 343
Robinson, Fred (tb) 249
Robinson, J. Russel (p) 82
Robison, Carson (g and v) 470
Robison, Willard (p and ldr) 219, 363, 396, 397, 419
Rockwell, "Doc" (comedian) 396
Rockwell, Tommy 194, 205, 210, 220, 222, 239, 266, 315, 376
Rodemich, Gene (p and ldr) 171
Rodgers, Richard 239
Roger, Alice 42
Rogers, Ruth (v) 435
Rogers, Will (humorist) 365

Rohlf, Wayne (t) 46, 49, 257, 259, 298, 335, 394
Rolfe, B. A. (t and ldr) 271, 305, 377, 378, 379, 381, 383, 384, 387, 388, 389, 390
Rollini, Adrian (bsx, gfs and hfp) 118, 133, 207, 208, 209, 211, 212, *214*, 215, 216, 217, 219, 220, 223, 352, 362, 363, 409, 416, 418, 419, 420, 421
Rollini, Arthur (ts) 223
Rollison, Fred (c) 119, 120
Rome, Lindell "Romey" (tb) 351
Roppolo, Leon (cl) 49, *50*, 51, 63, 67, 83, 87, 88, 99, 257, 344, 345, 348
Rose, George (g) 452
Royal Harmonists of Indiana, The 347
Rubin, Benny (comedian) 390
Russell, Charles "Pee Wee" (cl, as and ts) *142*, 145, 146, 147, 148, 166, 167, 169, 170, 308, 309, 324, 353, 354, 355, 356, 421, 471, 472
Russell, Mischa (vn) *252*, 253, 259, *261*, *275*, *277*, 283, 287, 288, 364, 421, 422, 423, 424, 425, 426, 427, 428, 429, 430, 431, 432, 433, 434, 435, 437, 438, 439, 440, 441, 442, 443, 444, 445, 446, 447, 448, 449, 450, 451, 452, 453, 454, 455, 456, 457, 458, 459, 460, 461, 462, 464, 465, 466, 467, 468, 469
Russin, Irving "Babe" (ts) 324, 398
Russin, Jack (p) 324
Ryan, John (v) 421
Ryker, Norma 167, 171, *177*
Ryker, Stanley "Doc" (as) 138, 139, *164*, 166, 167, 172, *175*, *177*, *178*, *182*, 186, 187, 196, *197*, *198*, 201, 207, 208, 211, 212, *336*, 351, 353, 356, 357, 358, 359, 407, 409, 410, 411, 412, 413, 414, 415, 416, 417

Sableman, Chester 160
St. Cyr, Johnny (bj) 39
St. Louis Dance Orchestra, The 171
Sanford, Herb (p) 233
Sannella, Andy (cl, as and stg) 369
Sargent, M. (vn) 345
Sarinson, Buck (bb) 394
Satterfield, Tommy (p and arr) 152, 209, 234, 235, 236, 237, 238, 239, *252*,

270, 355, 364, 422, 423, 424, 425, 426, 428, 432, 434, 435, 436, 438, 439, 440, 441, 443, 444, 445, 446, 447, 448, 450, 451
Savino, Domenico (arr) 424, 435
Savoy Bearcats, The 194
Sbarbaro, Tony (d) 82
Schantz, Harry 28
Schertzer, Hymie (cl and as) 308
Schoebel, Elmer (p and ldr) 71, 87, 88, 89, 193
Schoefner, "Dub" (t) 315, 318, 319, 398
Scholl, Warren W. 286, 376, 378, 384, 385, 387, 388, 390, 392
Schuller, Gunther 235
Schultz, John (as) 397
Schumann-Heink, Ernestine (v) 369
Schurr or Shears, Bob (vn) 46
Schutt, Arthur (p) 306, 310, 396, 397, 398
Scoville, Glenn (as) 87, 88, 348
Seaberg, Artie (cl) 83
Sears, Glenn (d) 393
Sears, Hal 345
Secrest, Andy (c) 264, 265, 267, 270, 271, *272*, *275*, 282, 287, 289, 297, 301, 302, 307, 308, 313, 376, 377, 379, 380, 382, 384, 385, 386, 390, 395, 463, 464, 465, 466, 467, 468, 469, 470
Seeman, William 380
Seiffert, Adele 19
Sells, Vic (c) *56*
Selvin, Ben (vn and ldr) 366, 368, 369, 452, 453
Serenaders, The 355
Servoss, Vic (tb) 397
Severance, Reggie (ts) 346
Severn, Reed 28
Sexton, Tal *50*, 86, 344
Shaffner, Bess 143, *144*, 147, 161, 169, 299, 354, 355
Shaffner, Estelle 143, *144*, 147, 154, 155, 162, 169, 229, 295, 299, *340*, 354, 355, 356
Shaffner, Ruth 143, *144*, 145, 146, 147, 148, 149, 150, 153, 154, 155, *156*, 157, 158, 159, 161, 162, 169, 204, 228, 229, 273, 295, 298, 299, 328, 337, *340*, 353, 354, 355, 356, 361, 364, 384, 394

# THE PLACES

# THE TUNES

509